MW01629119

PRAISE FOR *A HIS*... *THE RISE OF ISLAM*...

A History of the Middle East is a clear, well-balanced book introducing the Middle East by a well-experienced scholar.

—ERIK GOLDSTEIN, Boston University

A History of the Middle East is a fine, ambitious effort at covering 1,400+ years of Middle East political, religious, and cultural history in an engaging, accessible volume.

—ANDREW WENDER, University of Victoria

Lesch weaves together a rich and nuanced history of the Middle East. Both ambitious and rigorous, this book is an invaluable resource for seasoned scholars, students, and non-academic readers alike—a feat of scholarship.

—JASMINE K. GANI, University of St. Andrews

A History of the Middle East Since the Rise of Islam

David W. Lesch
Trinity University

OXFORD
UNIVERSITY PRESS

Oxford University Press is a department of the University of Oxford. It furthers the University's objective of excellence in research, scholarship, and education by publishing worldwide. Oxford is a registered trade mark of Oxford University Press in the UK and in certain other countries.

Published in the United States of America by Oxford University Press
198 Madison Avenue, New York, NY 10016, United States of America.

© 2023 by Oxford University Press

For titles covered by Section 112 of the US Higher Education Opportunity Act, please visit www.oup.com/us/he for the latest information about pricing and alternate formats.

All rights reserved. No part of this publication may be reproduced, stored in a retrieval system, or transmitted, in any form or by any means, without the prior permission in writing of Oxford University Press, or as expressly permitted by law, by license, or under terms agreed with the appropriate reproduction rights organization. Inquiries concerning reproduction outside the scope of the above should be sent to the Rights Department, Oxford University Press, at the address above.

You must not circulate this work in any other form and you must impose this same condition on any acquirer.

Library of Congress Cataloging-in-Publication Data
Names: Lesch, David W., author.
Title: A history of the Middle East since the rise of Islam / David W. Lesch, Trinity University.
Identifiers: LCCN 2022027311 (print) | LCCN 2022027312 (ebook) | ISBN 9780197587140 (paperback) | ISBN 9780197587188 (epub)
Subjects: LCSH: Middle East—History—1517—
Classification: LCC DS62.4 .L47 2023 (print) | LCC DS62.4 (ebook) | DDC 956—dc23/eng/20220614
LC record available at https://lccn.loc.gov/2022027311
LC ebook record available at https://lccn.loc.gov/2022027312

Printing number: 9 8 7 6 5 4 3 2 1
Printed by Sheridan Books, Inc., United States of America

CONTENTS

LIST OF MAPS

SPOTLIGHT BOXES

PREFACE

I have wanted to write this book for some time now. However, other more pressing book projects or endeavors always seemed to get in the way; not that I am complaining, but the stars were finally aligned for me to write this manuscript. The intent for this book is that it be accessible and useful both to an interested general public and college students. It is meant for those relatively uninitiated into the history of the Middle East, yet also it is for those who are culturally aware and open to learning about the history of a part of the world that seems to be in the news every day.

I believe this is the right size manuscript for the target audience. There have been both more limited and more expansive examinations of this roughly 1,400-year period in Middle East history. Hitting that sweet spot in terms of depth of information combined with accessibility is important, in my opinion, in order to reach the broadest possible audience with a volume that offers—as much as possible—an objective yet interpretive account. There is obviously some history triage applied in this book. Not every event, figure, dynasty, movement, or ideology that reared its head during this 1,400-year period will be covered; however, what I have determined to be the singular moments of this history—and the surrounding historical circumstances—will be featured, that is, those events, people, historical movements, and ideologies that shifted historical trajectories from what might have been to what actually happened. As I have taught university courses in medieval Islamic history and modern Middle East history for over thirty years, I think I have accumulated a body of knowledge in terms of breadth and depth to be able to choose what and what not to include. I may not satisfy all customers in this regard, but I try my best while attempting to keep the page count at a reasonable length and, therefore, an affordable price. For college students, hopefully this one volume will suffice, perhaps combined with some supplementary readings, instead of having to spend much more to purchase several books on different historical segments of the whole.

As in any book project, there are many people to thank. First, I want to thank Charles Cavaliere, executive editor at Oxford University Press, who I originally approached with this topic. This has been the second book project (the first one was *The Arab–Israeli Conflict: A History*, 2nd edition, 2019) on which I have worked with Charles, and on each occasion he has been encouraging, knowledgeable, and insightful. I also want to thank the Oxford staff, such as Katie Tunkavige and Sukwinder Kaur; copy editor Anne Sanow; and Steven Hall and his production team at Straive; without whom there would be no production process of which to speak. All of them made this book—and me—look much better than would have been the case otherwise. I also want to thank the reviewers of the book proposal and the manuscript, including Erik Goldstein, Boston University; Dr. Shahram Kholdi, University of Waterloo; Nicolas Trepanier, University of Mississippi; Pheroze Unwalla, University of Maryland; Jens Hanssen, Toronto University; and Andrew M. Wender, University of Virginia. As opposed to many in this business, I actually look forward to their constructive criticisms, remarks, and suggestions because I know it will only improve the final product. And of course I want to thank my research assistant, Jennifer Chiesa, who has been of inestimable help to me. She is copy editor, researcher, scheduler, reviewer, and overall helper all wrapped up into one. She is simply the best.

Finally, I want to thank Judy, the love of my life, for her unyielding and endless support and love—and for putting up with the piles of books, notes, papers, and documents that have been littering my office at home for about two years. I promise to clean it up soon . . . until the next mess with my next book!

NOTE ON THE TEXT

The transliteration of Arabic, Persian, Turkish, Mongolian, and Hebrew words into English varies quite a bit depending upon who or what publication is doing the translating. More often than not I selected the more recognizable version rather than a strict transliteration: for example, "Hussein" rather than "Husayn," "Nasser" rather than "Nasir," and "Faisal" rather than "Faysal." Sometimes the transliteration I utilize is different from that which appears in quotes from other sources in the text: for instance, I write "Hizbullah," whereas in newspapers it often is written as "Hezbollah." One also sees different spellings based on what Arabic spoken dialect is being transliterated. For instance, in Egypt it is most often transliterated into English as "Gamal" and "Naguib," taken from the Egyptian colloquial dialect, whereas in much of the rest of the Arab world those two names are spelled "Jamal" and "Najib." The word "ibn" means "son" in Arabic, and is most often seen as an element of a male's name, such as Khalid ibn al-Walid, literally meaning "Khalid, son of Walid." In the Persian Gulf region and in North Africa west of Egypt, typically the word "son" is written based on the spoken colloquial dialect, so "bin" (as in Osama bin Ladin) in the Gulf and "ben" in North Africa or the Maghreb. Again, I employ the more popularly utilized form, whether it be ibn, bin, or ben. Also, I have chosen not to indicate the important Arabic consonant *ʿayn*, even though it is one of the most frequently used consonants in the Arabic language. For instance, in the word "Arab," the first letter in Arabic is actually the ʿayn consonant followed by the letter "a" vowel. In these cases I do not utilize the diacritical mark, since its anglicized spelling is so commonly accepted in the English language. For other transliterated words, it might be more confusing than helpful to the uninitiated reader to include this and other (such as the glottal stop hamza) diacritical marks, so I have decided not to use them.

In addition, I have given a more neutral appellation to some references, particularly wars. The Arab–Israeli arena is still such a politically charged dynamic that oftentimes how a person designates a particular event says more about where he or she stands on the issue rather than being a reference to the event itself. As such, I simply refer to the war in 1967 as the "1967 Arab–Israeli war," rather than the "June War" or the "Six-Day War." Similarly, I refer to the 1973 conflict as the "1973 Arab–Israeli war," rather than the "Ramadan War," "Yom Kippur War," or "October War." The various sides of a conflict or a controversial issue often give different names to bodies of water or tracts of land. I have attempted to be as neutral and objective in this regard as possible. Hopefully but few exceptions have slipped through the cracks.

ABOUT THE AUTHOR

David W. Lesch is the Ewing Halsell Distinguished Professor of History in the Department of History at Trinity University in San Antonio, Texas. He received his MA and PhD in Middle East History from Harvard University.

He is the author or editor of 16 books and has over 140 publications. Among his books are the following: *Syria: A Modern History* (Polity Books, 2019); *The Arab–Israeli Conflict: A History* (Oxford University Press, 2009, 2019); *Syria: The Fall of the House of Assad* (Yale University Press, 2012, 2013); *The New Lion of Damascus: Bashar al-Asad and Modern Syria* (Yale University Press, 2005); *1979: The Year That Shaped the Modern Middle East* (Westview Press, 2001); his landmark volume, first published in 1996 and now, coedited with Mark Haas, in its 6th edition, *The Middle East and the United States: History, Politics and Ideologies* (Routledge, 2018); his coedited two-volume work (with Mark Haas), *The Arab Spring: Change and Resistance in the Middle East* (Westview Press, 2012) and *The Arab Spring: The Hope and Reality of the Uprisings* (Routledge, 2017); and *Syria and the United States: Eisenhower's Cold War in the Middle East* (Westview Press, 1992).

He has also published numerous articles in leading journals, chapters in books, and opinion essays in such noted publications as the *New York Times, Washington Post, Financial Times, Boston Globe, Foreign Policy*, and CNN.com.

Dr. Lesch has consistently met with and advised high-level officials in the United States, Europe, the Middle East, and the United Nations on diplomatic issues. He has testified in front of Senate and House committees. He has appeared frequently on national and international television and radio programs such as CNN, ABC, PBS Newshour, MSNBC, CNBC, Fox News, Al-Jazeera, NPR, and the BBC, and he has appeared in over a dozen documentaries, including those for The History Channel, the BBC, Frontline on PBS, and film productions by studios/news organizations in numerous countries.

He is on the board of a number of organizations involved in Middle East affairs, including the Syrian Studies Center (St. Andrews University, Scotland), the Damascus Foundation, and Cure Violence (Washington, DC). As a senior advisor to the Abraham Path Initiative (API), Dr. Lesch has spearheaded attempts to establish the API in Syria and Lebanon. The API is an ambitious multinational project sponsored by Harvard University to construct a touristic walking trail throughout the Middle East in order to enhance cross-cultural dialogue and understanding.

Dr. Lesch also initiated and developed (along with William Ury) the Harvard University-NUPI-Trinity University Syria Research Project, funded by the governments of Norway and Switzerland. He led a team of researchers in 2012–2013 to meet with most of the leading players involved in the Syrian civil war that began in 2011. The data provided necessary insights into the dynamics of the conflict in order to formulate possible pathways toward conflict resolution. In the fall of 2013 he completed an 850-page final report for the project and presented his findings at the highest levels in Europe, the United States, and at the UN. He completed phase 2 of the project in 2016, partnering in this phase with Conflict Dynamics International (Cambridge, Massachusetts). It was funded by the government of Denmark. Subsequently, he has been involved in several Middle East initiatives with the Carter Center (Atlanta, Georgia). He met regularly with Syrian President Bashar al-Assad between 2004 and 2009, in part as an attempt at the time to improve US–Syrian relations.

Dr. Lesch is actively engaged in the city of San Antonio politics and government in recent years, involved with the Violence Prevention Division and Stand Up SA program in the San Antonio Metropolitan Health District in city government. He has advised and been involved in several initiatives with the Mayor of San Antonio, Ron Nirenberg.

He was also the #1 draft pick of the Los Angeles Dodgers in the 1980 winter baseball draft as a pitcher and played in the minor leagues before a rotator cuff injury ended his career.

A HISTORY OF THE MIDDLE EAST SINCE THE RISE OF ISLAM

THE MIDDLE EAST AND CENTRAL ASIA TODAY

KAZAKHSTAN
UZBEKISTAN
KYRGYZSTAN
Tashkent
Bukhara
Samarkand
TURKMENISTAN
TAJIKISTAN
Ashkhabad
Mashhad
Tehran
Herat
Kabul
Islamabad
AFGHANISTAN
Isfahan
IRAN
PAKISTAN
QATAR
Dubai
Hyderabad
UNITED ARAB
EMIRATES
Muscat
OMAN
ARABIAN
SEA
0 km
250
500
0 miles
250
500

1

INTRODUCTION

"THERE WILL BE NO PROPHET AFTER ME . . ."

An expanded version of the above *hadith* (saying) attributed to the Prophet Muhammad goes as follows: "There will be no Prophet after me, but there will be caliphs who will increase in number."[1] This refers to the belief by most Muslims that the Prophet Muhammad was the Seal of the Prophets, the last in the line of prophets who appear in the Old and New Testaments. The *caliph* (successor) is a reference to those who will lead the *umma,* or Islamic community, following the Prophet's death. And there would be many caliphs and other leaders who dot the history of the Middle East since Muhammad's time—and many populations had to deal with the policies of these rulers. Some of them were righteous leaders and innovative thinkers, some of them less so. Together, however, for better or worse, they oversaw and guided the community, state, sultanate, empire, or caliphate. But there is much more to it than this. In this book I look at the movements, ideologies, struggles, and historical forces that existed in many ways independently of the rulers, for history is a multidimensional matrix requiring examination at the domestic, regional, and international levels simultaneously. It is a fascinating dynamic that has repeatedly changed the course of events in the Middle East, if not the world.

But what is the Middle East? This has been a question with many different answers, even during the course of my own professional lifetime. It is obviously a Eurocentric reference that began its life during the heyday of the British empire. The Near East, that is, nearest to Britain or Central and Western Europe, comprised the Balkans and the heart of the Ottoman Empire in present-day Turkey, and at various times may have also included the Mediterranean coast along the Levant (present-day Syria, Lebanon, and Israel/Palestinian Territories). The Far East referred to what most of us now term East Asia, including China, Japan, Korea, Southeast Asia, and even India. So what to call the lands in between the Near and Far East? But of course, the Middle East! It may have been British staffers in the British India Office in the 1850s who originally came up with the reference. "Middle East" was actually popularized, however, by an American, Alfred Thayer

Mahan (1840–1914). Mahan was better known—in fact widely known—as a US naval officer and historian who wrote a seminal book, *The Influence of Sea Power Upon History, 1660–1783*, which, along with a second volume, became one of the most important books on naval strategy in the modern era. He made his first mention of the "Middle East" in a 1902 article he wrote for a British magazine, although in his mind it was primarily a reference to the Persian Gulf region, which to him had fallen between the cracks of geography.

British diplomat Sir Mark Sykes, of whom we shall hear much more in chapter 10, started using "Middle East" frequently in his speeches during World War I. The term slowly began to expand to include Egypt and the Levant, and as the twentieth century wore on, it also encompassed North Africa and beyond as it became a political reference that included the Arab League countries, Turkey, Iran, and even Afghanistan in many instances, especially as the Arab–Israeli conflict, inter-Arab rivalries, and regional and international politics more and more linked these areas to each other by the 1970s. But "Middle East" is a product of the Occident—that is, Europe. The Near, Middle, and Far East made up the Orient. Amazingly enough, "Near East" or "Near Eastern" still can be found in the corridors of government and academia. Historians, area specialists, and geographers have tried over the years to come up with something a bit more neutral. For instance, the Middle East can be called Southwest Asia, to go with East Asia, Central Asia, Southeast Asia, and South Asia (India, Pakistan, and maybe or maybe not Afghanistan). Then there is the more inclusive Southwest Asia and North Africa, with the catchy acronym of SWANA, to refer to the countries in what we now think of as the Middle East, while others have utilized MENA, meaning Middle East and North Africa.

This is not even to speak of broader geographic references. If you are standing in what we most often call East Asia and gaze eastward, North and South America could be the Middle East with Europe as the Far East—or the Far West, if you turn around and look in the opposite direction. It all depended on who got dibs on naming things, and most often it was the one first to the plate, so to speak, at a certain confluence of historical events, which in this case happened to be Europe in the nineteenth and into the twentieth century. If China had been at that historical confluence, accepted geopolitical references today might look much different. Of course, we could go out even farther into space where geographic references and directions are perhaps meaningless. Who says the Northern Hemisphere is north and the Southern Hemisphere is south? With this in mind, the whole North–South divide—geographically, economically, and socioculturally—comes into question.

You get my point. The name "Middle East" is less a geographic designation than a political and sociocultural reference devised at a particular period of time when Europe and the United States enjoyed political, military, and sociocultural heft in a way that allowed them to monopolize and imbed the designation into the global consciousness. This is why the seminal work *Orientalism*, originally published in 1979 by Edward Said, a professor of English and comparative literature at Columbia University and a

Palestinian American, was critical to Middle East studies.[2] He helped reverse what had been for centuries the prevailing paradigm in the West (the "Occident") by which the Middle East (the "Orient") was viewed. In literature, art, culture, and historical studies the Middle East was depicted as static or underdeveloped: the "white man's burden," a patronizing attitude that directly and indirectly provided the intellectual foundation for imperialism, for which the indigenous peoples were actually expected to be grateful. But "Middle East" has become accepted into the lexicon of the day, even in the region itself. It is important, however, to note its historical evolution and that it is the product of a time and place. I remember meeting with the top foreign policy advisor to the Sultan of Oman back in the late 1990s. I had taken a class in graduate school at Harvard University titled "The Modern History of the Persian/Arabian Gulf," the word "Arabian" an apparent sop to the days of Arab nationalism when the Arab side of the Gulf frequently called the body of water that outlets into the Arabian Sea the "Arabian Gulf" and not the Persian Gulf. When I met with the Omani official, I thought I would be too smart for my own good and referred to that body of water or region as the Arabian Gulf. He immediately looked at me and asked, "Why did you call it that?" And he proceeded to tell me that they—the Omanis, and presumably other Arabs in the Gulf region—had long gotten over the "Arabian Gulf" reference. He said, "Just call it the Persian Gulf. All of us do. It's no big deal." So it is in the spirit of that flexibility and acceptance of reality that I use the term "Middle East."[3]

Speaking of the rest of the book, this volume focuses on historical events that occur over a long period of time (referred to as *la longue durée* in history circles) in the Middle East. This does not mean, however, that specific, individual actions are ignored. It can be quite to the contrary when the sources allow us to do so. As Middle East historian Richard Bulliet said, "Do not separate the *longue durée* from individual actions. Big history and personal agency are not incompatible."[4] I have chosen the rise of Islam as the general beginning point of this history of the Middle East. Although there are obviously millennia of salient history in the region that precede this period, there is an indelible link between the rise of Islam and the overall environment that exists today in the region. And it is the continuum of this chain of events that is the primary focus of my examination, hopefully specific enough to digest the flavor of particular periods, dynasties, movements, cultural markers, and ideological developments, yet general enough for the reader to be able to compare and contrast in one volume the totality of the progression of this history as elements of a distinct whole. After all, as I wrote in my book *1979: The Year That Shaped the Modern Middle East,* "Historians are indeed a kind of secular priesthood, seemingly endowed with the power and means to select what is and what is not important for the rest of us."[5]

In a thought-provoking work by Garth Fowden titled *Before and After Muhammad: The First Millennium Refocused,* the author contextualizes his approach to early Islam, examining the first one thousand years of the common era in the region as a whole rather than the typical Eurocentric periodization of history divided into late antiquity, then the European Middle Ages, followed by the Renaissance and Modernity.[6] His is a more inclusive history, examining Rome, Iran (Persia), and the Caliphate as integrated spokes of the same wheel and in a mutually affecting way. As he writes, "If Islam eventually touched everything, it is likely that everything touched Islam."[7] In his view, what followed the rise of Islam in the seventh century, particularly the Umayyad and Abbasid caliphates as well as other centers of Islamic culture to about the year 1000 CE, should be culled together as one overall nodal point during the first millennium. It is a different version of chronology, of historical narrative. It is the secular priesthood at work again. While I do not intentionally follow Fowden's periodization, I think in some ways I unconsciously do so simply by interpreting the history of the Middle East since the rise of Islam as one spoke of the wheel that influenced, was influenced by, and interacted on a consistent basis with Rome (i.e., the Mediterranean world from the time of Byzantium), and with Iran from the Sassanian period. This book goes beyond that history by adding another thousand years, linking the first and second millenniums of Middle East history.

For the most part, the chapters in the book are divided thematically, but in general follow a chronological narrative. In chapter 2, I examine first the environments in which Islam arose: the international setting of the Byzantine and Sassanian empires. Then I look at the local setting, that is, pre-Islamic Arabia. I then detail what we think we know about the life of the Prophet Muhammad and the origin story of Islam. Primary source material on this period—indeed, a good bit of early Islamic history—is lacking, to say the least, a subject I address in the chapters themselves. In chapter 3, I cover the trials, tribulations, and triumphs of early Islam following the death of Muhammad, a period of tremendous expansion and experimentation, all of which is accompanied by the typical growing pains that civilizations encounter during their early stages.

Chapters 4 and 5 deal with the Caliphate: the Umayyad empire/caliphate, or what may be seen as an Arab kingdom that was more a successor state to Rome, at least at first, than the crystallization of a new civilization. The latter, perhaps, became more apparent with the Abbasid caliphate, which was more of a broad-based Islamic empire and culture coming into its own. Chapter 6 details the different centers of power that emerged in and around the Middle East following the end of real Abbasid power in the middle of the tenth century. This chapter focuses primarily on the rise—and fall—of the Buyids in Iran, the Fatimids in North Africa (Maghreb) and Egypt, and various groups in Islamic Spain. Importantly, this is also a period that sees the real split in Islam between Sunnis and Shiites come into relief. In chapter 7, I examine the migration and entrance into the region of new groups from the East, the Seljuk Turks and the Mongols, and the West, mainly in the form of the European Crusades to the Holy Land, all of which had long-term repercussions at a number of different levels for the Middle East.

In chapter 8, I look at some of the more influential and long-lasting empires that arose in the wake of the breakup of the Mongol Empire in Eurasia: the Mamluks based in Egypt and Syria, the Ottomans based in Anatolia, the Balkans, and eventually into the heartland of the Middle East, and finally the Safavids in Iran. I shift my coverage primarily to the Ottoman Empire in chapter 9 because of its immediate and direct import to many of the long-standing issues in the Middle East to this day. I outline the empire's dynamic growth, territorially and institutionally, that reached its height under Sulayman the Magnificent (r. 1520–1566). The stresses and strains of the empire then become more apparent in the subsequent centuries, especially when confronting an assertive Europe through the eighteenth and nineteenth centuries. I conclude this chapter by examining the Ottoman responses to these challenges. Chapter 10 really begins our foray into the modern Middle East, a complex period to say the least, which is perhaps why this is the longest chapter in the book yet covers one of the shortest time periods. I start with what could be described as the Ottomans' last stand against Europe, coming to a climax with World War I, which immeasurably changed and propelled the region in all sorts of interesting directions, including the imposition of the European mandate system in the heartland of the area following the war, which is the last subject addressed in this chapter.

The final two chapters (11 and 12) analyze the post–World War II period in the Middle East. In chapter 11, I look at the multidimensional matrix in the region in the form of two intermingling cold wars: the inter-Arab one and the emerging superpower Cold War between the United States and the Soviet Union. Then we focus upon the increasing ferocity of the Arab–Israeli conflict, especially the run-up to and effects of the seminal 1967 Arab–Israeli war. Finally, I outline and analyze the primary-level events of 1979 in the Middle East—the Iranian revolution, the Egyptian-Israeli peace treaty, the taking of the Grand Mosque in Mecca by Islamic militants, and the Soviet invasion of Afghanistan—as a kind of culmination of different strands of modern Middle East history that separately and together produced a new Middle East going forward. The last chapter examines the region engaged in a struggle, sometimes with others, sometimes with itself. I begin by giving a brief history of the rise of twentieth-century Islamism or Islamic fundamentalism and how one vector in this process led to the catastrophic events of September 11, 2001 (9/11). What followed soon after was the US-led invasion of Iraq in 2003, with all of its problematic consequences. The last item of discussion in this chapter is the so-called Arab Spring that began at the end of 2010, when protests arose across the region against authoritarianism, corruption, and injustice, leading to the removal of several long-ruling regimes and the eruption of several civil wars, some of which still are raging as of this writing. On the surface these events do not portend a bright future for the Middle East, yet hope springs eternal that these multifarious, complicated, and vivid struggles can eventually be mitigated so that peace and prosperity become the norm rather than the exception. The people in the region deserve no less.

The Middle East isn't broken, as many people think. On the contrary, it has yet to come into its own in the modern post–nineteenth-century era. Politically, economically, and socioculturally the area's growth has been interrupted and stunted, often by external interference. War, extremism, authoritarianism, poverty, corruption, institutional immaturity, and weak or nonexistent national identities are the results of this process. Growing (and younger) populations combined with dwindling water resources and climate change compound existing problems. Perhaps the modern Middle East is simply an unfinished product—a product that was difficult to construct from the beginning of the twentieth century, due in good measure to imperialist and colonialist designs and actions, as the region was force-fed into the European-based nation-state system. Instead of going back to the drawing board, often an impossibility in an international environment, much of the region doggedly moved forward, but it did so on what in many ways was an artificial and weak edifice. Initial cracks in the edifice widened. Attempts to fix the manifold problems in the area have faced daunting challenges. Glue and duct tape have been applied more often than not to prevent total breakdown, but despite progress here and there, the entire foundation appears to be teetering on the edge.

Why do we care? The Middle East has a long and acutely consequential history. The rise and fluorescence of Islam is one of the great epochs of human history, without which the world—the West in particular—would look much different. The populations of the Middle East, as historian Michael Hamilton Morgan points out, are so much more than the common Western trope "they were once great, they invented arithmetic, but then they fell behind."[8] It also doesn't hurt that the Middle East today contains about two-thirds of the world's proven oil reserves. That alone would be enough in a combustion engine and carbon-based energy world to warrant sufficient attention. But there is much more. The over seventy-year Arab–Israeli conflict, despite being teased by comprehensive peace on occasion, still perseveres, albeit in a much different form than earlier manifestations. The heart of this conflict isn't in some out-of-the-way place, either; it is in the Holy Land, home to the three great Abrahamic religions of Judaism, Christianity, and Islam—it is not going to go unnoticed, and it hasn't been for millennia. It more than deserves our attention.

This book is patient. I do not rush the history being examined. I try to give something approaching equal weight to all of it. Some may wish I gave more prominence to one era over another, but, in my view, this does a disservice to the overall history itself. Books in the past that have roughly covered this time period often spend about a third of the book on what is typically categorized as the medieval and early modern period and then the remaining two-thirds on the modern era. This is uneven, and it undervalues *la longue duree* and how it informs and creates the links in the chain of history to the present day. I offer a comprehensive approach that will take the reader on what I hope is an informative ride through the Middle East since the period surrounding the rise of Islam. It will be done vertically in terms of historical periodization and thematic depth as well as horizontally in terms of geographic breadth, from Spain and the Atlantic shores of Morocco to the Central Asian mountain ranges of Afghanistan. As I mentioned in the preface, since I want to produce an affordable book dictated by a reasonable page limit, by necessity there is considerable historical triage. Every event, dynasty, empire, notable figure, movement, and ideology will not be examined—and sometimes not even mentioned. For that, my apologies; however, as a secular priest, an intermediary between history and those who read it, I have taken it upon myself to carefully and respectfully perform this triage and choose what to cover and what not to cover. This includes most especially what I have called the "bent rails" of history, those historical events and circumstances that sent history in one direction rather than the counterfactual—and hypothetical—other direction. [9]

By necessity due to being mindful of page count, I do not examine the butterfly effect in this regard, so unfortunately many elements of society do not get their just due in this volume, as I more often than not examine the decisions and actions more toward the end of the process of change rather than at the beginning. In addition, as Hossein Kamaly wrote, "Women's history is human history . . . in the past and today women have shaped many aspects of the history of Islam and deserve a more central place in the historical narrative."[10] Kamaly wrote an excellent book, *A History of Islam in 21 Women,* which I very much enjoyed reading; however, while doing so, I realized that there are not any books titled *The History of Islam in 21 Men* or the like. The choice of "21" is chosen for consistency with others works in the series examining twenty-one women in other cultures and places. The fact that we feel the necessity to even write such books admits the failure to include the important histories (and contributions) of individuals and groups who were forgotten or ignored. I attempt to rectify this in the narrative, but more so in a number of spotlight boxes that highlight the contribution of women in the Middle East over the centuries.

There is an Ottoman political aphorism and philosophy known as the Circle of Equity (often called the Circle of Justice) developed in the sixteenth century. While I mention this concept later in the book, essentially it assigns a role to various sectors of the empire's population that, in a circle, feed into each other in mutual support and dependency—it makes everything come together and work, or so it was thought. There are the sovereigns, the army, the people who provide the wealth (workers and peasants), and then justice underpinning it all. Broadening this concept to the period under examination in this book, I cover a good part of this circle over a roughly 1,500-year history but certainly not all of it. This is the nature of historical triage. Hopefully, I have chosen wisely.

NOTES

1 Muhammad Muhsin Khan, translator, *The Translation of the Meanings of Sahih Al-Bukhari, (Arabic-English) Volume 4* (Riyadh, Saudi Arabia: Darussalam Publishers & Distributors, 1997), p. 414. https://www.ahlesunnatpak.com/uploads/books/Saheh%20Al-Bukhari/english/SahihAl-bukhariVol.4-Ahadith2738-3648.pdf.
2 Edward W. Said, *Orientalism* (New York: Vintage Books, 1979).
3 For more on this topic, see Michael E. Bonine, Abbas Amanat, and Michael Ezekiel Gaspar, eds., *Is There a Middle East?: The Evolution of a Geopolitical Concept* (Stanford: Stanford University Press, 2011).
4 Richard W. Bulliet, Facebook post, January 30, 2021.
5 David W. Lesch, *1979: The Year That Shaped the Modern Middle East* (Boulder, CO: Westview Press, 2000), p. 25.
6 Garth Fowden, *Before and After Muhammad: The First Millennium Refocused* (Princeton, NJ: Princeton University Press, 2014), p. 3.
7 Ibid., p. 92.
8 Michael Hamilton Morgan, *Lost History: The Enduring Legacy of Muslim Scientists, Thinkers, and Artists* (Washington, DC: National Geographic Society, 2007), p. xv.
9 See Lesch, *1979.*
10 Hossein Kamaly, *A History of Islam in 21 Women* (London: Oneworld Publications, 2019), p. 2.

For additional digital learning resources please go to www.oup.com/he/lesch-middleeast-1e

2 THE RISE OF ISLAM

The International Setting

When examining such a dynamic movement as the rise of Islam in the seventh century CE (or any significant movement for that matter), it is important to look at the environment into which it expanded. More often than not, the empires or states being conquered were experiencing a series of convulsions, making them ripe for the picking. This is not in any way, shape, or form meant to diminish the tremendous success of the initial Islamic conquests, but typically rapid expansion is due not only to the motivation, fighting prowess, and organizational skills of the conquering power but also to the relatively dilapidated state of the conquered, who tend to be past their prime.

This was certainly the case in the 630s to 640s CE in the Middle East. The two superpowers of the day in the area—the Byzantine and the Sassanian empires, encompassing the territories that experienced the entire brunt of the initial Islamic conquests—were very much less than at their best when the Arabs exploded out of Arabia. It is important when reading this section of the chapter to keep in mind the generally accepted dates of the Prophet Muhammad's birth and death (570 and 632 CE, respectively). His successors almost immediately took on both the Byzantines and Sassanians after his death, decisions that perhaps can be viewed differently when weighed against the timing of the devastating wars fought between the two superpowers in the 610s through the 620s.

We take for granted today the so-called Arab world consisting of countries as far west as Morocco, as south as the Sudan in sub-Saharan Africa, and as far north and east as Syria and Iraq; however, at the time of the birth of Islam, the Arabs were essentially just in Arabia, which is why it was called Arabia. There were some nomadic seasonal migrations that brought Arabs into the northern reaches of the Arabian desert into what is today Jordan, Syria, and Iraq. Some Arabs may have settled into a region

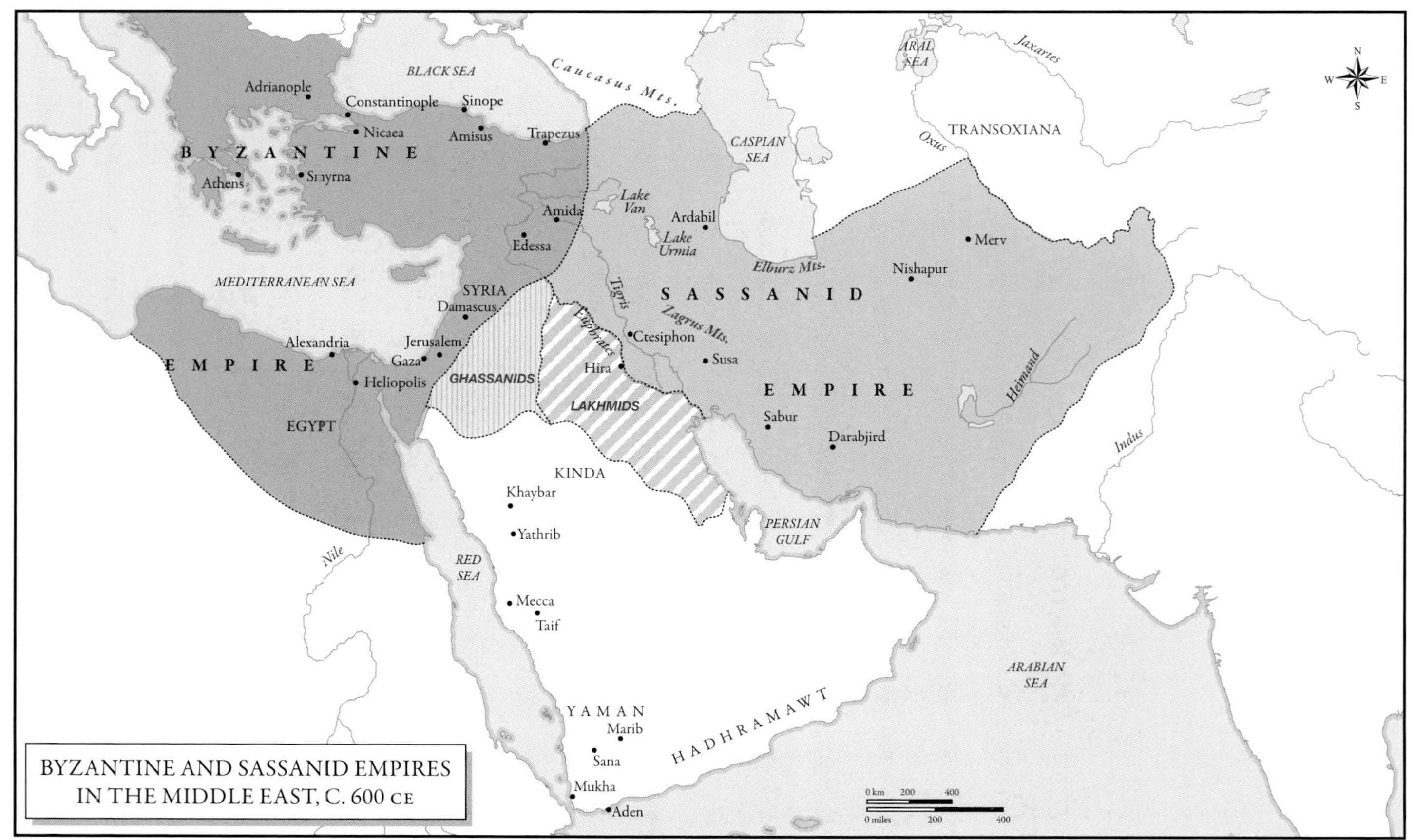

BYZANTINE AND SASSANID EMPIRES IN THE MIDDLE EAST, C. 600 CE

called the **Jazira**, which today is located along the border of Iraq and Syria. Jazira in Arabic means "island," which may seem to be an odd name for a land-locked area until one recognizes that it was located between the Tigris and Euphrates rivers, an island of land between the two waterways that gave life to the great civilizations of Mesopotamia. It was the Islamic conquests that brought the Arabs, their religion, and their language out of Arabia, which over time altered the ethnic, linguistic, and cultural landscape of the Middle East into that which exists today in the region.

Having said this, both the Byzantines and the Sassanians had during the second half of the sixth century CE reached certain arrangements with leading Arab clans on the fringes of each empire in the Middle East. For the Byzantines, the Ghassanids, located around where the Golan Heights exists today in Syria, played the role of frontier guard. Playing the same role for the Sassanians were the Lakhmids, located in what is today southern Iraq. Each acted as a kind of buffer against the other, but it shows that some Arabs did play important parts in the intensifying Byzantine-Sassanian drama. It also shows that both empires seemed to be relying more on frontier peoples for defense against the other rather than imperial forces. This can mean a number of things; one was that the reliance on both the Ghassanids and Lakhmids represented symptoms of change. This is not necessarily a sign of inevitable decline, but it does signal a change when taken together with everything else we know about what was going on inside each empire.

The Byzantine Empire was in fact the Eastern Roman Empire that survived the fall of Rome in the West in the fifth century. It is named after a small Greek fishing village founded by a man called Byzas, located near where Istanbul is today (or what before the twentieth century was called Constantinople), the capital of the Byzantines, on the European side of the Bosporus strait. No one really referred to the Byzantines by that name; to most everyone in the region it was still Rome (or Rum), and, with the Roman Empire's long and deep legacy in the region, it still carried the cachet of being "Rome," even when Byzantium was in precipitous decline. During and after reaching its territorial height under the Emperor Justinian (527–565 CE), the Byzantines suffered through a series of catastrophes that shook the foundation of the empire, especially that portion of it that existed in the Middle East.

In 541 the bubonic plague hit the empire, which may have killed up to a third of the population over the next decade or so (from a population of 30–34 million down to 17–20 million). There were also a number of devastating earthquakes that hit the Levant, the lands in the Middle East adjacent to the eastern Mediterranean, in the mid-500s, including one that destroyed Beirut; such was the "emptying out" of the local population in the Middle East due to these catastrophes (and ongoing war with the Sassanians) that a number of towns taken by the Arabs during the conquest were simply deserted.

The Byzantines also suffered through a series of invasions on both sides of the empire in the late 500s and into the early 600s. The Lombards retook most of the lands in Italy that Justinian had recaptured from the Visigoths; indeed, Justinian's attempts to make Rome whole again practically bankrupted the empire. Also, Slavic migrations into the Balkans placed additional pressure on the border regions of Byzantium. Finally, and most importantly, there were a series of very destructive invasions of the Syrian provinces of the empire by the Sassanians; there had been five wars between the Sassanians and the Byzantines since early in the sixth century, to the point where for almost an entire century through to the 620s, the heartland of the Middle East experienced almost constant conflict.

All of these setbacks had fundamental effects on the Byzantine Empire. The military was weakened with the loss of population and territory as well as the economy with the corresponding loss of tax base; at one point during the reign of Emperor Heraclius (r. 610–641), he appointed the head of the treasury as the commander of the military in order to ensure that the army was paid. Overall, the Byzantine Near East by the end of the sixth century had effectively lost its classical aspects and was going through a series of profound economic, political, and social change. It is against this background that the achievements of the initial Islamic conquests must be weighed. Timing is everything: if Islam had come on the scene a couple of generations earlier, during the heyday of Justinian's rule, the expansion out of Arabia most likely would have been less successful.

There were also a number of issues regarding the two primary territories of the Byzantine Near East into which the Muslim armies expanded: Syria and Egypt. Both regions were essentially lands of two cultures, the one urban, Greek-speaking, and centered around the cultural urban cities of Antioch in Syria and Alexandria in Egypt. The other culture was that which existed outside of the cities, encompassing the rural or pastoral areas or what some have described as the vernacular or native cultures, those who lived in these territories before the Greco-Roman era. In Egypt the vernacular culture was **Coptic**, taken from a seventeenth-century Latin word, "Coptus," which itself is derived from the Arabic word for the Copts, "qubt," referring to those native Egyptians going back to the age of the pharaohs—today it is a reference to the minority Christian group that resides in the modern nation-state of Egypt who make up about 10 percent of the population there; in Syria it was Aramaic, making up the Semitic ethno-linguistic group that also includes Hebrews and Arabs.[1] These rural peoples had little to no access to the traditions of the urban centers, and there often existed tensions between the two based on different backgrounds, status, and cultural practices. It has been said that they lived in almost mutual incomprehension of each other. But with the relative decline of the prosperity and population numbers of the urban centers, the pastoral world was in the ascendant and perhaps a bit more assertive. The rise of and reliance upon such groups as the Ghassanids and Lakhmids are emblematic of this.

The differences between the urban and rural peoples were also reflected in their respective variants of Christianity. During the sixth century the majority of the populations, especially outside of the cities, began to follow Monophysite

Christianity, whereas most of the practicing Christians in the urban areas followed Diophysite Christianity. The difference concerned the nature of Christ. **Diophysites** (meaning "two natures") believed that Christ had two complete natures, one human and one divine, miraculously fused into one. **Monophysites** (one nature) held that Christ had only one, divine nature. This difference may seem trivial, but it reflects fundamentally different religious traditions and cultural heritages. The Diophysites hark back to the Hellenistic tradition of humanizing the divine (Zeus, Athena, Hercules, etc.), whereas the Monophysites look back to aspects of the Jewish tradition with its deep distrust of any anthropomorphic representation of the divine, something that Islam shares.

These different forms of Christianity emerged from the central Christian question that was hotly debated for centuries: Who was Jesus Christ? There are many answers to this question (one bishop in the 300s counted over 150 heresies) ranging from the sublime to the ridiculous, but these were very serious issues.[2] What developed over time was the idea that Jesus was the Son of God, and that in God's oneness is triplicity (Father, Son, and Holy Spirit). To non-Christians (and even a number of Christians at the time) this smacked of polytheism. Finally, the Roman Emperor Constantine, who converted to Christianity himself, convened in 325 CE the bishops and other religious officials at Nicaea in present-day Turkey. At the time, the bishop of Rome ("Papa" in Latin, "Papas" in Greek, or "Pope" in English) presided over the Pentarchy, the five centers of the Christian church (Rome, Antioch, Constantinople, Alexandria, and Jerusalem). The bishops emerged with the Nicene Creed in hand, confirming God's oneness in his triplicity. The opening line, almost as if it was a rallying cry to convince the naysayers that Christianity is a monotheistic religion, begins with, "We believe in one God, the Father the Almighty, maker of heaven and earth. . . ."

After the fall of Rome, Byzantium was by and large able to control the lands of the five bishops, but it also inherited the debate concerning the nature of Christ, which persisted even after the Nicene Creed. Indeed, a fifth-century group called the Nestorians, named after Nestorius, were exiled from the Byzantine empire and branded heretics for believing in a slight variation of Diophysism. They relocated with the Sassanians, who welcomed them with the age-old foreign policy of "the enemy of my enemy is my friend." Interestingly, the Lakhmid Arab clan allied with the Sassanians became Nestorian Christians. Finally, in 451 at the Council of Chalcedon (just outside Constantinople on the Asian side of the Bosphorus), the Byzantines adopted Diophysite Christianity as the empire's official state religion and branded Monophysism as heresy. Coptics, Syrians, Armenians, Ethiopians, and others in the Middle East denounced Chalcedon as heresy. They formed the core of what became the Oriental orthodox churches, and for the most part they have been out of communion with the Roman Catholic and Greek Orthodox churches ever since. This situation became even more complicated when the Roman and Greek churches went their own separate ways in 1054 over a host of issues that were all really symptoms of a power struggle at the time between Rome and Constantinople.

Why have I gone over all these differences and variants? The significance of this is that it meant that a healthy portion of the populations in the Byzantine Near East, when the Muslim armies entered Syria and Egypt, were alienated from the ruling class both culturally and, because the church they were devoted to was regarded as heretical and subject to official sanctions, religiously. It is important, however, not to overestimate the significance of this. There is no evidence that a large number of either the Copts or the Monophysites of Syria actually cooperated with or fought on behalf of the Muslims. What can be said is that they felt little enthusiasm for the Byzantine cause and did not rise up en masse to protect Byzantium against the Islamic armies. If anything, they saw it as an opportunity to get rid of their oppressors, their fellow Christians. Perhaps some even saw the Muslims as liberators of a sort. This is especially the case because the Islam they encountered was much more ambiguous, nebulous, and fluid than the Islam that would develop over the subsequent decades and centuries. As an Abrahamic monotheistic religion, Islam probably seemed fairly familiar, and it was thus acceptable, especially since, for the most part, the new kids on the block were quite tolerant of local traditions and customs; the Muslim invasions allowed the Monophysites to much more freely practice their faith. Other Christians thought perhaps that the Arabs were an instrument of God, punishing them for sinful behavior, or even that they were a one-hit wonder, only to be taken over by the next movement in line. And for some, no doubt, it came down to one's pocketbook; Were taxes going to be more or less onerous, and could trade and commercial activity continue unabated and maybe even be enhanced under Muslim rule?

The long-term weaknesses of the Byzantine Empire were revealed and exacerbated in a series of defeats at the hands of the Sassanians in the early 600s, as the Persian dynasty penetrated into the heart of the Middle East, taking Antioch in 613 and Jerusalem in 614. All of the provinces of Syria, Palestine, and Egypt were taken amid intense conflict and widespread devastation, even into the Anatolian hinterland. However, Heraclius came to power in 610 as Byzantine emperor, and after initial setbacks, he began to fulfill the hopes of those who saw him as a much more competent leader. In 622 he set off from Constantinople and led an expedition through the Black Sea to begin a rear-guard action against the Sassanians, which proved to be very successful. He destroyed the bulk of the Persian armies and entered the Sassanian capital of Ctesiphon, in present-day Iraq, in 628. All of this was done at great expense to the Byzantines and caused a great deal of disruption in the Middle East.

The Sassanian empire of Persia (Iran) of the late sixth century was, like the Byzantines, the heir to an ancient imperial tradition going back to the great Achaemenid dynasty. The family dynasty came to power in the third century centered in the southern region of Iran known as Fars (from where is derived the term "Farsi," as

The Taq-i Kisra from the air, Ctesiphon, Iraq, 1925. Ctesiphon was the capital of the Sassanid Persian Empire. This great arch was the main portico of the audience hall of the imperial palace.
The Print Collector / Alamy Stock Photo

in the Farsi language, the Indo-European based—though Arabic scripted—dialect of Persian prevalent in Iran today). The Sassanians were the last in a long line of divinely guided monarchies in the ancient Middle East harking back all the way to the Sumerians, Akkadians, and Babylonians.

Despite the divine right to rule, however, the Sassanian royal house was challenged on occasion, none more so than in the 620s when dealing with the defeats at the hands of the Byzantines. There were at least ten different kings (shahs) in the four-year period from 628 to 632, not exactly the stability one would want in order to meet the onslaught of the Muslim armies entering into Iraq and Iran a few years later.

The Sassanian aristocracy was divided into many classes, but apart from the royal family, they were essentially divided into two groups: the first was the upper aristocracy composed of some powerful families who traced their lineage back to previous dynasties in Iran, such as the Parthians, the contemporaries of Rome. Some have suggested that the term "Shahanshah," king of kings, as the title of the Sassanian ruler was not so much a reflection of the unrivaled power of the Sassanian king but rather an indication of some ambiguity surrounding the actual authority of the Sassanian royal house over other royal houses descended from previous dynasties. This may suggest that political struggles at the top were a typical feature of Sassanian rule. The second group were the so-called lesser aristocracy of **dahaqin** (singular **dihqan**), who were a kind of landed nobility. They were often absentee landlords who formed a link between the peasantry and the central government. Many of the dahaqin were government administrators and tax collectors. It was the dahaqin who over time were the primary transmitters of Persian culture and administrative practices to the Arabs, since unlike the higher aristocracy and royal family, who for the most part were wiped out by the Islamic conquest, they survived and retained much of their power and purpose. In addition, until the Arabs developed their own distinct version of government and administration, in many of the newly conquered lands they simply grafted Islamic rule onto existing—and functioning—administrative systems. Well into the ninth century we find powerful administrators working for the Abbasid court who were descendants of the dahaqin, including one very influential family during the reign of the Caliph Harun al-Rashid in the late eighth century, a family we will encounter later in this book.

The Sassanians, like the Byzantines, also had their state religion, a monotheistic faith called Zoroastrianism, named after Zoroaster (or Zarathustra), who lived in the sixth century BCE. It was administered by a caste of priests called Magi, which is why the religion is sometimes referred to as Magian. It was a faith profoundly concerned with good versus evil, with fire temples established to worship the god, Ahura Mazda, although there were some lesser gods; so, as with Christianity, there was some question as to how monotheistic it really was. Zoroastrianism had a day of judgment as in Judaism, Christianity, and Islam, as well as a series of rituals and practices commonly found in the Middle East. But Zoroastrianism was never a very popular religion, seemingly confined to the upper classes and under the purview of a proprietary priesthood; it was probably a minority religion in the empire, challenged by an array of faiths, including Nestorian Christianity, Judaism, Manichaeanism, and a number of pagan belief systems.

This religious diversity was only exceeded by the linguistic and ethnic diversity in Sassanid lands. There were Kurds, Arabs, Daylamites, Baluchis, Aramaeans, and others; in terms of overall numbers at the height of Sassanian rule, the Persians may have been a minority within their own empire. For most of the people in Iraq and many people in Iran, the Sassanian empire and its state religion were alien and often seen as oppressive and hostile. Therefore, many if not most of the Sassanian population shared neither language, religion, nor custom with their rulers. As with the situation in the Byzantine Near East, it is not surprising that few of them, except in areas such as Fars, were prepared to defend and preserve the old order once the Muslim armies invaded, and especially after the Sassanian imperial army was defeated. As in Byzantium, the decades of wars with their counterpart, especially in the 610s and 620s, compounded short-term problems into long-term weaknesses. Again, a supposed superpower in the region was anything but by the time the Arabs emerged from Arabia.

Pre-Islamic Arabia

Perhaps the most significant factor in understanding the environment in which Islam arose is the setting in Arabia itself prior to the Prophet Muhammad's calling. As we shall see, Islam very much reflected and in many ways was a product of the conditions in pre-Islamic Arabia. As mentioned in the previous section, at the beginning of the seventh century the Arabs inhabited the Arabian Peninsula and parts of its northward extension into the Syrian desert, but little else.

The Arabs were generally united by a common language, although there were different dialects. They also developed a common poetic language employed especially in storytelling, which was a frequent form of not only entertainment, but also sharing information. Indeed, the Quran, the holy book of Islam, is structured and written in poetic form that reflects the oral-based communication system that permeated Arab life. The word "Quran" in Arabic means "recite," as in the command that God (Allah) gave Muhammad in his very first communication with the Prophet as transmitted to him by the Archangel Gabriel (Jibril), the same archangel who appears in the Christian New Testament. In other words, Allah directed Muhammad to "recite" what he is being told. The Quran is really intended to be recited, with rhythmic chants. It is meant to be heard, not read. This is a clear example of how Islam was developed by and tailored toward its Arab audience.

The possession of this common language was important in the development of Islam, as it meant that its fundamental teachings were accessible to the many different tribes that inhabited Arabia. This information was shared through the informal but mobile communication networks that existed in an area dominated by nomadic Bedouins. The spread of Islam would have been much more challenging if this had not been the case.

Despite linguistic and ethnic unity, the Arabs possessed no real political organization or formal government structures by the time of the Prophet Muhammad, even in the more settled areas such as Mecca. There had been Arab kingdoms in previous centuries; however, these were mostly located on the fringes of Arab life and owed their very existence to propinquity to trade routes in the Greco-Roman world. There was the Nabatean kingdom of Petra, located in southern present-day Jordan, which the Romans took over in 106 CE. And there was the third-century kingdom of Palmyra (Tadmur), located at an oasis in the desert of present-day south-central Syria. It, too, was a Roman client-state and way station on the land route between the Mediterranean world and the Persian Gulf leading out toward the Indian Ocean. Both states derived much of their wealth from control of the caravan routes and were heavily influenced by the Greco-Roman culture. Today, both Palmyra (although heavily damaged by the Islamic State in the Syrian civil war in the past decade) and Petra are two of the most spectacular and well-preserved archeological sites in the Middle East, if not the world. There were also some fairly advanced kingdoms in the southernmost region of Arabia, in Uman (Oman) and Yaman (Yemen), going back centuries and dependent once again upon trade based on the spice route (such a frankincense) into the heartland of the Middle East as well as the Greco-Roman world. However, by the second half of the sixth century CE, these kingdoms had been conquered by Ethiopian (Abyssinian) and Persian invaders.

On the whole, organized kingdoms were of marginal importance to those living in Arabia. Rather, for most Arabs, the tribe was the largest grouping to which they owed allegiance. The members of a tribe were considered to be the descendants of a remote common ancestor of some repute, someone who was thought to be a hero or otherwise a standout figure, usually regaled in poems and stories over the many years. So significant was this fact that tribal affiliations formed the basis of each member's name. For instance, the descendants of a reputable Arab named Shammar would be the Banu Shammar, the sons of Shammar (depending upon the location and dialect, "Banu" is the plural of ibn, bin, or ben, meaning "son"). The name can also refer to a geographic location, such as a city or region. The last element in an Arab's name who belonged to this tribe (in order to be identified with that tribe) would be "al-Shammar." The Banu Shammar today is still one of the largest tribes in the Arab world, mostly located in Iraq, Syria, and in the Arabian Peninsula. It is unclear whether the tribal name Shammar is taken from an individual or a place—or perhaps a place named after a notable individual.

Tribes in Arabia varied in size, and most never acted together as a unit. Those tribes that were more settled, such as the **Quraysh** in Mecca, the one into which Muhammad was born, did possess a considerable degree of group solidarity relative to their nomadic counterparts. The individual Bedouin Arab identified much more so with his or her clan or family. A tribe was made up of a number of clans going back a few generations or so, but there was no set number of clans that composed a tribe. Most tribes, especially the more nomadic ones, lacked any common leadership, unity, or purpose. For the most part, it was the clan that acted together as a unit.

The condition of "un-government" in Arabia made the kinship system vital to the daily lives of the Arabs. In other words, the group with which an individual Arab identified, particularly the clan or family, was the logical response to the lack of a formal social or political system. Genealogy, therefore, was important in pre-Islamic Arabia, and every clan—certainly every tribe—had what in effect was a genealogist in order to determine membership. This is why totemism, the veneration of ancestors, was so prevalent as a central form of worship or loose belief system in Arabia.[3] Also safety, mostly through the threat of retaliation, was provided by kinsmen since there was not any kind of enforcement agency in this environment of un-government. Because of this, the obligations of kinship were vitally important and one could not really survive without adherence to the kinship system. One of Muhammad's primary challenges, therefore, was to shift the devotion to kin to that of Allah and the rest of the Islamic community, the **umma**, that is, the community of believers. It was nothing short of an attempted social revolution. In this, however, he—and his successors—were not entirely successful.

Leadership in pre-Islamic society was both elective and hereditary. The tribal chiefs or shaykhs were usually chosen from a ruling lineage or family within the tribe, but within that ruling family the leader would be chosen because he was the most able and effective rather than the oldest son of the previous shaykh. There was no primogeniture within the ruling lineage. But the power of the shaykh was fairly limited, more *primus inter pares* (first among equals) than anything else. The primary functions of the shaykh were the following: 1) find adequate grazing ground for flocks of sheep, goats, or camels; 2) to arbitrate disputes within the tribe; 3) defend the livestock and the wells; and 4) entertain and be generous to visitors. This is another problem Muhammad would encounter: he accrued much more power than any typical shaykh, and it was resented by some—and many more after he died, as we shall see. The successors were left to deal with this problem, for at least the Prophet had the extra legitimacy of being the Messenger of God.

In pastoral tribal societies there was not that much difference in wealth between the shaykhs and others in the tribe, since large flocks of livestock or sums of money really did not provide any value added, and they were difficult to protect to boot. What was valued most often was a reputation for wisdom, generosity, and courage. This brought much more power and influence than anything else. This is why the early sources in Islamic history tend to focus on individual acts rather than the macro picture of an event such as a battle. This is what was valued in Arabian society rather than the overall strategic layout, disposition of forces, or even the chronology of an event or series of events. The tribal shaykh really had no coercive power either, no praetorian guard. After a shaykh would, in effect, render an opinion by arbitrating a dispute, it would be the weight of public opinion that would compel tribal members to honor the shaykh's decision. If a tribal member did not follow the shaykh's opinion, he or she would soon find themselves exiled from the tribe and therefore outside of the protection of the kinship system, which could be a virtual death sentence. But apart from these informal strictures, Arabs were fiercely independent. This would be another challenge Muhammad and the early Muslims faced when trying to impose an entirely new social and political system onto Arab society.

SPOTLIGHT

Pre-Islamic Arab Poetry

The poetry that developed and existed for centuries in the Arabian Peninsula before the rise of Islam is an art form. It laid the foundation for all subsequent poetry in the Arab world. It influenced the shape and structure of the Quran and facilitated Quranic exegesis. It provided a shared common language among the Bedouin Arabs, whether nomadic or settled, in Arabia, which was comprised of many different Arabic dialects. Unfortunately, very little written historical evidence exists to give us clues to how Arabic poetry developed its metrical and thematic structures. Instead, we encounter the first known works at what is considered to be the fully developed height of Arab poetry in the 150 years prior to the rise of Islam.

Poetry in Arabia before the rise of Islam played an important role in Arab society. The poet (*shair*) was also the historian, propagandist, and soothsayer of a particular family/clan or tribe. The poet would often praise his tribe and lampoon other tribes, which seemed to be quite popular at the time. Arab poetry was recited, not written down, with particular rhythms and chanting, again practices that were reflected in the Quran (the word "quran" means "recitation"). There were reciters (*rawis*) who actually vocalized—recited—the poems for the poet, the rawis themselves often becoming poets with their own set of young reciters.

The ode or *qasidah* is considered by scholars to be one of the distinguishing elements of Arabic poetry. It consists of about 15–80 lines in a monorhyme structure. A qasidah typically encompasses three different themes: 1) the *nasib,* which is a story of a failed relationship and home; 2) the *fakhr*, which is praise for a particular tribe or individual; and 3) the *rahil*, which describes a journey of some sort into the desert, usually involving camels—the journey would often have a heroic nature to it. Qasidahs also recount individual exploits through anecdotes, or what are called *akhbar* (today this word means "news reports"), focusing on revenge and blood sacrifice as a rite of passage. Overall, these poems reflected the values that were important in pre-Islamic Bedouin life, such as courage, hospitality, loyalty, and wisdom.

The primary examples of pre-Islamic Arab poetry came down to us in anthologies that were collected in the eighth century CE. One is called the *Muallaqat*, meaning the "hung or suspended poems," as they were hung up for all to read, specifically in Mecca from golden threads in or on the **Kaaba**, the very center of Islam. This suggests that they were either hung at the Kaaba when it was a pre-Islamic shrine in Mecca or that the popularity of Arab poems continued into the early years of Islam. The other collection is known as the *Mufaddaliyat*, named after the person who compiled the poems between 762 and 784, al-Mufaddal ibn Muhammad ibn Yalah, who appears to have been charged to do so by the Abbasid Caliph al-Mansur. The Muallaqat is made up of 126 poems, many of which are complete, while others are in fragments. This collection is considered the foremost example of Arabic poetry at its height in the century and a half before Islam.

It must be mentioned that there are some who have challenged the authenticity of the pre-Islamic Arabic poems that have come down to us. For instance, the Egyptian writer Taha Husayn claimed in his 1925 book *Concerning Pre-Islamic Poetry* that it was fabricated after the rise of Islam and therefore reflected the life of Muslims and not pre-Islamic Arabs; however, most scholars reject this notion, while acknowledging that pre-Islamic poetry was often edited for content, supplemented, and even changed by some early Muslims. This may have to do with the fact that the subject matter of many pre-Islamic Arab poems, especially those having to do with love, family relations, and other indulgences, may have been deemed inappropriate for the devout Muslim. In some ways this poetry represented a way of life—tribal-based—and system of thought that was contrary to that which was praised and valued in the early Islamic community.

Regardless, as literature professor Kamal Abd al-Malek purports, pre-Islamic poems played a role akin to social media today, as a form of communication that shared (and shaped) thoughts and ideas across society.

A very short example of a pre-Islamic Arab poem is the following, written by the shair (poet) Malik ibn al-Rayb:

> I thought who would weep for me, and none did I find to mourn
> But only my sword, my spear, the best of Rudainah's store,
> And one friend, a sorrel steed, who goes forth with trailing rein
> To drink at the pool, since Death has left none to draw for him.

Antarah Ibn Shaddad al-Absi (Najd, Arabia, 525–615), pre-Islamic Arabian poet and warrior, painting on glass, Damascus, Syria.
Photo by DeAgostini/Getty Images

Sources: Sanni Amidu, "Perspectives in a Religious System: The Role and Status of Poetry in Islam," *Islamic Studies* 29, no. 4 (1990): 339–352; Ludwig W. Adamec, *Historical Dictionary of Islam* (Lanham, MD: Rowman & Littlefield, 2016); Charles James Lyall, compiler, *The Mufaddaliyat: An Anthology of Ancient Arabian Odes* (Oxford: Clarendon Press, 1921); James Kritzeck, *Anthology of Islamic Literature* (New York: Holt, Rinehart and Winston, 1964), pp. 52–53; Rym Ghazal, "Arabic Treasures: Why Al Muaallaqat Is One of the Most-Cherished Literary Treasures of the Arab World," The National, January 31, 2017, https://www.thenationalnews.com/arts-culture/arabic-treasures-why-al-muaallaqat-is-one-of-the-most-cherished-literary-treasures-of-the-arab-world-1.51043?videoId=5754807360001 (accessed April 4, 2021). Poem appears in Kritzeck, *Anthology of Islamic Literature*, p. 62.

Although the sources are few and far between, it is believed that most Arabs in Arabia were pagans in terms of religious belief or leanings.[4] There were many forms of this paganism, but it is thought that it was pretty basic, with the worship of local idols being most prevalent; however, "worship" might be too strong of a word. The local idols, many of which revolved around sacred stones of some sort, were probably viewed more like what we would call today good luck charms, as they seem to have demanded favors and gifts rather than some sort of formal worship or commitment. The desert life also seems to have been conducive to superstition. Anyone who has spent evenings alone in the vastness of the Arabian desert can attest to the haunting sounds and even images that certainly can fuel superstition, if not semi-divine thoughts and ideas. In reality, for the Bedouin Arab it was the attachment to the honor of both individual and kin that was more important than any deity or rudimentary religion. The ideals mentioned earlier of generosity, wisdom, courage, formed what has been called a tribal humanism, which provided the foundational elements of an Arabian belief system.

Monotheistic ideas, however, were not foreign to many Arabs prior to the rise of Islam. For those few Arabs who followed a formal religion, Christianity was by far the most popular. For instance, as we have seen, the Lakhmids were Nestorian Christians. In addition, Abyssinia (Ethiopia), allied with the Byzantines but primarily Monophysite Christians, crossed over into Arabia and ruled much of South Arabia up to and through Mecca between 530 and 575 CE. Certainly from this, Christian ideas permeated through parts of Arabia, especially in its southern and western edges, including a good part of the Hijaz region, which includes Islam's holy cities of Mecca and Medina (Yathrib). There were also apparently a group of Judaized Arabs living in Yathrib prior to and during most of the lifetime of the Prophet Muhammad. No doubt, however, the Judaism and Christianity practiced in the periphery in Arabia was more ambiguous than that practiced in Jerusalem, Rome, or Constantinople. In addition, the primary occupation of Meccans was trade, including involvement in regular trade caravans to Syria, where both on the way and back they passed through the rich Judeo-Christian setting of the Holy Land. Finally, there are also indications that Arabs themselves in some areas of Arabia developed indigenous monotheistic faiths— again, very rudimentary and unstructured, but revolving around a single or primary deity reflecting the environment in which they lived. The point of all of this is to suggest that Islam did not develop in a religious vacuum. There were preexisting belief systems practiced by at least some Arabs and certainly known to most Arabs in the area. So when Muhammad began his ministry in Mecca in 610 CE and later in Medina, the messages he received and relayed were not completely foreign or incomprehensible to most Arabs.

Usually when one thinks of the physical setting in which Islam arose, thoughts of deserts, oases, camels, and palm trees come to mind. Ironically, the generally accepted scholarly picture is that Islam did not arise in a nomadic or even agricultural setting. Instead, as one of Muhammad's preeminent biographers, W. Montgomery

Watt, conjectures, it emerged in an atmosphere of high commerce and began as a thoroughly urban religion.[5] According to Watt, "The essential situation out of which Islam arose was the conflict and contrast between the Meccans' nomadic outlook and the new material environment in which they found themselves."[6] This statement is basically talking about change—changing conditions in Meccan society that perhaps produced societal fissures or augmented the changing status of some families as opposed to others in the city. It was a combustible setting that produced a receptive environment for another Semitic salvation religion.[7]

This general description is ultimately the best educated guess of medieval Islamic scholars because of the relative lack of primary documents from the Arabs themselves at the time of the rise of Islam. Since there was no formal government of which to speak, there were no official records, such as tax records, or court historians, who even though they typically embellish stories to favor the court employing them, can still offer valuable insights. Even the Quran is text without context. It is not a story of the Prophet Muhammad and the early Muslims, which even if embellished, would contain seeds of truth. Scholars such as Watt employed a variety of means with which to paint a reasonable picture of the environment in which Islam arose and the life of the Prophet Muhammad. There were documents written down well after the fact that were based on the oral transmission of data and stories about early Islam. Typically, historians frown upon the unreliability of oral transmission; however, for a society whose network of communication was based on oral transmission, its people probably got pretty good at it. While one must approach such sources with a healthy skepticism, they should not be so easily dismissed. In addition, extrapolation from and interpolation of the Quran can provide some reasonable scenarios. For instance, according to Islamic tradition, if Muhammad received a revelation from Allah during his Medinan period having to do with some basic procedural practice in society, a scholar can ask what the nature of society in Medina was at that time that necessitated that particular revelation. By continually deconstructing relevant revelations, particularly the more pedantic ones, and then reconstructing the conditions that produced these revelations, one can begin to piece together a general picture. Having said this, there is still plenty of room for alternative interpretations. Patricia Crone's *Meccan Trade and the Rise of Islam*, for instance, basically stands on its head the generally accepted version of early Islam that is presented in this book, calling into question the very notion that there was any significant prophet or movement at the time.[8] The reader should know that this may not be the definitive story by any stretch of the imagination, but it is a reasonable one based on the fragments of contemporary accounts from inside and outside of Arabia as well as important elements of Islamic tradition compiled after the fact.

So what was this change that Watt's passage implies? It is believed that for at least a millennium prior to the rise of Islam, Arabia was an important highway of trade that defined the lives of many Arabs, especially those in more settled and strategically located communities, such as Mecca. Trade in Mecca was apparently also tied into religious practice. Mecca was a religious sanctuary (**haram**) before Islam, housing local deities commemorated by both locals and visitors who had come via trade caravans. In the conditions of un-government and frequent hostility and raiding (*razzia*) between tribes, it was necessary to have some neutral ground on which members of different groups could meet safely to trade, exchange goods, and settle disputes. No doubt there were times of the year where there was more concentrated activity than others based on weather and seasonal migrations. Also, ideas, information, poetry, and other aspects of Arabian life were shared at these gatherings. Markets emerged around the haram where the property of merchants would be protected.

Mecca was thought to be a haram, perhaps the most important one in the Hijaz; the tribe of Quraysh most likely became the guardians of the haram in the first half of the sixth century. Under the guidance of the Quraysh, Mecca appears to have grown substantially as a commercial center. The primary reason for this, we think, had to do with the shifting trade routes along the Mediterranean to Persian Gulf corridor, the same corridor that sustained places like Petra and Palmyra. The trade routes shifted in the second half of the sixth century and into the seventh century due to the almost constant state of war between the Byzantines and the Sassanians in the heartland of the Middle East. Traders like stability. This way they know their goods can be safely transported. If there is instability, such as war or lack of centralized government control, traders can lose caravans or portions of caravans to raiders and therefore in order to reduce the possibility of this happening they have to provide more protection for these caravans. All of this costs money, and passing this cost onto potential customers makes their products less attractive.

As a result, the trade routes tended to shift down around the Arabian Peninsula and up through the Red Sea, where a place such as Mecca was strategically situated to reap the benefits of more trade coming its way. Over time, this increased commerce changed the socioeconomic setting in Mecca, where some clans benefitted much more than others—conditions that would cause societal fissures, especially among those clans who were the have-nots, or even the nearly-hads, which in the end may be even more frustrating. These changing socioeconomic conditions created the facilitating environment for a new belief system that focused more on spiritual rather than material satisfaction, which must have been music to the ears of those who felt dispossessed or disenfranchised.

The prosperity of Mecca—and of those clans who benefitted the most from the increased commerce—depended on the trade fairs connected with the religious sanctuary in the city. If someone or some movement came along that challenged the validity of the haram, if not the whole sociopolitical system on which it was based, the status quo powers that be would be none too happy as their position in the city would be jeopardized. This seems to be a plausible scenario that produced Muhammad's religious mission and the rise of Islam in Mecca.

Life of the Prophet Muhammad

No cask without an end stave or a head
E'er gaped so wide as the one shade I beheld
Cloven from chin to where the wind is voided
Between his legs his entrails hung in coils;
The vitals were exposed to view, and too
That sorry paunch that changes food to filth
While I stood there watching him
He looked at me and stretched his breast apart,
Saying: "Behold, how I split myself!
Behold, how mutilated is Mahomet!
In front of me the weeping Ali goes,
His face cleft through from forelock to the chin;
And all the others that you see about
Fomenters were of discord and schism;
And that is why they are so gashed asunder."

—Dante's *Inferno*, Canto 28

In explaining this passage, Harvard Divinity School Professor Harvey Cox writes how Dante places Muhammad in that "circle of hell stained by the sin" of being a schismatic, that is, from Christianity. Cox adds that "as a schismatic," according to Dante, "Muhammad's fitting punishment is to be eternally chopped in half from his chin to his anus, spilling entrails and excrement at the door of Satan's stronghold. His loyal disciple Ali, whose sins of division were presumably on a lesser scale, is sliced only from forelock to chin."[9]

Obviously, this is about as negative a depiction as one could write about anyone, but Dante was a product of his time and place. It is not a surprise that this characterization was written in the early 1300s (completed in 1320), so soon after the last Crusaders in the Holy Land had retreated back to Europe. As we shall see later in the book, the Crusades in the Middle East fanned misperceptions, mischaracterizations, and animus. After all, one doesn't write nice things about one's presumed enemy. What Dante wrote was a kind of culmination of a process that in many ways reflected the parameters for the Christian view of Muhammad and Islam for centuries, even to the present day in some quarters.

Yet some years ago, I was strolling through a bookstore and came across a book by a noted historian. Frankly, I forget the title of the book and even which noted historian wrote it, but it was a volume that listed the hundred most influential people in human history. Number one was Muhammad. For good measure, number two was Confucius and three was Jesus Christ. Now one can argue ad nauseam who should be number one, two, or three; it's akin to trying to determine whether Babe Ruth, Muhammad Ali, Michael Jordan, or someone else is the most influential athlete in American history. The point here is that regardless of any evaluative judgment about the Prophet Muhammad, it is safe to say he is one of the most influential people in human history. The Messenger of Allah, the progenitor of what is today the second largest organized religion in the world, certainly would be.

Having said this, we are faced with the same problem described in the last section regarding the dearth of primary source material. We are not even 100 percent certain Muhammad existed, although it is highly likely he did. One can find similar questions and doubts raised about Jesus Christ as well as a number of other prophets in the traditions of many religions. As mentioned, the Quran is really not much help other than through extrapolation and interpolation. It is the Word of God, not the story of Muhammad. It is not even organized chronologically, as it was compiled in a manner to facilitate memorization, especially for chanting; the longest passages in the Quran are at the beginning, when chronologically they probably were revealed to Muhammad during the last ten years of his life, the Medinan period. The shortest passages, on the other hand, were most likely revealed during his time in Mecca, yet they appear at the end of the Holy Book. The Quran is, however, helpful in terms of giving an indication on how the first Muslims saw themselves and saw themselves in relation to others—that is, as a social memory.

According to Islamic tradition, Muhammad was born into the clan of Hashim (**Hashimites**) in the tribe of Quraysh. There are some famous Hashimites today who trace their lineage back to the family of the Prophet, such as the king of Jordan (Hashimite Kingdom of Jordan) and the king of Morocco. It seems the family of Hashim at the time of the birth of the Prophet in 570 was a middling clan at best in Mecca, not one of the more powerful ones such as the Abd Shams (from whom emerged the Umayyads), which was probably the most dominant clan into Muhammad's adulthood.

Muhammad's grandfather was Abd al-Mutallib, who had four sons: al-Abbas (the namesake for the Abbasids), Abu Talib (Ali's father), Abu Lahab, and Abdullah (Muhammad's father). It was into this family that Muhammad ibn Abdullah ibn Abd al-Mutallib ibn Hashim was born. According to Islamic tradition, Muhammad had a difficult childhood, as his father died even before he was born, and he became an orphan when his mother died when he was six. Eventually his uncle, Abu Talib, took Muhammad in, assuring his upbringing and providing him protection; however, orphans were treated as outcasts in pre-Islamic Arabian society, so it is something Muhammad had to overcome as he grew older. It also may be why Islam is particularly sympathetic to orphans. But overcome them he did, as, like most able-bodied Meccans, Muhammad engaged in a life of trade and commerce, apparently even going on some trade caravans to Syria. He also acquired the reputation as a wise arbitrator, a skill of great value in pre-Islamic Arab life.

In or around 596 CE, Muhammad married a Meccan woman by the name of Khadija. She was a fairly wealthy Qurashyi widow, who according to Islamic tradition was fifteen years older than Muhammad, but she was likely only a few years his elder.[10] Interestingly, she employed him as her business manager, and *she* asked *him* to marry her. She had been married twice previously, one marriage ending in widowhood and the other either through widowhood or divorce. Muhammad and Khadija had five or six children, including their daughter, Fatima, who was the only one to survive and whose descendants would prove to be quite influential in Islamic history; there were no surviving male children, as they died very young, something not unusual in the harsh conditions of Arabia at the time. This would prove to be somewhat problematic when Muhammad died. The story of Khadija and Muhammad belies the common trope to this day that depicts Muslim women as passive, subservient, and subject to widespread misogyny. She was known to be—and, maybe more importantly, depicted—as a woman who was strong, smart, independent, and acquired considerable standing in Mecca. Some sayings or *hadiths* attributed to the Prophet seem to also paint a different picture: "Of worldly things, women and perfume are dearest to me"; and, "All people are equal as teeth of a comb. There is no claim of merit of an Arab over a non-Arab, or of a white over a black, or of a male over a female. Only God-fearing people will merit a preference with God."

It appears the emancipation of women in pre-Islamic society was very important to Muhammad, and women were fully involved in the umma from day one. Yes, Islamic society, as many others, was and remains a patriarchal one, but the position of women greatly improved with the establishment of the new Islamic rules and regulations. In pre-Islamic Arabia tribesmen "stigmatized womanhood and considered all things feminine to be weak, fragile, and generally inferior; a father who had daughters but no sons was called childless . . . and some even buried their infant daughters . . . having gotten rid of the shame of having fathered a girl."[11] It is important to remember that there is no widespread segregation or separation ordained in the Quran. These things evolved organically as a cultural development in a few parts of the Islamic world. There is also nothing specifically said about veiling or other aspects of female dress—it is vague at best and subject to interpretation. Veiling was actually a cultural adaptation copied from upper-class Byzantine and Sassanian women in urban areas. Islam, by Quranic prescription, was the first major religio-political system to recognize the existence of a judicial identity for women, long before it occurred elsewhere. It gave women the right of inheritance and divorce centuries before these rights were accorded to women in the West.

SPOTLIGHT

Veiling and Women in Islam

According to Quranic scripture, Muslim men and women are enjoined to dress modestly. The extent to which one should do so, especially with women, has been subjected to interpretation, reinterpretation, and controversy over the centuries, especially in relation to determining one's *awrah*, or that which is too shameful to be exposed publicly. This has been particularly the case in the twentieth and twenty-first centuries, where feminist movements in and outside of the Middle East have often viewed the *niqab* (face veil), *hijab* or *khimar* (head scarf), and *burka* or *chador* (full body length garment) as overt representations of the subordination and subjugation of women in Islamic societies. Even the terms used to describe these coverings are interpreted differently. Most scholars believe that *hijab*, mentioned in the Quran, was simply a reference to a curtain used to separate the Prophet Muhammad from his wives when visiting delegations met with him in Medina. Then there are different prescriptions for what exactly women should wear (or what should be covered up) in and outside the home, with family, friends, and strangers, and among fellow Muslims and non-Muslims. Most often these differences were and are due to local sociocultural norms and customs that developed over the years, as well as juridical decisions by religious scholars of the Quran and the Hadith.

Veiling did not begin with Islam. It has a long history going back to the various Persian empires that predated Islam as well as the Roman/Byzantine empire. The veil came to Arabia via contacts and trade with Syria and Iraq/Iran, where only the elite classes in Roman/Christian and Iranian cultures wore the veil; there has always been a hierarchical or class element regarding who should be wearing what. Some scholars believe that the hijab was only meant to protect the inviolability of Muhammad's wives and that no other Muslim women during the Prophet's lifetime wore head coverings; therefore, on religious grounds, veiling and head covering should not be compulsory. Other scholars believe that these views are seen through a contemporary lens and ignore carefully established precedent through the centuries that have detailed, if not ordained, various head and body coverings for Muslim women.

Depending on preference, state law, or social pressures and mores, Muslim women wear a variety of coverings—among those who choose to do so. Some "take the veil" (*darabat al-hijab*) to follow what they believe are the dress admonitions of modesty in the Quran and hadith. Others do it to be in accordance with state law, as in Iran, and are subjected to ill treatment by omnipresent morality police who bring those skirting (or tempting the boundaries of) the dress codes back into accordance with the law. Still others are following social convention, especially in the last 30–40 years, when a more conservative and traditional interpretation of covering has risen in popularity in many Muslim societies. This is more of the practical necessity argument, that they must conform to certain societal pressures in order to go to school, go to work, or enjoy life outside of the home. This way they can do so without being subjected to direct or indirect harassment or some other expressed form of disapproval. The growth of Islamist movements in general across much of the Middle East during this time period has in part fueled the decision by many more Muslim women to cover to some degree in public. Finally, there is a feminist argument for veiling, that it is actually freeing in the sense that women do not become sex objects and are not solely judged on appearance. In this way, people judge women on what is inside their heads and the nature of their personalities rather than what dress, jewelry, or make-up they are wearing.

Veiling has also become a sociopolitical issue in modern, secular states in Europe. France was the first European country in 2010 to ban the niqab in public, and a number of other countries in Europe have followed suit, usually with fines for violations. The variety of interpretations on the subject can be seen in a law passed by the Netherlands in 2019 that allowed the niqab on streets but banned it in educational and public institutions, hospitals, and in public transport. Whatever the case in the modern era, the wearing of the veil (and other coverings) has become a lightning rod in assessing the position of Muslim women and what type of freedoms they can and should enjoy as well as the nature of the societies in which they live.

A combination of pictures shows women wearing various coverings in Algiers, 2010.
REUTERS/Alamy Stock Photo

Sources: Leila Ahmed, *Women and Gender in Islam: Historical Roots of a Modern Debate* (New Haven, CT: Yale University Press, 1992); "Veiling and the Hijab," The Feminist Sexual Ethics Project, Brandeis University, https://www.brandeis.edu/projects/fse/muslim/veil.html, accessed January 18, 2022.

It is probably in 610, during the month of Ramadan, that Muhammad received the first of many revelations from Allah through the archangel Gabriel, the compendium of which would later be incorporated into the Quran. His early revelations tended to stress the glory and majesty of God, his mercy and generosity, the importance of doing good, the obligations of the rich to the poor, and the inevitability of the Day of Judgment. These revelations tended to be fairly dramatic and shorter in length. Within about a year after he received his first revelation, Muhammad began preaching, most likely to his family and friends first. He called on people to acknowledge the glory of God and prepare for the Last Day. This is certainly a common apocalyptic vision of prophets, of which there were many in the Middle East. They were there to call for social justice and warn the people to get their act together, repent, and do good before the end of times, which could be at any moment, in a few weeks, years, or decades. Usually there was an urgency to the message because typically the Day of Judgment was seen to be just around the corner.

William McNeill and Marilyn Waldman do a good job in their anthology of documents, *The Islamic World*, to separate the revelations into stages, befitting the changing role of Muhammad as well as the evolution of this nascent Islamic community.[12] The first stage encompassed the glory of God and the Day of Judgment. The second stage, probably also during the Meccan period but perhaps leaking into the Medinan period, were revelations that seemed to situate Islam more within its Judeo-Christian environment, the possible reasons for which will be described shortly. The final, third stage dealt primarily with establishing the rules and regulations of this new community—in other words, organizing the umma. These revelations tended to be longer and much more pedantic than earlier ones. This took place exclusively while Muhammad was in Medina. It is in Medina that what was in essence a religious cult in Mecca developed into a burgeoning state.

Khadija was Muhammad's first convert, followed by those close to him, including two slaves, Zayd and Bilal, as well as his cousin and future son-in-law (by Fatima), Ali ibn Abi Talib, who may be only second to the Prophet in terms of influence in Islamic history. Abu Bakr was an early convert as well, and he would become the first caliph, or successor, to the Prophet. Unusually at this early stage, Abu Bakr was from a different clan within Quraysh; however, most of the early converts were young men from the Hashimite clan. It was a pietistic movement at first, committed to living a righteous life amid sinfulness.[13] These first converts were expected to submit or surrender to Allah. This is the meaning of the verbal noun, "Islam," and "Muslim" is simply the active participle of that verbal noun, "someone who submits." Most Meccans, however, even within his clan, did not accept the validity of Muhammad's teachings; his family at this early stage probably just saw him as something of an embarrassment more than anything else. Others, perhaps, saw him as possessed by demons at worst or delusional at best. Because of this, there really was not much opposition to Muhammad at first because he was not yet seen as a threat.

But as the revelations became more specific and as he acquired more converts, the status quo elements in Mecca began to take notice. Any sort of monotheistic message, along with Muhammad's role as the Messenger of God, threatened the status of the haram and therefore the economic standing of those clans that benefitted the most from that status. As it turned out, Abu Sufyan, a leading figure in Mecca from the Umayyad clan, emerged as the leader of the opposition to Muhammad and the first Muslims.

There are three indications during the Meccan period that appear to confirm this rising opposition to the Muslims. At one point, Muhammad introduced what came to be called the "Satanic Verses." These were revelations that gave secondary status to some local deities, even though they were clearly subordinate to Allah. Muhammad soon recognized that he had been led astray, and that these were revelations from Satan and not Allah; they were later repudiated, confirming that Allah was the only God and that idols had no place in Islam. In retrospect, however, this could be seen as an attempt to assuage the local population by giving their idols some status, recognizing that rejecting them altogether was producing an uncomfortable level of opposition.

Also, most likely during the Meccan period, Muhammad began to receive messages that placed Islam more in line with Judaism and Christianity, which is the second stage of revelations. There could be many reasons for this, one of which is that Islam does not hide from its Jewish and Christian heritage. It is viewed as simply a natural evolution out of its previous Judeo-Christian milieu, correcting the mistakes that Jews and Christians are seen to have made in their own interpretations and practice of revelation. In this sense, then, bringing Islam more in line with these two other Semitic religions was to be expected at some point. However, by identifying Islam as an Abrahamic religion wherein Allah is the same God that Jews and Christians pray to and worship, and stating that Muhammad is the Seal of the Prophets, the last in a line going back to the prophets of the Old and New Testaments, such as Noah, Abraham, Moses, and Jesus, this could be interpreted as an attempt to make Islam more legitimate and acceptable to a population in Mecca that probably did have some awareness of both Judaism and Christianity.

Finally, around 615, a number of Muslims left Mecca and traveled to Ethiopia. Again, there could be a various reasons for this, one perhaps simply being an attempt to proselytize and spread the new faith to a people who were somewhat familiar to them from the time of Ethiopian rule in South Arabia. Surely, the Meccans had established some sort of network with Ethiopians in a way that was familiar to the Muslims; after all, the Ethiopians were monotheists as well, albeit Monophysite Christian. Perhaps the Muslims were seeking allies to help them offset the increasing opposition they were encountering in Mecca. It could also be that because of the more dangerous environment, Muhammad wanted to make sure the umma continued on somewhere if it was extinguished in his home city.

The most critical point for Muhammad to date, however, came in 619 when both Khadija died as well as Abu Talib, who as head of the clan protected the

Prophet. The Prophet called it his "year of grief." Abu Lahab became head of the clan, and he was not prepared to afford Muhammad the same level of protection. It is in this precarious position for Muhammad and the Muslims in Mecca that they prepared to make the migration or **Hijra** to Medina (Yathrib), located along the caravan route some 200 miles to the north.

What would become Medinat al-Nabi (City of the Prophet, or just Medina), Yathrib was an oasis town that was divided into two main tribes, the Aws and the Khazraj. In addition, there were three smaller tribes of Judaized Arabs: the Banu Qurayza, Banu Nadir, and Banu Qaynuqa. Apparently, the Aws and Khazraj had been feuding for years, so it was clearly a community in need of some mediation to put an end to the continuous conflict. Ideally, this arbitrator should come from outside of Medina in order to be acceptable to all sides. Enter Muhammad, who was helped by the fact that his clan may have had some distant relations with both tribes. Additionally, Medinans kind of thought of themselves as the stepsisters of Mecca, so any group the Meccans did not like was probably immediately looked upon with favor by the Medinans. And anything to annoy the Meccans, such as taking in the Muslims, was no doubt an attractive proposition. In any event, the Medinans obviously rode the right horse, for the city would indeed supersede Mecca, at least politically, soon enough. Amid increasing danger to the Prophet, the Muslims made careful preparations to move to Medina, which they did, some seventy in all, in 622. Those who made the Hijra were known as the **Muhajirun**, an exalted group throughout Islamic history. Muhammad and Abu Bakr were the last to depart.

The Prophet's Mosque at sunset, Medina, Saudi Arabia, July 12, 2014.
Ahmad Mortaja/Alamy Stock Photo

The Hijra was a major turning point in Islamic history, maybe the single most important event—so much so that the Islamic calendar begins with the Hijra. Everything changed, including the role of Muhammad. Until now, he had been just the religious leader of the umma. Upon the move to Medina, while still the Messenger of God, he also became the political and military leader. As such, Muhammad's power and authority increased dramatically. For the Muslims themselves, they could now practice their faith with an openness and safety that eluded them in Mecca. But by leaving Mecca they abandoned their tribal ties to the pre-Islamic kinship system. Now they were in the hands of and owed their allegiance to Allah and the umma.

With this a new form of social organization was needed, the basis of which was the so-called Five Pillars of Islam (*arkan al-Islam*). These are the five basic duties expected of every Muslim during the course of their lifetime. Although there is no formal entrance into the religion such as that which exists with the sacrament of baptism in Christianity, it would seem natural that the first is the **shahada**, bearing witness to God by saying, "There is no God but God [Allah], and Muhammad is his Messenger." This affirms the uncompromising monotheism of Islam and the role of the Prophet, although the latter portion of the shahada regarding Muhammad may have been inserted later during the Umayyad caliphate. The second pillar, **zakat**, is giving alms to the poor as a kind of purification of the soul, and in a number of Muslim societies it became an obligatory tax. Next is **salat**, or prayers, eventually settled on as five times a day (sunrise, noon, mid-afternoon, sunset, and evening), with the Friday noon prayer being a communal one when Muslims are encouraged to pray in a mosque with their fellow Muslims. Then there is **sawm,** the act of fasting during the ninth month of the Islamic calendar, **Ramadan**, the month, according to Islamic tradition, that Muhammad received his first revelation from Allah. As is the case with fasting in other religions, it is an act of spiritual renewal through self-denial while also putting you in a position to empathize with the poor. (Alms-giving is particularly prevalent during Ramadan.) Finally, there is the **hajj** to the Grand Mosque in Mecca, the center of Islam, that Muslims are enjoined to do at least once in their lifetime if they are able to do so. The Five Pillars helped bind the community together through collective religious rituals. Some Muslims may think one pillar is more important than others, or as one early Muslim leader was quoted as saying, "prayer carries us halfway to God, fasting brings us to the door of His praises, alms-giving procures for us admission."

At first, the Muhajirun were quartered in the homes of those Medinans who welcomed them, the latter known as the **Ansar** or Helpers, another important early group in Islamic history. But not everyone in Medina accepted Muhammad or the Muslims. One of the first things Muhammad had to do following the Hijra was to develop his authority in Medina, something that would take almost the remaining decade of his life to completely accomplish. But his primary objective was to take Mecca. Doing so would provide the bona fides for establishing his unquestioned authority and working out the rules and regulations of the community through the construction of a new social and political system. To take Mecca necessitated attracting as many allies as possible from surrounding tribes, because he would not be able to do it alone. But Mecca, indeed, had to fall. This was only practical because Mecca was the major prize in the region. Not conquering Mecca would be like trying to take New York state without taking New York City. For the Islamic movement to continue and grow, it needed the expertise, resources, and manpower of Mecca; otherwise, Islam would have remained a minor cult in a secondary city that probably would have faded into oblivion once Muhammad died. Furthermore, it was probably during the Medinan period that the haram in Mecca was identified through revelation as an Abrahamic shrine (*Kaaba*) that had been founded by Abraham and his son, Ismail (Ishmael), but it had been desecrated by idolaters for centuries. It was now the center of Islam, so it was imperative that it be taken. Until then, Muslims had recited their daily prayers in the direction (**qibla**) of Jerusalem, clearly revealing Islam's intimate relationship with Judeo-Christian heritage. The Prophet also needed to provide for his followers as well as attract new recruits, and what better way to do so than to successfully take on Mecca? Finally, it is important not to minimize the religious motivation during this volcanic period of the revolution. This was a very evangelical stage of the movement, so many Muslims must have been worried about the souls of their families and tribe they left behind in Mecca. Taking it therefore not only had a practical side to it, but also the Muslims wanted to save it by converting the pagans and eradicating sinfulness.

Muhammad seems to have begun the struggle against Mecca almost immediately, but Medina was not yet ready to attack it head-on. Instead, through raiding, the Muslims targeted the trade caravans that were the life-blood of Mecca. By doing so, they could diminish the commerce on which Mecca depended while also providing for his followers from the loot taken and the ransom paid for those who were captured. After several failed attempts—the Meccans were clearly aware of the potential danger Medina posed and beefed up security—the Muslims, in what was surely seen as an act of divine deliverance, successfully raided a Meccan caravan in 624 near the wells just outside Medina in the Battle of Badr. It came none too soon for Muhammad, because many of the doubters in Medina (the so-called Hypocrites or **munafiqun**) were beginning to more vocally voice their opposition to the Prophet. This victory by no means eliminated the Meccan threat, but it solved some of Muhammad's more immediate problems for the time being.

There were two more significant battles between the Meccans and Medinans. The first, about a year after Badr, was at Uhud, an agricultural field just outside of Medina, but it proved to be indecisive for both sides. Finally, in 627 in the Battle of the Khandaq (Trench), Mecca again marched on Medina; this time, the Medinans built a trench around the city to protect themselves from the Meccan cavalry.

After a few weeks of insults traded back and forth and a few small fights that broke out, the Meccans were forced to retreat. It seemed the Muslims in Medina were there to stay, and they could not be dislodged by Mecca.

At this point, I want to briefly address a very controversial subject: the Muslims' violent expulsion of all three of the Judaized Arab tribes in Medina, one after each of the three battles. As one can imagine, this has become periodic fodder on each side of the divide between Muslims and Jews, especially in modern times when otherwise what was often a cooperative and mutually reinforcing relationship over the centuries has been exacerbated by the Arab–Israeli conflict. At a practical level, the Jews in Medina could not accept Muhammad as political leader without accepting his position as the Messenger of God. This was not possible. The Jews were constantly seen by the Muslims as a potential fifth column, and Islamic tradition records attempts by the Meccans to subvert the Muslims in Medina through the Jewish tribes. As such, their expulsion, to Muhammad, was a strategic decision. And this is an important distinction. Muhammad was the political and military leader in Medina in addition to being the religious leader, so he had to make tough decisions that resulted in death and destruction. Too often in Western narratives about Muhammad, even into the twenty-first century, there has been a tendency to equate Muhammad's role with that of Jesus, to the point of even calling the religion Muhammadanism rather than Islam or Muhammadans rather than Muslims (in the manner of Christ, Christianity, and Christians).

But Muhammad, while certainly being seen throughout Islamic history as the perfect Muslim, was not viewed as—nor did he ever claim to be—divine. Indeed, there are groups of Muslims to this day who will passionately oppose any attempt to deify the Prophet. He was human, with human decisions to make and with human frailties. His role is more akin to Moses in the Jewish tradition rather than that of a sinless divine entity, such as the Son of God; the Islamic and Jewish traditions are much closer to each other theologically and juridically than either are to Christianity. There is also some indication that the whole affair with the Jewish tribes in Medina was an ex post facto insertion by Muslim sources into the Islamic tradition to confirm and amplify the distinctiveness of Islam from its Judeo-Christian roots. This is not unusual; after all, Christian apologists, evident especially in the Gospel of John, went to great lengths to separate an emerging Christianity from what was in its early stage simply a Christian variant of Judaism. In addition, Islam from the beginning always regarded Jews and Christians as wayward cousins. As such, they are to be protected peoples (*dhimmis*) and are seen as People of the Book (**ahl al-kitab**), people of previous revelation as told in the Old and New Testaments. Given all of this, if it happened at all, it is highly unlikely that Muhammad acted as he did based on purely religious grounds, so it is a shame that this episode has been utilized by both Jews and Muslims in recent history to support inimical agendas.

Through diplomacy more so than force, over the next two years after Khandaq, Muhammad was able to acquire a number of allies throughout Arabia, and by 629 he felt secure enough to attempt to make the hajj to Mecca. He was not able to do so on this occasion as he was forestalled by the Meccans, but an impractical truce between the two sides was worked out (the Treaty of *Hudaybiyya*). It did show, however, that the two sides were now negotiating rather than fighting. The Muslims did seem to have the upper hand. Many Meccans who saw the writing on the wall were willing to compromise, including the head of the Umayyad clan, Abu Sufyan, and two of the leading Meccan military commanders, who would become two of the foremost military leaders during the Islamic conquests, Khalid ibn al-Walid and Amr ibn al-As, after both converted to Islam. With opposition melting away, in 630 Muhammad led an impressive force (Islamic tradition says 10,000) and marched on Mecca. There was very little resistance or violence. In turn, Muhammad was extremely conciliatory. He was not out to destroy Mecca, but to incorporate it (or even save it from sinfulness) because he needed the Meccan elite to get on board, many of whom believed that power and leadership should accrue to them despite having opposed the Prophet. Some Muslims, particularly the Ansar of Medina, wanted to level Mecca. One can thus see some of the latent tensions here between the Ansar and the so-called Meccan elite (such as the Umayyads) that foreshadowed outright animosity after Muhammad died. To mollify the Ansar, who, with Mecca being the center of Islam now, were worried about their position, Muhammad decided to spend the remaining two years of his life in Medina, which effectively became the political capital of this new Muslim state. The Ansar could stomach the preeminence of the Muhajirun, but not the Johnny-come-lately Meccans.

It is a good thing Mecca was taken relatively peacefully. Within weeks there was an attack by a tribal confederation called the al-Thaqif from al-Taif, just south of Mecca, who mistakenly thought the Meccans were in disarray and a weakened condition. The Muslims were victorious in the Battle of Hunayn. The Thaqifis subsequently converted to Islam and would become notable in their own right in the Islamic conquests, especially against the Sassanians. By the end of Muhammad's life in 632, the Prophet had secured a measure of acknowledgment throughout most of the Arabian Peninsula. As events would soon show, however, it is unclear just how much these new converts really acknowledged the authority of Medina and how deeply held their Islam was. Some perhaps converted for the sake of expediency, either for economic or political reasons rather than religious commitment.

Muhammad made one last pilgrimage to Mecca in 632, called the Farewell Pilgrimage in Islamic tradition, which would hereinafter define the proper procedures for the hajj. A short time later upon returning to Medina, Muhammad became ill, while Abu Bakr led the umma in prayer in his place. He died a few days later in the home of his most influential wife, Aisha, who was a daughter of Abu Bakr's.

Muslim pilgrims circle the Kaaba and pray at the Grand Mosque ahead of the annual hajj pilgrimage in the holy city of Mecca, Saudi Arabia, August 2018.
REUTERS/Alamy Stock Photo

The umma had no parallels in Arab society, nor did Muhammad's status as the Prophet, his power having become vastly greater than any tribal leader. Another major difference with exclusive pre-Islamic religious cults, at least in theory, was Islam's universality. Anybody could join, and this aspect of Islam certainly accounted for much of its dynamism and attractiveness. Although Muhammad was not divine, as stated earlier, those who followed Muhammad's ways would surely live a blessed life. The way he lived was collectively known as the **Sunna**, the custom or tradition of the Prophet, from where the term "Sunni" is derived, today by far the largest sect in Islam. The sayings or *hadith* of the Prophet would be vetted through a chain of transmission (*isnad*) and compiled in written form a couple of centuries later, and as such were a kind of documentation of the Sunna. Together with the Quran as well as centuries of Islamic jurisprudence, the Sunna of the Prophet laid the foundation for almost every aspect of a Muslim's life, incorporated in various interpretations over the years into Islamic law, or *Sharia* (literally , "the path leading to the watering place").

Muhammad created a new basis for society. Religious excellence rather than wealth or breeding defined the elite class—in theory. However, as mentioned earlier, there were a number of underlying tensions in the umma and unanswered questions, first and foremost of which was who should succeed Muhammad and what type of power should this person have.

Chapter 2 Timeline

330–1453	Byzantine Empire, also known as the Eastern Roman Empire
224–651	Sassanian Empire
570	Generally accepted year of the birth of the Prophet Muhammad
596	Marriage of Muhammad and Khadija
610	According to Islamic tradition, the year Muhammad received the first revelations from Allah via the Archangel Gabriel
622	The Prophet makes the Hijra or emigration to Medina (Yathrib) along with seventy of his followers (Muhajirun). It also marks the first year of the Islamic calendar.
624	Battle of Badr
627	Battle of the Khandaq (Trench)
630	Muhammad and his followers take Mecca
632	Muhammad makes Farewell Pilgrimage and dies shortly afterward

Primary Sources

Thâbit: The Death of the Knight Rabia, Called Boy Longlocks

Rabia espied far way the stir of dust. Ride on fast! said he to the womenfolk with him; this is no friendly troop that follows us, I fear. Keep straight to the road; I will wait here till the dust clear and I spy who they be. If I see cause to fear aught for you women, I'll fall on them in yonder covert of trees, and draw them away from the road. We'll meet again at the Pass of Ghazal, or Usfan in Kadid; or if I do not meet you there, at least you will have won to our own country.

He mounted his mare, and rode back toward the dust. He shewed himself to the pursuers riding forth from the trees, as they were searching the tracks of his company; and when they saw him, they came on against him in a body, taking it for sure the women were beyond him. Now Longlocks was a famous archer; and he began to ply his arrows, till he had slain and disabled a good few men. So having given them something to do, he spurred his mare after the fleeing women; and when he came up with them bade press on faster still. But the clansmen of Sulaym followed him up; so he turned a second time to encounter them. And so he continued, urging on the women and turning to face his enemies, until his arrows all were spent. They won to the country of Kadid even as the sun was sinking.

But the horses black with sweat followed fast behind, and the riders in hate and rage, feverish for revenge. Then he turned once more, with spear and sword, and did great slaughter among them. But here Nubaysha son of Habib bore down on him and thrust him through with his lance. That thrust stopped him.

I have slain him! Nubaysha cried.

Thy mouth lies, Nubaysha, said Rabia. But Nubaysha smelt at the blade of his lance, and said: Thou art the liar; I surely smell the smell of thy vitals!

At this Rabia turned his mare, and galloped in spite of his wound until he came up with the women, in the mouth of the Pass of Ghazal. He cried to his mother: Drink! Give me to drink!

O my son! she answered him; if I give thee any drink, thou'lt die straightway, even here in this place; and we shall be taken. Endure then—we may escape them yet.

So: Bind up my wound, then, he said. She bound it with her veil; and while she worked he spoke a verse:

Bind the binding on me fast!
Ye lose a knight like burning gold:
A hawk who drove a troop like birds,
And stooped, and struck forehand and back.

His mother answered:

We are of Malik's stock, and Tha'laba's,
We are the world's tale without end.
Our folk fall, man after man;
Our life is loss, day after day.

Now go; and while thy strength lasts, smite!

So he turned back to face them once again, at the head of the pass, while the women hurried on with all the speed they might. Longlocks sat upright on his mare, barring the road; and when he felt his death coming on him, he stayed himself upon his spear; so he stood in the twilight. When the men of Sulaym descried him there, still sitting his mare, they flinched from another onset, and halted a long while, thinking not but that he was still a living man. At last Nubaysha, watching him steadily, said: His head droops on his neck! Yon's a dead man, I swear!

He bade a clansman of Khuza'a who rode with them shoot an arrow at the mare. The man shot; and the mare shied. Right forward on his face Boy Longlocks fell. So they came up and spoiled his body. But they were afraid to follow the women any further; for by this time they must be safe home, near the dwellings of their own people. A man of Sulaym rode close.

Thou foughtest for thy women in life and death both! he said; and so saying thrust the heel of his lance into Rabia's eye.

Source: from *Muhammad's People: A Tale by Anthology*, by Eric Schroeder (Portland, ME: The Bond Wheelwright Company, 1955, pp. 7–9).

Surah Al-Fatiha (The Opening)

Revealed at Mecca

1. In the name of God, the beneficent, the merciful.
2. Praise be to God, Lord of the worlds,
3. The beneficent, the merciful.
4. Owner of the day of judgment,
5. You (alone) do we worship; You (alone) do we ask for help.
6. Show us the straight path,
7. The path of those whom You have favored; not the (path) of those who earn Your anger nor of those who go astray.

Source: McAuliffe, Jane, ed. "Al-Fatiha." *The Qur'an*. New York: W. W. Norton & Company, Inc. 2017. Pg. 3.

Surah LXXV, The Resurrection

In the Name of God, the Merciful, the Compassionate
No! I swear by the Day of Resurrection.
No! I swear by the reproachful soul.
What, does man reckon We shall not gather his bones?
Yes indeed; We are able to shape again his fingers,
Nay, but man desires to continue on as a libertine,
asking, "When shall be the Day of Resurrection?"[1]
But when the sight is dazed
and the moon is eclipsed,
and the sun and moon are brought together,
upon that day man shall say, "Whither to flee?"
No indeed; not a refuge!
Upon that day the recourse shall be to thy Lord.
Upon that day man shall be told his former deeds and his latter;
nay, man shall be a clear proof against himself,
even though he offer his excuses.
Move not thy tongue with it
to hasten it;
Ours it is to gather it, and to recite it.
So, when We recite it, follow thou its recitation.
Then Ours it is to explain it.
No indeed; but you love the hasty world,
and leave be the Hereafter.
Upon that day faces shall be radiant,
gazing upon their Lord;
and upon that day faces shall be scowling,

25 thou mightiest think the Calamity has been wreaked on [them.
No indeed; when it reaches the clavicles
and it is said, "Who is an enchanter?"
and he thinks that it is the parting
and leg is intertwined with leg,
upon that day unto thy Lord shall be the driving,
30 For he confirmed it not, and did not pray,
but he cried it lies, and he turned away,
then he went to his household arrogantly.
Nearer to thee and nearer
35 then nearer to thee and nearer!
What, does man reckon he shall be left to
roam at will?
Was he not a sperm-drop spilled?
Then he was a blood-clot, and He created and formed,
and he made of him two kinds, male and female.
40 What, is He not able to quicken the dead?

---

[1] Acceptance of the Day of Resurrection and its implications for how life should be lived is central to the Qur'ân's demands. After this *sûra*, there follow some of the dramatic and graphic descriptions of the Day which characterize Muhammad's early Call.

Source: McNeill, William H. and Marilyn Robinson Waldman, eds. "LXXV, The Resurrection." *The Islamic World*. Chicago: University of Chicago Press, 1983. Pgs. 31–32.

NOTES

1. In Syria today, there is a largely Christian town called Maalula just to the northwest of Damascus that professes to be one of the last places in the region where Aramaic, the presumed language of Jesus Christ, is still spoken. It has become a tourist center for this reason as well as its dramatic topography connected to its Christian heritage.
2. Jonathan Kirsch, *God Against the Gods: The History of the War Between Monotheism and Polytheism* (New York: Penguin, 2004), p. 162.
3. Joseph Henninger, "Pre-Islamic Bedouin Religion," in Merlin L. Swartz, *Studies on Islam* (Oxford: Oxford University Press, 1981), pp. 3–22.
4. Most of the information on religion in pre-Islamic Arabia is gleaned from Henninger.
5. W. Montgomery Watt, *Muhammad: Prophet and Statesman* (Oxford: Oxford University Press, 1964), pp. 44–55.
6. Ibid., p. 48.
7. Premodern civilizations were based on a surplus of agricultural goods that depended on labor by peasants but primarily geared for the elite and their armies. Religion was a response to this development in the Axial age (700–200 BCE). It perhaps can be said that this process came later to the Arabs with the growing

unease at the inequity in Mecca due to the changing economic fortunes. See Jared Diamond, *Guns, Germs, and Steel: The Fates of Human Societies* (New York: Norton, 1999), pp. 277–281.

8. Patricia Crone, *Meccan Trade and the Rise of Islam* (Piscataway, NJ: Gorgias Press, 2004).
9. Harvey Cox, "Understanding Islam," *Atlantic Monthly*, January 1981, pp. 73–80.
10. The age of forty in ancient Middle Eastern literary traditions was a cipher of perfection and completion, so it is likely the age of Khadija when she was married to Muhammad was raised to this number in ex post facto treatments. Since she delivered five or six children (only one of which survived, Fatima, who was the youngest of four daughters, Zaynab, Ruqayya, and Umm Kulthum), it is highly unlikely at that particular time and place that she had multiple children past the age of forty. Hossein Kamaly, *A History of Islam in 21 Women* (London: Oneworld Publications, 2019), p. 12.
11. Ibid., p. 11.
12. William H. McNeill and Marilyn Robinson Waldman, *The Islamic World* (Chicago: University of Chicago Press, 1973), pp. 27–29.
13. Fred M. Donner, *Muhammad and the Believers: At the Origins of Islam* (Cambridge, MA: Harvard University Press, 2010), p. 67.

KEY TERMS

ahl al-kitab p. 35
Ansar p. 33
Coptic p. 12
dihqan p. 16
Diophysite p. 13
hajj p. 33
haram p. 24
Hashimites p. 26
Hijra p. 32
Jazira p. 11
Kaaba p. 20
Monophysite p. 13
Muhajirun p. 32
munafiqun p. 34
qibla p. 34
Quraysh p. 18
Ramadan p. 33
salat p. 33
shahada p. 33
Sunna p. 37
umma p. 18
zakat p. 33

For additional digital learning resources please go to www.oup.com/he/lesch-middleeast-1e

3 RASHIDUN

Succession and Ridda War

The **Rashidun**, or Rightly Guided Ones in Islamic tradition, were the first four **caliphs** or successors to the Prophet Muhammad following his death—Abu Bakr, Umar, Uthman, and Ali—and ruled from 632 to 661 CE. All four of the men were some of Muhammad's closest companions, which facilitated their rise. It is during this period that the general contours of a burgeoning Islamic empire came into being, particularly as a result of the initial Islamic conquests against the Byzantine and Sassanian empires. This is also a period when the young Islamic community experienced the growing pains of expansion and the formation of a functional state apparatus, which became manifest soon after the Prophet died with the so-called Ridda Wars, and especially during the caliphates of Uthman and Ali.

As often happens when the seminal figure in a rising movement dies, there is confusion, disorientation, and factionalism. The death of Muhammad raised a number of important questions about the nature and direction of the umma. One of the main problems, at least according to what would become the majority of Muslims, was that the Prophet did not appoint a generally acknowledged successor. In addition, since he was the Messenger of God, if not the Seal of the Prophets, who in the world could adequately fill his shoes? Even if his status was embellished after the fact, he was still most definitely the unquestioned leader of the community. The two questions that confronted the Muslims were who should lead the umma, and what powers and authority this new leader should have.

These questions were often answered by competing groups in the umma, which is at the root of the instability that began soon after the Prophet died. Was a new leader to be chosen by the umma in some sort of an elective process, or should it be hereditary succession within the Hashimite clan? The two strands of the pre-Islamic process of choosing a tribal shaykh appear to have persevered. This is the root cause of the split between Sunni and Shiite Islam, the two largest Islamic sects. No one called themselves a Sunni or a Shiite until well into the tenth century, but one can trace the origins of the split back to the different answers to the question of how the new leader should be chosen and who this should be. Shiites (*Shiatu Ali* or partisans or followers of Ali) believe that Muhammad did in fact choose a successor: his cousin and son-in-law, Ali. In what came to be called Sunni Islam, at least initially, the caliph would be chosen by an elective process—usually a committee of elders comprised of those who had been closest to the Prophet. It is only over time that the two sects acquired different ideological beliefs and rituals from what at its origins began as a question of political legitimacy; however, in the end, they are much more alike than they are different, perhaps lending more ferocity at times to Sunni–Shiite conflicts over the centuries precisely because they are so close and emerge from the same Arabian primordial soup. This is a development we will track throughout the volume.

It was indeed a very dynamic period. The leadership question was compounded and complicated by rapid expansion into surrounding territories once held by the Byzantines and the Sassanians. The Muslims were very much living by trial and error. As mentioned, it is reasonable to suggest that there was a great deal of confusion and political maneuvering almost immediately after the Prophet died. In this supposition, I am drawing from Wilferd Madelung's excellent work *The Succession to Muhammad: A Study of the Early Caliphate*.[1] Madelung, like Muhammad's biographer, W. Montgomery Watt, utilizes and examines accounts and stories that were recorded years later, some obviously apocryphal but others containing enough kernels of plausibility and truth. Combined with deductive reasoning and some common sense, he brings to life possible scenarios of this crucial episode.

The Ansar were concerned lest the Muhajirun ally with their relatives from the Quraysh, especially the Meccan elite such as the Umayyads, to utilize their joint strength to control the umma, if not Medina itself. According to this rendering, soon after Muhammad's death became known, the Ansar convened in order to elect one of their own to lead the community. However, within the Quraysh group of the Meccan elite and the Muhajirun there were important differences leading to competing claims. After all, the two had been fighting against each other for the better part of the past decade, and the latter had been shunned and exiled by the former. Then there was the unique case of Ali, Muhammad's son-in-law and cousin, the husband of his daughter, Fatima, and the father to his grandsons, Hassan and Hussein, who were very dear to their grandfather. There were those, reflecting tribal custom, who believed that since Muhammad had no surviving sons the leadership should by default go to Ali by way of Fatima, his eldest daughter.

Ali, however, was apparently assigned the honor of preparing the Prophet's body for burial while the various claimants to succession politically duked it out.

Madelung suggests that perhaps Ali was purposely pushed aside because of his high standing in the community, close relationship with Muhammad, and his popularity among the Ansar and non-Qurayshis in general—he was a serious threat to other Muhajirun, and especially the Meccan elite. It also may have been that Ali was seen to be too young, as compared with someone like Abu Bakr. He was, after all, thirty years younger than the Prophet, and perhaps as a case of ex post facto characterization by his enemies, was seen as being impetuous. Both the other Muhajirun and Meccan elite were loath to see the umma led by someone who might dilute Qurayshi dominance and direct power away from the Quraysh in general.

While the Ansar apparently debated, Umar ibn al-Khattab, who was a Muhajirun and close Companion of the Prophet (and who would become the second caliph), seized the initiative and declared his allegiance to Abu Bakr as the new leader of the umma. While Abu Bakr may have been called "caliph" (i.e., successor to Muhammad), it is more likely that he, as well as other caliphs well into the Umayyad period, were referred to as **amir al-mumineen** or Commander of the Faithful (or Believers). The authority of the new caliph was unclear at first. He could not be a prophet because Muhammad was the Seal of the Prophets, yet he could not be a king, which was too much of a secular designation and denied the religious basis of the umma.

Abu Bakr was the first caliph of the Rashidun period, so designated after the fact probably to distinguish the Companions of the Prophet from the widely despised Umayyad dynasty that followed. It has been said that Abu Bakr was the ideal selection because he was everyone's second choice. He appears to have been the most acceptable of the Muhajirun to the Ansar. He had a great deal of standing or precedence (**sabiqa**) in the umma because he was one of the first converts to Islam, even though he was from a different clan than Muhammad's. He was the only other person with Muhammad when the latter made the Hijra. Abu Bakr was also related to Muhammad by marriage since his daughter, Aisha, married Muhammad and would become his most influential wife in his later years. Because of this, she was active and influential in the umma itself, and she advocated strongly on her father's behalf—and against Ali and Fatima. Abu Bakr also led the community in prayers when Muhammad became ill before his death, a clear sign of his standing.

As an indication of how interpretations of history change over the years, when I was in graduate school, the picture of Abu Bakr that was presented to me was that of an old man who was basically disinterested in the affairs of state. He was akin to an aging gentleman whittling away on his front porch while delegating duties to others. Due to recent scholarly findings and interpretations, however, a different picture of Abu Bakr emerged: that he was fully engaged in the affairs of state, and was a fairly manipulative politician and forceful leader during his eventful two-year tenure in power.

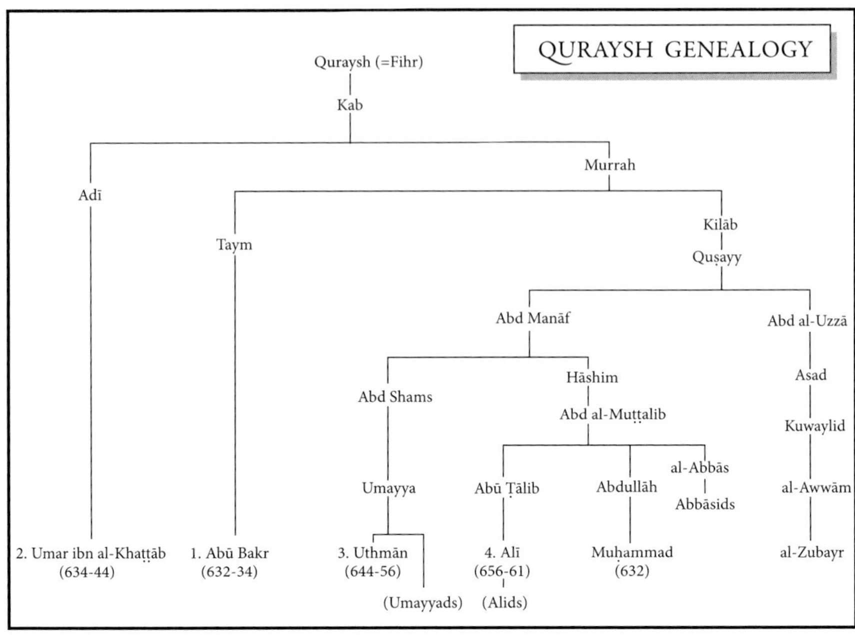

The various sources mined by Madelung strongly suggest that Abu Bakr did not like Ali, and that he, Umar, and Aisha did not want Ali to be caliph or the caliphate to stay exclusively within the Hashimite clan. They did not want the caliph to be non-Qurayshi, but within Quraysh the office of the caliph should be open to other clans. Abu Bakr's enmity for Ali may have stemmed from the tensions between Ali and Aisha, possibly caused by some unknown incident, maybe that Ali made it known that he believed Aisha was unworthy of the Prophet. Whatever the case, this deteriorating relationship would soon infect the umma as a whole. Abu Bakr, to the dismay of the Ansar and probably even the Muhajirun, appointed many members of the Meccan elite to important posts, including in the military. No Ansar appear to have been chosen, and only a few Muhajirun. It has been speculated that he may have done this at this very early stage to try to integrate different groups into the umma and acquire the buy-in of the important Meccan elite or Meccan aristocracy, who had to be won over and needed tangible reasons to support the movement and rationalize their recent conversion to Islam. But the decisions on which representatives from which group should be appointed to which positions became a gnawing sore in the side of the umma for years to come.

Abu Bakr wanted to maintain the Prophet's intended policies, which was clearly shown in the small military expedition he sent out in the direction of Syria soon after Muhammad died. It was something Muhammad had planned, and Abu Bakr wanted to demonstrate his commitment to the Prophet's vision. Syria had always been important to the Quraysh as the primary direction of trade caravans for the

Meccans. In addition, Abu Bakr and his advisers were almost certainly aware of the recent conflict between the Byzantines and the Sassanians as well as the related shifting sands of control in the heartland of the Middle East. An exploratory mission to assess the situation just north of Arabia thus made perfect sense, and indeed, soon enough under Umar, this would be the primary direction of the initial burst of Islamic conquest.

But not everyone was on board with this new Islamic state. Most Arabs had converted to Islam to a greater or lesser degree for a variety of reasons, as pointed out earlier. However, while they were willing to submit to the authority of Medina while Muhammad was alive, this was less the case following his death. Remember that the Arabs were fiercely independent and unaccustomed to rule by outsiders or a centralized government; even during Muhammad's time many Arabs' loyalty to the umma outside of the Hijaz was probably only skin deep. Without Muhammad's charismatic leadership, it would be difficult to maintain control over them. The rebellion by these elements has been called the Ridda Wars in Islamic tradition. Ridda has often been translated as "apostasy," or turning one's back on one's religion. This has serious consequences in Islam to this day, and perhaps it owes its sensitivity on this issue to the Ridda Wars. Whatever one calls it, this was Islam's first civil war. The term "Ridda" may be something of a misnomer, though. While there may have been some Arabs who renounced their Islam, which for them was at best an ambiguous proposition, most did not reject their new religion, but rather rejected government and the authority that governments try to impose, such as collecting taxes or conscripting armies. The independently minded Arabs would almost convulsively reject this.

Abu Bakr, however, would have none of this. He could not stand by and watch the umma unravel so soon after it had begun. Therefore, he ordered a series of military campaigns in Arabia led primarily by Khalid ibn al-Walid, to rein in the rebels by force if necessary to bring them back into the fold. And over the next two years, they were. As Madelung points out, the success of the umma was due primarily to the continued loyalty of Arabs in the Hijaz to Medina, primarily the Quraysh and the Thaqif and their allies. While the Hijazis remained united, their opponents were not, and the latter could then be defeated in a piecemeal fashion rather than having to face a united opposition. It is also important to remember that this was the volcanic period of this Islamic revolution. Certainly the diehards, the Muhajirun and Ansar, were ideologically motivated to prevail over the Ridda rebels. And the newly converted Meccan elite were no doubt motivated to maintain the lofty status and position they had acquired in their new reality.

In essence, the Ridda campaigns were the proving ground for the Islamic conquests that would soon follow. The wars allowed the Arabs to mobilize and organize troops as well as probe the borders of the Sassanian and Byzantine empires; indeed, the last stage of the Ridda Wars can be seen as the first stage of the Islamic conquests formally begun under the next caliph, Umar ibn al-Khattab.

Islamic Conquests

In 634, Abu Bakr died of natural causes, the only one of the four Rashidun caliphs to do so. The other three were assassinated or murdered, which kind of hints at the growing pains of early Islam. A close advisor to Abu Bakr, Umar ibn al-Khattab, became the next caliph. He appears to have faced very little opposition to his accession to power and was widely accepted. Umar had a great deal of sabiqa as well, and one of his daughters had married Muhammad, which put him on a par with Abu Bakr.

Umar comes down to us as the incorruptible leader who had an unparalleled devotion to Islam and the umma; throughout Islamic history Umar became the model caliph.[2] It was Umar who directed the initial Islamic conquests and established the early system of settlements that would form the basis of provincial governments. He also attempted to set up a system of payments that was based on merit in the cause of Islam, a salary rather than distributing lands to the victors. Umar also appointed many Muhajirun to important posts in his fledgling government and military structure, as he was most likely concerned with the growing power of the Meccan aristocracy that had occurred under Abu Bakr. This can best be seen in his replacement soon after he became caliph of Khalid ibn al-Walid. There is some ambiguity surrounding this incident, but the fact that this did not generate significant opposition from the Meccan aristocracy—or even an attempted military coup—suggests that Umar was not only politically shrewd but also that the Companions of the Prophet had a great deal of legitimacy and authority over and above other interest groups in the umma.

The Ansar were still basically shut out. Of the few within the Meccan aristocracy who were given positions, Umar tended to favor the Umayyad clan. A number of sources indicate that Umar's emphasis on sabiqa as a primary basis for reward and position was a backdoor attempt to reduce the power of the Meccan aristocracy, as the Muhajirun by default had the most sabiqa or precedence in Islam. His eventual appointment of an Umayyad, Muawiya ibn Abu Sufyan, as governor of Syria after its conquest seems to contradict this premise, but as we will discuss a little later, it appears that he had little choice but to do so when the time came because his initial appointments died unexpectedly of plague. It is a decision he would very much have regretted had he lived longer, for it would be Muawiya who would put an end to the Rashidun and inaugurate the Umayyad caliphate.

Again, when I was in graduate school, one of the theories regarding the conquests was that they were pretty much an accident—an extension of scouting and raiding parties that stumbled across two crumbling Middle Eastern empires. However, it has come to be accepted that for the most part, they were organized military expeditions led by an Islamic elite who were anxious to accomplish several things at once: 1) Enforce and maintain control over the Bedouin Arabs by directing their energies against an outside enemy rather than at each other. Some have called this an attempt to shift the common act of raiding (**razzia**) other Arab Muslims (*Dar al-Islam* or the Abode of Islam) to **jihad** (most often translated as "holy war," an armed struggle to spread the religion) against outsiders, *Dar al-harb* or the Abode of War; 2) Acquire more material wealth to divvy up the spoils of war. After all, for many Arabs, there had to be material incentive to not return to their previous life; 3) Establish new and secure old trade routes that had been disrupted by the Ridda wars as well as the conflicts between the Byzantines and Sassanians; and 4) Religious motivation, very much an evangelical movement in the beginning, meant that many Muslims were out to spread the faith as quickly as possible in order to save humanity before the end of times. Patricia Crone called them "missionary warriors," whereas in the Americas, for instance, the missionaries followed after the warriors to proselytize and save souls, the Muslims involved in the early conquests were in many ways one in the same.

Jared Diamond writes about a more systemic dynamic at work here that has occurred in almost every civilization: "Institutionalized religion brings two other benefits to centralized societies. First, shared ideology or religion helps solve the problem of how unrelated individuals are to live together without killing each other . . . by providing them with a bond not based on kinship. Second, it gives people a motive . . . for sacrificing their lives on behalf of others. At the cost of a few society members who die in battle as soldiers, the whole society becomes much more effective at conquering other societies or resisting attacks."[3] Sometimes this type of revolutionary ideology can lead to disaster, but for those who succeed, it can be quite useful even without intending it to be. The great Muslim historian and proto-sociologist Ibn Khaldun, who admired the early fervor of Islam, wrote that, "Vast and powerful empires are founded on religion. This is because dominion can only be secured by victory, and victory goes to the side which shows most solidarity and unity of purpose. Now, men's hearts are united and coordinated, with the help of God, by participants in a common religion."[4]

It is important to consider the word "jihad" here, as it has become such a volatile polemic in recent years, most certainly after 9/11. The term has been misinterpreted over the centuries not only by those in the Christian West but also by some Muslims themselves. Its original meaning is to struggle, and to most Muslims past and present, this is meant to indicate a personal struggle to be a better Muslim and a better overall human being, to live a good life, to be kind and giving, and to have courage in the face of evil. A **hadith**, or saying, attributed to the Prophet Muhammad talks about him telling the Muslims after the taking of Mecca that they had just performed the "lesser jihad" of conquest and now must embark upon the "greater jihad" of building a better Islamic community and becoming better Muslims. There are verses in the Quran, sometimes referred to as the "sword verses," which on the surface seem to legitimate warfare against unbelievers, particularly the following verse: "When the sacred months have passed, slay the idolaters wherever you find them, and take them, and confine them, and lie in wait for them at every place of ambush" (9:5). This has certainly been utilized by some Muslims over the centuries to countenance—if not encourage—war against infidels. Every religion has had to deal with such seemingly incongruous passages in the sacred texts. However, the next line of this verse is the following: "But if they repent and fulfill their devotional obligations and pay the zakat then let them go their way for God is forgiving and kind." There is also a passage here that appears to direct Muslims to fight only if first attacked. Taking all of this within context, many have put forth that the so-called sword verses actually refer to more of a defensive rather than offensive struggle as well as a call for peaceful relations.[5]

The conquests under Umar were directed against the Byzantines in Syria and Egypt and the Sassanians in Iraq and into Iran. Because of the lack of source material, however, there are many aspects of the military campaigns that are unknown or in doubt. And what little material we have from the Arab conquerors themselves tends to reflect what was valued in pre-Islamic Arabia: individual acts of heroism and courage. The disposition of forces and military strategy, even the sequence of battles and general chronology, are given short shrift, if any attention at all, so historians have once again been left to put forward their best guess.

The conquest of Syria was by far the primary focus of the Islamic leadership, especially the Quraysh. This was to be expected given the central role Syria played in Meccan trade. It seems to have taken place in phases, with the first expedition actually having been sent off by Abu Bakr during the last stages of the Ridda Wars; Abu Bakr sent four different expeditions under four different leaders, which M. A. Shaban says indicates that he did not expect a large confrontation initially against the Byzantines, perhaps aware of the situation in the immediate vicinity to the north in the wake of the Byzantine-Sassanian war.[6] In this sense, perhaps it was initially meant as a probing operation to reestablish trade routes, and subdue or gain more Arab allies to the north. It seems that once the nature of Byzantine defenses became known, Umar followed up upon these initial expeditions with a more formidable effort. One must remember that the Byzantine forces in the region, for obvious reasons, were arrayed against the Sassanians. The Sassanians were weakened considerably but they were still around, and the Byzantines certainly believed they had nothing to fear from the Arabs to the south, especially as earlier Arab raiding parties had been beaten back fairly easily by Byzantine forces in what is now southern Jordan.

What we know for sure is that between 634 and 637, three major battles occurred: Ajnadayn in southern Palestine, Fihl (Pella) in the Jordan Valley, and the biggest and most certainly the final one on the Yarmuk River around the present-day border between Syria and Jordan. The Battle of Yarmuk seems to have broken

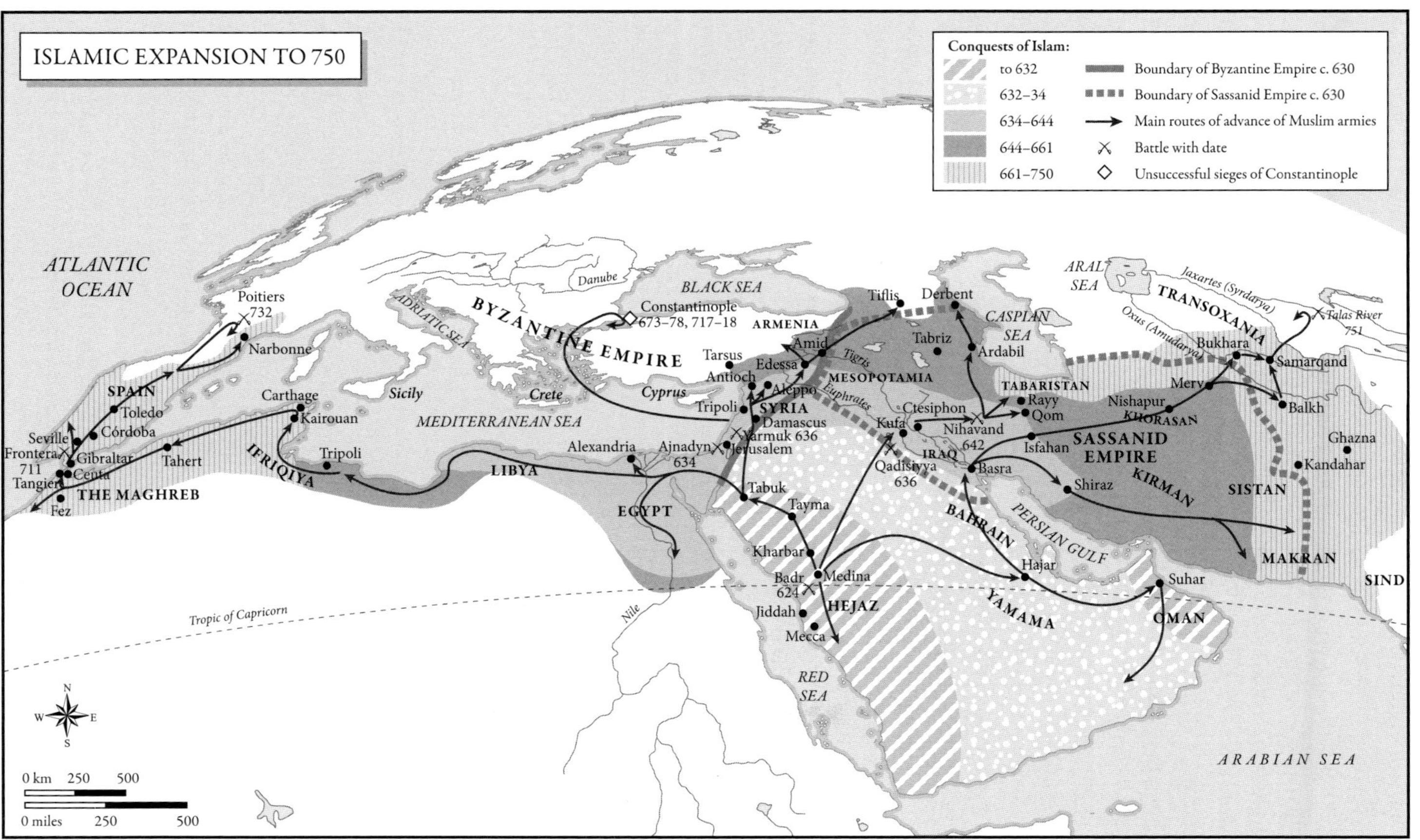

ISLAMIC EXPANSION TO 750
Conquests of Islam:
to 632
632–34
634–644
644–661
661–750
Boundary of Byzantine Empire c. 630
Boundary of Sassanid Empire c. 630
Main routes of advance of Muslim armies
Battle with date
Unsuccessful sieges of Constantinople
ATLANTIC OCEAN
Poitiers
732
Narbonne
SPAIN
Toledo
Córdoba
Seville
Frontera
711
Gibraltar
Ceuta
Tangier
Fez
THE MAGHREB
Tahert
Carthage
Kairouan
IFRIQIYA
Tripoli
Sicily
ADRIATIC SEA
BYZANTINE EMPIRE
Danube
Crete
MEDITERRANEAN SEA
LIBYA
Alexandria
EGYPT
Nile
BLACK SEA
Constantinople
673–78, 717–18
ARMENIA
Tarsus
Cyprus
Antioch
Tripoli
Edessa
Aleppo
SYRIA
Damascus
Yarmuk 636
Ajnadyn
634
Jerusalem
Amid
Tigris
Euphrates
MESOPOTAMIA
Tiflis
Derbent
Tabriz
Ardabil
CASPIAN SEA
TABARISTAN
Rayy
Qom
Ctesiphon
Kufa
Nihavand
642
IRAQ
Qadisiyya
636
Basra
Isfahan
SASSANID EMPIRE
KHORASAN
Nishapur
Merv
ARAL SEA
Jaxartes (Syrdarya)
Oxus (Amudarya)
TRANSOXANIA
Bukhara
Samarqand
Talas River
751
Balkh
Ghazna
Kandahar
SISTAN
KIRMAN
Shiraz
MAKRAN
SIND
Tabuk
Tayma
Kharbar
Badr
624
Medina
HEJAZ
Jiddah
Mecca
RED SEA
BAHRAIN
PERSIAN GULF
Hajar
YAMAMA
Suhar
OMAN
ARABIAN SEA
Tropic of Capricorn
N
E
S
W
0 km
250
500
0 miles
250
500

the back of the Byzantine resistance, even though many Arabs such as the Ghassanids, most of them Christian, actually fought on the side of Constantinople. There is some indication that many Arabs during the course of these campaigns switched their allegiance to the Islamic cause; in fact, the Banu Nadir, one of the Jewish Arab tribes in Medina, fought on the Muslim side because they hated the Byzantines more after Heraclius in 630 issued a decree forcibly converting Jews to Christianity. This also may cast some doubt on the veracity of the story that the Banu Nadir, along with the other two Jewish Arab tribes in Medina, were violently dealt with and kicked out by the Muslims.

After the conquest of Syria, Umar had to be very circumspect in how the conquerors and the conquered were treated, especially the Arabs who were already in Syria and who may or may not have fought for the Byzantines. The most telling characteristic of the conquest of Syria was the makeup of the Muslim army. The composition of the Muslim armies during the initial conquests would have far-reaching consequences for Islamic history. For Syria, the Muslim army was by and large exclusively—and intentionally—composed of Qurayshis. Conspicuous by their absence were Arabs from elsewhere in the Hijaz, such as the Thaqifis and the Ansar, and from other parts of Arabia. These non-Qurayshis would, in turn, lead the way in the conquest of Iraq and Iran from the Sassanians. But even among the Qurayshis there was a hierarchy of clans, and Umar appears to have been confronted with some of these inherent tensions over the spoils of war and the rewards of victory. Umar knew he needed the indigenous Arabs in the area to be assimilated into the new reality because he would need them against the Byzantines should the latter launch a counteroffensive. Therefore, the caliph gave some dissatisfied Muslim clans the Jazira along the present-day border of Syria and Iraq, where there had been some Arabs present in pre-Islamic times. Again, while mediating conflict in the immediate sense, this decision would have important repercussions later in Islamic history.

After considering other locations for the capital of this new Syrian province, Umar settled on Damascus, which for so long had been the dominant city in the area—it was a natural choice. Controversially only in retrospect, Umar settled on Muawiya as governor, which seems surprising given that the caliph had wanted to reduce the power of the Meccan aristocracy. But Umar had to deal delicately with Syria and the Arabs who were already in the area. Perhaps it is because of all of the Muslims, an Umayyad would be the most acceptable to those indigenous Arabs. The Umayyad family had been one of the leading trading families from Mecca with the Syrian hinterland; therefore, they were familiar with it, they were familiar to those in Syria, and they no doubt had developed a network of contacts, perhaps even owning property in Damascus and other nearby cities. Muawiya was probably not Umar's first choice, but in the near term, he may have been the only choice. Little did he know he would be setting up the basis for the Umayyad empire.

Al-Aqsa Mosque in Jerusalem, first established by the Caliph Umar in the late 630s and considerably expanded by the Umayyad Caliphs Abd al-Malik and his son al-Walid in the late seventh and early eighth centuries. "Al-Aqsa" means "the farthest" in Arabic and is a reference to a passage in the Quran that describes the Prophet Muhammad's famous "night journey" from Mecca to "the farthest mosque" in Jerusalem. Along with the Dome of the Rock, this complex on the Temple Mount or Haram al-Sharif (noble sanctuary) is considered by many Muslims to be the third holiest site in Islam (after Mecca and Medina).
Janek/Alamy Stock Photo

Now we come to the conquest of Egypt, which is shrouded in some mystery as to whether it was a part of Umar's greater strategy. We do know that the conquest was primarily due to the leadership of its commander, Amr ibn al-As. Some sources have Amr asking for permission from Umar to move against Egypt, perhaps because he and some lesser clans he represented were being crowded out of the victorious spoils of war by more powerful clans in and around Syria. Umar appears to have given grudging consent, maybe not wanting to split up the Muslim forces while the Byzantines could launch a counterattack, but he may have also realized that his authority wasn't so great, especially vis-à-vis someone from the old Meccan elite, that he could keep Amr from doing what he wanted. Shaban suggests that Amr just picked up and left to conquer Egypt without asking for permission.[7]

Whatever the case, Amr ibn al-As appears to have gone on some trade caravans to Egypt in pre-Islamic times, so he was somewhat familiar with the territory and probably knew that it was ripe for the picking, especially now that it was cut off by land from what had been Byzantine territory. The army he took with him was relatively small, around four thousand strong, with no leading Companions or Meccan elite accompanying him.[8] As in Syria, the back and forth of the recent Byzantine–Sassanian war had weakened the defenses in the area as well as the hold of the Byzantine government. And the entire rural population was Monophysite, so they were alienated from the provincial capital located in Alexandria and were by and large unwilling to defend it against the Muslims. This is also something of which Amr was most likely aware.

Egypt was taken relatively easily in 637–638, with Alexandria holding out until 642; located on the Mediterranean coast, it was able to be resupplied by sea. As in other areas conquered by the Muslims, settlement followed conquest. This was fairly small-scale in Egypt, where the Muslims remained for some time to come a minority ruling class, especially in the face of the tightly knit Coptic community; however, the Coptics probably saw the new situation under Islam as freeing them up from the persecution and oppression of their fellow (but Diophysite) Christians. They were allowed to maintain their customs and positions, could worship freely, and were relied upon for their local knowledge, skill set, and expertise. Guided by Umar's wise and conciliatory tone at this point, there was an agreement drawn up for those in the local population who did not want to convert to Islam, which was most of them at first. The agreement read as follows: "In the name of God, the merciful, the compassionate, this is the amnesty granted to the people of Egypt, to their religion, their goods, their churches and crosses, their lands and waters, nothing of which shall be touched or seized from them."[9] Why wouldn't they welcome the Muslims? A garrison town (*misr*, plural **amsar**) was established at Fustat (the tent), located about where Cairo is today, and this would become the provincial capital. The Arabic name for Egypt is *Misr*. Because there was very little Arab settlement in Egypt, the spread of Islam and the Arabic language was slow, which was the main reason why the province played a limited role in early Islam.

Now we come to the conquest of Iraq, which was decidedly different, especially in the makeup of the Muslims armies, than the conquest of Syria. As with Syria, the general outline of events is somewhat clear, although the chronology is less so. Iraq was always secondary in the minds of the Quraysh. The rich alluvial plains of the **Sawad** in central to southern Iraq, fed by an intricate canal and irrigation system based on the Tigris-Euphrates river valley, meant that agriculture was the primary occupation and revenue producer for civilizations going back millennia. The Quraysh were no farmers, however, which is why their focus was primarily toward Syria. Muhammad ordered no expeditions in the direction of Iraq, meaning "ancient" in Arabic, which is a reference to those civilizations located along the Tigris and Eurphrates river basin going back to the Sumerians, Akkadians, Babylonians, and Persians, among others. It was a colloquial reference that many centuries later stuck as the name of the modern nation-state of Iraq.

The first encounters against the Sassanians were a natural extension of the Ridda campaigns, and as such, the composition of the original Muslim army was quite different than the Muslim army in Syria. In Iraq there were few if any Quraysh, whereas there were a number of Thaqifis, Ansar, and non-Qurayshis from other parts of Arabia, all of whom had remained loyal to Medina during the Ridda wars. The Ridda rebels were conspicuous by their absence and were not allowed to participate at first. However, after the initial military thrust against the Sassanians experienced some setbacks, especially at the Battle of the Bridge in Iraq early in the campaign, Umar made the controversial—but militarily necessary—decision to include the Ridda rebels in the Muslim armies, simply in order to buffer up the number of soldiers against some tough resistance by the Sassanians. Following this, a decisive battle was fought in 637 at Qadisiyya, when the combined Muslim forces were victorious. This battle, much like the Battle of Yarmouk in Syria, broke the back of the Sassanians, and soon thereafter the Muslims marched into the Sassanian capital of Ctesiphon, which was soon renamed Mada'in, the plural of Medina. From there a separate army of Muslims from southern Iraq began to move into the southwestern Iranian province of Khuzistan, beginning the process of bringing Iran within Muslim rule over the next decade.

Umar then set about establishing amsar in Iraq, both on the edge of the desert: Kufa in central Iraq and Basra in the south. One of the main reasons for the establishment of amsar, especially in Iraq, was to maintain some level of control over the Bedouin Arabs who fought in the armies, as the Sassanians were not totally defeated yet and could still mount a counteroffensive. They could be more easily mobilized if kept together, even though within the amsar rule tended to be more tribal based initially rather than under the control of a provincial governor (*amir*). In addition, there was a fear that if left to themselves, the Arabs could assimilate into the dominant Persian culture they just conquered. They could lose their language, their culture, and ultimately even their religion if allowed to disperse throughout the region. This is not unusual in history. After all, very few spoke Visigothic or Lombardian after they took over the western Roman Empire—they assimilated for the most part into the dominant Latin and Christian traditions of the conquered. Finally, there may very well have been a sense by the Muslim leadership in Iraq that staying in amsar would better maintain the religious purity of the movement, allowing them to continue to live a righteous, pious life and not be poisoned by outside customs and traditions. Whatever the case, both Kufa and Basra, like most amsar, would grow into significant cities, and in Iraq would play a very important role in its history.

As in Syria, there were questions as to what to do with the land now under Muslim control and who should receive the lion's share of the spoils. In most of the territories conquered by the Muslims, who initially were without a governing system they could call their own, they essentially grafted Muslim rule onto preexisting governing systems: what could be called the equivalent of a civil service in each region and including such things as coinage and tax systems. In Iraq, land was to remain in the hands of the previous owners if they had not fled, and they would continue to pay taxes to the Muslims as they had to the Sassanians. There were somewhat complicated tax systems in the newly conquered territories; however, for our purposes the two most important for the residents of Iraq were a land tax (*kharaj*) based on the area and type of crops cultivated, and a poll tax (**jizya**) to be paid by non-Muslims as protected peoples (*dhimmis*) and, for the most part, considered People of the Book (*ahl al-kitab*).

Lands that had been abandoned by the Sassanian royal family, the upper aristocracy, and the Zoroastrian priesthood were to come under the control of the umma, but in reality it was very provincially based. These lands essentially became crown lands (**sawafi**), but the administration of these lands and the wealth derived from them would become an area of great contestation, especially between the provincial capitals and Medina. The local government would collect the revenues from taxes and then redistribute them as a salary (**ata**) to the victorious soldiers, settlers, and administrators, although the exact nature of this system varied from place to place. Umar, however, attempting to create the Islamic meritocracy that he believed Muhammad would have wanted, used the principle of sabiqa, or precedence, to calculate what each Muslim would be paid.

One can readily see that while the intent was altruistic, this system of ata based on sabiqa could—and did—produce enormous tensions in early Islam. This was the case for those who conquered Iraq. They believed they should receive higher salaries, especially those who remained loyal during the Ridda wars; however, later converts to Islam would make less simply because they had only been a Muslim for a few years and did not participate in the military campaigns. This would be particularly galling to the later convert or latecomer if in the pre-Islamic tribal hierarchy they belonged to a much more notable tribe or group than, for instance, the Thaqifis or the Ansar.

The amirs, as expected, tended to represent the interests of their local constituents rather than concern themselves too much with the demands from Medina. Umar tried to pressure the provincial governors to return surplus revenues to Medina—that is, those funds that were left over after the local ata had been paid. The amirs, however, believed that it was their right to spend these funds in the way they determined, focusing on local needs rather than have Medina decide this for them. It was a classic situation of state versus federal authority. This fiscal autonomy in the provinces would prove to be a source of conflict soon enough. Although by the end of Umar's rule in 644 Islam had spread rapidly and had defeated two empires, and the umma had been kept intact when it could have broken up into independent kingdoms, there were two very important areas of tension that would erupt into civil war about a decade later: group status, which determined your salary or ata; and who controlled surplus revenues.

Fitna

The word "fitna" has been translated into civil war or civil strife. There are typically religious undertones to these terms in Islamic tradition, as was the case with "ridda." In this context, fitna refers to being seduced or tempted from righteousness, possibly by Satan himself. It is certainly not a positive reference, and refers to a series of civil wars and civil strife that marked the caliphates of Uthman ibn al-Affan and Ali ibn Abi Talib, the last two caliphs in the Rashidun.

Since sabiqa determined one's salary in terms of service to the cause in the case of Iraq, it was important for individual Arabs to be identified with groups with more sabiqa, and being a part of a more powerful group was jealously defended. During and after the conquest of Iraq, three groups emerged that would help shape the politics there for a generation. One group was the *ahl al-ayyam* (those who fought the battles, i.e., against the Sassanians); the second one was the *ahl al-Ridda*, those who were Ridda rebels, so this was a group with which one really did not want to be identified; finally, there was the *ahl al-Qadisiyya*, those who fought in this seminal battle in 637 against the Sassanians. This last group included both the ahl al-ayyam and the ahl al-ridda, following Umar's important decision to include the Ridda rebels in the Muslim armies in Iraq.

As you can imagine, the ahl al-ayyam did not particularly like being grouped with the ahl al-ridda. After all, they had remained loyal to Medina throughout, and they believed they should not be grouped with rebels—in essence, apostates. As such, they adopted another group title, *ahl al-qurra*, which according to Shaban roughly translates to "those of the villages."[10] There is some ambiguity surrounding the exact meaning or reference, but it may be that the Qurra (and we will just refer to them in this fashion from here on out) were self-identifying as those who were not from some grander tribes in pre-Islamic times. The Qurra were essentially the ahl al-ayyam, but after the Battle of Qadisiyya. They settled into the central Iraqi capital of Kufa and came to dominate the politics of the city with one of their own as amir.

The Caliph Umar was assassinated by a Persian slave in Medina in 644. There seems to have been no political motivation behind it, and it may have been some sort of personal matter; however, it is also tempting to suggest that perhaps it may have been an early signal of dissatisfaction with the dominant position of the Arabs in early Islam. Ultimately, we really do not know. Umar stayed alive long enough after the stabbing to appoint a **shura**, a committee, to choose a successor. Apparently the shura had six members, all of them Muhajirun. Conspicuous by their absence were the Ansar, many of whom were no longer in Medina and were now a part of the Qurra, or any of the more recent converts, some of whom no doubt resented the continued domination by the Quraysh.

Two candidates emerged upon Umar's death: Ali and Uthman. Uthman was an early convert to Islam, but he was from the Umayyad clan, which endeared him to Muhammad, as the rest of the Umayyads were adamantly opposed to the nascent Muslim movement. Two of Muhammad's daughters married Uthman, which put him on a par with Ali, who married Fatima, the Prophet's eldest daughter by Khadija. Ali and Fatima probably married a year after the hijra at the Prophet's urging. Ali, as mentioned, was very close to Muhammad and for the most part grew up within his household. Fatima was between nine and nineteen when she married Ali, the exact age made murky by the lack of attention to such family details in even Islamic sources, as the chroniclers in later decades and centuries were more interested in

Muhammad's religious, military, and political affairs. As with Khadija, Fatima is said to have been a very strong, active, and independently minded person with whom—against tribal custom—the Prophet consulted frequently, often siding with her when she voiced her opinions on various issues.[11] It appears she was quite vocal on behalf of Ali when he did not become caliph immediately after the Prophet died, but unfortunately for Ali's supporters, perhaps the loudest and most authoritative voice on the subject died within a year or so after her father. It is interesting to speculate what would have happened had this dynamic person lived longer.

In the pre-Islamic tribal scale of things, the tribal shaykh's daughter marrying someone gave the son-in-law higher status than someone whose daughter married the shaykh, so in this context Ali and Uthman were of higher status than Abu Bakr and Umar, whose daughters married Muhammad. This may have been why Uthman was put up as caliph, as only he had the necessary credentials to take on Ali, who many of the Muhajirun and Meccan elite opposed. It was not because Uthman was known as a great leader; he has been described as kind of a goofball who made Muhammad laugh because of his clumsiness. This may be polemics at work or ex post facto revisionist history, but subsequent events seemed to prove this to be at least partially true.

Madelung writes that Ali may have actually been offered the caliphate, but only if he would guarantee the continued dominance of the Quraysh. As we have already seen, Ali had become a champion of non-Qurayshi groups, and he probably believed that the continued grip on power of the Quraysh would divide and ultimately weaken a quickly expanding umma. He felt that power should be open to others, which many Muhajirun believed would be the Ansar, as Ali had developed close links with them in Medina.

Whatever the case, Uthman did indeed become caliph, and he came to power with a clear political program: to ensure that this new Islamic state remained under the control of the Quraysh. His caliphate has been described as very nepotistic, as he naturally turned to his own Umayyad clan to fill many posts. Many of the old Islamic elite were either dead or too old, so a number of new faces were brought into leadership positions. It seems that Umar's Islamic meritocracy was over before it had much of a chance to take hold. Uthman—and certainly his closest advisor, his cousin, Marwan ibn al-Hakam, who seems to have despised the Companions—believed in the centralization of power in Medina, which meant that amirs or governors were to be chosen by the central government and not necessarily be from the province itself. In addition, this meant that all financial affairs were to be determined by Medina and not by provincial governments. One can readily see the roots of discontent and eventual conflict, focusing again on group status and surplus revenues. An important element of Uthman's centralization of power was the development of a definitive version of the Quran rather than having different readings of the Holy Book floating around. According to Islamic tradition, Muhammad's revelations had been written down either during his life or shortly after his death, so having one government ordained reading was necessary to order society according to an accepted set of precepts.

SPOTLIGHT
The Quran

The Quran (often mistakenly transliterated into English as "Koran") is the Holy Book of Islam. It is sacred, revealed scripture, and Muslims consider it to be the very word of God (*Allah*). The word "quran" itself means "recitation"; the book is meant to be recited, even rhythmically chanted, reflecting the oral tradition of pre-Islamic Arabia. It is taken from the very first word, "recite," that according to Islamic tradition, Allah spoke to the Prophet Muhammad via the Archangel Gabriel (*Jibril*) in 610 CE—the same archangel who appears in the Christian New Testament. Muhammad is charged to recite or tell others that which is being communicated to him from Allah. The verses that would make up the Quran were written down by his followers on various materials such as stones and palm branches. One Companion of the Prophet by the name of Zayd ibn Thabit collected these materials and apparently jotted them down on sheets of parchment, which he handed over to the second caliph, Umar. The collection then passed down to the next caliph, Uthman, upon Umar's death in 644. It was under Uthman (644–656) that an authoritative version of the Quran was produced in order to eliminate the many versions of it that had spread throughout Arabia. It is generally thought that it was this version that became the standard one to this day.

The Quran is much shorter than the Hebrew Bible and even the New Testament. The Bible has about 800,000 words, whereas the Quran has about 77,400 words, which is about four-fifths the length of the New Testament. It is divided into 114 chapters (*surahs*) and composed of 6,236 verses (*ayat*). Other than the opening surah, *al-Fatiha* (meaning "The Opening"), which is recited during each of the five daily prayers in Islam, the chapters are ordered in decreasing length rather than chronologically—longest to shortest—probably to facilitate oral transmission and memorization. As with al-Fatiha, the chapters are known by names, such as "The Cow" (chapter 2) or "The Poets" (chapter 26); however, the title has less to do with the meaning of the chapter with which it is associated and more to do with a word that stands out in the text of that chapter. The longest chapter is the second one (The Cow), which has 286 verses; the shortest has three verses. Each surah (except the ninth) begins with the phrase "In the name of Allah, the most merciful and most gracious" (*Bismillah al-rahman al-raheem*). The Quran is often divided into thirty roughly equal parts (*juz*), allowing devout Muslims to read one passage per day per month, which is especially important during the month of fasting (*Ramadan*).

The Quran provides the foundation for Islamic law (**sharia**), although sharia is also derived from the *hadith* (plural *ahadith*), or sayings of the Prophet Muhammad. The Quran can be quite difficult to decipher. It is written in an elliptical style, and it admits to the multiple or hidden meanings of some words and phrases, an esoteric knowledge known only to Allah. It is also difficult to place the Quran within a historical context, for it is not the history of a religious community, as recorded in the Old Testament (Hebrew Bible), nor is it like the Gospels of the New Testament (i.e., biographical stories of a particular prophet, in this case Jesus Christ). It is not about the life of Muhammad, whose name barely appears in the text, or the rise of Islam itself. However, many of the places, names, events, and stories in the Old and New Testament appear in the Quran, such as Adam (*Adam*), the Day of Judgment, Noah (*Nuh*), Abraham (*Ibrahim*), Moses (*Musa*), the Virgin Mary (*Maryam*), and Jesus (*Isa*). Jesus is called the Messiah in the Quran, and has disciples, performs miracles, and ascends to Heaven, but is not divine. Many of these stories, however, do not exactly correspond to what is written in the Bible. Interestingly, the name Mary appears more in the Quran than in the New Testament, especially as the name Jesus is often followed by "son of Mary"; Mary is the only female name cited in the Quran. But included in the text of the Quran are also exclusively Arabian prophets who do not appear in the Bible.

The Quran has been translated into over forty languages; however, regardless of their nationality, Muslims are enjoined to learn, read, and recite it in Arabic, the original and sacred language of the Holy Book. Because of the preeminent position of the Quran is Islamic society, copies of the Book are often quite ornately decorated, and the calligraphy associated with the written word in the Quran has come to be considered one of Islam's highest art forms. In a Muslim house, the Quran is prominently placed on a specially designed bookstand called a *rahla*.

The ornate pages of a Quran, dated 1689, Syria.
INTERFOTO/Alamy Stock Photo

Despite these simmering issues, the state continued to expand under Uthman. Expeditions were sent to Nubia (what is today the Sudan) and into North Africa from Egypt. In addition, the Muslims began to develop a naval capability and brought much of the eastern Mediterranean under its control, forcing Cyprus to pay tribute and defeating the Byzantines at sea, although the sailors, ships, and commanders of the Muslim navy were probably only a little over a decade earlier fighting for, rather than against, Constantinople. Almost all of Sassanian Iran as well came under Muslim control, although primarily through tribute rather than settlement, as local conditions and systems of governance continued virtually untouched.

But it is the uprising against and assassination of Uthman in 656 that is of such import, so it is necessary to speculate as to the nature of the opposition and immediate causes for the assassination itself. There were three main regions of discontent against Uthman and his method of governance: Kufa, Egypt, and in Medina itself.

We know that Kufa had been dominated by the Qurra. Their power and wealth were based on their sabiqa during Umar's time as well as their control of the sawafi or crown lands. The decentralized nature of Umar's government did not threaten their position, and there is no evidence that they returned any surplus revenue to Medina. This changed under Uthman, who almost immediately sent a Qurayshi to Kufa to become governor, and he was not sympathetic at all to the so-called early-comers such as the Qurra, who in the eyes of Medina had become too comfortable in their privileged position. From now on, surplus revenue in the province was to be sent to Medina to be disbursed how the caliph pleased.

The position of the Qurra was also threatened by continued immigration from Arabia into Iraq from latecomers to Islam. They were not allowed to immigrate to Syria, since that was clearly a Qurayshi enterprise and off-limits. Many of these latecomers were from powerful pre-Islamic tribes, and the shaykhs of these tribes resented the privileged position of the Qurra, who they may have looked down upon in the pre-Islamic tribal hierarchy. To them, the world had been turned upside down. They put pressure on Uthman and his governors to abolish distinctions between the groups in Iraq, and they found sympathetic ears. As a result, the Qurra began to organize opposition to Uthman and Medina. Led by Malik al-Ashtar, in 655 about three thousand of them refused to allow the Uthman-appointed governor back into Kufa and replaced him with one of their own. They then marched on Medina in 656 to confront Uthman directly.

Egypt had similar problems to Kufa. The original Arab conquerors, now "Egyptians," also enjoyed Umar's decentralized system. But that changed with Uthman, who almost immediately deposed Amr ibn al-As as governor, and his new governor, as in Kufa, was committed to undermining the power of the original Islamic ruling elite in Fustat. According to the story, about 400–600 of these Egyptians marched on Medina as well to express their grievances directly to Uthman. They were assuaged initially and embarked to return home; however, on the way back a message from Uthman (Madelung suggests that Marwan ibn al-Hakam probably wrote it) was intercepted, the message telling the new Egyptian governor to treat the 400–600 harshly upon their return. The Egyptians turned right around, now in an angrier mood, and marched back to Medina, surrounding Uthman's house.

With two groups of malcontents parked outside of Uthman's home, one gets the impression that it was a very confusing—if not entirely weird—situation for those involved, with most of them not really knowing what to do next. And Uthman had very little support by then in Medina itself. Those left of the Islamic elite, including the Mother of the Faithful, Aisha, who was—perhaps conveniently—on a pilgrimage to Mecca at the time, were increasingly critical of Uthman's policies and did little to support him (although Aisha reportedly said on one occasion that "Uthman's fingertip" was still better than the whole of Ali, which gives one the clear sense of the level of animosity between Ali and Aisha).[12] Certainly those Ansar who were still in Medina, many of whom were allied with former Ansar now in the Qurra, would not come to Uthman's aid. Finally, many within Quraysh had been upset at Uthman's heavy reliance on the Umayyad clan. In the end, his manipulative cousin, after doing so much to fan the flames to begin with, could not save him. Uthman appears to have not been a very good politician nor a diplomat after all.

After weeks of sitting around, a group of Egyptians besieged Uthman's home, broke in, and killed the caliph while he sat alone, reading the Quran. As we shall see, at least two more caliphs in medieval Islam were killed in this manner. It is probably an apocryphal image, but it is most likely meant to convey two things: that the caliph has lost all support and was isolated and alone; and despite his being abandoned, in the end he was still a true Muslim, reading the Holy Book even at the point of death, a touch of ex post facto salvaging of a reputation for a Companion of the Prophet in spite of his limitations.

This was Islam's first true political trauma, one that begot many others. Uthman tried to centralize too soon, and he did not have the wherewithal, either personally or in terms of supporters, to do it—and he paid the ultimate price.

With Uthman dead, Ali finally got his chance as caliph. There was no shura, but with the Qurra still in Medina and Ali's traditional support from the Ansar, there was really no other choice; however, from the beginning Ali's position was fraught with challenges, including claims by opponents of illegitimately becoming caliph. Although Ali did indeed have his own political program and approach, he had very little space in which to implement his vision, with opposition from a number of quarters from the start.

Elements within the Quraysh were the first to challenge Ali, led by a Muhajirun by the name of al-Zubayr ibn al-Awwam as well as the Prophet's widow, Aisha. Muhammad probably married Aisha, a daughter of Abu Bakr, within two years after the Hijra. She was between five and nine years old, possibly a bit older, but as with most medieval sources, ages were mostly symbolic; in this case, because of her young age, she was depicted as pure and innocent.[13] As with Fatima and Khadija,

Aisha was someone on whom the Prophet relied upon a great deal for counsel, especially toward the end of his life when she was older, and most sources claim that Muhammad had a special affection for her over his other wives. According to tradition, it was in her lap that the Prophet drew his last breath. As with Fatima, she was an activist and quite opinionated, to the point that over two thousand hadith reports are traced back to her, although only a fraction of them made it into the most widely accepted hadith volumes a century and a half later. Revisionist history within Islam itself constructed her as a very controversial figure, in some ways recasting her as acting somewhat out of place—conservative Muslims to this day, whether Sunni or Shiite, sometimes use her as an example of why women should be kept out of politics, or what Fatima Mernissi called "opportune traditions."[14]

Like Uthman, al-Zubayr was one of the Muslims sent to Ethiopia in 615 and he and Ali were the scouts who discovered the Meccan caravan prior to the Battle of Badr. He also married a daughter of Abu Bakr, and as Aisha was a daughter of the first caliph, there was an immediate kinship. And by now there weren't many Muslims left who were associated with the origin story of Islam, so he was a definite threat to Ali. Al-Zubayr and Aisha did not support Uthman or the Umayyads either, but they also did not want power to escape the hold of the Quraysh entirely, which is what they feared would happen if Ali remained caliph.

According to the shreds of information that came down about what happened in Medina, apparently al-Zubayr and Aisha claimed Ali was responsible for the death of Uthman, knowing he wasn't. But they were saying so in order to gain political advantage by attempting to discredit Ali. Ali's mistake in the whole Uthman affair was that he became directly involved in it by trying to diplomatically resolve the situation, but that's apparently who he was. He was not someone who stood on the sidelines; however, by directly implicating himself, he opened himself up to all sorts of accusations by his opponents. The gambit did not work for al-Zubayr and Aisha, but it provided grist for the mill for the Umayyad family in their opposition to Ali.

For some unknown reason al-Zubayr and Aisha went to Basra to build up an army. Ali could not stay in Medina and make the same mistake Uthman did. In any event, the Qurra had returned home, and Ali knew they strongly supported him, so he followed his opponents to Iraq, but instead went to Kufa. Ali was able to attract a much larger army in Kufa, and in late 656 he marched on Basra and defeated al-Zubayr and Aisha in the Battle of the Camel, the former being killed in battle while the latter was forced into virtual retirement. Supposedly the battle is called the "Camel" after the camel that Aisha sat on in the middle of her army as Ali's forces closed in on her. Again, this is probably apocryphal, but it is a very dramatic scene.[15] Regardless, the gates of fitna had been opened and they would be very difficult to close, as subsequent history would show. Showing respect for the Mother of the Faithful, Ali sent Aisha back home to Medina, where she died years later in 678.

Muhammad's widow, Aisha, battling the fourth caliph Ali in the Battle of the Camel. Sixteenth-century miniature.
UtCon Collection/Alamy Stock Photo

Following the Battle of the Camel, Ali in effect made Kufa the new capital in place of Medina. His authority was accepted in Basra, and he was able to appoint a new governor in Egypt; however, in Syria it was a different story. The main reason for this is that the governor was an Umayyad. Muawiya ibn Abu Sufyan had by then been the governor of Syria for about two decades, and as such he had built up an effective army and loyal power base that could not be easily removed. Even though he had really done nothing to protect his kinsman in Medina, the moral obligation to avenge Uthman's murder fell to Muawiya, and he adroitly used this claim against Ali. His demand that he would not acknowledge Ali as caliph unless the new ruler turned over those responsible for the death of Uthman was made that much easier because the Mother of the Faithful herself, Aisha, held Ali at least partially responsible for the debacle in Medina.

The problem for Ali is that he was dependent on the support of the very group, the Qurra, who were seen by many, especially Ali's opponents, as being primarily responsible for Uthman's death. Muawiya was a cunning and ruthless politician, and he knew that his vengeful claim would place Ali in quite a pickle. It was a brilliant move. Another problem for Ali was that he became entangled in the politics of Kufa, especially the increasing antagonism between the late comer immigrants to the area, some of whom grouped themselves as the **Ashraf** (plural of sharif), as many had been tribal leaders in pre-Islam, and the entrenched Qurra. Somehow Ali had to convince both groups that it was in their interest to march on Syria and confront Muawiya. After all, from the perspective of the Qurra, Muawiya was simply fighting for the same type of provincial autonomy for which they had just successfully fought. As for the Ashraf, why would they support an action that if successful could only increase the power of those who were seen to be in their way: Ali and his primary supporters, Malik al-Ashtar and the Qurra?

This was a difficult situation for Ali, especially as he comes down to us as something of a charismatic leader but not much of a politician. It seems that to Ali it was important that the caliph be a religious inspiration who cut across different groups by stressing the equality of believers and his role as a spiritual leader, an **Imam**, and not so much "a tyrannical tax gatherer and guardian of vested interests."[16] After the tumult of the preceding few years, Ali seemed determined to bring the purity of the umma back to where it had been under Muhammad.

Ultimately, Ali was able to muster up an army to march up the Euphrates into Syria, reaching Siffin, just outside of Raqqa, in 657. It seems at first the combatants were reluctant to shed Muslim blood or weaken the state with the Byzantines no doubt licking their chops, but a battle did eventually develop, with Ali's forces gaining the clear advantage. It was at that point, according to the narrative, that Muawiya's army placed leaves of the Quran on their lances, appealing for arbitration to resolve the dispute. Some in Ali's retinue, no doubt Malik al-Ashtar and other Qurra, wanted to finish off Muawiya. In retrospect Ali probably should have, but the caliph was perhaps moved by the spiritual outpouring, so he agreed to arbitration, which turned out to be a fatal error.

Muawiya used the arbitration process to buy time and manipulate the negotiations in a way that benefitted him, particularly in dealing with Ali as a perceived equal. Amr ibn al-As was chosen by Muawiya to be his arbitrator. Ever since he was kicked out of Egypt by Uthman, Amr took up shop in Damascus with the Syrian governor, becoming his closest advisor; a year after Siffin, Muawiya returned Amr to Egypt as governor for the remaining five years of his life. This was not a bad comeback for Amr, as he definitely chose the right horse to back. On the other hand, with Malik al-Ashtar being totally unacceptable to Muawiya, Ali felt compelled to appoint a leading member of the Ashraf as his arbitrator, who was not exactly someone totally committed to Ali's cause.

The arbitration severely weakened Ali's position among his supporters. A number of them, as we know, were against the decision to negotiate with Muawiya. A portion of these started to question Ali's leadership and rebelled against the caliph in what in effect was a civil war within a civil war. This opposition came to be known as the Khawarij (singular Khariji, which is why they have become more commonly known as the Kharijites). The appellation is taken from the Arabic verb **kharaja**, which means to go out or withdraw, in this case perhaps because they withdrew from Ali's coalition. The Kharijites became the oldest sect in Islam, and the first group to break away officially from the mainstream. Ali persuaded some to come back to the fold, but the rest were defeated in battle, scattering them to other places in Iraq and especially down into the eastern coast of Arabia. There they set up little commune-like Islamic towns characterized by their version of the righteous community, where they developed a belief that it was a sin to follow a corrupt ruler and it was their duty to overthrow them. Their influence in early Islamic history far outweighed their small numbers.

With the Kharijites breaking away and the less-than-enthusiastic support of the Ashraf, Ali's position in Iraq seemed like it was becoming more vulnerable by the day. Probably by 660, Muawiya was now openly claiming the caliphate for himself. But Ali's fortunes began to turn around as rumors of Muawiya's ruthlessness in gaining supporters by applying coercive force in Arabia and elsewhere began to concern and then win over the Ashraf and others who had heretofore been lukewarm to Ali's leadership. Even Basra seemed ready to support Ali and join Kufan forces to finally put an end to the recalcitrant governor of Syria. As fate would have it, though, the new army never got the opportunity to move on Syria. Ali was assassinated in a mosque in Kufa in 661—not by one of Muawiya's henchmen, but by a Kharijite.

Ali was a complicated and controversial leader, despised by some but loved by many. His well-intended sincerity and concern for Islam won him plaudits throughout the centuries. His political naivete in the face of the master politician from Syria alienated many of his supporters, but as the years went by and as opposition to Umayyad rule increased, this naivete began to be seen as an earnestness that was long missing in Islamic society, and almost a collective guilt developed for not having supported him more vigorously when he needed it. In the end, his charismatic spiritual leadership as an Imam became a beacon, eventually inspiring some to distinguish themselves as *Shiatu Ali*, followers of Ali, otherwise known today as Shia or Shiites, the second largest sect in Islam comprising today about 15 percent of Muslims worldwide (Sunnis being the other 85 percent). They are the majority in Iran, Iraq, and Bahrain, the largest religious sect in Lebanon, and are significant minorities in a host of other Middle Eastern countries.

In the short term it was not only a victory of Muawiya over Ali, but also a victory for the Quraysh, specifically the Umayyad clan. Perhaps giving himself too much credit, Muawiya reportedly said, "I triumphed over Ali because I held my secrets close while he revealed his, because the Syrians obeyed me while his followers disobeyed him, because I spent my wealth generously while he was miserly with his."[17] In addition, it was a victory of Syria over Iraq, and within Iraq itself, of the Ashraf over the Qurra. But the conflicts were anything but decided and would continue on in some form or fashion for almost the next century. I will end this section with a rather long quote from Madelung. It is a pretty harsh assessment of what transpired with the victory of Muawiya over Ali, but many Muslims at the time would probably have wholeheartedly agreed with it—sentiments that would eventually lay the foundation for the dismantlement of the Umayyad dynasty, so in the end, maybe Ali had the last laugh.

> In a wider historical perspective, Islam was now taken over by the state. Just as three centuries earlier Roman-Byzantine despotism appropriated Christianity, strangled its pacifist religious core, and turned it into a tool of imperial domination and repression, so now it appropriated Islam, strangling its spirit of religious brotherhood and community and using it as an instrument of repressive social control. . . . The Roman emperor, in pagan times deified . . . had since Constantine become head of the Christian church, the Vicar of Christ on earth, a Christ transformed from a Saviour and brother of man into a grim Pantocrator and Judge. The Umayyad caliph, a rival and successor of the Roman emperor in all but name, became the Viceregent of God on earth, a God who now primarily commanded absolute obedience and unquestioning submission to His arbitrary Decree and Ordainment. The Arabs had now what most of them had dreaded and vigorously resisted for so long. They had lost their freedom and tribal autonomy . . . They had now, as Ali had warned them, the rule of Caesar.[18]

Chapter 3 Timeline

632–661	Rule of the *Rashidun* Caliphs
632–634	Caliphate of Abu Bakr and the Ridda Wars
634–644	Caliphate of Umar ibn al-Khattab
636	Muslim army defeats the Byzantines at the Battle of Yarmuk
637	Muslim army defeats Sassanians at the Battle of Qadisiyya
637–638	Muslim conquest of Egypt
644–656	Caliphate of Uthman ibn al-Affan; authoritative version of the Quran produced
656–661	Caliphate of Ali ibn Abi Talib; the First *Fitna*

Primary Sources

The Battle of Ajnadin (or Ajnadain)

The battle of Ajnadin ensued. In this battle about 100,000 Greeks [i.e., Byzantine troops] took part, the majority of whom were massed one band after the other by Heraclius [Hirakl], the rest having come from the neighboring districts. On that day, Heraclius was in Hims [Emesa]. Against this army, the Moslems fought a violent battle, and Khalid ibn-al-Walid particularly distinguished himself. At last, by Allah's help, the enemies of Allah were routed and shattered into pieces, a great many being slaughtered.

Those who suffered martyrdom on that day were 'Abdallah ibn-az-Zubair ibn-'Abd-al-Muttalib ibn-Hashim, 'Amr ibn-Sa'id ibn-al-'Asi ibn-Umaiyah, his brother Aban ibn-Sa'id (according to the most authentic report. Others, however, claim that Aban died in the year 29), Tulaib ibn-'Umair ibn-Wahb ibn-'Abd ibn-Kusai (who fought a duel with an "unbeliever" who gave him a blow that severed his right hand making his sword fall down with the palm. In this condition he was surrounded and killed by the Greeks. His mother Arwa, daughter of 'Abd-al-Muttalib, was the Prophet's aunt. His surname was abu-'Adi), and Salamah ibn-Hisham ibn-al Mughirah. According to others, Salamah was killed at Marj as-Suffar. Other martyrs were: 'Ikrimah ibn-abi-Jahl ibn-Hisham al-Makhzumi, Habbar ibn-Sufyan ibn-'Abd-al-Asad al-Makhzumi (who, according to others, was killed in the battle of Mu'tah), Nu'aim ibn-'Abdallah an-Nahham al-'Adawi (who, according to others, was killed in the battle of al-Yarmuk), Hisham ibn-al-'Asi ibn-Wail as-Sahmi (who is also supposed by others to have been slain in the battle of al-Yarmuk), Jundub ibn-'Amr ad-Dausi, Sa'id ibn-al-Harith, al-Harith ibn-al-Harith, and al-Hajjaj ibn-al-Harith ibn-Kais ibn-'Adi as-Sahmi. According to Hisham ibn-Muhammad al-Kalbi, an-Nahham was killed in the battle of Mu'tah.

Said ibn-al-Harith ibn-Kais was slain in the battle of al-Yarmuk; Tamim ibn-al-Harith, in the battle of Ajnadin; his brother, 'Ubaidallah ibn 'Abd-al-Asad, in al-Yarmuk; and al-Harith ibn-Hisham ibn-al-Mughirah, in Ajnadin.

When the news of this battle came to Heraclius, his heart was filled with cowardice and he was confounded. Consequently, he took to flight to Antioch [Antakiyah] from Hims [Emesa]. It was mentioned by some-one that his flight from Hims to Antioch coincided with the advance of the Moslems to Syria. This battle of Ajnadin took place on Monday twelve days before the end of Jumada I, year 13. Some, however, say two days after the beginning of Jumada II, and others two days before its end.

After that, the Greeks massed an army at Yakusah, which was a valley with al-Fauwarah at its mouth. There the Moslems met them, dispelled them and put them to flight with a great slaughter. Their remnants fled to the cities of Syria. The death of abu-Bakr took place in Jumada II, year 13, and the Moslems received the news in al-Yakusah.

Source: Gordon, Matthew S. "The Battle of Ajnadin (or Ajnadain)." *The Rise of Islam*. Indianapolis: Hackett Publishing Company, Inc. (paperback version), 2008. Pgs. 123–124. Original source *The Origins of the Islamic State*, vol 1, translated by Philip Khuri Hitti (New York, 1916).

Tabarî: "The Death of 'Uthmân," from *The History of Prophets and Kings*

Then Muhammad b. Abû Bakr came to 'Uthmân.[1] He threatened Ibn al-Zubayr and Marwân, and they fled;[2] Muhammad b. Abû-Bakr then came to 'Uthmân and seized him by his beard. He said, "Let go of my beard—your father did not take hold of it." Muhammad let it go. But the people rushed upon him, some striking him with the iron tips of their scabbards, others striking him with their fists. A man came at him with a broad iron-tipped arrow and stabbed the front of his throat, and his blood fell on the Koran.[3] Yet (even) when they were in that state they feared killing him. 'Uthmân was old and he fainted. Others came in and when they saw that he had fainted they dragged him by the legs and (his wife) Nâ'ila and his daughters wailed loudly. Al-Tujîbî[4] came, drawing his sword to thrust it into his belly. When Nâ'ila protected ('Uthmân), he cut her hand. Then he leaned with his sword upon his chest; and 'Uthmân (Allâh bless him) was killed before sundown. A crier went about calling that his blood and property were forbidden. But the people sacked everything and then proceeded to the public treasury . . . .

Muhammad said: Al-Zubayr b. 'Abd-Allâh related to me from Yûsuf b. 'Abd-Allâh b. Salam,[5] who said:

"Uthmân looked upon the people while he was under siege and they were surrounding the house in every direction, and he said: 'I beseech you by Allâh (to Him belong glory and power), do you know that when the Commander of the Faithful, 'Umar b. al-Khattâb[6] (Allâh bless him), was (fatally) wounded, you prayed to Allâh asking Him to bless you and unite you in choosing the best among us (to succeed him)? What do you think of Allâh? Do you say that you were of so little consequence to Him, that he did not heed your prayer at a time when you were the only upholders of His truth among his creatures, and had not yet disagreed about it? Glory to Allâh! Allâh is far above such imperfection! Or do you say that His religion was of so little value to Him that He did not care who had charge of it, at a time when the religion is the way that people unite in worshipping Allâh? Submit yourselves to Allâh or you will be vanquished and punished. Or do you say that the selection was not done through consultation—you are very proud!—and that God appointed the community to act, if it disobeyed him!—and that you did not take counsel in choosing the *imâm*[7] and did not exert yourselves to learn his weaknesses? Or do you say that Allâh did not know how I would conduct my affairs? In some of my acts I did good and the Faithful approved. Since then, in the conduct of my affairs I have not committed any acts which you condemn that Allâh did not know of on the day that he chose me and clothed me with the robe of His glory (glory to Allâh! Allâh is far from such imperfection). I beseech you by Allâh, do you know that Allâh has made me witness over his Truth (and to fight for Allâh against His enemies is the Truth), which every man coming after me should confess that I possess? Do not kill me. For killing is allowed in only three cases: a man may be killed for committing adultery, for disbelieving after accepting Islam, or for murdering another person except in retaliation. If you kill me you will be putting your necks under a sword which Allâh (to Him belong glory and power) will not remove from you until the Day of Judgment. Do not kill me, for if you kill me you will never pray together again after I am gone, and you will never divide the booty among you again, after I am gone, and Allâh will never settle your disagreement again.'

"They replied. 'As for what you have mentioned concerning the people's appeal for Allâh's guidance (to Him belong glory and power) in appointing a guardian to succeed 'Umar (Allâh bless him) and your selection with Allâh's guidance, we answer that all the actions of Allâh are the best of actions, but Allâh (glory to Allâh! Allâh is above imperfection) has sent your case upon His people as a trial. As for what you have mentioned concerning your seniority, and priority with the Messenger of Allâh (Allâh's blessing and peace upon him), you used to have seniority and precedence with him and were worthy of the highest office; but since then you have changed and have innovated in the way you already know. As for what you have mentioned concerning the affliction which would befall us if we killed you, the fear of a rebellion ought not to sway us from upholding the truth against you. As for your belief that killing is forbidden except on three grounds only, we find in the Book of Allâh [i.e., the Qur'ân] other lawful killings than those which you have named—the killing of one who has spread corruption in the land; the killing of one who swerves from the path of justice and prevents its execution and fights against it and scorns it. You acted in tyranny; and you have prevented the executions of justice and have swayed from its path and been scornful of it, refusing to punish yourself in recompense for those whom you have deliberately oppressed. You have held fast to the Caliphate over us, and you have gone astray in your rule and your oath. You claim that you did not treat us with scorn and that those who defended you and prevented us from reaching you were fighting without your command. But they are fighting because of your tenacious hold upon the Caliphate. If you had abdicated they would not have fought to defend you.'"

Notes

[1] Muhammad b. Abû Bakr: son of the first Caliph Abû Bakr (r. 632–634).
[2] Meccan companions of 'Uthmân.
[3] Variant spelling of "Qur'ân."
[4] One of the assassins, probably one of a group of Arab tribesmen from Egypt who felt they had been double-crossed by 'Uthmân.
[5] The transmitters in this chain (*isnâd*) would have been sympathetic to 'Uthmân.
[6] 'Umar b. al-Khattâb: the second Caliph (r. 634–644) who had appointed the *shûra* or council which chose 'Uthmân. 'Umar did so on his deathbed, having himself been stabbed by a madman.
[7] *Imâm*: originally indicating the leader of Muslim prayer, it came to mean the leader of the community with the implication of religious authority. During the time of the first four Caliphs, it was synonymous with Caliph.

Source: McNeill, William H. and Marilyn Robinson Waldman, eds. "Tabari: 'The Death of Uthman,' from the History of Prophets and Kings." *The Islamic World*. Chicago: University of Chicago Press, 1983. Pgs. 76–79.

NOTES

1. Wilferd Madelung, *The Succession to Muhammad: A Study of the Early Caliphate* (Cambridge: Cambridge University Press, 1997), pp. 1–56.
2. Fadi Azzam, "In Syria, the World's Democracies Failed Us," *New York Times,* September 18, 2017. https://www.nytimes.com/2017/09/18/opinion/syria-democracy-fail.html.
3. Jared Diamond, *Guns, Germs, and Steel: The Fate of Human Societies* (New York: Norton, 1997), p. 278.
4. Quoted in Richard Fletcher, *Moorish Spain* (Berkeley: University of California Press, 1992), p. 106.
5. For instance, see John L. Esposito, *Unholy War: Terror in the Name of Islam* (Oxford: Oxford University Press, 2002), p. 35.
6. M. A. Shaban, *Islamic History: A New Interpretation, A.D. 600–750* (Cambridge: Cambridge University Press, 1971), p. 25
7. Shaban, *Islamic History*, p. 36.
8. Afaf Lutfi Al-Sayyid Marsot writes that there were 8,000 "horsemen" in the army that conquered Egypt. *A History of Egypt: From the Arab Conquests to the Present* (Cambridge: Cambridge University Press, 2007), p. 1.
9. Ibid., p. 2.
10. Shaban, *Islamic History*, p. 23.
11. Hossein Kamaly, *The History of Islam in 21 Women* (London: Oneworld Publications, 2019), p. 23.
12. The animus between the two appears to stem from a claim by someone in Medina, perhaps looking to discredit the Prophet, that having been mistakenly left behind from a caravan in the desert, there may have been an inappropriate relationship between Aisha and the man who found her and brought her back to Medina. According to tradition, the Prophet vehemently backed his wife in denying the claim, choosing not to divorce, beat or at worst, kill Aisha. Quite to the contrary, Muhammad used the incident to condemn those who brought false witness against a woman in this regard, with a hadith saying that "Those who slander married women without producing four witnesses, flog them with eighty stripes; and reject their evidence ever after, for they are wicked transgressors." Quoted in Kamaly, *History of Islam in 21 Women*, p. 32.
13. Ibid., p. 29.
14. Ibid., p. 36. See also Fatima Mernissi, *The Veil and the Male Elite: A Feminist's Interpretation of Women's Rights in Islam* (Reading, MA: Addison-Wesley, 1991), p. 78. As Kamaly writes, however, "we should bear in mind that most narratives about this formative period of Islam were all carefully reworked to establish some political or theological point." Kamaly, *History of Islam in 21 Women*, pp. 36–37.
15. Again, Aisha's role has been touted as a prominent example of the active part women played in early Islam, counter to popular stereotypes in the West; however, her defeat was also used by later Muslim polemicists as an argument or warning

against women in politics. Nikki R. Keddie, *Women in the Middle East Since the Rise of Islam* (Washington, DC: American Historical Association, 2007), p. 4.

16. Madelung, *Succession to Muhammad*, p. 310.
17. Quoted in R. Stephen Humphreys, *Mu'awiya ibn Abi Sufyan: From Arabia to Empire* (Oxford: Oneworld, 2006), p. 9.
18. Madelung, *Succession to Muhammad*, pp. 326–27.

KEY TERMS

Amir al-mumineen p. 45
amsar p. 54
Ashraf p.65
ata p. 56
caliph p. 43
hadith p. 49
Imam p. 65
jihad p. 49
jizya p. 56
kharaja p. 66
Rashidun p. 43
razzia p. 49
sabiqa p. 45
Sawad p. 54
sawafi p. 56
sharia p. 59
shura p. 57

For additional digital learning resources please go to www.oup.com/he/lesch-middleeast-1e

4 ARAB KINGDOM

Sufyanids

After the death of Ali, Muawiya ibn Abu Sufyan was in the catbird seat. He proclaimed himself caliph and he was acknowledged by enough to actually become caliph. By default, the capital became Damascus, with Syria as the engine for a new era in early Islam. With what in effect was now an empire in all but name, one that comprised pretty much all of the former Sassanian territory and all of the Byzantine Near East, the capital could not revert back to a remote desert oasis in western Arabia with its lack of resources to support a government and an army. There was probably very little if any thought given to Iraq, which in any case had too many **Alids**, or supporters of Ali (we cannot yet speak of Shiites).

But Muawiya inherited a very troubled state of affairs. Three of the last four caliphs had been assassinated, and the umma had been wounded and divided by at least two civil wars. It would take a great deal of energy and political acumen to keep this fractured entity together in a way that would allow it to continue to grow. As it turned out, Muawiya was the right man for the job. He was not a brilliant general or charismatic religious leader, but he was a master politician and tactician. He is said to have possessed the quality of *hilm,* or equanimity—he was calm under pressure. He tried to cultivate the image of a tribal shaykh rather than an authoritarian dictator, although his actions at times perhaps resembled more the latter than the former. As medieval Islamic historian Chase Robinson described him, "He was, then, very much the product of the same world that produced Muhammad himself: a Qurashi schooled in the ways of tribal politics of Mecca, he would practice those skills among the Arabs of Syria. Of state and empire building, he would have known relatively little—and this only relatively late. Faced with the difficult task of managing a small Muslim elite riven by divisions and disagreements resulting from the conquests, he fell back upon that which he knew best."[1]

He was ruthless when he had to be, but he typically tried first to persuade or bribe in order to get his way. He reportedly said on one occasion, "I never use my voice if I can use my money, never my whip if I can use my voice, never my sword if I can use my whip, but if I have to use my sword, I will."[2] To Muawiya, money was as important a weapon as the Syrian army. The problem with this type of approach is that it really only papers over problems, without addressing the root causes. Such a clever politician as Muawiya could get away with it, even thrive in it; however, if his successors were not so endowed with his political skill set, serious problem could—and did—become manifest.

The most serious problems that faced Muawiya immediately were in Iraq, where the death of Ali had not dampened pro-Alid sentiments nor growing opposition to Umayyad rule. Fortunately for Muawiya, the continuing intra-Muslim fissures in Iraq, particularly the divisions between the Ashraf and Qurra, prevented the development of a unified opposition movement against the Umayyads. In a decision that would change early Islamic history and actually lay the foundation decades later for the fall of the Umayyads, in 671 CE Muawiya arranged for the resettling of approximately 50,000 Muslims in Iraq to the far northeast in Iran to the province of Khurasan, an attempt to relieve the pressure building in Iraq from continued immigration there from Arabia. Khurasan actually had more Muslims than any other province outside of Iraq and Syria. This seems to have worked in the short term, and in combination with Muawiya's political acumen, for the remainder of his rule until 680, Iraq remained relatively quiet.

Muawiya's power base was obviously in Syria; however, we have less information about the Umayyad caliphs than Kufan amirs, as much of the history of the Umayyad period was written under Abbasid rule, which was naturally hostile toward Syria and tended to focus on points east. We do know that Muawiya had a wide base of support in Syria, and that he drew as much support from Christian Arab tribes as he did from the Muslims, lending more credence to the ecumenical nature of early Islam as more of an eclectic Believers movement than as yet a distinct religion. The caliph used this support to continue military expansion, especially in the Mediterranean. The Umayyads took the island of Rhodes off of the Anatolian coast in 672 and Crete in 674 from the Byzantines, thus extending their control over the eastern Mediterranean. During the final years of Muawiya's caliphate the Umayyad army, under the leadership of his son, Yazid, even attempted (unsuccessfully it turns out) to take Constantinople. Ultimately, Muawiya probably saw himself and his empire as more of a Caesar and successor to Rome rather than tribal shaykh from western Arabia. But what all of this showed was that under Muawiya there occurred a transition from expansion driven by evangelicalism to one that became institutionalized state policy for military-strategic and economic reasons—or even prestige, in the case of trying to take Constantinople.

But the Umayyad caliphate was still fairly decentralized, with provinces making only sporadic contributions to the central treasury in Damascus. Military expansion was something of a necessity in order to keep the soldiers happy and be able to fund various government projects. Other than when Muawiya intervened with his special brand of carrot and stick policies, the cities and provinces outside of Syria remained for the most part under local control and operated under localized administrative systems that had existed under Byzantine and Sassanian rule.

A couple of issues arose during Muawiya's reign that would have serious repercussions for the Umayyads after his death. One was the increasing number of **mawali** (singular *mawla*), who were non-Arab converts to Islam. As the state expanded, more non-Arabs began to see the benefits of conversion, either for spiritual or for material reasons, the latter having to do with no longer paying the *jizya,* or poll tax that non-Muslims were required to pay. The provincial and central governments came to depend on the jizya as a revenue builder, so it would create quite a hole in the budget if large sections of non-Arabs all of sudden converted. As we shall see, however, if mawali were prevented the benefits of conversion, a whole new set of antagonisms would be created, which is exactly what would happen under Muawiya's successors.

Another problem was Muawiya's choice to succeed him—his son, Yazid. This sort of hereditary succession had not happened yet in Islam, and many Muslims were vociferously opposed to the idea, instead preferring a shura to help select the next caliph. They accused Muawiya of trying to set up a hereditary monarchy, which was anathema to the religious nature of the umma for a number of Muslims. As one typically anti-Umayyad diatribe written under the Abbasids put it:

> There is Muawiya's disdainful attitude toward the religion of God, manifested by his calling God's servants to (acknowledge) his son Yazid (as heir apparent), that arrogant drunken sot, that owner of cocks, cheetahs, and monkeys. With furious threats and frightful intimidation, he forced the best of Muslims to give the oath of allegiance to Yazid, although he was aware of Yazid's stupidity and was acquainted with his ugliness and viciousness . . . his drunkenness, immorality and unbelief.[3]

This seems rather harsh, but it was emblematic of anti-Umayyad bias among large sections of Muslims, and the personal nature of the attack was also fairly typical in medieval Islamic history. To the contrary, Yazid appears to have been a quite capable military leader well-liked by his soldiers. In any event, if Yazid became caliph it would further secure Syria as the base of Islam to the exclusion of those in Iraq or the Qurayshis in the Hijaz, who had been effectively excluded from power by Muawiya. In the end, Muawiya was able to bribe or threaten enough people to accept Yazid as his successor, but without his father's political acumen, he would face a whole new set of challenges. Whatever one thinks of Muawiya's methods, he kept Islam together at a time when it could have easily broken up, and although he became an iconic figure as time went by, especially in Syria, one wonders whether the relatively politically naïve Ali could have been as successful, someone who could not even keep his own coalition together and was in the end assassinated by one of his own.

After Muawiya died in 680, some Iraqis, especially those in Kufa who held to the memory of Ali, saw an opportunity to put things right. Ali's eldest son, Hassan, apparently had no appetite for politics, and he abandoned any leadership claims to the Family of the Prophet. Perhaps it was polemical, but there were some who said he was bribed by Muawiya to stand down—and even a suggestion or two that he was poisoned at the order of Muawiya.

Regardless, Ali and Fatima's second son, Hussein, was willing to take up the Alid banner. Upon receiving word of the caliph's death, Hussein, along with some family members and a few supporters, left Medina to head toward Kufa, just as his father had done. He never made it there, however. Just outside of Kufa in Iraq at a place called Karbala, on the tenth *(ashura)* day of the month of Muharram in 680, after several days of confrontation and increasing starvation and thirst, Umayyad forces attacked in what has been called a massacre. Hussein, certainly in the minds of Alids and later to Shiites, was martyred. The attempt to raise the Alid banner was a puny affair as far as battles go, and it was obviously a pathetic failure in terms of its immediate objectives. But oftentimes these seemingly small events are embellished and become bigger than life, acting as a rallying cry for later generations. This was definitely the case here, as today the so-called Ashura holiday is by far the most intense passion play in all of Islam, as Shiites relive the martyrdom of Hussein, killed by the godless Umayyads. As someone who had been near and dear to his grandfather, the Prophet Muhammad, Hussein's death created a collective guilt among Alids that they had not done more to come to his aid. Hussein became a symbol for the suffering of all those who were weak and defenseless, and his martyrdom would play an important role in the development of a distinct Shiite sect centuries later.

In the immediate sense, however, Yazid faced an even bigger problem in the Hijaz. A number of Muslims in Mecca and Medina refused to take the *baya,* or oath of allegiance, to the new caliph. The opposition was led by Abdullah ibn al-Zubayr, the son of Zubayr ibn al-Awwam who, with Aisha, had marched against Ali. Rebellion seemed to run in the family. Known simply as Ibn al-Zubayr, he was reportedly the firstborn of the Muhajirun in Medina soon after the Hijra, so in a sense he could be considered a Companion of the Prophet. He held that the caliphate should not be the exclusive property of the Umayyads, but that the ruler should be chosen from all of the Quraysh, the traditional refrain from non-Umayyad Qurayshis.

Ibn al-Zubayr established himself in Mecca, which became the center of opposition to Yazid. The Abbasid-based diatribes against Yazid had nothing on Ibn al-Zubayr's, as he reportedly said in a sermon the following, with considerable accusations of sexual perversion: "Yazid of liquors, Yazid of whoring, Yazid of panthers, Yazid of apes, Yazid of dogs, Yazid of wine-swoons, Yazid of barren deserts."[4] Umayyad forces first occupied Medina after defeating the Muslims there in the

Battle of Harra in 683, a lava field just east of the city. The city was apparently sacked. Next, they marched on Mecca itself. None of these attacks endeared the Umayyads any more to their detractors. Reportedly the Umayyad forces included a number of Christian Arabs, which is consistent with the eclectic nature of support behind Muawiya, a Believers movement. The Christian Arabs may have carried crosses and other Christian symbols into battle, which may or may not have antagonized the Meccans further.

As the story goes, Umayyad forces were in the process of attacking a last stand of Ibn al-Zubayr at the Kaaba itself when word came of the death of Yazid by natural causes, most likely disease, which would frequently run rampant in a city such as Damascus. Umayyad forces, who were probably never enthusiastic to begin with in attacking Medina and Mecca, withdrew, leaving Ibn al-Zubayr to fight another day—and indeed he would.

By prior arrangement, Yazid was succeeded by his son, Muawiya II, but he was sickly and died after only a few weeks. This created a deep crisis in the Umayyad caliphate, as Yazid's other sons were too young, while at the same time Ibn al-Zubayr used the respite to regroup and rebuild his forces, soon to be on the march again. As it turned out, another line within the Umayyad family would come to the rescue, led by that redoubtable cousin of Uthman, now an old man: Marwan ibn al-Hakam.

Marwanids I

Marwan ibn al-Hakam seems to have been chosen as the next caliph in 684 based on his seniority within the clan and his long-time connection with the origin story of the movement as the right-hand man to Uthman. Most of his connections were in the Hijaz, not Syria. But he appears to have had the support of one section of Muslims in and around Syria, the Yamani tribe (also called the Kalb), as opposed to the Qays-Mudar (Qaysi or Qaysite), which opposed him.

This is a bit confusing, mostly because we do not have a great deal of information on the subject. But apparently by the time Marwan became caliph, the Arabs in Syria—and eventually with Arab Muslims throughout the empire—had begun to identify themselves with two supertribes rather than to the specific one to which they actually belonged. It seemed to be as much a political choice based on common interests as genealogical. Shaban compares this division to the Whigs and Tories in English history.[5] Chase Robinson maintains that with the disruption of the old way due to the mobility of Arab tribesmen with the initial conquests and then the settling that followed, many took up different occupations, including the military, and therefore "tribal loyalties ceased to make much sense."[6] As a result, Arabs began to identify with various factions rather than their preexisting tribal affiliations. There was a need for many Arabs to forge new social links in the post-conquest environment. The state tended to reinforce this binary division by typically favoring one side or the other. And with the breakdown of Umayyad authority during the transition from Sufyanid to Marwanid rule, many of the emerging differences began to manifest themselves.

The Yamanis touted their glorious pre-Islamic past and claimed to be descended directly from Ismail, the concubine son of Abraham by Hagar, who began the Arab line (Isaac, by Sarah, began the Hebrew line according to this narrative). Despite Marwan's rather negative image that comes down to us, the Yamani platform, if you will, was rather farsighted. It called for a drawing down or end to expansion in order to focus more on domestic affairs, in addition to the fact that as time went by many Syrian soldiers were just flat-out tired of constant military campaigns. Yamanis could also be called assimilationist, that is, they believed there should be a more inclusive political, social, and economic environment for non-Qurayshis and non-Arabs in general. It is certainly a policy of which Ali would have approved.

The Qays, on the other hand, included the Quraysh among their lot; thus, in a case of the past being superimposed on the present, they promoted themselves and their ancestors as being primarily responsible for the rise of Islam. As far as their political program, Qays wanted the borders of Islam to continue to expand while also making sure that only their "supertribe" remained in power, so they could be considered to be exclusivist while the Yamanis were inclusivist.

Upon Marwan's assumption of power, a man by the name of al-Dahhak ibn Qays, a leader of the Qays-Mudar (as the last element in his name clearly indicated, which was probably artificially attached just to show his affiliation), took up opposition to the new caliph; he recognized Ibn al-Zubayr as the rightful caliph. He was located in the Jazira, which became a primary base for the Qays in Syria, many of whom were likely descended from the original core group of Arab conquerors sent by Umar following the initial conquest. Apparently Muawiya had allowed Arab immigration into the Jazira, but not the rest of Syria, which the Qays increasingly resented. The scene was thus set for war.

Just nine months after the death of Yazid, in July 684, the Qays and Yamanis met in a very bloody battle at Marj Rahit, just north of Damascus. With Ibn al-Zubayr still out there, this was yet another civil war within a civil war, in this case allowing the Zubayrids to regroup. The Yamanis were decisively victorious, with numerous dead from both sides on the battlefield. However, the intensity of the conflict only solidified rather than resolved the tribal division, and the Qays-Yamani dispute would expand and continue on for the remainder of the Umayyad dynasty, ultimately being one of the primary factors in its fall. Marwan was an old man, probably in his sixties, so he very well could have died of natural causes in 685 after a short reign, although there is one delightfully juicy story on what may have been the cause.[7] Regardless, he is considered one of the architects of Umayyad rule.

Marwan's son, Abd al-Malik, succeeded him. Next to Muawiya, he is the most important—or at least impactful—of all the Umayyad caliphs. However, when he took office, one cannot underestimate the challenges that faced him. Ibn al-Zubayr was still around after the reprieve he received with Yazid's death. He used the

Qays-Yamani dispute in Syria to his advantage, rebuilding his forces and extending his reach. As Robinson points out, it would not be wrong at all to say that Abd al-Malik was the rebel now, opposing the generally acknowledged caliph in the Islamic world, Ibn al-Zubayr, especially as the latter had the two Holy Cities, Mecca and Medina, under his control.[8] Such was the extent of his acceptance as caliph that if some alien from outer space had come down and viewed the Islamic world at that moment, it would conclude that it was the Zubayrid and not the Umayyad caliphate.

Abd al-Malik also understood that the most immediate threat was the Byzantine empire bordering Syria to the north, and it was a Byzantine empire that was probably eager to retake some of the territory it lost in the Middle East after witnessing all the distress and turmoil in Islamic lands of late. As such, the Umayyad caliph entered into a rather humiliating treaty with Byzantium in order to keep them off his back. It was a classic case of one step backward for now, two steps forward later. The promise of tribute paid to Constantinople would buy him some breathing space.

The Umayyads, though, experienced a bit of good luck flowing in their direction for a change. The social tensions in Iraq that led to the death of Uthman and Ali's problems had not really subsided; with troubles in Syria, the tensions in Kufa increased as one would expect. Perhaps Abd al-Malik took some satisfaction in the knowledge that it would fall to Ibn al-Zubayr to deal with the incessant problems of Iraq rather than the Umayyads. Similarly, Zubayrid attention toward Iraq would do for the Umayyads what the Qays-Yamani dispute did for the Zubayrids: buy even more time and breathing space to regroup. In addition to the old disputes in Kufa around the question of status, a new problem emerged: more and more of the local non-Arab population had been converting to Islam. As mentioned earlier, these non-Arab converts were called *mawali.* This meant that conversion could mean a substantial loss of revenue because once a taxpayer became a Muslim, at least in theory, that person would no longer pay the jizya or poll tax. Mawali, however, tended to be denied the fiscal benefits of conversion, which they adamantly resented. This not only had strict monetary repercussions, but it also had to do with political power and social status; under some of the stricter moments of Umayyad rule, mawali could not live in the same areas as Arab Muslims and were also denied certain social activities enjoyed by Arab Muslims. The Ashraf, acting much as the Qurra once viewed them, saw mawali as a threat to their power base and thus eagerly supported Umayyad policy on this front. As usual, these tensions would come to a head in Kufa.

There was still pro-Alid sentiment in Iraq, especially in Kufa. Some had been professing support for Ali, Hussein's son (Ali ibn Hussein ibn Ali), while others got behind Muhammad ibn al-Hanafiyya, who was a half-brother of Hussein (Ali ibn Abi Talib was his father, but not by Fatima). Both were located in the Hijaz and reluctant to get involved in politics, and after seeing what happened to Hussein and his father, one couldn't blame them. By default, the leadership of the opposition movement in Kufa devolved to a man by the name of Mukhtar ibn Abi Ubayd. In 685, Mukhtar and his Alid supporters drove out of town the governor sent by Ibn al-Zubayr and proclaimed Muhammad ibn al-Hanafiyya not just caliph, but the **Mahdi**, a divinely guided messiah or savior who would—with Allah's support—establish justice for all Muslims. This could be a case of Judeo-Christian messianic influence seeping into Islam, and this was the first time in any significant way that this term appeared in Islamic history. What is interesting about all this is that there is some ambiguity as to whether or not Muhammad ibn al-Hanafiyya was even aware that he had been proclaimed caliph, much less the Mahdi. But from the point of view of the Alids, it had become something of an article of faith that only someone from the Family of the Prophet Muhammad had the necessary insight, spiritual guidance, and tools to lead the umma, so Muhammad ibn al-Hanafiyya got tapped for the job whether he wanted it or not.

At this moment there were three main poles of attraction in Islam: the Umayyads in Syria, the Alids in Kufa, and the Zubayrids basically everywhere else. Because of the recent history in Iraq as a source of serious problems, Ibn al-Zubayr probably saw the revolt by Mukhtar as more threatening to his position than Abd al-Malik's. Ibn al-Zubayr dispatched his brother, Musab, with an army to take care of Kufa, which he did in short order in 687, including the killing of Mukhtar. In the end, the Kufan revolt really wasn't that big of a deal on the surface, and it was dealt with relatively quickly. However, it is of great importance because of some of the ideas it introduced into Islam and what the revolt represented. It was the first—and certainly not the last—time that the mawali, feeling discriminated against despite conversion, would play an important role in Islamic history. Second was the introduction of the idea of a mahdi, something that would inspire a number of later Islamic movements over the centuries. Finally, Muhammad ibn al-Hanafiyya, as mentioned earlier, was directly descended from Ali but not from the Prophet Muhammad, thus elevating the former's stature at the same time that it widened the definition of who legitimately could be said to be from the Family of the Prophet. In a way, the revolt led by Mukhtar was something of a dress rehearsal for the Abbasid revolution that would come some sixty-five years later, preparing the ideological and practical ground for what would put an end to the Umayyad caliphate.

With Mukhtar out of the way, Abd al-Malik and Ibn al-Zubayr came face to face. The troubles in Iraq allowed Abd al-Malik to rebuild and regroup his experienced Syrian army. He personally led the forces that moved into Iraq in 691 and defeated the Zubayrid army led by Musab at a place called Dayr al-Jathaliq, just north of present-day Baghdad on the Tigris River. He entered triumphantly into Kufa shortly thereafter. All that was left was to dispatch his celebrated right-hand man, al-Hajjaj ibn Yusuf al-Thaqifi, to Mecca in 692. There, the Zubayrids were decisively defeated, with Ibn al-Zubayr, probably around age seventy, dying in the fighting.

One of the interesting achievements of the Umayyads during the Zubayrid period was the building of the Dome of the Rock in Jerusalem. It is one of the earliest and greatest architectural structures in medieval Islamic history. The Dome was completed in 692; however, Abd al-Malik ordered its construction shortly after he came to power. The Dome of the Rock consecrates Muhammad's famous Night Journey from Mecca to heaven. The rock, located on the Temple Mount or **Haram al-Sharif** (Noble Sanctuary), was the metaphorical halfway point on his way to heaven. Monumental architecture is certainly a way to project power and wealth in all societies, and this may have partly been the case here for the Umayyads despite their condition at the time. In addition, building the Dome of the Rock on the Temple Mount—the center of Judaism and near the epicenter of Christianity—can perhaps be seen as a coming out party of sorts announcing that Islam was here to stay, utilizing monumental architecture as a way to separate itself from its Judeo-Christian environment, a representation of replacing and superseding previous revelation.

One interesting possibility suggested by historian G. R. Hawting is that since Mecca and Medina were outside of Umayyad control at the time, Abd al-Malik ordered the Dome of the Rock to be built as an alternative hajj site.[9] We know that Jerusalem was important to the Umayyad family going back to pre-Islamic times; Muawiya was "crowned" caliph there instead of in Damascus. It is interesting to ponder what would have happened to Islam if the Zubayrids and Umayyads continued to exist side-by-side for some time. Would the Muslim world have been bifurcated into two related but separate parts? I think that inevitably one or the other had to prevail completely, which is what happened. Perhaps the civil war and the battle of religious authenticity that went along with it accelerated the emergence of a distinct Islam under Umayyad leadership. One wonders also what would have happened had the Zubayrids won the war: Would the Believers movement begun by Muhammad have continued, with some form of syncretic Abrahamic religion coming into being in the Middle East?

SPOTLIGHT

The Dome of the Rock

The Dome of the Rock in Jerusalem is the most recognizable architectural feature in the fabled city. It has also over the years become a symbol of the competing claims for the city between Muslims and Jews and the focal point for Israeli–Palestinian rallies, protests, and violence. The Dome of the Rock commemorates the halfway point in the Prophet Muhammad's miraculous night journey from Mecca before ascending through the seven heavens. During the course of this journey he met with and sought advice from preceding prophets, such as Moses, Jesus, Abraham, and John the Baptist, before entering into the presence of God (Allah) himself. The Rock contains Muhammad's footprint where he ascended into the heavens. It is located on the platform of the Temple Mount (or what Muslims refer to as the Haram al-Sharif, the Noble Sanctuary), the location of the Jewish temple built originally by Solomon around the year 950 BCE, situated on the site where Jews believe Abraham almost sacrificed his son Isaac. The First Temple was destroyed by Babylonian King Nebuchadnezzar in 586 BCE. Following the seventy-year Babylonian captivity of the Jews, the Second Temple was built in 515 BCE, only to be destroyed once again by the Roman legions in 70 CE following the Great Jewish Revolt that began in 66 CE. The Western Wall on one side of the Temple Mount is all that remains of the Second Temple, and it is considered the holiest site in all of Judaism. To many Jews, Israel itself is considered to be the Third Temple.

Some Muslims believe that Muhammad's night journey actually occurred, whereas others believe that it was more of a visionary experience rather than a physical one. Regardless, it displays the centrality of Jerusalem in Islam, making it the third holiest site for most Muslims (after Mecca and Medina). The night journey also positioned Islam in the pantheon of the Judeo-Christian experience and tradition, where Muhammad is seen by Muslims as the Seal of the Prophets, the last in the line of Old and New Testament prophets who received revelations from God. Jerusalem was the *qibla* or direction of prayer for Muslims in years immediately after Muhammad began receiving revelations from Allah through the archangel Gabriel; through revelation, the qibla was changed to the Kaaba in Mecca later in Muhammad's life, and this has remained the direction of prayer for Muslims ever since.

Umar ibn al-Khattab, the second caliph or successor to the Prophet Muhammad and one of the Prophet's closest companions, directed the initial wave of the great Islamic conquests. In 638 CE, after the defeat of Byzantine armies in the region, Umar entered the conquered city of Jerusalem. Since Jews and Christians are considered to be *ahl al-kitab*, or People of the Book, (i.e., the Bible), and therefore protected peoples, Umar ordered that all three Abrahamic faiths should coexist peacefully. According to Islamic tradition, Umar refused to pray in the Church of the Holy Sepulchre built by the Roman Emperor Constantine in the fourth century CE, which contains the site of Jesus Christ's crucifixion and tomb; if he had done so, Umar was afraid the Muslims would have wanted to transform the church into a mosque. Umar even invited a number of Jewish families to return to Jerusalem, for the Christian Byzantines did not allow Jews to establish a permanent residence in the city. The Caliph Umar apparently found the Temple Mount to be desecrated as a garbage dump, a place for refuse and ruins. He was sufficiently horrified and ordered it to be cleaned up. He reconsecrated the plateau at the top of the Temple Mount, building a relatively simple mosque that became the site of what today is called the al-Aqsa (Farthest) Mosque.

Western and Egyptian tourists visiting the Dome of the Rock in 1890, before the Dome received its gold-plated makeover that is so recognizable today.
mideastimage.com

It was left to the Caliph Abd al-Malik (685–705 CE) during the Umayyad caliphate in Damascus to build the Dome of the Rock on the Temple Mount. Begun in 687 CE, it was completed together with its magnificent golden dome four years later. There is some speculation that Abd al-Malik built the Dome of the Rock as a possible alternative pilgrimage site and direction for prayer for Muslims, since at the time of the decision to erect the structure both Mecca and Medina were under the control of a rival caliphate led by Ibn al-Zubayr, the son of Zubayr ibn al-Awwam, who was a companion of the Prophet and who himself rebelled against the caliphate of Ali ibn Abi Talib, the son-in-law and cousin of Muhammad. However, by the time the Dome of the Rock was completed, Mecca and Medina had been restored to Umayyad control.

Since that time the Dome of the Rock has been restored and embellished by a number of different rulers, the latest being the replacement of the rusting and worn gold dome in 1993 paid for by Jordan's King Hussein. It is a popular tourist site today, as are the other related structures on and around the Temple Mount/Haram al-Sharif, but it is also a source and symbol of the passion that nourishes the Arab–Israeli conflict.

Abd al-Malik had won. Now he could consolidate power and extend his authority. Borrowing liberally from the imperial tradition of the Romans and Sassanians, he would centralize power in a way that no previous caliph had done. Uthman tried, but he was woefully unprepared to succeed. Gone would be Muawiya's decentralized system, in which Muawiya had fashioned himself as a glorified tribal shaykh; Abd al-Malik was king and conqueror, and his political and administrative centralization would provide the model for many caliphs to come, including the Abbasids.

One of the main ingredients of centralization was developing a standard Arabic coinage to replace the imitation Byzantine and Sassanian coinage used up to this time, so that tax collecting and monetary transactions could be systematized and become more efficient. Getting more money into the treasury in Damascus was vital to any policy of centralization, first and foremost to pay the soldiers so that they could enforce government policy if necessary. And since there was no social media at the time or billboards along the side of the road, what appeared on coins was often the best way to propagandize. Typically, these newly minted coins would have the *shahada*, or Muslim profession of faith, imprinted on them, but it was at this time that the double shahada starts to appear more often: "and Muhammad is his Messenger" was added to the first part, "There is no God but Allah." Along with the Dome of the Rock and similar inscriptions appearing on the inside of the Dome, this may have been when Islam started to become a distinct religion and when individuals began to refer to themselves as Muslims and not simply Believers.[10] There were no more Christian crosses appearing on coins. Instead, along with the religious invocations, a mock-up of the caliph appeared on one side, usually with a fierce posture and portrayal depicting strength, if not fear; encouraging, if not demanding, submission to more than just Allah. This process was not put in place overnight, and local conditions continued to prevail for a time, but this is when the change began. The Iraqis had lost their battle to retain revenues of the rich Sawad alluvial plains in their own hands, and there was no longer any doubt that surplus revenues made their way back to Damascus.

Syrian gold dinar of the Umayyad caliph Abd al-Malik, 694–695.
agefotostock/Alamy Stock Photo

Along with the standardization of coinage went the Arabization of the administration. Before Abd al-Malik, local languages typically prevailed in places like Iran and Iraq (Persian), or Coptic or Greek in Egypt and along the Mediterranean coast in Syria and Palestine. From this point on, in whatever part of the empire you were, Arabic was the language of government and commerce, and this marked the beginning of Arabic becoming the dominant language in much of the Middle East. As Robinson states:

> Christians and Jews alike had gotten along fine as linguistic schizophrenics, reading, writing and speaking a variety of languages and scripts, translating scripture from one language to the next. Muslims were altogether more ambitious; they were hardly the first linguistic imperialists, but they were the first to insist that the language spoken by God and those delegated by Him (caliphs, governors, commanders, etc.) should be the language of the mundane job of ruling—the language of receipts, bills, orders, contracts, coins, weights, measures, passports, sealings and the like. Language therefore functioned both as a powerful tool of political integration and as a token of cultural and religious superiority.[11]

In addition, Abd al-Malik improved the postal system as well as the system of roads. This made communication much faster, and it allowed for soldiers, commerce, and orders to be transported more efficiently, all important elements of centralization. In Iraq, though, is where the caliph employed his loyal right-hand man, al-Hajjaj ibn Yusuf al-Thaqifi. It is no surprise that Abd al-Malik essentially made him lord of the eastern half of the empire. Iraq was always the troublesome spot, and al-Hajjaj ruthlessly bludgeoned it into submission, almost goading Iraqis into rebellion with some of his draconian policies in order to bring them out of hiding so that he could crush them. The following is a quote attributed to al-Hajjaj after he, disguised, snuck into a mosque in Kufa full of rebellious types, ripped off his cloak, and defiantly threatened them; while he may or may not have actually said it, it seems to accurately reflect his approach based on the policies he implemented:

> By God, I shall make evil bear its own burden; I shall shoe it with its own sandal and recompense it with its own like. I see heads before me that are ripe and ready for plucking, and I am the one to pluck them, and I see blood glistening between the turbans and the beards . . . The Commander of the Faithful emptied his quiver and bit his arrows and found me the bitterest and hardest of them all. Therefore he aimed me at you. For a long time you have been swift to sedition; you have lain in the lairs of error and have made a rule of transgression. By God, I shall strip you like bark, I shall truss you like a bunder of twigs, I shall beat you like stray camels. . . . By God, what I promise, I fulfill; what I propose, I accomplish; what I measure, I cut off.[12]

By 702, under al-Hajjaj's guidance, a military garrison (misr) was established about halfway between Kufa and Basra at a place called Wasit, which in Arabic means "middle." Here a permanent Syrian standing army presence would be in place, and for the foreseeable future it would be the arbiter of power in Iraq, which the Iraqis bitterly resented. By the time Abd al-Malik died of natural causes in 705 at the age of sixty, the decentralized Sufyanid system had effectively been replaced by the Marwanid centralized system in the Qaysite style. But it was a system that was dependent ultimately on the power of the Syrian army, and both for the soldiers themselves as well as the population in general, it would be a form of heavy-handed rule that would generate weariness and opposition over time among friend and foe alike. Abd al-Malik was smoothly succeeded by his son, al-Walid, who would rule for a decade. His time in power would be relatively peaceful and prosperous. Expansion continued on both ends of the empire, with most of the Iberian Peninsula falling under Islamic control following the invasion of Spain in 711, and on the eastern end, from their base at Merv in Khurasan, Umayyad armies moved past the

Umayyad Mosque, Damascus, Syria, 2010. The site was a temple dedicated to the Roman god Jupiter then a Byzantine cathedral before the Caliph Walid I between 705 and 715 had the mosque built. Considered by many Muslims to be the fourth holiest site in Islam (after Mecca, Medina, and the Dome of the Rock), it also contains what many believe to be the head of John the Baptist, enshrined inside the mosque, as well as the location where Jesus (Isa) will appear at the end of times.
Erdal Şükrü Akan/Alamy Stock Photo

Oxus River and secured the submission of Bukhara, Samarqand, Khwarazm, and Farghana between 706 and 713.

Al-Hajjaj remained as loyal to al-Walid as he was to his father. However, when the overlord of the east died in 714 and the caliph died the following year in 715, there appeared to be an opportunity for the Umayyads to go in a different direction, perhaps adopting a more Yamani style of rule in place of what had effectively been Qaysite policies.

Marwanids II

Another son of Abd al-Malik, Sulayman, succeeded his brother. Sulayman was governor of Palestine, which was dominated by Yamanis, therefore offering some hope that he might lean in that direction with regard to his policies. It's difficult to tell what his inclination actually was, because he was only in power for a couple of years, was not regarded as a very pious caliph (as was the case with most of the Umayyads), and had a reputation for living a decadent and debauched life. However, his choice of Umar II as his successor seems to suggest that he leaned toward the Yamanis. Umar II would be the exception to the rule thus far when he became caliph in 717 following Sulayman's death from illness. Choosing the name of Umar indicates where he wanted to go in terms of policy direction, returning to the type of religious-based and incorruptible leadership for which his namesake was famous. Even though much of the polemical history of the Umayyads was written by the Abbasids—or by historians in Abbasid times—the Islamic tradition is unanimous in depicting Umar II as different, a complete contrast to other Umayyad caliphs who were usually described as tyrannical, impious, or corrupt and degenerate. After the Abbasids entered Damascus, all the Umayyad caliphs' tombs were violated except for that of Umar II.

Umar II saw the rising tensions between mawali and the government, especially in Iraq, where under al-Hajjaj they did not enjoy the fruits of conversion. The resentment over their economic and political exclusion along with the stigma of sociocultural discrimination had grown exponentially. To counter this, Umar II introduced a new fiscal policy and administration that would tax and treat mawali as the Muslims they in fact were. But as one can imagine, his policies threatened too many established interests and these policies came to a premature end when he himself came to a premature end in 720, most likely after being poisoned. His successor, Yazid II, was a caliph in the Qaysite tradition—and gone was the hope raised by Umar II.

Yazid II only lasted four years, and he was succeeded by Hisham, who although also Qaysite leaning, was thought to be much more competent. This proved to be the case, and he ruled for nineteen years until 743. Hisham displayed Muawiya-like qualities in terms of being an able politician. He was able to paper over differences, encourage compromise, and on the whole was conciliatory. Importantly, like most

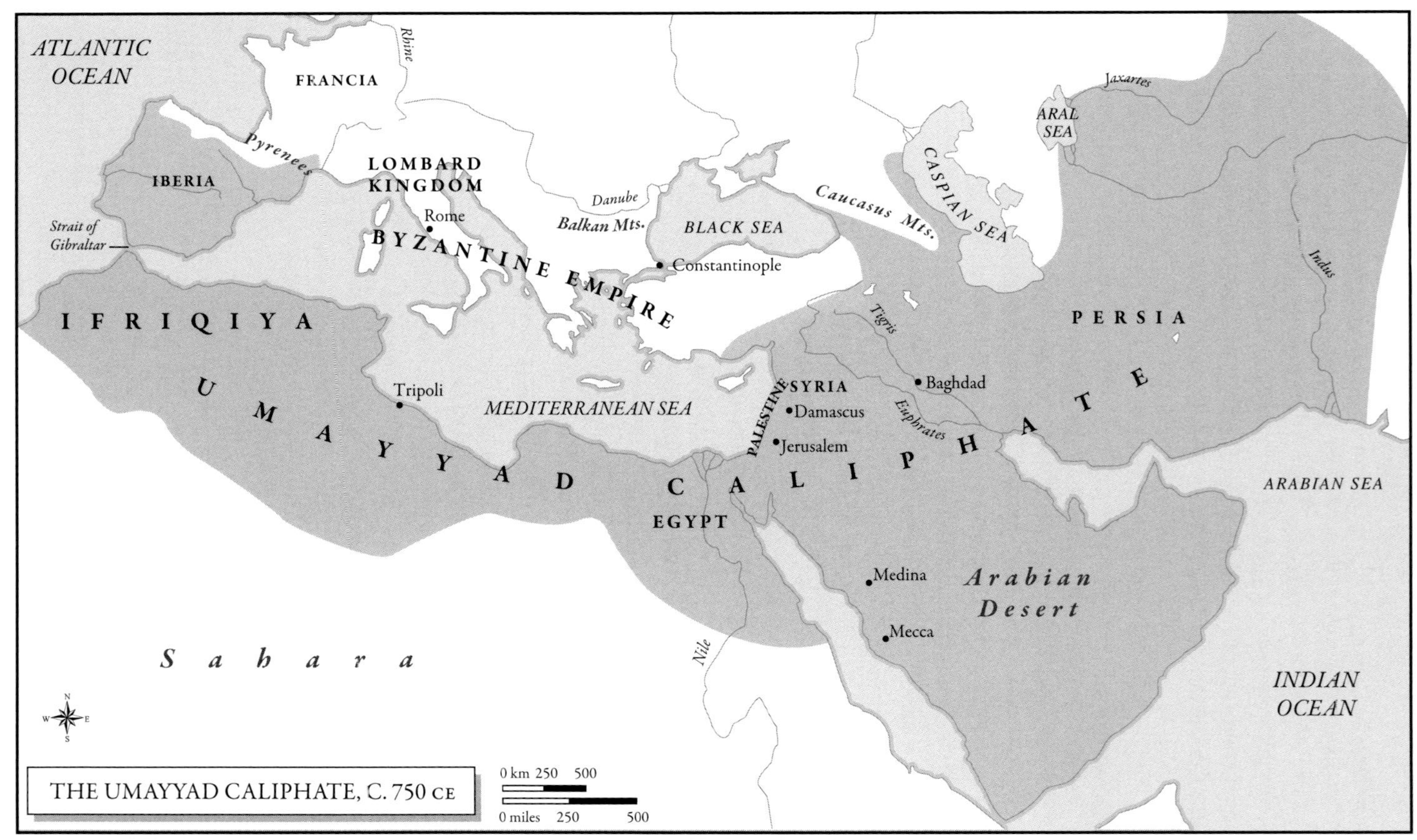

THE UMAYYAD CALIPHATE, C. 750 CE

successful Umayyad caliphs, he was able to stay above the Qays-Yamani dispute and avoid major confrontations on this front. There was very little internal opposition, especially in the heartland of the Islamic world, during his time in power.

Hisham's primary problems, however, were on the fringes of the empire, where recalcitrant groups in North Africa and invasions by Turkish-based tribal confederations just outside the north and northeast regions of the empire drained the central treasury over time, as well as the morale of the Syrian army. The first threat came from the independently minded Berbers in North Africa. While most had converted to Islam, like the early Arabs, they were almost convulsively resistant to outside control—and some were egged on by Kharijite missionaries from the Persian Gulf. Repeated attempts by the Umayyads to reign them in usually failed or were pyrrhic victories, and a very loose live-and-let-live type of existence emerged in North Africa away from the Mediterranean coast. In the end, Umayyad rule really did not extend past Qayrawan in present-day Tunisia; thus Spain was effectively cut off by land.

In the Caucasus region west of the Caspian Sea a Turkish group called the Khazars were stirring up trouble, and only with great difficulty were Umayyad armies able to push them back into their own territory in the lower Volga area by 738. Finally, beyond the eastern border of Khurasan, a Turkish tribal confederation known as the Turgesh threatened the settled areas in Bukhara and Samarqand, located in present-day Uzbekistan. The Umayyad armies were victorious by 737 in pushing them back, although the depredations of war in the area helped mobilize opposition to Umayyad rule in Khurasan—something that would have important repercussions soon enough.

All of this effort sapped the strength and morale of the Syrian army, which seemed to have to be everywhere at the same time to deal with multiple threats. When Hisham died in 743, the peace and prosperity that seemed to exist on the surface throughout much of the empire hid some important tensions and issues lying in wait underneath. It was not inevitable that the Umayyad caliphate should fall only seven years later, but it was a situation that called for strong, farsighted leadership. Unfortunately for the Umayyads, this is not what happened.

Hisham was opposed to al-Walid II (Yazid II's son) succeeding him, as al-Walid was known to have been incompetent and had a reputation for luxurious living. But oftentimes within a family line, the choice of the successor is a community decision based on internal politics as much as competency and leadership skills. It is telling that someone such as Hisham, who was in power for almost two decades, could not dictate who would succeed him. As it turned out, al-Walid II confirmed all of Hisham's worst fears. He has been described as the playboy par excellence of the Umayyads. He seldom could be seen in Damascus, which many caliphs wanted to increasingly avoid anyway due to the prevalence of plagues, but he paid very little attention to administrative affairs wherever he was. He wasted funds building half-baked and half-finished palace projects, and he seemed to party more than politic.

In the end, he was killed by elements of a weary Syrian army, tired of campaigning. Like Uthman, al-Walid II was killed sitting alone, reading the Quran. And just as the assassination of Uthman led to the end of the Rashidun, so did the murder of al-Walid II lead to the unraveling and eventual end of Umayyad rule. Without strong and sagacious leadership, the Qays-Yamani feud broke open with renewed vigor. One of al-Walid II's sons, who adopted the name of Yazid III, took over as caliph, and it appeared that he recognized the rising problems and committed to follow the Yamani line, reportedly declaring that a caliph could be Quraysh or non-Quraysh, Arab or non-Arab, and that the umma had the right to remove an unjust ruler, which was very Kharijite in tone.[13] As with Umar II, however, his policies barely got to see the light of day before he died under suspicious circumstances in 744 after only six months in power.

In 744 alone there were four different Umayyad caliphs—not exactly the stability one would want to see with so many underlying problems existing and with rising opposition maturing into a serious movement in Iraq and especially in Khurasan, which would turn into the Abbasid revolution. Finally, the Umayyad family settled on Marwan ibn Muhammad (Marwan II), the grandson of Marwan ibn al-Hakam, as the next caliph. At some other point during the Umayyad caliphate, Marwan probably would have done just fine, as he was a strong, capable military leader who was popular with his troops. He was known as al-Himar, or the "Ass" in Arabic, which in this context suggests he exhibited traits akin to the strength and stubbornness of a mule. His stubbornness in following Qaysite policies, however, was the beginning of the end for him and the Umayyads. Someone such as Umar II might have been able to turn things around, if he in fact had the internal support necessary to do so, but a return to Qaysite policies is exactly what the empire did not need at the time. He was backed by a faction of the Syrian elite, particularly the Qaysites from the Jazira; he effectively relocated the capital from Damascus to Harran in the Jazira.

Marwan II seemed to constantly be putting down rebellions, especially in Iraq, during his tenure in power. He was mostly successful in doing so, but there was a cloud on the horizon in the form of a rebellion in Khurasan that would morph into the Abbasid revolution. That this movement was led initially by Abu Muslim Abd-Rahman ibn Muslim almost says it all with regard to the nature of the growing opposition to Umayyad rule. Abu Muslim was Persian, so he was a mawla, a non-Arab convert to Islam. The Muslim name he adopted translates into "father of a Muslim, servant of God, and son of a Muslim," so there is no doubt that he was emphasizing a return to a purer Islamic way of life and leadership and a more equitable distribution of power and wealth among Arab and non-Arab Muslims.

Abu Muslim established himself and his army in Merv by 748, having driven out the Umayyad governor. He moved into Iraq the following year and occupied Kufa, naming a member of the Abbasid family as the new caliph, Abu al-Abbas al-Saffah. Not about to shrink from this challenge, Marwan II mustered up his troops and marched into Iraq. In February 750 the two armies met at the Zab River, a tributary of the Tigris, and Abu Muslim and the Abbasids were victorious. The Yamanis in Damascus opened their gates to the Abbasids. Marwan fled to Egypt where he was soon caught and killed, and the Syrian-based Umayyad caliphate had reached its end.

The Umayyads probably are treated too harshly by their contemporaries and those, such as the Abbasids, who immediately followed them. After all, the victors were not going to say they overthrew an enlightened, far-sighted dynastic family. The Umayyads were described as corrupt, tyrannical, and impious. Some were, some weren't. The Umayyads could not offer the type of leadership that many Muslims wanted, which maybe was impossible considering the fact that there were a number of different types of government and leadership that Muslims wanted. Also, Umayyad rule increasingly looked like Syrian rule, and other regions, especially Iraq, resented this. Overall, non-Arabs were excluded from leadership positions and the benefits of converting to Islam, and this created tremendous tensions over what was probably the majority of the population in Umayyad lands. It was, as Julius Wellhausen put it in the title of his book *Das Arabische Reich und Sein Sturz* ("The Arab Empire and Its Fall"), an Arab kingdom.[14] But it was an Arab kingdom in which Arabic became the dominant language and when Islam continued to spread, where being a part of the Muslim elite was desirable.

Islam was on the verge of breaking up following upon the assassinations of Uthman and Ali. If that had happened, Arab culture and the Islamic religion may have been gobbled up by the dominant Byzantine and Sassanian cultural milieus. The fact that Arabic is the dominant language and Islam the dominant religion in the Middle East today is in large measure due to the Umayyads being in power at a critical moment in early Islamic history and to the leadership skills of caliphs such as Muawiya, Abd al-Malik, and Hisham.

Chapter 4 Timeline

661–750	Umayyad Caliphate
661–680	Rule of Muawiya ibn Abu Sufyan
680	Death of Ali's son, Hussein at Karbala
681–692	Zubaryid Period
685–705	Rule of Umayyad Caliph Abd al-Malik
685–687	Alid uprising in Kufa led by Mukhtar ibn Abi Ubayd
692	Completion of the Dome of the Rock in Jerusalem
706–713	Umayyad expansion beyond Oxus River
711	Start of Umayyad invasion of the Iberian Peninsula
750	Defeat of last Umayyad Caliph, Marwan II, at the Battle of the Zab River by Abbasid forces led by Abu Muslim

Primary Sources

The Death of al-Husayn ibn Ali

Selection from Ta'rikh al-Rusul wa'l-Muluk of Muhammad ibn Jarir al-Tabari

According to Abu Mikhnaf: A young lad came out against us. His face was young like the first splinter of the moon, and there was a sword in his hand. He was wearing a shirt and a waistcloth, and a pair of sandals, one of whose straps was broken—as I remember, it was the left. Amr b. Sa'd b. Nufayl al-Azdi said to me, "By God! Let me attack him." I said, "Praise be to God! What do you want to do that for? Is it not enough for you that these people who, you see, have surrounded them should do the killing?" But he insisted, "By God! Let me attack him." So he rushed against him and did not turn back until he had struck his head with his sword. The young lad fell face downward as he called out, "O uncle!" Al-Husayn [his uncle] showed himself just like the hawk shows itself. He launched into attack like a raging lion and struck Amr [b. Sa'd b. Nu-fayl] with his sword. That man tried to fend off the blow with his arm, but his arm was cut off from the elbow; he gave a great shriek. As al-Husayn turned away from him, the cavalry of the Kufans attacked in order to save Amr [b. Sa'd b. Nufayl] from Husayn. Their horses collided against Amr with their chests, their hooves kicked out and they galloped with their riders over him so that they trampled him to death. The dust fell; there was al-Husayn standing by the head of the young lad; the lad had his feet stretched out on the ground. Husayn was saying, "May the people who killed you perish, for the one who will oppose them on the Day of Resurrection on your behalf will be your grandfather. By God! It is hard on your uncle that you called him and he did not answer you, or rather he answered but your cry did not help you, for, by God, those who kill his relatives are many but those who help him are few." Then he carried him.

It is just as if I can see the two feet of the boy leaving tracks in the ground while Husayn held his breast close to his own. I asked myself what he would do with him. He brought him and put him with his son Ali b. al-Husayn and the other members of his family who had been slain. I asked about the boy and was told that he was al-Qasim b. al-Hasan b. Ali b. Abi Talib.

Al-Husayn remained there for a long time during that day. Whenever one of the people came against him, he would turn aside from him and was unwilling to be responsible for his death and such a dreadful sin. A man from the Banu Badda' of Kindah called Malik b. al-Nusayr came against him and struck him on the head with his sword. Al-Husayn was wearing a hooded cloak. The sword cut through [the hood of] the cloak and wounded his head. The cloak became covered with blood. Al-Husayn declared, "Because of that may you never eat and drink with your hand. May God gather you on the [Day of Judgment] with those people who are wrongdoers." He threw down the cloak and called for a cap. He put on the cap and wound a turban around it. He was tired and had become less active.

The man from Kindah had managed to take the cloak, which was made of silk. Later, when he brought it to his wife, Umm 'Abdallah bt. al-Hurr—she was the sister of Husayn b. al-Hurr al-Baddi—he began to wash the blood from the cloak. His wife said to him, "Have you brought plunder from the son of the daughter of the Apostle of God into my house? Take it away from me." His colleagues mentioned that he remained poor as a result of the wicked action until he died.

According to Abu Mikhnaf: Abu Ja'far Muhammad b. Ali b. al-Husayn told me that the blood of his family was on the hands of us from Banu Asad. I said: "Is it my fault? May God have mercy on you." Then I asked him what our guilt was. He answered, "Al-Husayn was brought his young child; he was on his knee. Then one of you, Banu Asad, shot an arrow that slaughtered the child. Al-Husayn caught the blood [in his hand]. When the palm of his hand was full, he poured the blood onto the ground and said, 'O Lord, if it be that You have kept the help of heaven from us, then let it be because Your purpose is better than [immediate] help. Take vengeance for us on these oppressors.'"

Source: Gordon, Matthew S. "Document 12, The Death of al-Husayn ibn Ali." *The Rise of Islam*. Indianapolis: Hackett Publishing Company, Inc. (paperback version), 2008. Pgs. 144-146. Reprinted by permission from *The History of al-Tabari*, vol. 19, *The Caliphate of Yazid b. Muawiyah A.D. 680-683/A.H. 60-64*, translated by I.K.A. Howard. New York: The State University of New York Press, 1991.

Hasan Al-Basri: Letter to 'Umar II

Beware of this world with all wariness; for it is like to a snake, smooth to the touch, but its venom is deadly. Turn away from whatsoever delights thee in it, for the little companioning thou wilt have of it; put off from thee its cares, for that thou hast seen its sudden chances, and knowest for sure that thou shalt be parted from it; endure firmly its hardships, for the ease that shall presently be thine. The more it pleases thee, the more do thou be wary of it; for the man of this world, whenever he feels secure in any pleasure thereof, the world drives him over into some unpleasantness, and whenever he attains any part of it and squats him down upon it, the world suddenly turns him upside down. And again, beware of this world, for its hopes are lies, its expectations false; its easefulness is all harshness, muddied its limpidity. And therein thou art in peril: or bliss transient, or sudden calamity, or painful affliction, or doom decisive. Hard is the life of a man if he be prudent, dangerous if comfortable, being wary ever of catastrophe, certain of his ultimate fate. Even had the Almighty not pronounced upon the world at all, nor coined for it any similitude, nor charged men to abstain from it, yet would the world itself have awakened the slumberer, and roused the heedless; how much the more then, seeing that God has Himself sent us a warning against it, an exhortation regarding it! For this world has neither worth nor weight with God; so slight it is, it weighs not with God so much as a pebble or a single clod of earth; as I am told, God has created nothing more hateful to Him than this world, and from the day He created it He has not looked upon it, so much He hates it. It was offered to our Prophet with all its keys and treasures, and that would not have lessened him in God's sight by so much as the wing of a gnat, but he refused to accept it; and nothing prevented him from accepting it—for there is naught that can lessen him in God's sight—but that he knew that God hated a thing, and therefore he hated it, and God despised a thing, and he abased it. Had he accepted it, his acceptance would have been a proof that he loved it; but he disdained to love what his Creator hated, and to exalt what his Sovereign had debased. As for Muhammad, he bound a stone upon his belly when he was hungry; and as for Moses, the skin of his belly shewed as green as grass because of it all: he asked naught of God, the day he took refuge in the shade, save food to eat when he was hungered, and it is said of him in the stories that God revealed to him, "Moses, when thou seest poverty approaching, say, Welcome to the badge of the righteous! and when thou seest wealth approaching, say, Lo! a sin whose punishment has been put on aforetime." If thou shouldst wish, thou mightest name as a third the Lord of the Spirit and the Word (Jesus), for in his affair there is a marvel; he used to say, "My daily bread is hunger, my badge is fear, my raiment is wool, my mount is my foot, my lantern at night is the moon, my fire by day is the sun, and my fruit and fragrant herbs are such things as the earth brings forth for the wild beasts and cattle. All the night I have nothing, yet there is none richer than I!" And if thou shouldst wish, thou mightest name as a fourth David, who was no less wonderful than these; he ate barley bread in his chamber, and fed his family upon bran meal, but his people on fine corn; and when it was night he clad himself in sackcloth, and chained his hand to his neck, and wept until the dawn; eating coarse food, and wearing robes of hair. All these hated what God hates, and despised what God despises; then the righteous thereafter followed in their path and kept close upon their tracks.

Source: McNeill, William H. and Marilyn Robinson Waldman, eds. "Hasan al-Basri: Letter to Umar II." *The Islamic World*. Chicago: University of Chicago Press, 1983. Pgs. 79–81. Reprinted with permission from *Sufism* by Arthur J. Arberry. London: Allen & Unwin, 1950. Pp. 33–35.

NOTES

1. Chase Robinson, *Abd al-Malik* (London: Oneworld Publications, 2005), p. 65.
2. Quoted in G. R. Hawting, *The First Dynasty of Islam* (Carbondale: Southern Illinois University Press, 1987), pp. 42–43.
3. Quoted in R. Stephen Humphreys, *Mu'awiya ibn Abi Sufyan: From Arabia to Empire* (Oxford: One World, 2006), p. 6.

4. Quoted in Fred M. Donner, *Muhammad and the Believers: At the Origins of Islam* (Cambridge, MA: Harvard University Press, 2010), p. 180.
5. M. A. Shaban, *Islamic History: A New Interpretation* (Cambridge: Cambridge University Press, 1990), p. 121.
6. Robinson, *'Abd al-Malik*, p. 70.
7. One probably apocryphal story but perhaps fitting end to Marwan is the following: Apparently Umm Khalid, who was the widow of Yazid I and wanted her son, Khalid, to succeed Marwan instead of Marwan's son, Abd al-Malik, was incessantly ridiculed by Marwan publicly, especially her rather rotund derriere. As the ultimate act of revenge for the relentless humiliation, one afternoon while Marwan was napping she snuck into his room, climbed up on the bed, and suffocated Marwan with that part of her body of which he used to make so much fun. Again, stories like this, meant to denigrate someone, were often circulated; however, Madelung, no doubt with the wink of his eye, suggests that it's one of those stories that is so ridiculous it might actually be true. Wilferd Madelung, *The Succession to Muhammad: A Study of the Early Caliphate* (Cambridge: Cambridge University Press, 1997), p. 351.
8. Robinson, *'Abd al-Malik*, pp. 34–37.
9. Hawting, *First Dynasty of Islam*, pp. 59–61.
10. See Donner, *Muhammad and the Believers*, pp. 234–235.
11. Robinson, *'Abd al-Malik*, p. 125.
12. Quoted in Thabit A. J. Abdullah, *A Short History of Iraq: From 636 to the Present* (New York: Pearson-Longman, 2003), p. 15.
13. Hawting, *First Dynasty of Islam*, pp. 95–96.
14. Julius Wellhausen, *Das Arabische Reich und Sein Sturz* (Berlin, Germany: De Gruyter, 1960), p. 180.

KEY TERMS

Alids p. 73
Haram al-Sharif p. 81
Mahdi p. 80
mawali p. 75

For additional digital learning resources please go to www.oup.com/he/lesch-middleeast-1e

5 ISLAMIC EMPIRE

Revolution and Consolidation

The Umayyad caliphate was overthrown by a movement in favor of rule by someone from the Family of the Prophet, sometimes referred to as the *ahl al-bayt*, or those from the house, the House of the Prophet Muhammad. That someone who would be selected to rule was referred to as *al-rida min Al Muhammad*, the Chosen One from the Family of Muhammad, or simply called *al-rida*, the Chosen One. Since the death of Ali, it had become something of an axiom among Alids, and even just your average everyday Muslim who opposed the Umayyads, that only someone from the Family of the Prophet had the necessary tools to right the injustices of Umayyad rule and restore the stability of the umma after so many years of instability and civil war. This person, an Imam or even a Mahdi, would be divinely guided and would be able to perform **ijtihad**: the ability to interpret divine will, taken to be the Quran and the Sunna, in order to meet the ever-changing environment of Muslim life during such a dynamic period.

The only problem with this idea is that it was not entirely clear who made up the Family of the Prophet, nor how the leader should be chosen from the many different lines that had emerged from the Hashimite clan in the century-plus since the Prophet died and nine decades since the death of Ali. In later centuries, when a distinct Shiite Islamic sect emerged, it became generally accepted that the rightful rulers of the umma should be from the descendants of Ali and Fatima through their son, Hussein. However, in Umayyad times, the parameters and composition of the Family were much more ambiguous. We discussed in the last chapter how the designation of Muhammad ibn al-Hanifiyya as the Mahdi by the Kufan revolt led by Mukhtar had widened the definition of the Family, since the so-called Mahdi was directly descended from Ali but not Muhammad. Therefore, the Abbasid family, descended from the Prophet's paternal uncle, al-Abbas, could, in the climate of the times, claim to be from and of the *ahl al-bayt.* This was the case even though al-Abbas reportedly never converted to Islam, which after the Abbasids ascended to power was used against them to discredit their claim. But the Abbasids spread the idea that any Hashimite had the right to rule, which included the Alids and the Abbasids but pointedly excluded the Umayyads.

There were a number of ideas floating around in the decades prior to the Abbasid revolution regarding the appropriate criteria for choosing who from the Family of the Prophet should lead. One was hereditary succession in the line of Ali and Fatima through Hussein, which would become the gold standard in centuries to come. At the time, though, for a number of Muslims, any Hashimite would suffice. Another was the concept of **nass**, or designation by the previous Imam. Still another was what came to be termed the Zaydi view: that the Imam should be someone from the Family who was prepared to take up arms to right the wrongs of the Umayyads. This was named after Zayd bin Ali ibn Hussein ibn Ali, the great grandson of Ali ibn Abi Talib. In Kufa in 740 he led a rebellion against Umayyad rule. It was easily put down, but among some Alids there it became popular to believe that the proper Imam was simply the one who had the courage to oppose the oppressors. Those who continued to believe this also began to follow the progeny of Zayd, and they would become to this day the Zaydis or Fivers—the latter designation because they broke off from the main Twelver Shiite line of Imams (to be discussed later in the next chapter) at the fifth one. The Twelvers followed Zayd's brother Muhammad, who is the fifth Imam in that line.

The Abbasid's claim was a combination of these possible criteria, saying they more or less met all three. They were obviously descendants of Hashim, which met the broadened definition of the Family of the Prophet at the time. In around 716–717, the son of Muhammad ibn al-Hanifiyya, Abu Hashim, inherited the claim of Iman from his father and began what was called the Hashimiyya movement based in Khurasan. When he died, the Abbasids claimed that Abu Hashim had designated (*nass*) a member of the Abbasid family, Muhammad ibn Ali ibn al-Abbas (grandson of al-Abbas), as the next Imam. There appear to have been others who claimed that Abu Hashim had designated them as the next Imam, so there is some ambiguity here. Regardless, the Abbasids used this claim to connect with anti-Umayyad groups in Iraq as well as in Khurasan; however, it is not a criterion the Abbasids emphasized too much, because of its specious nature. Finally, the Abbasids joined and eventually led the opposition to the Umayyads and took up arms against them. They were obviously able to translate this opposition into success, so they certainly met this criterion; after displacing the Umayyads, the Abbasids tended to emphasize this Zaydi view because it was the most unambiguous.

As we shall see, Alids tended to sour fairly quickly on the Abbasids and questioned their legitimacy to rule, but by the standards of the day they had a pretty good claim to lead the umma. Obviously, enough Muslims felt the same way at the time of the Abbasid revolution.

In a practical sense, the Abbasid revolution was a success because of the backing of the Muslims of Khurasan under the leadership of Abu Muslim Abd al-Rahman ibn Muslim. There is some question regarding the exact makeup of the armies that Abu Muslim led across Iran and into Iraq, but most assuredly it was a mix of Arabs and Persians, including descendants of the Arabs who had settled in Khurasan some eight decades earlier and by now had assimilated into their dominant Persian environment. The Khurasanis had long resented what they considered to be almost alien rule from Damascus, and like many provinces under Umayyad rule wanted more independence, including keeping their revenues in the province rather than sending them back to Syria. The Abbasids took great pains after coming to power to connect their clandestine opposition to the Umayyads and position in Khurasan with similar actions taken by the Prophet Muhammad when he was opposed by his fellow Meccans (including the Umayyads at the time). Although probably apocryphal, relating the past to the present, especially in terms of a connection with the Prophet, was important to Abbasid propaganda.[1] For instance, according to this narrative, around 718–719 the Abbasid family, from what is now Jordan, sent twelve representatives (*naqibs*) to advance their interests in Khurasan, just as Muhammad is said to have done in sending twelve naqibs to Medina to represent Muslim interests there before the Hijra. It would not be a surprise to see Muslims in Khurasan turn to the Family of the Prophet for guidance if not leadership, but it appears to only be after the failure of Zayd ibn Ali's revolt in Kufa in 740 that they turned to the Abbasid family. In any event, attachment to the Alid cause in Khurasan was no doubt less than it was in Kufa, therefore opening up some space for the Abbasids.

The Abbasid revolution was at the very least an *attempt* to remake the Muslim world, to reintegrate rulers and ruled under the leadership of the Family of the Prophet. Soon enough, however, it would fall far short of that objective in many people's eyes. However, in the beginning hope was high. As Jacob Lassner writes, "the restructuring of society attempted by the Abbasids seems radical and far-reaching. Whether one speaks of new networks of social relationships, a complete overhaul of the military structure, innovations in provincial administration, of the creation of highly centralized and massive bureaucracy, encased by monumental architecture and reflected in lavish court ceremony, the changes instituted by the Abbasids represented an ambitious departure from both the style and substance of Umayyad rule."[2] Lassner talks about how the Arabic word "dawlah" ("to turn" or "come about") was contemporaneously used to described the event to depict the changing order of things—that is, a revolution.[3] There were even messianic and apocalyptic overtones to the revolution, supposedly ushering in a new era of justice. The black banners they adopted reflected the messianic nature of the movement and linked back to the Prophet's grandfather's wearing of black in opposition to the ancestors of the Umayyads, similar to the Biblical account of the underdog David wearing black when he stood up to the seemingly invincible Goliath, as they were now doing to the "monstrous" Umayyads.[4]

The Abbasid family latched on to an opposition movement of Khurasanis that already existed. The former, through propaganda, good luck, and some clandestine activities, were able to place themselves in a position with and appeal enough to the latter to be chosen as the rightful leaders of the Family of the Prophet. In a way, the Abbasids provided the religious legitimacy to Khurasani muscle. The Abbasids did not participate in the long march of the armies led by Abu Muslim across Iran nor in the battles against the Umayyads. Perhaps that was not their calling, but one cannot underestimate the disadvantageous power position the Abbasid family was in compared to the Khurasani military leaders, especially Abu Muslim, once the Umayyads were vanquished. Abu Muslim and his Khurasani army marched into Kufa in 748, kicked out the Umayyad governor and other officials, and in 749 proclaimed Abu al-Abbas al-Saffah as the new caliph, with official recognition being conferred after the victory at the Zab River in 750. As mentioned in the last chapter, Marwan II was hunted down and killed (and dismembered), in Egypt; most of the Umayyad family was rooted out and brutally put to death by the Abbasid armies. The brutality of the virtual exorcism of Umayyad rule from the Islamic body as well as the collective yearning for someone from the Family of the Prophet to lead the umma suggests just how disliked the Umayyads were—or more to the point, the nature of Umayyad rule—and how frustrated many Muslims were with how far many believed Islam had strayed from its origins. It was very much what we would call today a fundamentalist movement: an attempt to get back to the original principles of the movement itself.

The primary challenge for the Abbasids at this point was to make sure they did not become the puppets of the Khurasani military, or what became known as the **Khurasaniyya**. Were the Abbasids to rule as well as reign? Was the virtual dictatorship of the Syrian army simply to be replaced by that of the Khurasaniyya? As is typically the case in an immediate postrevolutionary atmosphere, the leading elements of the revolution that brought about success tended to bicker and fight among each other over who should have power. That the Abbasids were able to assert themselves and rule as well as reign is mainly due to the efforts of one man: the brother of Abu al-Abbas al-Saffah and the caliph's main advisor, Abu Jafar, who would take the name of al-Mansur when he became the next caliph upon his brother's death in 754.

Al-Mansur is the most important caliph of the entire Abbasid caliphate. He is in many ways a combination of what Muawiya and Abd al-Malik were to the Umayyads: the person who really established Abbasid rule and the one who set up the centralized governing structure that would last several generations. A key to Abbasid success at first was a decision made under Abu al-Abbas al-Saffah and affirmed under al-Mansur to leave Khurasan in the hands of Abu Muslim and the Khurasaniyya. In other words, Khurasan was essentially an autonomous province, one of the objectives for which the indigenous folks had fought in the first place. But this could only last so long, especially considering Abu Muslim's popularity

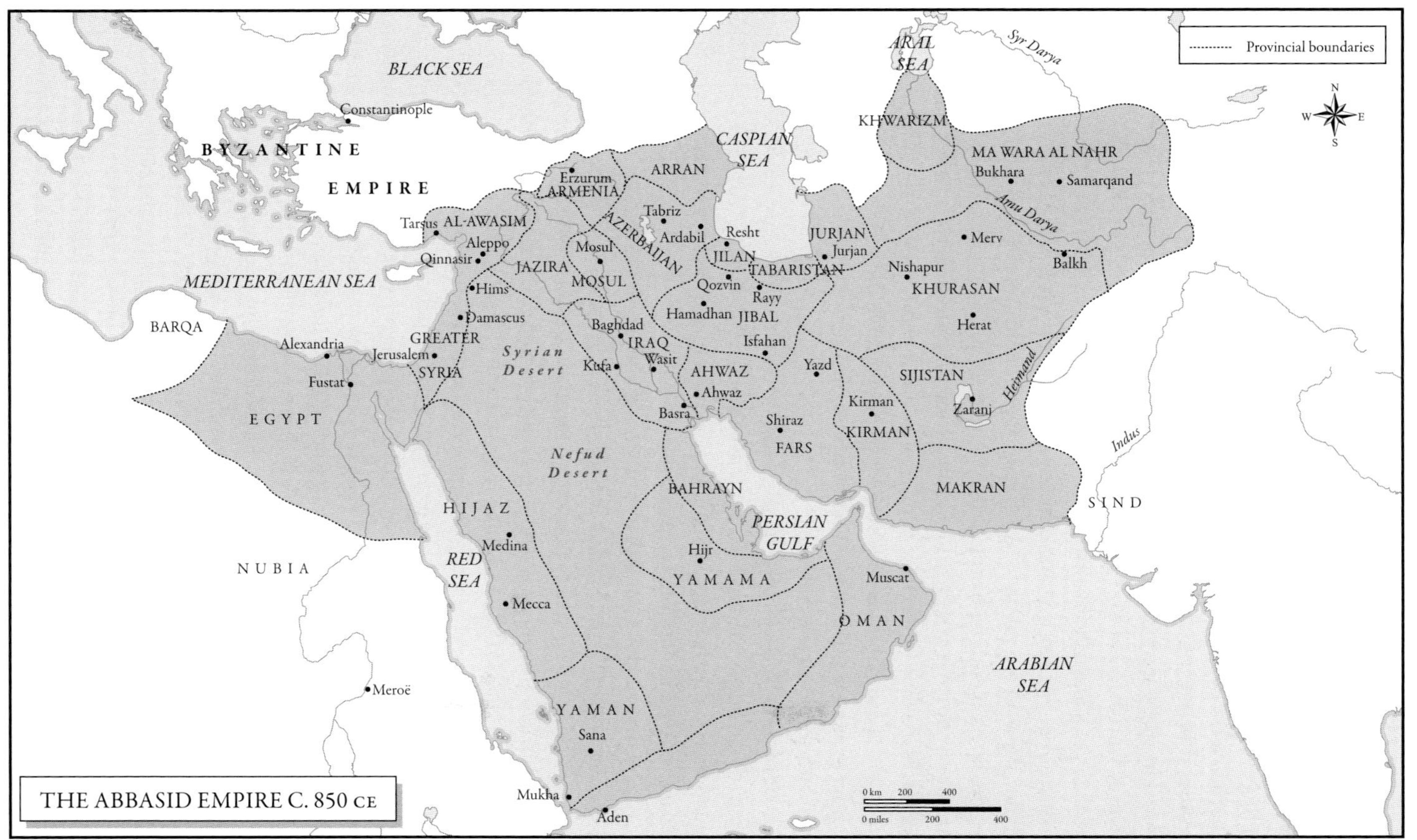
Provincial boundaries
N
W
E
S
BLACK SEA
Constantinople
BYZANTINE
EMPIRE
ARAL SEA
Syr Darya
KHWARIZM
MA WARA AL NAHR
Bukhara
Samarqand
Amu Darya
CASPIAN SEA
ARRAN
Erzurum
ARMENIA
Tarsus
AL-AWASIM
Aleppo
Qinnasir
Tabriz
Ardabil
AZERBAIJAN
Resht
JILAN
JURJAN
Jurjan
TABARISTAN
Merv
Nishapur
KHURASAN
Balkh
Mosul
JAZIRA
MOSUL
MEDITERRANEAN SEA
Hims
Qozvin
Rayy
Hamadhan
JIBAL
Herat
Damascus
BARQA
Baghdad
IRAQ
Isfahan
GREATER
Syrian
Desert
Alexandria
Jerusalem
SYRIA
Kufa
Wasit
AHWAZ
Yazd
SIJISTAN
Helmand
Fustat
Ahwaz
Kirman
Zaranj
Basra
Shiraz
KIRMAN
EGYPT
FARS
Indus
Nefud
Desert
MAKRAN
BAHRAYN
SIND
HIJAZ
PERSIAN
GULF
Medina
RED
SEA
Hijr
NUBIA
YAMAMA
Muscat
Mecca
OMAN
ARABIAN
SEA
Meroë
YAMAN
Sana
THE ABBASID EMPIRE C. 850 CE
Mukha
Aden
0 km 200 400
0 miles 200 400

and position there and with the Khurasaniyya, the men who made up most of the armies that carried out the Abbasid revolution—and the fact that he was, as Hugh Kennedy calls him, the regime's "ruthless enforcer."[5] From the point of view of the Abbasids, to rely exclusively on the Khurasaniyya would relegate them to being puppets in the hands of the military.

It really came down to a contest between the leading individuals in the new Abbasid realm, which inevitably meant a stand-off between al-Mansur and Abu Muslim. Al-Mansur actually had to fend off some challenges from within his own family who believed they should become the new caliph, especially his uncle, Abdallah. Al-Mansur brilliantly used Abu Muslim to successfully counter this threat, which then just left the two of them to find, if possible, a workable arrangement. From the vantage point of al-Mansur, there could not be one. Abu Muslim had to go, but it had to be handled delicately, given his popularity. It may seem on the surface a supreme gesture of ingratitude for the Abbasids to get rid of the person most responsible for them coming to power, but if al-Mansur was really going to be the type of caliph he wanted to be, he could not leave the eastern half of the empire under someone else's leadership nor have such a popular pole of attraction lording his authority over the Abbasids.

Soon after he became caliph, al-Mansur would make his move. Abu Muslim had visited Iraq but refused to heed al-Mansur's request to see him.[6] Abu Muslim and his advisors apparently thought it might be a trap, so they were obviously aware of al-Mansur's possible intentions. Against his better judgment, however, and maybe as a sign of his arrogance or underestimation of al-Mansur's ruthlessness, Abu Muslim visited the caliph's camp before heading back to Khurasan. There, according to the story, al-Mansur's guards reluctantly agreed to kill Abu Muslim. Certainly they were fearful of the repercussions, especially what the Khurasaniyya might do upon learning of the perfidy. As Kennedy describes it, "The murder of Abu Muslim was an immense gamble."[7] There was sporadic resistance from some of Abu Muslim's troops, but al-Mansur went to great lengths to reconcile with the Khurasaniyya and his other supporters in Khurasan. This is when the province of Khurasan and its tax revenues remained in the hands of the Khurasaniyya, and many of Abu Muslim's top commanders would soon be found in the caliph's service on what no doubt were lucrative salaries and benefits. With the carrot and the stick, al-Mansur was able to not only survive the killing of Abu Muslim, but also, as he intended, consolidate his own position and the authority of the Abbasid family.

One problem that reared its head during the middle of al-Mansur's tenure in power was the Alid rebellion of Muhammad ibn Abdullah (Muhammad the Pure Soul) in Medina and his brother, Ibrahim, in Basra in 763. They were from the Hassanid branch of the Alid family: descended from Hassan, the eldest son of Ali ibn Abi Talib. The rebellion in and of itself was a puny affair. Abbasid troops made their way to Medina and in short order put down the revolt and killed Muhammad the Pure Soul, despite the latter's digging of a trench around Medina as the Prophet had done. Ibrahim was killed shortly thereafter in Basra. What this Alid uprising did show was early dissatisfaction with the direction of Abbasid rule: that to at least some Alids it was not the reshaping of the Islamic polity and looked increasingly like Umayyad rule, especially with al-Mansur's centralizing policies amid some stories of his personal fear and hatred of the Alids. A stickler for detail and clear lines of authority, al-Mansur himself admitted that the Abbasids owed a debt of gratitude to Umayyad caliphs such as Abd al-Malik and Hisham for establishing the model of government within the Islamic world for the proper centralization of power. Nevertheless, the Hassanid revolt would be the last significant Alid uprising for decades amid the consolidation of Abbasid rule and at least some serious attempts by caliphs from time to time to appeal to and placate members of the Family of the Prophet.

Al-Mansur's lasting legacy was his decision to build a new capital of the Abbasid caliphate near the old Sassanian capital of Ctesiphon and a small village by the name of Baghdad, whose name stuck. In a way, it was al-Mansur's signal for a new beginning. Kufa had too much of a history of turmoil and sedition, and it became associated too much with Alid sentiment. There was no way anyplace in Syria would work, because it would have been associated too closely with the Umayyads. And Khurasan was not a consideration, because it was on the fringes of the caliphate, and maybe most importantly, this was at a time when the caliph was trying to distance himself and the family from all things Khurasan. North of Kufa on the Tigris River, the site was chosen and it would become one of—if not the—greatest city in the world soon enough. And while the Abbasid state structure may have taken on the veneer of the Umayyad's, the location of the capital in Iraq shifted the orientation of the center of the Islamic world. While Damascus and Syria were oriented toward the Mediterranean, Baghdad and Iraq were more oriented to points east, more of an Asian empire than a Mediterranean one. Baghdad would become the center of commerce, thought, science, philosophy, and power. But it depended on the economic foundation of the Sawad and the intricate canal-based irrigation system that allowed for the agricultural fertility of its alluvial plain—more specifically, the taxes from the agricultural production that would enrich the central treasury. It became an axiom that as the Sawad went, so did the Abbasids. So important was this area to the well-being of Abbasid rule that one of the main canals was called the Abu al-Jund, or Father of the Army, in that the revenues from the immense yields would first and foremost go toward paying the army, which in the end was the ultimate expression of Abbasid authority.

The Abbasid revolution also represented a change in the nature of the elite. The Umayyad caliphate had essentially been by the Arabs and for the Arabs. At a time when most Muslims were Arab, this is not surprising. But by the time of the Abbasid revolution, as we know with the growth of the mawali, this was a point of contention. The Abbasid ruling class was still somewhat Arab-centric but it was much more varied, especially as time went on. In an important way, the transition from Umayyad to Abbasid marked a shift from an Arab empire to more of an Islamic

"Baghdad in the Days of Mansur," painting by Edmund Sandars, 1915. This aerial view of the walled city of Baghdad depicts how it might have appeared in the eighth century CE.
The Print Collector/Alamy Stock Photo

empire, where Persians, Kurds, Turks, Berbers, and other ethnicities started to play more important roles. Some have suggested in the past that the geographic shift toward Persia/Iran was akin to a Persian revival. It is clear now that this was not the case; after all, the Abbasid family was Arab. However, Persian culture, customs, and families were to play a more important role than in the past, seeping into the fabric of Abbasid life and ways of governance.

In addition, the establishment of Baghdad by 762 was also intended to provide a base for the Khurasaniyya. Though they were far from their homeland, they were close to the center of power and still relied on surplus revenues from their home province to line their pockets and provide them with their living. The land was obviously cheaper in the undeveloped area of Baghdad initially than in Kufa, and it was clear that the caliph could keep them close by—for good or ill.

Al-Mansur died in 775 while on pilgrimage to Mecca. He left a caliphate that was sound and secure, and he established the foundation for all that would come after him. He named one of his sons as his successor, thus establishing the parameters for the same sort of family dynasty as the Umayyads. His son would take the name of al-Mahdi, itself a sign that he wanted to reverse the inimical relationship between his family and the Alids that had risen during his father's time in power. To a large degree, he would succeed.

Of Golden Primes and Civil War

In many ways al-Mahdi's caliphate was a continuation of his father's. He continued to rely heavily on the Khurasaniyya as his primary base of support. There were some subtle changes, however, the most obvious being his attempts to reconcile with the Alids after the latter's challenging relationship with al-Mansur. Adopting the caliphal name of al-Mahdi, one that especially resonated with Alids, was the most outward sign that Alids would once again be welcome members at court. It was largely successful, as there were no significant Alid uprisings during his time in power.

There were some developments during his caliphate that did have important near and long-term repercussions, and not all of them were good. We have seen succession become an issue during the Umayyad caliphate. This would be no less the case during Abbasid times. Al-Mahdi adopted what has been called the "heir and a spare" approach to succession, meaning the naming of his eldest son, Musa, as his immediate successor and then the spare, Harun. Harun would become caliph either right after his elder brother died or right after his father if his elder brother predeceased him. The names of al-Mahdi's sons were not chosen by coincidence. Musa is "Moses" in Arabic, while Harun is "Aaron." As one may recall from the Old Testament book of Exodus narrative, Aaron succeeded his brother Moses as the leader of the Jewish nation following the latter's death. Again, this is an example of bringing the past into the present, at least symbolically, as a sign of legitimacy, if not fate.

This also marked a period of the increasing centralization of government reach and authority, a process begun by al-Mansur. In particular, the civilian bureaucracy grew substantially, to the point where it was a pressure group within the ruling apparatus in and of itself. The civilian bureaucrats were called the *kuttab*, from one of the Arabic words for secretary or administrator, **katib**, itself a derivative from the word for book, *kitab*. The complexities of the revenue collection from the Sawad—and elsewhere—necessitated an increase in civilian administrators, especially with the entrance into the Middle East of paper from China, so now records, payrolls, receipts, and so on could more easily be logged and kept. This was a transitional period in the Islamic world when a large portion of the revenues were now based on taxes on people, products, and land rather than coming from that which was produced by conquest and the spoils of war.[8] This financial efficiency allowed for the building and upkeep of infrastructure as well as monumental architecture. Aiding in the centralization process was the development of a wide-ranging postal system, the *barid*—a kind of Abbasid version of the pony express, where orders and intelligence could be more easily sent and received.[9]

One particular family of administrators came to lead the kuttab during the time of al-Mahdi and his sons—the Barmakids. The Barmakid family was led by Yahya ibn Khalid al-Barmak, who had become al-Mahdi's right-hand man during the future caliph's time as governor of the province of Rayy in Iran. Yahya was a personal tutor to Harun and became something of a surrogate father to him. The Barmakids were of Persian origin and most likely descended from a family of bureaucrats from the days of the dahaqin in the Sassanian empire. They were well positioned and experienced, and one could say that the times finally caught up with them to create this opportune moment.

Competing for power and access is common in just about every governing system. This was no less the case during Abbasid times. Even the palace servants, with their control of access to the caliph, became at times an important pressure group. With the rise of the kuttab, however, the military, which had till now enjoyed almost unfettered political power and access, began to feel threatened, especially with the Barmakids' close relationship with al-Mahdi and his son, Harun. As a result, tensions developed between the kuttab and the military, which would become a recurring theme of Abbasid rule for over the next century and a half. Since the civilian administrators collected the taxes which paid the soldiers' salaries, there was definitely room for disagreement. Oftentimes the kuttab and the military backed different members of the Abbasid family, hoping to align themselves with the next caliph—or even help bring about a succession that was favorable to one or the other. This became apparent right away, as Musa (Caliph al-Hadi) was backed by the military, and Harun (Caliph Harun al-Rashid) was backed by the kuttab.

These tensions began to play out when al-Mahdi was killed in 785 in the Zagros mountains in Iran due to a hunting accident. According to one version, the caliph was chasing a gazelle. The gazelle entered a house, whose door was presumably open, and the caliph on his horse rode into the entryway to the house to give chase. One problem: al-Mahdi apparently forgot to duck, and hit his head on the wall above the doorway and died instantly. This is one of these stories that may or may not be true, and one doesn't really know if it is flattering or damning; he showed resolve and bravery to chase the gazelle into the house, but on the other hand he was not smart enough to duck. Whenever a caliph or leading official died out of sight of the public, there was always the so-called harem intrigue version of events that presupposed some sort of foul play. Enough conspiracy did occur in Islamic history to give credence to just about any particular claim of foul play. Then there is the idea that it was fate, that it was just his time to go, and the oddity of how he died only reaffirmed to some that it was predestined. Whatever the case, according to the succession arrangement, al-Hadi became the next caliph.

Al-Hadi's reign is something of an enigma because he was only in office for thirteen months, so there was not much of a record to go on. He apparently tried to replace Harun as his successor, but with the staunch opposition of the Barmakids, he was unable to do so. He died in 786 under mysterious circumstances. In this case the "harem intrigue" story could be correct, as there was every incentive for the Barmakids and their allies to bring about his premature death (perhaps by poison, which was a tried and true tactic) because the longer al-Hadi stayed in power the more precarious the position of the kuttab—and Harun and the Barmakids specifically—would have become.

Al-Mahdi's succession arrangement continued in force, and Harun al-Rashid became the next caliph at the age of twenty-one. Even though many may not know it, he is the most famous Abbasid caliph in the West. Anyone who has seen film adaptations (cartoon or otherwise) of the stories in the famous Arab literary work *A Thousand and One Nights* or *Tales of the Arabian Nights* has come across him, as he is the caliph during the period covered by the book. Equally, almost in every case—and in typical Orientalist fashion—the caliph is something of a caricature, portrayed more often than not as old, with a white beard, and short and fat, as if to depict slovenliness and decadence. The real Harun al-Rashid was a warrior caliph who was on campaign with his troops for most of his first decade in power, and he was only forty-six when he died, so he may have never had white hair or a white beard at all.

As just mentioned, the caliph was often on campaign on the Byzantine frontier operating from his base in Raqqa in Syria. This was a very caliphal thing to do, especially against what was still considered Rome; perhaps it was also an attempt to establish a better relationship with the military. In addition, Harun al-Rashid apparently hated Baghdad, calling it the "steam room" because of its dense humidity. He also went on the hajj more than any other Abbasid caliph, eight times in all—another caliphal thing to do that shored up his religious credentials. While in the Holy Cities he showered dinars and gifts on the descendants of the Muhajirun and even the Ansar in order to curry favor—and to keep them satisfied and quiet. The caliph essentially left the running of the empire to the Barmakid family, who next to the Abbasids were the most powerful family in the empire, so much so that in some scholarly works the 790s are called the decade of the Barmakids. They implemented a level of political centralization and monetary efficiency that probably had some longing for the good old days of the Umayyads. Governors were changed so often that the records fail to mention many of their names.

Something inevitably had to give. The Barmakids, from the point of view of Harun al-Rashid, appeared to acquire too much power—and to some they flaunted their power. In a very dramatic episode in 803 that had many contemporaries confused as to how and why it happened,[10] soon after Harun al-Rashid's return to Baghdad, the caliph suddenly and decisively moved against the family, one being killed in a rather gruesome fashion and others imprisoned. It was a shocking moment, but thereafter the caliph was more on his own, perhaps having grown into the position. For the remaining six years of his caliphate he concentrated on securing his own succession scheme between two of his sons, al-Amin and al-Mamun, especially as it related to the unique arrangement with the province of Khurasan.

As we know, from the time of the Abbasid revolution the province had been ruled by the Khurasaniyya military who had taken up residence in Baghdad. By the time of Harun al-Rashid, however, it was primarily the descendants of the

Khurasaniyya, who enjoyed this privilege and status. They referred to themselves as the *abna al-dawlah*, the sons of the revolution (**abna** is the plural of "ibn," or son), or simply as the abna. This group wanted to continue the arrangement that al-Mansur had set up with regard to the revenues from Khurasan being brought to Baghdad to provide for their salaries and pensions. They were akin to absentee landlords. Noble families in Khurasan, particularly one by the name of the Tahirids, firmly objected to this arrangement, as they wanted more revenues to stay in the province itself. This, of course, was totally unacceptable to the abna. The special position of Khurasan had now come back home to roost, which was perhaps inevitable.

It was fitting, then, that Harun al-Rashid died of natural causes on a trip in 809 to Khurasan, the only reigning caliph ever to visit the province, which is curious considering the role it played in bringing the Abbasids to power. In light of his own checkered history with the heir-and-a-spare succession scheme, it is surprising that Harun made similar arrangements for two of his sons. However, he laid out the arrangements in meticulous detail. Under his version Muhammad al-Amin would become caliph upon his death, and one of his other sons, Abdullah al-Mamun, would become the governor of Khurasan and would succeed his brother. But this succession scheme would turn out to be disastrous.

Harun al-Rashid's tenure in power is often depicted, even by contemporaries, as the golden age or golden prime of the Abbasid caliphate, if not of all of medieval Islam. However, in this instance it is as much a recognition of what came after Harun al-Rashid as what happened during or before he came to power. As we know from the Barmakid episode, everything was not copacetic under Harun. But when set against the brutal civil war fought between his sons and for the most part the steady deterioration of Abbasid rule thereafter, it seems like a golden prime, when the lands from Ifriqiyya in the west to India in the east were under the real control of the caliph. It is a time when the central treasury was bursting with dinars, which were invested in monumental architecture and infrastructural projects as well as showered upon poets, artists, scientists, philosophers, and the literati. The House of Wisdom (*bayt al-hikma*) in Baghdad was at the time perhaps the center of learning in the entire world, where tremendous discoveries and advancements were made in astronomy, medicine, mathematics, philosophy, and navigation. Leading thinkers from all over the world would congregate in the great city of Baghdad. It was a propitious time to be in the Abbasid empire.

SPOTLIGHT

The House of Wisdom

The House of Wisdom (*Bayt al-Hikma*) was a renowned center of learning located in Baghdad; for a time during the height of the Abbasid Empire it was probably the foremost center of scholarship and scientific inquiry in the world.

It helped that it was located in one of the leading cities of the medieval period at a crossroads of civilizations that connected East and West through trade, commerce, and scientific and intellectual exchange. The House of Wisdom appears to have been established by the Caliph al-Mansur, the second of the Abbasid caliphs who ruled from 754 to 775 CE. He strongly encouraged Muslims to study sciences (nature), something that is a basic injunction in Islam. He collected books from Persia, Greece, and India to be translated, all of which probably formed the foundation of the library that would become the House of Wisdom. It developed over time, and some Abbasid caliphs patronized the institution more than others. Under the Caliph Harun al-Rashid, the House of Wisdom grew by leaps and bounds, supplemented in many ways by the expanded collection of manuscripts acquired through conquest.

The House of Wisdom probably reached its height in many ways under the caliphate of al-Mamun (813–833 CE). Al-Mamun was perhaps the most intellectual of the early to mid-period Abbasid caliphs. He was keenly interested in science, research, and debate, and was deeply engaged in Greek philosophy and reason. He was particularly interested in astrology, the practitioner of which had to be well-versed in complex trigonometric functions, reflection and refraction, precision instrumentation, time keeping, and star tables. Because of this, the caliph became very supportive of these and other scientific endeavors, which in many ways gave rise to the modern scientist.

Over time the House of Wisdom included a library, a translation bureau, and a scientific academy composed of scholars from across the empire and beyond. It was located, we think, in the palace area of the caliph until the time of al-Mamun. Because of its growth, the library was moved to the other side of the Tigris River in Baghdad, in an area known as al-Rusafa, along with a newly built astronomical conservatory. The introduction of paper (from China) to the Abbasids greatly accelerated the production and spread of manuscripts. The first mention of a paper factory in Baghdad was recorded in 795 CE, a time when Christian Europe was still wedded to animal skins that produced parchment. Over about a century and a half, the House of Wisdom played a key role in the Arab translation of Greek works in science and philosophy, as Arabic became the universal language of scientific inquiry.

Some of the greatest scientists and philosophers associated with the House of Wisdom included the following: Al-Biruni, who has been called the Leonardo de Vinci of the Islamic world for the breadth and depth of his knowledge; Muhammad ibn Musa al-Khwarizmi, an astronomer and mathematician who built upon existing ideas from India and is known as the father of algebra, the word in English taken from the Arabic word "al-jabr" ("balancing") which appeared in the title of his famous book, *Kitab al-jabr wa al-muqabala* ("The Book of Restoring and Balancing"); Abu Ali al-Hussein ibn Abdallah ibn Sina, better known in the West as Avicenna (970–1037 CE), who became one of the most prominent philosophers and physicians in the Islamic world and produced the famous book *Canon of Medicine*, which influenced European medical practices into the 1600s; and Abu Yusuf ibn Ishaq al-Kindi, who was known as a mathematician but was also the first person to introduce Aristotelian philosophy to the Arabs.

It is important to note that some scholars believe the House of Wisdom did not exist as a distinct institution or building, and that the lack of primary source evidence or ruins (you can thank the Mongols for this when they destroyed Baghdad in 1258) suggest that it may rather have been a reference to the overall larger academic and scholarly community in Baghdad. This is a minority view, but regardless, what is indisputable is the extremely important scientific and philosophical legacy the Islamic world bequeathed to posterity. To begin to understand the impact of Islamic scientific contributions, one only has to read National Geographic's *1001 Inventions: The Enduring Legacy of Muslim Civilization* edited by Salim T. S. al-Hassani (Washington, DC: National Geographic Society, 2012) or Michael Hamilton Morgan's *Lost History: The Enduring Legacy of Muslim Scientists, Thinkers, and Artists* (Washington, DC: National Geographic Society, 2007).

Source: Much of this is gleaned from Jonathan Lyons, *The House of Wisdom: How Arab Learning Transformed Western Civilization* (London: Bloomsbury, 2009).

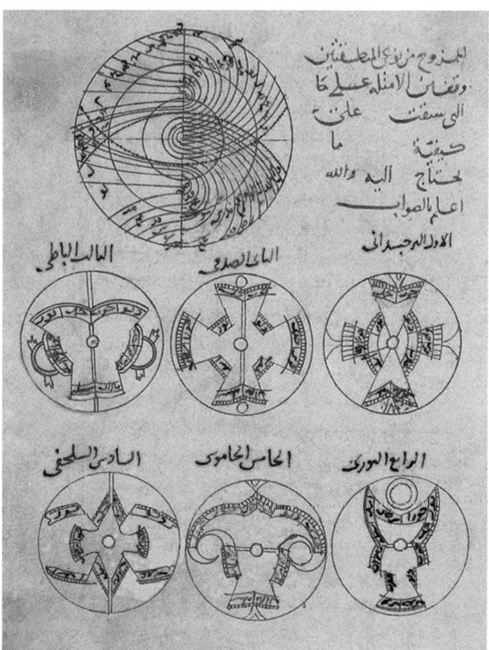

"Treatise on the Astrolabe," a Seljuk-illustrated Arabic manuscript copied by Mahmud bin Muhammad al Mushi, Sivas, Turkey, dated 1231.

Science History Images/Alamy Stock Photo

But just when things seem at their best, trouble often follows. This was clearly the case with the heightening tensions between al-Amin and al-Mamun over the status of Khurasan. The abna began to put immediate pressure on al-Amin to make sure the revenues from the province made their way back to Baghdad and into their pockets. The Tahirid family and their allies in Khurasan, backed at first by a reluctant al-Mamun, demanded their right to the revenues. It is no surprise that civil war ensued. Al-Mamun was put forth as a rightly guided Imam and not just a caliph, and as such should be the leader of the umma and not al-Amin. The two armies—minus the two brothers—met at Rayy in Iran in 811, with the Tahirid-led forces decisively victorious, after which Mamun was officially proclaimed caliph/imam from Khurasan. Al-Amin desperately tried to raise another army from Baghdad without much success, and by 812 the Tahirid army had surrounded the Abbasid capital. After over a year of blockading and bombarding the city by siege engines, with the subsequent famine taking hold in Baghdad amid some very ugly scenes of survival and the destruction of whole quarters of the capital, the forces of al-Mamun and the Tahirids breached the outer walls, entered the city amid hand-to-hand fighting, and killed al-Amin. Many argue that the death of al-Amin, as with the murder of Uthman that led to the end of the Rashidun or the assassination of al-Walid II that led to the dismantling of the Umayyads, similarly diminished Abbasid rule—from which it never fully recovered. The years between the death of al-Amin and al-Mamun's eventual return to Baghdad in 819 saw prolonged fighting between various groups competing for power and resources amid the vacuum of power created by the death of the caliph—especially in and around Iraq—that permanently scarred the prestige and reputation of the Abbasid family.

Mamun was an intellectual. Raised by the Barmakids, he was exposed to Aristotelian philosophy and *kalam*, the technique of dialectical argumentation and speculative reasoning, especially, in his case, with regard to religion.[11] He argued that it was the caliphate that was the true heir to Greek philosophy and science rather than Byzantium.[12] Al-Mamun and the brother who would succeed him, al-Mutasim, became associated with the rationalist theological ideology called **Mutazilism**, which is from the Arabic root which means "to separate from" or "withdraw." Mutazilites concerned themselves with the nature of authority, the question being how far a caliph or an imam could go in interpreting and expanding upon revelation and tradition, the Quran and the Sunna: in effect, how much could this person perform *ijtihad*, divine interpretation, in order to meet the changing needs of the community. In many ways it is a quite progressive philosophy that brings reasoning into the equation of deciphering what is not answered by the Quran or the Sunna. In this regard it is very close to the Alid point of view, or what would become Shiite Islam in the next century, and it may have been yet another attempt to reconcile with the Alids. Mutazilism held that the Quran was created, in distinction to those who believed it was eternal with Allah. If it was created at a particular time, then it could be modified to suit different circumstances at different times subject to the God-guided judgment of the imam. At the same time, it was also a philosophy that enhanced the power of the caliph by giving his word theocratic force and even religious authority over Islamic scholars (**ulama**). In so doing, those who opposed Mutazilism feared it created a power imbalance whereby the caliph would no longer be subject to Islamic law, but above it. Mutazilism was introduced into the mainstream by al-Mamun, but it would be his brother who would forcibly implement it.

As such, it is not surprising that in 817, while he was still ruling from Khurasan, al-Mamun named an Alid, Ali ibn Musa, more commonly known as Ali al-Rida (the Chosen One), as his successor. Al-Mamun apparently believed that the caliph or imam (the title with which he preferred to be called) could be an Abbasid or an Alid, which would not only appeal to Alids, particularly in Iraq where he had very few other supporters, but also to Iranians and non-Arabs in general, many of whom gravitated to the Alid point of view. In practical terms, al-Mamun had alienated just about the entire Abbasid family because of his actions that led to the civil war with al-Amin and resulted in so much damage to the fabric of Abbasid rule. He was, as historian Michael Cooperson put it, "a ruler without a dynasty."[13] He had little choice but to go outside of the family, especially if it jibed with his political and religious philosophy. Since Ali al-Rida was not a young man it was perhaps mostly a symbolic move, as he would most likely predecease al-Mamun. Regardless of the rationale it proved to be a disaster, especially for Ali al-Rida, as he may have been poisoned while traveling with al-Mamun, and he died in 818. If so, it was most likely done at the orders of elements in the Abbasid family whose proprietary role as caliphs they hoped to preserve.[14] Ali al-Rida burial place in Meshhad in Iran is a popular Shiite shrine today, as he is the eighth Imam in the Twelver Shiite line.

Following this, al-Mamun finally relented and returned to Baghdad in 819, a move no doubt designed as a compromise and reconciliation with the Abbasid family. For the remainder of his time in power he continued to promote Mutazilism and oversaw a process of change in the nature of the elite in the empire, particularly as the abna were neutered and even the presence and influence of some of the most important Arab families from Syria, Iraq, and Arabia were diminished. New groups with new ideas and customs began to enter into positions of authority under al-Mamun, none more important than his brother, al-Mutasim, who became governor of Egypt in 829 and then succeeded to the caliphate (or Imamate) in 833 upon his brother's passing.

Al-Mutasim implemented and advanced what al-Mamun had started. It was a period of change in some ways as important as the Abbasid revolution itself, and the caliphates of al-Mamun and al-Mutasim are often seen as the dividing point between the early and middle Abbasid periods. But while the Abbasid revolution was a broad-based movement, al-Mutasim's was one that was really implemented from the top-down, encompassing a fairly small group that enjoyed virtually no mass support. They were more concerned with preserving—perhaps even reinvigorating—Abbasid rule. To do this, al-Mutasim initiated a kind of inquisition (*mihna*) that forced the adoption of Mutazilism by pain of death if necessary. In order to carry all of this out, he needed a new army as well as a new capital.

Al-Mustasim's decision to build a new capital at Samarra, about eighty miles north of Baghdad on the Tigris River, was probably made for many of the same reasons that al-Mansur decided to abandon Kufa to establish the new capital of

Baghdad. No doubt the symbolism of the move was potent: a new beginning, a new era. In addition, he needed a place he could design to his satisfaction to house his new army, much as al-Mansur needed space for the Khurasaniyya. Land was also cheaper in the new locale as opposed to Baghdad, which had become well-developed, if not overcrowded, over the past seven decades.

The new army would be made up primarily of **mamluks**, or what some have termed "slave soldiers." They typically were Turks captured in battle or even purchased, converted to Islam if they were not already Muslim, and then trained, manumitted, and integrated into the ruling apparatus, especially the military. Al-Mutasim surrounded himself with a Turkish mamluk militia while governor of Egypt, one that he used and expanded upon once he became caliph. Not all of the mamluks were Turks, but most of them were—or at the very least were called Turks even if they were another ethnicity. This recruitment of peoples from the margins of the empire to form a military elite was common to many cultures in the

This tile fragment was covered with a white glaze, fired, painted with metallic pigments in three colors, refired, and then polished. Designers of the Abbasid period put this new glazing technology, known as luster painting, to innovative use at Samarra.
The Metropolitan Museum of Art

past. The real change was that the military was now composed of different minority groups, whether they were Turks, Circassians, Armenians, or Berbers, rather than from Arab sources in Iraq, Syria, or Arabia. The military became separate from the rest of society ethnically and in terms of customs and tradition. Many Arabs in Baghdad resented the Turks, believing them to be uncouth barbarians unfit for the cultured society they had built.[15] Perhaps this was another reason for building the new capital. The mamluks and Baghdadis simply did not get along.

Al-Mutasim's policies generated a good deal of opposition in Baghdad and elsewhere in Iraq. A group of so-called Traditionalists emerged in Baghdad diametrically opposed to Mutazilism. They believed that humankind should solely rely upon divine revelation and tradition of the Quran and Sunna. Humans are sinful and fallible, and therefore they should in no way be entrusted with divine reinterpretation. The Traditionalists were led by Ahmad ibn Hanbal, who asserted the absolute inviolability of the Quran and Sunna, and determined that no Imam—or anyone else for that matter—could reinterpret them. About the **Hanbalis** or Hanbalism, Cooperson would write: "This increasingly powerful literalist movement eventually developed into what is today called Sunnism."[16] This is why they are often called proto-Sunnis. Al-Mamun and al-Mutasim were therefore "enemies of the faith."[17] As one can see, the theological positions of Sunni and Shiite Islam were starting to form. It was al-Mamun's and al-Mutasim's promotion of Mutazilism that went a long way toward bringing the two opposing views on this issue into greater relief.

Al-Mutasim died in 842 at the age of forty-six. His nine-year reign produced a highly centralized system with power in the hands of a small group of army officers and civilian administrators, what has been called the Samarra elite. Little did al-Mutasim know, however, that by bringing in mamluks to man the armies he was setting up a trap, if not a prison, for future Abbasid caliphs under the thumb of military/mamluk rule. He was succeeded by his son, Harun al-Wathiq, who ruled for about five years. He basically continued, even intensified, his father's policies, and the nature of the government remained the same.

Following Harun al-Wathiq's death in 847, he was succeeded by another son of al-Mutasim's: al-Mutawakkil. The new caliph was thought to be someone who would continue his father's and brother's policies. Certainly this is what the mamluks believed at first, as they were instrumental in arranging his rise to power. However, al-Mutawakkil turned out to be anything but a supplicant. Over time he systematically set about tearing down the system that his predecessors established. It would in the end usher in a period of intense instability in the empire, as Abbasid rule would break down across the board in a way that would threaten the survival of the caliphate itself.

Breakdown

The caliphate of al-Mutawakkil can be seen in retrospect as the long-expected reaction to the policies implemented by the previous three caliphs, as there had been years of simmering opposition to the inquisition as well as the seeming impunity of the mamluks. One of the first things al-Mutawakkil did was to begin replacing mamluk officers with members of the Abbasid family and other loyal groups. He was able to get his people in as governors of provinces and other important official positions. It was not easy, and it did not happen overnight, but it was a systematic process that generally was successful in the short term. Once again Alids were unwelcome at court and generally repressed, as the figure of Ali was cursed from the pulpits and the tombs of many of the Alid Imams were destroyed. On the flip side, al-Mutawakkil reconciled with the Hanbalis and promoted the idea of the inviolability of the Quran and Sunna. He even moved the capital for a time just north of Samarra to get away from the Turks (interestingly, he had wanted to go to Damascus at first, but there was still too much association with the Umayyads).

Al-Mutawakkil ruled until 861, and it was mostly a stable and peaceful period. However, the mamluks certainly were not happy with their deteriorating position. In the end, as often happens, the most drastic of actions was taken to rectify the situation from their perspective. It was not so much that they were in such a powerful position that they could indiscriminately kill a caliph; on the contrary, it was an act of desperation to protect the position and power they had left. Al-Mutawakkil was killed in his palace by a cabal of Turks. One narrative has one of his sons, al-Muntasir, helping the mamluks because he had been ridiculed by his father for years. And it would be the weak and pliable al-Muntasir who would become the next caliph, in essence a puppet of the mamluks.

As with the murder of previous Rashidun and Umayyad caliphs, it led to a period of instability and political chaos. The assassination of al-Mutawakkil ushered in what has been called the "nine-year night of anarchy," when paralysis and weakness at the center allowed for provincial dissent to emerge with intense vigor. There was even open conflict between Samarra and Baghdad that further damaged the delicate ecosystem of the Sawad. During this period between 861 and 870 there were four caliphs, at least three of whom were murdered via assassination or rebellion. Such was the degree of long-term instability generated by the assassination of al-Mutawakkil that the great medieval historian Muhammad ibn Jarir al-Tabari, in his voluminous work on Islamic history, titled his chapter covering this period "Incipient Decline"—the beginning of the end. And in many important ways, it was the beginning of the end of Abbasid power. The caliph seemed nothing more than a pawn in the power games played by rival Turkish military factions.

The weakness at the center encouraged groups inside and on the fringes of the empire to assert themselves. This is the beginning of the fragmentation of Abbasid rule, when we start to hear names like Saffarids, Hamdanids, Qaramita (Carmathians), Tulunids, Zanj, Samanids, and others, as they usurp the authority of the Abbasid caliphate if not outright try to destroy it. The Abbasid-Tahirid partnership in Khurasan and eastern Iran by 873 was shattered by the Saffarids from Sistan. Not willing to accept the Abbasid offer to establish the cooperative relationship the caliphate had enjoyed with the Tahirids, the Saffarids actually marched on Baghdad. It was only the sitting caliph's brother, al-Muwaffaq, who was able to defeat the

Saffarids in 876 outside of Baghdad and save the caliphate. He was the one member of the Abbasid family who was popular and close with the military. Unfortunately, being the son of a concubine wife, he was not able to become caliph, but he would repeatedly save the Abbasid realm when it seemed on the brink of collapse. The Saffarids would continue to rule in Khurasan and they would grudgingly acknowledge the Abbasid caliph, but they were essentially independent and returned little if any revenues to Iraq, and there was nothing the Abbasids could do about it.

In the other direction, a son of a mamluk who had been captured during the time of al-Mamun, Ahmad ibn Tulun, left Iraq in 868 (during the nine-year night of anarchy) and, in the spirit of Amr ibn al-As, was either appointed or made himself the governor of Egypt until his death in 884. He brought mamluks with him and built up an impressive army in Egypt that was able to extend Tulunid authority into Syria; it would be Tulunid armies that kept the Byzantines at bay in northern Syria, not the Abbasids. Fortunately for the Abbasid caliph, Ahmad ibn Tulun never ceased to acknowledge his sovereignty, and he utilized the natural wealth of Egypt to return surplus revenues from time to time to the central treasury.

As opposed to the Saffarids or Tulunids, with whom a level of cooperation was possible, the Abbasids faced a more profound challenge right underneath their noses in Iraq from a group with whom no compromise was possible. This was the so-called Zanj slave revolt in southern Iraq near (and soon in) the city of Basra. The **Zanj** was the name given to the slave population that worked primarily on land reclamation projects in the marshy areas in southern Iraq, especially where the Tigris and Euphrates rivers meet to form what is called today the Shatt al-Arab waterway, a confluence of the two rivers that outlets into the Persian Gulf. It was largely a black African population from the eastern portion of Africa, possibly Zanzibar. This was pretty much the only area in Islam where large scale agricultural slavery occurred. There is also no doubt that these slaves lived in terrible conditions, and there were several minor revolts in this area by slaves during the Umayyad caliphate.

This revolt was out to flip on its head the entirety of Abbasid society. The slaves were going to be the masters and the masters were going to suffer. What made this revolt so threatening was not only the content and vitality of its messaging, but also the fact that a number of nonslave elements disappointed in Abbasid rule joined the uprising. The rebellion was led by one of these nonslave elements, an Arab man by the name of Ali ibn Muhammad. Starting his prophetic opposition movement in eastern Arabia, he soon found a ready-made support base of rebellion in southern Iraq among the Zanj. He claimed he was a member of the Alid family, which would be more appealing in Iraq in general.

The rebellion broke out in 869, during the nine-year night of anarchy. It was very successful, and for over a decade the Zanj movement went basically unchallenged. The Abbasids could do little to quell the rebellion, and after some efforts failed they essentially adopted a live-and-let-live policy until a time when they were ready to confront the Zanj. In the meantime, Ali ibn Muhammad and his forces took Basra in 871, and the slaves' hatred of their former masters became manifest in the fact that the city was virtually destroyed and most of the inhabitants massacred in brutal fashion. It is said that Basra never fully recovered from this, and it was the economic outlet to the Persian Gulf and Indian Ocean for Baghdad. Trade routes were disrupted and began to shift, as traders and merchants sought more stable routes and economic centers elsewhere; one can see this as the acceleration of the shift away from Iraq as the economic center of the Islamic world.

Ali ibn Muhammad founded his own capital called Mukhtara ("chosen") on a canal east of Basra. He minted his own coins, and after taking Basra he proclaimed himself the mahdi, a natural progression for his largely Alid-leaning followers. Finally, it fell again to al-Muwaffaq to save the day. In 883 he led an Abbasid army that laid siege to Mukhtara, taking it in hand-to-hand fighting, with Ali ibn Muhammad being killed in the battle. But the damage to the caliphate—and in particular Iraq—had been done. As the Sawad went, so did the Abbasids. And the Sawad, Baghdad, Basra, and other parts of Iraq had seen much better days. The Abbasid caliphate was now in inexorable decline, and it would end in financial ruin.

After the Zanj were defeated, the main objective of the Abbasids was to increase revenues, which required more control over more territory in order to derive wealth from the taxes on people, produce, and land in those territories. It was a kind of chicken and egg conundrum: they needed more territory to increase revenues, but they needed more revenues to pay the army to take back territory and the kuttab to more efficiently collect taxes. Some sort of new, more expedient, and more viable financial system had to be constructed or else groups of soldiers would continue to mutiny for back pay and undermine the ability of the Abbasids to reextend their control, first and foremost in Iraq and the immediately surrounding areas such as the Jazira, the Byzantine frontier, and western Iran. Other areas were left on their own as long as the local rulers continued to show at least some deference to the Abbasid caliph. One important case was the Samanids in eastern Iran and Khurasan, who had replaced the Saffarids but were essentially independent. Even the Jazira and the Syrian desert in general were difficult for the Abbasids to control by the 890s because of the presence of the Qaramita, named after Hamdan ibn Qarmat, who was an Ismaili Alid/Shiite or Sevener, a follower of the Ali-Fatima through the Hussein line of Imams that broke off of the main line (soon to become Twelver Shiism) at the seventh Imam. Whereas the Twelvers followed one son of the sixth Imam, Jaafar al-Sadiq, by the name of Musa al-Kazim, the Seveners followed his older brother, Ismail, who had predeceased Musa. The Qaramita were loosely organized groups of Bedouin Arabs roaming the Arabian and Syrian deserts disrupting not only trade but also the hajj route from east to west. By 904 the Abbasids were able to largely subdue the Qaramita, but once again only after great effort and expense.

Money was a priority after each and every one of these challenges. The accumulation of them made the financial situation dire. The Abbasids and the kuttab would attempt to implement a variety of measures, often at the same time, in the hope of increasing revenues. Unfortunately, most attempts to do so may have provided some short-term relief but in the end did more damage to Abbasid authority than helped it. It was a military bureaucracy with a cost well out of proportion to the Abbasids ability to pay for it. There was an increase in direct taxation, something called tax farming, and other methods. Usually this resulted in rapacious tax collectors or overlords who would use their positions to exploit the people and the land under their purview in order to return as much money to the central treasury as possible. While generating immediate returns, it usually alienated the population and harmed the fertility of the land through overharvesting in order to generate more revenue.

Increasingly, the method adopted was the **iqta** system. This was the granting of territory, usually to a military commander, but also at times to an administrative official. The iqta-holder was assigned the task of revenue-collecting in his territory. In return, he would send an agreed sum of money to Baghdad and provide troops if and when called upon to do so. For the most part it was the latter rather than the former. This method was a better solution in the sense that the iqta-holder had a vested interest in the land, especially as he could typically pass it on to his sons; therefore, it would be counterproductive to exploit the population and the land. He would take on all of the administrative duties of government in the territory as well. This way, the central treasury was relieved of the burden of paying for a large salaried army as well as some administrators. At first, the iqtas were assigned near the fringes of the empire in order to more immediately meet the need of defense against invasion from the outside if necessary and to maintain order in areas far removed from the metropole. But financial need compelled the Abbasids to grant more and more iqtas in the interior, even in Iraq itself. While the iqta system seemed to work, it was truly a temporary palliative, especially with regard to actual Abbasid authority. Over time the iqta-holders became more independent, essentially rulers of their own fiefdoms, and in essence what was being created were mini-dynasties. In the end, it led to the dispersion and diffusion of Abbasid power rather than concentration of it. It also brought the military directly into the fiscal and administrative structures of the caliphate.

With financial need such a priority for the Abbasids, the kuttab still played an important role despite the ascendance of the mamluks. The battles between the kuttab and the military continued unabated. We have already seen that different military factions often maneuvered against each other. These rivalries existed within the kuttab as well, as powerful bureaucratic families would battle each other for prominence within the administration.[18] These divisions among the kuttab only complicated their ability to govern in a consistent manner and to keep the military at bay.

The high point of kuttab power in the early tenth century came when a member of the Abbasid family they backed became caliph in 908. He took the name al-Muqtadir. He has been described as a tool of the bureaucrats, but by being so, the link that some previous caliphs—and al-Muwaffaq—had established with the military had been broken. Even so, al-Muqtadir enjoyed a relatively long tenure in power. Similar to the situation with al-Mutawakkil, however, the Turkish mamluks felt their hard-won position within the Abbasid empire was threatened. In 932, some Turks once again murdered a caliph. This signaled the final takeover of government by the military. From now on it would be military commanders of one sort or another who were the real power, keeping the Abbasid caliphs on as figurehead rulers. In 935 they had their personally chosen caliph create the office of the **amir al-umara**, commander of commanders. The amir al-umara was the de facto head the state.

This chain of events, especially after the murder of a caliph, led to further instability in the empire amid growing financial crisis. Egypt was lost again shortly after the death of al-Muqtadir. Northern Iraq and the Jazira were in the hands of a group called the Hamdanids. And half of Iran by the 940s was taken over by a family of Daylamites known as the Buyids. None of these made any financial contributions to the state. The ultimate problem for the Abbasids was a lack of money. The only question that remained was if one of these breakaway groups would take over Baghdad itself. If they did so, would they keep the caliphate—and keep it within the Abbasid family. The Abbasid caliphate, such as it was, had essentially shrunk to that of Baghdad and some immediately surrounding areas in Iraq. One of the aforementioned groups, the Buyids, would enter Baghdad in 945, rendering the Abbasids essentially vestigial.

As a kind of epitaph to the Abbasid caliphate, Hugh Kennedy wrote the following:

> The Abbasid caliphate was the last polity to use the resources of Mesopotamia to support a great empire. Since the third millennium BC a succession of powers, Sumerians, Babylonians, Assyrian, Achaemenid Persian and Sassanian Persia, had used the fertility generated by the Tigris and Euphrates to create great civilizations and world empires. The Abbasids were to prove the last representatives of this ancient tradition. By the tenth century, the broken and desolate landscapes, exploited by corrupt and grasping administrations and ravaged by marauding bands of unpaid soldiers, could support nothing more than small-scale principalities. The real powers in the Muslim world were to be based in Egypt, Iran and, later, Turkey.[19]

It is to the Buyids in Iran, the Fatimids in Egypt, and later the Seljuk Turks that we now turn.

Chapter 5 Timeline

750	Abbasid Caliphate established
754–775	Caliphate of Abu Jafar al-Mansur
762	Foundation of the Abbasid capital of Baghdad
786–809	Rule of Caliph Harun al-Rashid
809–813	Abbasid Civil War between Al-Amin and Al-Mamun
833–842	Caliphate of Al-Mustasim and the beginning of the Samarra Period
861	Assassination of the Caliph al-Mutawakkil
861–869	Nine-Year Night of Anarchy at Samarra
868	Tulunid dynasty established in Egypt
869–883	Zanj Revolt
873	Saffarid rule established in Khurasan
908–932	Caliphate of al-Muqtadir
945	Buyids take control of Baghdad

Primary Sources

Harun al-Rashid and the Succession Arrangement

Selection from Ta'rikh al-Rusul wa'l-muluk of Muhammad ibn Jarir al-tabari

He related: [The caliph] Harun [al-Rashid] made the Pilgrimage, accompanied by [his two sons], Muhammad and 'Abdallah, and by his military commanders, ministers and judges, in the year 802. He left behind at al-Raqqah Ibrahim b. 'Uthman b. Nahik al-'Akki in charge of his womenfolk, the treasuries and material wealth, and the army, and he dispatched his son al-Qasim to Manbij and then installed him there with the military commanders and soldiers whom he had attached to al-Qasim's side.

When he had accomplished the rites of the Pilgrimage, he composed for his son 'Abdallah al-Ma'mun two letters, over the composition of which the religious lawyers and judges had expended intensively their intellectual efforts. One of them comprised stipulations laid upon Muhammad setting forth the conditions which Harun had imposed on him regarding Muhammad's faithful adherence to the arrangements in the document concerning the handing over of the administrative regions for which 'Abdallah was to assume responsibility, and he conveyed to him estates, sources of revenue, jewels, and wealth. The other was the documentary text of the oath of allegiance which the Caliph had extracted from the nobles and commoners alike, and that of the obligations due to 'Abdallah and incumbent upon both Muhammad himself and those nobles and commoners.

[Harun al-Rashid] placed the two documents in the Holy House [the Ka'bah in Mecca] after he had extracted the oath of allegiance to Muhammad and after he had called to witness in his favor regarding the terms of the oath, God, His angels and all those who were with him in the Ka'ba, comprising the rest of his children, his family, his [clients], his military commanders, his ministers, his secretaries, and so forth. The act of witness to the succession oath and the (other) document took place in the Holy House, and he ordered the doorkeepers to guard the two documents and to prevent anyone from taking them away and making off with them. 'Abdallah b. Muhammad, Muhammad b. Yazid al-Tamimi, and Ibn al-Hajabi have mentioned that al-Rashid was present and that he summoned the leading members of the Hashimite family, the military commanders and the religious lawyers. They were taken into the Holy House, and he ordered the document to be read out to 'Abdallah and Muhammad, and made the whole of those present bear witness to the attestation of the two of them to the document. Then he thought it fitting to hang up the document in the Ka'bah, but when it was lifted up in order to attach it for suspension, it fell down, and people commented that this arrangement would speedily be dissolved before it could be carried through completely.

The text of the document was as follows:

In the name of God, the Merciful, the Compassionate One. This is a document composed by the servant of God Harun the Commander of the Faithful, which Muhammad son of Harun the Commander of the Faithful has written out in a state of soundness of mind and full exercise of his powers, willingly and unconstrainedly. The Commander of the Faithful has appointed me as his successor after him and has imposed acknowledgment of allegiance to me on the whole of the Muslims. He has appointed 'Abdallah the son of Harun the Commander of the Faithful as his successor and as caliph and as the one responsible for all the affairs of the Muslims after myself, with my full agreement and freely conceded by me, willingly and unconstrainedly. He has given responsibility for Khurasan, its frontier regions and its districts, for the conduct of warfare there and its army, its land tax, its official textile workshops, its postal relay system, its public treasuries, its poor-tax, its religious tithe, the sums collected as tribute, and all its administrative divisions, both during his own (i.e., Harun's) lifetime and afterwards. I have accepted the obligation laid on me by the servant of God Harun the Commander of the Faithful with my full agreement and a contented mind, that I will faithfully fulfill and hand over to my brother 'Abdallah b. Harun the right of succession, the executive power, the caliphate and the affairs of the whole of the Muslims, which Harun the Commander of the Faithful has granted to him after me.

Source: Gordon, Matthew S. "Document 5, Harun al-Rashid and the Succession Arrangement." *The Rise of Islam*. Indianapolis: Hackett Publishing Company, Inc. (paperback version), 2008. Pgs. 128–130. Reprinted by permission from *The History of al-Tabari*, vol. 30, *The Abbasis Caliphates of Musa al-Hadi and Harun al-Rashid A.D. 785-809/A.H. 169-193*, translated by C.E. Bosworth. New York: The State University of New York Press, 1989.

NOTES

1. For more on this connection see Jacob Lassner, "The Abbasid *Dawlah*: An Essay of the Concept and Praxis of Revolution in Early Islam," in Frank Clover and R. Stephen Humphreys, eds., *Tradition and Innovation in Late Antiquity* (Madison: University of Wisconsin Press, 1989).
2. Ibid., p. 5.
3. Ibid.
4. Ibid., p. 25.
5. Hugh Kennedy, *When Baghdad Ruled the World: The Rise and Fall of Islam's Greatest Dynasty* (Cambridge, MA: De Capo Press, 2004), p. 8. See also Amira K. Bennison, *The Great Caliphs: The Golden Age of the Abbasid Empire* (New Haven, CT: Yale University Press, 2009), p. 26.
6. For the story of Abu Muslim's assassination, see Kennedy, *When Baghdad Ruled the World*, pp. 17–21.

7. Ibid., p. 21.
8. Bennison, *The Great Caliphs*, p. 28.
9. Ibid.
10. For some possible explanations, none of which are definitive, see Kennedy, *When Baghdad Ruled the World*, pp. 71–77.
11. Michael Cooperson, *Al Ma'mun* (Oxford: Oneworld Publications, 2012), pp. 28–29.
12. Garth Fowden, *Before and After Muhammad: The First Millennium Refocused* (Princeton, NJ: Princeton University Press, 2014), p. 149. It was said at the time that Aristotle had appeared to al-Mamun in a dream. Ibid., p. 157.
13. Ibid., p. 56.
14. In Shiite tradition as it developed later on, many accused al-Mamun of murdering Ali al-Rida, and when they enter the eighth Imam's shrine in Mashhad, many curse the name of al-Mamun, even though he sympathized with the Alids perhaps more than any other Abbasid caliph. See Cooperson, p. 70. For Shiites, as they emerged as a distinct sect in the tenth century, it became accepted fact that all of their Imams had been murdered.
15. Kennedy, *When Baghdad Ruled the World*, p. 218.
16. Cooperson, *Al Ma'mun*, p. 67. Hanbali Sunni Islam would become the most strict of the four generally accepted religious schools of Islamic law or Shari'a.
17. Ibid., p. 68.
18. For an excellent book detailing these kuttab battles, particularly in the early 900s between the Banu al-Jarrah and the Banu al-Furat, see Harold Bowen, *The Life and Times of Ali ibn Isa: The Good Vizier* (Cambridge: Cambridge University Press, 1928). Ali ibn Isa was from the Banu al-Jarrah family.
19. Kennedy, *When Baghdad Ruled the World*, pp. 295–296.

KEY TERMS

abna p. 108
amir al-umara p. 119
Hanbalis p. 114
ijtihad p. 97
iqta p. 118
katib p. 105
Khurasaniyya p. 100
mamluks p. 113
Mutazilism p. 111
nass p. 98
ulama p. 112
Zanj p. 116

For additional digital learning resources please go to www.oup.com/he/lesch-middleeast-1e

6 FRAGMENTATION

Buyids

It is at this point in the semester of my Medieval Islamic History class that I tell my students that the course begins to fragment, as is readily apparent in the syllabus. The first half of the semester has about three to four class meetings on the life of the Prophet Muhammad and the Rashidun, then three classes on the Umayyads, and then three to four more classes on the Abbasids up to 945 CE. Essentially, the syllabus simply reflects what happened in the Islamic world following the disintegration of Abbasid rule. Other groups and dynasties begin to enter the pages of history, either contesting or usurping the power of the Abbasid caliph. We have already seen groups such as the Saffarids, Tulunids, Qaramita, and the Zanj. In this chapter we begin to encounter even more powerful dynasties as the Abbasid center continues to weaken. For most of the tenth century there were three publicly acknowledged caliphs in the Islamic world: the Umayyad caliph in Cordoba, Spain; the Fatimid caliph in Cairo, Egypt; and, of course, the Abbasid caliph still in Baghdad. It just so happens that several of these new dynasties are Shiite or Shiite-leaning, creating facilitating environments for the development of distinct types of Shiism amid the majority Muslim presence of the *ahl al-sunna*, those of the Sunna—or what would soon become Sunni Islam. Although we have already touched upon some Shiite groups, such as the Qaramita and the Hamdanids, it is the Buyids and the Fatimids that really come to dominate the tenth century in the heartland of the Middle East—a period that because of this is often called the Shiite Century. And then in far-off Spain, the Islamic presence reached its zenith under a surviving branch of the Umayyad family. With this fragmentation we begin to see what some have called the establishment of an Islamic commonwealth. This was not necessarily a bad thing, as it encouraged—indeed in important ways facilitated—commercial and intellectual exchange that often heightened civilizational discourse and development.

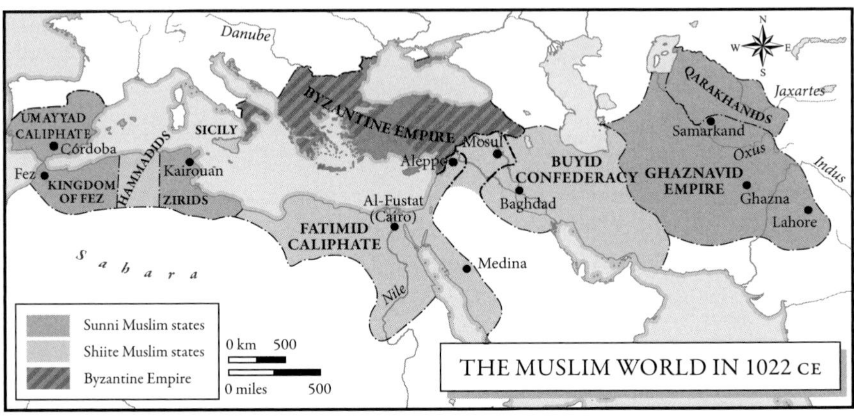

The Buyids (or Buwayhids) are a Persian family of Daylamites who emerged from the province of Daylam in the mountainous areas of northern Iran just south of the Caspian Sea in the first half of the tenth century. Groups such as the Buyids who lived in mountainous, hard-to-reach places typically maintained a good deal of independence from the established power due to their relative isolation. It was hazardous at best for Umayyad or Abbasid armies to enter into the forbidding landscapes nor was there much if any Arab settlement, so there tended to be a live and let live relationship between the metropole and these isolated pockets of autonomy. In these places, local peoples maintained their preexisting indigenous customs and belief systems and those who converted to Islam more often than not adopted heterodox forms of it, sometimes in and of itself an expression of independence. The Buyids were one of these groups.

It appears that Alid missionaries from the Zaydi branch of the family began to convert a number of people in Daylam to Islam, but not everyone was so persuaded in the region. One rather unusual individual took advantage of the problems and distractions of the Abbasid caliphate to assert himself in the 920s and 930s. This was a man by the name of Mardavij ibn Ziyar, whose followers were called, appropriately, the Ziyarids.[1] Much like the Zanj, Mardavij wanted to eliminate the Abbasid caliphate entirely. Unlike the Zanj, he was not and never became Muslim. Quite to the contrary, he wanted to bring back Zoroastrianism as the state religion and restore a Persian monarchy with a revival of the Persian language and culture. He even wanted the old Sassanian palaces in Ctesiphon to be rebuilt to await his arrival. Ultimately, his ambition would outreach his capability, but for a short time this presented a serious threat to the Abbasids.

The Buyid brothers joined the Ziyarid movement, led by the eldest, Ali ibn Buya, and his two younger brothers, Hasan and Ahmad. They would not stay with Mardavij for long, as the Buyids were independently minded themselves, and they also probably adhered to a vague form of Zaydi Islam, which would naturally put them at odds with the Ziyarids. As such, in 932 the Buyid brothers and several hundred of their followers made their way south to the Iranian province of Fars. Apparently, there were some wealthy and powerful families in Fars who were less than enamored with an exploitative Turkish warlord in charge of the province. This created the opportunity by 934 for a symbiotic relationship with the Buyid brothers, who provided the muscle to Farsi money, launching the province in a different, much more prosperous, and powerful direction in the Islamic world.

The Buyids did not even have to deal with Mardavij before gaining fame and fortune, because he was reportedly killed by some of his disillusioned followers in 935, thus opening the door for further Buyid expansion in Iran. A number of Ziyarids shifted their allegiances to Ali ibn Buya and his two siblings. Over the next decade Ali consolidated his position in Fars, while Hassan became the overlord of the province of Rayy in central Iran. Ahmad, on the other hand, made his way to Baghdad in an attempt to secure Iraq under Buyid control. The Buyids were not out to overthrow the Abbasid caliphate. Rather, they attempted to derive some legitimacy from it by receiving the sanction of the Abbasid caliph. As outsiders in the Islamic world practicing a heterodox form of Islam, the Buyids had virtually no religious standing of which to speak. They were obviously not descended from the Prophet's family, nor were they Arab. And even though the Abbasid caliphate was virtually powerless anywhere outside of the immediate environs of central Iraq, the office and position of the caliph still had, at the very least, religious standing and a level of acceptance among most of the population, as it had been around for almost three hundred years by this time. Getting rid of it was seen as much more trouble than it was worth, especially in a province (Iraq) that was in many ways marginal to the Buyids; after all, it was the *youngest* Buyid brother who was sent to Baghdad. After about a year of threats and persuasion, Ahmad was able to force the Abbasid caliph to name him the amir al-umara, effectively usurping the role previously assigned to Turkish mamluks and becoming the real power in Baghdad, where the Abbasid caliph was powerless for the time being to do anything about it and was kept under what was effectively house arrest.[2] As Marshall Hodgson wrote in the last line of his multivolume work *The Venture of Islam*, "The caliphal state had ceased to exist as an actual independent empire."[3] Ironically, though, the Buyids never established control over their hinterland, Daylam, rather settling for uneasy alliances for the duration of their time in power.

Thus the Buyid confederacy formally began. As the name implies, this was not a centralized empire. Officially, the Buyid brothers were appointed to their positions by the Abbasid caliph and given honorific titles to boot in order to enhance their stature. Ali was Imad al-Dawla (Support of the State), Hassan became Rukn al-Dawla (Pillar of the State), and Ahmad was given the title of Muizz al-Dawla (Glorifier of the State).[4] Fars was always the most important province in the confederacy, but it did not rule over the other Buyid provinces; it was a very decentralized political construct. Ali ibn Buya was also given the grandiose title of **shahanshah** (king of kings) within the confederacy, but it was really a first among equals, and they were anything but kings; however, the title is interesting because of its link to the Persian monarchical tradition. The Ziyarid movement revealed a yearning for a resuscitation of Persian customs and traditions, so the Buyids had to respect that. Perhaps the title was something of a sop thrown to their Persian subjects.

The problem historians have in examining the Buyid period is similar to that which existed under the Umayyads: the historical record emerged from Baghdad, therefore events in Iraq tend to be emphasized during the Buyid period at the expense of Rayy and Fars, even though Iraq was perhaps the least important, certainly in economic terms. Events in Baghdad during the Buyid confederacy are important, however, because it is here that Twelver Shiite Islam emerges as a distinct sect with unique religious beliefs and rituals that separate it from mainstream Islam at the time.

Even though the condition in Baghdad had deteriorated considerably over the previous decades, it remained a center of intellectual activity, especially with regard to Islamic discourse. As Iraq had always been a center for Alid activity, it is not surprising that discussions surrounding the Imams and the Imamate occurred in Baghdad. And it is here where the idea of the Hidden Imam developed, even well before the arrival of the Buyids. But it became crystallized during the Buyid period. Contributing to this was the fact that the Buyids were practicing an amorphous brand of Zaydi Islam, so Baghdad under Buyid watch created a more propitious environment for intellectual activity on such matters. And it was the idea of the Hidden Imam that doctrinally separated Twelver Shiite Islam from its ahl al-sunna dominant landscape. What came into focus during the Buyid period was the idea that the eleventh imam, Hassan al-Askari, died in Samarra in 874. He had a son who then went into hiding or occultation (*ghaybah*) and never died. At some point in the future the Hidden Imam would return as the Mahdi to establish the just rule of Islam. In the meantime, he left representatives in the world who were in some way guided or inspired by the Hidden Imam and could lead the flock until his return. This is why it became known as Twelver Shiism (or *ithna ashr* Islam, Arabic for the number twelve). The first imam is Ali, then his eldest son Hassan, with Hussein as the third imam. The remaining Twelver Imams all are of the Husseinid line. There is no consensus on why the idea of the Hidden Imam emerged when it did. The sixth imam, Jaafar al Sadiq, established a quietist form of Alid opposition to the Abbasids that was much safer, as previous imams in the Twelver line had typically been killed. It was akin to *taqiyya* or pious dissimulation, which was viewed as necessary by many Alids/Shiites in order to survive in a world that was often dangerous for them. Perhaps the Hidden Imam, from the historian's point of view, was the ultimate fruition of this trend. As Roy Mottahedeh put it, "It was a good moment for the Twelvers to put aside their aspirations for worldly power."[5] In any event, non-Shiites would be much more willing to tolerate Twelvers if they had no living imam and maintained the more passive posture laid down by Jaafar Sadiq.[6]

Whatever the case, this definitely marked the evolution of a more mature Shiism from what had existed beforehand. In addition, there also developed during this time, again under the more forgiving Buyid environment, rituals that came to distinguish Shiites from the ahl al-Sunna. One was the public denigration of the first three caliphs—Abu Bakr, Umar, and Uthman—who were seen by Shiites as having usurped the caliphal rights of Ali, who should have succeeded Muhammad. The flip side of this was the development of exclusive Shiite public festivals, such as that of the **Ghadir Khumm** on the 18th day of the Islamic month of Dhu al-Hijja, when, according to Shiites, the Prophet Muhammad, at the well of Ghadir Khumm located outside of Medina, appointed Ali as his successor. Unfortunately for Shiites—and for Ali—there was no one else present to witness this. What some have called the "big bang" of Shiite Islam, the martyrdom of the Imam Hussein at Karbala in 680, became the most important annual commemoration for Shiites, celebrated as the Ashura (number 10 in Arabic) on the tenth day of the Islamic month of **Muharram**. Finally, tombs of the twelve imams were developed as shrines and acted as centers of pilgrimage for Shiite Muslims.[7] All of these things contributed to the development of what historian Heinz Halm called a strengthened Shiite "sense of identity."[8]

It was a crisis in Baghdad in 973–974 that really cemented the division between Shiites and those who would later identify as Sunnis.[9] It revolved around a resurgent

The Shah-Cheragh Sanctuary in the Iranian city of Shiraz, 2017. It is the burial place of Amir Ahmad (d. 835) and Mir Muhammad, brothers of Shiite Imam Reza, who found refuge in Shiraz before an Abbasid persecution. The double mausoleum is one of the most famous Shiite pilgrimage sites in Iran.

dpa picture alliance/Alamy Stock Photo

Byzantine Empire that had made some inroads into northern Syria. Muslims in the area now looked to the Buyids to deal with the situation. The Buyid amir al-umara in Baghdad (Ahmad ibn Buya had died in 967) subsequently called for a jihad against the infidel Byzantines; however, Turkish mamluks in and around Baghdad, who had always resented the Buyids taking over their role in the Abbasid caliphate, instead called for a jihad against the Buyids. In essence, they were calling the Buyids infidels and heretics. The Buyids were forced out of Baghdad by the Turks. While the Buyids were able to reestablish themselves in Iraq in short order, the damage had been done. The so-called Turkish crisis of 973–974 hardened the already differentiating religious opinions and practices between Shiites and the ahl al-Sunna (Hanbalis) to the point where they began isolating themselves in exclusively Shiite and anti-Shiite/proto-Sunni quarters in the city, or as Hugh Kennedy writes, "armed political groupings."[10] This is what often happens when there is a breakdown of government or society: people tend to retreat into their subidentities, be they sectarian or ethnic fortresses, in order to preserve their cultural identity and to simply survive amid the chaos. These divisions soon spread to other parts of Iraq and places beyond over time.

In response to this situation in Baghdad, by the end of the tenth century, the Caliph al-Qadir (991–1031) started to position the caliphate as anti-Shiite. Buyid power in Iraq had weakened considerably by then, while Turkish mamluks were reasserting themselves. In addition, powerful, mostly Turkish groups to the east of the Buyids, such as the Ghaznavids and the Seljuks, were making themselves felt on the fringes of Buyid territory, and all of them were ardently anti-Shiite. Al-Qadir was able to carve out a functional position for the Abbasid caliph that had not previously existed, as a religious rather than political leader; if one examines the tenure of power of the remaining Abbasid caliphs until the Mongols sacked Baghdad in 1258, what is readily noticeable is the rather long length of time almost all of the remaining Abbasid caliphs rule. This can be due to one of two reasons: they once again become all-powerful in the tradition of al-Mansur or the like, or they become politically impotent to the point of becoming irrelevant except for their symbolic religious leadership. It is the latter that prevailed. But by adopting a nonpolitical role and aligning the caliphate's position with powerful new Sunni groups on the horizon, al-Qadir bought the Abbasids over two more centuries in Baghdad. It is with some irony that this happened. As you may recall, the Abbasids came to power in 750 as representatives of the Family of the Prophet, adopting a position that was favorably disposed toward the Alids. Primarily under al-Mamun and al-Mutasim and their implementation of Mutazilism, the Abbasid caliphate came closest to becoming essentially a Shiite Imamate. The Abbasid caliph under al-Qadir and his successors had thus come full circle, vehemently opposed to Shiism. Muhammad the Pure Soul was probably saying in his grave, "I told you so."

The Buyids reached their peak under the leadership as shahanshah of Fanakhusrau, who was accorded the title of Adud al-Dawla (also meaning "pillar of the state"). He ruled from Fars and died in 983. During his time in power most areas of the confederacy, especially Fars, became agriculturally prosperous and became a center of commercial and urban development.[11] From then on, however, the Buyid confederacy slowly but surely began to disintegrate amid constant dynastic disputes as well as the increasing pressure from Turkish tribal conglomerates to the east, most notably the Seljuks. In addition, while Fars replaced Iraq as an economic and trade center in the area and experienced significant economic growth, Iraq continued to be a source of instability for the Buyids, as the Turkish crisis in 973–974 showed—and they never really could reconcile with the Turks. They could never get Iraq under control nor revive its economic fortunes as a central fiscal source in the region, as it had been for generations under the Abbasids, but this may have been beyond the control of anyone by this point. As such, the Buyids resorted to the iqta system much as the Abbasids did, with similarly short-term benefits and long-term negative repercussions.[12] The Byzantine frontier frequently drained Buyid resources, and they could never entirely reel in the Hamdanids in Syria and the Jazira in a way that would supplement Buyid rule in Iraq. Kurdish tribes in northern Iran and Iraq also began to assert themselves against the weakening façade of Buyid rule into the eleventh century.

What one observes is a steady deterioration of Buyid power and control until someone stronger came along to put a formal end to it. The inherent benefits of a confederal system perhaps preordained that it would not have the military or financial resources—nor the unified purpose, leadership, or response—to deal with a new power on the horizon.

Fatimids

As we know from chapter 3, following the conquest of Egypt by Amr ibn al-As and his army, there was very little Arab settlement there. Essentially, Muslim rule was grafted onto the existing Byzantine structure, with the tightly knit Coptic community maintaining their religious customs and practices in the face of what was likely a very vague and amorphous brand of Islam at the time. This is even more so if it was truly just a Believers movement that did not encroach upon the sensibilities of the dominant local Christian population. Conversion to Islam was a very slow process. As such, even though Egypt had long been a wealthy country and breadbasket for multiple Mediterranean civilizations, in the early Islamic period its economic well-being based on the fertility of the Nile Valley did not translate to political power. There was no ready-made block of Arabs or Muslims that could help catapult a would-be dynast to power in the wider Muslim world beyond Egypt itself.

It wasn't really until forces entered Egypt from the outside once again a couple of centuries later that it began to acquire commensurate political clout and more economic centrality. This began to develop with the arrival of Ahmad ibn Tulun and his mamluk army in 868, thus beginning the short-lived Tulunid dynasty. Although ostensibly Tulun remained loyal to the Abbasid caliph, he expanded his territory to include most of Syria and Palestine up to the Byzantine frontier. This had become something of an axiom of Egyptian dynasties going back to the pharaonic period—that it was deemed necessary to hold onto the Levant for strategic and economic reasons. The Levant, strategically, acted as a necessary buffer to would-be invaders from the east, while economically, it provided an alternative agricultural source in times of famine in Egypt that typically followed upon excessive flooding of the Nile River. The Tulunid dynasty brought Egypt into the mainstream of the Islamic world, especially as the Abbasids in Iraq were experiencing a host of challenges and disruptions stemming from the nine-year night of anarchy in Samarra. Following the demise of the Tulunids in 884, the powers that be in Egypt continued to engage in the Islamic world even though for a time after the Tulunids, as Egyptian historian Afaf Lufti Marsot wrote, "The population of the country was treated like a conquered people by the invaders while plunder and extortion brought low a state that had so recently enjoyed an unprecedented degree of wealth and prosperity. For the next thirty years government of Egypt at the hands of Turkish governors and their willful and undisciplined armies was a mockery."[13]

Unlike the Tulunids, who cooperated with and acknowledged the suzerainty of the Abbasid caliph, the Fatimids were out to completely overthrow the Abbasids and essentially replace them with their new Islamic order. It would be the Berber population in northwest Africa who would play the critical role in the rise of the Fatimid Empire, even though the ruling family was Arab, descendants of Ali and Fatima through Hussein. It would be the Prophet's daughter whose name was appropriated by the Fatimid movement to emphasize its Alid orientation. For the Fatimids themselves, they preferred to refer to their movement as the *dawlat al-haqq* or the legitimate or true (*haqq*) state or dynasty, as opposed to what they believed to be the illegitimate Abbasid caliphate.

The Berbers of North Africa, as we saw during a major rebellion against Umayyad rule, were never particularly agreeable to centralized government. They steadily resisted the Aghlabids, an Arab dynasty in Qayrawan in modern day Tunisia, through whom the Abbasids attempted to extend some level of control in North Africa. As with the Buyids, the Berbers tended to adopt heterodox forms of Islam as something of an expression of their independence. Ismaili missionaries had found a receptive audience in the Kabyle mountains in Morocco, particularly with a tribal bloc called the Kutama Berbers. As we know, Ismailis are Alids/Shiites who broke off from the Twelver Shiite line of imams following the death of the sixth imam, Jaafar al-Sadiq. Ismailis believe that Jaafar's eldest son, Ismail and his progeny, should be the rightful leaders of the community even though he predeceased his father. While Twelvers follow his younger brother, Musa, who was designated by his father as the seventh Imam, Ismailis continued to follow the line of Ismail, ergo the name of this Shiite sect as Ismailis or Seveners.

The founding father of the Fatimid movement is a man by the name of Said ibn al-Hussein, who is better known as Abdullah al-Mahdi. In some sources he is known as Ubayd Allah. The difference may simply be due to the fact that both "Abdullah" and "Ubayd Allah" mean "servant of God," although in the latter case it has been translated as well as "little servant of God." And by attaching "al-Mahdi" to his name, it certainly elevated his intentions and his station. Whatever the case, Abdallah al-Mahdi claimed descent from Muhammad ibn Ismail, the grandson of Jaafar al-Sadiq and son of Ismail. Abdullah al-Mahdi's acclaimed connection to Muhammad ibn Ismail is somewhat clouded, but obviously a critical mass of followers believed it eventually. In addition, his rise to prominence and how he got from Syria to North Africa is shrouded in mystery and, no doubt, embellished narratives. In a way, the mystery and harrowing circumstances of his journey add a certain aura that all prophets need.

According to the story, in 899 Hamdan Qarmat (of Qaramita fame) broke away from what would become the Fatimid line. Abdallah al-Mahdi continued in Salamiyya, but in 902 some missionaries in Syria called on Qaramita Bedouin tribes to acknowledge Abdallah al-Mahdi. In the process they revealed his location, however, so he had to flee for fear of Abbasid forces coming to hunt him down. After deciding not to go to Yemen, where there were also some Ismaili communities, he ventured across into the *Maghrib* or North Africa (*Ifriqiya*) and landed in the Sijilmasa oasis in Morocco, an important way station for trade in the region.[14] Kharijites 150 years earlier had founded the oasis and converted many in the area to Islam, so the Muslim populace there by the time Abdallah al-Mahdi arrived were already of the rebellious type. He and his disciples, particularly one Abu al-Abbas al-Shii, who had been proselytizing in North Africa since 893, found a receptive audience to the Ismaili calling (*dawa*) among the Kutama Berbers, beginning a partnership that would carry the Fatimids to power. In an important way, Ifriqiya was to the Kutama Berbers what Khurasan was to the Khurasaniyya. And the Kutama Berbers were to Abdallah al-Mahdi and his lineage what the Khurasaniyya were to the Abbasids, the primary military support for the movement.[15]

The Fatimids shifted from a fringe movement to a regional power when they took Qayrawan from the Aghlabids in 909. Abdallah al-Mahdi became the first Fatimid caliph, beginning the dynasty. Since this was a movement of expansion, particularly at the expense of the Abbasids, the Fatimids always had their eyes turned eastward, and the initial prize in this direction was Egypt. Between 909 and 969 the Fatimids tried on a couple of occasions to conquer Egypt, but the Turkish-based dynasties there, namely a group called the Ikhshidids, were more than up to the task as they had restored some order and stability in Egypt following a period of instability after the Tulunids. There was also the occasional Berber revolt to the west that occupied their attentions. It was not until 969 that the Fatimids, under the Caliph al-Muizz, were successful in finally taking the province that came to be geographically synonymous with the dynasty. By that time, a number of important Egyptian families were ready to welcome a stabilizing force that could settle things down in a way in which trade and commerce could once again flourish. Soon after taking Egypt the caliph built a new capital to consecrate his victory, al-Qahira al-Muizziya, or what soon was just referred to as al-Qahira (the victorious), more popularly known in its anglicized form today, Cairo.[16] It was built a few miles to the north of the provincial capital of Fustat primarily to house the government as well as the Ismaili Kutama Berbers—and to keep the latter separate from the indigenous Sunni Muslim and Coptic inhabitants in Fustat.[17] Over time Cairo came to envelope Fustat, which essentially disappeared as a distinct city.

Like the Tulunids, the Fatimids extended their control to Syria and Palestine, and they also moved into the Hijaz, where their control of the two holy cities of Mecca and Medina—and the hajj itself—added to their religious credentials as the true dynasty of the Islamic world. But Syria and Palestine were a different story for the remainder of the Fatimid time in power. While Egypt was relatively peaceful, Syria and Palestine were almost always problematic, a constant drain on Fatimid resources. This was because Fatimid forces had to contend with a bewildering set of challenges, if not outright foes, including the Hamdanids, the Qaramita, the Byzantines, and eventually the Seljuks, who were diametrically opposed to the Fatimids—as well as the rather odd intrusion of the Crusades. In addition, the Berber forces in Syria could never really integrate or ingratiate themselves into the population, and Turkish elements were always battling against the Berbers for position and power in the area.

Egypt, though, was quite a different story for the Fatimids. Already rich agriculturally, under the Fatimids, Egypt became a transit route for trade between the Indian Ocean and Mediterranean worlds.[18] Trade advanced significantly at this time because of the relative decline of the economy in Iraq and the instability of the overland trade route from the Persian Gulf to the Mediterranean. Traveling around the Arabian peninsula and then up the Red Sea and a short trek over to the Nile (or at times even a canal), Cairo was well-situated to take advantage of the shifting trade routes. The Fatimids built up a navy that could not only increase their territorial hold along North Africa and up the Levant, but also protect the commerce and trade on which they so depended. Trade with Christian Europe began in earnest—with a Europe that was finally free around the year 1000 of the Viking raids that had so bottled up the continent. Many have pointed out the contrast during the Fatimid heyday of the rich, luxurious state of affairs in Cairo versus the relative poverty of Baghdad; as Kennedy notes: "Essentially, Cairo took over the role of Basra, reduced by the instability of Iraq."[19] So much so, in fact, that there was a talent drain from Iraq to Egypt where there existed much more opportunity: most notably the famous kuttab family of the Banu al-Furat, who had served the Abbasid caliph al-Muqtadir, made their way to Cairo.

The financial health of Fatimid Egypt seemed to trickle down to the populace as well. There was an artistic and architectural boom associated with society's economic well-being. As Hodgson wrote:

> The brilliance of Fatimi high society shows most readily in its fine arts. Egyptian commercial prosperity was not based only on the transit trade.

> Egyptian handicraft industry was itself an important element in the trade. Among other things, fine fabrics were made, especially in certain towns near the coastline or actually on it, where the air was conducively humid. These industrial arts were inherited from the pre-Islamic Coptic times. They were controlled by the government, which absorbed a large part of the product. The rest went to the luxury markets everywhere between the Nile and the Oxus, and far beyond.[20]

As the treasury was usually full, there were no mutinies by irate troops demanding to be paid, which seemed to become a feature of life during the middle Abbasid period. Kennedy writes: "If the Abbasid caliphate was destroyed by the economic collapse in Iraq, the Fatimid caliphate was in a sense created by the economic prosperity of Egypt."[21] The relative political stability for over a hundred years after Cairo was founded was also due to the nature of succession in the Fatimid caliphate. As opposed to the Umayyads or the Abbasids, where different lines of the family or sons of the sitting caliph competed for power and were often backed by different interest groups, the Fatimid dynasty had a fully developed method of succession based on the Ismaili emphasis on primogeniture. It doesn't mean there were no disputes at the top, but they were few and far between. Even if a member of the ruling family became caliph as a child, there were but few challenges from other family members or powerful interest groups; there were no civil wars between brothers such as that which occurred between the Abbasid caliphs al-Amin and al-Mamun. In addition, members of the Fatimid ruling family for the most part did not involve themselves in governance or in the military. These were the preserve of mostly Berbers and Turks, so the ruling family played very little role in politics; therefore, members of the family did not become powerful in their own right in a way separate from the caliph, and they did not become popular commanders of the army or provincial governors from which they could develop independent bases of power to pressure or even overthrow the caliph.

The height of the Fatimid Empire is generally considered to have been reached in the last quarter of the tenth century and into the first half of the eleventh century. It just so happens that the most colorful character of the Fatimid Empire was caliph during this time, although he was so eccentric, if not bizarre, according to most reports, that one wonders if this boon occurred in part because of his policies or despite them due to the momentum of success and institutional strength of the Fatimid state. This is the caliph al-Hakim, who succeeded to power in 996 at the age of eleven. He has been described as psychopathic by some, prescient by others. All agree he was nonconformist at the very least. He was something of an ascetic, symbolized by his riding on a simple donkey when he ventured out into the city. Al-Hakim appears to have also been an Ismaili puritan, at least at first, which was in contrast to the overall tolerance for non-Ismailis during Fatimid times, aided in part by the fact that the Ismaili ruling structure basically kept to themselves.

To try to impose the Ismaili rite would have generated such opposition from the majority of the population as to make it ill-advised at best. But the famous mosque of al-Azhar ("radiant one," a reference to Fatima) built in Cairo as a center of Ismaili religious thought and intellectual activity was, along with other institutions of learning, put to good use by al-Hakim.[22]

SPOTLIGHT

Al-Azhar in Cairo

Al-Azhar mosque was built in the new Fatimid capital of *al-Qahira* (Cairo) in 970 CE, a year after Egypt was taken by the Fatimids. The name itself is an allusion to the Prophet's daughter, Fatima, who was also called *al-Zahra* (the luminous), and her name was borrowed as one of the references—and eventually the dominant one—to what became the Fatimid dynasty in the tenth century CE. The mosque was built by Jawhar al-Siqilli, the Fatimid general who conquered Egypt on behalf of his ruler, the Caliph al-Muizz. It was first intended to be the main mosque for Friday prayers in Cairo, but a generation later in 988 it was transformed into a university of religious learning. The basic program of studies was—and still is today—Islamic law, theology, philosophy, and Arabic language. The curriculum at first was informal, and there were no entrance requirements nor any degrees conferred upon completion of the program.

Having been established by the Fatimids, al-Azhar was at first a center of Ismaili Shiite learning. When the Fatimids were replaced by Salah al-Din al-Ayyubi (Saladin) in the late twelfth century, al-Azhar fell into some disuse primarily because the new Ayyubid ruler and dynasty were Sunni. The Mamluk dynasty, however, which rose to power in Cairo in the 1250s and 1260s, revived al-Azhar and restored its educational role as well as its architectural splendor. The Mamluks, as primarily a warrior class, have not often in history been associated with learning and architecture but they were surprisingly prolific in both areas, all of which gave al-Azhar a new lease on life. Under Mamluk stewardship and sponsorship, it became a leading center of Sunni learning in the Islamic world.

Al-Azhar continued as a prominent center of Islamic education after the Mamluks—and Cairo—fell to the Ottomans in 1517. By the end of the sixteenth century it was considered by many to be the fifth most important mosque in the Islamic word, following upon those in the Holy Cities (Mecca and Medina), the al-Aqsa mosque in Jerusalem, and the Umayyad mosque in Damascus. Over time is also became a sanctuary and a focus of resistance against local authorities or external overlords. For instance, when the French took over Egypt in 1798, al-Azhar became a center of protest and opposition to the invaders, to the point where the French troops bombed the mosque/university and it was closed for a period of time.

The mosque rose again in the aftermath of the French departure in 1801, under Ottoman suzerainty once again as well as the more direct influence of the local dynast, Muhammad Ali. Al-Azhar became home to two very important Islamic philosophers who helped develop the ideas of Islamic modernism in the late nineteenth century, Jamal al-Din al-Afghani and his influential disciple, Muhammad Abduh, both about whom you will hear more of later in the book. Under President Gamal Abd al-Nasser in the early 1960s al-Azhar became more of a formal university with faculties in medicine, business, agriculture, and engineering in addition to the more traditional religious programs. Women were even allowed admission in 1962. Today, Al-Azhar University (*Jamiat al-Azhar*) is considered by most Muslims to be the foremost center of Islamic and Arabic learning in the world, located in what is now called the medieval quarter of modern Cairo.

Al-Azhar Mosque in Cairo.
Pavel Chonya/Alamy Stock Photo

Al-Hakim was described as being very cruel to anyone who might possibly challenge his authority, and many officials surrounding him were killed during periodic purges over the course of his tenure in power. His puritanism extended to restrictions on women, non-Muslims (*dhimmis*), and on various social activities, such as drinking wine.[23] In 1009 he inexplicably ordered the destruction of the Church of the Holy Sepulchre in Jerusalem, Christianity's holiest site. While this was used in Europe to drum up support for the Crusades toward the end of the century, no one knows exactly why he did this. Some of his apologists suggest it might have been in order to placate Muslims who were becoming disturbed by the improving economic and societal positions of Christians. But other behaviors were more difficult to explain, including dictating unusual dietary restrictions and keeping the lights on all night in the city when he traveled about town. What generally began to be of most concern was the inconsistency and unpredictability of his policies. Finally, one evening in 1021 al-Hakim apparently went off into the desert and was never heard from again—he simply disappeared. There are more sinister—and probably correct—explanations of what happened to him, such as the suggestion that he was killed and unceremoniously disposed of by a member of his family or others in the ruling hierarchy who grew tired of his eccentric behavior. The mysterious nature of his death only added to the story. During al-Hakim's lifetime, a man by the name of Muhammad ibn Ismail al-Darazi had proclaimed the caliph to be God. Al-Darazi was murdered, perhaps even at al-Hakim's orders, but his doctrine lived on among some of his followers. Over the course of the next centuries, these followers tended to settle down in the mountainous areas of what is now Lebanon and Syria, developing an esoteric doctrine that has as one of its tenets that al-Hakim disappeared in 1021 but would return one day as the Mahdi. They became known by the name of al-Hakim's erstwhile disciple, al-Darazi, better known today as the Druze.

By the end of the eleventh century, the Fatimid Empire was experiencing a slew of challenges that led to a slow but inexorable decline. As stated previously, Syria was always a drain on resources. The Fatimids began to lose territory to the Turkish Seljuks, who entered Baghdad in 1055 and who were committed to extinguishing the Fatimid threat on behalf of the Abbasid caliph. They did not do a very good job at first because the Fatimids took and occupied Baghdad in 1058 for a couple of years before the Seljuks began to pay more attention to this and expelled them for good—and they did not stop there, moving into Syria and Palestine as well, even taking Jerusalem in 1071. Then Sicily was lost, also in 1071, to European (Frankish) pressure, which in retrospect was something of a precursor to the Crusades. Beginning in 1095, the Crusaders established city states in the Levant out of what had for the most part been Fatimid territory. The Fatimid elan began to dissipate as time went on, and the mercenary nature of the military, particularly the near-constant bickering between Turks and Berbers, began to weaken Fatimid resolve and military capabilities. And there was also pressure from the West in the form of other Berber tribal conglomerations that would actually be more keenly felt in Islamic Spain.

All of these conditions combined to create a situation in Egypt not unlike that which existed prior to when the Fatimids entered in 969. The general population, including powerful merchant and commercial families, was ready for something else, someone else, to come in and restore stability and prosperity. Perched ready to do so was Salah al-Din al-Ayyubi, known in the West as Saladin. A devout Sunni Kurd who never ceased to acknowledge his loyalty to the Abbasid caliph, he entered Cairo in 1171, formally putting an end to the Fatimid caliphate and inaugurating the Ayyubid dynasty. This placed him in an advantageous position to do even bigger and better—certainly more famous—things over the next couple of decades, especially encountering the Frankish Crusader states in the Holy Land, but that is the subject of a different story to be covered later.

Islamic Spain

Hadith in Islam are primarily thought to be the sayings or reports of the Prophet Muhammad.[24] In Sunni Islam some hadith are attributed to his Companions, while in Twelver Shiite Islam, in addition to the Prophet are added the *ahl al-bayt* (those of the House, of the Prophet's House), the Twelve Imams, and Fatima, the Prophet's daughter. Hadith are second only to the Quran in terms of being a source of moral guidance and religious law. Since it appears that the hadith were transmitted orally for about a hundred years before actually being recorded, authentication of individual reports or sayings became an important matter in Islam, so much so that it became a field of study unto itself. Islamic law scholar Joseph Schacht described the relationship between the Sunna (custom or tradition of the Prophet) and hadith by saying that hadith is the "documentation of the Sunna."[25] A massive effort of authentication of hadith took place in the late eighth and into the ninth centuries under Abbasid auspices. The critical element to this authentication process was the chain of transmission (*isnad*) over the generations from the time and place of the Prophet Muhammad. Of the thousands upon thousands of possibilities, some were considered authentic via rigorous examination, while others were considered likely authentic or not authentic. There were many that could not possibly be authentic, often constructed contemporaneously to sanction or legitimate a particular action, person, or policy. For any single hadith, the chain of transmission constituted the first part and the actual report itself the second part. Two important bodies of hadith in the early ninth century were compiled, one under the name of Sahih al-Bukhari (d. 870) and other under Sahih al-Muslim (d. 875), both of whom were disciples of Ahmad ibn Hanbal. They are generally considered to be the most reliable and have the highest status. Together the two volumes are known as the *Sahihayn* (two truths).

One patently inauthentic hadith that was suddenly "found" in the tenth century went along the lines of the following, and I am paraphrasing: it is allowed in Islam to have multiple caliphates only if they are separated by a large body of water. This is a reference to the fact that by the middle of the tenth century there were three caliphates: the Abbasids, the Fatimids, and, since 929, the Umayyad caliphate in Spain. The body of water separating the caliphates was the Mediterranean Sea. If this supposed hadith even existed, it was probably constructed by an Abbasid official to account for the caliphal fragmentation in the Islamic world at the time. The newest player at the table was the caliph residing in the world class city of Cordoba in al-Andalus: Islamic Spain.

The Muslim conquest of Spain was an Arab and Berber exercise, the latter comprising most of the troops and initial settlers. To the Muslims, these new conquered territories in the Iberian Peninsula were referred to as al-Andalus. There is no consensus on this term, which is still used today in reference to southern Spain along the Mediterranean coast, or Andalucia. Largely disregarded now is any etymological link to the Vandals, who had ravaged southern Spain in the fifth century. The idea was put forth that Andalus could come from Vandalucia, land of the Vandals. Then there is another postulation, again largely dismissed these days, that Andalus could have emerged from Atlantida or Atlantic, a reference to Jazirat al-Andalus, "island of the Atlantic," or even Atlantis. More recently put forward by Heinz Halm, with more scholarly acceptance, is that al-Andalus comes from the post-Roman Visigothic term for allotted or inherited land in the area, *landahlauts*, which phonetically to the Arabs could sound like "landalus" or al-Andalus.[26]

Whatever the case, it was a Berber military commander by the name of Tariq ibn Ziyad, who pretty much on his own led a few thousand of his troops across from North Africa into Spain in 711. An island and strait at the nearest point (only some twelve miles wide at its closest) between North Africa and Spain bears his name, *Jebel Tariq* or Tariq's mountain, more commonly known in its anglicized form, "Gibraltar." This was not some leap in the dark for the Berbers. There had been a number of smaller exploratory expeditions or raids into southern Spain prior to this time. The land, climate, and topography of southern Spain was quite similar to that which existed in North Africa, only a better version of it in almost every sense, so it was a very attractive prize in and of itself.[27] Tariq's army was not terribly large, only a few thousand or so light cavalry and infantry, and most of them were Berber, a name derived from the Latin word "barbari," a term the Romans used to refer to barbarians or outsiders, which was indiscriminately applied to many different ethnicities but somehow stuck with the tribal peoples of North Africa. They marched north toward the Baetis River, which the Arabs referred to as al-Wadi al-Kabir (great river or river valley), or what the Spanish call to this day, derived from the Arabic, the Guadalquivir River.[28] The Visigothic King Roderic (Rodrigo) marched from his capital of Toledo to meet Tariq's forces. The two armies met just east of Cadiz, and the invaders from North Africa were decisively victorious, with Roderic being killed in battle.

Tariq's superior, Musa ibn Nusayr, who was the Arab governor of Ifriqiya, getting wind of his commander's successes, quickly rallied together his own force and crossed over into Spain in 712. Utilizing the Roman roads that helped Rome maintain control of Spain, the Arab-Berber force moved about quickly and freely, with most of the Iberian Peninsula taken by 716, including Visigothic Septimania in southern France stretching from the Pyrenees to Provence. The centralized nature of Visigothic Spain, a heritage of imperial Rome, added to the speed with which it was taken; the remainder of Spain fell largely in line once the head was cutoff. While the Muslims only held Septimania for a couple of decades, it did alert Frankish forces elsewhere in France to the looming threat, particularly Charles Martel, the strongman of the Merovingian dynasty. In 732 he defeated a Muslim raiding party at the Battle of Tours (or Poitiers), outside of Paris. European chauvinism has been behind the depiction of this battle as one of the turning points in Western civilization; Martel turned back the Muslim onslaught. But it was actually much less than that. It really was a raiding party, not a Muslim army set on conquering Europe in which they had little to no interest, especially as European culture was relatively crude and barbaric to the Muslims with little to offer them. If anything, it had more long-term effects for Frankish politics and the development of the Merovingian dynasty and the subsequent dynasty of the Carolingians under his grandson, Charlemagne.

Ostensibly, the taking of Spain was done on behalf of the Umayyad caliph back in Damascus, al-Walid I, and his successor, Sulayman. Musa ibn Nusayr even returned to Damascus shortly after the initial conquest to show off some of his treasure, including some Visigothic lords. For the Umayyads, it may have been one way to keep the Berbers occupied and somewhat under control instead of constantly rebelling against Arab rule.[29] In actuality, however, because of sheer distance alone if nothing else, it was always partially to fully autonomous from Damascus and later Baghdad under the Abbasids, no matter who did what in any caliph's name. Umar II, the reforming Umayyad caliph, even considered removing all Muslim forces from Spain because it was so isolated.[30] Even if he gave the order, it is doubtful that it would have been followed to the letter. The motivations for the Arab-Berber enterprise were similar to that of the Arabs during the initial Islamic conquests. Some were religiously motivated to spread the word, but just as many if not more were most likely motivated by the treasures available, especially that held in Christian churches, and the potential of improving one's position through conflict by acquiring land, riches, status, and glory. This was a powerful draw to Arab and Berber military men and their families alike.

It is estimated that about 150,000–200,000 Arab and Berber warriors made their way to Spain during the initial conquest, and if most were later accompanied by families, clients, and slaves, the number rises by a factor of four or five at the least. Given that the entire population of the Iberian Peninsula was about four to five million by the time of the conquest, this introduced a drastically new demographic reality into Spain.[31] Most of the population was Christian European, with a not insignificant number of Jews, who most likely welcomed the Muslim invaders, as their lot most definitely improved under them given the strict repressive policies of the Visigoths. Conversion to Islam, as in Egypt, Syria, and elsewhere, was gradual: perhaps only 8 percent of the population were Muslim by the year 800, and with the bare majority of the population Muslim by about 950, growing to 75 percent by 1000.[32] The more advanced Islamic culture was very seductive to the Spanish Christians, and many became what has been called *mozarabs,* or Arab on the outside—fashion, language, and so on. As Hodgson wrote, "But these cultural fashions were so much more attractive than what the Spaniards had been used to, that they were readily adopted by all the population. The leading Christian elements in the Muslim-ruled areas tended to share Islamicate culture, learning Arabic more than Latin. But they did not lose the consciousness of belonging to a wider Christendom. Their church continued its ties to Rome."[33] Only in the far north in Asturias did some Christian principalities survive the initial invasion somewhat intact, often having to deal with Muslim raids and paying tribute to nearby Muslim provinces. They were not much of a threat in the beginning, but they did provide a bridgehead of sorts for the eventual Christian reconquest (*Reconquista*) of Spain in ensuing centuries. Between this strip of poorer Christian areas in the north and the richer, more developed Muslim center in the south lay what has often been described as the frontier zone, which was a fluctuating stretch of territory that was more often than not on a war footing and was not wholly controlled by either Muslims or Christians.

In theory, governors ruling from Cordoba were appointed by the Umayyad caliph in Damascus. In reality, the first one to rule over the newly conquered land was Musa ibn Nusayr's son, Abd al-Aziz. The topography of Spain was quite fragmented, one of the most mountainous regions in all of Europe. As such, unified rule was difficult to obtain, and rulers, including the new Arab-Berber military class, had to strike deals with local city bosses in order to nominally extend their control. By necessity it evolved into a decentralized system that differed in character from city to city and from region to region depending on a host of local circumstances. Two events in the late 730s to 750 contributed even more so to Islamic Spain's isolation and fragmentation. First, there were a series of Berber rebellions in North Africa in the late 730s into the 740s that we briefly discussed when examining Hisham's caliphate in Damascus. This spilled over into disruption and political and economic factionalism in Spain, as it was cut off even more so from the east. Second was the Abbasid revolution in 750, which shifted the center of Islam even farther to the east once Iraq (and Baghdad) became the capital of the new Arab dynasty. It seemed as if Islamic Spain would have to develop on its own terms.

This became more likely when one of the few surviving members of the Umayyad family, Abd al-Rahman, escaped the Abbasid massacre. He made his way to northwest Africa where he had some family ties on his mother's side with the Berbers, and soon thereafter in 756 he ventured to Spain, where he established himself—and was accepted for the most part—as the Umayyad amir of Spain based in Cordoba. Ostensibly an amir served at the pleasure of the Abbasid caliph, but this was but an illusion. Spain was developing its own character and ruling class, and Abd al-Rahman was but one of a large cast of local rulers in a decentralized polity. Despite this political fragmentation, Spain developed economically, especially in terms of agricultural growth and the establishment of prosperous trading networks with the rest of the Muslim world, something the Visigoths did not enjoy—nor could they. This was especially the case in the south, and Cordoba, under Umayyad tutelage, quickly became the preeminent city in Spain, if not all of Europe. It seemed as if Islamic Spain was on the verge of reaching its zenith under Muslim rule, and the Umayyad family in Cordoba was well placed to lead the charge.

Abd al-Rahman III became amir in 912 and began a long tenure in power until his death in 961. The assimilation of the Arab-Berber settlers into their Spanish environment is embodied in Abd al-Rahman III, who was probably three-quarters Spanish, or Hispano-Basque, due to his mother and grandmother having been local Christians in origin; he was light-skinned, had blue eyes, and he reportedly dyed his reddish hair black to look more like an Arab.[34] In 929, however, he upped his game considerably. He proclaimed himself *amir al-mumineen,* the caliph of all Islam, thus beginning the Umayyad caliphate in Spain. Although the exact reason for doing so is unknown, it is most likely in response to the rise of the Fatimids in

North Africa. As you may recall, the Fatimids took Qayrawan in Tunisia in 909, and they were seen as a preeminent threat by Cordoba, contesting for the hearts and minds of the Berbers in North Africa as well as the economy of the central and western Mediterranean world—as Richard Fletcher notes, Abd al-Rahman wanted to get to the Berbers before they were "poached" by the Fatimids.[35] As it turns out, once the Fatimids moved east to Egypt in 969 and established Cairo as their new capital, their attentions were firmly focused on the Abbasids rather than the Umayyads of Spain, thus ceasing to be a direct threat, but for a time the competing caliphates diluted caliphal authority in the Islamic world as a whole but allowed an opportunity for the Umayyads to reassert themselves.

The reign of Abd al-Rahman III and his immediate successors is generally considered to be the height of a unified Spain under Islamic rule. Underscoring this was the building in 936 of a new resplendent palace called *Madinat al-Zahra* (the "radiant city," with *al-Zahra* being a reference to Fatima), located a few miles west of the city. This vast palace complex was "the architectural counterpart of the adoption of the caliphal title."[36] The caliph applied the wealth of his amirate to fund his army, which he then used liberally to subdue—or threaten to subdue—many of the semi-independent provinces south of the Christian principalities to the far north. This centralization of power continued under those caliphs who followed

Columns of Court of the Lions at Alhambra of Granada, built in the thirteenth century and derives its name from the Arabic word *al-hamra*, or "the red one."
Javier Sánchez Mingorance/Alamy Stock Photo

him, but especially under Abu Amir Muhammad ibn Abi Amir al-Maafari, who took the name of Almanzor (al-Mansur in Arabic, which means "victorious"). He was not a caliph but a vizir (wazir), who essentially ran the government under the weak caliph Hisham II from 981 to 1002. Echoes of the Barmakids come to mind, although for different reasons. Almanzor was even more aggressive with his army, leading it on many occasions. The pinnacle—or at least the most notable—of his military exploits was the taking (and sacking) of the city of Santiago de Compostela, the center of the shrine of St. James, in 997, a major Christian pilgrimage site; this episode was also utilized as a constant rallying cry during the Christian Reconquista, and the bells taken from the shrine to Cordoba by Almanzor were not returned until Cordoba was taken by Christian forces in 1236.

The power and wealth of the Umayyad caliphate translated to a growing and largely prosperous population, especially in al-Andalus. This is reflected in the grandeur of Cordoba, as it became a bustling center of commerce, science, and intellectual pursuits, much as Baghdad was in its heyday. The contemporary chronicler, Ibn Hawkal, wrote the following about the capital of Islamic Spain:

> The biggest city in Spain is Cordoba, which has no equal in the Maghrib, and hardly in Egypt, Syria or Mesopotamia, for the size of its population, its extent, the space occupied by its markets, the cleanliness of its streets, the architecture of its mosques, the number of its baths and caravanserais. Natives of Cordoba who have travelled to Mesopotamia say that it is about the same size as one of the divisions of Baghdad.[37]

As Fletcher points out, this would put Cordoba at about the size of Constantinople and several times bigger than the largest cities elsewhere in Europe in the tenth century.[38]

Almanzor's campaigns cost a lot of money and brought into Spain many more Berbers as mercenaries, who were loyal to their leader as well as his son who succeeded him, but unfortunately to no one thereafter. The Berbers became an uncontrollable lot who fueled the increasingly fragmented and antagonistic politics that once again arose in al-Andalus. It became a chaotic environment as rival pretenders to the caliphate went back and forth, bringing about discord and dysfunction in which the citizenry suffered the most. By 1031 the last Umayyad caliph had been pushed aside, bringing to an end what has been called the Andalusian *fitna* since the death of Almanzor's son in 1008. It allowed for Christian kings in the north to reassert themselves and become more involved in the life and politics of the provinces to their south.

What emerged in the aftermath of this fitna was a period referred to as the *muluk al-tawaif* in Arabic (*reyes de taifas* in Spanish), or the "party kings." This appellation is meant to convey the existence in Islamic Spain of a series of statelets in the aftermath of Umayyad rule, each mostly independent but frequently allying with one or more against one or more of the others—and it was not always exclusively Muslim versus Christian. For some, especially those located on the fringes, it was simply a continuation of the loose administrative arrangement they had enjoyed under the Umayyad caliphate. For others, it was a new reality in which mini-dynasties emerged in places like Granada and Seville. All in all, between 1010 and 1040 there were three dozen or so of these statelets, where smaller ones were often swallowed up by larger ones.[39] While there were some states that flourished culturally under less ominous centralized rule, generally it was an unstable period marked by internecine conflict that allowed for Christian advances at Muslim expense. It seemed to portend the beginning of the end for the dominant Muslim presence in Spain, although some powerful Islamic movements in North Africa would intervene to save the day for Islam in Spain—but it was a very different type of movement than that which originally crossed over in 711.

A number of Muslim provincial leaders during the muluk al-tawaif period reluctantly contemplated appealing to a new Berber force in North Africa to come over and save them from total Christian reconquest. The turning point in this seems to have been the taking of Toledo by King Alfonso VI of Leon-Castile. Muslims in Spain were not ignorant of the nature of the Berber force on the horizon. The ruler of Seville at the time pretty much captured their dilemma, reportedly saying that he "would rather be a camel-driver in Morocco than a swineherd in Castile."[40] This

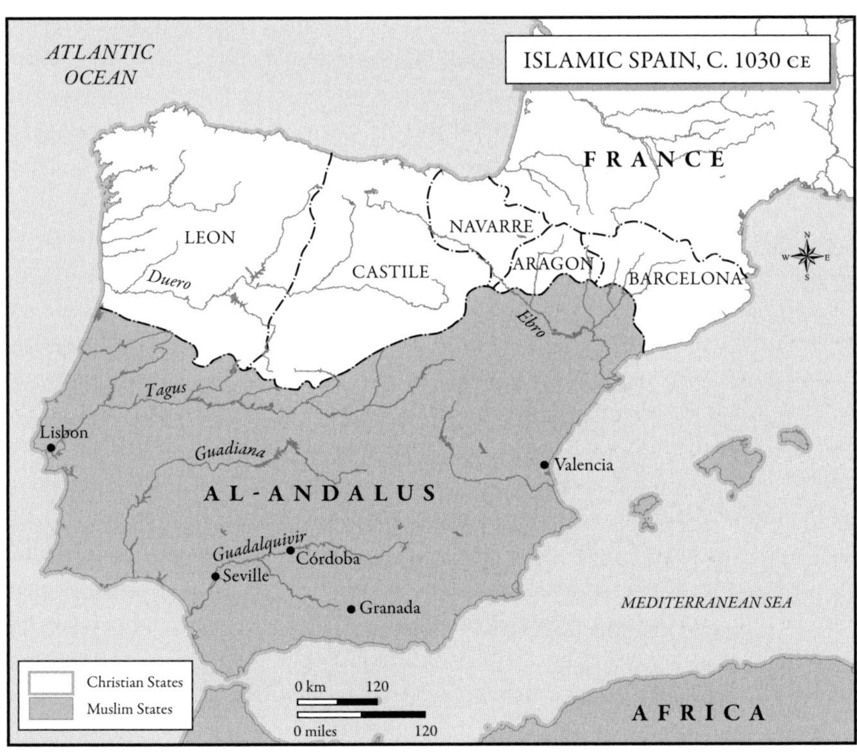

new Berber power was founded and led by a man by the name of Ibn Yasin, who led a group of puritanical Muslims to establish a *ribat* or jihad war outpost in 1056, backed by the Lamtunah Berber tribe. The movement was called the *al-Murabitun,* devotees of the ribat. Al-Murabitun has been anglicized as Almoravids, which is how they are more commonly known in the West. They established Marrakesh in present-day Morocco as their capital. This was what many would call a fundamentalist movement: they were committed to rooting out all of the decadence and corruption they believed had seeped into Islam.

They crossed over in 1086 and reunited al-Andalus in a way that it had not been since the tenth century, taking one *taifa* state after another. They ruled not from the Spanish hinterland, but from Marrakesh, sending governors to Spain to rule on their behalf. It was like trying to fit a square peg in a round hole. The al-Murabitun's more restrictive policies toward non-Muslims only exacerbated the enmity toward Islam by Spain's Christian population, if not the European Christian world beyond Spain; both sides became more aggressive toward the other. They also hit the Christian mini-kingdoms in the pocketbook, as many of them depended on tribute paid to them by surrounding Muslim statelets. That income suddenly disappeared. The rigorous brand of Islam they brought with them along with their repressive policies did not sit well with a number of Muslims in Spain either. As such, slowly but surely, opposition from a number of quarters in Spain mounted against the al-Murabitun. In addition, as in most self-described revolutionary movements, once the volcanic period of it subsides the esprit de corps tends to dissipate, with corresponding political factionalism becoming the natural state of Spain. By the 1120s al-Murabitun rule in al-Andalus was disintegrating, so much so that some have called this period to the 1140s a second Spanish *fitna*. Furthermore, their base in Morocco was under attack from a new Berber movement that would soon replace it, the *al-Muwahhidun,* more commonly known in its anglicized form as the Almohads.

The al-Muwahhidun were founded and led by Muhammad ibn Tumart, backed in this case by the Masmudah Berber tribal bloc. Educated in Islam during his travels to the heartland of the Islamic world, his movement was intended as a purification of Islam, including that of the al-Murabitun, whose views he thought were too sectarian. The driving force of the al-Muwahhidun was the unification of humankind to Allah via Islam; this is the meaning of *muwahhidun*, unitarians. Leading the way toward this divine unity, Ibn Tumart was proclaimed the Mahdi by his followers in 1121. Although Ibn Tumart died in 1130, his successors continued to push onward, defeating and taking over al-Murabitun territory by the 1140s, which weakened the latter's hold over Spain. It was in 1146 that the al-Muwahhidun crossed over into Spain in what seemed to be a repeat Berber performance, as once again a number of Muslim rulers invited the new force over to keep the advancing Christians at bay.

The al-Muwahhidun were more organized than the al-Murabitun, however, and perhaps a touch less rigorous in the application of their rule and brand of Islamic zeal. Because of this, by the last quarter of the twelfth century al-Andalus was once again firmly united under Islamic rule and the al-Muwahhidun were able to last a bit longer than their predecessors. But the Christian reconquest had picked up too much momentum by then; the Crusading zeal that fueled Christendom's jihad in the Middle East over the preceding two centuries (to be covered in the next chapter) had more than made its way to Spain. And a good bit of the reforming zeal of the initial al-Muwahhidun movement had, as with the al-Murabitun, dissipated by the early thirteenth century. Christian Spain and Islamic Spain seemed to be going in two different directions. This became manifest in 1212 when King Alfonso VIII and a conglomeration of Spanish and French Christian forces decisively defeated the al-Muwahhidun in the battle of Las Navas between Madrid and Cordoba. This was the turning point for the al-Muwahhidun and the Islamic presence as a whole in Spain. Cordoba fell in 1236 and Seville in 1248. All that was left was the tiny Nasrid kingdom of Granada established in 1230, paying tribute to the Christians—and building the magnificent Alhambra palace complex—until it was also extinguished, in 1492.

In Spanish Christian lore, the *Reconquista* began the day after Tariq ibn Ziyad defeated King Roderic. We know now that it really did not begin to pick up steam until after the end of the Umayyad caliphate in 1031, marked by the taking

Interior ornamentation of Umayyad Mosque and Cathedral in Cordoba, Spain. The mosque was first built under the order of Abd al-Rahman I in 785. It was converted to a cathedral in 1236 upon the fall of Cordoba to Christian forces, and the Gothic-style cathedral was built in the center of the mosque in the sixteenth century.
Diego Grandi/Alamy Stock Photo

of Toledo in 1085. The al-Murabitun and the al-Muwahhidun stymied this advance for over a century, but by 1212, the Christian reconquest of Spain was inexorably headed toward success. Spain thus experienced by the middle of the thirteenth century a process of re-Christianizing as well as unification, particularly after the merging of Leon and Castile in 1230. The taking of Cordoba and Seville followed soon thereafter. The marriage of King Ferdinand of Aragon and Isabella of Castile in 1469 united the crowns of these two kingdoms and sealed the fate of what was left of Islamic rule in Spain in Granada, which finally fell to Christian forces in 1492.

The Christian reconquest of Spain was an ugly process, however. Although Muslim rule over a largely Christian Spanish population certainly had its rough edges, there were just as many instances of wonderful synthesis between Muslims, Jews, and Christians in the form of everyday life to tremendous works of art and architecture and boundless intellectual and scientific achievement, all of which made their way into Europe and, along with similar transference of knowledge via Sicily, Italy, and the Crusades in the Holy Land, was critical toward fueling the European Renaissance. Much of this Islamic—and Jewish—heritage in Spain was purposely glossed over, if not buried, following the fall of Granada; from the Alhambra itself, Queen Isabella signed a decree expelling all Jews from Spain (to become the Sephardic Jews), never to return. In 1499 Queen Isabella's confessor, Cardinal Ximenez de Cisneros, began a campaign of forced conversion of Muslims to Christianity and an eradication of the Arab-Berber enterprise in Spain with the burning of Arabic language books. The Inquisition was soon implemented, with both Muslims and Jews in Spain feeling the brunt of Christianity's wrath.

Those Muslims who remained in Spain were called Moriscos, Spanish for "little Moors." The English term "Moor" is derived from the West African nation of Mauretania, and its inhabitants called "Mauri," which is presumably of Phoenician (i.e., Carthaginian) origin meaning "western," in this sense the peoples of western North Africa. In Spanish this word is "Moros," which is why the Muslim population in the Philippines discovered by the Spanish explorer Magellan in 1521 are stilled called Moros to this day. The Moriscos were mostly of Spanish descent, and many became crypto-Muslim, professing Christianity on the outside but Islam at home and adopting Christian names in public but Islamic or Arabic names in private. Such was the state of things. For the most part, Christian rule in Spain was much less tolerant or forgiving than Muslim rule. In 1501, a royal decree was issued declaring that all Muslims in Leon and Castile must recant and become Christian or leave Spain. This process soon spread over the entire peninsula. The final order of expulsion was signed by King Philip III in 1609. Between the fall of Granada in 1492 and the first decades of the seventeenth century, it is estimated that over three million Muslims were banished from Spain—or killed. Spain became the conspicuous exception to what had become a rule: that where Islamic civilization was planted, there it stayed.

Maybe there is no finer example of the duality of the Christian–Muslim experience in Spain—between cooperation and antagonism and between synthesis and awkwardness—than the Grand Mosque of Cordoba. Originally built as a mosque atop the ruins of a church by the early Muslim rulers in Cordoba, it initially welcomed both Muslims and Christians inside its doors. As the Muslim population grew, it was expanded in 786 as solely a mosque with a unique brand of splendid architecture, consisting of its arcaded hypostyle hall with 856 columns connected by double arches with its famous red and white *voussoirs* in order to allow for higher ceilings. Its architectural influence would be felt throughout Europe thenceforward.[41]

However, the mosque was converted back into a church when Cordoba fell to the Reconquista in 1236. Then, in the middle of the sixteenth century, a Christian cathedral was inserted smack into the middle of the mosque, producing one of the most interesting yet awkward combinations of architectural—and cultural—styles in any structure the world over. When one visits the site today, it is as if you are passing through some sort of portal to another place and time. Even though you are warned of what you are about to see, it is still difficult to aesthetically comprehend. For me personally, after walking around the cathedral part so common to me as a Western Christian, I felt ultimately more comfortable reentering the double arches of the mosque. For a brief instant, I felt a bit what a Christian must have felt like upon encountering Islam in the early eighth century, and what perhaps a Morisco would have felt like in trying to maintain the cultural duality of his or her existence in Spain following the Reconquista. It has taken centuries for Spain to come to terms with its Islamic and Jewish heritage. It was only in 1992 upon the quincentennial of the fall of Granada and the discovery of the Americas by Columbus that Spanish King Juan Carlos began to publicly acknowledge and reconcile with this past. There is still a long way to go.

Yet the influence of Arabo-Islamic culture in Spain, and via Spain the Americas, is omnipresent. I live in San Antonio, Texas (Tejas), which is replete with Spanish-Mexican culture as expressed through its architecture, language, art, cuisine, and institutions, much of which originally came from the Middle East. Soon after I moved here I visited a local museum. I was taking a break, sitting on the side of a fountain in the courtyard, when a small group of tourists came in led by a museum guide. The guide proceeded to inform the group that the courtyard was a prime example of Spanish design. Gazing at the blue arabesque mosaic tiles, the arched doorways, and the position of the fountain, I recognized it as a classic example of Arabo-Persian design as expressed and brought over to the New World through Islamic Spain. It was but a small example of the how the influence of Middle Eastern-Islamic culture has been appropriated and subsumed by neglect, ignorance, and intent. On the drive home I passed a restaurant that is named after a small city just on the Mexican side of the Rio Grande across from the Texas city of Brownsville: Matamoros, a Spanish word that means "killer of Moors."

Chapter 6 Timeline	
874	According to Twelver Shiite theology, Twelfth Imam enters into occultation
909	Fatimid Caliphate established in North Africa by Abdallah al-Mahdi
929	Establishment of the Umayyad Caliphate in Spain by Abd al-Rahman III
945	Abbasid Caliph recognizes Buyid rule in Baghdad
969	Fatimid Caliph al-Muizz conquers Egypt and soon thereafter establishes new capital of al-Qahira (Cairo)
996–1021	Fatmid Caliphate of al-Hakim
1031	End of Umayyad Caliphate and political fragmentation in Islamic Spain
1055	Buyid rule ended in Baghdad by the Turkish Seljuks
1086–1147	Al-Murabitun (Almoravids) rule in Islamic Spain
1171	Fatimid Caliphate ends with Salah al-Din al-Ayyubi's takeover of Egypt
1147–1212	Al-Muwahhidun (Almohads) rule in Islamic Spain
1492	Conquest of Nasrid kingdom of Granada by Christian forces

Primary Sources

The Cities of Egypt: Alexandria and al-Fustat

Selection from Ahsan Al-Taqasim fi Ma'rifat al-Aqalim of al-Muqaddasi

Al-Iskandariyya (Alexandria) is a delightful town on the shore of the Romaen Sea [i.e., the Mediterranean]. Commanded by an impregnable fortress, it is a distinguished city with a goodly [populace] of upright and devout people. The drinking water of the inhabitants is derived from the Nile, which reaches them in the season of its flood via an aqueduct and fills their cisterns. It resembles Syria in climate and customs; rainfall is abundant; and every conceivable type of product is brought together there. The countryside round about is splendid, producing excellent fruits, and fine grapes. It is a clean town, and their buildings are of the kind of stone suited for maritime construction; it is also a source of marble. It has two mosques. On their cisterns are doors which are secured at night so that thieves may not make their way up through them. The remaining towns here are very well developed; and in the surrounding area grow locust, olives, and almonds, and their cultivated lands are watered by the rain. It is near here that the Nile [lets out] into the Romaen Sea. It is the city founded by Dhu al-Qarnayn (Alexander the Great), and has, indeed, a remarkable citadel.

Al-Fustat is a metropolis in every sense of the word; here are together all the departments of government administration, and moreover, it is the seat of the Commander of the Faithful. It sets apart the Occident [i.e., Egypt and North Africa] from the domain of the Arabs, is of wide extent, its inhabitants many. The region around it is well cultivated. Its name is renowned, its glory increased; for truly it is the capital city of Egypt. It has superseded Baghdad, and is the glory of Islam, and is the marketplace for all mankind. It is more sublime than the City of Peace [Baghdad]. It is the storehouse of the Occident, the entrepôt of the Orient, and is crowded with people at the time of the Pilgrimage festival. Among the capitals there is none more populous than it, and it abounds in noble and learned men. Its goods of commerce and specialities are remarkable, its markets excellent as is its mode of life. Its baths are the peak of perfection, its bazaars splendid and handsome. Nowhere in the realm of Islam is there a mosque more crowded than here, nor people more handsomely adorned, no shore with a greater number of boats. It is more populous than Nishapur, more splendid than al-Basra, larger than Damascus. Victuals here are most appetizing, their savories superb. Confectioneries are cheap, bananas plentiful, as are fresh dates; vegetables and firewood are abundant. The water is palatable, the air salubrious. It is a treasury of learned men; and the winter here is agreeable. The people are well-disposed, and well-to-do, marked by kindness and charity. Their intonation in reciting the *Qur'an* is pleasant, and their delight in good deeds is evident; the devoutness of their worship is well-known throughout the world. They have rested secure from injurious rains, and safe from the tumult of evildoers. They are most discriminating in the selection of the preacher and of the leader in prayer; nor will they appoint anyone to lead them but the most worthy, regardless of expense to themselves. Their judge is always dignified, their *muhtasib* [market inspector] deferred to like a prince. They are never free from the supervision of the ruler and the minister. Indeed were it not that it has faults aplenty, this city would be without compare in the world.

The town stretches for about two-thirds of a *farsakh*, in tiers one above the other. It used to consist of two quarters, al-Fustat and al-Jiza, but later on, one of the [Abbasid caliphs] had a canal cut around a portion of the town, and this portion became known as al-Jazira (the island), because of its lying between the main course of the river and the canal. The canal itself was named the "Canal of the Commander of the Faithful," and from it the people draw their drinking water. Their buildings are of four storeys or five, just as are lighthouses; the light enters them from a central area. I have heard it said that about two hundred people live in one building. In fact, when al-Hasan bin Ahmad al-Qarmati arrived there, the people came out to meet him; seeing them, as he considered, like a cloud of locusts, he was alarmed, and asked what this meant. The reply was: "These are the sightseers of Misr [the city]; those who did not come out are more numerous still."

I was one day walking on the bank of the river, and marveling at the great number of ships, both those riding at anchor, and those coming and going, when a man from the locality accosted me, saying: "Where do you hail from?" Said I, "From the Holy City [i.e., Jerusalem]." Said he, "It is a large city. But I tell you, good sir—may God hold you dear to Him— that of the vessels along this shore, and of those that set sail from here to the towns and the villages—if all these ships were to go to your native city they could carry away its people, with everything that appertains to it, and the stones thereof and the timber thereof, so that it would be said: 'At one time here stood a city.'"

Source: Gordon, Matthew S. "Document 7, The Cities of Egypt: Alexandria and al-Fustat." *The Rise of Islam*. Indianapolis: Hackett Publishing Company, Inc. (paperback version), 2008. Pgs.132–135. Reprinted with permission from *The Best Divisions for Knowledge of the Regions* by al-Muqaddasi and translated by Basil Collins. Reading, UK: Garnet Publishing, 2001.

Abd al-Rahman III of al-Andalus

'Abd al-Rahman [III] died at [his palace] al-Zahra on the second or third day of the month of Ramadhan of the year 961, of a paralytic fit, at the age of seventy-three. He was born in the year 890, and was only twenty years old when his father Muhammed was put to death. His mother's name was Muznah. In addition to the honourable appellation of al-Nasir li-din-illah (the defender of the true faith), 'Abd al-Rahman received from his subjects the surname of *Abu al-Mutarrif* (the victorious). Never was the [Islamic realm] more prosperous, or the true religion more triumphant, than under his reign. The infidels of Andalus [Islamic Spain] were driven back to the mountainous districts of the north, where they insured their safety only by paying tribute to the Commander of the Faithful. Commerce and agriculture flourished; the sciences and arts received a new impulse, and the revenue was increased ten-fold. Notwithstanding the costly magnificence with which 'Abd al-Rahman surrounded his person—the unusual number of troops which he constantly kept in his pay, the multitude of eunuchs, Slavs, and other servants employed about his palace, the bounteous gifts which he distributed to the learned, and the splendid buildings which he caused to be erected in various parts of his extensive dominions, in Africa as well as in Andalus—it is said that when he died he left in the coffers of the treasury the enormous sum of five millions of dinars.

The amount of the revenue under this reign has been estimated by several contemporary writers at six million, two hundred and forty-five thousand dinars; namely, five million, four hundred and eighty thousand arising from the land-tax levied in the towns and districts, and seven hundred and sixty-five thousand being the amount of indirect taxation, and duties imposed upon goods. As to the sums which entered the royal coffers, being the fifth of the spoil taken from the infidels, they were beyond calculation, and cannot be estimated, as no precise account of them was kept in the treasury books.

Of this immense sum one-third went to pay the troops and the public officers; another third was destined for ['Abd al-Rahman's] own use; and the remainder was spent in public buildings. Many, indeed, were the works of public utility which this just and enlightened monarch caused to be erected in various parts of his extensive dominions. As to his capital, Cordova, he is well known to have embellished it and widened its precincts, so that it equaled, if it did not surpass, in size and splendour the proud metropolis of the ['Abbasids] [i.e., Baghdad]. His addition to the great mosque of Cordova, and the construction of the palace of al-Zahra in the vicinity of that capital, are two splendid erections, which will transmit the name of 'Abd al-Rahman to posterity. Of both those buildings we have elsewhere given as accurate a description as it was in our power; and therefore we need not now return to the subject.

It is said that after the death of 'Abd al-Rahman a paper was found in his own hand-writing in which those days which he had spent in happiness and without any cause of sorrow were carefully noted down, and on numbering them they were found to amount only to fourteen. O man of understanding! Wonder and observe the small portion of real happiness the world affords, even in the most enviable position! The Caliph al-Nasir, whose prosperity in mundane affairs and whose widely spread empire became proverbial, had only fourteen days of undisturbed enjoyment during a reign of fifty years, seven months, and three days. Praise be given to him, the Lord of eternal glory and everlasting empire! There is no God but He! The Almighty, the giver of empire to whom-soever he pleases!

As previously stated, 'Abd al-Rahman was the first sovereign of the Umayyad house in Andalus who assumed the title of *Amir al-Mu'minin* (Commander of the Faithful). The authors of the time say that when 'Abd al-Rahman saw the state of weakness and abjectness to which the ['Abbasid] Califate had been reduced, and perceived that the Turkish freedmen in the service of the ['Abbasids] had usurped all authority and power in the state—when he heard that the Caliph al-Muktadir had been put to death, in the year 929, by one of his freedmen, called Munis al-Muzaffar—he no longer hesitated to assume the insignia of the Caliphate, and call himself *Amir al-Mu'minin*.

Source: Gordon, Matthew S. "Document 15, Abd al-Rahman III of al-Andalus." *The Rise of Islam*. Indianapolis: Hackett Publishing Company, Inc. (paperback version), 2008. Pgs. 151–153. Original source: *The History of the Mohammedan Dynasties in Spain*. Translated by Pascual de Gayangos. London, 1840.

NOTES

1. See Hugh Kennedy, *The Prophet and the Age of the Caliphates: The Islamic Near East from the Sixth to the Eleventh Century* (New York: Longman, 1986), pp. 213–217. Most of this section is based upon Kennedy's more extensive treatment in his chapter on the Buyids in this excellent book, which is one of the few in depth narratives I have found in the literature on the subject. Also, Roy Mottahedeh, who

was one of my advisors at Harvard University, wrote a classic book that also examines the Buyid period, *Loyalty and Leadership in an Early Islamic Society* (Princeton, NJ: Princeton University Press, 1980). This section also relies on his work.

2. Amira K. Bennison, *The Great Caliphs: The Golden Age of the Abbasid Empire* (New Haven, CT: Yale University Press, 2009), p. 42.
3. Marshall G. S. Hodgson, *The Venture of Islam, Vol. 1: The Classical Age of Islam* (Chicago: University of Chicago Press, 1974), p. 495.
4. Kennedy, *The Prophet*, p. 218.
5. Mottahedeh, *Loyalty and Leadership*, p. 16.
6. Ibid.
7. Kennedy, *The Prophet*, pp. 227–229.
8. Heinz Halm, *The Shiites: A Short History* (Princeton, NJ: Markus Weiner Publishers, 2007), p. 96.
9. Kennedy, *The Prophet*, p. 230.
10. Ibid., p. 227.
11. Ibid., p. 233.
12. See Mottahedeh, *Loyalty and Leadership*, pp. 36–37.
13. Afaf Lutfi Al-Sayyid Marsot, *A History of Egypt: From the Arab Conquest to the Present* (Cambridge: Cambridge University Press, 2007), p. 11.
14. Heinz Halm, *The Fatimids and their Traditions of Learning* (New York: I. B. Tauris, 1997), pp. 8–9.
15. Kennedy, *The Prophet*, p. 316.
16. Marsot writes that it was al-Muizz's astrologers that determined that Egypt had been taken when the planet Mars (*Al-Qahir* in Arabic) was in ascendancy; therefore, the new capital was named al-Qahira. Marsot, *History of Egypt*, p. 15.
17. Ibid., p. 319.
18. Ibid., pp. 343–344.
19. Ibid., p. 344.
20. Marshall G. S. Hodgson, *The Venture of Islam, Vol. 2: The Expansion of Islam in the Middle Periods* (Chicago: University of Chicago Press, 1974), p. 25.
21. Kennedy, *The Prophet*, p. 344.
22. Ironically, today the al-Azhar mosque and associated school is what most consider to be the leading Sunni religious institution of learning in the world.
23. Hodgson, *Venture of Islam*, p. 27.
24. The plural of *hadith* in Arabic is *ahadith*, but in English hadith is often used as both the singular and plural depending upon the context.
25. Joseph Schacht, *The Origins of Muhammadan Jurisprudence* (Oxford: Oxford University Press, 1950), p. 3.
26. Heinz Halm, "Al-Andalus und Gothic Sors," *Welt des Oriens* 66 (1989): 252–263.
27. Brian A. Catlos, *Kingdoms of Faith: A New History of Islamic Spain* (New York: Basic Books, 2018), p. 22.
28. Ibid.

29. Richard Fletcher, *Moorish Spain* (Berkeley: University of California Press, 1992), p. 20.
30. Catlos, *Kingdoms of Faith*, p. 25.
31. Fletcher, *Moorish Spain*, pp. 25–26.
32. Ibid., p. 37–38.
33. Hodgson, *Venture of Islam, Vol. 1: The Classical Age of Islam* (Chicago: University of Chicago Press, 1974), p. 309.
34. Fletcher, *Moorish Spain*, p. 53.
35. Maribel Fierro, *Abd al-Rahman III: The First Cordoban Caliph* (Oxford: Oneworld Publications, 2005); p. 28. See also Fletcher, *Moorish Spain*, p. 55.
36. Fierro, *Abd al-Rahman III*, p. 113.
37. As quoted in Fletcher, *Moorish Spain*, p. 65. The monumental architecture was especially evident in Abd al-Rahman III's building of a new palace west of the city, the magnificent Madinat al-Zahra.
38. Ibid.
39. Ibid., p. 85.
40. Quoted in ibid., p. 111.
41. For more on the influence of Islamic architecture in Europe, see Diana Darke, *Stealing from the Saracens: How Islamic Architecture Shaped Europe* (London: Hurst, 2020).

KEY TERMS

Muharram p. 127 Ghadir Khumm p.127 shahanshah p. 125

For additional digital learning resources please go to www.oup.com/he/lesch-middleeast-1e

7 FROM EAST AND WEST

The Seljuks

Many world historians claim that the most seismic global event between the ninth century and the seventeenth century was the rise and migration from the east of the Turco-Mongolian peoples over much of the Eurasian landmass. This period is typically split into three phases: 1) ranging from about 800 to 1200, the first phase encompasses the entrance into the Middle East en masse of Turkish peoples first as mamluks under such Abbasid caliphs as al-Mamun and al-Mutasim in the 800s and ending with a Turkish family, the Seljuks, becoming masters of much of the region by the middle of the eleventh century; 2) the rise and fall of the Mongol Empire in the thirteenth century; and 3) from the disintegration of the Mongol Empire at the end of the thirteenth century to about 1600, the rise of a slew of powerful dynasties from central Asia through the Middle East and into the Balkans in Europe in the aftermath of the Mongol breakup, in particular the Ottoman, Mamluk, Timurid, Mughal, and Safavid Empires. We will take on the Ottomans, Mamluks, and Safavids in the next chapter. Unfortunately, because of historical triage—in addition to their mostly non–Middle East location—I will leave out the Timurid and Mughal Empires but for a mention here and there. In this chapter, however, we will examine the Seljuks and Mongols as well as the rather strange saga of the Crusades, an unwelcome interloper to the region from the opposite direction.

The Turks and Mongols belong to the Ural-Altaic ethno-linguistic group—those largely nomadic tribes who lived in the great steppes between the Urals, the range of mountains traditionally taken to separate Europe from Asia, and the Altai mountains in Siberia. The origins of the term "Turks" (often referred to as "Turcoman" or "Turkmen") is somewhat clouded in mystery. It may have its origins in a Chinese reference to those peoples, "Tu Kiu." We know it was the collective name that Arabs gave to nomadic tribal peoples from Central Asia, with whom they had come into contact as Islam spread during the Umayyad caliphate, which had to struggle to defend itself against various Turkish tribal conglomerates.

Whatever the case, the Turks increasingly made their presence known within the Islamic world during Abbasid times, becoming an integral part of the political and military administration of the state in the 800s and 900s to the point of playing the role of king- or caliph-maker on a number of occasions. They were essentially pagan or polytheistic, but those who encountered Muslim armies and settlers tended to convert to Islam—or they were converted after being captured or purchased and brought into caliphal service. Like most nomadic tribal peoples, the Turks, to the extent they had any organized political structure, were very decentralized. As with the Arabs, certain families within tribes were able to establish themselves as ruling clans, but their power was always limited: typically primus inter pares, first among equals, rather than authoritarian. The Seljuks were one of these Turkish families that established a leadership position within their tribal conglomerate, but their authority would be challenged more often than not—and mostly by their fellow Turks. The transition from tribal leader to settled ruler was typically a wrenching one and often unsuccessful. We saw this struggle with both Muhammad and the first caliphs during the early years of Islam—and we will see it later in this chapter and the next. But enter the region the Turks did, and through both the front and back doors they became part and parcel of—indeed shaped—the landscape of the medieval Middle East, a position that has not changed since.

The Seljuk (or Seljukid) family did not lead this mass migration of Turks into the Middle East. They were caught up in it, but they emerged as the most successful of them all at the time. The Seljuks were part of a Turkish tribal conglomerate known as the Ghuzz or Oghuz. This conglomerate was divided into nine tribes so in Turkish it was also known as the Dokuz Oghuz ("dokuz" is Turkish for the number nine). They had migrated into the area of the lower Syr Darya (Jaxartes) near the Aral Sea at the beginning of the eleventh century, which is also apparently when the Seljuks converted to Islam. The Seljuk family at this time was under the leadership of Qutlumush, the grandson of the eponymous Seljuk.

It is at this time that the Seljuks began their advance into the Middle East. Actually, it was more of a retreat than a forceful entrance into the region due to more powerful groups pushing them westward. First it was the Ghaznavids, led by Mahmud of Ghazna, located in present-day Afghanistan and northeastern Iran who forced the Seljuks and their allies in 1030 west along the southern flanks of the Caspian Sea in Daylam and Azerbaijan. It was after this that the Seljuks split into two, one group going to the northwest into what is today near the border of eastern Turkey around Lake Van, while the other one made its way into northern Iraq around Mosul before being defeated by a mostly Kurdish army in 1044. The Seljuk initial onslaught of the Middle East was anything but planned and executed. It was the path of least resistance into a crumbling Abbasid Empire and a by-then fragmenting Buyid confederacy. It was only when more Seljuks and other Turks arrived in the region that this Turkish family was able to construct an empire.

The reinforcements came in the form of the Qutlumush's cousin, Tughril Beg, who in 1040 cleared the road to join up with his comrades by defeating the Ghaznavids at the battle of Dandanqan near Marv in Khurasan. First and foremost, this gave Tughril and his cohorts a great deal of legitimacy, which acted as a tool for more recruitment but also opened up Iran to Seljuk expansion. By the early 1050s Tughril and his Seljuk army settled around Isfahan in central Iran, which would turn out to be the capital of the empire they were in the process of building. It is at this time that Tughril entered into negotiations with the Abbasid caliph in Baghdad, who was eager to finally get rid of the Buyids and cement the Sunni direction of Abbasid rule with the Sunni Seljuk Turks. Most of Buyid Iran had fallen to the Seljuks by 1053. They were definitely the new power on the horizon; indeed, they were at the Abbasid doorstep.

As we know from the last chapter, the Abbasid caliphate had by now long identified itself as the champion of the *ahl al-sunna*, what was becoming Sunni Islam. The Seljuks had openly aligned themselves with this position. Tughril Beg formalized this association in 1055 by entering Baghdad, declaring his intention of attacking the heretical Fatimids, and announcing his plans to make the hajj (Mecca was in Fatimid hands at the time). Much like the Buyids, the Seljuks were outsiders seeking religious legitimacy to their rule by receiving the sanction of the Abbasid caliph. They were not out to overturn the existing order but to derive power and benefits from it. In return for caliphal recognition, the Seljuks became champions of Sunni Islam; much as the Buyids created the facilitating environment for the formalization of Twelver Shiite Islam, the Seljuks did the same for what became popularly known as the Sunni Revival, which in actuality was simply the mainstream Islamic reaction to the Shiite century in which the ahl al-sunna began to formalize their own distinctive practices and belief system.

The main question that confronted the Seljuks now is the same one that had confronted previous successful tribal movements: Were they going to continue to ravage the landscape they just conquered for all that it was worth, or were they going to become settled rulers who would establish institutions and norms that would protect the population over which they now ruled? They chose the latter role, but it would be anything but easy to implement, and ultimately the Seljuks were unsuccessful in doing so.

The Seljuk Sultan, Tughril Beg, assumed most temporal authority over the lands that were nominally still the Abbasid Empire, while the Abbasid caliph continued to be a figurehead with some residual spiritual authority. They settled into Isfahan as the capital; the Seljuks and their cohorts in government assimilated into their dominant Persian Islamic environment, adopting Persian as the language of administration, bringing into government Persian ministers, and elaborating upon Persian traditions and customs, a process that had begun under the Buyids. Some have commented on how Arabic and Arabs virtually disappeared in some parts of the Seljuk domain, especially in ruling circles, to the point where it almost became a derogatory reference in that part of the Middle East.

What was Seljuk Sultan Tughril Beg to do with the Turkmen who were primarily responsible for bringing the Seljuks to power but who also wanted to continue pillaging and plundering? The answer seemed to be to get rid of them as fast as possible, but this was easier said than done. These were independently minded Turkish tribal elements not keen on taking orders. The Seljuk sultans used both carrot and stick to try to both lure and force them into areas outside of their control, and maybe in the process even extend their territory in the same way it was created in the first place. In order to do this, they needed a salaried army in order to push the Turkmen out if need be—that is, if they failed to convince them of the glory and gain that could be had going elsewhere. The Seljuks wanted them to head west and southwest toward the Fatimids, their declared primary enemy; let the Fatimids deal with them and in doing so become spent in the process. Unfortunately for the sultans, the Turkmen for the most part preferred to go north and northwest into Anatolia, whose topography and climate was closer to home and much preferable to the arid land and deserts of Syria, Arabia, and Egypt.

There emerged two major problems with this that would affect Seljuk history from here on out. First, how was the Seljuk administration going to have enough money to pay for a salaried army on a consistent basis? They did not yet have a central fiscal source, such as the Sawad, that could fund the central treasury. And they did not yet have the administrative capacity or control to raise these funds through an efficient tax system. Both of these elements had long been missing, ever since the middle Abbasid period. It may well have been beyond the capacity of anyone at this point to reverse the economic course that had been in motion for two centuries. The solution? The one that had also been around for almost two centuries: the **iqta** system. As before, this would relieve the central treasury of the burden of paying for a standing army by allocating parcels of land to military commanders

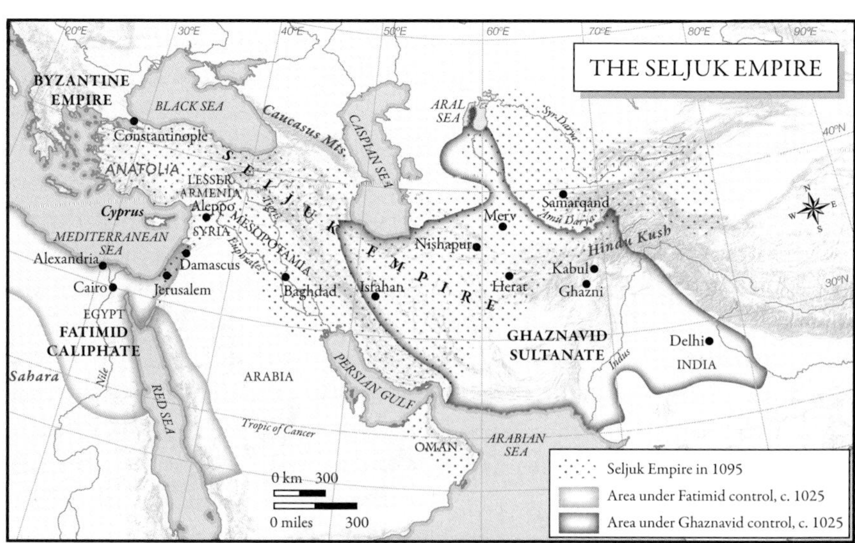

and administrators in return for their service, particularly providing troops when needed—and maybe even some surplus revenues from time to time. While this worked in an immediate sense, over the long term, as we have seen previously, this led to the fragmentation of power in Seljuk lands as these iqta holders became powerful in and of themselves, often starting mini-dynasties within the heartland of Seljuk rule, especially when the latter started to itself fragment.

The second problem was the repercussions of the Turkmen choosing to migrate into Anatolia, hooking up in some cases with the descendants of the group under Qutlumush who had entered the region a generation earlier near Lake Van. This naturally aroused the concern and consternation of the Byzantine emperor, and it only accelerated under the centralizing policies of the next Seljuk Sultan, Alp Arslan, who came to power in 1063. This is not what the sultan wanted. He wanted them to head toward the hated Fatimids and even hoped to ally with the Byzantines or even the Crusader states against the heretics in Cairo. But this was not to be. Byzantine Emperor Romanus Diogenes could not just leave the immigration doors wide open—he had to protect the eastern doorway to Byzantium. He therefore gathered his armies and marched into Anatolia. Alp Arslan was compelled to meet him in battle.

This he did in 1071 at the Battle of Manzikert (Malazgird) in eastern Anatolia north of Lake Van. It was a decisive victory for the Seljuks in what many history books call one of the most influential battles in history, for it opened the floodgates of Turkish immigration into Anatolia, which was slowly but surely transitioning from a bastion of Greek culture and language as well as Greek (and Armenian) Orthodox Christianity into the land of the Turks and Islam. And along with the Seljuk takeover of Jerusalem in the same year, it helped lay the foundation for the call to the Crusades in Europe a generation later, ostensibly to help the Byzantines get back what they had lost. The way was now paved for a Turkish takeover of Anatolia, the emergence around two centuries later of the Ottoman Empire, and eventually the fall of Byzantium. It is why today the area comprising Anatolia is called "Turkey." It is not where the Turks originated; it is where some tribal branches of Turks ended up. Fortunately for the Byzantines, Alp Arslan did not follow up the victory at Manzikert with further imperial expansion into Anatolia because his primary focus was still on the Fatimids, which was amply on display with the subsequent conquest of Jerusalem.

Alp Arslan died during a campaign in 1072 and was succeeded by his son, who adopted the title of Malik Shah. His full name was Jalal al-Dawla Muizz al-Dunya al-Din Abu al-Fath ibn Alp Arslan, one full of titles and references. We are glad, therefore, he chose the rather economical "Malik Shah," which literally means "King King," with "malik" being the Arabic version and "shah" the Persian variant. It is interesting to speculate that this may have been his attempt to assuage both Arabs and Persians under Seljuk rule. Whatever the case, his reign (1072–1092) is generally known as the high point of the Seljuk Empire. Fairly young upon his father's death, much of the day-to-day business of ruling fell to his chief minister, Abu Ali Hasan Ibn Ali Tusi, who is better known by his honorific title, Nizam al-Mulk, which means "order of the realm." He is the most famous of all of the medieval Islamic **wazirs** (*vizirs,* singular vizir) in any dynasty, and having served Malik Shah's father for years, he was in an advantageous position to dominate the politics of the Seljuk Empire for two decades.

Two aspects of Nizam al-Mulk's legacy are of particular note. One was the establishment of religious schools (*madrasas*) named after him, Nizamiyyah. They were located throughout Seljuk lands in such cities as Isfahan, Nishapur, Herat, Mosul, and the most famous one in Baghdad. In some ways they have been described as the precursors to the university system in Europe; in other ways, it was an attempt to reinforce Muslim orthodoxy, Sunnism, in the wake of the Shiite century, what some have termed the "Sunni revival." As historian Roy Mottahedeh wrote, "most of the new regimes of the fourth century [in the Islamic calendar, the tenth century CE] were Shi`i [i.e., Buyids and Fatimids]. And most of them were founded by men from peripheral areas of the Near East, nomads or mountain dwellers, who had little interest in the fine points of the religion of their city-dwelling subjects. The *ahl al-sunna* saw that in the presence of alien and occasionally hostile governments they had to rely largely on themselves to preserve the achievement of earlier consensus-minded Muslims, and to prevent deviant speculation from pulling the community in so many directions that it would be irretrievably rent."[1] In addition, as a testament to the mostly successful methods of governance that he established in the empire, he was directed by the Sultan to write what came to be known as the *Siyasatnama*, the Book of Government. His was so valued that it essentially became a kind of constitution for the state, having discussed the role of government, justice, and even such things as state surveillance and establishing a pervasive espionage network in order to maintain power and authority and keep at bay enemies in and outside of Seljuk lands.[2]

SPOTLIGHT

Sufism, al-Ghazali, and Rabia al-Adawiyya

Sufism, known as *tasawwuf* ("being or becoming a Sufi") in the Muslim world, has also been referred to as Islamic mysticism or asceticism and in modern times, populist Islam.[1] In its most developed form, it means to practice strict self-denial as a measure of discipline and commitment. As such, many believe the word "Sufism" comes from "suf" ("wool"), a reference to the simple wool garments typically donned by ascetics and mystics (i.e., Sufis), as they shed the material trappings of life for the bare minimum in order to get closer to Allah and the truth. When it actually began is up for some debate; however, scholars point to increasing dissatisfaction with dogma in early Islam toward a more personal and therefore less dogmatic form of the religion, perhaps even taking some cues from early mendicants among Christians in Byzantium. Sufism is not an Islamic sect. Rather, it is a form or dimension of Islam, or even a way of practicing Islam; therefore, any brand of Muslim—Sunni, Shiite, Ismaili—can be a Sufi.

Sufi orders or *tariqahs*, have been quite influential throughout Islamic history. They quickly became social organizations where the members of one particular tariqah would meet periodically to recite prayers, poems, or selections from the Quran. In addition, Sufis might dance and chant (*dhikrs*) aloud, often accompanied by music in order to reach a level of consciousness, a trance-like condition in which individual Sufis can transport themselves from the material world and come closer to Allah. The form and structure of the dhikrs differed from order to order and were often determined by the spiritual leader or guide of the order (*murshid* or *pir*), to be followed by his disciples (*murid*). An order was usually named after the founder of the tariqah, as we shall see in chapter 8 with the Safavid empire, originally a Sufi order called the Safaviyya, named after the Safavid family member who founded it. Maybe the most famous of the dhikrs is performed by the so-called whirling dervishes ("dervish" taken from the Persian word for poor or poverty) of the Mevlevi Order founded in the thirteenth century by the famous poet, Mevlana Rumi. The Mevlevi spiritual home is in Konya in Anatolia, where Rumi's tomb is located, but it remains an important tariqah to this day in the modern Republic of Turkey. Tariqahs are still popular throughout the Islamic world, where they have provided social cohesion in an increasingly mobile society as well as interregional association.

One other famous Sufi was the Persian mathematician and poet Omar Khayyam (1048–1131 CE), who along with Rumi produced some of the world's most beloved poems and literature. Another Sufi was the influential Islamic philosopher and scholar known as al-Ghazali (1056–1111 CE). He studied and wrote about many different forms and interpretations of Islam, particularly his discourse on Aristotelian and Avicennian (Ibn Sina) logics and metaphysics, but he eventually came to embrace Sufism. His attempts to resolve the apparent contradictions between reason and revelation became accepted by later Muslim theologians, and through the work of Ibn Rushd (Avveroes, 1126–1198) in Spain made its way into Europe and had a significant influence on medieval European religious thought, such as the work of St. Thomas Aquinas.

Having worked for the Seljuk Sultan Malikshah as well as the Abbasid caliph still nominally ruling in Baghdad, al-Ghazali became the most important intellectual of his day, and in becoming such played an important role in the so-called Sunni revival following upon and in response to the so-called Shiite century. However, he soured on working for the state and a life in politics. In 1096 he arrived in Tus in eastern Iran and founded a small Sufi school. For most of the rest of his life he became an ascetic living in relative poverty while composing his masterwork, *The Revival of Religious Science* (*Ihya Ulum al-Din*), which criticizes the dogmatic practices of the Islamic scholars of his time as being too concerned with ritual and politics.

His lasting legacy was to mainstream Sufism into everyday Islam as a way to legitimately seek divine truth.

Rabia al-Adawiyya (c. 717–801) is the best-known female Sufi. She is a somewhat mythic figure who was born in Basra, Iraq. There are no primary sources on her life, and what we have learned of her comes from legends, poems, and biographies. As Rkia Elaroui Cornell stated, "The various depictions of her—as a deeply spiritual ascetic, an existentialist rebel and a romantic lover—seem impossible to reconcile, and yet Rabi`a has transcended these narratives to become a global symbol of both Sufi and modern secular culture."[2] A manumitted slave as a girl, Rabia is said to have preached in mosques in her native Iraq, using poems to express her intense love of Allah, uniquely speaking of the divine in loving terms, which in such turbulent times was meant to calm the anxieties of the population. In one of her poems she said the following: "O Lord, should I worship you for fear of punishment, then burn me in hellfire. Should I worship you for reward, then keep me out of Paradise. But I worship you only for you. So, do not withhold from me your Eternal Beauty."[3] As with most Sufis, she called on people to live a simple and humble life, free from worldly attachments and materials things.

Rabia is still regarded highly to this day, with famous modern singers, such as the revered Umm Khulthum in the twentieth century, singing verses attributed to the ascetic in some of their music. Her family name reflects a heritage connected to the Prophet's tribe, the Quraysh, which gave her some added legitimacy; however, her legacy has been interpreted in a variety of ways, sometimes used to minimize the contribution of women to Islamic history, but as Hossein Kamaly writes, "By holding Rabia in highest esteem, Sufism shattered misogynistic clichés and opened a space for women's active spiritual presence in the history of Islam."[4]

Whirling dervishes performing at Galata Mevlevi Museum, Istanbul, Turkey.
Stefano Politi Markovina/Alamy Stock Photo

Today most Sufi orders are known as bastions of pluralism and tolerance. Often throughout Islamic history Sufi orders were very locally based and inculcated local practices and rituals into their own. Because of all this, they have frequently been criticized—if not violently attacked—by Islamic extremists who view Sufism as an impure, if not heretical, form of Islam. One hopes the predominant view of Sufism as a symbol of peace and tolerance becomes the norm.

---

[1] See "Sufism," in *The Oxford Dictionary of Islam* edited by John L. Esposito, Oxford Islamic Studies Online, http://www.oxfordislamicstudies.com/article/opr/t125/e2260.

[2] Rkia Elaroui Cornell, *Rabi`a from Narrative to Myth: The Many Faces of Islam's Most Famous Woman Saint, Rabi`a al-Adawiiya* (London: Oneworld Publishing, 2019), https://oneworld-publications.com/rab-a-from-narrative-to-myth-hb.html.

[3] Hossein Kamaly, *A History of Islam in 21 Women* (London: Oneworld Publications, 2019), p. 43.

[4] Ibid., p. 46.

The beginning of the end for the Seljuk dynasty is often seen as happening in 1092, when both Malik Shah and Nizam al-Mulk died. The circumstances surrounding the death of each man is shrouded in mystery and intrigue, with the Assassins of Alamut sometimes being blamed for both. The so-called **Assassins** were Nizari Ismailis who had split from the main Fatimid branch in Cairo, having chosen to follow one offspring, Nizar, of the previous caliph rather than the other, who

Depiction of the assassination in 1092 of Nizam al-Mulk, vizir of the Seljuq Empire, from a fourteenth-century manuscript.
The History Collection/Alamy Stock Photo

Ruins of Alamut Castle, fortress of the so-called Assassins, northeast of Ghazvin, Iran.
John Warburton-Lee Photography/Alamy Stock Photo

became the next Fatimid ruler. As happens with schismatics, they often find refuge in isolated, mountainous areas. One branch of Nizaris took up shop in northwestern Syria, led by a man the Crusaders called the "Old Man of the Mountain," whose actual name was Rashid al-Din Sinan. In Iran, the Nizaris established themselves in the Elburz mountain range in north central Iran just south of the Caspian Sea. This branch was led by Hassan al-Sabah, and it eventually (by 1091) took over the mountain fortress of Alamut, which was almost impregnable, only falling—like just about everything else at the time—to the Mongols in 1256.

As the Seljuks were ardent Sunnis who had received caliphal sanction to root out Shiism whenever and wherever it stood, the Ismailis, among other Shiites, were on the defensive. They could not take on the powerful Seljuk army in a pitched battle, so as often happens, the weaker party adopts tactics that in modern times might be called terrorism. It is not that the Assassins were the first terrorists; far from it, but they had some spectacular successes that lent an aura to their cause and methodology that has, with considerable embellishment, established a reputation that has lasted to this day, as one can readily see in the Assassins video games and movies very loosely based on them. The term "assassin" is an English corruption of the Arabic word "hashishiyyun," those who smoke or somehow ingest hashish. According to lore, Nizari assassins, blindly obedient to Hassan al-Sabah, would infiltrate the camp, retinue, or palace of their target and when the time was right would typically attempt to kill him with knives. Before they embarked upon their mission the assassins would smoke hashish, perhaps in order to acquire the medieval equivalent of "Dutch courage." How much of this is true is left to conjecture, but their tactics and at least minimal level of success was such that many Seljuk leaders (and non-Seljuk luminaries such as Saladin) went to extraordinary lengths to protect themselves against infiltration, even to the point of wearing a coat of armor while sleeping just in case one slipped through the cracks. Even so, the Nizaris were never a serious threat to overturn the established order but they were an influential pinprick—especially if they were responsible for one or both deaths.[3]

It is also possible that Nizam al-Mulk was killed on the orders of Malik Shah because the former had become too powerful for the latter to stomach. We have heard a similar story previously with Harun al-Rashid and the Barmakids. In this telling, Nizam al-Mulk's allies took revenge and summarily assassinated Malik Shah in retaliation—or maybe he was poisoned on the orders of the Abbasid caliph at the time because he suspected the sultan wanted to replace him with a Seljuk. While these versions have been deemed unlikely, the deaths of both the sultan and his chief wazir in the same year did have a chilling effect on the empire. There immediately ensued a succession struggle that was never fully resolved, and without the towering authority and skill set of Nizam al-Mulk, the Seljuks were ill-prepared to deal with the aftermath. Slowly but surely the combination of various branches of the family competing with one another, along with the dispersion of power preordained by the iqta system, prevented the Seljuks from once again consolidating the power they enjoyed under Alp Arslan and Malik Shah. A son of Malik Shah, Sinjar, became the next generally acknowledged Sultan, and on the surface he appears to have been successful, having ruled until 1157, which is often the date given for the end of the Seljuk Empire. But as we have seen before, longevity does not always equate to power and authority. Sinjar oversaw the breakup of Seljuk power through compromise and retreat, having to negotiate his way as a first among equals in order to maintain the illusion of leadership. The Seljuks were long past having any central fiscal resource that could really buffer a Sultan with a paid and pliant army. The empire had become a mishmash of statelets ruled by Seljuk princes and atabegs, while lands in the west and east were taken by the stronger dynasties that seem to always be at the ready to pounce. As we have seen previously, what were once successful dynasties go out with a whimper rather than a bang.

The Mongols

Perhaps there is no other dynasty or movement accompanied by so much disinformation and misinformation as that which exists with the Mongols, whose fame and fortune in the thirteenth century constitutes the second stage of the advance of the Turco-Mongolian peoples.[4] Much of the blame for this lay at the feet of the Mongols themselves. They were astute propagandists and experts at psychological warfare, so much so that many of the myths surrounding the Mongols last to this day. They were bigger, badder, crueler, and more numerous than any of their

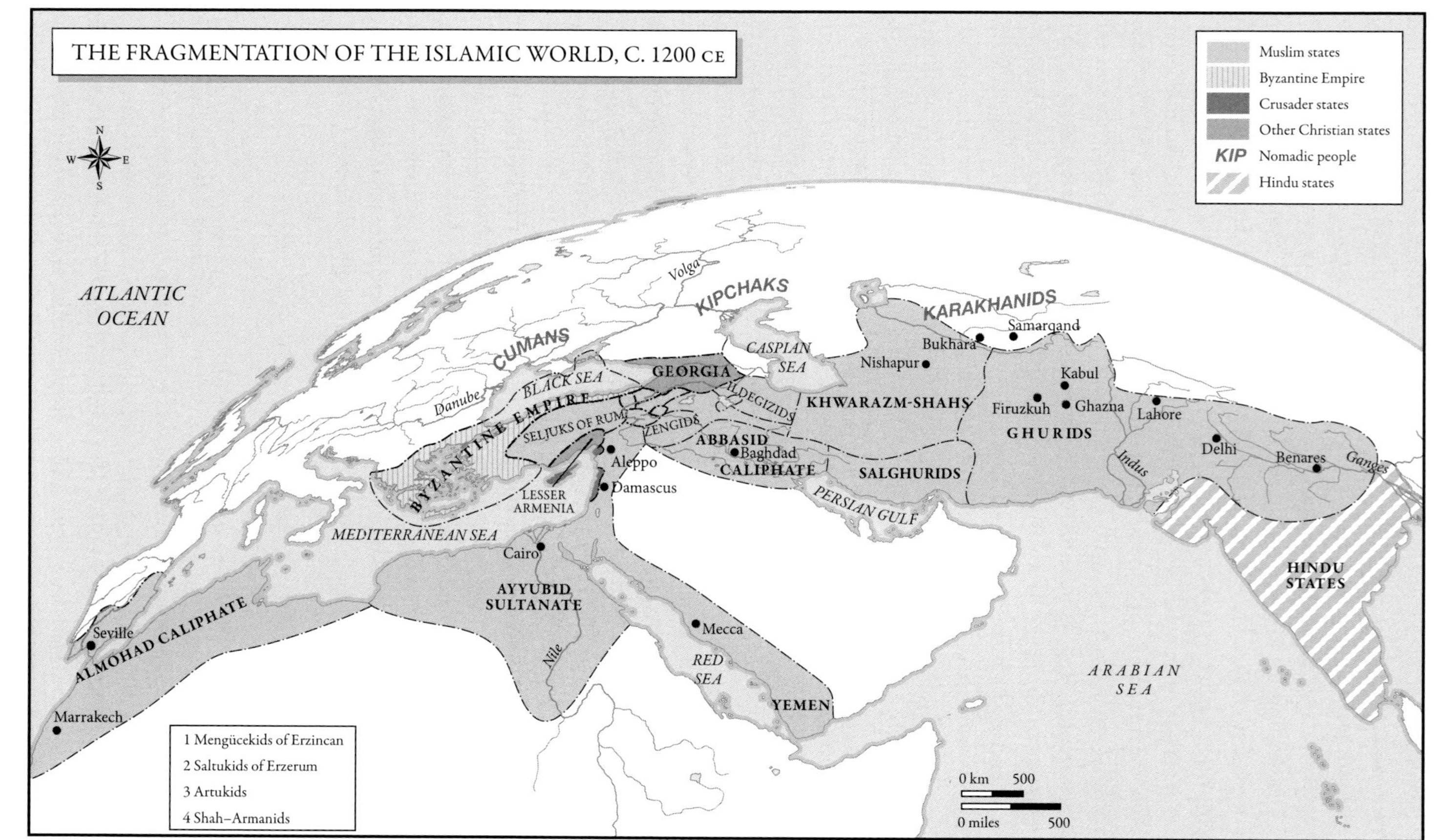
THE FRAGMENTATION OF THE ISLAMIC WORLD, C. 1200 CE
Muslim states
Byzantine Empire
Crusader states
Other Christian states
KIP Nomadic people
Hindu states
N
W
E
S
ATLANTIC OCEAN
KIPCHAKS
Volga
CUMANS
KARAKHANIDS
Samarqand
Bukhara
Nishapur
CASPIAN SEA
GEORGIA
BLACK SEA
Danube
BYZANTINE EMPIRE
SELJUKS OF RUM
ZENGIDS
ILDEGIZIDS
KHWARAZM-SHAHS
Kabul
Firuzkuh
Ghazna
Lahore
GHURIDS
Delhi
Benares
Ganges
Indus
ABBASID CALIPHATE
Baghdad
SALGHURIDS
Aleppo
Damascus
LESSER ARMENIA
PERSIAN GULF
MEDITERRANEAN SEA
Cairo
AYYUBID SULTANATE
Nile
Mecca
RED SEA
YEMEN
HINDU STATES
ARABIAN SEA
ALMOHAD CALIPHATE
Seville
Marrakech
1 Mengücekids of Erzincan
2 Saltukids of Erzerum
3 Artukids
4 Shah–Armanids
0 km 500
0 miles 500

contemporaries, or so the legend has it. I always ask my students at the beginning of this section to conjure up the images they have of the Mongols. Most often the pictures that come to their minds are of millions and millions of them running roughshod over the Eurasian landmass, towers of heads as examples of their ruthlessness, or barbarous warriors of great repute in the art of warfare. They were good propagandists, but the imagery they tried so hard to project has colored our collective view of them over the centuries to the point that the now outdated categorization of races into Caucasoid, Negroid, and Mongoloid hatched in Germany in the eighteenth century is naturally Eurocentric, casting both the Negroid and Mongoloid races as inferior to the Caucasoid race. This pejorative imagery extended even further when, until recently, those suffering from Down syndrome were called Mongoloid children. The history of the Mongols is actually more nuanced, with much more positive influence than has been traditionally portrayed. We primarily encounter them when they enter the Middle East and put a final end to the Abbasid caliphate in Baghdad in 1258.

One cannot talk about the Mongols without focusing first and foremost on Genghis Khan (also spelled Chinggis or Jenghiz), one of the great conquerors in world history. His birth name was Temujin (Temuchin), which means something close to "smith," as in the occupation. It is generally accepted that he was born in 1167, although various other years of birth have been offered. Not much of his childhood is known, and most of what is known is the stuff of legend.[5] Most likely he emerged from rather modest beginnings, but he slowly built up his reputation in war and diplomacy, maintaining a loyal following that helped him to eventually combine most of the Mongol tribes into one unit, which was the foundational key to his career of military expansion.

In 1206, an assembly (or *quriltai*) of Mongol tribal chiefs proclaimed Temujin to be the supreme head of his people with the title of Genghis Khan, which in one definition means "ruler of the universe" (another translation has it as "ocean-like ruler," as in ruling from ocean to ocean). Whatever the exact meaning, Genghis almost did become ruler of the known universe. As anthropologist Jack Weatherford points out, "In twenty-five years, the Mongol army subjugated more lands and people than the Romans had conquered in four hundred years."[6] After uniting the people of the "felt-walled tents," he was now in a position to engage in his life-long occupation: conquest. He reportedly said on one occasion that "man's highest joy is in victory, to conquer one's enemies, to pursue them, to deprive them of their possessions, to make their beloved weep, to ride on their horses, and to embrace their wives and daughters."[7] Whether or not he actually said this, the quote reflects the typical pillaging and plundering attitude of tribal warriors.

The question that many have asked is how Genghis Khan was the one tribal leader who went on to conquer most of the Eurasian landmass with the exception of its extremities, creating the largest contiguous land empire in world history. This is an especially intriguing question when one understands that contrary to Mongol propaganda and popular myth, there were in fact not that many of them. There were probably about one million Mongols overall (men, women, and children). Out of that number Genghis Khan probably assembled, by most estimates, a maximum of 100,000–125,000 Mongol warriors, which is woefully insufficient on the surface to conquer as much territory as he and his successors did. It was not just Mongols who did the conquering, as Genghis and his cohorts frequently added to their ranks mostly Turkish allies along the road of conquest, beefing up their numbers here and there. Regardless, the question still stands: How was he uniquely able to accomplish this?

Most of the answers to this question revolve around the nature of the Mongols themselves as rugged, hearty warriors along with their strategy and tactics. First was the fact that similar to most nomadic tribal warriors, as we saw with the Arabs in the initial Islamic conquests, the Mongols' daily life was a constant rehearsal for military campaigns. They lived off the land, and their skills in the hunt, acquired from an early age, are well-known, especially their incomparable mounted archers and their compound bows, which allowed them to harass and attack foes from a relatively safe distance. They were capable of riding for several days in a row with little rest and food, and this mobility, as many scholars have remarked, introduced *blitzkrieg* tactics into the thirteenth century. These tactics are usually the purview of armies who are numerically less than their opponents; if not, they could just overwhelm their enemies with sheer numbers. On some occasions this was no doubt the case with the Mongols, but mostly they relied on movement and tactics to wear

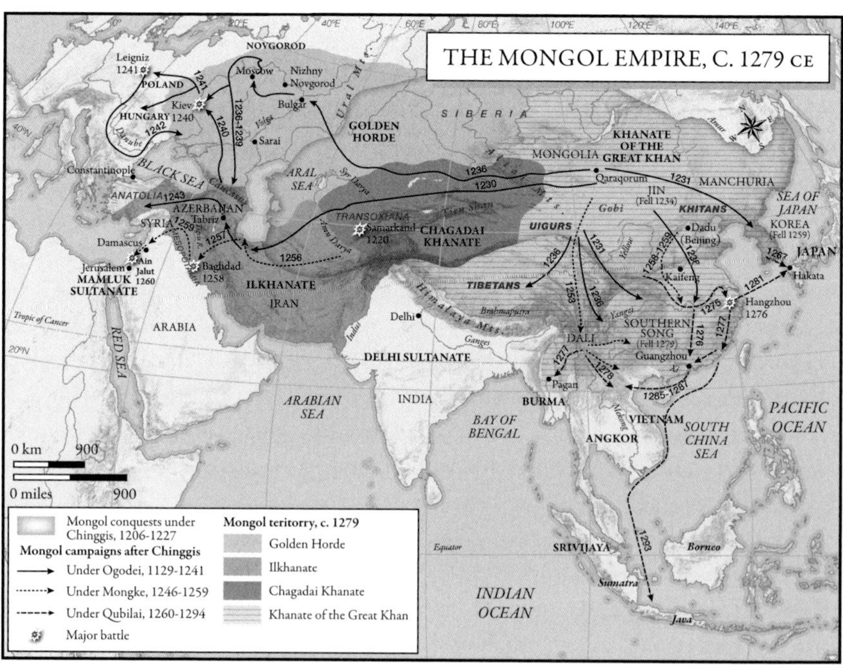

down and defeat the enemy. Most of their tactics revolved around deception, either luring a foe into a strategically disadvantageous position (or ambush) or by doing things to make it seem as if there were many more Mongols than there actually were, such as tying branches to the tails of horses to stir up dust to give the impression there was a large army on the horizon or mounting dummies or even dead bodies on spare horses to accomplish the same objective.

There is a story, certainly apocryphal, that has Genghis Khan and his army confronting a fortified city for the first time in China. He did not have the appropriate siege equipment, so he lit the tails of one thousand cats and ten thousand swallows on fire and sent them to the city, which subsequently burnt down. What this story indicated was the fact that the Mongols needed siege materials in order to take cities, adapting to and adopting Chinese siege tactics, showing that the Mongols were keen to integrate new ways and means into their overall military modus operandi. Perhaps another moral to this story is that the "ruler of the universe" could actually command the fauna of this world to do his bidding, embellishing his already growing reputation.

The Mongols were also experts at espionage and psychological operations. They would infiltrate towns and cities to find out everything they could about their enemies before going on campaign, acquiring knowledge about the nature of the armies they might face, fortifications, morale, and the topography of potential battle sites in a way that could be used to their advantage. These spies would also spread demoralizing tales of the might of the Mongol armies as well as spread terror among urban populations about the Mongols' ruthlessness. The hope was that these cities would surrender without a fight. In some cases most of the inhabitants of a city would be massacred with the intention that nearby towns and cities would then hear of this and choose not to put up a fight. Much of this strategy was because of the low number of Mongols—so the less fighting in which they actually engaged, the better they could preserve their men and materiel. An example of a much more direct, intimidating entreaty to encourage submission can be found in the letter in 1260 that Hulegu Khan, the grandson of Genghis, sent to the Mamluk Sultan Qutuz, based in Egypt. It read as follows:

> From the King of Kings of the East and West, the Great Khan. To Qutuz, the Mamluk, who fled to escape our swords. You should think of what happened to other countries . . . and submit to us. You have heard how we have conquered a vast empire and have purified the earth of the disorders tainting it. We have conquered vast areas, massacring all the people. You cannot escape from the terror of our armies. Where can you flee? What road will you use to escape us? Our horses are swift, our arrows sharp, our swords like thunderbolts, our hearts as hard as the mountains, our soldiers as numerous as the sand. Fortresses will not detain us, nor arms stop us. Your prayers to God will not avail against us. We are not moved by tears nor touched by lamentations. Only those who beg our protection will be safe. Hasten your

> reply before the fire of war is kindled. . . . Resist and you will suffer the most terrible catastrophes. We will shatter your mosques and reveal the weakness of your God, and then we will kill your children and your old men together. At the present you are the only enemy against who we have to march.[8]

This is an intimidating letter, and by 1260 there were enough instances of Mongol might and cruelty to back up the claims Hulegu was making. Although the threats worked pretty well against Qutuz, they did not frighten the person who would actually come to lead the Mamluks, and as we shall soon see, it ended in a notable Mongol defeat.

Genghis Khan was also intent on overcoming his nomadic neighbors before taking on established dynasties. He was well aware of the traditional divide and rule strategy of the Chinese to "use barbarians to control barbarians," and he would incorporate warriors and other skilled personnel from those he conquered in order to buffer his forces. But the main reason for Genghis Khan's unparalleled success was that he arrived at the right historical moment. We saw this with the initial Islamic conquests against the weakened Byzantine and Sassanian empires. In addition to looking at the military prowess and motivation of the conquerors, one also has to examine the condition of those who were conquered, and more often than not they are well past their prime. This is not to diminish the Mongol conquest but rather to explain how it happened so quickly over such an expanse of territory.

At the beginning of the thirteenth century, China was divided into three kingdoms. Had it been united under one dynasty, the Mongols probably would not have been as successful against them. Genghis by 1215 had conquered most of China. Manchuria fell in 1216 and Korea in 1218, and then he set his sights to the west. The Turkish empire of the Kara-Khitai fell in 1219, and between 1219–1221 the Mongols defeated what had been the powerful Khwarzmshahs based in Transoxiana with Samarqand as its capital. Had either of these two states been at their height, the outcome might have been different, but now the Mongols were perched to eventually enter the heartland of the Middle East. After their exploits in Central Asia, the Mongols headed northward into the Caucasus, defeating Georgian and Russian armies in 1223. Genghis Khan was then compelled to return east to put down a Tibetan revolt, during which time he died in 1227.

The campaigning did not end, however, with the Great Khan's death. Genghis's son, Ogodai, was acknowledged as the new Great Khan by 1229, and during his reign to 1241 the military campaigns continued across the breadth of the Eurasian landmass, five thousand miles apart. Another of Genghis's grandsons, Batu, led a force of Mongols and Turks into the Ukraine, where the foundations of the Golden Horde were laid, and then in 1241 straight into the heart of central Europe, defeating a German army in Silesia after having moved into Poland and Hungary, reaching the Adriatic coast after capturing Zagreb. Mongol armies were thus operating from the Sea of Japan to the Mediterranean.

Statue of Genghis Khan in Sukhbaatar Square, Ulaan Baatar, Mongolia.
i on the world/Alamy Stock Photo

It was only a matter of time before the Mongols would invade a long-past-its-prime Abbasid Empire. By the mid-1250s there was really nothing in the area to stop them. In 1258, Hulegu, the brother of the Great Khan Mongke, captured Baghdad, killing most of the inhabitants in the process, including the last Abbasid caliph, al-Mustasim.[9] Some members of the Abbasid family were able to escape, taking up shop with the Mamluks in Egypt, where the caliphate under the Abbasids continued for another two and half centuries as religious figureheads serving the Mamluk sultans.

I want to point out something in the accepted dates in power of the Great Khans since the death of Genghis in 1227: Ogodai, 1229–1241; Guyuk, 1246–1248; Mongke, 1251–1259; and Kublai, 1260–1294. Notice the intervals—sometimes lengthy interregnums—following the death of a Great Khan and the assumption of power of the next one. This was due to the typical infighting between the descendants of Genghis, often to the precipice of civil war. Whenever a Great Khan died, members of the family on campaign would usually at the very least pause; often they headed back toward the capital of Karakorum in Mongolia with a healthy portion of their army in order to participate in the choice of who would come next. Some say that this is what saved western Europe from Mongol destruction: when Batu was advancing in eastern and central Europe, he suddenly had to return to Mongolia upon the death of Ogodai in 1241. This is also what happened in 1260, a year after the death of Mongke.

As we saw earlier with the quote, Hulegu was advancing into Syria. All that was left to oppose him in the region was a just-emerging Mamluk Empire, centered in Egypt but extending into Syria. Even though the letter referenced earlier came from Hulegu, he was not actually at the inevitable battle between the Mongols and Mamluks in 1260 at Ain Jalut (Well of Goliath) in Palestine north of Jerusalem. He had returned to Karakorum with some of his forces. The battle of Ain Jalut has been considered by many historians in the past to have been one of the most consequential battles in world history primarily because it stopped the Mongols in their tracks—they were finally defeated, and thus the Levant and North Africa were spared the wrath of the Great Khan. While the battle was certainly important (if nothing else for the psychological factor of proving the Mongols were not invincible and in essence really giving birth to the Mamluk Empire), there is some question as to whether the Mongols would have been interested in the arid and desert regions of the Levant and Arabia, much less North Africa. Hulegu may have just wanted to protect his western flank before settling down to rule in Iran. The Mongols were not at full strength at Ain Jalut. Similarly, there are questions as to whether the Mongols would have been interested in the dense forest terrain, where they were less mobile, and the relative poverty further into central and western Europe was likely unappealing, even had Batu not felt compelled to retreat upon the death of Ogodai in 1241. They wanted good pastureland for their horses and loot. On the contrary, the Muslim empires and dynasties of the Middle East and Central Asia were quite desirable as one of the richest, most educated, and most advanced areas in the world. These are hypotheticals, but there were a host of other reasons the Mongol Empire was destined not to last.

For one thing, it was just too big, and there were not enough Mongols to man the gates. The Mongols may have been outnumbered by those over whom they ruled by a thousand to one.[10] It almost had to break up into its constituent parts, especially when the centrifugal forces of inevitable dynastic disputes became a common feature of political life—something we have seen time and again, most recently in this chapter with the Seljuks. The Mongol dispersion resumed the old pattern of the barbarian outsiders conquering and then becoming absorbed into the more established and dominant cultures of the civilizations they had conquered, especially as they became more sedentary after the death of Genghis. While the Arabs had a language and religion that eventually superimposed itself on most of the territories they conquered, the Mongols really did not have either as they expanded, and in a way over time they lost their identity outside of Mongolia itself. For instance, Kublai Khan moved the Mongol capital from Karakorum to Beijing, where he started the Yuan dynasty. But he became more and more of a Chinese emperor, ruling from a palace of Chinese design and adopting the Confucian ways that dominated Chinese culture at the time. Many in the Golden Horde (gold was considered an imperial color by the Mongols, and Genghis Khan and his relatives were often referred to as the Golden Family),[11] located in Central Asia up through into the Ukraine and the Caucasus, became Orthodox Christians. Hulegu, who settled in Tabriz in Iran as the ruler of the Il-Khanate, subject to the Great Khan, became more of a Persian overlord rather than Mongol, adopting the Persian language and customs; by the 1290s the Il-Khanate became a Muslim state. Perhaps one only has to look at the religious persuasions of Hulegu himself over the course of his life: he began, as most Mongols did, as a Shamanist; then he became a Nestorian Christian upon entering Iraq, then he converted to Shiite Islam, and ultimately toward the end he became a Sunni Muslim. The only pure Mongols left into the fourteenth century seemed to be in Mongolia itself, where Buddhism came to prevail soon enough.

The legacy of the Mongol conquests is often associated with negative consequences. There can be no doubt that the Mongols destroyed many a city and their inhabitants, but historians have traditionally postulated that because Western Europe was able to escape the destruction of the Mongol conquests, it was in a much better position to advance scientifically, militarily, and culturally than eastern Europe. The Mongol conquests are also the reasons given for the relative backwardness of the Middle East and Central Asia compared to places such as Japan and Western Europe. Weatherford notes that "the Mongols became scapegoats for other nations' failures and shortcomings."[12] Reality is more nuanced.

The Mongol Empire was extremely tolerant of other religions; Karakorum at the time may have been the most religiously tolerant city on earth.[13] Some even suggest that the Mongols' separation of church and state or perhaps state control of religion influenced the growth of this concept later in Europe. The Mongols did not engage, in terms of criminal law, in any kind of torture akin to that which existed in contemporary (and future) Europe as ordained by both church and state, such as burning at the stake, disemboweling, or the rack.[14] In any event, Mongols thought of themselves as Mongol first before any religious identification. In addition, Genghis Khan established a society based on law to which even the Great Khan was subject; the rule of law over the individual was a central premise under the Mongols.[15] Education and literacy were extremely important, and Genghis decreed that all children should learn how to read. It was a merit-based society where farmers and peasants became generals, and there was no doubt that Genghis himself was simply a mortal human and not a god of some sort. Although men had more overall rights than women, the latter were much more highly valued and integrated into society than other contemporary civilizations. Selling a woman into marriage against her will, as well as the kidnapping of women, were against the law. Women played prominent roles in government administration and public life and fought in battles; it is said that the mother of Genghis Khan was quite influential, urging him that unity would be the key to Mongol expansion and the success of her son, an admonition he certainly took to heart. The bottom line is that the Mongol Empire united much more than it divided, and for a period of time created a virtual global network of trade and the exchange of ideas—what some term a Pax Mongolica—in many ways inaugurating an intellectual and scientific revolution of which succeeding civilizations and dynasties would reap the benefits. As Weatherford states, "The Europeans received all the benefits of trade, technology transfer, and the Global Awakening without paying the cost of the Mongol conquest."[16] The empire served as the "basic information circuit" in the Eurasian landmass.[17] It has also been called the "Genghis exchange," analogous to the "Columbus exchange," denoting the intrusion and long-term consequences of the Europeans into the Americas.[18]

As David Morgan (whose book *The Mongols* is a standard in the field) puts forward, however, there was some long-term destruction in the Middle East, but it was much less due to the burning of cities to the ground and massacring of populations, which for the most part was primarily felt in Transoxiana and Khurasan, than to the disruption of the intricate *qanat* (underground canal) and surface irrigations systems in Iran and Iraq. The relocation if not decimation of peasant populations, of whom the Mongols thought no better than animals grazing in pastures, also diminished the very workforce who maintained these delicate irrigation systems. This is something, as we know, that waxed and waned depending upon the political stability at any particular time, but the Mongol onslaught might have been the final blow that debilitated the ability of generations to reestablish fully functioning and integrated agrarian-based societies.[19]

Whether one is more positive or negative about the Mongol era, it was spectacular, and the world would look drastically different today had Genghis Khan not entered the history books.

The Crusades

I usually ask my students how they were taught about the Crusades in high school. I have been surprised—but maybe should not be—that over the years there still remain a variety of responses to this question, ranging from a largely positive depiction to a mostly negative one. There still is no general consensus in most circles in the West about the history of the Crusades. Even though in recent decades the Crusades have been revealed as something of a Christian jihad marked by senseless killing and massacres perpetrated by European Christians in the Middle East (and in the Balkans as well), it is not so negative as to force some of those same high schools to remove the word "Crusaders" as their nicknames. It is not yet considered so pejorative as to informally ban its usage as something of a galvanizing term, as in "a crusade to eradicate poverty" or the like. History, of course, is more nuanced. While there can be little doubt that the actual Crusaders to the Holy Land perpetrated untold atrocities that went against everything the person for whom they were supposedly fighting (Jesus Christ) is said to have believed, the overall repercussions for Europe in terms of the transfer of knowledge and goods from east to west were positive. In my mind, however, the price of all this was too steep during and after the period of the Crusades. In many ways it cemented misperception and animus to this day, for as Garth Fowden put it, "the Islamic world . . . represents not an economic challenge but something more insidious, a moral and spiritual competitor offering different norms of conduct and a variant and vision of man and God unnervingly close—yet at the same time a challenge, as the Qur`an makes explicit—to the values espoused by Judeo-Christian civilization."[20] The encounter with the Crusades not only antagonized civilizations but also antagonized history, beginning a psychological rupture that unnecessarily separated what should have been obviously similar.

So went the encounter between the Franks and the Saracens: "Franks," meaning the French, because most of the Crusades to the Middle East were French or French-dominated. The original call to Crusade by Pope Urban II was in France. The dominant language of the Europeans living in the Crusader states established in the Middle East was French. Even the most famous Crusader of them all, King Richard I (the Lionheart) of England, spent most of his European life in Aquitaine and spoke French, spending all of about six months of his entire reign in England. The origin of the word "Saracens" is considerably more jumbled. There are many versions of the story, some of them quite colorful, but it is most likely of Greek root or a mangled pronunciation of the Arabic word for "east," which is "al-sharq," or "al-sharqiyyah," which means "eastern." Whatever the case, by the time of the Crusades, "Saracens" was a common European reference to Arabs or Muslims in general, with a tinge of derogatory meaning to it.

Europeans in general had been inflamed about the Holy Land, specifically Jerusalem, being in Muslim hands for some time prior to the First Crusade in the 1090s. There had been several affronts in the minds of many Europeans perpetrated by Muslims against Christian symbols and shrines over the previous century. The shrine of St. James (Santiago) in Spain was desecrated by Muslims in 997; the Reconquista in Spain, which made some headway in the eleventh century, animated the ideological, moral, and theological justification for Crusade. In addition, the epicenter of Christianity, the Church of the Holy Sepulcher in Jerusalem, had been destroyed in 1009 under the orders of the Fatimid Caliph al-Hakim. There had been numerous stories, many of them embellished, that made thier way back to Europe of Christian pilgrims to the Holy Land having been robbed, tortured in gruesome fashion, and killed. While no doubt some were, this was more a function of the general fragmentation in that part of the Middle East and accompanying insecurity. A great many Muslim pilgrims were also preyed upon. There was no systemic, concerted campaign by Islam to attack Christians; as we have seen, Christians were by and large protected peoples, many of whom played active roles in Muslim society.

The turning point for general Christian angst in Europe over the fate of the Holy Land into a call for Crusade came in 1071 with two events, both involving the Seljuk Turks. We have examined the first one already with the Seljuk defeat of the Byzantines at the Battle of Manzikert, which opened the floodgates to Turkish and Islamic immigration into Anatolia and more pressure on the quickly receding territory of Greek Orthodox Byzantium. This led to pleas for help from Constantinople to Latin Christendom to stem the tide, and in the 1090s one specific cry for assistance from the Byzantine emperor to the Latin pope. Later in the same year the Seljuks took Jerusalem from the Fatimids, and the Sunni Turks were much more restrictive of Christian practice and pilgrimage traffic than the caliphs in Cairo had been. Even though the Fatimids would recover Jerusalem soon enough, the damage had been done in the eyes of Christendom.

The Byzantine emperor would rue the day he called for help, as we shall see. At the Council of Clermont in southern France in 1095, Pope Urban II made the call to Crusade to liberate the Holy Land from the infidels, in the process of which persecuted Christians in the Middle East would be liberated and those making the Crusade would acquire salvation, wealth, and power in the "land of milk and honey." The pope argued that it was better to slaughter Muslims than fellow Christians, and if a Christian died in the process he would receive a plenary indulgence, exempting the Crusader from the necessity of rendering satisfaction for sins; essentially, it was a get out of jail for free card promising immediate entry into heaven. It was also one of the main things that Martin Luther railed against a few centuries later, as by then a plenary indulgence could be purchased by making a proper donation to the church. As you may have already noticed, helping the Byzantine Empire survive the so-called onslaught of Islam wasn't enough. Taking (or perhaps saving) Jerusalem had to be added to the equation in order to really fire up the passions of European Christians.

There was the medieval equivalent of a propaganda campaign associated with the call to Crusade in order to recruit not only those willing to travel to the Middle East and fight, but also the financial sponsorship to enable the whole enterprise. Robert the Monk attended Pope Urban's speech at Clermont, and he relayed what the pope uttered. While it is probably not a word-for-word transcription, it no doubt captures the tone:

> They [the Muslims] have completely destroyed some of God's churches and they have converted others to the uses of their own cult. They ruin the altars with filth and defilement. They circumcise Christians and smear their blood from the circumcision over the altars or throw it into the baptismal fonts. They are pleased to kill others by cutting open their bellies, extracting the end of their intestines, and tying it to a stake. Then, with flogging, they drive their victims around the stake until, when their viscera having spilled out, they fall dead on the ground. They tie others, again, to stakes and shoot arrows at them; they seize others, stretch out their necks, and try to see whether they can cut off their heads with a single blow of a naked sword. And what shall I say about the shocking rape of women?[21]

These were just some of the shocking stories circulated in certain parts of Europe. As Crusade specialist Thomas Madden points out, "for knights steeped in a culture of militant Christianity, there were stories to make the blood boil."[22] The pope's vicars of the Church, bishops and priests, helped spread the call by using the supposed words of Christ himself as articulated in the New Testament: "If any man will come after me, let him deny himself, and take up his cross, and follow me" (Matthew 16:24), and "everyone that hath forsaken houses, or brethren, or sisters, or father, or mother, or wife, or children, or lands, for my name's sake shall receive a hundredfold, and shall inherit everlasting life" (Matthew 19:29).[23] In essence, the Crusaders were being called to action by Christ himself, especially as, symbolically, He was being crucified all over again, this time by Muslims.[24] This was a religiously fired-up age, so when Crusaders embarked on their quest in this frame of mind it is little wonder they perpetrated such regular violence against anyone in their way.

Europe was an armed camp at the time, especially following the Viking era of constant raiding along the coasts of the continent. The Crusades were in one respect a way to turn militant Christianity outward toward a convenient foe. As a sign of the militancy in Europe in the eleventh century, there was a Truce of God movement that attempted to outlaw warfare on Sunday and holidays.[25] There were two trends that helped lay the foundation for Crusade: lay piety and lay sanctity. One did not need the Church if they took control over their religious lives. And the culture of nobility in the eleventh century was one of public displays of piety. Crusade proved the means to turn a talent for warfare into individual salvation through this very public display of piety.

The motives for going on Crusade for both the Church and individual Crusaders varied, and not all of them were altruistic. For the papacy, which was a political office in those days, the Crusades offered the pope the opportunity to reinforce his leadership position in Europe, especially against rising secular forces. It also offered the opportunity to heal the breach between Latin and Greek Christianity that had so recently occurred in 1054. (As we shall see, the Crusades, if anything, cemented the breach.) The Crusaders themselves were motivated by one or more of the following: true spiritual concerns; plenary indulgence, which frequently opened a Pandora's Box to the worst of the lot (i.e., those who needed absolution the most); material gain; the lure of adventure; an escape from the daily lot of their lives and to enhance their stature; and to participate in activity, especially for the knights, that quickly became fashionable in parts of Europe.

But there were also overall or systemic reasons why this fairly peculiar episode in European and Middle Eastern history occurred at this time. First, between about 900 and 1300 there was a 50 percent increase in the population of Europe that fueled a period of tremendous economic growth. It is almost as if Europe was bursting at the seams after what had been a period of relative isolation, reaching a critical mass demographically and economically that compelled it to break out—all it needed was a convenient justification, and religious passion provided the fuel.

In addition, the Viking raids ended about the year 1000, which made it safe for Europe to send massive armies elsewhere rather than keeping the warriors at home for defense. Finally, the increased commerce emerging from the economic growth created the need to control the trade routes of the Mediterranean, as in the days of the Roman Empire. It was a favorable historical moment for success, as there was a power vacuum at the time in that part of the Middle East, and had the Crusader movement begun a couple of decades earlier they would most likely have been defeated by a Seljuk Empire at its height.[26]

I will not be covering each and every Crusade that occurred over a two-hundred-year period, but I will highlight the most notable ones. The actual first Crusade was an unofficial one. When the Byzantine emperor requested assistance from the pope, he apparently just wanted some equipment and maybe a few hundred knights to help protect his eastern flank. Instead, the first batch of Crusaders in 1096 came in the form of what is commonly referred to as the Peasant's Crusade led by an ascetic by the name of Peter the Hermit. It was a hodgepodge of mostly commoners, some of whom were fired up by the hopes of founding a New Jerusalem, but it was also composed of brigands and other lesser lights angling for that plenary indulgence. It was a group devoid of military experience or proper equipment. That did not stop them from killing Jews and Gypsies in the Balkans as they made their way to Constantinople; many Jews refer to the entire Crusader period as the "first Holocaust," as they paid almost as high a price in death and destruction at the hands of the Christians as the Muslims did. The Byzantines wanted to get rid of them as fast as possible and shipped them over to Anatolia, where most of them were massacred by the Turkish army of the sultan of Nicaea, one of the many Turkish principalities that now dotted the Anatolian landscape.

A much more impressive effort was launched later in 1096, which has been termed the real First Crusade, or the Crusade of Princes. Many of Europe's most illustrious princes led this Crusade, leading a rather large army of some 50,000–60,000 soldiers, including thousands of knights as well as thousands of accompanying noncombatants. The massive force trudged its way across Anatolia, being harassed the entire time by Turkish forces. They headed into the Middle East from what is now southern Turkey into Syria. It was this group that established the four Crusader states along the Levantine coast: Edessa and then Antioch in 1098, then Tripoli early the following year, with the grand prize, Jerusalem, by mid-summer of 1099. To say that the Crusaders used hook or crook to conquer or enter the main city in each state would be an understatement; they were agitated, especially after such a long trek in hostile territory. Nothing was going to get in their way, so in Edessa they tricked and then beheaded the Armenian Christian ruler, and in Antioch, after a seven-month siege, the Crusaders killed all of the Muslims and Jews in the city, including many non-Latin Christians. But they saved their worst for last in Jerusalem, where after such hardship and scorched-earth tactics on the part of the locals, they must have really been fired up when they gazed upon the walls

CRUSADER STATES, c. 1140 CE
Byzantine territory
Cilician Kingdom of Armenia
County of Edessa
Principality of Antioch
County of Tripoli
Kingdom of Jerusalem
Major castle
N
W
E
S
SELJUK SULTANATE OF RUM
Tigris
Bira
Edessa
Turbessel
Euphrates
Antioch
Aleppo
Ma'rrat An-Nu'man
Saone
Latakia
Hamah
Tortosa
Homs
Krak des Chevaliers
Cyprus
Tripoli
Beirut
Baalbek
Sidon
Damascus
Belfort
Tyre
MEDITERRANEAN SEA
Tiberias
Acre
Bostra
Caesarea
Jaffa
Jerusalem
Ascalon
Krak des Moabites
Damietta
Montreal
FATIMID CALIPHATE
Cairo
Nile
0 km
100
200
0 miles
100
200

of the holy city. Depending upon the source, several tens of thousands of people in Jerusalem were massacred in a cathartic rage: Muslims, Jews (many of whom were burned alive in the synagogue to which they retreated), and Christians. It is forever a stain on Christendom, but they got their city.

Devoid of the bloodshed—which is frankly hard to separate—it was quite the military accomplishment for a relatively backward Europe to send an army to the east and establish a 500-mile strip along the eastern Mediterranean. Its success certainly inspired succeeding Crusades. One of the primary reasons for its success, however, was the fragmentation of power in that part of the Middle East. At their height the Umayyad or Abbasid Empires could have easily dismissed the Crusaders, as could a Fatimid Empire some eighty years earlier. But the Crusaders took advantage of the political disintegration in the area, and their continued success depended on that part of the Muslim world remaining disunited; oftentimes a Muslim dynast in the area would ally with a Crusader state against another Muslim dynast. Again, timing was everything. As the new political landscape evolved, it was not as black and white—Christian versus Muslim—as it would seem to appear on the surface, at least not until Salah al-Din al-Ayyubi (Saladin) entered the picture a little less than a hundred years into Crusader history.

At first, maintaining and defending these outposts of European Christianity became an overriding concern for all involved. Military orders developed, such as the Templars and the Hospitallers, to protect the pilgrimage route as well as the Crusader states themselves. These knights typically distinguished themselves in battle, but they also perpetrated some unspeakable atrocities—they were Christianity's version of missionary warriors. Associated with this, imposing castles were built in the area, the best in the Middle East, located at particularly strategic points along trade and military transportation routes. The Crac de Chevaliers (referred to as Qaalat al-Hosn in Syria), located about halfway between the city of Homs and the coastal city of Tartous, is the most magnificent—and best preserved—of them all; so imposing is this fortress that it was actively used for defense by both opposition and government forces at different times during the recent Syrian civil war—it held up even against modern armaments. To get more European Christians to the Crusader states, especially the city-state of Jerusalem, subsidies and cheap land were offered to induce Europeans to take up shop in the Middle East and help offset the demographic disadvantage.

It was only by the mid-twelfth century that some Muslim forces in the immediate area turned their attentions toward the Crusader states. There was a group called the Zenghids (Zangids), named after the putative governor of Mosul province in northern Iraq that also stretched into Syria, Imad al-Din Zenghi (Zangi). Ostensibly he served at the pleasure of the Abbasid caliph, but he acted independently, though he always nominally recognized the authority of the caliph because his blessing and sanction still carried some weight, especially at a time when Sunni Islam was really solidifying its position in the Islamic world following the Seljuk

Crusader Castle, Crac des Chevaliers, Syria, built in the eleventh century.
Paul Gapper / Alamy Stock Photo

presence. The Zenghids captured Edessa in 1144, the first such Crusader city-state to fall, beginning dreams in the heartland of the Middle East that Jerusalem could perhaps be retaken as well in the near future.

This did not sit well in Europe and elicited the call for another Crusade, which became the Second Crusade (1147–1149) led by King Louis VII of France and the Emperor Conrad III of Germany. For some as yet unknown reason, the objective of the Second Crusade was not to take back Edessa but rather to capture Damascus—which did not make much sense, because it had been a fairly neutral player on the scene. The Crusade was a disaster, as much of the army was annihilated as it moved through Anatolia, and it never got near Damascus. Instead, the Zenghids, now led by Zenghi's son, Nur al-Din, after his father was killed by one of his own slaves in 1146, took Damascus, placing it firmly in the hands of someone interested in getting closer and closer to Jerusalem. Nur al-Din was known as an impressive leader. He hired well, especially in the military, some of whom were family members of Saladin who had also served Zenghi. Saladin's rise to the top did not begin at the bottom. He was already close to power through family connections. He was well trained by his family (and Nur al-Din) and gained valuable experience along the way.

In the 1160s, Nur al-Din sent Saladin to Cairo ostensibly to work under the last Fatimid caliph of a crumbling Fatimid Empire, who desperately needed help, even from Sunni elements. By 1169, Saladin, at age thirty-one, had risen to the post of vizir and essentially became the ruler of Egypt, something that was more formalized in 1171 when he had the caliph removed from power, officially ending the Fatimid Empire. He still in theory served under Nur al-Din, who was now in

Damascus, and for the Abbasid caliph, for whom Saladin never forswore his ultimate allegiance no matter how frustrating a powerless caliph could be at times. As John Man wrote, Egypt kind of "fell into Saladin's lap."[27] The increasing power of Saladin potentially put him at odds with Nur al-Din, but we will never know because the latter died in 1174, perhaps of natural causes and perhaps not. In any event, Saladin was the natural successor, and with meticulous diplomacy marked by the graciousness and magnanimity for which he would become famous, he acquired Syria, and he moved the (now) Ayyubid Empire's center to Damascus. This is what the Crusader states had always feared: a unified Islamic power at their doorstep and led by a popular and capable leader, although Saladin still minted coins in the Abbasid caliph's name.[28] Crusader success depended on Islam's continued fragmentation, but this was no longer the case.

After more diplomacy and military forays, by 1187 Saladin had assembled an impressive army and was ready to move on Jerusalem. First, he defeated a large Crusader army in the Battle of Hattin located in present-day northern Israel near the Sea of Galilee/Lake Tiberius. The Muslims were decisively victorious over the thirsty and rundown Crusader army. A few months later Saladin laid siege to Jerusalem, and after about a month it was taken when the inhabitants sued for terms. As opposed to the First Crusade's conduct against Muslims and Jews in Jerusalem when it fell, Saladin treated the Christians with mercy and graciousness, even though some of his advisers wanted revenge. As Man wrote regarding the taking of Jerusalem, "Islam was victorious twice over, militarily and morally."[29]

Christendom could not let this defeat stand. Another Crusade was called, the third one. This included some of the most illustrious European leaders of any Crusade, primarily the thirty-three-year-old King Richard I (the Lionheart) of England. King Philip II of France and the Holy Roman Emperor Frederick Barbarossa were also along for the ride. It was a fairly uncoordinated effort, with Frederick drowning after being thrown off his horse with all his armor in a river in Anatolia before ever reaching the Holy Land. What remained of his army soon dissolved after reaching Antioch. Philip and Richard took the city of Acre in Lebanon in 1191, after which Philip returned home. Richard guided his remaining forces down the coast of present-day Israel in order to have access to supplies via the sea, toward Jaffa, where he set up shop. Richard's and Saladin's forces skirmished every now and then, and there were a number of on-again, off-again negotiations between the two sides to come to some sort of an arrangement, as both appeared less than enthusiastic about engaging in a final pitched battle for Jerusalem. Sick, tired, and worried that his brother John (of Magna Carta fame) was stealing away with the English crown while he was gone, Richard wanted to end this, and so his and Saladin's negotiators agreed to the Treaty of Jaffa in 1192, which allowed Christian pilgrims into Jerusalem along with protection of Christian properties.[30] Richard then headed home toward a whole other set of adventures until his death in 1199, but the Third Crusade was now over. Saladin died of natural causes six months later in 1193, so historians have speculated if Richard had just remained in the area until then, it may have been possible to militarily take Jerusalem after all.

The Treaty of Jaffa did not sit well back home in Europe, so Pope Innocent III called for the Fourth Crusade (1202–1204) to do what the last one had not: take Jerusalem. This Crusade is only noteworthy because it was the most disreputable of the lot, which is saying something. The Crusaders embroiled themselves in a Byzantine succession dispute in Constantinople and then basically sacked and pillaged the city, massacring many along the way.[31] They established the Latin Kingdom of Constantinople in 1204, which lasted until 1261. They never did get to the Middle East. The irony of ironies is that this whole Crusader endeavor that originally began as an effort to protect the Byzantine Empire ended up fatally damaging it. The seat of Byzantium moved to Trebizond in Anatolia on the Black Sea coast until the Byzantines were able to retake Constantinople in 1261. But the empire had been severely weakened, and it limped along for two more centuries until the Ottomans finished it off.

The egregiously corrupt and inept Fourth Crusade did not diminish the crusading fever in Europe, although in some ways subsequent Crusades were different in form and character.[32] There were none of any particular military significance, and the last Crusader outpost in the Middle East, Acre, fell to the Mamluks in 1291.

As in any historical event that makes its way into the history books, there were plusses and minuses to the Crusades, with the latter perhaps ultimately outweighing the former. Overall, the Crusades failed in their objective of taking and keeping the Holy Land for Christendom. In attempting to do so there was a heavy price in lives paid by all, especially by unsuspecting Muslims and Jews, which pretty much undercut the stated spiritual motives of the Crusaders of whom many were much less than altruistic in their real reasons for going on Crusade. Nor did the Crusades heal the breach between Greek Orthodox and Latin Christianity; if anything, it only deepened the fracture. The Crusader movement also exacerbated already simmering hostility between Christians and Muslims, particularly with the anti-Muslim propaganda campaign in Europe (as seen in the passage from Dante on the Prophet Muhammad in chapter 2) that still infects Western perceptions of Islam and the Middle East. W. Montgomery Watt outlined this long-term effect of the Crusades, the negative image of Islam propagated in the West, by listing four common misperceptions of Islam that still persist to this day, coming to life again unfortunately in some circles after the tragic events of September 11, 2001: 1) that Islam is a false religion; 2) that it is a religion of the sword; 3) that it is a religion of self-indulgence and sexuality; and 4) that Muhammad is the anti-Christ.[33]

The beneficial aspects of the Crusades are primarily of an economic and cultural nature. Europe was exposed to Islamic high culture. The heightened contact between the Middle East and Europe enhanced commercial activities in commodities such as spices, perfumes, and textiles. European cuisine was altered for the better, which one could also say about Europe's general cleanliness, as soap was brought from the Middle East. New trade routes were established and new avenues for the exchange of ideas opened up, all of which helped fuel Europe's Renaissance and Enlightenment. Such things as improvements in shipbuilding and banking, including the use of letters of credit and bills of exchange, were all brought back by Crusaders, which helped fuel the overall economic upsurge already underway in Europe that provided, for better or worse, the foundation (ideologically and materially) for overseas expansion in coming centuries.[34] And perhaps there was a little less fighting in Europe itself, since most of its knights were busy trying to get to or around the Middle East.

In my estimation it is overall a very sad chapter in the Christian-Muslim experience, but nonetheless, it is a chapter of history. Time to turn the page.

Chapter 7 Timeline

1055	Tughril Beg establishes Seljuk rule in Baghdad
1071	Seljuks defeat Byzantine army at the Battle of Manzikert; Seljuk takeover of Jerusalem from the Fatimids
1072–1092	Rule of Seljuk Sultan Malik Shah
1096–1099	First Crusade
1144	Fall of the first Crusader state (County of Edessa) to the Muslims (Zengids)
1147–1149	Second Crusade
1157	Death of Sultan Sinjar and the collapse of Seljuk power in the Middle East
1187	Saladin captures the city of Jerusalem from Crusaders soon after defeating them at the Battle of Hattin
1189–1192	Third Crusade
1204	Fourth Crusade
1227	Death of Genghis Khan
1258	Mongols conquer Baghdad ending the Abbasid Caliphate
1260	Mamluk defeat Mongols at the battle of Ain Jalut
1291	Last Crusader outpost in Middle East, Acre, taken by Mamluks

Primary Sources

Selections from *The Muqaddimah* by Ibn Khaldun

It should be known that history, in matter of fact, is information about human social organization, which itself is identical with world civilization. It deals with such conditions affecting the nature of civilization as, for instance, savagery and sociability, group feelings, and the different ways by which one group of human beings achieves superiority over another. It deals with royal authority and the dynasties that result in this manner and with the various ranks that exist within them. Also with the different kinds of gainful occupations and ways of making a living, with the sciences and crafts that human beings pursue as part of their activities and efforts, and with all the other institutions that originate in civilization through its very nature.

Untruth naturally afflicts historical information. There are various reasons that make this unavoidable. One of them is partisanship for opinions and schools. If the soul is impartial in receiving information, it devotes to that information the share of critical investigation the information deserves, and its truth or untruth thus becomes clear. However, if the soul is infected with partisanship for a particular opinion or sect, it accepts without a moment's hesitation the information that is agreeable to it. Prejudice and partisanship obscure the critical faculty and preclude critical investigation. The result is that falsehoods are accepted and transmitted.

Another reason making untruth unavoidable in historical information is reliance upon transmitters. Investigation of this subject belongs to (the discipline) of personality criticism.[1]

Another reason is unawareness of the purpose of an event. Many a transmitter does not know the real significance of his observations or of the things he has learned about orally. He transmits the information, attributing to it the significance he assumes or imagines it to have. The result is falsehood.

Another reason is unfounded assumption as to the truth of a thing. This is frequent. It results mostly from reliance upon transmitters.

Another reason is ignorance of how conditions conform with reality. Conditions are affected by ambiguities and artificial distortions. The informant reports the conditions as he saw them, but on account of artificial distortions he himself has no true picture of them.

Another reason is the fact that people as a rule approach great and high-ranking persons with praise and encomiums. They embellish conditions and spread their fame. The information made public in such cases is not truthful. Human souls long for praise, and people pay great attention to this world and the positions and wealth it offers. As a rule, they feel no desire for virtue and have no special interest in virtuous people.

Another reason making untruth unavoidable—and this one is more powerful than all the reasons previously mentioned—is ignorance of the nature of the various conditions arising in civilization. Every event (or phenomenon), whether (it comes about in connection with some) essence or (as the result of) action, must inevitably possess a nature peculiar to its essence as well as to the accidental conditions that may attach themselves to it. If the student knows the nature of events and the circumstances and requirements in the world of existence, it will help him to distinguish truth from untruth in investigating the historical information critically. This is more effective in critical investigation than any other aspect that may be brought up in connection with it.

Students often happen to accept and transmit absurd information that, in turn, is believed on their authority. Al-Mas'ûdî, for instance, reports such a story about Alexander. Sea monsters prevented Alexander from building Alexandria. He took a wooden container in which a glass box was inserted, and dived in it to the bottom of the sea. There he drew pictures of the devilish monsters he saw. He then had metal effigies of these animals made and set them up opposite the place where building was going on. When the monsters came out and saw the effigies, they fled. Alexander was thus able to complete the building of Alexandria.

It is a long story, made up of nonsensical elements which are absurd for various reasons. Thus, (Alexander is said) to have taken a glass box and braved the sea and its waves in person. Now, rulers would not take such a risk. Any ruler who would attempt such a thing would work his own undoing and provoke the outbreak of revolt against himself and be replaced by the people with someone else. That would be his end. People would not wait one moment for him to return from the risk he is taking.

Furthermore, the jinn are not known to have specific forms and effigies. They are able to take on various forms. The story of the many heads they have is intended to indicate ugliness and frightfulness. It is not meant to be taken literally.

All this throws suspicion upon the story. Yet, the element in it that makes the story absurd for reasons based on the facts of existence is more convincing than all the other arguments. Were one to go down deep into the water, even in a box, one would have too little air for natural breathing. Because of that, one's spirit[2] would quickly become hot. Such a man would lack the cold air necessary to maintain a well-balanced humour of the lung and the vital spirit. He would perish on the spot. This is the reason why people perish in hot baths when cold air is denied to them. It also is the reason why people who go down into deep wells and dungeons perish when the air there becomes hot through putrefaction, and no winds enter those places to stir the air up. Those who go down there perish immediately. This also is why fish die when they leave the water, for the air is not sufficient for a fish to balance its lung. The fish is extremely hot, and the water to balance its humour is cold. The air into which the fish now comes is hot. Heat, thus, gains power over its animal spirit, and it perishes at once. This also is the reason for sudden death, and similar things.

Al-Mas'ûdî reports another absurd story, that of the Statue of the Starling in Rome. On a fixed day of the year, starlings gather at that statue bringing olives from which the inhabitants of Rome get their oil. How little this has to do with the natural procedure of getting oil!

Another absurd story is reported by al-Bakrî. It concerns the way the so-called Gate City was built. That city had a circumference of more than a thirty days' journey and had ten thousand gates. Now, cities are used for security and protection. Such a city, however, could not be controlled and would offer no security or protection.

Then, there is also al-Mas'ûdî's story of the "Copper City." This is said to be a city built wholly of copper in the desert of Sijilmâsah which Mûsâ b.

Nuṣayr[3] crossed on his raid against the Maghrib. The gates of this city are said to be closed. When the person who climbs its walls, in order to enter it, reaches the top, he claps his hands and throws himself down and never returns. All this is an absurd story. It belongs to the idle talk of storytellers. The desert of Sijilmâsah has been crossed by travellers and guides. They have not come across any information about such a city. All the details mentioned about it are absurd. They contradict the natural facts that apply to the building and planning of cities. Metal exists at best in quantities sufficient for utensils and furnishings. It is clearly absurd and unlikely that there would be enough to cover a city with it.

There are many similar things. Only knowledge of the nature of civilization makes critical investigation of them possible. It is the best and most reliable way to investigate historical information critically and to distinguish truth from falsehood. It is superior to investigations that rely upon criticism of the personalities of transmitters. Such personality criticism should not be resorted to until it has been ascertained whether a specific piece of information is in itself possible, or not. If it is absurd, there is no use engaging in personality criticism. Critical scholars consider absurdity inherent in the literal meaning of historical information, or an interpretation not acceptable to the intellect, as something that makes such information suspect. Personality criticism is taken into consideration only in connection with the soundness (or lack of soundness) of Muslim religious information, because this religious information mostly concerns injunctions in accordance with which the Lawgiver (Muhammad) enjoined Muslims to act whenever it can be presumed that the information is genuine. The way to achieve presumptive soundness is to ascertain the probity (*'adâlah*) and exactness of the transmitters.

On the other hand, to establish the truth and soundness of information about factual happenings, a requirement to consider is the conformity (or lack of conformity of the reported information with general conditions). Therefore, it is necessary to investigate whether it is possible that the (reported facts) could have happened. This is more important than, and has priority over, personality criticism. For the correct notion about something that ought to be can be derived only from (personality criticism), while the correct notion about something that was can be derived from (personality criticism) and external (evidence) by (checking) the conformity (of the historical report with general conditions).

If this is so, the normative method for distinguishing right from wrong in historical information on the grounds of inherent possibility or absurdity is to investigate human social organization, which is identical with civilization. We must distinguish the conditions that attach themselves to the essence of civilization as required by its very nature; the things that are accidental and cannot be counted on; and the things that cannot possibly attach themselves to it. If we do that, we shall have a normative method for distinguishing right from wrong and truth from falsehood in historical information by means of a logical demonstration that admits of no doubts. Then, whenever we hear about certain conditions occurring in civilization, we shall know what to accept and what to declare spurious. We shall have a sound yardstick with the help of which historians may find the path of truth and correctness where their reports are concerned.

1. Both Bedouins and sedentary people are natural groups

It should be known that differences of condition among people are the result of the different ways in which they make their living. Social organization enables them to cooperate toward that end and to start with the simple necessities of life, before they get to conveniences and luxuries.

Some people live by agriculture, the cultivation of vegetables and grains; others by animal husbandry, the use of sheep, cattle, goats, bees, and silkworms, for breeding and for their products. Those who live by agriculture or animal husbandry cannot avoid the call of the desert, because it alone offers the wide fields, pastures for animals, and other things that the settled areas do not offer. It is therefore necessary for them to restrict themselves to the desert. Their social organization and cooperation for the needs of life and civilization, such as food, shelter, and warmth, do not take them beyond the bare subsistence level, because of their inability (to provide) for anything beyond those (things). Subsequent improvement of their conditions and acquisition of more wealth and comfort than they need, cause them to rest and take it easy. Then, they cooperate for things beyond the bare necessities. They use more food and clothes, and take pride in them. They build large houses, and lay out towns and cities for protection. This is followed by an increase in comfort and ease, which leads to formation of the most developed luxury customs. They take the greatest pride in the preparation of food and a fine cuisine, in the use of varied splendid clothes of silk and brocade and other (fine materials), in the construction of ever higher buildings and towers, in elaborate furnishings for the buildings, and the most intensive cultivation of crafts in actuality. They build castles and mansions, provide them with running water, build their towers higher and higher, and compete in furnishing them (most elaborately). They differ in the quality of the clothes, the beds, the vessels, and the utensils they employ for their purposes. "Sedentary people" means the inhabitants of cities and countries, some of whom adopt the crafts as their way of making a living, while others adopt commerce. They earn more and live more comfortably than Bedouins, because they live on a level beyond the level of bare necessity, and their way of making a living corresponds to their wealth.

It has thus become clear that Bedouins and sedentary people are natural groups which exist by necessity, as we have stated.

2. The Bedouins are a natural group in the world

We have mentioned in the previous section that the inhabitants of the desert adopt the natural manner of making a living, namely, agriculture and animal husbandry. They restrict themselves to the necessary in food, clothing, and mode of dwelling, and to the other necessary conditions and customs. They do not possess conveniences and luxuries. They use tents of hair and wool, or houses of wood, or of clay and stone, which are not furnished (elaborately). The purpose is to have shade and shelter, and nothing beyond that. They also take shelter in caverns and caves. The food they take is either little prepared or not prepared at all, save that it may have been touched by fire.

For those who make their living through the cultivation of grain and through agriculture, it is better to be stationary than to travel around. Such, therefore, are the inhabitants of small communities, villages, and mountain regions. These people make up the large mass of the Berbers and non-Bedouins.

Those who make their living from animals requiring pasturage, such as sheep and cattle, usually travel around in order to find pasture and water for their animals, since it is better for them to move around in the land. They are called "sheepmen," that is, men who live on sheep and cattle. They do not go deep into the desert, because they would not find good pastures there. Such people include the Berbers, the Turks, the Turkomans and the Slavs, for instance.

Those who make their living by raising camels move around more. They wander deeper into the desert, because the hilly pastures with their plants and shrubs do not furnish enough subsistence for camels. They must feed on the desert shrubs and drink the salty desert water. They must move around the desert regions during the winter, in flight from the harmful cold to the warm desert air. In the desert sands, camels can find places to give birth to their young ones. Of all animals, camels have the hardest delivery and the greatest need for warmth in connection with it. (Camel nomads) are therefore forced to make excursions deep (into the desert). Frequently, too, they are driven from the hills by the militia, and they penetrate farther into the desert, because they do not want the militia to mete out justice to them or to punish them for their hostile acts. As a result, they are the most savage human beings that exist. Compared with sedentary people, they are on a level with wild, untamable animals and dumb beasts of prey. Such people are the Bedouins. In the West, the nomadic Berbers and the Zanâtah are their counterparts, and in the East, the Kurds, the Turkomans, and the Turks. The Bedouins, however, make deeper excursions into the desert and are more rooted in desert life because they live exclusively on camels, while the other groups live on sheep and cattle, as well as camels.

It has thus become clear that the Bedouins are a natural group which by necessity exists in civilization.

3. Bedouins are prior to sedentary people. The desert is the basis and reservoir of civilization and cities

We have mentioned that the Bedouins restrict themselves to the bare necessities in their way of life and are unable to go beyond them, while sedentary people concern themselves with conveniences and luxuries in their conditions and customs. The bare necessities are no doubt prior to the conveniences and luxuries. Bare necessities, in a way, are basic, and luxuries secondary. Bedouins, thus, are the basis of, and prior to, cities and sedentary people. Man seeks first the bare necessities. Only after he has obtained the bare necessities does he get to comforts and luxuries. The toughness of desert life precedes the softness of sedentary life. Therefore, urbanization is found to be the goal to which the Bedouin aspires. Through his own efforts, he achieves what he proposes to achieve in this respect. When he has obtained enough to be ready for the conditions and customs of luxury, he enters upon a life of ease and submits himself to the yoke of the city. This is the case with all Bedouin tribes. Sedentary people, on the other hand, have no desire for desert conditions, unless they are motivated by some urgent necessity or they cannot keep up with their fellow city dwellers.

Evidence for the fact that Bedouins are the basis of, and prior to, sedentary people is furnished by investigating the inhabitants of any given city. We shall find that most of its inhabitants originated among Bedouins dwelling in the country and villages of the vicinity. Such Bedouins became wealthy, settled in the city, and adopted a life of ease and luxury, such as exists in the sedentary environment.

All Bedouins and sedentary people differ also among themselves in their conditions of life. Many a clan is greater than another, many a tribe greater than another, many a city larger than another, and many a town more populous than another. . . .

4. Bedouins are closer to being good than sedentary people

The reason for this is that the soul in its first natural state of creation is ready to accept whatever good or evil may arrive and leave an imprint upon it. Muhammad said: "Every infant is born in the natural state. It is his parents who make him a Jew or a Christian or a heathen." To the degree the soul is first affected by one of the two qualities, it moves away from the other and finds it difficult to acquire it. When customs proper to goodness have been first to enter the soul of a good person, and his (soul) has thus acquired the habit of (goodness, that person) moves away from evil and finds it difficult to do anything evil. The same applies to the evil person.

Sedentary people are much concerned with all kinds of pleasures. They are accustomed to luxury and success in worldly occupations and to indulgence in worldly desires. Therefore, their souls are coloured with all kinds of blameworthy and evil qualities. The more of them they possess, the more remote do the ways and means of goodness become to them. Eventually they lose all sense of restraint. Many of them are found to use improper language in their gatherings as well as in the presence of their superiors and womenfolk. They are not deterred by any sense of restraint, because the bad custom of behaving openly in an improper manner in both words and deeds has taken hold of them. Bedouins may be as concerned with worldly affairs as (sedentary people are). However, such concern would touch only the necessities of life and not luxuries or anything causing, or calling for, desires and pleasures. The customs they follow in their mutual dealings are, therefore, appropriate. As compared with those of sedentary people, their evil ways and blameworthy qualities are much less numerous. They are closer to the first natural state and more remote from the evil habits that have been impressed upon the souls (of sedentary people) through numerous and ugly, blameworthy customs. Thus, they can more easily be cured than sedentary people. This is obvious. It will later on become clear that sedentary life constitutes the last stage of civilization and the point where it begins to decay. It also constitutes the last stage of evil and of remoteness from goodness. Clearly, the Bedouins are closer to being good than sedentary people. . . .

5. Bedouins are more disposed to courage than sedentary people

The reason for this is that sedentary people have become used to laziness and ease. They are sunk in well-being and luxury. They have entrusted the defence of their property and their lives to the governor and ruler who rules them, and to the militia which has the task of guarding them. They find full assurance of safety in the walls that surround them, and the fortifications that protect them. No noise disturbs them, and no hunting occupies their time. They are carefree and trusting, and have ceased to carry weapons. Successive generations have grown up in this way of life. They have become like women and children, who depend upon the master of the house. Eventually, this has come to be a quality of character that replaces natural disposition.

The Bedouins, on the other hand, live apart from the community. They are alone in the country and remote from militias. They have no walls or gates. Therefore, they provide their own defence and do not entrust it to, or rely upon others for it. They always carry weapons. They watch carefully all sides of the road. They take hurried naps only when they are together in company or when they are in the saddle. They pay attention to the most distant barking or noise. They go alone into the desert, guided by their fortitude, putting their trust in themselves. Fortitude has become a character quality of theirs, and courage their nature. They use it whenever they are called upon or roused by an alarm. When sedentary people mix with them in the desert or associate with them on a journey, they depend on them. They cannot do anything for themselves without them. This is an observed fact. (Their dependence extends) even to knowledge of the country, the directions, watering places, and crossroads. Man is a child of the customs and the things he has become used to. He is not the product of his natural disposition and temperament. The conditions to which he has become accustomed, until they have become for him a quality of character and matters of habit and custom, have replaced his natural disposition. If one studies this in human beings, one will find much of it, and it will be found to be a correct observation.

6. The reliance of sedentary people upon laws destroys their fortitude and power of resistance

Not everyone is master of his own affairs. Chiefs and leaders who are masters of the affairs of men are few in comparison with the rest. As a rule, man must by necessity be dominated by someone else. If the domination is kind and just and the people under it are not oppressed by its laws and restrictions, they are guided by the courage or cowardice that they possess in themselves. They are satisfied with the absence of any restraining power. Self-reliance eventually becomes a quality natural to them. They would not know anything else. If, however, the domination with its laws is one of brute force and intimidation, it breaks their fortitude and deprives them of their power of resistance as a result of the inertness that develops in the souls of the oppressed, as we shall explain.

When laws are (enforced) by means of punishment, they completely destroy fortitude, because the use of punishment against someone who cannot defend himself generates in that person a feeling of humiliation that, no doubt, must break his fortitude.

When laws are (intended to serve the purposes of) education and instruction and are applied from childhood on, they have to some degree the same effect, because people then grow up in fear and docility and consequently do not rely on their own fortitude.

Thus, greater fortitude is found among the savage Arab Bedouins than among people who are subject to laws. Furthermore, those who rely on laws and are dominated by them from the very beginning of their education and instruction in the crafts, sciences, and religious matters, are thereby deprived of much of their own fortitude. They can scarcely defend themselves at all against hostile acts. This is the case with students, whose occupation it is to study and to learn from teachers and religious leaders, and who constantly apply themselves to instruction and education in very dignified gatherings. This situation and the fact that it destroys the power of resistance and fortitude must be understood.

It is no argument that the men around Muhammad observed the religious laws, and yet did not experience any diminution of their fortitude, but possessed the greatest possible fortitude. When the Muslims got their religion from Muhammad, the restraining influence came from themselves, as a result of the encouragement and discouragement he gave them in the Qur'ân. It was not a result of technical instruction or scientific education. The laws were the laws and precepts of the religion that they received orally and which their firmly rooted belief in the truth of the articles of faith caused them to observe. Their fortitude remained unabated, and it was not corroded by education or authority. 'Umar said, "Those who are not (disciplined) by the religious law are not educated by God." 'Umar's desire was that everyone should have his restraining influence in himself His certainty was that Muhammad knew best what is good for mankind.

(The influence of) religion, then, decreased among men, and they came to use restraining laws. The religious law became a branch of learning and a craft to be acquired through instruction and education. People turned to sedentary life and assumed the character trait of submissiveness to law. This led to a decrease in their fortitude.

Clearly, then, governmental and educational laws destroy fortitude, because their restraining influence is something that comes from outside. The religious laws, on the other hand, do not destroy fortitude, because their restraining influence is something inherent. Therefore, governmental and educational laws influence sedentary people, in that they weaken their souls and diminish their stamina, because they have to suffer them both as children and as adults. The bedouins, on the other hand, are not in the same position, because they live far away from the laws of government, instruction, and education. . . .

7. Only tribes held together by group feeling can live in the desert
It should be known that God put good and evil into the nature of man. Thus, He says in the Qur'ân: "We led him along the two paths."[4] He further says: "And inspired the soul with wickedness as well as fear of God."[5]

Evil is the quality that is closest to man when he fails to improve his customs and when religion is not used as the model to improve him. The great mass of mankind is in that condition, with the exception of those to whom God gives success. Evil qualities in man are injustice and mutual aggression. He who casts his eye upon the property of his brother will lay his hand upon it to take it, unless there is a restraining influence to hold him back. The poet thus says:

Injustice is a human trait. If you find
A moral man, there is some reason why he is not unjust

Mutual aggression of people in towns and cities is averted by the authorities and the government, which hold back the masses under their control from attacks and aggression upon each other. They are thus prevented by the influence of force and governmental authority from mutual injustice, save such injustice as comes from the ruler himself.

Aggression against a city from outside may be averted by walls, in the event of unpreparedness, a surprise attack at night, or inability (of the inhabitants) to withstand the enemy during the day. Or it may be averted with the help of government auxiliary troops, if (the inhabitants are) prepared and ready to offer resistance.

The restraining influence among Bedouin tribes comes from their *shaykhs* and leaders. It results from the great respect and veneration they generally enjoy among the people. The hamlets of the Bedouins are defended against outside enemies by a tribal militia composed of noble youths of the tribe who are known for their courage. Their defence and protection are successful only if they are a closely knit group of common descent. This strengthens their stamina and makes them feared, since everybody's affection for his family and his group is more important (than anything else). Compassion and affection for one's blood relations and relatives exist in human nature as something God put into the hearts of men. It makes for mutual support and aid, and increases the fear felt by the enemy.

Those who have no one of their own lineage (to care for) rarely feel affection for their fellows. If danger is in the air on the day of battle, such a man slinks away and seeks to save himself because he is afraid of being left without support. Such people, therefore, cannot live in the desert, because they would fall prey to any nation that might want to swallow them up.

If this is true with regard to the place where one lives, which is in constant need of defence and military protection, it is equally true with regard to every other human activity, such as prophecy, the establishment of royal authority, or propaganda. Nothing can be achieved in these matters without fighting for it, since man has the natural urge to offer resistance. And for fighting one cannot do without group feeling, as we mentioned at the beginning.

---

[1] "Personality criticism" (*al-jarh wa-t-ta'dîl*) is concerned with investigating the reliability or unreliability of the transmitters of traditions. Ibn Khaldûn often has occasion to refer to it.

[2] The "vital spirit," which according to Galenic and Muslim medicine, was believed to originate in the left cavity of the heart.

[3] The great general (640–716/17 CE) who completed the conquest of the Muslim West.

[4] Qur'ân 90. 10 (10).

[5] Qur'ân 91. 8 (8).

Source: Rosenthal, Franz, trans. and N.J. Dawood, ed. Ibn Khaldun, *The Muqaddimah, an Introduction to History*. Princeton: Princeton University Press, 1967. (First Princeton/ Bollingen Paperback Printing, Fifth Printing, 1981.) Pgs. 34–38 and 91–98

Ibn Al-Athir: from *The Great History*

Account of the Outbreak of the Tartars into the Lands of Islam Under the year A.H. 617 (A.D. 1220–1221)

For some years I continued averse from mentioning this event, deeming it so horrible that I shrank from recording it, and ever withdrawing one foot as I advanced the other. To whom, indeed, can it be easy to write the announcement of the death-blow of Islam and the Muslims, or who is he on whom the remembrance thereof can weigh lightly? O would that my mother had not born me, or that I had died and become a forgotten thing ere this befell! Yet withal a number of my friends urged me to set it down in writing, and I hesitated long; but at last came to the conclusion that to omit this matter from my history J could serve no useful purpose.

I say, therefore, that this thing involves the description of the greatest catastrophe and the most dire calamity (of the like of which days and nights are innocent) which befell all men generally, and the Muslims in particular; so that, should one say that the world, since God Almighty created Adam until now, hath not been afflicted with the like thereof, he would but speak the truth. For indeed history doth not contain aught which approaches or comes nigh unto it. For of the most grievous calamities recorded was what Nebuchadnezzar inflicted on the children of Israel by his slaughter of them and his destruction of Jerusalem; and what was Jerusalem in comparison to the countries which these accursed miscreants destroyed, each city of which was double the size of Jerusalem? Or what were the children of Israel compared to those whom these slew? For verily those whom they massacred in a single city exceeded all the children of Israel. Nay, it is unlikely that mankind will see the like of this calamity, until the world comes to an end and perishes, except the final outbreak of Gog and Magog. For even Antichrist will spare such as follow him, though he destroy those who oppose him; but these [Tartars][1] spared none, slaying women and men and children, ripping open pregnant women and killing unborn babes. Verily to God do we belong, and unto Him do we return, and there is no strength and no power save in God, the High, the Almighty, in face of this catastrophe, whereof the sparks flew far and wide, and the hurt was universal; and which passed over the lands like clouds driven by the wind. For these were a people who emerged from the confines of China, and attacked the cities of Turkistan, like Kashghar and Balasaghun, and thence advanced on the cities of Transoxiana, such as Samarqand, Bukhara and the like, taking possession of them, and treating their inhabitants in such wise as we shall mention; and of them one division then passed on into Khurasan, until they had made an end of taking possession, and destroying, and slaying, and plundering, and thence passing on to Ray, Ramadan and the Highlands, and the cities contained therein, even to the limits of Iraq,[2] whence they marched on the towns of Adharbayjan and Arraniyya, destroying them and slaying most of their inhabitants, of whom none escaped save a small remnant; and all this in less than a year; this is a thing whereof the like hath not been heard. And when they had finished with Adharbayjan and Arraniyya, they passed on to Darband-i-Shirwan, and occupied its cities, none of which escaped save the fortress wherein was their King; wherefore they passed by it to the countries of the Lan and the Lakiz and the various nationalities which dwell in that region, and plundered, slew, and destroyed them to the full. And thence they made their way to the lands of Qipchaq, who are the most numerous of the Turks, and slew all such as withstood them, while the survivors fled to the fords and mountain-tops, and abandoned their country, which these Tartars overran. All this they did in the briefest space of time, remaining only for so long as their march required and no more.

Another division, distinct from that mentioned earlier, marched on Ghazna and its dependencies, and those parts of India, Sistan and Kirman which border thereon, and wrought therein deeds like unto the other, nay, yet more grievous. Now this is a thing the like of which ear hath not heard; for Alexander, concerning whom historians agree that he conquered the world, did not do so with such swiftness, but only in the space of about ten years; neither did he slay, but was satisfied that men should be subject to him. But these Tartars conquered most of the habitable globe, and the best, the most flourishing and most populous part thereof, and that whereof the inhabitants were the most advanced in character and conduct, in about a year; nor did any country escape their devastations which did not fearfully expect them and dread their arrival.

Moreover they need no commissariat, nor the conveyance of supplies, for they have with them sheep, cows, horses, and the like quadrupeds, the flesh of which they eat, [needing] naught else. As for their beasts which they ride, these dig into the earth with their hoofs and eat the roots of plants, knowing naught of barley. And so, when they alight anywhere, they have need of nothing from without. As for their religion, they worship the sun when it arises, and regard nothing as unlawful, for they eat all beasts, even dogs, pigs, and the like; nor do they recognise the marriage-tie, for several men are in marital relations with one woman, and if a child is born, it knows not who is its father.

Therefore Islam and the Muslims have been afflicted during this period with calamities wherewith no people hath been visited. These Tartars (may God confound them!) came from the East, and wrought deeds which horrify all who hear of them, and which thou shalt, please God, see set forth in full detail in their proper connection. And of these [calamities] was the invasion of Syria by the Franks (may God curse them!) out of the West, and their attack on Egypt, and occupation of the port of Damietta therein, so that Egypt and Syria were like to be conquered by them, but for the grace of God and the help which He vouchsafed us against them, as we have mentioned under the year 614 (A.D. 1217–18). Of these [calamities], moreover, was that the sword was drawn between those [of the Muslims] who escaped from these two foes, and strife was rampant [amongst them], as we have also mentioned: and verily unto God do we belong and unto Him do we return! We ask God to vouchsafe victory to Islam and the Muslims, for there is none other to aid, help, or defend the True Faith. But if God intends evil to any people, naught can avert it, nor have they any ruler save Him. As for these Tartars, their achievements were only rendered possible by the absence of any effective obstacle; and the cause of this absence was that Muhammad Khwarazmshah[3] had overrun the [Muslim] lands, slaying and destroying their Kings, so that he remained alone ruling over all these countries; wherefore, when he was defeated by the Tartars, none was left in the lands to check those or protect these, that so God might accomplish a thing which was to be done.

It is now time for us to describe how they first burst forth into the [Muslim] lands.[4]

> "Stories have been related to me," he says, "which the hearer can scarcely credit, as to the terror of them [i.e., the Mongols] which God Almighty cast into men's hearts; so that it is said that a single one of them would enter a village or a quarter wherein were many people, and would continue to slay them one after another, none daring to stretch forth his hand against this horseman. And I have heard that one of them took a man captive, but had not with him any weapon wherewith to kill him; and he said to his prisoner, 'Lay your head on the ground and do not move'; and he did so, and the Tartar went and fetched his sword and slew him therewith. Another man related to me as follows: 'I was going,' said he, 'with seventeen others along a road, and there met us a Tartar horseman, and bade us bind one another's arms. My companions began to do as he bade them, but I said to them, "He is but one man; wherefore, then, should we not kill him and flee?" They replied, "We are afraid." I said, "This man intends to kill you immediately; let

us therefore rather kill him, that perhaps God may deliver us." But I swear by God that not one of them dared to do this, so I took a knife and slew him, and we fled and escaped.' And such occurrences were many."

---

[1] They are properly called Tatar (by the Arabs), or Tatar (by the Persians). The European form was dictated by a desire to connect them with Tartarus, on account of their hellish deeds and infernal cruelty. (Tr.)
[2] Mesopotamia, or 'Iraq-i-'Arab as it is now called to distinguish it from 'Iraq-i-'A;am. (Tr.) All the place-names which precede and follow simply describe the rapid westward progress of the Mongols from northern China to western Iran.
[3] The last Muslim defender in Iran against the Mongols. At the beginning of the thirteenth century, the empire of the Khwarazmshah included nearly the whole of Persia.
[4] This was written nearly thirty years before the crowning catastrophe, to wit, the sack of Baghdad and the extinction of the Caliphate, took place; for this happened in February, 1258, while Ibn al-Athir concludes his chronicle with the year . . . 1230–31, and died two years later. Nor did he witness the horrors of which he writes, but only heard them from terrified fugitives, of whose personal narratives he records several under the year with which his chronicle closes. (Tr.)

Source: McNeill, William H. and Marilyn Robinson Waldman, eds. "Ibn al-Athir: From Great History; Account of the Outbreak of the Tartars into the Lands of Islam Under the Year A.H. 617 (A.D. 1220-1221)." *The Islamic World.* Chicago: University of Chicago Press, 1983. Pgs. 249–253. Reprinted with permission from *A Literary History of Persia* by Edward G. Browne. Cambridge: Cambridge University Press, 1902. Vol. 2, pp. 427-431.

JUVAINI: FROM *THE HISTORY OF THE WORLD CONQUEROR*

OF THE LAWS WHICH CHINGIZ-KHAN FRAMED AND THE YASAS WHICH HE PROMULGATED AFTER HIS RISE TO POWER

God Almighty in wisdom and intelligence distinguished Chingiz-Khan from all his coevals and in alertness of mind and absoluteness of power exalted him above all the kings of the world; so that all that has been recorded touching the practice of the mighty Chosroes[1] of old and all that has been written concerning the customs and usages of the Pharaohs and Caesars was by Chingiz-Khan invented from the page of his own mind without the toil of perusing records or the trouble of conforming with tradition; while all that pertains to the method of subjugating countries and relates to the crushing of the power of enemies and the raising of the station of followers was the product of his own understanding and the compilation of his own intellect. And indeed, Alexander, who was so addicted to the devising of talismans and the solving of enigmas, had he lived in the age of Chingiz-Khan, would have been his pupil in craft and cunning, and of all the talismans for the taking of strongholds he would have found none better than blindly to follow in his footsteps: whereof there can be no clearer proof nor more certain.

---

[1] Chosroes (Cyrus) Nushirwan (531–579), Persian king of Sassanian dynasty.

Source: From *The History of the World Conqueror* by 'Ala-ad-Din 'Ata-Malik Iuvaini Translated from the text of Mirza Muhammad Qazvini, trans. by John Andrew Boyle (Manchester: Manchester University Press, 1958, vol. I), pp. 23–34, 153, 159–164, 201–207.

Robert the Monk's Account of Pope Urban II's Call to Crusade

In 1095 a great council was held at Auvergne, in the city of Clermont. Pope Urban II, accompanied by cardinals and bishops, presided over it. It was made famous by the presence of many bishops and princes from France and Germany. After the council had attended to ecclesiastical matters, the pope went out into a public square, because no house was able to hold the people, and addressed them in a very persuasive speech, as follows:

> O race of Franks, O people who live beyond the mountains [that is, from Rome], O people loved and chosen by God, as is clear from your many deeds, distinguished over all other nations by the situation of your land, your catholic faith, and your regard for the holy church, we have a special message and exhortation for you. For we wish you to know what a grave matter has brought us to your country. The sad news has come from Jerusalem and Constantinople that the people of Persia, an accursed and foreign race, enemies of God, "a generation that set not their heart aright, and whose spirit was not steadfast with God" [Ps. 78:8], have invaded the lands of those Christians and devastated them with the sword, rapine, and fire. Some of the Christians they have carried away as slaves; others they have put to death. The churches they have either destroyed or turned into mosques. They desecrate and overthrow the altars. They circumcise the Christians and pour the blood from the circumcision on the altars or in the baptismal fonts. Some they kill in a horrible way by cutting open the abdomen, taking out a part of the entrails and tying them to a stake; they then beat them and compel them to walk until all their entrails are drawn out and they fall to the ground. Some they use as targets for their arrows. They compel some to stretch out their necks, and then they try to see whether they can cut off their heads with one stroke of the sword. It is better to say nothing of their horrible treatment of the women. They have taken from the Greek empire a tract of land so large that it takes more than two months to walk through it. Whose duty is it to avenge this and recover that land, if not yours? For to you more than to other nations the Lord has given the military spirit, courage, agile bodies, and the bravery to strike down those who resist you. Let your minds be stirred to bravery by the deeds of your forefathers, and by the efificiency and greatness of Charles the Great, and of Louis his son, and of the other kings who have destroyed Turkish kingdoms and established Christianity in their lands. You should be moved especially by the holy grave of our Lord and Savior which is now held by unclean peoples, and by the holy places which are treated with dishonor and irreverently befouled with their uncleanness.
>
> O bravest knights, descendants of unconquered ancestors, do not be weaker than they, but remember their courage. If you are kept back by your love for your children, relatives, and wives, remember what the Lord

> says in the Gospel: "He that loveth father or mother more than me is not worthy of me" [Matt. 10:37]; "and everyone that hath forsaken houses, or brothers, or sisters, or father, or mother, or wife, or children, or lands for my name's sake shall receive a hundredfold and shall inherit everlasting life" [Matt. 19:29]. Let no possessions keep you back, no solicitude for your property. Your land is shut in on all sides by the sea and mountains and is too thickly populated. There is not much wealth here and the soil scarcely yields enough to support you. On this account you kill and devour each other, and carry on war and mutually destroy each other. Let your hatred and quarrels cease, your civil wars come to an end, and all your dissensions stop. Set out on the road to the holy sepulcher, take the land from that wicked people and make it your own. That land which, as the scripture says, is flowing with milk and honey, God gave to the children of Israel. Jerusalem is the best of all lands, more fruitful than all others, as it were a second paradise of delights. This land our Savior made illustrious by his birth, beautiful with his life, and sacred with his sufifering; he redeemed it with his death and glorified it with his tomb. This royal city is now held captive by her enemies, and made pagan by those who know not God. She asks and longs to be liberated and does not cease to beg you to come to her aid. She asks aid especially from you because, as I have said, God has given more of the military spirit to you than to other nations. Set out on this journey and you will obtain the remission of your sins and be sure of the incorruptible glory of the kingdom of heaven.

When Pope Urban had said this and much more of the same sort, all who were present were moved to cry out with one accord, "It is the will of God, it is the will of God." When the pope heard this he raised his eyes to heaven and gave thanks to God, and, commanding silence with a gesture of his hand, he said: "My dear brethren, today there is fulfilled in you that which the Lord says in the Gospel, 'Where two or three are gathered together in my name, there I am in the midst' [Matt. 18:20]. For unless the Lord God had been in your minds you would not all have said the same thing. For although you spoke with many voices, nevertheless, it was one and the same thing that made you speak. So I say unto you, God, who put those words into your hearts, has caused you to utter them. Therefore let these words be your battle cry, because God caused you to speak them. Whenever you meet the enemy in battle, you shall all cry out, 'It is the will of God, it is the will of God.' And we do not command the old or weak to go, or those who cannot bear arms. No women shall go without their husbands, or brothers, or proper companions, for such would be a hindrance rather than a help, a burden rather than an advantage. Let the rich aid the poor and equip them for fighting and take them with them. Clergymen shall not go without the consent of their bishop, for otherwise the journey would be of no value to them. Nor will this pilgrimage be of any benefit to a layman if he goes without the blessing of his priest. Whoever therefore shall determine to make this journey and shall make a vow to God and shall offer himself as a living sacrifice, holy, acceptable to God [Rom. 12:1], shall wear a cross on his brow or on his breast. And when he returns after having fulfilled his vow he shall wear the cross on his back. In this way he will obey the command of the Lord, 'Whosoever doth not bear his cross and come after me is not worthy of me'" [Luke 14:27].

When these things had been done, while all prostrated themselves on the earth and beat their breasts, one of the cardinals, named Gregory, made confession for them, and they were given absolution for all their sins. After the absolution, they received the benediction and permission to go home.

Source: "Urban II's Call for a Crusade," (pp. 35–7) in *The Crusades: A Reader*, 2nd edition, edited by S.J. Allen and Emilie Amt, © University of Toronto Press 2014. Reprinted with permission of the publisher.

Ibn al-Athir, X, 185–190, 193–195

THE FRANKS SEIZE ANTIOCH (IBN AL-ATHĪR, X, 185–8)

The power of the Franks first became apparent when in the year 478/1085–86 they invaded the territories of Islām and took Toledo and other parts of Andalusia, as was mentioned earlier. Then in 484/1091 they attacked and conquered the island of Sicily[1] and turned their attention to the African coast. Certain of their conquests there were won back again hut they had other successes, as you will see.

In 490/1097 the Franks attacked Syria. This is how it all began: Baldwin, their King,[2] a kinsman of Roger the Frank who had conquered Sicily, assembled a great army and sent word to Roger saying: "I have assembled a great army and now I am on my way to you, to use your bases for my conquest of the African coast. Thus you and I shall become neighbours."

Roger called together his companions and consulted them about these proposals. "This will be a line thing both for them and for us!" they declared, "for by this means these lands will be converted to the Faith!" At this Roger raised one leg and farted loudly, and swore that it was of more use than their advice.[3] "Why?" "Because if this army comes here it will need quantities of provisions and fleets of ships to transport it to Africa, as well as reinforcements from my own troops. Then, if the Franks succeed in conquering this territory they will take it over and will need provisioning from Sicily. This will cost me my annual profit from the harvest. If they fail they will return here and be an embarrassment to me here in my own domain. As well as all this Tamīm[4] will say that I have broken faith with him and violated our treaty, and friendly relations and communications between us will be disrupted. As far as we are concerned, Africa is always there. When we are strong enough we will take it."

He summoned Baldwin's messenger and said to him: "If you have decided to make war on the Muslims your best course will be to free Jerusalem from their rule and thereby win great honour. I am bound by certain promises and treaties of allegiance with the rulers of Africa." So the Franks made ready and set out to attack Syria.

Another story is that the Fatimids of Egypt were afraid when they saw the Seljuqids extending their empire through Syria as far as Gaza, until they reached the Egyptian border and Atsiz[5] invaded Egypt itself. They therefore sent to invite the Franks to invade Syria and so protect Egypt from the Muslims.[6] But God knows best.

When the Franks decided to attack Syria they marched east to Constantinople, so that they could cross the straits and advance into Muslim territory by the easier, land route. When they reached Constantinople, the Emperor of the East refused them permission to pass through his domains. He said: "Unless you first promise me Antioch, I shall not allow you to cross into the Muslim empire." His real intention was to incite them to attack the Muslims, for he was convinced that the Turks, whose invincible control over Asia Minor he had observed, would exterminate every one of them. They accepted his conditions and in 490/1097 they crossed the Bosphorus at Constantinople. Iconium and the rest of the area into which they now advanced belonged to Qilij Arslān ibn Sulaimān ibn Qutlumísh, who barred their way with his troops. They broke through[7] in rajab 490/July 1097, crossed Cilicia,[8] and finally reached Antioch, which they besieged.

When Yaghi Siyān, the ruler of Antioch, heard of their approach, he was not sure how the Christian people of the city would react, so he made the Muslims go outside the city on their own to dig trenches, and the next day sent the Christians out alone to continue the task. When they were ready to return home at the end of the day he refused to allow them. "Antioch is yours," he said, "but you will have to leave it to me until I see what happens between us and the Franks." "Who will protect our children and our wives?" they said. "I shall look after them for you." So they resigned themselves to their fate, and lived in the Frankish camp for nine months, while the city was under siege.

Yaghi Siyān showed unparalleled courage and wisdom, strength and judgment. If all the Franks who died had survived they would have overrun all the lands of Islam. He protected the families of the Christians in Antioch and would not allow a hair of their heads to be touched.

After the siege had been going on for a long time the Franks made a deal with one of the men who were responsible for the towers. He was a cuirass-maker called Ruzbih[9] whom they bribed with a fortune in money and lands. He worked in the tower that stood over the river-bed, where the river flowed out of the city into the valley. The Franks sealed their pact with the cuirass-maker, God damn him! and made their way to the water-gate. They opened it and entered the city. Another gang of them climbed the tower with ropes. At dawn, when more than five hundred of them were in the city and the defenders were worn out after the night watch, they sounded their trumpets. Yaghi Siyān woke up and asked what the noise meant. He was told that trumpets had sounded from the citadel and that it must have been taken. In fact the sound came not from the citadel but from the tower. Panic seized Yaghi Siyān and he opened the city gates and fled in terror, with an escort of thirty pages. His army commander arrived, but when he discovered on enquiry that Yaghi Siyān had fled, he made his escape by another gate. This was of great help to the Franks, for if he had stood firm for an hour, they would have been wiped out. They entered the city by the gates and sacked it, slaughtering all the Muslims they found there. This happened in jumada I (491/April/May 1098).[10] As for Yaghi Siyān, when the sun rose he recovered his self control and realized that his flight had taken him several *farshakh*[11] from the city. He asked his companions where he was, and on hearing that he was four *farsakh* from Antioch he repented of having rushed to safety instead of staying to fight to the death. He began to groan and weep for his desertion of his household and children. Overcome by the violence of his grief he fell fainting from his horse. His companions tried to lift him back into the saddle, but they could not get him to sit up, and so left him for dead while they escaped. He was at his last gasp when an Armenian shepherd came past, killed him, cut off his head and took it to the Franks at Antioch.

The Franks had written to the rulers of Aleppo and Damascus to say that they had no interest in any cities hut those that had once belonged to Byzantium. This was a piece of deceit calculated to dissuade these rulers from going to the help of Antioch.

THE MUSLIM ATTACK ON THE FRANKS, AND ITS RESULTS (IBN AL-ATHĪR, X, 188–90)

When Qawām ad-Daula Kerbuqā[12] heard that the Franks had taken Antioch he mustered his army and advanced into Syria, where he camped at Marj Dabiq. All the Turkish and Arab forces in Syria rallied to him except for the army from Aleppo. Among his supporters were Duqāq ibn Tutūsh,[13] the Atabeg Tughtikīn, Janāh ad-Daula of Hims, Arslān Tash of Sanjār, Sulaimān ibn Artūq and other less important amīrs. When the Franks heard of this they were alarmed and afraid, for their troops were weak and short of food. The Muslims advanced and came face to face with the Franks in front of Antioch. Kerbuqā, thinking that the present crisis would force the Muslims to remain loyal to him, alienated them by his pride and ill-treatment of them. They plotted in secret anger to betray him and desert him in the heat of battle.

After taking Antioch the Franks camped there for twelve days without food. The wealthy ate their horses and the poor ate carrion and leaves from the trees. Their leaders, faced with this situation, wrote to Kerbuqā to ask for safe-conduct through his territory hut he refused, saying "You will have to fight your way out." Among the Frankish leaders were Baldwin,[14] Saint-Gilles, Godfrey of Bouillon, the future Count of Edessa, and their leader Bohemond of Antioch. There was also a holy man who had great influence over them, a man of low cunning, who proclaimed that the Messiah had a lance buried in the Qusyān, a great building in Antioch:[15] "And if you find it you will he victorious and if you fail you will surely die." Before saying this he had buried a lance in a certain spot and concealed all trace of it. He exhorted them to fast and repent for three days, and on the fourth day he led them all to the spot with their soldiers and workmen, who dug everywhere and found the lance as he had told them.[16] Whereupon he cried "Rejoice! For victory is secure." So on the fifth day they left the city in groups of five or six. The Muslims said to Kerbuqā: "You should go up to the city and kill them one by one as they come out; it is easy to pick them off now that they have split up." He replied: "No, wait until they have all come out and then we will kill them." He would not allow them to attack the enemy and when some Muslims killed a group of Franks, he went himself to forbid such behaviour and prevent its recurrence. When all the Franks had come out and not one was left in Antioch, they began to attack strongly, and the Muslims turned and fled. This was Kerbuqā's fault, first because he had treated the Muslims with such contempt and scorn, and second because he had prevented their killing the Franks. The Muslims were completely routed without striking a single blow or firing a single arrow. The last to flee were Suqmān ibn Artūq and Janāh ad-Daula, who had been sent to set an ambush. Kerbuqā escaped with them. When the Franks saw this they were afraid that a trap was being set for them, for there had not even been any fighting to flee from, so they dared not follow them. The only Muslims to stand firm were a detachment of warriors from the Holy Land, who fought to acquire merit in God's eyes and to seek martyrdom. The Franks killed them by the thousand and stripped their camp of food and possessions, equipment, horses and arms, with which they re-equipped themselves.

THE FRANKS TAKE MA'ARRAT AN-NU'MĀN (IBN AL-ATHĪR, X, 190)

After dealing this blow to the Muslims the Franks marched on Ma'arrat an-Nu'mān and besieged it. The inhabitants valiantly defended their city. When the Franks realized the fierce determination and devotion of the defenders they built a wooden tower as high as the city wall and fought from the top of it, but failed to do the Muslims any serious harm. One night a few Muslims were seized with panic and in their demoralized state thought that if they barricaded themselves into one of the town's largest buildings they would be in a better position to defend themselves, so they climbed down from the wall and abandoned the position they were defending. Others saw them and followed their example, leaving another stretch of wall undefended, and gradually, as one group followed another, the whole wall was left unprotected and the Franks scaled it with ladders. Their appearance in the city terrified the Muslims, who shut themselves up in their houses. For three days the slaughter never stopped; the Franks killed more than 100,000 men and took innumerable prisoners. After taking the town the Franks spent six weeks shut up there, then sent an expedition to 'Arqa, which they besieged for four months. Although they breached the wall in many places they failed to storm it. Munqidh, the ruler of Shaizar, made a treaty with them about 'Arqa and they left it to pass on to Hims. Here too the ruler Janāh ad-Daula made a treaty with them, and they advanced to Acre by way of an-Nawaqir. However they did not succeed in taking Acre.

THE FRANKS CONQUER JERUSALEM (IBN AL-ATHĪR, X, 193–95)

Taj ad-Daula Tutūsh[17] was the Lord of Jerusalem hut had given it as a feoff to the amīr Suqmān ibn Artūq the Turcoman. When the Franks defeated the Turks at Antioch the massacre demoralized them, and the Egyptians, who saw that the Turkish armies were being weakened by desertion, besieged Jerusalem under the command of al-Afdal ibn Badr al-Jamali.[18] Inside the city were Artūq's sons, Suqmān and Ilghazi, their cousin Sunii and their nephew Yaquti. The Egyptians brought more than forty siege engines to attack Jerusalem and broke down the walls at several points. The inhabitants put up a defence, and the siege and fighting went on for more than six weeks. In the end the Egyptians forced the city to capitulate, in sha'bān 489/August 1096.[19] Suqmān, Ilghazi and their friends were well treated by al-Afdal, who gave them large gifts of money and let them go free. They made for Damascus and then crossed the Euphrates. Suqmān settled in Edessa and Ilghazi went on into Iraq. The Egyptian governor of Jerusalem was a certain Iftikhār ad-Daula, who was still there at the time of which we are speaking.

After their vain attempt to take Acre by siege, the Franks moved on to Jerusalem and besieged it for more than six weeks. They built two towers, one of which, near Sion, the Muslims burnt down, killing everyone inside it. It had scarcely ceased to burn before a messenger arrived to ask for help and to bring the news that the other side of the city had fallen. In fact Jerusalem was taken from the north on the morning of Friday 22 sha'bān 492/15 July 1099. The population was put to the sword by the Franks, who pillaged the area for a week. A band of Muslims barricaded themselves into the Oratory of David and fought on for several days. They were granted their lives in return for surrendering. The Franks honoured their word, and the group left by night for Ascalon. In the Masjid al-Aqsa the Franks slaughtered more than 70,000 people, among them a large number of Imams and Muslim scholars, devout and ascetic men who had left their homelands to live lives of pious seclusion in the Holy Place. The Franks stripped the Dome of the Rock of more than forty silver candelabra, each of them weighing 3,600 drams, and a great silver lamp weighing forty-four Syrian pounds, as well as a hundred and fifty smaller silver candelabra and more than twenty gold ones, and a great deal more booty. Refugees from Syria reached Baghdād in ramadan, among them the qadi Abu Sa'd al-Hárawi. They told the Caliph's ministers a story that wrung their hearts and brought tears to their eyes. On Friday they went to the Cathedral Mosque and begged for help, weeping so that their hearers wept with them as they described the sufferings of the Muslims in that Holy City: the men killed, the women and children taken prisoner, the homes pillaged. Because of the terrible hardships they had suffered, they were allowed to break the fast.

---

[1] This date clearly refers to the end of the Norman conquest.

[2] This Baldwin (*Bardawīl*) is a mythical character, compounded of the various Baldwins of Flanders and Jerusalem; or else the first Baldwin is mistakenly thought to have been already a king in the West.

[3] It is disagreeable to find the great Count acting like a barbarian on the very first page, but the passage is characteristic of the contemptuous crudity with which the Muslims usually spoke of their enemies, as well as giving a fairly accurate picture of Roger's political acumen.

[4] The Zirid amīr of Tunisia Tamīm ibn Mu'ízz.
[5] A general of the Seljuqid Sultan Malikshāh, who in 1076 attacked Egypt from Palestine.
[6] The Fatimids were also Muslims, but they were heretics and so opposed to the rest of *sunni* Islām.
[7] At Dorylaeum.
[8] Literally "the land of the son of Armenus," as the Arab writers call the Lesser Armenia of the Cilician Roupenians.
[9] *Firūz* is an alternative reading.
[10] June 3 according to European sources.
[11] One *farsakh* (parasang) is about four miles.
[12] The Turkish amīr of Mosul.
[13] The Seljuqid Lord of Damascus, soon to be succeeded by his general, the Ata-beg Tughtikīn, whose name comes next on the list and who was to be one of the most active and tenacious opponents of the Crusades during this first phase of conquest.
[14] Baldwin of LeBourg, later Baldwin II.
[15] The Church of St. Peter in Antioch, called in Byzantine sources *Κασσινός* and in Arabic sources *Qusyān*, from the name of the man whose son was raised from the dead by St. Peter.
[16] The Finding of the Sacred Lance, at the instigation of Peter Bartholomew, seen through rationalistic Muslim eyes.
[17] A Syrian Seljuqid, Malikshāh's brother.
[18] The Fatimid vizir.
[19] If this date were correct the connection with the fall of Antioch would no longer exist. In fact the date given here is wrong: the Egyptians took Jerusalem in August 1098.

Source: Francesco Gabrieli, "Ibn al-Athir, X, 185–190, 193–195." In *Arab Historians of the Crusades* (Berkeley: University of California Press, 1969), pp. 3–11.

"Imad al-Din al-Asfahani relays Salah al-Din"

Ṣalāḥ al-Dīn, *he wrote*, invited the king to sit beside him, and when Arnat entered in his turn, he seated him next to his king and reminded him of his misdeeds: "How many times have you sworn an oath and then violated it? How many times have you signed agreements that you have never respected?" Arnat answered through an interpreter: "Kings have always acted thus. I did nothing more." During this time, Guy was gasping with thirst, his head dangling as though he were drunk, his face betraying great fright. Ṣalāḥ al-Dīn spoke reassuring words to him, had cold water brought, and offered it to him. The king drank, then handed what remained to Arnat, who slaked his thirst in turn. The sultan then said to Guy: "You did not ask my permission before giving him water. I am therefore not obliged to grant him mercy."

After pronouncing these words, the sultan smiled, mounted his horse, and rode off, leaving his captives in terror. He supervised the return of the troops, then came back to his tent. He ordered Arnat brought there, advanced towards him, sword in hand, and struck him between the neck and shoulder-blade. When Arnat fell, he cut off his head and dragged the body by its feet to the king, who began to tremble. Seeing him thus upset, the sultan said to him in a reassuring tone: "This man was killed only because of his maleficence and his perfidy."

Source: Amin Maalouf, "Imad al-Din al-Asfahani relays Salah al-Din." In *The Crusade Through Arab Eyes* (London: Al Saqi Books, 1984), pp. 193, 194.

NOTES

1. Roy P. Mottahedeh, *Loyalty and Leadership in an Early Islamic Society* (Princeton, NJ: Princeton University Press, 1980), pp. 23–24.
2. See A. K. S. Lambton, "The Internal Structure of the Seljuq Empire," in *The Cambridge History of Iran*, Vol. 5 (Cambridge: Cambridge University Press, 1968); and P. M. Holt, *The Age of the Crusades: The Near East from the Eleventh Century to 1517* (New York: Longman, 1986), pp. 67–81.
3. For more on the Assassins, see Marshall G. S. Hodgson, *The Order of the Assassins* (The Hague: Mouton & Co., 1955); Bernard Lewis, *The Assassins* (Oxford: Oxford University Press, 1967); and on Alamut and other castles of the Assassins, see Peter Wiley, *The Castles of the Assassins* (London: George G. Harrap & Co., 1963).
4. Often the word "Mongols" was used interchangeably with "Tatars," who are altogether separate although close geographically, and many of them were taken into Mongol ranks in the army and governing structures.
5. David Morgan, *The Mongols* (New York: Basil Blackwell, 1986), p. 55.
6. Jack Weatherford, *Genghis Khan and the Making of the Modern World* (New York: Three Rivers Press, 2004), p. xviii.
7. John K. Fairbanks, Edwin O. Reischauer, and Albert M. Craig, *East Asia: Tradition and Transformation* (Boston: Houghton Mifflin Company, 1973), p. 164.
8. David W. Tschanz, "History's Hinge: Ain Jalut," *Aramco World* 58, no. 4 (July/August 2007), pp. 24-33.
9. There are many different versions on how the Abbasid caliph died. Various accounts have him being put to death by starvation, by the sword at the hand of Hulegu himself, having had molten gold poured down his throat, or rolled in a carpet and trampled to death. Nassima Neggaz argues that "the accounts are replete with symbolism targeting their specific audiences, and that the choices made by the historians on the manner of the Caliph's death were meant to offer commentaries on—and evaluation of—Abbasid rule." Most contemporary descriptions point to the rolled-up-in-a-carpet version, but these are largely Arab and Persian (and anti-Mongol) accounts meant to preserve the dignity and martyrdom aspect of the Abbasid caliph. As the story goes, it was traditional and based on superstition not to shed the blood of royalty—and certainly not a caliph—because it could lead to some calamity against the perpetrator, such as an earthquake. The other accounts tend to be more pro-Mongol and were chronicled mostly by Armenian and Georgian sources (and one notable Persian source) that were later picked up and embellished as anti-Islamic propaganda in the West. These accounts tend to focus on suitable punishment (starvation, molten gold) for the corruption and greed of the Abbasid caliph, and was a way to humiliate him. Death by Hulegu's sword has been seen as both pro and anti-Abbasid caliph (depending on how dignified he died) and in either case depicting the cruelty of the Mongols. As we saw with the Caliph

Uthman, the story of how a caliph died often had little to do with reality and more with perception and creating social memory. See Nassima Neggaz, "The Many Deaths of the Last Abbasid Caliph al-Musta'sim bi-Ilah (d. 1258)," *Journal of the Royal Asiatic Society* (August 18, 2020), pp. 585-612.

10. Weatherford, *Genghis Khan*, p. 247.
11. The Golden Horde was also known as the *Dasht-i-Kipchak*, the westernmost portion of the Mongol Empire. Justin Marozzi, *Tamerlane: Sword of Islam, Conqueror of the World* (Cambridge, MA: De Capo Press, 2004), pp. 72–75.
12. Weatherford, *Genghis Khan*, p. xxvi.
13. Ibid., p. 69.
14. Ibid., p. 201.
15. Ibid., p. 70.
16. Ibid., p. 234.
17. Peter Jackson, *The Mongols & the Islamic World* (New Haven, CT: Yale University Press, 2017), p. 5.
18. Ibid., p. 6.
19. Morgan, *The Mongols*, pp. 79–82.
20. Garth Fowden, *Before and After Muhammad: The First Millennium Refocused* (Princeton, NJ: Princeton University Press, 2014), p. 2.
21. As quoted in James A. Brundage, *The Crusades: A Documentary Survey* (Milwaukee: Marquette University Press, 1962), p. 18. It is taken from the recorded account by Robert the Monk, *Historia Hierosolimitana.*
22. Thomas F. Madden, *The New Concise History of the Crusades* (New York: Rowan and Littlefield Publishers, 2006), p. 9.
23. As quoted in Madden, *New Concise History*, p. 9.
24. If you visit museums in Europe and view medieval paintings of the crucifixion, the Roman soldiers are sometimes replaced by soldiers wearing the turbans of a Muslim, which only fired that much more the passions against Muslims.
25. Madden, *New Concise History*, p. 6.
26. Afaf Lutfi Al-Sayyid Marsot, *A History of Egypt: From the Arab Conquest to the Present* (Cambridge: Cambridge University Press, 2007), p. 23.
27. John Man, *Saladin: The Sultan Who Vanquished the Crusaders and Built an Islamic Empire* (New York: De Capo Press, 2016), p. 61.
28. Ibid., p. 71.
29. Ibid., p. 181.
30. Ibid., p. 223.
31. See Brenda Skalcup, *The Crusades* (San Diego: Greenhaven Press, 2000), pp. 32–34.
32. For instance, the so-called—and misnamed—Children's Crusade in 1212 was made up primarily of commoners and clergy, not warriors, in an attempt to get back to the pristine, religious and spiritual motives of Crusade. Like many other Crusader efforts, it never made it to the Holy Land. (See Madden, *New Concise History*, pp. 136–138.)

33. W. Montgomery Watt, *The Influence of Islam on Medieval Europe* (Edinburgh: Edinburgh University Press, 1994), p. 73.
34. For instance, one of the primary objectives for Christopher Columbus was to discover new routes and find new mines of gold that would enable Europe to generate another Crusade to take Jerusalem. Skalcup, *The Crusades*, p. 183.

KEY TERMS

Assassins p. 163 iqta p. 158 wazirs p. 160

For additional digital learning resources please go to www.oup.com/he/lesch-middleeast-1e

8 IN THE WAKE OF THE MONGOLS

The Mamluks

There were a number of dynasties across the Eurasian landmass that filled the voids created by the disintegration of the Mongol Empire toward the end of the thirteenth century. Many of them were still Mongol and Turkish, some of whom sought to recapture the power and grandeur of Genghis Khan. Most did not, and they became footnotes of history, becoming known more as precursors to other dynasties that enjoyed more long-term success. Because we are geographically limiting ourselves to the Middle East in this volume, I will focus on three important empires that did so much to transition the area from the medieval period to the modern: the Mamluks and Ottomans, who emerged roughly contemporaneously in the middle to late thirteenth century and who were charter members of the third stage of the rise of the Turco-Mongolian peoples discussed in the last chapter, and then later the Safavids, who forever altered Iranian history when they came to power in the early sixteenth century.

We have already encountered the Mamluks at the battle of Ayn Jalut in 1260, where they defeated the Mongol forces of Hulegu. Even though Mamluk warrior chiefs had established themselves as the real rulers in Cairo upon the disintegration of the Ayyubid dynasty and the assassination of the last Ayyubid ruler, Turanshah, in 1250, the legitimacy acquired by defeating the Mongols at Ayn Jalut in many ways birthed the Mamluk Empire. Mamluks had been continually brought into the Middle East since the ninth century. These were warriors captured or purchased, usually from the fringes of the Abbasid Empire, and most of them were Turkish. Mamluks were often recruited from the Black Sea area slave markets, signed up by an agent of a general or officer, and then transported to Egypt, usually by Christian Italian merchants.[1] Their masters trained them, mostly as cavalry; converted them to Islam; and often manumitted them after a certain amount of time and service. After being freed, these former slaves would then recruit more mamluks, and so the cycle was self-perpetuating, creating a kind of "slave oligarchy that lasted for centuries."[2] Mamluks tended to belong and remain loyal to the houses and families they served, until they might form a household of their own over time. We have seen some of them already rise to great heights in Abbasid times as amir al-umaras, as kingmakers, or as the de facto ruler of Egypt in the person of Ahmad ibn Tulun and the Tulunid dynasty in the ninth and tenth centuries. Even when other groups from the outside and different ethnicities ruled over Egypt (and Syria), such as the Berber-based Fatimids or the Kurdish-Arab Ayyubid dynasty, Turkish mamluk warriors and mamluk houses remained, and they usually played an important role in political and military affairs. They would continue to do so in Egypt long past the expiration date of the Mamluk Empire in 1517.

To say that the Mamluk **sultans**—the rulers—were chosen in a way akin to *Game of Thrones* would be an understatement. It was typically regicidal, where the most common word to describe the succession of one Mamluk sultan to the next would be "usurpation." The machinations and maneuvering of mamluks and their houses against each other was a constant. A few Mamluk sultans were able to acquire legitimate authority and enjoy relatively long reigns, even to the point of establishing a short-term hereditary dynasty by arranging for their sons to succeed them. But most of the sultans were viewed by other leading Mamluks, referred to as "magnates" by historian P. M. Holt, as firsts among equals rather than some semidivine figure from whom one should keep his distance. Holt describes them as often playing the role of an "electoral college" in choosing the next sultan.[3] The sultans had to earn their keep, which usually meant—especially in the earlier stages of the Mamluk Empire—showing a high level of military aptitude, political cleverness, and ruthlessness when necessary. The Mamluk Empire is usually divided into

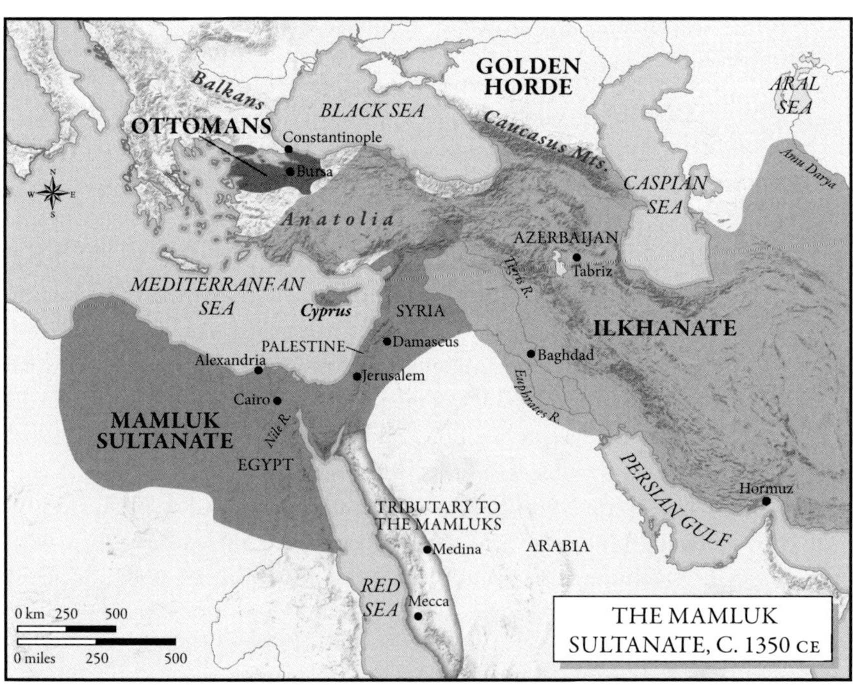

THE MAMLUK SULTANATE, C. 1350 CE

two periods reflecting the different ethnic origin of those in power. The first group was the so-called *Bahri* or River Mamluks who ruled from 1250 to 1382 (their main barracks was located on an island in the Nile River). The second is the *Burji* or Citadel Mamluks, who ruled from 1382 to the fall of the empire at the hands of the Ottomans in 1517. The Bahri Mamluks were mostly Turkish, whereas the Burji Mamluks were predominantly Circassian. Many of them never bothered to learn Arabic and often remained separate from the indigenous population.

When examining the origins of the Mamluk Empire one has to focus on Baybars al-Bunduqdari, a Kipchak from the Ural mountains, who became the most famous and consequential of all the sultans; when one travels in Egypt and the Levant, one hears about (and sees in the form of architectural evidence) the exploits and achievements of Baybars just as much as, if not more than, Saladin. He was a mountain of a man about whom the populace wrote stories and sang songs for centuries. He is the one who really established the empire after having played a prominent role leading the Mamluks to victory at Ayn Jalut. Baybars had also played a role earlier in the assassination of Turanshah, the last Ayyubid leader, which brought the Bahri Mamluks to power under its first sultan, al-Muzaffar Qutuz. Qutuz and Baybars simply could not exist in the same power spectrum for too long, especially with the increasing popularity of Baybars after Ayn Jalut. Not too long after the battle, Baybars and some of his mamluks murdered Qutuz outside of Cairo on the latter's return from a hunting expedition. This set an unsavory precedent of succession in the Mamluk Empire that would be repeated often.

As with many a dynasty and empire before him, Baybars was intent on controlling Syria. Ironically, the Mongols did the Mamluks something of a favor by occupying much of Syria before Ayn Jalut, therefore weakening potential Ayyubid and other forms of opposition that Baybars most likely would have encountered. After Ayn Jalut, Syria essentially fell into his lap, although as with the Fatimids before him controlling it was easier said than done. It would remain an irritant to Baybars and most of his Mamluk successors; for the remainder of Baybars's rule his primary foreign policy preoccupations centered on keeping the Ilkanate Mongols of Hulegu at bay while also trying to further reduce the Crusader presence along the coast. In 1271 he was able to take the mightiest Crusader castle, Crac de Chevaliers, in Syria, leaving the Crusaders but a couple of coastal cities in present-day Lebanon. Internally, Baybars consolidated power and developed a centralized state that long outlasted him, and he established an oligarchic regime that set the pattern of political life, with competing Mamluk magnates proceeding to develop their own corps of imported military slaves (i.e., their own mamluk households).[4] Because the Mongols were just about everywhere else in the Middle East, Mamluk Egypt in many ways became the center of Islamic civilization for a time.[5]

As we know from the last chapter, the Mongols had killed the Abbasid caliph in Baghdad in 1258. A few members of the family were able to escape the carnage and one found his way to Cairo, where Baybars installed him as Caliph al-Mustansir in 1261, and the Mamluk sultan gave him *baya* or an oath of allegiance. We have seen previously with the Buyids and the Seljuks that keeping the Abbasid caliph around had its benefits, especially in conferring religious legitimacy and political authority to those who were outsiders. In turn, the caliph recognized and invested Baybars not only with Egypt and Syria but much of the rest of the Middle East, as the "universal sultan of Islam" and the "universal deputy of the universal caliph."[6] The Abbasid caliph had only nominal power, and the position would remain in Cairo until the Ottoman conquest in 1517.

Baybars died in Damascus in 1277—some say by natural causes, others that he was poisoned. He had attempted to set up a hereditary monarchy of sorts. But as typically happened, the son of the previous sultan was too young and inexperienced to take on more powerful Mamluk magnates, even within his father's own household. By 1279, one of those mamluks who has worked his way up the ranks, Qalavun (Kalavun), was able to push aside the young sultan with the help of the mamluks of his household. It was quite the game of chess to position your own mamluks in important roles in order to facilitate one's rise to the top, and Qalavun played the game well. He often pitted the mamluks of the new household against older mamluk households associated with former sultans and magnates. One of the most important occurrences during Qalavun's rule was that he recruited a different ethnic group of mamluks from the Caucasus region: Circassians from the east coast of the Black Sea region. Perhaps the Sultan wanted to build up an outside force only loyal to him and his household. They were housed in the barracks of the Citadel of Cairo, the location of the Sultan and center of government; therefore, these Circassians became known as the *Burji* or Citadel Mamluks. They would continue to play an important role in Mamluk politics to the point where they would eventually usurp the power of the Bahri Mamluks altogether.

Qalavun died in 1291 while the Mamluks were campaigning to rid the Middle East of the last vestiges of the Crusader presence. His son, who took the name of al-Malik al-Ashraf (also known as al-Ashraf Khalil), continued on and saw the final Crusader city, Acre, fall later in the same year. Sultan Malik was not considered a very apt or strong leader—even his own father doubted his abilities. As such, for the most part he became a powerless pawn in the hands of Mamluk magnates. Malik al-Ashraf was murdered by mamluks from another household, and the magnates eventually agreed on the next Qalavunid sultan from their lot, al-Nasir Muhammad, who succeeded at about the age of nine.

It is indicative of the Mamluk saga that al-Nasir Muhammad ruled from 1293 to 1341, with a couple of periods during his long reign where he was forced out. The constantly competing Mamluk households, especially when the Sultan was young, removed al-Nasir from office yet also allowed him the opportunity to return to power—twice. In doing so, however, and managing not to get himself killed, al-Nasir successfully learned the game. He was eventually able to surround himself with a loyal group of mamluks and rule as an autocrat for the last thirty years or so of his reign. The fact that both the Crusader and Mongol threat had receded considerably allowed him to focus on the internal affairs of the empire; he spent very little time on campaign in Syria, which had been a hallmark of previous sultans.[7] Due to this stability, in the manner of the Fatimids, it is during this time that the Mamluk Empire really began to enjoy the fruits of the Egyptian economy and of its strategic positioning in the Mediterranean for commercial activity and as a transit point toward the Indian Ocean.

The societal momentum of this period lasted for forty years after Qalavun's death in 1341; however, bereft of the political authority al-Nasir accumulated as well as his political acumen, the game of thrones of the magnates once again foisted itself onto the course of events. During those forty years there were twelve different sultans, a clear indication of political infighting and the inability of the Bahri Mamluks to solidify their power. Waiting in the wings were the Burji Mamluks, ready to pounce on an opportunity at the right time and behind the right leader. This they found in the person of Barquq, who like many who had preceded him had worked his way into position carefully and ruthlessly. In 1382 he was able to push aside a nine-year-old sultan and assume the position himself with the concurrence of the other Mamluk magnates, thus beginning the reign of the Burji Mamluks, which lasted to the end in 1517. Like most of the more successful Mamluk sultans, such as Baybars, Qalavun, and al-Nasir Muhammad, Barquq was able to develop an operational military power base before coming to power, which helped him not only rise but to stay in the top spot for an extended period.[8] Barquq died in 1399, and although he too tried to establish a hereditary monarchy, like the other sultans, he was unable to do so against the current of Mamluk political life. From here on in it is safe to say that there were no other notable Mamluk sultans of the caliber of Barquq or some of those in the Bahri Mamluk era. As we have seen before, political uncertainty begot economic and military weakness. The increasing militarization of the civilian administration as a result did not help matters much, as was evident in the middle Abbasid period as well. The Mamluks early on implemented something we have also seen before: the iqta system, land parcels in return for military service and, hopefully, tax revenue. As with the Abbasid period, there are many drawbacks to the iqta system, mostly the dispersion of power over time; however, the Mamluks made it work to their advantage over the first half of the empire's existence via the centralization of the system. It was carefully parceled out, monitored, and controlled, and for the most part the Mamluks did not allow the iqtas to become hereditary.[9] But as the authority of the sultan and the efficiency of government diminished in Cairo, the iqta system only fed into the already existing independent nature of the Mamluk magnates, fraying the power structure at a time when they could ill afford it.

Why could they ill afford it? For one, Timurleng (Tamerlane), based in Samarqand, was in the midst of his attempts to recreate the Mongol Empire. To secure his western flank against potential troublesome foes, the Mamluks and especially the increasing power of the Ottomans in Anatolia, he turned his attentions in that direction. The timing could not have been worse for the Mamluks, because this occurred shortly after Barquq died in 1399. Aleppo and Damascus were taken by the Timurids in 1400. Fortunately for the Mamluks, Timur turned his attentions northward toward the Ottomans, defeating them at the Battle of Ankara in 1402; for a time this reduced the Ottomans to that of a principality, therefore mitigating the threat to the Mamluks themselves.[10] After Timur secured his western flank and returned to Central Asia, the Mamluks were able to take over Syria again—but it was now a Syria that would cause increasing problems for Cairo, as the Timurid interlude encouraged a number of would-be dynasts to increase their independence, if not break away entirely from the Mamluks.

SPOTLIGHT

Ibn Khaldun

Ibn Khaldun was one of the most colorful characters of his time. He was a famous intellectual even during his lifetime, fought in battles, was imprisoned for sedition (while some of his friends and his brother were executed for it), traveled widely, served under several rulers, and tried—unsuccessfully—to negotiate with one of world history's greatest conquerors, Timurleng (Tamerlane) to save the city of Damascus from destruction. He was a hands-on type of intellectual who wanted to involve himself in history, not just study it from afar; he was the Indiana Jones of his day. Wali al-Din Abd al-Rahman ibn Muhammad ibn Abu Bakr ibn al-Hasan ibn Khaldun was born in Tunis, Tunisia, in 1332 and died in Cairo in 1406. He is considered the greatest historian and sociologist in Arab history, and one of the greatest the world over. He developed a philosophy of history, outlined in his masterpiece "Muqaddimah" ("Introduction"), that influenced all who came after him.

Ibn Khaldun constantly involved himself—or became involved in—political intrigue, as he frequently served in high-level positions for several different rulers, from the Sultan of Morocco, Abu Inan, to the Sultan of Granada in Islamic Spain, Nasrid Muhammad V, to Mamluk Sultan Barquq in Cairo. As most of the dynasties for which he worked were marked by political instability, Ibn Khaldun's lot in life tended to wax and wane with that of those he served, leading to a number of interesting adventures. Being a part of history gave Ibn Khaldun some unique insights. Perhaps it helped him develop what twentieth-century English historian Arnold Toynbee described as "a philosophy of history which is undoubtedly the greatest work of its kind that has ever yet been created by any mind in any time or place."[1] He outlined this philosophy in his lengthy "Muqaddimah," the introductory volume to his *Kitab al-Ibar* ("The Book of Precepts"), though the two are often treated as separate works.

In the "Muqaddimah" Ibn Khaldun delineates what he sees as repetitive cycles to history, where certain nomadic or barbarian peoples, who naturally have a great deal of group solidarity (**asabiyyah**) and relatively little material culture to lose, invade and conquer more settled and urbanized civilizations. These more civilized societies have wealth and culture, but they have lost their martial spirit and social cohesion and have become weak through self-indulgence. But then the barbarian conquerors assimilate into civilized society, and the same thing happens to them. They lose their asabiyyah and become weak and therefore objects to be preyed upon by the next round of nomadic warrior peoples—and the cycle keeps repeating itself throughout history.

Ibn Khaldun (1332–1406) depicted on a 10 dinar 2005 banknote from Tunisia.
Georgios Kollidas/Alamy Stock Photo

In the late 1300s Ibn Khaldun arrived in Egypt, where he started teaching at Al-Azhar, the famous Islamic university first established by the Fatimids. Soon enough Barquq, one of the more famous and successful of the Mamluk rulers, got wind of Ibn Khaldun, and the sultan appointed him to be chief judge of the Maliki *madhab*, one of the four different rites of Sunni Islam. The next Mamluk sultan, al-Nasir, directed Ibn Khaldun in 1400 to travel to Damascus to take part in negotiations with Timur (Timurleng), who had arrived from Central Asia (Samarqand was his capital) to deal with the growing Ottoman threat to his rear flank. Over the course of seven weeks, the great historian tried to convince Timur to spare Damascus. While Ibn Khaldun did secure the safety of the civilian employees in Damascus and safe conduct for his own return to Egypt, the city was sacked by Timur's forces on his way toward defeating the Ottomans at the Battle of Ankara a couple of years later; however, the rest of the Mamluk domains were spared.

Ibn Khaldun's fame long survived him. President Ronald Reagan once cited him, and Facebook founder Mark Zuckerberg picked "Muqaddimah" as one of his book club choices. Despite his fame, he tended to admire and long for a simpler time. To him Islam's golden age was not the height of the Abbasids, but rather it was during the time of Muhammad and the first four caliphs (Rashidun), as things were much more simple, and it was a time when the Arab nomadic peoples, enjoying strong asabiyyah, were conquering civilized societies. While he wrote on a great many subjects—music, literature, economics, pedagogy—his lasting legacy remains his cyclical interpretation of history.

[1] Arnold Toynbee, *A Study of History, Volume 3* (London: Oxford University Press, 1948), p. 322.

The nature and quality of the Mamluk military also changed—and not for the better. With a few exceptions, we have seen that the Mamluk sultans, beginning with al-Nasir Muhammad, became less warrior chief and more chief executive of the state. This decreased from the top down the established esprit de corps of the infamous Mamluk cavalry. Peace and stability bred prosperity and also some military complacency, yet it did not do away with the power-seeking infighting between Mamluk households. A set-in-their-ways approach to military innovation prevented the Mamluk military from adequately integrating gunpowder into their weaponry and tactics; they rarely utilized hand guns and only used cannons in siege warfare, unlike the Europeans and the Ottomans, who were fully exploiting the new military technology. Even more than the weaponry of war, what severely hurt the Mamluk Empire in the fifteenth century was plague; whereas in Europe in the fourteenth century over a third of the population died, perhaps over half the population in Egypt died. There were twelve epidemics between 1416 and 1513.[11] Not only did this thin the ranks of the Mamluks themselves, with the imperial Royal Mamluk guard being cut at least in half (from 12,000 to 6,000), but it decimated the countryside and the peasantry that worked the land, reducing the amount of crop that could be produced and taxed. The economic effects were devastating. In addition, by 1498 the Portuguese, led by explorer Vasco de Gama, circumnavigated the Cape of Good Hope in Africa and discovered an alternative trade route for European commercial ships sailing back and forth to the Indian Ocean world. As we shall see in the next section, this deleteriously affected the Ottomans as well, but in a way that led them to look rapaciously at Mamluk territory to confront the economic and territorial challenge posed by the Europeans.

It seemed inevitable that the Turkish Ottoman Empire would come into competition—and fight a war—with the Mamluks. There had been a number of skirmishes between the two in northern Syria in the late 1400s. The Mamluks gave refuge to and supported a brother of Ottoman Sultan Bayezid II in the former's attempts to orchestrate his way to power, thus incurring the everlasting suspicion and enmity of many in the Ottoman family and capital city, Constantinople. It finally came to a head when a new, more aggressive Ottoman Sultan Selim I came to power in 1512. Often when new sultans came to power they immediately went on campaign to secure their legitimacy and appease the military, and this was certainly the case with Selim I, who wanted a return to the expansionist policies of earlier Ottoman sultans (something from which his father, Bayezid II, had shied away). After successfully dealing with a threat from Safavid Iran in 1514, Selim I turned his attention toward Syria. The Mamluks were no match on the battlefield, and the Ottomans easily defeated them at the Battle of Marj Dabiq, just north of Aleppo, in August 1516. The fact that some elements of the Mamluk army betrayed their sultan and went over to the Ottomans was only the military representation of the factiousness of the magnates that permeated Cairo. Selim followed up his victory and triumphantly entered Cairo in January 1517, thus formally putting an end to the Mamluk Empire.

A citadel in Aleppo, Syria, rebuilt by the Mamluks in the fifteenth century over existing ruins of a fortress built, rebuilt, and occupied by many dynasties dating back to the 3rd millennium BCE.
Wojciech Wójcik/Alamy Stock Photo

Like the Mongols, the Mamluks are often given short shrift by historians in terms of anything other than their military prowess. They were, after all, mamluks. However, their legacy goes far beyond that, as the wealth of Egypt, periods of peace and prosperity, and a number of competent, far-sighted sultans allowed for the building of religious schools, hospitals, and centers of learning and philosophy throughout Egypt and Syria, not to mention some of the impressive structures built under their watch, such as the striking Mamluk citadel in Aleppo. More so, it was the political legacy of the Mamluks that prevailed over the next three centuries. Because of distance, the breadth of their own empire, and eventually pressure from other directions the Ottomans could only rule indirectly in Egypt, usually through garrisons holed up in citadels and a select group of appointed officials. The real power in and outside of the cities in Egypt still lay with the mamluk households, who would continue to compete with each other, often over such things as recognition by the Ottoman overlords, into the early nineteenth century.

The Ottomans

The Ottomans were a Turkish family. The name is a Europeanized (Italian) version of the name "Osman," which in itself is the Turkish version of "Uthman" (which is why in a few texts the Ottomans are referred to as the "Uthmanlis"). Osman is considered the founder and first sultan of the dynasty that became the Ottoman Empire. The Ottoman movement led by Osman began in the 1290s. There is some ambiguity regarding the exact beginning because there wasn't really any seminal moment such as a battle, revolution, or death that allows us to more accurately pinpoint the year of birth.[12] It was simply a tribal movement led by Osman and his family that noticeably appeared on the scene in Anatolia, which was pockmarked by numerous Turkish principalities by the end of the thirteenth century.

As we have already noted, there are usually two (or more) versions of the rise of a successful movement or dynasty. There is something close to what actually happened, and then there is the version extolled by the successful movement or dynasty—one that obviously embellishes reality to almost mythical levels in order to enhance its reputation, as if it was destined to succeed. The Ottomans preferred the version that had their ancestors entering Anatolia with the Seljuks as military commanders two centuries earlier. Closer to the truth, they probably entered Anatolia at some point following Manzikert in 1071 as rootless nomads who sold their services to the highest bidder. They fought and negotiated their way toward western Anatolia, where they were able to finally set up shop.

It was Osman who began the policy of expanding the territory under Ottoman control against the Byzantines to the west rather than against their Turkish neighbors to the east. This policy would soon take the Ottomans into southeastern Europe (i.e., the Balkans or Rumeli, as it was more often called), although I doubt the Ottomans thought in terms of being a European versus an Asian up-and-coming power. Once they did entrench themselves in the Balkans, Europe was always first and foremost in the minds of the sultans rather than their holdings in the Middle East, even after they expanded much farther in the direction of the latter in the early 1500s. In a way, the foreign policy priority of the modern Republic of Turkey to join the European Union had its embryonic beginning with Osman's decision. It was also an attractive recruitment tool for others, mostly Turks, to join the Ottoman movement. They were **gazi (ghazi)** warriors, akin to mujahideen or holy warriors, fighting the infidel Christians and, most importantly, against Byzantium (i.e., Rome), which if successful would bring a significant amount of cachet to the enterprise. Nothing helps a movement more than success, and more tribal warriors began to attach themselves to the Ottomans, motivated by religion, lure of adventure, material gain, and the acquisition of prestige and position. The Ottoman movement at this point has been described as a "predatory confederacy" made up of both Muslims and Christians perhaps less concerned with holy war than pillaging, plundering, and loot; as Ottoman history Caroline Finkel points out, at this stage "Turcoman fighters were in the minority: the rapid pace of conquest required willing and indiscriminate acceptance of large numbers of Christians into the Ottoman fold to meet the shortage of manpower available to create and administer the fledgling state."[13]

Two events in large measure created the space for the Ottomans to establish themselves in western Anatolia and begin their quest for more. First was the Fourth Crusade, which as we saw in the last chapter expelled the Byzantines from Constantinople from 1204 to 1261. Although the Byzantines were able to move back into their capital city it severely weakened them overall, making them vulnerable to Turkish Muslims in Anatolia if any of the latter could coalesce into a real threat. The second was the Mongol defeat of the Seljuks of Rum at the Battle of Kosedagh in 1243. The Seljuks of Rum, descended from Qutlumush, became the most powerful Turkish principality. Located in south-central Anatolia, Konya (Iconium) was the capital, and they established themselves there in 1107. Following Kosedagh, the Seljuks of Rum were reduced to vassal state status paying tribute to the Mongols. They limped along until officially done in 1307, but for the time being there was no Turkish bully on the block who could inhibit the Ottomans. Even with this, the Ottomans certainly saw the path of least resistance to the west rather than the east. By the early 1300s, Byzantium was crumbling and the Serbian and Bulgarian empires in the Balkans were past their prime.

Osman was succeeded by his son, Orhan, in 1326. Shortly after taking power, Orhan took the city of Bursa in western Anatolia. This became the first true city that fell under Ottoman control, and as such it became their first generally recognized capital. The Ottomans were no longer the tribal-based movement controlling a principality with ambiguous borders. Now they had a capital city ruling over something resembling a state, as well as a developing but rudimentary administrative apparatus to govern over it.[14] We have seen before with the Arabs (following the death of the Prophet), the Seljuks, and others that the transition from nomadic warriors to settled rulers is often painful and unsuccessful. Given the fact that the Ottoman Empire lasted until shortly after World War I in the early twentieth century suggests that they were much more successful at this transition than the Seljuks. Even so, as we will see, it wasn't without some growing pains and potentially devastating opposition.

As the Ottomans pushed the Byzantines out of Anatolia by 1337 and began to sporadically raid into the Balkans, to the point of sometimes involving themselves as mercenaries in Byzantine succession disputes, Orhan and his followers saw firsthand the dilapidated condition of Byzantium and other Balkan kingdoms, and they must have been eager to move in. The Ottomans officially crossed over into Europe in 1354, expanding up the Gallipoli (Gelibolu) peninsula into Thrace and beyond (although Turks had been camping out in Gallipoli as early as 1352). It became a somewhat strange situation in that the Ottomans had completely surrounded Constantinople, which is essentially what the entire Byzantine Empire consisted of at this point. But the city held out against the Ottomans for another hundred years. This was due to a number of reasons, primarily the very high and thick walls that encircled Constantinople, making it almost impossible to take by land force. In addition, strategically located as it was astride the Sea of Marmara with access to the Black Sea to the north through the Bosphorus Strait and to the Mediterranean to the south though the Dardanelles, it could easily be resupplied by its European allies desperate to keep it afloat against the unwelcome Turkish Muslims. The fact that the Ottomans did not yet have any sort of sufficient naval capacity of their own allowed the Byzantine Empire to live a little longer. The Europeans would have helped more directly at the time, but they were in the throes of the Black Plague that was decimating a third of Europe's population, and distracted by the Hundred Years War. In addition, the demand was often made that the Byzantines must first abandon their schismatic ways and accept the Church of Rome before any aid would be forthcoming.

In the span of two sultans, father and son, the size of the Ottoman state had doubled. The Ottomans were clearly committed to expansion in Europe, and in 1361 Orhan shifted the capital from Bursa to Edirne (Adrianople), located to the west of Constantinople in Thrace. It would be Orhan's son, Murad (Murat), who succeeded upon his father's death in 1362, to really expand Ottoman territory in Europe to include the rest of Thrace, Macedonia, Bulgaria, and Serbia. Murat also solidified the Ottoman position in the western third of Anatolia, moving back and forth between Europe and Asia as needed. Although it did not trouble the Ottomans too much at this time, it did reveal a problem that would become more acute later on: that the Ottoman state consisted of a one-front military apparatus that often had to fight on two fronts. When the sultan and his army were in Europe, Asian foes of the Ottomans would often stir up trouble—and vice versa.

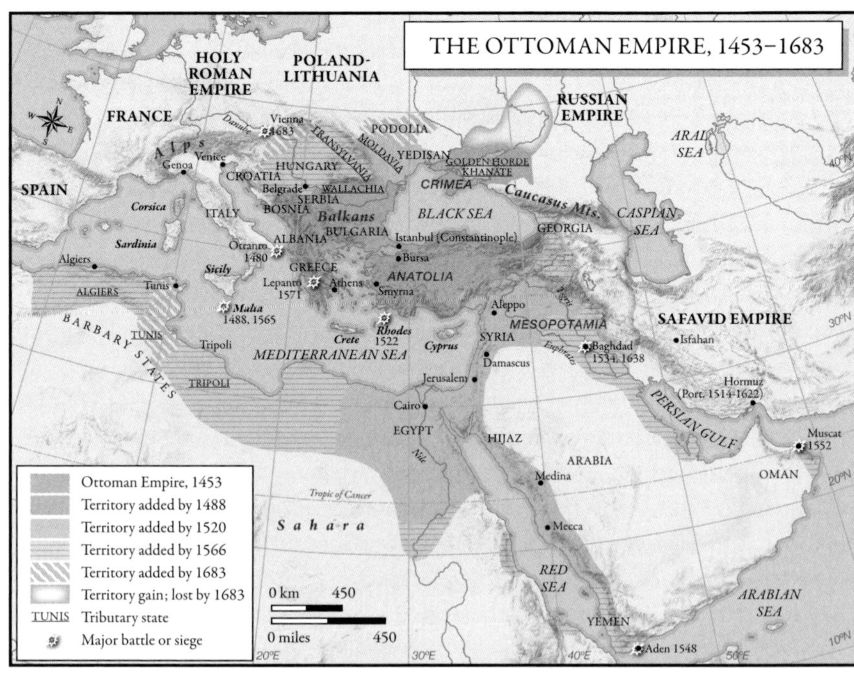

Toward the end of the fourteenth century, elements in the Balkans coalesced enough with the formation of the Balkan Union to mount a military campaign to push the Muslim Turks back into Asia. The culmination of this was the Battle of Kosovo in Serbia in 1389, a conflagration that still resonates in the region to this day. The Ottomans won the battle decisively, their first major victory over a significant European foe. It essentially established Ottoman control over the Balkans for the next five hundred years, save for one short interlude, and it opened up central Europe to Ottman designs, namely Hungary and Austria. Although they lost, over the years Serbians constructed a martyrdom mythology surrounding the battle that rallied them against the Ottomans for centuries—even to the point of Serbian militias fighting NATO in the 1990s following the break-up of Yugoslavia, wearing arm patches bearing the names of many of the Serbian princes and commanders who fought at Kosovo in 1389.[15] To many Serbs, Kosovo became a Serbian Jerusalem, and it is part of the reason why they fought so hard to keep it even when up against US-led NATO forces.

It appears that Murat was killed, possibly assassinated by a Serb, sometime during the Battle of Kosovo or just afterward.[16] In either event, his son Bayezid (Bajazet) took over as sultan, and he ruled until 1402. He had his brother Yakub killed upon coming to power, which appears to be the first case of fratricide in the Ottoman dynasty, a practice that would become more typical as time went on. Bayezid inherited a burgeoning empire that now had Serbia and Bulgaria firmly under Ottoman control. Bayezid was a fascinating character. Ruthless when he felt he had to be, he was also quite the progressive thinker. He saw himself as a universal ruler and advocated a religious eclecticism, apparent in the names of his four sons: Muhammad (Mehmet in Turkish), Isa (Jesus), Musa (Moses), and Sulayman (Solomon). Musa was appointed to the highest legal position in the state and was someone who wanted to combine Islam, Christianity, and Judaism into one religion, following upon his father's religious egalitarianism. This reflected the tolerant nature of Ottoman society. As the Ottomans expanded into Europe the majority of their territory and subjects were Christian, so in a sense they *had* to be tolerant lest they end up ruling over a population that felt repressed and alienated.

Although the state religion was Sunni Islam, the Ottomans practiced the most tolerant or least rigid interpretation of Islamic law (Sharia), Hanafi Sunni Islam. In addition, informally before the taking of Constantinople in 1453 (and formally afterward), around the time of the establishment of Edirne as the capital the Ottomans implemented what was called the **millet** system. "Millet" in Turkish means "nations," and it was an attempt to meet the demands of a multireligious, multiethnic population, especially as the majority was non-Muslim. Essentially each significant non-Muslim religious denomination was a millet, in which Greek Orthodox Christians, Armenian Orthodox Christians, Jews, and Catholics only had to look to their own authorities and courts in dealing with family or religious matters. This generated a good deal of religious autonomy, which kept a potentially restless population largely quiescent—and kept them paying the poll tax, which was the single largest contributor to the Ottoman treasury. Although these were not geographic designations, they often did correspond to pockets of majority populations in certain regions. This was a very progressive and far-sighted policy, if only by necessity, but it also contributed to some problems in the nineteenth century, as we shall see. Islam was not categorized as a millet, since it was the state religion.

With Bayezid keen on expansion following Kosovo, there were again stirrings of a European Crusade to beat back the Turkish threat. Knights from all over Europe heeded the call to Crusade of Pope Boniface IX, and in 1396 they marched down the Danube and met the Ottoman armies at Nicopolis, located in northern Bulgaria. The Crusader effort was ill-planned and arrogant, with many of the knights, as popular legend has it, engaged in festivities and nonchalant behavior before the battle. The Ottomans under Bayezid crushed the Christian force, with thousands of Crusaders drowning in the Danube while retreating. As a result, Ottoman prestige soared following the victory, leading to more recruits joining the army. Bayezid then quickly moved his troops into Anatolia to defeat a military force from the Turkish principality of Karaman in south-central Anatolia. Although the Karamanids would become a vassal state for the remainder of Bayezid's time in power, it would remain a thorn in the side of the Ottomans for another two generations. So fast was Bayezid in moving his troops back and forth between the two fronts that he was given the nickname of Yildirim, or Lightning Bolt.

But Bayezid was perhaps too successful. By extending Ottoman control farther into Anatolia, he aroused the consternation of Timurleng (Tamerlane). The Timurid ruler did not want to leave his western flank vulnerable to a new threat while trying to further his own expansion in central Asia and into India, so he marched his army to Anatolia and met Bayezid's forces at the Battle of Ankara in 1402. Timurleng was victorious, with Bayezid taken prisoner and later dying in captivity the next year. What had become an Ottoman Empire was reduced to vassal status to the Timurid Empire, and it seemed just to be a matter of time before the Ottomans went the way of the Seljuks, Mongols, and others—about a hundred-year good run, and then disappearing from the history books.

Bayezid had alienated many of the Turkish elements in the military and beyond because of his attempts to centralize power more in Edirne, the common problem of tribal-based movements transitioning to settled rulers. In addition, the recruitment system into the military and administration that developed under his father, Murad, had tended to favor Christians in the Balkans over the traditional Turkish families who had helped bring the Ottomans to power in the first place. This was the so-called **devshirme**, which literally means a gathering of youths. The make-up of the Ottoman army had evolved over the decades. The core that comprised the bulk of the original Ottoman armies were Turcoman horsemen organized into clans and tribes. But Orhan found that undisciplined Turkish tribal warriors, interested in pillaging and plundering, were more trouble than they were worth, especially as the sultan in his capital of Bursa was committed to protect the population over which he now ruled. Orhan began to organize a salaried army to move away from reliance upon Turcomans.

Murad, however, found this to be too expensive, and in any event he did not particularly like the fact that these troops served the state for money instead of loyalty to the Sultan. He began a system of recruitment called the **kapikullari**, literally "slaves of the Porte." "Porte" is a reference to the **Sublime Porte**, the office of the Sultan. The Porte itself refers to the door (porte) that led into the inner sanctums of the sultan, and keeping with tribal tradition, the sultan (or tribal chief) would periodically meet his subjects just outside the porte and dispense adjudication and wisdom (sublime), so Sublime Porte became almost synonymous with the sultan himself. The kapikullari came to the sultan as his share of captured enemy or slaves purchased, this way he could build up an army directly under his command. They would be brought to the capital, converted to Islam if they were not already Muslim, and educated in Turkish and the Ottoman way. They would be given military training and organized as infantry into the **Janissary** (*Yeni Ceri* or "new force") corps or as cavalry (**sipahis**). It would be primarily the Janissaries who led the Ottomans into Europe rather than the Turkish tribal warriors or salaried forces. Some of the kapikullari would also be brought into administration if they showed a talent for it. Regardless of whether they were men of the pen or the sword, the commanders and top officials would be awarded land grants (**timars**) in return for their service, which sounds a lot like the iqta system.

Murad tweaked the kapikullari system as time went on because there was not always a readily available supply of slaves won in battle or purchase, the latter being expensive as well. He instituted a more regularized form of recruitment through periodic conscriptions or levying of Christian boys, primarily in the Balkans and usually between the ages of eight and thirteen, with the best and brightest entering the military and palace service. In a way it systematized the kapikullari. There was no fixed time period for the levies, as it was only done when needed. And there were a number of exemptions, such as if a family only had one son or various types of hardship. A family could also buy their son's way out of the levy if they could afford to do so. Opponents of the Ottomans would have you believe that the boys were dragged from their homes kicking and screaming by bands of marauding soldiers hunting down recruits. This may have happened sometimes, but after understanding the upward mobility this could provide their sons—and the family itself—a number of families began to want to buy their son's way *into* the devshirme. Only five of the first forty-eight grand viziers (the CEO of the state) were Turkish, much to the displeasure of the Turkish notables, so much so that the latter derisively called the Imperial Council of the sultan and grand vizir the "slave market." In the end, the devshirme only levied a very small part of the population.[17] The officials and military officers recruited through the devshirme also helped the Ottomans deal with Balkan entities, as they could speak the requisite Slavic languages and in some cases were even related to Balkan notables.

The reliance that Murad and especially Bayezid developed on Christians did not sit well with the aristocratic Turkish families. As one palace official stated, "There are few native-speaking Turks in the palace because the Sultan finds himself more faithfully served by Christian converts who have neither hearth nor home nor parents nor friends. They conceive such an affection for his service that if it were in their power they would voluntarily expose a thousand lives for the life of his person and the increase of his empire."[18] Many of the Turkish forces at Ankara abandoned the Sultan on the battlefield, bought off in some cases by Timur; others just got up and left. It was the current and former Christian elements of the army who stayed with Bayezid to the end. Historian Peter Sugar put it well:

> The leading Turkish families, descendants of the first successful *gazi* leaders and of those who allied themselves with the Ottomans early and had achieved wealth and leading positions, resented the sultan's increasingly "Byzantine" tendencies: the growing centralization of power, a court that was more and more "imperial," and several new influences including slaves in the ruling and decision-making process, all of which diminished their positions. Both of these groups accused Bayezid not only of abandoning the *gazi* tradition, but even of being a bad Muslim because he was too strongly under the Christian influence of his mother, wife, and European friends.[19]

Following Bayezid's death, his four sons competed with one another during the Interregnum from 1402 to 1413 when the Ottomans were reduced to principality status following the defeat at Ankara. Two things kept the Ottomans from fading into oblivion. One was that Timur died in 1405, leaving his vast empire to his sons, who bickered and fought each other over the inheritance and diminishing and weakening the Timurid Empire along the way, something we have seen previously following the deaths of Ahmad ibn Tulun and Saladin. The second is that the preponderance of powerful merchant and trading families *wanted* the Ottoman Empire to recover. They did not agitate on the whole for the return of the Byzantine, Serbian, or Bulgarian empires.[20] To them, the Ottoman system worked. It had tried and true state institutions and a tolerant system of governing that was attractive to those groups who prized stability and security above all else. Fortunately for the Ottomans they had established an institutional template well before Bayezid's defeat, and since it had proven to be largely successful once already there was no reason to not resuscitate it, which also meant bringing back the Ottomans themselves.

The horizontally organized millet system and the clear vertical hierarchy the Ottomans had in place in terms of the segmentation of government allowed for a workable combination of space and boundaries for indigenous populations.[21] Not everyone was on board, but a critical mass wanted the Ottoman system back. At the top of the pyramid was the Ottoman royal family itself, but power as a whole at the top was encapsulated in the Imperial Council (**Divan al-Humayun**), which was akin to a presidential cabinet or council of ministers. The Imperial Council was overseen by the sultan, but as affairs of state became more complex or the sultan was away on campaign or became further removed from governance, it was run by the grand vizir, who was in essence the prime minister in charge of the everyday state of affairs.[22]

Below the Imperial Council were the provinces (**beylerbeyiks** or *vilayets*), led by the provincial governors (*beylerbeys* or *valis*). The provincial governors usually sat on the Imperial Council along with other ministers of state. Below the provinces were the districts (*sanjak,* plural *sanajik*) led by district heads (*sanjakbegs*). A varying number of districts would make up a province depending upon geography and the size of the local population. A number of timars would typically be included in a district, with the size and amount varying depending upon location. There would be frequent cadastral surveys organized by the government to determine and confirm boundaries as well as who owed what in terms of timariot (timar holders) services. There was a clear line of authority that was reinforced by the success of the sultans and their enterprises, all of which mitigated against the dispersion of power that we have seen with the iqta system of the middle Abbasid period and with the Seljuks. In this sense, the transition from a simple tribal structure to a fairly sophisticated governing system was smoother than previous attempts—although it was not without some significant hiccups, as Bayezid discovered.

Muhammad I (Mehmet) finally won out over his three brothers in an at times vicious battle for the throne. He ruled from 1413 to 1421, and his job was a holding action, basically to secure things after so much disruption and trying to gain—largely successfully—recognition in the region as the new Ottoman sultan. He was smart to cultivate better ties with the Turkish aristocracy after they had rejected the European ways of his father, behavior that was seen as being contrary to Islamic norms; simply going to war with other Muslims such as the Karamanids and the Timurids was seen as ill-advised. There were many reasons to be unenthusiastic about Bayezid from the perspective of the Turkish nobility, but most of all, his centralization policies impinged on their autonomy.

It would be under Murad II (1421–1451) that the Ottoman Empire really began to recover lost territory—in a way, it was the second Ottoman Empire.[23] Murad II was something of a reluctant sultan, having voluntarily abdicated twice to his young son in order to concentrate on his intellectual pursuits—and twice was brought back to successfully deal with an impending crisis. The Ottomans regained the territory they had lost in Serbia by 1438, but they could not make inroads in Hungary, where popular Hungarian hero John Hunyadi was able to hold them off. In 1444, however, threatened by a recent accord between the Orthodox and Catholic Christian churches—making Crusade more likely—Murad II was compelled to return to power, and he led his forces to a decisive victory over a combined Crusader effort at the battle of Varna, located near the Black Sea in Bulgaria. Varna did for the second Ottoman Empire what Kosovo in 1389 did for the first: secured Ottoman control in the Balkans, but this time it would last for over four hundred years. It also pretty much sealed the fate of Byzantium, for there would be no more significant European attempts to save the fading Christian outpost in Constantinople.

Murad II died in 1451, and his son Muhammad II (Mehmet II) took over at nineteen years old. He was no longer the young boy he had been when he assumed power for his abdicated father in the 1440s: dominated by more powerful elements in the capital, particularly the grand vizir at the time, Chandarli Halil Pasha. Muhammad's goal was simple: take Constantinople once and for all, something his father failed to do—and Muslims in general had failed to do on twelve prior occasions. As a young man surrounded by powerful personalities, he needed the prestige and legitimacy that would accrue from this tremendous victory, allowing him to consolidate his rule and return to military expansion, in the process of which the Ottomans would truly become a world empire. The requirements of empire also necessitated the control over and profits from Mediterranean trade and taxation that Constantinople traditionally commanded. Since he is known in history as Muhammad the Conqueror (*Fatih*), he was obviously successful, and although this seems to characterize him as a warrior-sultan first and foremost he was actually very well educated and spoke several languages—future sultans went to the best schools. After a trying seven-week siege in 1453, the Ottoman army finally breached the walls of Constantinople with cannon fire, and after pouring into the city they pillaged and plundered it for a couple of days. The city's population had

The fall of Constantinople. Panorama 1453 History Museum, Istanbul, Turkey.
Zhanna Tretiakova/Alamy Stock Photo

shrunk to about 30,000–50,000 by 1450, but it still had its history and legacy—as well as its cachet as the seat of the Roman Empire. Muhammad entered the magnificent Church of the Hagia Sophia (Aya Sofia), the Church of the Holy Wisdom, and converted it to a mosque. He would build the Topkapi Palace or New Palace as the home to the sultans and their retinues, which would house them until the nineteenth century. Soon after taking Constantinople, the sultan had Chandarli Halil Pasha executed. The Janissary corps were kept happy by the campaign, which sultans were well advised to ensure after taking office.

Secure in power, Muhammad could engage in military expansion: eighteen campaigns in all, in which he personally participated. There are three conquests of note, more for their future repercussions than for any changes they wrought at the time. First, the Ottomans took Athens in 1458, and with it most of Greece was absorbed into the empire, which was important in terms of controlling the Aegean Sea and its passage into the Mediterranean Sea, especially against Venetian ships. From a very early period this was a fraught relationship, ultimately leading to the Greek war of independence in the nineteenth century and a long heritage of Turkish-Greek animus that still exists to this day. Next, in 1468, the pesky Karamanids finally fell once and for all, opening up the rest of Anatolia to the Ottomans and, importantly, clearing the road for further expansion into the Middle East. Finally, the Crimea submitted to Ottoman authority in 1475, making the Black Sea a virtual Ottoman lake and connecting Constantinople with Central Asia. This also brought the Ottoman Empire smack up against the Russian heartland, and although Russia was not yet the imperial threat it would soon become under the czars, the Ottoman–Russian confrontation within two centuries would become the single most important dynamic in terms of the question of Ottoman survival as well as Constantinople's evolving relationship with Europe—a geostrategic paradigm that would lead straight to World War I.

Muhammad the Conqueror died in 1481, and there ensued a potentially devastating succession struggle between his two sons, Bayezid and Jem (Cem). This was not unusual, as we have already seen. The main reason for this is that there was no set system of succession within the Ottoman family; it was not primogeniture. Surviving sons of a just-deceased sultan essentially duked it out with one another, and to the winner went the spoils. This competition, the maneuvering against one another, would often begin long before the father died. The winner was typically the most cunning, politically able, and ruthless. In addition, most of the sons of the sultan were given political (mostly as provincial governors) or military positions. In these capacities each son gained experience, political know-how, and bastions of support when the time came to move against his brothers or his father. This survival of the fittest succession process appears to have worked despite itself. Every sultan from Osman through Sulayman the Magnificent (d. 1566) acquitted himself well in the role. I cannot think of another line in one dynasty that produced such good, far-sighted leaders one after another without any duds. It was brutal and the price was sometimes high, as the Ottomans were on the verge of (or actually in) civil war before one son ultimately emerged on top, but one cannot argue against the results. A change in this so-called method of succession (or lack thereof) in the early 1600s is often seen as the reason for a series of incompetent sultans, which is important because the shift came at a time when the Ottomans desperately needed sound leadership.

Bayezid II emerged as the victor over Jem, although the latter took up shop with Ottoman foes and for a time constricted his brother's options; Bayezid feared opening the door for Jem's return if he left Constantinople to go on campaign. Bayezid's long time in power (1481–1512) is often characterized as a status quo reign, mostly because it was devoid of a spectacular military campaign, especially when compared to his predecessor. But this doesn't mean that nothing of note happened. Ottoman historian Justin McCarthy contends that Bayezid gave the empire some "breathing space" after the exhausting years of conquest of his father, further noting that "Bayezid generally gave his empire peace, improved and regularized the state's tax system, and reduced inflations, the sort of good government that is seldom celebrated by historians, who love a good war as much as the next person, but it was essential for reunification of the empire. He left the empire in fine financial shape, ready for renewed expansion."[24]

Two events occurred during Bayezid's rule that were outside of his control, yet they would have important repercussions for his son and successor, Selim I.[25] First, in 1497 the Portugese explorer Vasco de Gama circumnavigated the Cape of Good Hope in Africa, finding an alternative trade route for Europe to the Indian Ocean. In a more immediate sense this was threatening to the Mamluk Empire, but the deleterious economic hit on the Ottoman economy also did not go unnoticed. Secondly was the rise of the Safavid Empire in Iran in 1501, which will be discussed in more detail in the next section. Even though the Safavi royal family was Persian, their first capital was Tabriz in Azerbaijan, close to Anatolia. Located there, the Safavids recruited heavily among Turkish tribes in Anatolia to make up the bulk of the Safavid army. Many Turks in eastern Anatolia saw the Ottomans as looking to the European West, especially after moving into the Balkans and taking Constantinople, and therefore looked themselves to the East.[26] It was also a Shiite Islamic state, which while not in itself a cause for war between the Ottomans and the Safavids, certainly fanned the flames. It was a growing, dynamic movement in the beginning that had encroached on Ottoman territory, and Constantinople certainly saw this as a threat.

It would be Selim I (also known as Yavuz or "the Grim") who would have to deal with all this. As per usual, there was a great deal of maneuvering by Bayezid II's sons, bordering on civil war. Bayezid actually fought against Selim, who was eager to push aside his father, who was akin to Murad II—the reluctant sultan who was more an intellectual, indeed a Sufi ascetic, than warrior chief. Selim the Grim was aggressive and ambitious, and he eventually forced his father to abdicate in 1512. Selim arranged for accession gifts to the Janissaries to keep them placated, and then he planned for military expansion. The Safavids were the immediate threat. Selim marched eastward with his army in 1514. The Mamluks, who had fought several skirmishes with the Ottomans under Bayezid II, were clearly on the defensive, expecting Selim to turn his attentions toward Syria. Instead, Selim met the Safavids in eastern Anatolia in the Battle of Chaldiran. It was a bloody conflagration, but the Ottomans were victorious and soon after entered Tabriz. The Safavid threat was turned back, but it was not extinguished completely simply because of the distance from home and lack of resources, as the Safavids in retreat carried out a scorched-earth policy. They would continue to confront the Ottomans from time to time for the next two centuries, although they ceased to be an existential threat. With this, Iraq and the Persian Gulf were open to Ottoman expansion.

Next, Selim decided to finally deal with the Mamluks, the culmination of a dispute that had been long in coming. This was in addition to Vasco de Gama's circumnavigation of Africa in 1497, which threatened the Mamluks as well as the Ottomans, the latter realizing they had best try to regain control of the trade routes to the east; Bayezid II's involvement in Mamluk affairs set the foundation for his son's efforts. As we know, the Mamluk Empire was well past its prime and ripe for the picking, even though it was, like the Ottomans, a Sunni Muslim state. However, as often happened in Islamic history, some sort of rationalization, usually a religious ruling, could be conveniently found to legitimize military action against supposedly fellow Muslims—in this case, a rather specious claim that the Mamluk sultan had been conspiring with Shah Ismail did the trick by implying that someone who connived with a heretic was himself a heretic. In 1516 Selim again marched his troops eastward, this time keeping the Safavids on the defensive by thinking he was coming for them. On this occasion the Ottomans did enter Syria, and with the muskets, pistols, and cannon the Mamluks were so reluctant to utilize, the former decisively defeated the latter at the Battle of Marj Dabiq, located near Aleppo. Soon thereafter, in early 1517, despite some reluctance to do so, Selim marched into Cairo itself, thus formally ending the Mamluk Empire and incorporating its territory into the Ottoman Empire. Included in this were the holy cities of Mecca and Medina. This meant that the caliphate that had been in Cairo was now transferred to Constantinople in the person of the sultan—or sultan-caliph, although the caliphate was not something the Ottomans emphasized or utilized until the eighteenth century.[27]

The Ottoman Empire was now clearly a Middle Eastern as well as a European empire, with all of the important repercussions of this development for centuries to come—including, for the first time, a majority Muslim population. Selim had placed the empire on the precipice of reaching its golden age, which his son, Sulayman, would oversee.

The Safavids

The Safavid Empire is named after the Safavi family, which also lent its name to the Safaviyya Sufi order.[28] They were most likely a Persian family (with perhaps some Kurdish, Arab, and Turkish DNA), but it was definitely an Iranian based empire, although as we shall see, there was a heavy Turkish presence as well. The family emerged from the city of Ardabil in eastern Azerbaijan. It was in a mountainous region, which worked to their advantage in terms of being able to begin their movement in relative isolation, which as we know from prior chapters (such as with the Buyids) was also fertile ground in which to adopt heterodox forms of Islam. It was an area that consisted of religious diversity and political fragmentation, with the Safavids ebbing and flowing within the political environment of Turco-Mongolian principalities that popped up following the breakup of the Mongol Empire.

It would be Shaykh Safi al-Din, born in 1252, who put the Safavids on the map. At around the time Osman was starting what would become the Ottoman Empire, Safi al-Din linked up with the Sufi leader Shaykh Zahid al-Gilani, who was the *murshid-i kamil,* or perfect spiritual head of the Zahidiyya Sufi order. The tolerant religious atmosphere overseen by the Mongol Empire allowed for such religious diversity to flourish. Safi was Zahid's disciple for twenty-five years, but when the latter died in 1301, Safi inherited the leadership position and renamed the Sufi order (*tariqah*) to the Safaviyya. The movement grew quite a bit under Safi's guidance and became a popular Sufi order in the area. Under his leadership and that of his son's (Sadr al-Din, 1304–1391), the Safaviyya order began to recruit from Turcoman tribes in eastern Anatolia and elsewhere, which would later arouse the consternation of the Ottomans. This period in Safavid history was very much one of ups and downs, trying to navigate the terrain dominated by Mongol mini-dynasties such as the Qara Quyunlu (Black Sheep) and the Aq Quyunlu (White Sheep) as well as survive the onslaught of Timurleng's campaigns in the 1380s and 1390s. That they survived is a testament to the popularity of their calling (*dawa*) as well as the continued support and loyalty of their disciples (*murids*).

Junayd took over in 1447, and he introduced a new militant tone into the Safavid movement, calling for expansion—jihad. The movement changed from a Sufi order to a militant political one. This aroused opposition from surrounding powers, and in 1460 Junayd was killed in battle by the Qara Quyunlu. His son Haydar succeeded as head of the order, and like his father, he too was killed in battle in 1488, this time by the Aq Quyunlu. The Safavid movement seemed destined to fail. Under Haydar, however, the Safavid army came into shape as Turcoman, mostly recruited from Anatolia. They wore a distinctive scarlet headgear and therefore became known as the *qizilbash*, or "redheads," and would form the backbone of the Safavid army for decades to come.

One of Haydar's sons, Ismail, escaped the Aq Quyunlu's attempts to extinguish the Safavid line. He was a young boy at the time, and reportedly went through a number of adventures and close calls in order to survive (much of the story probably embellished after the fact). That he lived to tell the tale is mostly due to a group of seven close advisors known as the *ahl al-ikhtisas*, those who were special or assigned special duties—in this case educating, training, and keeping alive the future shah. In 1500, Ismail, at the head of a Turkish tribal army, which included the Qajar family (who later ruled Iran in the nineteenth and early twentieth century), defeated the Aq Quyunlu, gaining control of Azerbaijan and taking over the city of Tabriz. It was here in 1501 that Ismail—as the fourteenth Safavid leader—was crowned shah, probably at the age of fourteen, and as history tells it thus begins the Safavid Empire.

You may have noticed the number seven and its multiples (14) appearing quite often in the Safavid historical narrative, whether true or apocryphal. These numbers have traditionally been important in Shiite circles over the centuries, so the fact that they are associated with the Safavids added an aura of destiny to their claims. The power and legitimacy of the Safavid shahs typically depended on three sometimes interrelated claims that were emphasized at one time or another: 1) the divine right of Persian kings or the "Shadow of God on Earth." They asserted that Hussein, Ali's younger son, had married into the Sassanian royal family by marrying the daughter of Yazdgird III, the last Sassanian shah, thereby linking the ancient Iranian monarchical tradition and divine right of kings to the family of Ali; 2) the earthly representatives of the Hidden Imam in Twelver Shiism, or on occasion even the Mahdi himself. The Safavids traced their lineage back to the seventh Shiite Imam, Musa al-Kazim; and 3) the murshid al-kamil, the head of the Safaviyya Sufi order, which in Iran had been closely tied to Shiism. Twelver Shiism was the one thing that linked all of these concepts.

It is not a surprise then that soon after assuming power, Ismail declared Twelver Shiite Islam to be the Safavid state religion. Even though we take for granted today that Iran is a Twelver Shiite Islamic Republic, the problem in Iran at this time was that it had a predominantly Sunni population. But Ismail was determined. He thought of himself as a divine reincarnation of sorts, and in this volcanic, successful beginning of the Safavid state, his followers by and large believed him and were motivated to enforce his dictate. He imposed a kind of inquisition and through pain of death forced conversion to Shiism. He brought Shiite scholars into Iran, many from Lebanon, to help with the transition and expropriated endowments (*awqaf,* singular **waqf**) of Sunni ulama to reduce their authority and power.[29] On the positive side, the imposition of Shiism produced an identity of its own, which reinforced the dynamism of the state and gave the central government a galvanizing ideology.

One problem in the inherent bureaucratic structure of the Safavid state was the split and frequent antagonism between the Iranian (*Tajik)* elements of society and the Turcoman tribal forces comprising the qizilbash. Although not exclusively, the Tajiks were typically the men of the pen and the Turks, the men of the sword. We saw this problem in the middle Abbasid period between the kuttab and the mamluk-dominated military. Each thought the other was unworthy. Their relationship has been described like oil and water, and only a strong shah could paper over the antagonisms and maintain a semblance of governmental unity. Ismail tried to appease both groups by appointing at various different times representatives of each to important posts.

The Safavids had two traditional enemies for most of their time in power: the Uzbeks (Ozbegs) and the Ottomans. Ismail was able to defeat the Uzbeks in 1510, thereby securing most of Iran under Safavid control. This only heightened Ismail's popularity, as he was pretty much worshipped as invincible by his followers. That did not last. The Safavids also engaged in successful military actions in Anatolia, which caught the attention of Selim the Grim. We already know the outcome of this confrontation in 1514 at the Battle of Chaldiran: like the Mamluks, the Safavids eschewed gunpowder-based weaponry, while the Ottomans did not, the latter emerging victorious because of it.

Ismail is said to have retreated into seclusion, wearing black robes and engaging in decadent behavior for the rest of his life. He became a shattered man, as he seemed to actually believe in his semidivine stature and invincibility. More importantly, the qizilbash ceased to continue to believe in the shah's divinity, and even the murshid–murid relationship dissolved. The qizilbash tribal chiefs began to behave more independently of the government and the shah, clashing among themselves without the legitimacy of the shah to keep them together. Ismail died in 1524 at the age of thirty-seven.

Ismail's eldest son, Tahmasp, succeeded as shah at the ripe young age of ten. Without a strong and entrenched leader the qizilbash took matters into their own hands, and for the next decade different factions of them competed with each other for power and control. To say it was a chaotic situation would be an understatement, and territories were lost to their enemies when they sensed the opportunity. Once again it seemed

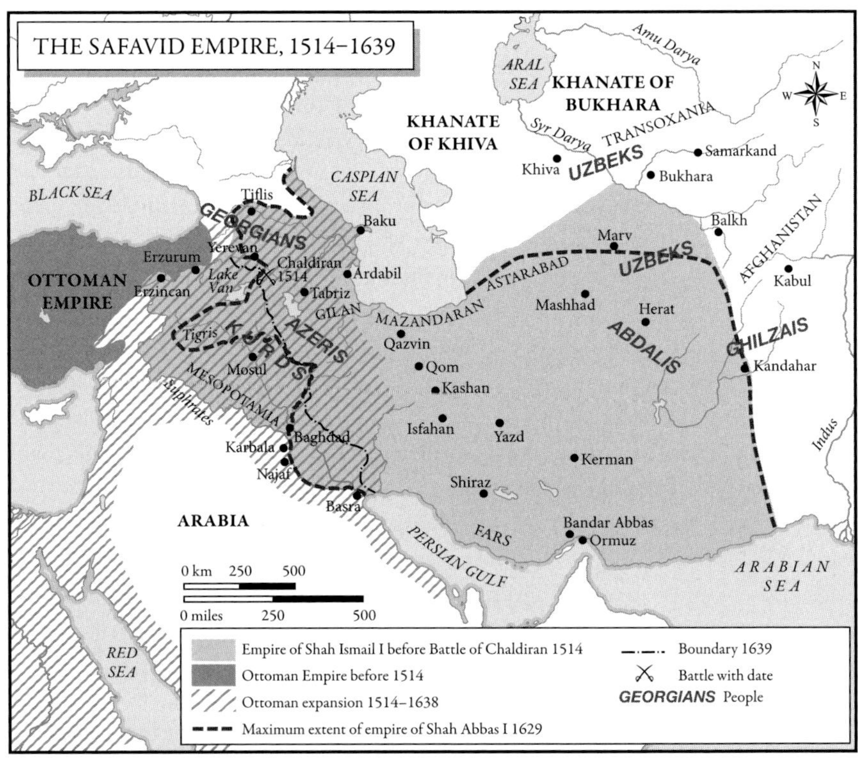

THE SAFAVID EMPIRE, 1514–1639

as if the Safavids were destined to depart from the history books, but distance from the centers of power of both the Ottomans and the Uzbeks helped save the Safavids.

In 1533, however, Tahmasp showed his mettle. He had to move against the qizilbash, and he did so spectacularly by executing the qizilbash leader, Hussein Beg Lala Shamlu. Shamlu was a cousin of the shah as well as the guardian (lala) to his son, so the fact that Tahmasp was willing to get rid of him showed the other qizilbash tribal leaders that he was ready to rule as well as reign. For the next decade Tahmasp held the empire together when it could have easily broken up into a hodgepodge of Turkish principalities. By 1540 he had built up enough authority and loyalty from the qizilbash that he embarked on a series of military campaigns in the Caucuses, which is really all that he could do since he still was reluctant to go up against the Ottomans or Uzbeks. Safavid forces did bring back to Iran thousands of Georgian, Circassian, and Armenian prisoners, which later would have important repercussions for Safavid society and politics. Much like mamluks in other Middle East societies, these *Ghulam* (*Ghulaman-i khassa-yi sharifa* or slaves of the royal household) were given special training, and those that made it through would in time be placed in the military, the royal household, or the administration. It would be the children of these original Ghulam who would play such an important role for later shahs.

Tahmasp died in 1576, having kept things together for forty years, which was no minor accomplishment given the circumstances under which he took power. His two sons who succeeded him one after the other would not be so fortunate. Ismail II had been kept in prison by his father for twenty years prior to becoming the next shah, because his father suspected him of plotting against him. What this did was make for an inexperienced, unprepared, and possibly mentally deranged successor. Upon coming to power Shah Ismail II killed or blinded anyone who could conceivably challenge him—except for one brother who was blind anyway, which is the only reason he survived the slaughter. Ismail confirmed his father's worst fears: he was interested in ruthlessly maintaining power and pretty much nothing else, although he did try to reimpose Sunnism on the populace. This suggests that the conversion in Iran to Shiism was incomplete; regardless, this plan did not go far because the qizilbash soon realized Ismail was not the man for the job and they had him poisoned in 1577, replaced by his blind brother, Muhammad.

Although well-intentioned, Muhammad was no more effective than his brother. He was weak and under the thumb of the qizilbash. He tried to curry favor with lavish gifts, which depleted the treasury. The Ottomans and the Uzbeks again took advantage of the situation, with the former (already having taken over Iraq earlier) taking the city of Tabriz in 1585, while the latter captured Herat and Mashhad. Fortunately for the Safavids, Tahmasp had moved the capital to the southeast in Qazvin. With things deteriorating quickly, some qizilbash guardians of one of Muhammad's sons, Abbas, pushed aside his father and placed in power as a seventeen-year-old shah who would become known as Abbas the Great. Indeed he was "great," ushering in the height of Safavid power, but it did not come easily or quickly.

The situation was dire. Half the empire had been lost. The treasury was empty amid continuing pressure from the outside and intertribal qizilbash rivalries on the inside—along with the continuing antagonisms between Tajik and Turk that divided the administration and military. The manner in which Abbas dealt with all this revealed his pragmatism and farsightedness. He adopted a similar approach to that of the Umayyad Caliph Abd al-Malik, who also came to power on the verge of an empire in dissolution. Abbas took one step backward and then two steps forward. To get the Ottomans off his back he entered into a humiliating peace treaty with them in 1589, ceding some of Iran's richest provinces (Azerbaijan, Georgia, Kurdistan, Luristan) to Constantinople.

He then set about corralling the qizilbash—who had to be controlled, or else the shah would never be able to really rule. As we have seen previously, when wanting to push aside an unruly force that also comprises the core element of the military, one has to create another military—a standing army. Looking for that standing army, Abbas found a ready-made alternative in the Ghulam, or what became known as the "third force." He established Ghulam regiments, totaling some 40,000 troops, which enabled the shah to deal with any opposition or malcontents, especially among the qizilbash. It is one thing to create a standing army, of course, but it is quite another to pay for it. This is where short-term expediency wins out over long-term policy.

Before Shah Abbas, the government in the provinces for the most part was allotted to qizilbash chiefs in land grants known as *tiyul*, similar to the Ottoman timars. The tiyul holder consumed most of the revenue produced by his land while promising to levy and deliver troops to the shah when called upon. Provinces organized in this manner were called *mamalik* lands (the plural of mamluk), which would supply very little to the central treasury. Most of the funds going to the central treasury under this system came from what were called *khassa* or crown lands (owned by the state). Abbas's solution to paying the Ghulam standing army was to convert mamalik into khassa, where these new crown provinces would often be administered by Ghulam; over time, about half of the provincial governors were Ghulam, and most of the provincial revenue went directly into the central or state treasury. Abbas killed two birds with one stone with increased state revenues while also reducing the power of the qizilbash.

In the short term, all of this worked and Shah Abbas was able to push out the Uzbeks by 1602. By 1607 the Safavids were able to recapture all of the territory they lost to the Ottomans as defined in the 1555 Treaty of Amasya, retaking Azerbaijan and Shirvan. The Safavids took Qandahar from the Mughals of India and moved more stoutly into the Persian Gulf, taking Bahrain and then forcing the Portuguese out of the Gulf by 1622, thereby enhancing the empire trade access and capabilities. The highlight of renewed Safavid military strength against the Ottomans was the taking of Baghdad in 1624, which had been in Ottoman hands for ninety years. As a sign of the rebirth of the empire the capital was moved from Qazvin to Isfahan, the latter becoming one of the great cities in the world under Abbas's watch. It was more centrally located in a strategic sense, but also economically, as it became a center of commerce and had better access to the robust trade of the Persian Gulf. Abbas built more roads to connect the major cities of Iran, and the wealth of the state was reflected in the architecture of Isfahan, highlighted by the Masjid-i Shah imperial mosque. This became the symbol of Abbas's efforts to implant Twelver Shiism in the empire along with the creation of religious endowments, all of which had the long-term effect of increasing the power of the Shiite *mujtahids*, the ultimate fruition of which came to pass in the 1979 Iranian revolution that created a Shiite Islamic republic. Nonetheless, Isfahan flourished. In their travel logs, Europeans marveled at the splendor and wealth of the capital city during the time of Shah Abbas the Great.[30]

The reforms of Shah Abbas had long-term negative repercussions, however. Perhaps it is a case of having to do what was necessary at the time—the difference between looking backward and living forward—but his policies hampered succeeding shahs. First, the qizilbash did not exploit the land or population in their tiyuls, as they saw these as long-term investments that their sons would inherit. The Ghulams, on the other hand, were out to raise as much money as possible in

Dome of the Madar-e Shah Madrasah or Chahar Bagh, seventeenth–eighteenth centuries, Safavid era, in Isfahan, Iran.
PRISMA ARCHIVO/Alamy Stock Photo

their khassa provinces through heavy taxation, which made for a restless populace as well as long-term decline in provincial prosperity, as the land was also exploited for all of its worth. In addition, although the Ghulam were capable soldiers, as the territorial recovery showed, the qizilbash were, quite simply, better. They would more vigorously defend their lands (and the empire that provided them with it). It is telling that in the years to come, qizilbash would often be reappointed as provincial governors in times of crisis, an admission of their military capability in and of itself. Overall, Abbas's reforms weakened the empire economically and militarily, especially under less than capable shahs who did not have the power and authority to maintain the delicate balance of the state between Tajik and Turk and between qizilbash and Ghulam. Another reform of Abbas almost guaranteed that his successors would be wanting. He incarcerated his sons, the royal princes, in the harem. He remembered how he came to power and wanted to maintain a close eye over his own sons just in case; however, because of this, they did not acquire field experiences nor establish their own bases of power, and they were often mentally impaired from living under such paranoid conditions their whole lives.

Despite the flaws in the system, the restructuring of the state under Abbas continued under its own momentum for several decades after the great shah died in 1629. But the graph line was inexorably headed downward. Abbas was succeeded by his grandsons, Shah Safi (1629–1642) and then Abbas II (1642–1666), both of whom basically continued the polices of Abbas I. They accelerated the transfer of mamalik to khassa lands, except in times of war when the lands would switch back, a process that was cumbersome and ineffective because the different systems of government could not be instantly transformed. As a sign of the deteriorating situation, Baghdad was recaptured by the Ottomans in 1638, only fourteen years after Shah Abbas the Great had taken it. Qandahar was also retaken by the Mughals in the same year. After Abbas II, whose excessive drinking probably led to his premature death in 1666, the Safavid Empire entered a period of steep decline under Shah Sulayman. The shah no longer actually ruled. So bad was the situation for Sulayman that he changed his throne name from Safi II to Sulayman about a year and a half into his tenure to indicate a fresh new start. Although he stayed in power for twenty-eight years, this was more a reflection of his diminishing relevance rather than any reassertion of the legitimacy of the shah.

The Ottomans, Afghan Sunni tribes, and even the Russians recognized the weakness of the Safavid state, and all of them made territorial inroads into what had been Safavid territory. Such was the state of deterioration that it only took a force of some 20,000 Afghans to compel the last generally acknowledged Safavid shah, Sultan Hussein, to surrender the city of Isfahan in 1722. After Abbas II probably any outside power could have occupied the capital and ended the Safavid Empire, but it seems only the Afghans were interested in doing so some six decades later.

Chapter 8 Timeline	
1107–1307	Seljuks of Rum rule from Konya
1250–1517	Mamluk Empire
1290s	Ottoman expansion begins in western Anatolia under Osman
1354	Ottoman Expansion into Europe under Orhan
1389	Battle of Kosovo establishes Ottoman control over Balkans
1402	Ottoman Sultan Bayezid defeated at the Battle of Ankara by Timurleng
1453	Ottomans under Muhammad the Conqueror capture Constantinople
1501	Safavid Empire founded by Shah Ismail
1514	Ottoman victory over Safavids at the Battle of Chaldiran
1516–1517	Ottoman army under Selim I defeats Mamluks at Marj Dabiq and enters Cairo in early 1517, thus ending the Mamluk empire
1588–1629	Reign of Shah Abbas I (the Great)

Primary Sources

Kritovoulos: From *The History of Mehmed the Conqueror*

Position and Orders Given the Generals

§215. Then the Sultan mounted his horse and went around to all the other divisions, reviewing them and giving his orders to all in general and each in particular. He encouraged them and stirred them up for the battle, especially the officers of the troops, calling each one by name. Then, having passed along the entire army, along the wall from sea to sea, and having given the necessary orders and encouraged and incited all for the fight, and having urged them to play the man, he ordered them to have their food and rest until the battle-cry should be given and they should see the signal. And after doing all this, he went back to his tent, had his meal, and rested.

§216. Now the Romans, seeing the army so quiet and more tranquil than usual, marveled at the fact and ventured on various explanations and guesses. Some—not judging it aright—thought this was a preparation for withdrawal. Others—and this proved correct—believed that it was a preparation for battle and an alert, things which they had been expecting in the near future. So they passed the word along and then went in silence to their own divisions and made all sorts of preparations.

§217. The hour was already advanced, the day was declining and near evening, and the sun was at the Ottomans' backs but shining in the faces of their enemies. This was just as the Sultan had wished; accordingly he gave the order first for the trumpets to sound the battle-signal, and the other instruments, the pipes and flutes and cymbals too, as loud as they could. All the trumpets of the other divisions, with the other instruments in turn, sounded all together, a great and fearsome sound. Everything shook and quivered at the noise. After that, the standards were displayed.

§218. To begin, the archers and slingers and those in charge of the cannon and the muskets, in accord with the commands given them, advanced against the wall slowly and gradually. When they got within bowshot, they halted to fight. And first they exchanged fire with the heavier weapons, with arrows from the archers, stones from the slingers, and iron and leaden balls from the cannon and muskets. Then, as they closed with battleaxes and javelins and spears, hurling them at each other and being hurled at pitilessly in rage and fierce anger. On both sides there was loud shouting and blasphemy and cursing. Many on each side were wounded, and not a few died. This kept up till sunset, a space of about two or three hours.

§219. Then, with fine insight, the Sultan summoned the shield-bearers, heavy infantry and other troops and said: "Go to it, friends and children mine! It is time now to show yourselves good fighters!" They immediately crossed the moat, with shouts and fearful yells, and attacked the outer wall. All of it, however, had been demolished by the cannon. There were only stockades of great beams instead of a wall, and bundles of vine-branches, and jars full of earth. At that point a fierce battle ensued close in and with the weapons of hand-to-hand fighting. The heavy infantry and shield-bearers fonght to overcome the defenders and get over the stockade, while the Romans and Italians tried to fight these off and to guard the stockade. At times the infantry did get over the wall and the stockade, pressing forward bravely and unhesitatingly. And at times they were stoutly forced back and driven off.

§220. The Sultan followed them up, as they struggled bravely, and encouraged them. He ordered those in charge of the cannon to put the match to the cannon. And these, being set off, fired their stane balls against the defenders and worked no little destruction on both sides, among those in the near vicinity.

§221. So, then, the two sides struggled and fought bravely and vigorously. Most of the night passed, and the Romans were successful and prevailed not a little. Also, Giustinianni and his men kept their positions stubbornly, and guarded the stockade and defended themselves bravely against the aggressors.

§226. Sultan Mehmed saw that the attacking divisions were very much worn out by the battle and had not made any progress worth mentioning, and that the Romans and Italians were not only fighting stoutly but were prevailing in the battle. He was very indignant at this, considering that it ought not to be endured any longer. Immediately he brought up the divisions which he had been reserving for later on, men who were extremely well armed, daring and brave, and far in advance of the rest in experience and valor. They were the elite of the army: heavy infantry, bowmen, and lancers, and his own bodyguard, and along with them those of the division called Yenitsari [Janissaries].

§227. Calling to them and urging them to prove themselves now as heroes, he led the attack against the wall, himself at the dead until they reached the moat. There he ordered the bowmen, slingers, and musketeers to stand at a distance and fire to the right, against the defenders on the palisade and on the battered wall. They were to keep up so heavy a fire that those defenders would be unable to fight, or to expose themselves because of the cloud of arrows and other projectiles falling like snowflakes.

§228. To all the rest, the heavy infantry and the shield-bearers, the Sultan gave orders to cross the moat swiftly and attack the palisade. With a loud and terrifying war-cry and with fierce impetuosity and wrath, they advanced as if mad. Being young and strong and full of daring, and especially because they were fighting in the Sultan's presence, their valor exceeded every expectation. They attacked the palisade and fought bravely without any hesitation. Needing no further orders, they knocked down the turrets which had been built out in front, broke the yardarms, scattered the materials that had been gathered, and forced the defenders back inside the palisade.

§229. Giustinianni with his men, and the Romans in that section fought bravely with lances, axes, pikes, javelins, and other weapons of offense. It was a hand-to-hand encounter, and they stopped the attackers and prevented them from getting inside the palisade. There was much shouting on both sides—the mingled sounds of blasphemy, insults, threats, attackers, defenders, shooters, those shot at, killers and dying, of those who in anger and wrath did all sorts of terrible things. And it was a sight to see there: a hard fight going on hand-to-hand with great determination and for the greatest rewards, heroes fighting valiantly, the one party struggling with all their might to force back the defenders, get possession of the wall, enter the City, and fall upon the children and women and the treasures, the other party bravely agonizing to drive them off and guard their possessions, even if they were not to succeed in prevailing and in keeping them.

§230. Instead, the hapless Romans were destined finally to be brought under the yoke of servitude and to suffer its horrors. For although they battled bravely, and though they lacked nothing of willingness and daring in the contest, Giustinianni received a mortal wound in the breast from an arrow fired by a crossbow. It passed clear through his breastplate, and he fell where he was and was carried to his tent in a hopeless condition. All who were with him were scattered, being upset by their loss. They abandoned the palisade and wall where they had been fighting, and thought of only one thing—how they could carry him on to the galleons and get away safe themselves.

§231. But the Emperor Constantine besought them earnestly, and made promises to them if they would wait a little while, till the fighting should subside. They would not consent, however, but taking up their leader and all their armor, they boarded the galleons in haste and with all speed, giving no consideration to the other defenders.

§232. The Emperor Constantine for bade the others to follow. Then, though he had no idea what to do next—for he had no other reserves to fill the places thus left vacant, the ranks of those who had so suddenly deserted, and meantime the battle raged fiercely and all had to see to their own ranks and places and fight there—still, with his remaining Romans and his bodyguard, which was so few as to be easily counted, he took his stand in front of the palisade and fought bravely.

§233. Sultan Mehmed, who happened to be fighting quite near by, saw that the palisade and the other part of the wall that had been destroyed were now empty of men and deserted by the defenders. He noted that men were slipping away secretly and that those who remained were fighting feebly because they were so few. Realizing from this that the defenders had fled and that the wall was deserted, he shouted out: "Friends, we have the City! We have it! They are already fleeing from us! They can't stand it any longer! The wall is bare of defenders! It needs just a little more effort and the City is taken! Don't weaken, but on with the work with all your might, and be men and I am with you!"

Source: William H. McNeill and Marilyn Robinson Waldman, eds., "Kritovoulos: From *History of Mehmed the Conqueror*." In *The Islamic World* (Chicago: University of Chicago Press, 1983), pp. 327–331.

LETTERS FROM SELÎM AND ISMÂ'ÎL

1. Selîm to Ismâ'îl (undated, c. 1514)

> It is from Solomon and it is: "In the Name of God, the Merciful, the Compassionate. Rise not up against me, but come to me in surrender." [Qur'ân XXVII:30–31] God's blessings upon the best of his creatures, Muhammad, his family, and his companions all. "This is a Scripture We have sent down, blessed; so follow it, and be godfearing; haply so you will find mercy." [Qur'ân VI: 156]

This missive which is stamped with the seal of victory and which is, like inspiration descending from the heavens, witness to the verse "We never chastise until We send forth a Messenger" [Qur'ân XVII: 15] has been graciously issued by our most glorious majesty—we who are the Caliph of God Most High in this world, far and wide; the proof of the verse "And what profits men abides in the earth" [Qur'ân XIII: 17] the Solomon of Splendor, the Alexander of eminence; haloed in victory, Farîdûn[1] triumphant; slayer of the wicked and the infidel, guardian of the noble and the pious; the warrior in the Path, the defender of the Faith; the Champion, the conqueror; the lion, son and grandson of the lion; standard-bearer of justice and righteousness, Sultân Selîm Shâh, son of Sultân Bayezîd, son of Sultân Muhammad Khân—and is addressed to the ruler of the kingdom of the Persians, the possessor of the land of tyranny and perversion, the captain of the vicious, the chief of the malicious, the usurping Darius[2] of the time, the malevolent Zahhâk[3] of the age, the peer of Cain, Prince Ismâ'îl.

As the Pen of Destiny has drawn up the rescript "Thou givest the kingdom to whom Thou wilt" [Qur'ân III: 26] in our sublime name and has signed it with the verse "Whatsoever mercy God opens to men, none can withhold" [Qur'ân XXXV: 2], it is manifest in the Court of Glory and the Presence of Deity that we, the instrument of Divine Will, shall hold in force upon the earth both the commandments and prohibitions of Divine Law as well as the provisions of royal proclamations. "That is the bounty of God; he gives it unto whomsoever He will." [Qur'ân LVII: 21]

It has been heard repeatedly that you have subjected the upright community of Muhammad (Prayers and salutations upon its founder!) to your devious will, that you have undermined the firm foundation of the Faith, that you have unfurled the banner of oppression in the cause of aggression, that you no longer uphold the commandments and prohibitions of the Divine Law, that you have incited your abominable Shî'î faction to unsanctified sexual union and to the shedding of innocent blood,[4] that like they "Who listen to falsehood and consume the unlawful" [Qur'ân V:42] you have given ear to idle deceitful words and have eaten that which is forbidden:[5]

> He has laid waste to mosques, as it is said, Constructing idol temples in their stead, that you have rent the noble stuff of Islâm with the hand of tyranny, and that you have called the Glorious Qur'ân the myths of the Ancients. The rumor of these abominations has caused your name to become like that of Hârith deceived by Satan.[6]

Indeed, as both the *fatwas* of distinguished *'ulamâ'*[7] who base their opinion on reason and tradition alike and the consensus of the Sunnî[8] community agree that the ancient obligation of extirpation, extermination, and expulsion of evil innovation must be the aim of our exalted aspiration, for "Religious zeal is a victory for the Faith of God the Beneficent"; then, in accordance with the words of the Prophet (Peace upon him!) "Whosoever introduces evil innovation into our order must be expelled" and "Whosoever does aught against our order must be expelled," action has become necessary and exigent. Thus, when the Divine Decree of Eternal Destiny commended the eradication of the infamously wicked infidels into our capable hands, we set out for their lands like ineluctable fate itself to enforce the order "Leave not upon the earth of the Unbelievers even one." [Qur'ân LXXL: 26] If God almighty wills, the lightning of our conquering sword shall uproot the untamed bramble grown to great heights in the path of the refulgent Divine Law and shall cast them down upon the dust of abjectness to be trampled under the hooves of our legions, for "They make the mightiest of its inhabitants abased. Even so they too will do" [Qur'ân XXVII: 34] ; the thunder of our avenging mace shall dash out the muddled brains of the enemies of the Faith as rations for the lion-hearted *ghâzîs*. "And those who do wrong shall surely know by what overthrowing they will be overthrown." [Qur'ân XXVI: 227]

> When I the sharp-edged sword draw from its sheath,
> Then shall I raise up doomsday on the earth.
> Then shall I roast the hearts of lion-hearted men,
> And toast the morning with a goblet of their blood.
> My crow-feathered arrow will fix the eagle in his flight;
> My naked blade will make the sun's heart tremble.
> Inquire of the sun about the dazzle of my rein;
> Seek news of Mars about the brilliance of my arms.
> Although a Sûfî[9] crown you wear, I bear a trenchant sword:
> The owner of the sword will soon possess the crown.
> O Mighty Fortune, pray grant this my single wish:
> Pray let me take both crown and power from the foe.

But "Religion is Counsel," and should you turn the countenance of submission to the *qibla* of bliss and the Ka'ba[10] of hope—our angelic threshhold, the refuge of the noble—moreover, should you lift up the hand of oppression from the heads of your subjects ruined by tyranny and sedition, should you take up a course of repentance, become like one blameless and return to the sublime straight path of the Sunna[11] of Muhammad (Prayers and salutations upon him and God's satisfaction upon his immaculate family and his rightly-guided companions all!). For "My companions are like the stars: whomever you choose to follow, you will be guided aright."[12] And finally should you consider your lands and their people part of the well-protected Ottoman state, then shall you be granted our royal favor and our imperial patronage.

> He whose face touches the dust of my threshold in submission
> Will be enveloped in the shadow of my favor and my justice.
> How great the happiness of him who complies with this!
> On the other hand, if your evil, seditious habits have become a part of your nature, that which has become essential can never again be accidental.
> What avail sermons to the black-hearted?

Then, with the support and assistance of God, I will crown the head of every gallows tree with the head of a crown-wearing Sûfî and clear that faction from the face of the earth—"The party of God, they are the victors" [Qur'ân V: 56] ; I will break the oppressors' grip with the power of the miraculous white hand of Moses, for "God's hand is over their hands." [Qur'ân XLVIII: 10] Let them remove the cotton of negligence from the ears of their intelligence and, with their shrouds on their shoulders, prepare themselves for "Surely that which you are promised will come to pass." [Qur'ân VI: 134] The triumphant troops "As though they were a building well-compacted" [Qur'ân LXI: 4] crying out like fate evoked "When their term comes they shall not put it back a single hour nor put it forward" [Qur'ân VII: 34] and maneuvering in accordance with "Slay them wherever you find them" [Qur'ân IV: 89], will wreak ruin upon you and drive you from that land. "To God belongs the command before and after, and on that day the believers shall rejoice." [Qur'ân XXX: 4] "So the last roots of the people who did evil were cut off. Praise be to God, the Lord of the Worlds." [Qur'ân VL: 45]

II. Ismâ'îl to Selîm (undated, c. 1514)

May his godly majesty, the refuge of Islâm, the might of the kingdom, he upon whom God looks with favor, the champion of the sultanate and of the state, the hero of the faith and of the earth, Sultân Selîm Shâh (God grant him immortal state and eternal happiness!) accept this affectionate greeting and this friendly letter, considering it a token of our good will.

Now to begin: Your honored letters have arrived one after another, for "No sooner has a thing doubled than it has tripled." Their contents, although indicative of hostility, are stated with boldness and vigor. The latter gives us much enjoyment and pleasure, but we are ignorant of the reason for the former. In the time of your late blessed father (May God enlighten his proof!) when our royal troops passed through the lands of Rûm[13] to chastise the impudence of 'Alâ' al-Dawla Dhû'l-Qadr,[14] complete concord and friendship was shown on both sides. Moreover, when your majesty was governor at Trebizond [i.e., before his accession] there existed perfect mutual understanding. Thus, now, the cause of your resentment and displeasure yet remains unknown. If political necessity has compelled you on this course, then may your problems soon be solved.

Dispute may fire words to such a heat
That ancient houses be consumed in flames.

The intention of our inaction in this regard is twofold:

(1) Most of the inhabitants of the land of Rûm are followers of our forefathers (May God the All-Forgiving King have mercy upon them!).

(2) We have always loved the *ghâzî*-titled[15] Ottoman house and we do not wish the outbreak of sedition and turmoil once again as in the time of Tîmûr.

Why should we then take umbrage at these provocations? We shall not.

The mutual hostility of kings is verily an ancient rite.
Should one hold the bride of worldly rule too close,
His lips those of the radiant sword will kiss.

Nevertheless, there is no cause for improper words: indeed, those vain, heretical imputations are the mere fabrications of the opium-clouded minds of certain secretaries and scribes. We therefore think that our delayed reply was not completely without cause for we have now dispatched our honored personal companion and servant Shâh Qulî Âghâ (May he be sustained!) with a golden casket stamped with the royal seal and filled with a special preparation for their use should they deem it necessary. May he soon arrive so that with assistance from above the mysteries concealed behind the veil of fate might be disclosed. But one should always exercise free judgment not bound solely by the words of others and always keep in view that in the end regrets avail him naught.

At this writing we were engaged upon the hunt near Isfahan;[16] we now prepare provisions and our troops for the coming campaign. In all friendship we say do what you will.

Bitter experience has taught that in this world of trial
He who falls upon the house of 'Alî[17] always falls.

Kindly give our ambassador leave to travel unmolested. "No soul laden bears the load of another." [Qur'ân VI: 164; LIII: 38]

When war becomes inevitable, hesitation and delay must be set aside, and one must think on that which is to come. Farewell.

---

1 An ancient and celebrated king of Persia, who began to reign about 750 BCE.

2 Darius: Probably Darius III (r. 336–330 BCE), who was defeated three times by Alexander the Great before his assassination by the satrap of Bactria. Selîm is alluding to current Ottoman-Safavid relations.

3 Zahhâk: A mythological king of Irân, notorious for blood-thirstiness.

4 Reference to uncanonical practices, such as temporary marriage. The shedding of blood could be a reference to Shî'î massacres of Sunnîs at Tabrîz and elsewhere.

5 Further reference to uncanonical (from Sunnî perspective) practices condoned by Shî'ites.

6 Hârith: Possibly a reference to Hârith ibn Suwayd, who pretended to convert to Islâm in Muhammad's time, apostasized, and was ordered executed by Muhammad when he tried to rejoin the young Muslim community. Selim is alluding to parallels between Hârith's and Ismâ'il's career.

7 ***Fatwas***: legal opinions; ***'ulamâ'***: learned men.

8 Sunnî community: those who follow the practice of Muhammad; i.e., not those like Shî'îtes who followed 'Alî.

9 Allusion to Safavî origins as mystical order. The "crown" was their special headgear. Though the meter is that of the old famous ***Shâhnâmeh*** of Firdawsî, such topical references mark it as contemporary composition.

10 ***Qibla-***, direction of prayer for Muslims; i.e., the Kaaba or holy building in Mecca.

11 ***Sunna***: practice, example, custom of the Prophet Muhammad.

12 Reference to Shî'î practice of cursing the first three caliphs.

13 Rûm; i.e., Anatolia. Selîm's father was Bayezîd II (r. 1481–1512).

14 'Alâ' al-Dawla Dhû'l-Qadr: ruler of partially Shî'ite Dhû'l-Qadr Turkomans in Elbistan and Mar'ash, buffer state between Ottomans and Safavids. Ismâ'îl had attacked them in 1507.

15 An allusion to the Ottoman origin as frontier warriors for the faith.

16 City in Persian Irâq, later (1598) to become the Safavid capital.

17 House of 'Alî; i.e., the Shî'îtes.

Source: McNeill, William H. and Marilyn Robinson Waldman, eds. "Letters from Selim and Ismail." *The Islamic World.* Chicago: University of Chicago Press, 1983. Pgs. 338–344. From *Asnâd va nâmehâye tarîkhî va ijtimâiyye dowreye safavîyye*, edited by Z. Sabitiyân (Tehran: Ibn-i Sinâ, 1964), pp. 112–117. Translated especially for this volume by John Woods.

NOTES

1. William Ochsenwald and Sydney Nettleton Fisher, *The Middle East: A History* (New York: McGraw Hill, 2011), p. 137.
2. Afaf Lutfi Al-Sayyid Marsot, *A History of Egypt: From the Arab Conquests to the Present* (Cambridge: Cambridge University Press, 2007), p. 33.
3. P. M. Holt, *The Age of the Crusades: The Near East from the Eleventh Century to 1517* (New York: Longman, 1986), pp. 82–129.
4. Marshall G. S. Hodgson, *The Venture of Islam, Vol. 2: The Expansion of Islam in the Middle Periods* (Chicago: University of Chicago Press, 197), p. 418.
5. Ochsenwald and Fisher, *The Middle East*, p. 137.
6. Holt, *Age of the Crusades*, p. 93.
7. Ibid., p. 114.
8. Ibid., p. 139.
9. Ibid., pp. 146–147.
10. Marsot, *A History of Egypt*, p. 41.
11. Ibid., p. 194. Also see Marsot, *A History of Egypt*, p. 38, who adds that a number of plagues in the fourteenth century also destabilized the Mamluks.
12. The year 1299 CE is often used as the beginning of the Ottoman dynasty, perhaps because the year corresponds, in the Islamic calendar, to 699–700, which means in both the Christian and Islamic calendars the centuries turned, and as Caroline Finkel points out, "What more auspicious year to mark the founding of an empire that spanned Europe and the Middle East?" Caroline Finkel, *Osman's Dream: The History of the Ottoman Empire* (New York: Basic Books, 2005), p. 2.
13. Finkel, *Osman's Dream*, p. 10.
14. The oldest surviving Ottoman coins go back to this point (i.e., the taking of Bursa), and some contend that this is when the Ottoman state becomes an independent entity rather than a tributary state to the Mongol Ilkhanid empire based in Iran. Finkel, *Osman's Dream*, p. 7.
15. One mythical story has the commander of the Balkan Union, Serbian Prince Lazar, having had a last supper the night before the battle with his twelve generals. This equates Lazar's "night before" with that of Jesus Christ's Last Supper. In a way, then, the Serbs viewed the Turks as something akin to Christ-killers, which just added to the antipathy.
16. Stanford J. Shaw, *History of the Ottoman Empire and Modern Turkey: Volume I: Empire of the Gazis; The Rise and Decline of the Ottoman Empire, 1280–1808* (Cambridge: Cambridge University Press, 1976), p. 22.
17. In Bulgaria in the early 2000s, legislation was offered that would forcibly convert Muslims back to Christianity because it was believed that their ancestors only became Muslim in the first place because they were forcibly converted to Islam through the devshirme. Fortunately, the legislation never got too far, but it is

emblematic to this day of the often-fraught relationship between Christians and Muslims in the Balkans dating back to the Ottoman Empire.

18. Quoted in Philip Mansel, *Constantinople: City of the World's Desire, 1453–1924* (New York: St. Martin's Press, 1995), p. 18.
19. Peter F. Sugar, *Southeastern Europe under Ottoman Rule, 1354–1804* (Seattle: University of Washington Press, 1977), pp. 23–24.
20. Ibid., p. 24.
21. On the political, military, and social institutions of the Ottoman Empire, see Shaw, pp. 22–30.
22. If you visit the Topkapi palace in Istanbul, long the home of the Ottoman sultans after Constantinople was taken, you will want to find an intrepid guide who can bring you on a tour of the secret passageways where the sultan could remain unseen while listening in on the proceedings of the Imperial Council just to make sure everyone remained loyal and were following his orders.
23. Shaw, *History of the Ottoman Empire*, p. 12. Shaw was the first that I read who divided the Ottoman Empire into a first and second one, divided by the defeat at the hands of Timurleng and the succeeding interregnum.
24. Justin McCarthy, *The Ottoman Turks: An Introductory History to 1923* (London: Longman, 1997), pp. 79–80.
25. See Norman Itzkowitz, *Ottoman Empire and Islamic Tradition* (Chicago: University of Chicago Press, 1972), pp. 30–31.
26. Finkel, *Osman's Dream*, p. 96.
27. At the time it was done to counter Russian claims of their right to protect Christians in Ottoman lands by implicitly claiming to oversee Muslims in Russia (Finkel, *Osman's Dream*, p. 111). In the late nineteenth century, Ottoman sultans would also emphasize their role as caliph in order to gain leverage against predatory European powers who had large number of Muslims either in their countries or in their colonies, especially Russia, France, and Britain.
28. Unless otherwise noted, much of this history is derived from Roger Savory, *Iran Under the Safavids* (Cambridge: Cambridge University Press, 1980).
29. Ochsenwald and Fisher, *The Middle East*, p. 216.
30. Ibid., pp. 222–224.

KEY TERMS

asabiyya p. 214
beylerbeyik p. 225
devshirme p. 222
Divan al-Humayun (Imperial Council) p. 224
Gazi (Ghazi) p. 218
Janissary (Yeni Ceri or New Force) p. 223
kapikullari p. 223
millet p. 221
sipahis p. 223
Sublime Porte p. 223
sultan p. 210
timars p. 223
waqf p.231

For additional digital learning resources please go to www.oup.com/he/lesch-middleeast-1e

9 RISE, RESISTANCE, RETREAT, AND REFORM

The Age of Sulayman the Magnificent

So-called golden ages are a funny thing: once one is reached, the graph line of success thereafter can only inexorably head downward. And this is not just the ruminations of historians looking backward. Oftentimes those living in a time of prosperity, power, and security recognize that what they are experiencing is a golden age. This tends to mimic the human condition: we are born, we reach our peak, and then we decline and die. This is how civilizations were thought to progress. After the peak is perceived to have been reached, even within civilizations themselves there appears a literature of decline, some of it saying that things must change drastically in order to stay on top—or even afloat. Others take a more conservative approach, wanting to hark back to the past in order to recreate that which brought about the peak period in the first place—society has veered off course, away from the principles that enabled success; it's broken, and it just needs to be fixed. This has been a common scholarly approach to the history of the Ottoman Empire. It is generally agreed that the Ottomans reached their peak under Sulayman (Suleiman) the Magnificent, who ruled for forty-six years after coming to power in 1520, the longest of any Ottoman sultan. His legacy dominated Ottoman life for another hundred years. Yet the empire lasted for some 350 years after he died in 1566, all the way until just after World War I in the twentieth century. Surely there is a more nuanced approach to examining the course of the Ottoman Empire than an analogy to the human body. And there is. As Garth Fowden writes, it is more accurate to "see humankind constantly, across the ages, adjusting bit by bit not to decline, either slow or precipitate, but to gradual transformations."[1] While certainly not discounting the mounting losses on the battlefield to European foes beginning in earnest in the seventeenth century and the economic woes of the empire when compared to parts of Europe, in this chapter we will chart the progression of the Ottoman Empire within a paradigm of crisis and adaptation rather than decline and death, and not as a passive recipient of pernicious European designs.[2] Reality is more complex.

Sulayman was destined for greatness. After all, he was the tenth sultan, born in the tenth year (1494) of the tenth century in the Islamic calendar. There were ten parts to the Quran, ten closest Companions of the Prophet Muhammad, and Ten Commandments in the Old Testament or Pentateuch.[3] Surely this was no accident. He was the biggest and baddest of his era, outshining Charles V, the Holy Roman Emperor of the Habsburgs, Henry VII or Elizabeth I of England, Ivan the Terrible of Russia, or Francis I of France. And he knew it. Just look at how he addressed the Grand Master of the Knights of St. John on the island of Rhodes, one of his early targets for conquest, in the salutation of his letter: "Suleiman the sultan, by the grace of God, kind of kings, sovereign of sovereign, most high emperor of Byzantium and Trebizond, very powerful king of Persia, of Arabia, of Syria, and of Egypt, supreme lord of Europe, and of Asia, prince of Mecca and Aleppo, lord of

Sultan Suleyman I (1494–1566), also known as "Suleyman the Magnificent" and "Suleyman the Lawmaker," was the tenth and longest reigning sultan of the Ottoman Empire.
CPA Media Pte Ltd/Alamy Stock Photo

Jerusalem, and ruler of the universal sea, to Philip de L'Isle Adam, Grand Master of the island of Rhodes, greetings."[4] He followed this up with a less than subtle threat to Philip, hoping he would just surrender the island (he did not), and this was only in his first year as sultan.

As mentioned in the last chapter, soon after ascending to the throne, sultans often went on military campaign to buffer their bona fides as well as satisfy the military with the promise of glory and booty—it was their accession gift to the army. Sulayman was no different. He had two initial strategic objectives: to take Belgrade in Serbia, which would be the gateway to Hungary and eventually the grand prize, Vienna; and take the Island of Rhodes in the Mediterranean just off the coast of southwest Anatolia. Rhodes became even more important after the taking of Egypt in 1517. Ottoman control over the eastern and central Mediterranean could not be secured until the marauding pirates of the Knights of St. John, who raided the coastline and feasted on commercial ships to and from Constantinople, were eliminated. In fairly short order, Sulayman achieved both objectives. In 1521 he occupied Belgrade, and in 1522, albeit with great difficulty and heavy loss of men, he took the heavily fortified island of Rhodes. In the 1526 Battle of Mohacs, the Ottomans captured the cities of Buda and Pest (today's Budapest) in Hungary, which began a century-and-a-half conflict with the Habsburgs for European supremacy. At the time it seemed inevitable that Vienna would fall next, but in the 1529 siege winter came early and hard, and Sulayman was forced to retreat, a blot on an otherwise spotless record.

The Habsburgs did appear to be the last line of defense against the Ottomans in Europe. The Ottoman leadership always thought of themselves as European, and by advancing into central Europe it became part and parcel of European diplomacy; witness Charles V's attempt to ally with the Safavids to outflank the Ottomans and Francis I's seeking an alliance with Constantinople in an attempt to outflank the Habsburgs. While not a lot came of these, it was a portent of things to come for the Ottomans. For the Habsburgs and the Ottomans, the centralized bureaucracies developed by then in Constantinople and Madrid were the engines of warfare, fueled in the Habsburg case by the bullion beginning to arrive from the Americas. As historian Roger Crowley writes, the two empires could "raise taxes, levy men, dispatch ships, organize supplies, manufacture cannon and mill gunpowder with a comparative efficiency unimaginable in the handmade wars of the Middle Ages."[5] Or as historian Norman Itzkowitz put it, with considerable Eurocentrism, the confrontation took on the shape of "a contest for world supremacy."[6] They had the wherewithal to confront each other, and they did, both on land and at sea.[7]

Sulayman also could not ignore the continuing threat of the Safavids to the east, especially as his military priorities often had him deep into Europe. On two separate campaigns he inflicted a series of defeats on the Safavids in 1533 and 1548, eventually compelling the Iranian dynasty to sue for peace in the fairly humiliating Treaty of Amasya in 1555. But the Safavids survived to fight another day.

The Ottomans were a one-front army fighting on multiple fronts, and although they continued to be successful in both directions as well as across North Africa, it was increasingly coming at a higher cost—and higher opportunity costs as well. What was becoming more apparent during Sulayman's reign is that the Ottomans were reaching their logistical limits in terms of expansion, what with the limits in communication and transportation of the day. Ottoman suzerainty in North Africa was typically little more than nominal and really only along the coastline, with a garrison stationed in the main cities and an Ottoman governor and other officials appointed by Constantinople. During Sulayman's later years, victory still came but at higher cost. One of Sulayman's last campaigns was an attempt to take the island of Malta in 1565. It ended in a virtual draw, with the Ottomans losing some 40,000 soldiers. If consistent expansion ended, the Ottoman system would have to adjust in terms of raising revenues, the structure of the state and military apparatus, and the Ottomans own self-image. This would be a persistent challenge.

At home, the sultan was known as Sulayman the Lawgiver (*kanuni*), as he went to great lengths to codify the laws. He did much to clarify the corpus of law in terms of taxation, land tenure, and civil and commercial law. The institutional momentum that kept the empire going after Sulayman died was in large measure due to his efforts in codifying the disparate legal mechanisms of the state. As Ottoman historian Justin McCarthy wrote, "Sulayman transformed the state into an organization of rules and set procedures, a feat as important in the long run as important as his military conquests."[8] The wealth of the state also allowed Sulayman to sponsor the architectural exploits of Sinan, whose work dots the landscape of the Middle East, none more spectacular than the Sulaymaniyah mosque in Constantinople/Istanbul. The power of the Ottomans under Sulayman was felt at many different levels and throughout the empire. It is a shame to hear, then, the lamentations of Sulayman toward the end of his rule as he became more of an ascetic and wrote poetry reflecting his tenor. He hated being sultan by that time, due to his weariness with constant harem intrigue, the premature death of his favorite son, and the constant pressure of meeting the high standards he had set for himself. On one occasion he wrote, "Listen my heart, don't crave silver and gold like a highwayman. ... Don't stand there stiff, chest puffed up like a wrestler's lion. Never cherish wealth or high office. You might conquer far flung lands and seas and rule them as their sultan or king. Even if your reign on the imperial throne comes everlasting, don't be taken in. One day a hostile wind is bound to blow and bring to your land of beauty heaven's misfortune and worst suffering. Don't blow up your chest like a proud sail. Shun arrogance and malice. If you aspire to God's compassion, kindness should come from you too. If you hope to reach the garden of paradise to find love and grace instead of terrifying destruction. When the end comes to you, humble yourself like a skirt, blow at the sage's feet, and rub your face."[9]

As mentioned earlier, golden ages are hard acts to follow. The Ottoman Empire did begin to experience challenges that altered their relationship with

Sulaymaniyyah Mosque in Istanbul, Turkey, built in the 1550s by the famous Ottoman architect, Sinan.
mastix/Alamy Stock Photo

Europe—and often not in a good way. They were not the only ones to have to deal with these changing circumstances, as there were global forces afoot by the sixteenth and seventeenth centuries that in many ways caught the Ottomans—and others—on the outside looking in. There is usually no one single reason for the apparent decline of an empire when compared to some others; it is usually a confluence of reasons that together present challenges that are too difficult to overcome. And as discussed previously, "decline" is too general a word to use. Some indices of decline for the government, such as decentralization, might actually improve the lives of those living on the periphery of the empire. Less expansion through conquest seems to indicate a weakened empire, but it was probably a good thing for many of those who would have been levied into the army and who would have died or been maimed in battle—not to mention the resources expropriated by the government for war that could be earmarked in other directions. It is not so simple an equation. However, to say that the Ottoman Empire was not experiencing serious difficulties by the 1600s is to be blind to reality. It was not a graph line inexorably headed downward, but the general condition of the empire in terms of economic and industrial output, technological advancement, and losses on the battlefield and in territory in relation to Europe, especially northwestern Europe, was less than ideal.

One overall cause of this given by historians over the years was the end of conquests by the Ottomans. Despite surges every now and then by an energetic sultan or grand vizir, they had effectively reached their logistical limits by the end of Sulayman's reign. As Itzkowitz wrote, the end of expansion "for a polity and society predicated upon, committed to, and organized for conquest, was to have far-reaching and eventually devastating consequences."[10] While end of expansion doesn't necessarily in and of itself lead to disaster—after all, it lasted another 350 years after Sulayman—for the Ottomans at the time it had some negative cascading effects, mostly resulting from a system that had to adjust to the new reality devoid of constant expansion. It just did not do so in a timely or effective manner—or at least not effectively enough. One adjustment was that the empire shifted from acquiring revenues mainly through conquest to internal sources, such as taxes, a process that was typically inefficient and sporadic. With the loss of territory, mostly to European powers, also went the loss of a tax base, population centers, and resources (especially when these losses eventually came in the Balkans, the most heavily populated and resource-rich areas of the empire). For instance, in 1675 the Ottoman Empire consisted of 1.47 million square miles; in 1850 it was 1.14 million, in 1900 it was 910,000, and by the beginning of World War I in 1914, it had shrunk to 690,000 square miles.[11] In the span of about 240 years, the size of the empire was reduced by over 50 percent, resulting in less of just about everything that helped grow and maintain the empire during its first three hundred years. All of this put a great deal of stress on the treasury. As a result, to use but one example, the funds that were used to maintain the frontier against the Safavids could not be provided for by a depleted imperial treasury, so the government used the revenues from provinces in Anatolia and Syria to pay for the expense—funds that were normally earmarked for the imperial treasury, a substantial portion of which was used to pay the imperial army in the capital or for infrastructure.[12]

Another reason for the increasing challenges to the Ottoman Empire is the population explosion in the sixteenth century, perhaps by 40 percent in Egypt, Syria, and Anatolia alone. Historians are unsure of the causes, although natural population recovery after the Black Death of the fourteenth century could be a cause along with improving techniques in agriculture, which made it possible to grow and feed a larger population. The growing population at the same time the empire was shrinking territorially and economically led to a growing landless and restless peasantry, many of whom swelled the ranks of the brigands and bandits roaming the countryside, which only put more strain on the government to try to restore a level of security and stability—with less and less resources to do so. The Jelali (Celali) revolts in Anatolia in the late 1500s and early 1600s were emblematic of this problem, especially as many of the unemployed were former soldiers with training, making them that much more difficult to subdue. In some ways the situation is similar to the disaffected former Iraqi soldiers who made up the core of the shock troops for the Islamic State (ISIS) in its initial successful offensives in Iraq in 2014–2015. It may also be that the Jelali revolts were a product of a prolonged period of climate change, the Little Ice Age, that occurred at the time. It led to frequent droughts, frosts, floods, famines, and epidemics, all of which particularly decimated the rural areas hit hard by the fall in agricultural production. Only with great effort and strain on the imperial treasury were the Jelali revolts put down in what may have been the clearest sign yet of the end of the so-called Ottoman golden age, as the Sultan's power over the provinces was severely circumscribed with two centuries of increasing de-centralization to follow.[13]

An additional cause given by historians is that of Ottoman complacency.[14] This suggests that at a critical moment, Ottoman leadership had a certain smug belief in the superiority of their own civilization to even bother taking a look at others. Despite what appeared to be technological advances in Europe, which became manifest first and foremost on the battlefields on land and at sea, the Ottomans stuck to what was familiar. There were Ottoman writers and officials in the 1600s who were advocating for more openness to new ideas, even from Europe, which most Ottomans over the centuries considered to be backward and uncouth. There is also the convulsive, almost reflexive reaction in challenging times to make a conservative shift—to harken back to societal norms when things were good, or in the parlance of a supporter of US President Donald Trump in his successful 2016 presidential campaign, "Make the Ottoman Empire Great Again." The answer is staring everyone right in the face: fix what has become broken rather than adopt new ideas and ways. This is fairly typical. The problem for the Ottomans was that this general response came at a time of unprecedented growth in Europe, and the old ways could only do so much.

Related to this complacency, Ottoman leadership was also lacking at a critical moment when they needed strong and innovative sultans. The reason for this was the change in the method of succession during the reign of Sultan Muhammad III (1595–1603). We have seen the fratricidal survival of the fittest method of succession to the office of the sultan up until this time. As we know, even though it was haphazard and oftentimes brutal, it produced a terrific line of sultans. Sultan Muhammad III, knowing the history of how on many occasions the sons moved against the father, kept his own sons in what have been called *kafes* or cages: not actual bird cages or jails, but they were kept in the harem area of the palace under the watchful eye of the father. This way they could be kept in check and could not pose a threat. But it also meant that the sons did not acquire any experience as provincial governors or military commanders, and they did not gain any bases of support to enhance their claims. Instead, what emerged were often mentally deranged, paranoid, and inexperienced sultans who were not fit for office. We saw this happen to the Safavids with a similar change put in place by Shah Abbas the Great. That significant periods in the late 1550s and 1600s in the Ottoman Empire are referred to by historians as the Sultanate of the Women (wives, mothers, consorts of the sultans) and the Kuprili era, named after a family of grand viziers, is testament to the fact that there were a series of young, weak, or incapacitated sultans—and at a time when strong leadership was needed.

SPOTLIGHT

Sufiye Sultan and Sultanate of the Women

In just about every patriarchal society where the official leadership positions were mostly or entirely confined to men, women have played important roles at the top as well—and not just operating behind the throne. The Ottoman Empire was no different, particularly from the mid-1500s to the mid-1600s. Women connected to the sultan began to gain more agency under the reign of Sulayman the Magnificent (1520–1566). He was the first sultan to officially get married, whereas before his time the sultans had relations and children (heirs) with a slew of concubines. Sulayman married a woman known later as Hurrem Sultan, who probably was originally from Poland ("Hurrem" means "joyful" in Turkish, apparently a reference to her cheerful demeanor). The wife of the sultan would be known by the title of Haseki Sultan, as the wife's identity was still defined in relation to her husband (or mother to her son). It was under Sulayman that an imperial harem was established in the palace, and it was at a time when the sultan began to spend more time at the palace rather than constantly on campaign, thus propinquity and access allowed for more influence by those who were close to the sultan. Subsequent Haseki Sultans and mothers (known as Valide Sultans) of the sultans would become quite influential as a result, especially in pushing for the building of public works projects, charitable foundations, and hospitals, schools, and mosques.

With the change in the method of succession in the early seventeenth century, the series of young or incompetent sultans who took over only increased the power of the Haseki and Valide Sultans, often in opposition to the grand viziers, who tended to resent the sway they might have with their husbands or sons. On occasion, foreign ambassadors or other dignitaries, realizing where real power would lie at times, would even correspond directly with the Haseki or Valide Sultan (rather than the sultan or grand vizir) in order to communicate a particular action or request.[1]

Sufiye Sultan (1550–c. 1619) was a Christian Albanian woman who was married to Sultan Murad III (r. 1574–1595).[2] As with other wives of sultans, she was presented as a slave girl or concubine to Murad when he was a prince, and she wound up in the royal harem where she received the name of "Sufiye," meaning "purely chosen." Following Murad's death, she orchestrated the accession of her son, Mehmed III, to sultan, and her role shifted from the Haseki Sultan to that of Valide Sultan. It is said that she outshone her son, two grandsons, and a great-grandson, all of whom succeeded each other and all of whom were rather incompetent—or even deranged—sultans. When Sufiye was Haseki Sultan she often tussled with the Valide Sultan, especially over who should be chosen as heir and whether or not the sultan should have children with concubines to increase the pool of possibilities. In turn, when Sufiye became Valide Sultan she often clashed with the Haseki Sultans of her son, grandson, and great-grandson over similar issues as well as a host of domestic and foreign political challenges facing the empire. When she had to, she would deal with these situations in a ruthless manner.

Sufiye Sultan also became an advocate—as much as she could—for women's rights. One of the first things she did when she became Valide Sultan was to suspend the sentence of drowning women accused of adultery, informing the mayor of Istanbul that he should confine himself to governing the city and not killing women. She engaged in high-level diplomacy as well, carrying on a correspondence with Queen Elizabeth I of England. There is a well-circulated portrait of Elizabeth wearing Turkish clothing that may very well have been gifted to her by Sufiye. A Venetian diplomat once remarked that she was "a woman of her word, trustworthy, and I can say that in her alone have I found truth in Constantinople." As with many others in the Sultanate of the Women, Sufiye's patronage and funding of public works projects, architectural monuments, and humanitarian facilities had lasting beneficial effects for her Ottoman subjects.

---

[1] On this subject see Leslie Pierce, *The Imperial Harem: Women and Sovereignty in the Ottoman Empire* (New York: Oxford University Press, 1993).

[2] Information on and quotes from Sufiye Sultan found in Hossein Kamaly, *A History of Islam in 21 Women* (London: Oneworld Publications, 2019), pp. 117–123.

Her Imperial Majesty the Empress consort Hürrem Sultan of the Ottoman Empire, known to Europeans informally as simply Roxelana (c. 1500–1558), was the wife of Sülayman the Magnificent of the Ottoman Empire. Anonymous eighteenth-century painting.

CPA Media Pte Ltd/Alamy Stock Photo

Finally, and maybe most importantly, was the monetary revolution of the sixteenth century in Europe that caused an inflationary spiral in the Ottoman Empire that damaged the Ottoman economy in a way that did not happen to northwestern Europe (France, England, and the Netherlands). There is no doubt about how inflation in Europe trickled into the Ottoman Empire, and to other areas in the Mediterranean and beyond. There are some differences in opinion over the causes, from the demographic explosion in Eurasia (the same one that affected the Ottomans) to the prevalence of the cash economy combined with enormous state expenditures that required frequent debasing of the currency. The explanation that makes reasonable sense is somewhat more complicated, and it has to do with events and shifting forces happening in Europe rather than in the Ottoman Empire.[15] In this scenario, the inflation that hit Europe was caused by the influx of silver and gold into Europe from the Americas. This caused prices on basic commodities to rise precipitously in Europe, causing what some would call a great sucking sound out of the Ottoman Empire of these commodities through smuggling and other means searching for higher prices—and therefore profits for Ottoman merchants and traders. This disrupted what had been a mostly closed, self-sufficient Ottoman economy, with fewer resources for the artisanal guilds, with the craft industry being immeasurably hurt and the central government and cities across the empire losing customs revenues on these products in addition to just having less of them to support local manufacturing and infrastructural needs. In reaction, the Ottomans attempted a number of short-term expedients such as devaluing the currency, raising taxes, and seizing estates, most of which had long-term negative repercussions. The Ottoman economy was further disrupted when the inflationary trend hit it more directly.

The question is why northwestern Europe didn't suffer as badly. There are various responses to this. The one that offers the best explanation has to do with the price-wage-rent differential in certain countries in Europe. For instance, in England in the sixteenth and seventeenth centuries prices rose by 256 percent, wages by 145 percent, and rents rose at a slower rate, so of the entrepreneurs, laborers, and landlords, it was the entrepreneur who prospered the most from the inflation. The entrepreneurs, rather than utilizing their wealth as a way to enter the upper elite class and a life of luxury, as frequently happened in the Mediterranean basin, plowed their surplus capital back into the economy—into their mining ventures, commercial enterprises, and industrial establishments. The difference in the basic items of Mediterranean versus North Atlantic trade is a telltale sign. The former was based on luxury items (such as spices, perfumes, and silks) that only appealed to and could be bought by the upper classes. North Atlantic trade, on the other hand, was based on bulk items geared for the masses such as lumber, grain, and fish.

The entrepreneurs and merchants in northwestern Europe who got wealthy remained entrepreneurs and merchants because they were often already tied into the political class through their alliances with the national monarchies (to provide the kings and queens with the money to make or purchase bigger cannons to blow away the feudal barons hiding in their castles). They had status, wealth, and power while essentially remaining in their occupations and not retiring to the countryside in their chateaus and attending galas full time. They wanted to get richer, or as English economist John Maynard Keynes noted, these are the years when modern capitalism was born. Then the competitive national monarchies accelerated the advances in business techniques, overseas enterprises, and trading companies (e.g., the British East India Co. and Dutch East India Co.), as well as naval technology, especially in military applications that ultimately led to the control of the seas. A seminal event symbolizing the shift from the Mediterranean basin to the North Atlantic was the British defeat of the Spanish armada in 1588.

Northwestern Europe had the industrial and manufacturing base to absorb the effects of inflation; the Ottoman Empire did not. What happened eventually was what economic historian Omer Lutfi Barkan called the "penetration of the high-pressure dominant economy, the Atlantic economy, into the Ottoman low tension economy."[16] This produced a severe inflationary trend in the Ottoman Empire with all of the concomitant negative repercussions that forever disrupted what had been a close, self-sufficient economic system. The Ottoman economy (and many others around the globe) became peripheralized, more and more dependent upon the growing Atlantic economy. The Ottoman system could not adequately adjust to this new global economy increasingly dominated by northwestern Europe. It's not as though the graph line for the Ottoman economy and system was headed downward; it was just not rising nearly as fast as the countries of the Atlantic economy.

By the mid-1600s the Ottomans knew they were in trouble. With an empty treasury, rampant corruption, mounting losses on the battlefield, and poor leadership, a man by the name of Muhammad Kuprili (Koprulu) rose to the office of grand vizir in 1656 and inaugurated what came to be called the Kuprili era; for most of the remainder of the century members of the Kuprili family succeeded each other as grand vizir, attempting to reverse the deterioration of the empire. Muhammad Kuprili enacted a policy of sociopolitical fundamentalism or going back to the basics, fixing what had gone wrong in the empire and looking back to the past to see what had been done right. They did not have to look back too far to determine that the Age of Sulayman needed to be recreated to make the Ottoman Empire great again. As mentioned earlier, conservative responses in these circumstances are typical in any society.

The Circle of Equity (or Justice), an "all-encompassing formulation that embodied the ethical, political, and social values" of the Ottomans, was broken and needed to be fixed.[17] It was a political philosophy that essentially stated that every class of Ottoman society fed into each other in a circle of purpose and function. If the circle was broken, the state could not function well and the whole system could break down. It needed to be reconstructed, or so the Kuprilis thought. In what has been described as a dictatorship, Kuprili was ruthlessly successful in rooting out corruption, reforming the military and administration, rebuilding the fleet, and putting down internal opposition and revolts. As an indication of the success of the Kuprilis, the Ottomans were able to go on campaign again and lay siege to Vienna in 1683. Although it came close, it ultimately failed. As opposed to Sulayman's ordered retreat and residual military strength following his own failed attempt to take Vienna in 1529, this time the Ottoman army collapsed like a house of cards. The Ottomans were obviously feeling good about themselves to even engage in this military campaign, but the bottom line was that the Kuprili reforms were only superficial and did not address the fundamental problems and changes the Ottomans were encountering. The Europeans pressed onward after Vienna, inflicting losses on the Ottomans in central and southeastern Europe, with proportionate disarray at home in Istanbul with sultans, grand viziers, and other officials being removed, imprisoned, or executed as scapegoats amid continuing economic decline. Finally, on retreat in 1699, the Ottomans agreed to the Treaty of Karlowitz (in Croatia) with a coalition of European states led by the Habsburgs. It was the first time in any significant fashion that the terms of a treaty were dictated to the Ottomans rather than the other way around, and when territory that had been Ottoman for centuries had to be relinquished. Many have traditionally viewed Karlowitz as the beginning of the end for the Ottomans, particularly with regard to territorial conquest.

By looking backward to the Age of Sulayman the Magnificent, it is possible that the Kuprilis stifled the progress or growing pains of progress, especially along the European model, which would have enabled the empire to properly reform and regain its strength and stability. On the other hand, as we will see later in this chapter, an Ottoman sultan some 150 years later attempted to do just that—reform along the European model—and he was removed and summarily assassinated for his efforts by status quo forces. Perhaps the Kuprilis engaged in the only policies that were realistically available to them given the mindset of the Ottoman ruling class and conservative forces in the empire.

European Pressure

During the sixteenth and seventeenth centuries the Habsburg empire centered in Vienna, Austria was the European standard bearer against the Ottoman Empire. As head of the house of Habsburg, Charles V (r. 1516–1556) was also the Holy Roman Emperor and ruler of a number of other states in Europe, including Spain. He was a contemporary of Sulayman the Magnificent as they fought against each other for control of central Europe and the Mediterranean. Ottoman defeat at the naval battle of Lepanto in 1571 and at Vienna in 1683 signaled a shift in the balance of power between the Ottoman Empire and its European competitors. After the Treaty of Karlowitz in 1699, it was less the Habsburgs and increasingly Czarist Russia that became the foremost antagonist of the Ottomans, a confrontational relationship that would intermittently continue until World War I in the early twentieth century (1914–1918). Along the way other European powers would become involved in Ottoman affairs, which usually ended up at times with some of them taking Ottoman territory themselves or at other times through political and military assistance helping peoples break free from effective Ottoman control. The Ottomans had long wanted to be thought of as a European power. By the nineteenth century, however, they clearly had become more involved in European affairs than they perhaps wanted to be. To the Europeans, the Ottomans became the centerpiece of what was called the "Eastern Question": what to do about what was perceived to be a crumbling empire.

Czarist Russia's primary interest in the Ottoman Empire was strategic. Russia traditionally wanted year-round access to warm water ports, as their own were icebound for portions of the year. With the Ottoman Empire this meant gaining control of the Black Sea, which had outlets through the Turkish straits (the Bosphorus on the north side of the Sea of Marmara, and the Dardanelles on the south side) into the Aegean Sea and then to the Mediterranean. As Russian power grew under Ivan the Terrible (r. 1547–1584), Peter the Great (r. 1682–1725), and especially Catherine the Great (1762–1796), their appetite for this access through the Turkish straits became bigger and bigger. In order to truly be a great power, unimpeded access through or control of the straits was considered a military and economic imperative. In addition, the czars took it upon themselves to act as the protectors of Eastern (Greek) Orthodox Christians in the Balkans and in the Middle East, claiming this right in the Treaty of Kucuk Kainarja (Kaynarja) signed with (or rather imposed on) the Ottomans in 1774. It was during the reign of Catherine the Great that Russia started to inflict significant losses on the Ottomans. Russians considered St. Petersburg to be the "third Rome," following the fall of Rome in Italy and then Constantinople to the Ottomans. As Russian Orthodox Christians, it was incumbent upon them to protect other Orthodox Christians—after all, "czar" in Russian means "caesar." Although most have considered this simply to be a convenient wedge to interfere in the affairs of the heartland of the Middle East, one should not devalue how real they believed their religious obligations were. Finally, there was the ethnic factor, in that most Russians (certainly in leadership circles) were Slavic—so there was definitely an awareness, if not concern, for Slavs living under Ottoman rule in the Balkans. By the nineteenth century many of these Slavic peoples, often egged on by the czars, were agitating for more autonomy or outright independence from the Ottomans, which happened to fit with Russian strategic designs in the area.

The French were interested in the Ottoman Empire relative to their concerns about the British and the Russians. In addition, going back to the time of the Crusades, France had particular interests—religious, economic, strategic—in the Levant, especially the coast of what is today Syria and Lebanon. This manifested itself most dramatically elsewhere in the region in 1798, when none other than Napoleon Bonaparte led a military takeover of Egypt, then under nominal Ottoman suzerainty, that lasted but three years. Ostensibly the French, in true Orientalist fashion, entered Egypt to save it, almost as a moral obligation. In a critique leveled against the Islamic era in Egypt, the French framed their invasion as restoring the greatness of Egypt to that of the Pharaonic times, as that classical civilization had degenerated ever since. It was the typical European rationalization for imperialism: the "white man's burden," degeneracy that could be cured only through liberty and modernity.[18] Behind all this nonsense lay strategic and economic reasons for taking Egypt. To gather support for his military endeavor, Napoleon wrote French foreign minister Talleyrand a note in 1797: "The time is not far away that we will feel that, in order truly to destroy England, we must take Egypt. The vast Ottoman Empire, which dies every day, lays an obligation on us to exercise some forethought about the means whereby we can protect our commerce with the Levant."[19] Unsurprisingly, the French had misread what they thought would be a more welcoming Egyptian population, soon being seen as foreign occupiers. And by essentially decapitating the Ottoman-Egyptian state in the one month it took to do so, the French unleashed unforeseen forces in the country that along with British assistance, compelled the French to leave in 1801.[20] Napoleon, perhaps seeing the writing on the wall, had already returned to France to launch the more historically well-known part of his career.

While the French entry into Egypt was ultimately a failure, it did elicit British concern; the British also kept a close eye on the constant Russian pressure on the Ottomans. London correctly saw the French incursion as an attempt by Paris to be the first in line in the Middle East if the Ottoman Empire fell apart, thus gaining a strategic advantage over the British in the process. There were even fears in London that Napoleon's landing in Egypt was an attempt to establish a bridgehead to eventually take India, Britain's most important colonial possession, and Britain viewed the Middle East as its lifeline to India, to be protected at all costs. The best way—or at least the most efficient way—that Britain could protect this lifeline would be to maintain the integrity of the Ottoman Empire by keeping it afloat.[21] On occasion the British would directly intervene militarily to protect the Ottomans, as was the case with the Crimean War in 1854–1856 when Britain and France came to the empire's rescue against the Russians. With balance of power politics the order of the day on the European continent, keeping the Ottoman Empire together would protect the Europeans from themselves. Otherwise, its breakup would cause a free-for-all feeding frenzy upon the carcass of the Ottoman Empire, therefore upsetting the balance of power in Europe in a way that could lead to an all-European conflict—which essentially is what happened with World War I less than a century later.

It is important to remember that for the European powers the Ottoman Empire was clearly secondary in their calculations relative to events in Europe and relations among themselves, and this dynamic continued right up to and through World War I. As historian M. E. Yapp wrote regarding the European powers, "their main concern was that the changes in the distribution of power in the Middle East should not affect the balance of power in Europe."[22] But this is where Europe's dual-track policy toward the Ottomans undermined the goal of keeping the empire intact. By this I mean that one track was to maintain the integrity of the empire, but this meant much more than just saying it or committing troops and naval ships every now and then. It also meant supporting changes in the Ottoman system of government that would facilitate its continued existence. We will examine more closely Ottoman attempts to reform in the nineteenth century, but suffice it to say that within this context most of the European powers believed that in order to strengthen the empire so it could survive there should be more Ottoman government control: a centralization of power that would enable Constantinople to sufficiently raise and collect taxes, reform the military and administration, modernize the state, and build an Ottoman identity above and beyond ethnic, geographic, or religious subnational identities.

The problem is that this attempted centralization of power and reform efforts—encouraged and aided by the Europeans—ran smack into the demands of many groups, especially Christians in the Balkans, for more autonomy if not outright independence. Nationalism had been catching on in Europe ever since the French Revolution in 1789, and it was increasingly linked to ethnicity, with a group of people identifying themselves as a nation for one reason or another and wanting a state for themselves. In the Balkans these groups were mostly Christian, with whom the sympathies of Christian Europe usually lay when weighed against the Muslim Ottoman Empire. Therefore, in a second policy track toward Ottoman lands, European powers directly and indirectly tended to support these nationalist claims, all of which worked to undermine the first track, maintaining the integrity of the empire. Yapp put it well when writing that "the essence of the Eastern Question during the nineteenth century was the conflict between Ottoman rulers and their Christian subjects, primarily in the Balkans, the demand by those subjects for autonomy or outright independence, the Ottoman resistance to those demands and the efforts of the major European powers to find a resolution to the conflict which would accommodate the desires of both Ottomans and Christians and which would not upset the balance of power in Europe."[23] This was quite a tall task, to say the least, and one could add from the British and French perspective the additional objective of keeping Russia (and each other) from becoming a dominant power in the Middle East. In the end they all failed in trying to walk this delicate line, and when push came to shove, especially along the fringes of the empire, they simply took Ottoman territory directly for strategic reasons.

The contradiction in the dual-track policy revealed itself first in the Greek civil war of the 1820s that led to Greek independence from the Ottomans in 1830. Awash in pan-Hellenism amid sympathies for the putative birthplace of democracy, combined with antipathy toward the Turks and Muslims, most in Europe strongly supported Greek independence, and a number of Europeans (and some

Americans) actually traveled there to fight on the side of the Greeks. It would have been difficult for their governments to support Ottoman integrity directly. Muhammad Ali, a Circassian Albanian who had risen from an officer in the Ottoman army in 1801 that pushed the last vestiges of the French out of Egypt to become the de facto ruler of Egypt by 1805, tried to help the Ottomans keep Greece. The effort failed overall, but the Egyptian dynast thought he still deserved the gratitude of the sultan, who was unwilling to give it with the loss of Greece. As a result, Muhammad Ali sent his forces north and took Syria, and it was only with British assistance that he did not go further. Syria remained under the de facto rule of Egypt for most of the 1830s until the Ottomans reasserted themselves there in 1839. On this occasion it was an internal threat to Ottoman rule, although it was precipitated by the Greek civil war.

In 1830 the French took Algeria, which was incorporated as a province of France, and it remained so until the Algerian revolution in 1954 led to independence in 1962. The dual-track system was blown open in 1878 at the Congress of Berlin. The Europeans would frequently hold these conferences following a Russo-Ottoman war in order to try to keep the Ottoman Empire as intact as possible while not upsetting the European balance of power. With the exception of the Crimean war Russia was typically the winner, and it expected and was awarded territorial concessions by the Ottoman Empire. The other European states would simply try to contain Russian ambitions as much as possible. At the Berlin conference it was decided that Serbia, Romania, and Montenegro would become independent. France moved into Tunisia in 1881, whereas the British took over Cyprus in 1878 and then Egypt in 1882 to directly protect the Suez Canal, which opened up in 1869, built by the French and the British and owned and operated by British and French companies. The Suez Canal became the lifeline to India for the British.

Following the instability caused by the Young Turk revolution in the Ottoman Empire in 1908, Bulgaria, Bosnia, and Herzegovina became independent. Late to the imperial game after unification in the 1880s, Italy poached Libya from Ottoman hands in 1911. The consistent loss of territory for the Ottomans had deleterious consequences—lower population, fewer resources, and less tax base and revenues, as well as the ignominy of presiding over a steadily shrinking empire. By World War I the Ottoman Empire had shrunk by more than half. In terms of population, before 1850 about 50 percent of all Ottoman subjects lived in the Balkans; by 1906 it only constituted 20 percent of the total, and even less so after losing more territory in the Balkans in 1908.[24] After the Congress of Berlin in 1878 the Eastern Question was no longer how to keep the Ottoman Empire together and viable; now it was how to oversee the orderly break-up of the empire. It appeared to be a fait accompli that the empire would disintegrate. How were the Europeans going to maintain the balance of power in the face of this? It ultimately proved to be an insurmountable task, and blew up in everyone's faces with the onset of World War I.

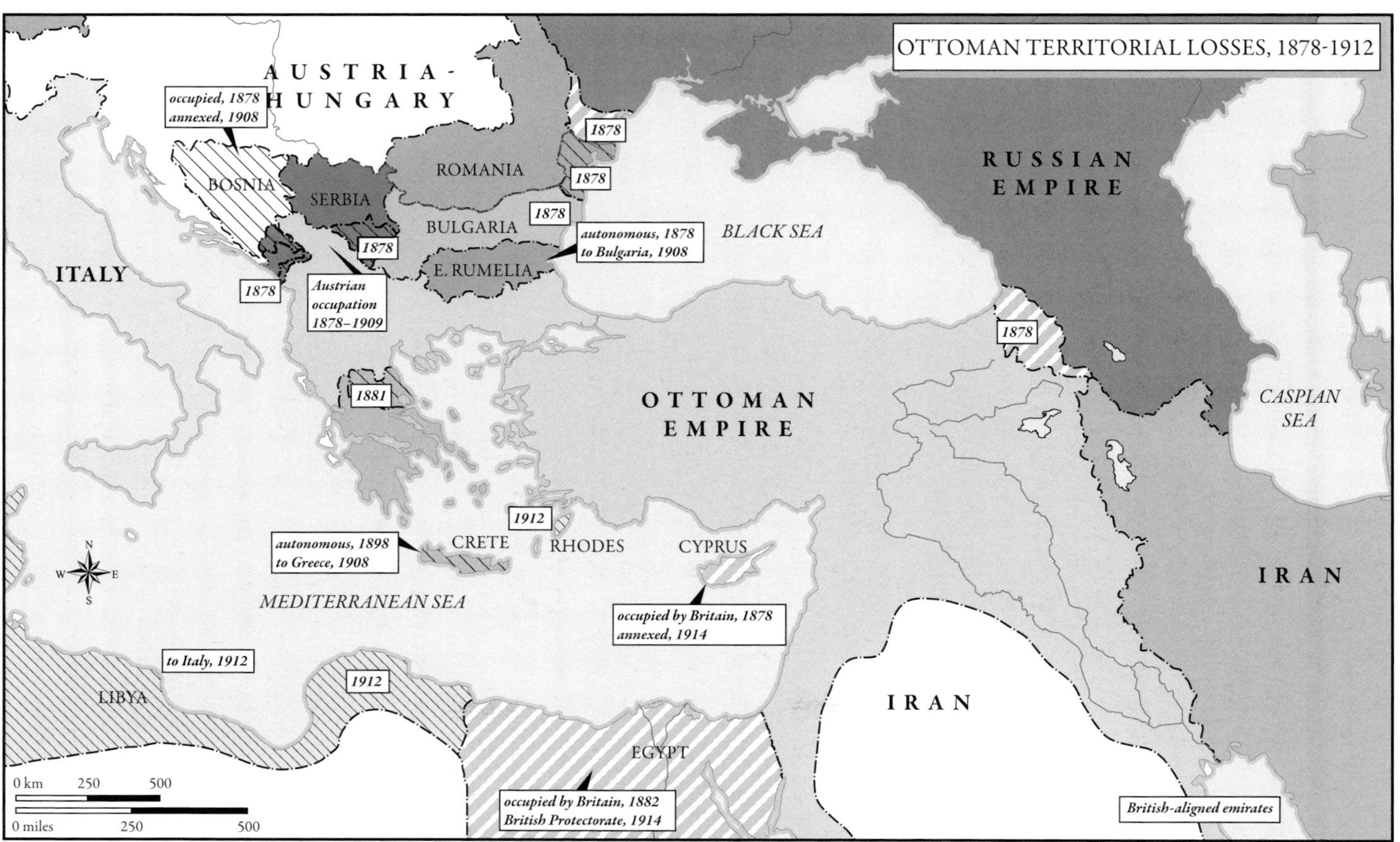
OTTOMAN TERRITORIAL LOSSES, 1878-1912
AUSTRIA-HUNGARY
occupied, 1878
annexed, 1908
BOSNIA
SERBIA
ROMANIA
BULGARIA
E. RUMELIA
1878
1878
1878
1878
1878
autonomous, 1878
to Bulgaria, 1908
Austrian occupation 1878–1909
ITALY
BLACK SEA
RUSSIAN EMPIRE
1878
CASPIAN SEA
1881
OTTOMAN EMPIRE
1912
autonomous, 1898
to Greece, 1908
CRETE
RHODES
CYPRUS
MEDITERRANEAN SEA
occupied by Britain, 1878
annexed, 1914
IRAN
to Italy, 1912
1912
LIBYA
EGYPT
IRAN
occupied by Britain, 1882
British Protectorate, 1914
British-aligned emirates
0 km 250 500
0 miles 250 500

This section of the chapter has focused on the international aspects of the Ottoman Empire primarily regarding its relations with the Europeans powers. It tends to reinforce the "sick man of Europe" image of the empire that was cultivated in the West, that it was this passive recipient of European designs. Not too long ago it would primarily be through this Eurocentric prism that students first encountered the Ottomans. But internally the Ottomans were an active, reforming state that was not somehow destined for the trash heap of history. There were dramatic institutional, economic, and sociocultural changes made as the Sublime Porte finally decided to modernize along the European model. Although ultimately losing, the Ottomans acquitted themselves admirably well in wars against Russia in 1828 and in 1877, the Italians in Libya in 1911, and in the early stages of World War I—all testament to their efforts. What did in the Ottomans in the end was prolonged conflict because of the lack of resources; they just could not sustain such efforts for very long against the European powers. It is now time to examine the other side of the coin.

Ottoman Reform Movement

By the late 1700s, the Ottoman Empire was not in particularly good shape. Sultan Mustafa III captured the moment fairly well shortly before his death in 1774 when he wrote the following quatrain:

> The world is turning upside down, with no hope for better during our reign,
> Wicked fate has delivered the state into the hands of despicable men,
> Our bureaucracy are villains who prowl through the streets of Istanbul,
> We can do nothing but beg God for mercy. [25]

It wasn't just the loss of productive capacity, smaller domestic markets, and reduced population from losing territory to the Europeans—as well as the unpredictability of war itself—but also the enhanced economic pressure directly from Europe that made the acquisition of revenue more challenging for the Ottoman state treasury. The manufacturing capacity of European factories resulted in machine-made sweaters from Lancashire, England being cheaper than ones sold in Aleppo made down the street by a local loom. This devastated the local craft and small business economy throughout the empire, which reduced the tax revenue coming from heretofore productive sectors—not to even speak of the social costs. The Ottoman economy was primarily provisionist, not one based on mass production. The cost of war and modernization led to continuous budget deficits (and ultimately bankruptcy). The final humiliating blow came in the form of capitulations, which included reduced customs duties and tariffs for European goods, which also harmed the domestic economy in the Ottoman Empire and made local products less competitive with their European counterparts. Something had to be done.

SPOTLIGHT

Turkish Carpets

One of my prized possessions is a Turkish *Hereke* silk prayer rug. I value it not only for the object itself, which is the finest of all silk carpets, but also because of the time—four days—it took me upon one of my earliest visits to Istanbul to negotiate the price of the carpet down to what I thought was a reasonable amount at a store in the Grand Bazaar.

Turkish and Persian carpets have been around for centuries prior to the medieval and early modern periods. But under the Ottoman and Safavid (as well as Mughal) empires, carpet weaving was "transformed from a minor craft based on patterns passed down from generation to generation into a statewide industry with patterns created in court workshops."[1] Carpets were made in quantities never before seen, and they were valuable items of trade to Europe and the Far East. The carpets were often placed on the ground, but they were also valued as wall hangings, covers for furniture, and as tablecloths. The finest of carpets typically found their way to royal households.

Turkish carpet weaving with looms, usually located in individual households, had been an art form with geometric motifs since the eleventh century. Italian (Venetian) traders had been importing Turkish carpets since the fourteenth century, long before Persian carpets hit the international markets; Turkish carpets can be found in the paintings of some of Europe's leading artists in the sixteenth and seventeenth centuries. Having the finest Turkish (and Persian) carpets became something of a status symbol in Europe. But Turkish rugs had been discovered centuries before as far east as Siberia in the Altai region, which is where the Turks originated before many of them migrated westward across Eurasia. It was in Ottoman Turkey that new weaving patterns and techniques were incorporated following the empire's conquests in the early sixteenth century of Safavid Persia and Mamluk Egypt. What had been a primary Turkish design of stylized animals and geometric patterns was transformed through this cultural exchange into one that focused on a central medallion with flowing *saz*-styled vegetation.[2]

The carpets themselves are woven textiles produced by knotting colored threads on the warp, compressed by the weft. All hand-knotted and hand-woven carpets have warps and wefts. The warps are the foundation yarn from fringe to fringe that runs top to bottom, and the wefts run left to right. The primary structural difference between Turkish and Persian carpets is in the knots. The Turkish (Gordes-symmetrical) knot is wrapped around two warps, and the Persian knot (Sine-asymmetrical) around a single warp. This makes the Turkish carpet stronger and more durable, while the Sine knot allows for the weaving of more variety of patterns. Most of the better carpets are still woven on looms in homes located in villages around Turkey, with the name of the carpet reflecting the name of the village. Young girls about ten years old make for the best weavers given their small hands and fingers, which allow them to tie smaller and tighter knots—some 800–1,000 knots per hour by the best of them.[3]

To determine the size of knot—and thus the quality and cost of the carpet—you must run your fingers on the back of the carpet. Even if you do not know what you are doing, at least it looks like you know how to evaluate a carpet.

Turkish carpets started to decline in the seventeenth century under the Ottomans, not so much because of any innate downsizing of the industry but rather because Persian carpets were entering the international trade market with more vigor. Even the Ottoman sultans preferred the more complex compositions of Persian carpets.[4] This was due to the fact that Safavid Shah Abbas the Great (1588–1629) in the late sixteenth and early seventeenth centuries entered into a number of trade treaties with European countries to enhance his empire's economy, especially the floundering textile industry, which led to the exporting of more Persian carpets. As some have said, this is when Persian carpets really acquired their fame. Soon Europeans were

Carpet with Triple-Arch Design c. 1575–1590. One of the earliest carpets to include a triple-arched gateway, its design probably originated in the Ottoman imperial workshop. The combination of this carpet's imagery, high quality, and relatively small size suggest that it was used as a prayer rug by a member of the Ottoman courtly elite.
The Metropolitan Museum of Art

buying more Persian rather than Turkish carpets, and the former rather than the latter were appearing in the paintings of Europe's premier artists.

The Hereke Turkish carpets are the finest silk carpet in perhaps the entire the world. Someone told me—probably the shopkeeper who sold me my Hereke carpet in Istanbul—that they are the Rolls Royce of carpets. They are made in the Turkish village of Hereke, a town about sixty kilometers east of Istanbul. Hereke carpets often have intricate designs of birds and trees woven in pale pastel colors, and they contain anywhere between 360,000 and 1.2 million knots per square meter, with a typical prayer rug taking five to six months to weave.[5] They were often known as "palace carpets" because they found their way into the royal palaces of the sultans and their inner circles. Carpets woven in Kayseri in Turkey are the most numerous of Turkish carpets, woven with cotton, wool, and silk. The colors are usually ground in red, blue, and deep blue, with white, black, grey, and purple often infiltrating the base colors. Whatever the case, the carpets often told a story of some sort, and they have been called communication devices delivering messages—and beautiful artwork—from the past to the present.

---

[1] (Marika Sardar, "Carpets from the Islamic World, 1600–1800," in *Heilbrunn Timeline of Art History online*. New York: Metropolitan Museum of Art, 2003, http://www.metmuseum.org/toah/hd/crpt/hd_crpt.htm.

[2] Ibid.

[3] https://www.nytimes.com/1981/11/22/travel/anatolia-s-magic-carpets.html.

[4] Ibid.

[5] Ibid.

It would be Sultan Selim III (1789–1807) who first tried to implement systemic reform along the European model in order to try to reverse the course of the empire. In 1791 he officially inaugurated the **Nizam-i Jadid** or New Order, meaning a new system. Since the Ottomans had never really bothered to understand what was happening in Europe, the first order of business for Selim and subsequent reformers was to gather information. This they did by opening embassies for the first time in many European countries, which could act as information collection centers. In addition, European military, financial, and administrative advisers were brought in to help reorganize the government to make it look more like those that existed in Europe, creating appropriate ministries and departments. Perhaps the most important element was reform of the military, since it was getting defeated on the battlefield against European foes on a regular basis. Many have called the overall Ottoman reform efforts as military-led reform, or sometimes defensive developmentalism; the ultimate objective of the reform movement was for the empire to survive against European predations.

Others have called this process of reform as modernization from above, meaning initiated from the top down, fueled by the bureaucracy. As such, the reform movement was not organically grown from the bottom up. There was no social, political, or economic impulse from below. Because of this, Sultan Selim III had to have the support of the most powerful sectors of the state, including the religious classes (ulama) and the military. This he did not have. He was opposed by the ulama as well as the Janissaries, both of whom saw their privileged positions threatened by military reform (replete with European style uniforms) and educational reform, the latter focusing on establishing a more European-style educational system, which obviously would supplant the religious-based schools (*madrasas*) controlled by the ulama. Selim was summarily removed as sultan in 1807 by the Janissaries, and then was assassinated shortly thereafter under house arrest. Apparently it was still too soon to try this type of wide-ranging reform. The situation would have to get even worse before it stood a chance of getting better. Two types of systems comingling could not work; one had to win out. As historian M. Sukru Hanioglu writes, "the challenges of the new era produced duality in every field: a modern, European style army alongside a stubbornly conservative corps of Janissaries; an increasingly monetary economy together with the medieval timar system; glimmerings of fiscal responsibility yet multiple budgets; modern academies boasting libraries ... along with Ottoman *medreses* (madrasas) whose curricula had not changed for centuries. It was this inherent tension between the old and the new which issued in the violent rupture of 1807."[26]

Supported by the ulama, the Janissaries hand-picked the next sultan, Mustafa IV, who was known to be against the Nizam-i Jadid. But there were still powerful pockets of pro-reformists, especially rural notables (**ayan**) in the European provinces of the empire, who saw firsthand the need for Westernized reform. One in particular, Alemdar Mustafa from Rumelia, possessed a very strong army himself (maybe the strongest single army in the empire at the time). He marched on Istanbul intent on placing Selim III back on the throne, but the latter was executed before he could do so. Regardless, Sultan Mustafa IV was forced from office and his son, Mahmud II, was placed in power as sultan with a mandate to engage once again in reform. For his efforts, Alemdar Mustafa was appointed grand vizir.

The reactionary elements were not yet ready to pack it in, however. Groups of Janissaries rose up against the new sultan, and in the process Alemdar Mustafa was killed. This was a serious blow to the reformists, and many of them were forced from office or executed. The newly formed European-style army of the Nizam-i Jadid was disbanded, and it seemed the status quo ante was restored. It was a very chaotic time with the back and forth by pro and anti-reform forces, and a young sultan not yet ready for prime time caught in the middle. He would have to tread very carefully.

One thing Mahmud II learned from the violence of 1807–1808 was that if the empire was going to reform along the European model, he would have to proceed carefully until he garnered enough support to take appropriate action. Adroitly, the sultan and the reformers would frame specific reformist policies in the name of Islam, for instance quoting a hadith from the Prophet Muhammad or a Quranic verse to sanction a particular policy in order to assuage the ulama as well as a general public that was still for the most part traditional and conservative.[27] And he would not try to establish a parallel European-style army as Selim III had done—at least until he was ready.

By the mid-1820s, Mahmud II had built enough support for his final onslaught on the Janissaries. The efficiency of Muhammad Ali's European-style army fighting in Greece as well as his centralizing policies in Egypt proved to be an encouraging example for one and all to see. In 1826 the sultan began to form a new army corps. As expected, the Janissaries prepared to rebel by gathering in one of the main squares near the palace, calling Mahmud II the "infidel sultan." But the infidel sultan was ready, obtaining a religious ruling (*fatwa*) approving the killing of Janissaries, and many were slaughtered in the square and beyond. The tide had turned in what has become known as the **Auspicious Incident**. Soon thereafter the sultan formed a European-style army corps known as the Victorious Troops of Muhammad (*Asakir-i Mansure-i Muhammadiye*), composed of infantry and cavalry under one unified command with units established in the provinces, and the preexisting provincial armies, such as those of Alemdar Mustafa had, were disbanded. It is interesting that even in victory, the new army corps was named after the Prophet Muhammad, a clear sign that traditional opposition remained.

As one might expect, following the chaos of the Auspicious Incident and considering the time it would take to effectively build up a replacement to the Janissaries, some of the foes of the Ottoman Empire were seeing a prime opportunity to expand at the latter's expense. It is then not a surprise that the Greek rebellion emerged successful shortly thereafter, or that the Russians launched another war in the Balkans against the empire in 1826, ending in the Ottomans suing for peace in the Treaty of Turkomanchai in 1828. A dissatisfied Muhammad Ali was able to take over Syria from the Ottomans in the 1830s. It was certainly one step backward; Mahmud II was hoping that it would ultimately result in two steps forward.

Bereft of support from the now abolished Janissary corps, the conservative ulama were also on the defensive against Mahmud II's reforms. The sultan accelerated the secularization of the education system while also extending state control over the ulama, co-opting many of them as part of the system so that they were less likely to move against it. This was not a separation of church and state, but rather more state control of religion. Student missions were sent to Europe, and Ottomans working in the newly revamped Ministry of Foreign Affairs needed to learn European languages—all part of acquiring the necessary information to reform as well as the tools of diplomacy. The foreign embassies that were closed after Selim III was removed were reopened in 1834, a year after the Translation Bureau was created, the influence of which would be felt by a new generation of European-leaning officials over the next few decades.

Mahmud II also attempted to curtail the power of the provincial notables (ayan), part of which was done through the reorganization of the military and by

(a)

Lithograph showing Ottoman soldiers, 1600–1805.
mccool/Alamy Stock Photo

(b)

Ottoman Army officers in 1895. Vintage illustration by Henri Meyer.
Chris Hellier/Alamy Stock Photo

default with more centralized control, trying to reverse a process of decentralization in the provinces that had been in motion since the days of Sulayman the Magnificent. As Hanioglu wrote, "The Ottoman order could only survive if the seepage of power from the center to the periphery was reversed. ... Certainly, a loosely-bound association of disparate, semi-independent territories could not expect to survive long in the Napoleonic era."[28] It was an effort that was not entirely successful, as the ayan remained influential at the local level. The ayan had developed into quasi-independent local rulers who sometimes worked with Ottoman authorities and sometimes did not. Typically, large landowners and religious or family and tribal leaders would also act as important intermediaries between the Ottoman government and the local populations, carving out critical roles for themselves that in one form or another would last well into the twentieth century, especially in the Arab provinces of the empire. The ebb and flow of the relationship between the ayan and the central government is one of the more important features of modern Ottoman history.

Mahmud II died in 1839, but his hard-won reformist agenda was continued by his successor, Abd al-Majid (1839–1861). He made reform public by giving the process a formal title: the **Tanzimat**, from the same root as *nizam* and translated as "reorganization." The Tanzimat was essentially just giving name to what had already begun under Mahmud II. The overall goal of the reform movement may have been imperial survival, but the state now delineated more specific ways to get there.

These included a more centralized state that went beyond military and administrative reform to include such things as a state newspaper to better control the flow of information; postal services so that government orders, decrees, and policies could go out faster and information and intelligence from the provinces could be received more quickly and efficiently; and something as simple as putting up more portraits of the sultan in order to consciously and subconsciously remind the population of who was in charge.[29] The whole system needed to modernize, which included a professional bureaucracy based on merit, uniform and more efficient taxation, a state police force to ensure security, and the end of the monopoly of privilege by the ayan.

One of the more ambitious goals of the Tanzimat was what was called Ottomanization: to encourage if not compel the population to think of themselves as Ottoman citizens first and foremost, before their subnational identities. In other words, they were Ottoman—not Serbian, Syrian, Bosnian, Turkish, Muslim, Christian, or Jewish. This was intended to foster an Ottoman nationalism that would help unify the empire to counter European pressure that often supported internal separatist tendencies, but it also flew in the face of the millet system, which unintentionally systematized separation over the centuries rather than unity. All one had to see was the dozen or so languages in which Ottoman edicts were often published to understand the lack of a national identity. This would be a hard nut to crack, however. Many in the empire reflexively retreated into these subnational identities even more. A true national identity is forged organically over decades, if not centuries, not imposed top-down by government fiat. In addition, some of the more privileged millets, such as Greek Orthodox Christians, who willingly accepted their secondary status to the Muslims, largely opposed Ottomanization because now they would be on equal footing with such "lesser" millets as the Jews or Armenian Orthodox, an unofficial hierarchy of religion and race that developed over the years. They wanted to preserve their hard-earned status, not have it diminished. As a result, in terms of its intended objective, Ottomanization may in the end have done more harm than good.

From the outside looking in, the Tanzimat period was symbolized by three government documents: the Khatt-i Sherif of Gulkhane in 1839; the 1856 Khatt-i Humayun (also known as the Islahat Fermani); and the Ottoman constitution of 1876. The first two documents essentially translate as "Imperial Rescript," a government or sultanic decree or policy edict ("Gulkhane" is the name of the garden adjacent to the sultan's Topkapi palace in Istanbul where the rescript was signed). They also are very similar documents in content, with the latter basically reaffirming the former. They were really statements of principles, almost like a bill of rights for Ottoman citizens calling for "security of life, honor and prosperity," along with a reaffirmation of religious liberty and equality to all non-Muslim subjects. The Ottoman constitution, based on the Belgian model, is self-explanatory, creating a European-style parliamentary system of government overseen by the sultan. Ottoman constitutionalists had been pressing for this for some time as the ultimate expression of European-style modernization. In practice, without the balancing forces of the Janissary corps and ulama as in the past, the arbitrary power of the sultan (in this case Abd al-Aziz, who succeeded Abd al-Mejid in 1861) had grown unabated. Abd al-Aziz had fifteen grand viziers during his reign. Constitutionalists believed that the autocratic state had failed at protecting the empire against European encroachment; having a constitution would somehow magically strengthen that state and demonstrate to the Europeans that they were "civilized members of the world community rather than carcasses to be picked clean by various imperialists powers or nationalist movements."[30] However, there was no impulse from below for a parliamentary form of government. It was once again top-down, led in this instance by Midhat Pasha, who, like many other constitutionalists, had received at least some European-style education. It was almost seen as a prerequisite to being thought of as a modern European state. It was the end game but without the necessary elements of civil society: educational and social development over many decades that underpin the successful formation of a truly representative system of government. One constitutionalist described the traditional Ottoman system as a "Bedouin government in the heart of Europe, exercising a form of absolutism fit only for tribes."[31]

But as M. E. Yapp writes, "the real, efficient Tanzimat was the drive for a modernized, centralized state; the unreal, decorative Tanzimat was the professions of unrealizable ideals made necessary by the need for some measure of European consent."[32] The second part, the "decorative Tanzimat," is the section upon which to focus. What Yapp means by this is that we should look at the timing of the three symbols of the Tanzimat. The Khatt-i Sherif was promulgated in 1839, shortly after European support to push back Muhammad Ali. The Khatt-i Humayun came about in 1856 right after another European intervention against Russia in the Crimean war. The Ottoman constitution followed upon Ottoman bankruptcy to mostly European banks in 1875, as well as heightening tensions with Russia that would soon result in another Russo–Ottoman war. The European governments who came to the aid of the Ottomans—mainly the British and French—had their own publics to assuage. These publics as well as their parliamentarians were unlikely to countenance losing their human and material national treasure so that their governments could save an anachronistic, authoritarian, and repressive empire. Yet if it had been a modernizing, reforming state that was increasingly based on the European model of government and establishing a Rights of Man–like social contract with its citizenry, then perhaps Europeans in general would support the effort. It was all window dressing, however, to impress the Europeans and make it easier for European governments to come to the aid of the Ottomans. The Khatt-i Humayun was essentially dictated to the sultan by the British ambassador in Istanbul.

So the Tanzimat ultimately failed. Ottoman territories kept breaking away from European intervention and pressure, a major escape occurring in 1878 with the

Congress of Berlin, just two years after the constitution was adopted. There were successes, but they were limited due to lack of trained personnel, continued European military and political interference, and the continued opposition of conservative elements in the empire who were threatened by the reforms—such as the peasants facing higher taxes, ulama whose traditional role was undermined, and the ayan, whose power was being circumscribed. Maybe the most important reason was the lack of money. Military reform and modernization are expensive, and in the end the Ottoman government simply did not have enough of it, leading to debts and bankruptcy in 1875, partly because of the global depression of 1873. Making weapons, roads, and railroads as part of the centralization process required enormous expenditures.[33]

The government attempted a rudimentary form of import-substituting industrialization (ISI), which is meant to move an economy dependent on imports to an industrial footing. Not only is this supposed to generate a more robust local economy, but it also means less economic—thus political—dependence on outside powers. Too often, though, in an effort to industrialize quickly, governments establish end-product factories that are intended to create backward linkages, feeder industries to provide the basic materials to the end-product factory, thus establishing a fully integrated economy—or so it was thought.[34] The problem in almost every case was the government neglect of the agricultural center. In the Ottoman Empire and other states in the twentieth century that attempted ISI, agriculture was by far the biggest revenue producer for the state from taxes on produce and earnings. In the nineteenth century, 80 percent of the Ottoman Empire of some thirty million was rural. By neglecting or economically smothering the agricultural sector the governments were cutting off their nose to spite their face; they were undermining their own customer base, those who would purchase the products to keep the factories operating at full capacity. Pretty soon the only people who could afford the products whose prices had risen due to economies of scale were the upper classes, thus exacerbating the unequal distribution of wealth and the development of distinctly different cultures or classes in mutual incomprehension of each other. Without the necessary income and the lack of foreign exchange from inferior or pricey products, the Ottomans went hunting for loans from European banks, most of which ended up being earmarked toward servicing the debt. When they could not even pay the interest on the loans, that meant bankruptcy—and ultimately even more dependence on the European powers.

Maybe the ultimate legacy of the Tanzimat is that it did establish something of a foundation of modernization for future use, inspiring an important cadre of Turks who wanted to enter the European world at every level, none more important than the founder of the modern Republic of Turkey, Mustafa Kamal Ataturk. Not that it was an easy process of change and modernization following World War I when he became Turkey's first president, but without the Tanzimat, he quite possibly could not have even tried.

Chapter 9 Timeline

1520–1566	Reign of Ottoman Sultan Sulayman the Magnificent
1529	Failed Ottoman siege of Vienna
1571	Ottoman naval defeat at Lepanto
1656	Muhammad Kuprili becomes Grand Vizir of the Ottoman Empire, inaugurating the so-called Kuprili era
1683	Second Ottoman siege of Vienna ends in disaster
1699	Ottomans agree to Treaty of Karlowitz
1789–1807	Sultan Selim III initiates reforms in the Ottoman Empire
1798	French army under Napoleon Bonaparte occupies Egypt
1808–1839	Rule of Sultan Mahmud II
1826	Destruction of the Janissaries in what is known as the Auspicious Incident
1830	Greece gains independence from Ottoman Empire; French conquest of Algeria
1839–1876	Era of the Tanzimat
1878	Congress of Berlin

Primary Sources

Poem written by Sulayman the Magnificent to his wife, Hurrem Sultan (Roxelana)

Roxelana

Throne of my lonely niche, my wealth, my love, my moonlight.
My most sincere friend, my confidant, my very existence, my Sultan
The most beautiful among the beautiful ...
My springtime, my merry faced love, my daytime,
  my sweetheart, laughing leaf ...
My plants, my sweet, my rose, the one only who does not distress me
  in this world ...
My Istanbul, my Caraman, the earth of my Anatolia
My Badakhshan, my Baghdad and Khorasan
My woman of the beautiful hair, my love of the slanted brow, my love of eyes
  full of mischief ...
I'll sing your praises always
I, lover of the tormented heart, Muhibbi of the eyes full of tears, I am
  happy.

Quoted in the film, *Sulayman the Magnificent*, produced for The National Gallery of Art and Metropolitan Museum of Art, 1987. Directed and produced by Suzanne Bauman.

The Gülhane Proclamation, 1839

All the world knows that in the first days of the Ottoman Monarchy, the glorious precepts of the Koran and the Laws of the Empire were always honored. The Empire in consequence increased in strength and greatness, and all her subjects, without exception, had risen in the highest degree to ease and prosperity. In the last 150 years a succession of accidents and diverse causes have arisen which have brought about a disregard for the sacred code of Laws, and the Regulations flowing therefrom, and the former strength and prosperity have changed into weakness and poverty; an Empire loses all its stability so soon as it ceases to observe its Laws.

These considerations are ever present to our mind, and, ever since the day of our advent to the Throne, the thought of the public weal, of the improvement of the state of the Provinces, and of relief to the peoples, has not ceased to engage it. If, therefore, the geographical position of the Ottoman Provinces, the fertility of the soil, the aptitude and intelligence of the inhabitants are considered, the conviction will remain that, by striving to find efficacious means, the result, which by the help of God we hope to attain, can be obtained within a few years. Full of confidence, therefore, in the help of the Most High, assisted by the intercession of our Prophet, we deem it right to seek by new institutions to give to the Provinces composing the Ottoman Empire the benefit of a good Administration.

These institutions must be principally carried out under three heads, which are:

1. The guarantees insuring to our subjects perfect security for life, honor, and fortune.
2. A regular system of assessing and levying Taxes.
3. An equally regular system for the levy of Troops and the duration of their service.

From henceforth, therefore, the cause of every accused person shall be publicly judged in accordance with our Divine Law, after inquiry and examination, and so long as a regular judgment shall not have been pronounced, no one can, secretly or publicly, put another to death by poison or in any other manner.

No one shall be allowed to attack the honor of any other person whatsoever.

Each one shall possess his Property of every kind, and shall dispose of it in all freedom, without let or hindrance from every person whatever; thus, for example, the innocent Heirs of a Criminal shall not be deprived of their legal rights, and the Property of the Criminal shall not be confiscated.

These Imperial concessions shall extend to all our subjects, of whatever Religion or sect they may be; they shall enjoy them without exceptions.

We therefore grant perfect security to the inhabitants of our Empire, in their lives, their honor, and their fortunes, as they are secured to them by the sacred text of our Law.

As all the Public Servants of the Empire receive a suitable salary, and that the salaries of those whose duties have not, up to the present time, been sufficiently remunerated, are to be fixed, a rigorous Law shall be passed against the traffic of favoritism and of appointments (*richvet*), which the Divine Law reprobates, and which is one of the principal causes of the decay of the Empire.

Original source cited: Edward Herslet. The Map of Europe by Treaty. (London: Butterworth, 1875–1891), vol. II, pp. 1002–1005.

Jamal al-Din al-Afghani, "Commentary on the Commentator"

He who does not look upon things with the eye of insight is lost and to be blamed.

Man is man because of education. None of the peoples of mankind, not even the savage, is completely deprived of education. If one considers man at the time of his birth, one sees that his existence without education is impossible. Even if we assumed that his existence were possible without education, his life would in that state be more repulsive and vile than the life of animals. Education consists of a struggle with nature, and overcoming her, whether the education be in plants, animals, or men.

Education, if it is good, produces perfection from imperfection, and nobility from baseness. If it is not good it changes the basic state of nature and becomes the cause of decline and decadence. This appears clearly among agriculturalists, cattle raisers, teachers, civil rulers, and religious leaders. In general, good education in these three kingdoms [human, animal, and plant] is the cause of all perfections and virtues. Bad education is the source of all defects and evils.

When this is understood, one must realize that if a people receives a good education, all of its classes and ranks, in accord with the natural law of relationships, will flourish simultaneously and will progress. Each class and group among that people, according to its rank and degree, tries to acquire the perfections that are appropriate to it, and does obtain them. The classes of that people, according to their rank, will always be in a state of balance and equilibrium with each other. This means that just as great rulers will appear among such a people because of their good education, so there will also come into existence excellent philosophers, erudite scholars, skilled craftsmen, able agriculturalists, wealthy merchants, and other professions. If that people because of its good education reaches such a level that its rulers are distinguished beyond the rulers of other peoples, one can be certain that all its classes will be distinguished above the classes of other countries. This is because perfect progress in each class depends on the progress of the other classes. This is the general rule, the law of nature, and the divine practice.

When, however, corruption finds its way into that people's education, weakness will occur in all its classes in proportion to their rank and to the extent of the corruption. That is, if weakness appears in the ruling circles, this weakness will surely overtake the class of philosophers, scholars, craftsmen, agriculturalists, merchants, and the other professions. For their perfection is the effect of a good education. When weakness, disorder, and corruption are introduced into a good education, which is the causative factor, inevitably the same weakness, disorder, and corruption will enter into the effects of that education. When corruption enters a nation's education it sometimes happens that, because of the increase of corruption in education and the ruin of manners and customs, the various classes, which are the cause of stability, and especially the noble classes, are gradually destroyed. The individuals of that nation, after removing their former clothes and changing their name, become part of another nation and appear with new adornments. This happened to the Chaldeans, the Phoenicians, the Copts, and similar people.

Sometimes Eternal Grace aids that people, and some men of high intelligence and pure souls appear among them and bring about a new life. They remove that corruption which was the cause of decline and destruction, and rescue souls and minds from the terrible malady of bad education. And through their own basic luster and brightness they return the good education and give back life once more to their people. They restore to them greatness, honor, and the progress of classes.

This is why every people who enter into decline, and whose classes are overtaken by weakness, are always, because of their expectation of Eternal Grace, waiting to see if perhaps there is to be found among them a wise renewer, experienced in policy, who can enlighten their minds and purify their souls through his wise management and fine efforts, and do away with the corrupt education. By the policies of that sage they could return to their former condtion.

There is no doubt that in the present age, distress, misfortune, and weakness besiege all classes of Muslims from every side. Therefore every Muslim keeps his eyes and ears open in expectation—to the East, West, North, and South—to see from what corner of the earth the sage and renewer will appear and will reform the minds and souls of the Muslims, repel the unforeseen corruption, and again educate them with a virtuous education. Perhaps through that good education they may return to their former joyful condition.

Since I am certain that the Absolute Truth *(haqq-i mutlaq)* will not destroy this true religion and right *shari'a,* I more than others expect that the minds and souls of the Muslims will very soon be enlightened and rectified by the wisdom of a sage. For this reason I always want to keep abreast of the articles and treatises that are now appèaring from the pens of Muslims, and be thoroughly acquainted with the views of their authors. I hope that in these readings I may discover the elevated ideas of a sage who could be the cause of good education, virtue, and prosperity for the Muslims. I would then hope, to the extent of my ability, to assist him in his elevated ideas and become a helper and associate in the reform of my people.

In the course of discussions and investigations about the ideas of the Muslims, I heard of one of them who, mature in years and rich in experience, took a trip to European countries. After much labor and effort he wrote a Commentary on the Koran in order to improve the Muslims. I said to myself, "Here is just what you wanted."

And as is customary with those who hear new things, I let my imagination wander, and formed various conceptions of that commentator and that commentary. I believed that this commentator, after all the commentaries written by Traditionists, jurists, orators, philosophers, Sufis, authors, grammarians, and heretics like Ibn Râwandî[1] and others, would have done justice to that subject, unveiled the truth, and achieved the precise goal. For he had followed the ideas of both Easterners and Westerners. I thought that this commentator would have explained in the introduction to his commentary, as wisdom requires, the truth and essence of religion for the improvement of his people. That he would have demonstrated the necessity of religion in the human world by rational proofs, and that he would have set up a general rule, satisfying the intellect, to distinguish between true and false religions. I imagined that this commentator had undoubtedly explained the influence of each of the prior, untrue religions on civilization and the social order and on men's souls and minds. I thought he would have explained in a philosophical way the reason for the divergence of religions on some matters, along with their agreement on many precepts, and the reason for the special relation of each age to a particular religion and prophet.

Since he claims to have written this commentary for the improvement of the community, I was certain he had in the introduction of his book described and explained in a new manner, with the light of wisdom, those divine policies and Koranic ethics that were the cause of the superiority and expansion of the Arabs in every human excellence. I was sure he had included in his introduction those precepts that were the cause of the unity of the Arabs, the transformation of their ideas, the enlightenment of their minds, and the purification of their souls; and all that when they were in the extremity of discord, savagery, and hardship.[2]

When I read the commentary I saw that this commentator in no way raised a word about these matters or about divine policy. In no manner are Koranic ethics explained. He has not mentioned any of those great precepts that were the cause of the enlightenment of the minds and purification of the souls of the Arabs. He has left without commentary those verses that relate to divine policy, support the promulgation of virtuous ethics and good habits, rectify domestic and civil intercourse, and cause the enlightenment of minds. Only at the beginning of his commentary does he pronounce a few words on the meaning of "sura," "verse," and the separate letters at the beginning of the suras. After that all his effort is devoted to taking every verse in which there is mention of angels, or *jinns*,[3] or the faithful spirit [Gabriel] , revelation, paradise, hell, or the miracles of the prophets, and, lifting these verses from their external meaning, interpreting them according to the specious allegorical interpretations of the heretics of past Muslim centuries.

The difference is that the heretics of past Muslim centuries were scholars, whereas this unfortunate commentator is very ignorant. Therefore he cannot grasp their words correctly. Taking the subject of man's *nature* as a subject of discourse, he pronounces some vague and meaningless words, without rational demonstrations or natural proofs. He apparently does not know that man is man through education, and all his virtues and habits are acquired. The man who is nearest to his nature is the one who is the farthest from civilization and from acquired virtues and habits. If men abandoned the legal and intellectual virtues they have acquired with the greatest difficulty and effort, and gave over control to the hands of nature, undoubtedly they would become lower than animals.

Even stranger is the fact that this commentator has lowered the divine, holy rank of prophecy and placed it on the level of the *reformer*.[4] He has considered the prophets to be men like Washington, Napoleon, Palmerston, Garibaldi, Mister Gladstone, and Monsieur Gambetta.

When I saw the commentary to be of this kind, amazement overtook me, and I began to ask myself what was the purpose of this commentator in writing such a commentary. If the goal of this commentator is, as he says, the improvement of his community, then why does he try to end the belief of Muslims in the Islamic religion, especially in these times when other religions have opened their mouths to swallow this religion?

Does he not understand that if the Muslims, in their current state of weakness and misery, did not believe in miracles and hell-fire, and considered the Prophet to be like Gladstone, they undoubtedly would soon abandon their own weak and conquered camp, and attach themselves to a powerful conqueror? For in that event there would no longer remain anything to prevent this, nor any fear or anxiety. And from another standpoint the prerequisites for changing religion now exist, since being like the conqueror, and having the same religion as he, is attractive to everyone.

After these ideas and reflections, it first occurred to me that this commentator certainly believes that the cause of the decline of the Muslims and of their distressed condition is their religion itself, and that if they abandoned their beliefs they would restore their former greatness and honor. Therefore, he is trying to remove these beliefs, and because of his motivation he could be forgiven.

Having reflected further, however, I said to myself that the Jews, thanks to these same beliefs, rescued themselves from the humiliation of slavery to the pharoahs and rubbed in the dust the pride of the tyrants of Palestine. Has not the commentator heard of this.

And the Arabs, thanks to these same beliefs, came up from the desert lands of the Arabian peninsula, and became masters of the whole world in power, civilization, knowledge, manufacture, agriculture, and trade. The Europeans in their speeches referred aloud to those believing Arabs as their masters. Has not this fact reached the ears of this commentator? Of course it has.

After considering the great effects of these true beliefs and their followers, I looked at the followers of false beliefs. I saw that the Hindus at the same time that they made progress in the laws of civilization, and in science, knowledge, and the various crafts, believed in thousands of gods and idols. This commentator is not ignorant of this. The Egyptians at the times when they laid the foundations of civilization, science, and manufactures, and were the masters of the Greeks, believed in idols, cows, dogs, and cats. This commentator undoubtedly knows this. The Chaldeans, at the time that they founded observatories, manufactured astronomical instruments, built high castles, and composed books on agricultural science, were worshippers of the stars. This is not hidden from the commentator. The Phoenicians, in the age that they made manufacture and commerce on land and sea flourish, and colonized the lands of Britain, Spain, and Greece, presented their own children as sacrifices to idols. This is clear to the commentator.

The Greeks, in that century that they were rulers of the world, and at the time that great sages and revered philosophers appeared among them, believed in hundreds of gods and thousands of superstitions. This is known to the commentator. The Persians, at the time when they ruled from the regions of Kashgar to the frontiers of Istanbul, and were considered incomparable in civilization, had hundreds of absurdities engraved in their hearts. Of course the commentator remembers this. The modern Christians, at the same time as they acknowledged the Trinity, the cross, resurrection, baptism, purgatory, confession, and transubstantiation, assured their domination; progressed in the spheres of science, knowledge, and industry; and reached the summit of civilization. Most of them still, with all their science and knowledge, follow the same beliefs. The commentator knows this well.

When I considered these matters I realized that the commentator never was of the opinion that faith in these true beliefs caused the decline of the Muslims. For religious beliefs, whether true or false, are in no way incompatible with civilization and worldly progress unless they forbid the acquisition of science, the earning of a livelihood, and progress in sound civilization. I do not believe that there is a religion in the world that forbids these things, as appears clearly from what has been said above. Rather I can say that the lack of faith results only in disorder and corruption in civil life, and in insecurity. Reflect—this is *Nihilism!*[5]

If the lack of faith brought about the progress of peoples, then the Arabs of the Age of Ignorance would have had to have precedence in civilization. For they were mostly followers of the materialist path, and for this reason they used to say aloud: "Wombs push us forth, the earth swallows us up, and only time destroys us." They also always used to say: "Who can revive bones after they have decomposed?"[6] This despite the fact that they lived in the utmost ignorance, like wild animals.

After all these various thoughts and considerations, I understood well that this commentator is not a reformer, nor was his commentary written for the improvement and education of the Muslims. Rather this commentator and this commentary are for the Islamic community at the present time like those terrible and dangerous illnesses that strike man when he is weak and decrepit. The aim of his modifications has been demonstrated above.

The goal of this commentator from this effort to remove the beliefs of the Muslims is to serve others and to prepare the way for conversion to their religion.

These few lines have been written hastily. Later, by the power of God, I will write in detail about this commentary and the aims of the commentator.

---

[1] Ibn Râwandî: ninth-century heretic who criticized prophecy in general and Muhammad's prophecy in particular.

[2] Afghânî believed in the Muslim religion as a basis for political unity among Muslims of his day.

[3] Spirits.

[4] In English. (Tr.)

[5] In English. (Tr.)

[6] Qur'ân XXXVI:77. (Tr.)

Source: McNeill, William H. and Marilyn Robinson Waldman, eds. "Jamal al-Din al-Afghani, 'Commentary on the Commentator.' " In *The Islamic World.* Chicago: University of Chicago Press, 1983. Pgs. 423–431. From *An Islamic Response to Imperialism; Political and Religious Writings of Sayyid Jamâl ad-Dîn "al-Afghâni,"* edited and translated by Nikki R. Keddie. Originally published by the University of California Press, 1968, pp. 123–129.

NOTES

1. Garth Fowden, *Before and After Muhammad: The First Millennium Refocused* (Princeton, NJ: Princeton University Press, 2014), p. 53.
2. As R. Matthee wrote with regard to the Safavids, "In today's academic climate, skeptical about (non-Western) decline and especially averse to decline as a moral category, one is almost forced to reject this type of interpretation out of hand and to focus on manifestations of continued vitality in the form or artistic expression, religious disputation, or overlooked provincial initiative. But to do so would be to

ignore the many unmistakable signs of trouble." *Persia in Crisis: Safavid Decline and the Fall of Isfahan*, as quoted in Fowden, *Before and After Muhammad*, p. 53.

3. Roger Crowley, *Empires of the Sea: The Final Battle for the Mediterranean, 1521–1580* (London: Faber and Faber, 2008), p. 10.
4. Ibid., p. 9.
5. Ibid., p. 51.
6. Norman Itzkowitz, *Ottoman Empire and Islamic Tradition* (Chicago: University of Chicago Press, 1972), p. 34.
7. Ottoman Admiral Khair al-Din Barbarossa (Red Beard) became quite famous for his successful naval raids, including a significant naval victory in 1538 inflicted on the Venetians off the coast of Greece, thus securing Ottoman suzerainty in the Mediterranean for several decades until the 1571 Battle of Lepanto, again off the coast of Greece, which resulted in a combined European victory, shattering Ottoman control of the Mediterranean Sea. See Ann Williams, "Mediterranean Conflict," in Metin Kunt and Christine Woodhead, eds., *Suleyman the Magnificent and His Age: The Ottoman Empire in the Early Modern World* (London: Longman, 1995), pp. 39–54.
8. Justin McCarthy, *The Ottoman Turks: An Introductory History to 1923* (London: Longman, 1997), p. 87.
9. Quoted in the film *Sulayman the Magnificent*, the National Gallery of Art and Metropolitan Museum of Art, 1987. (I transcribed the quote directly from listening to my own personal copy of the film, which at times is a bit garbled, so one or two words may be off as well as some of the punctuation.)
10. Itzkowitz, *Ottoman Empire and Islamic Tradition*, p. 63.
11. McCarthy, *The Ottoman Turks*, p. 199.
12. Omer Lutfi Barkan and Justin McCarthy, "The Price Revolution of the Sixteenth Century: A Turning Point in the Economic History of the Near East," *International Journal of Middle East Studies* 6, no. 1 (January 1975): 5.
13 For the effects of climate change on the Ottomans around 1600, see Andrea Duffy, "What the Ottoman Empire Can Teach Us About the Consequences of Climate Change—and How Drought Can Uproot Peoples and Fuel Warfare," *The Conversation*, June 8, 2021, https://source.colostate/what-the-ottoman-empire-can-teach-us-about-the-consequences-of-climate-change-and-how-drought-can-uproot-peoples-and-fuel-warfare/.
14. Itzkowitz, *Ottoman Empire and Islamic Tradition*, pp. 96–97.
15. For this, please see Barkan and McCarthy, "The Price Revolution," as well as Itkowitz, *Ottoman Empire and Islamic Tradition*, pp. 94–95, and James Gelvin, *The Modern Middle East: A History* (Oxford: Oxford University Press, 2005), pp. 38–46.
16. Barkan and McCarthy, "The Price Revolution," p. 7.
17. Itzkowitz, *Ottoman Empire and Islamic Tradition*, p. 88.
18 Juan Cole, *Napoleon's Egypt: Invading the Middle East* (New York: Palgrave-Macm. illan, 2008), p. 29.

19. Quoted in ibid., p. 13.
20. In his excellent book on the French invasion of Egypt, Juan Cole, who wrote it in 2007, was making a not-so-subtle analogy to the then contemporaneous problems the United States-led coalition was encountering in Iraq following its 2003 invasion and decapitation of the Iraqi state, generating political and economic chaos as well as a lethal indigenous insurgency against the US presence.
21. "Maintaining the integrity" of the Ottoman Empire isn't just a catchphrase. In 1833 Foreign Minster Palmerston sent instructions to his representatives in Egypt, writing that "H. M.'s Government attach great importance to the maintenance of the integrity of the Ottoman Empire, considering that state to be a material element in the general balance of power in Europe." Quoted in M. E. Yapp, *The Making of the Modern Near East, 1792–1923* (London: Longman, 1987), p. 71.
22.. Ibid., p. 91.
23. Ibid., p. 59.
24. Donald Quataert, *The Ottoman Empire, 1700–1922* (Cambridge: Cambridge University Press, 2000), p. 54.
25. Ahmed Ataullah, *Tarikh-I Ata'nun Esar Fashna Dair Olam Dorduncu Cildidir* (Istanbul, 1876), p. 67, as quoted in M. Sukru Hanioglu, *A Brief History of the Late Ottoman Empire* (Princeton, NJ: Princeton University Press, 2008), p. 6.
26. Hanioglu, *A Brief History*, p. 53.
27. This reminds me of what King Faisal of Saudi Arabia did in the early 1970s in order to get the powerful Saudi ulama on board with the introduction of a Western innovation: television. He told the ulama that with television they could reach a broader audience and could preach and read the Quran 24/7 over the airwaves. They heartily agreed, but by introducing television within an Islamic paradigm, Faisal was able to overcome initial opposition to television. Once television became an accepted part of life, the programming could be tweaked and tweaked until popular television shows from US networks were shown (although censored at times).
28. Hanioglu, *A Brief History*, p. 40.
29. For more on the daily reproduction of nationalism through various symbols and inputs into routine consciousness, see Michael Billig, *Banal Nationalism: Theory, Culture, and Society* (Thousand Oaks, CA: SAGE Publications, 1995).
30. Gelvin, *The Modern Middle East*, pp. 143–144. Japan having a Western-style constitution in 1874 showed that non-Western states could have a representative parliamentary system of government.
31. Quoted in Hanioglu, *A Brief History*, p. 114.
32. Yapp, *The Making of the Modern Near East*, p. 114.
33.. Alan Richards and John Waterbury, *A Political Economy of the Middle East* (Boulder, CO: Westview Press, 1996), p. 40.
34. For instance, to use a more modern example: an end-product factory would be a textile company. It needs a sewing machine factory to provide the sewing machines to knit the clothes. This backward links to the necessity for a steel factory to pro-

vide the steel to the sewing factory to make the sewing machines, which then creates the need for an iron-ore factory to make the steel, and so on.

KEY TERMS

Auspicious Incident (1826) p. 269

ayan p. 268

Nizam-i Jedid (1791) p. 267

Tanzimat p. 270

For additional digital learning resources please go to www.oup.com/he/lesch-middleeast-1e

10 INFLECTION POINT

The Hamidian Era and the Young Turks

Following upon bankruptcy in 1875 and heightening tensions with Russia, a group of reformist officials removed Sultan Abd al-Aziz from power. A week later he apparently committed suicide in his apartment, his wrists slashed. Such was the state of things that his successor, Murat V, had a nervous breakdown three months later and was kicked out of office.[1] Almost by default, Abd al-Hamid II, at the age of thirty-three, came to power as sultan in 1876. The challenges that lay before him were numerous and complicated, to say the least. That he remained in office until the so-called Young Turk revolution in 1908 was no small feat. But things looked very bad for him at first, especially after another Russo–Ottoman war in 1877–1878 that led to the Congress of Berlin, which peeled away from the Ottoman Empire the states of Serbia, Romania, and Montenegro. It seemed to be at that point just a matter of time before the empire would implode, causing a feeding frenzy of European powers battling for territories in a chaotic competition that would upset the balance of power in Europe, pushing it toward an all-out conflict. This is essentially what happened with the onset of World War I in 1914.

Abd al-Hamid II was thought to be a reformist when he was placed in power—if he were not, he would have been bypassed. It was during his initial year as sultan that the constitution was promulgated and a parliamentary system of government enacted. That he suspended the constitution and disbanded parliament in 1878 has branded him as anti-reformist in a number of critical analyses since then; again, reality is more nuanced. He was pro-reform, but he believed—and he was not alone—that the reformist ministers and parliamentary form of government had helped bring about the disasters of the second half of the 1870s. He would not be the first authoritarian ruler to believe he knew best how to reform and save the country.

Under the pressure of the Russians bearing down on him in the 1877–1878 war, Abd al-Hamid II was taken to task by some parliamentary representatives. He reacted by summarily placing them under house arrest, dissolving parliament, and suspending the constitution. This certainly set the tone for the remainder of his time as sultan. He had to endure the loss of Tunisia to the French in 1881, and following Egyptian bankruptcy, he watched as the British seized control of Egypt the following year.[2] To his credit, the sultan kept the empire from further dismemberment until the 1908 Young Turk revolution.

Part of the price for this relative stability in the empire was that it degenerated into a police state. Newspapers were heavily censored, opponents were imprisoned or exiled, and a suffocating formal and informal security apparatus was constructed to keep tabs on everything and everyone. Opposition groups had to go the clandestine route for their activism, and as a result a number of secret societies formed throughout the empire. We call many states in the Middle East today *Mukhabarat* (security) states because of the overweening presence and power of intelligence agencies. Abd al-Hamid II's rule can be seen as an early form of the Mukhabarat state. This is why the Hamidian era is often viewed as reactionary against the Tanzimat, but reform continued, although the style was different. It is not as though the Tanzimat reformers were true democrats anyway.

Abd al-Hamid saw himself as an enlightened, legal autocrat, which by then many in the empire wanted to see or felt was needed in order to restore stability and fend off the Europeans. This was still a conservative population overall, and many were comfortable with the idea of a strong, independent ruler. The European-style reforms, despite some tangible progress, were an affront to many on cultural terms and in the end did not keep the Europeans at bay. One of the things the sultan did differently than his immediate predecessors was to emphasize his role as caliph much more, something that had been minimized previously, especially when sultans had tried to Ottomanize the citizenry. Abd al-Hamid encountered a more receptive audience for this simply because after 1878 the empire was much more Muslim: approximately 75 percent by the late 1890s. He also hoped that by appealing to Muslims worldwide in his role as caliph he would acquire some political advantage in his dealings with the European powers. What the Russians, French, and British feared was the potential for the Ottoman sultan-caliph to call for a jihad against them, which could make life very difficult for the British in such places as Egypt or India, for the French in North Africa, and the Russians in their central Asian provinces. This would be an important concern for Europe all the way up to World War I, as we shall see in the next section.

Abd al-Hamid took advantage of the changing sentiments in the empire to frame reform within an Islamic veneer, harkening back to the Mahmud II approach. As M. E. Yapp wrote, "Islam served to socialize the Tanzimat reforms without changing their nature."[3] Overall the sultan began to promote a form of Pan-Islamism that reinforced his governing approach. Pan-Islamism was an Islamic nationalistic response using the vehicle of Islam as the primary unifying element in the empire, and Abd al-Hamid employed it to rally support for the sultanate and

Ottoman Sultan Abd al-Hamid II, Nineteenth century. Artist: George J. Stodart.
The Print Collector/Alamy Stock Photo

to turn sentiments against Europe. One of the main progenitors of Pan-Islamism at this time was Jamal al-Din al-Afghani, who laid the foundations for an activist Muslim response in the Middle East to their increasingly weak condition. He was welcomed at the court of Abd al-Hamid II, as they mutually supported each other's positions and shared the same overall goal of protecting the Muslim world against European mischief. In a way, al-Afghani advocated a nationalistic ideological response not unlike that which was occurring contemporaneously in Europe, although rather than the unifying element of the nation being language, ethnicity, or a shared heritage, it was Islam.[4]

From within this construct began to emerge in the last quarter of the nineteenth century what became known as the *salafiyya* movement. **Salafiyya** is taken from the phrase "al-salif al-sahih" (pious ancestors). It was an Islamist movement that sought to unify and strengthen Islam through a rediscovery of what made the original Muslims from the Prophet Muhammad's time so successful. Those who came to define the salafiyya movement have often been called Islamic modernists, in the sense that ultimately they did not totally reject European-based modernization if it could be shown to be helpful; after all, Islam is not at all anti-scientific or against technological progress.[5] A small intellectual group called the Young Ottomans (led by Namik Kemal) were influential in establishing and spreading the ideas of Islamic modernism. They would agree with al-Afghani that the Islamic world needed a unifying ideology—Islamic principles—but they also advocated for a constitution and parliament as an outgrowth of the Islamic concept of *shura* or "consultation." This is an idea that has its roots in the origins of Islam, and which is why today many so-called representative legislative bodies in the Arab world are called *Majlis al-Shura* or "consultative assembly," even though most are but rubber stamps to the powers that be. There was an odd constellation of forces that helped bring in the Ottoman constitution—each mistakenly convinced this was all the empire needed to stave off Europe.

During the salafiyya, however, many Arabs who supported it made their own rediscovery: the role the Arabs played in the birth, growth, and height of the medieval Islamic era. In many ways over the previous centuries the Arabs had become somewhat marginalized within the general environment they themselves created, giving way to Persians and Turks. As such, what has been called a kind of proto-Arab nationalism began to percolate, laying the foundation for a more mature Arab nationalism in the twentieth century. One of the unfortunate repercussions of the salafiyya movement, however, was that as with the Tanzimat, it was seen by a number of Muslims to have failed, especially with the European-dominated mandate system imposed on much of the Middle East following World War I. The failure of the Islamic modernists, who accepted an accommodation with the West even while trying to fight it off, led to a more virulently anti-Western and anti-modern form of Islamism in the twentith century, the results of which we will examine later in the book.

Another thought that gained some momentum during this time was that Abd al-Hamid had committed a crime by suspending the constitution. There were a number of groups of liberal constitutionalists who believed that a constitution and representative government could save the empire, not going back to the absolutism of prior centuries that the sultan seemed to resurrect. By 1900 the most prominent of these groups became known as the Young Turks, which was a conglomeration of different parties, the most influential of which was called the **Committee of Union and Progress (CUP)**. The fact that the CUP took its name from two of the main elements of French intellectual Auguste Comte's philosophy of positivism—unity and progress—says something about the European orientation of its membership. Comte's philosophy, which was popular in certain intellectual circles in the Middle East, held that societies go through stages, from religious-based, to philosophical-based, and then to scientifically based. This offered hope for Middle Eastern societies that they could reach the level of Europe, if properly guided by technocrats (*savants*) and intellectuals (*mutanawwir*).[6]

The CUP was a secret society, one with cells of civilians and military throughout the empire, but it tended to be concentrated in the Balkans, particularly in Macedonia, Thrace, and Albania. On July 8, 1908, a CUP officer led a few hundred like-minded soldiers from the Ottoman Third Army to demand the restoration of the 1876 constitution.[7] Apparently their cell had been uncovered by authorities anyway, so they decided to throw caution to the wind, fully expecting to die in the process. Instead of launching what they thought would be their own heroic demise, they ended up starting the Young Turk revolution. This CUP cell had obviously underestimated the appeal of their action, including among most other elements of the Ottoman Third Army, which soon thereafter marched on Istanbul to make their demands on the sultan in force. Abdul Hamid II saw the writing on the wall, and on July 24 said somewhat sheepishly and disingenuously that he would "follow the current. The constitution was first promulgated under my reign. I am the one who established it. For reasons of necessity, it was suspended. I now wish for the ministers to prepare a proclamation restoring it."[8]

Hope sprung eternal across the empire with the return of constitutional government. However, the Young Turks were young, so they mistakenly allowed most of the existing officials to run things, and Abd al-Hamid II, though his power was circumscribed, surely was not going to passively lay down to these newcomers on the block. And he did not. He and his supporters attempted a counterrevolution in April 1909 that lasted about two weeks, once again suspending the constitution and dissolving parliament. The Third Army sprang into action again, and this time they finally deposed Abd al-Hamid II and replaced him with a puppet sultan clearly subservient to the restored constitutional government.

These liberal constitutionalists hoped that by clearly displaying their modern European and civilized form of government, they would mute the predatory dispositions of the European powers. But they would be gravely disappointed with the results of the Young Turk revolution. Bulgaria and Bosnia-Herzegovina took advantage of the political chaos in Istanbul to break away in 1908. Italy took Libya in 1911. Because of the valiant attempt by the Ottoman military to ward off the Italians in Libya, more opportunities for various entities in the Balkans were opened up, beginning what came to be called the First Balkan war in 1912 with Serbia, Greece, Montenegro, and Bulgaria declaring war on the Ottoman Empire. As a result, Albania, Macedonia, and Thrace were able to break free from Ottoman rule. The Ottomans were able to regain some of this valuable territory in the Second Balkan war in 1913, mostly because Bulgaria, Serbia, and Greece turned on each other.

In the process of all this, leaders among the Young Turks finally decided to take full control of things themselves, buffeting their claims to power with the restoration of some lost territory in the Second Balkan War. They engaged in an even more heightened level of centralized rule to stem what seemed to be impending disintegration. This is when the percolating ideology of Pan-Turkism or Turkish nationalism started to really find its way into the halls of power. Not only was the Ottoman Empire becoming more Muslim by the first part of the twentieth century, it was also becoming more Turkish. A triumvirate of Young Turks widely known as Talat Pasha, Enver Pasha, and Jamal (Cemal) Pasha, took matters into their own hands and began a final authoritarian spasm of Ottoman rule. To their names was added the honorific title of "pasha," which was the highest grade in both military and civilian service.[9] Officially, Enver was minister of war as well as the most powerful general in the military; Talat was minister of the interior, thus heading the intelligence services; and Jamal was mayor of Istanbul. They implemented what has been called Turkification policies as part of the centralization of power, which rubbed those non-Turks in the empire the wrong way, especially in the remaining Arab territories of the empire still under real Ottoman control (essentially by this time only Syria). Such edicts as requiring the Turkish language in local government and in schools in Syria began to produce or in some cases reinforce a growing proto-Arab nationalism complete with its own line-up of secret societies, such as al-Fatat, founded in 1909 by Syrian Muslims living in Paris.[10] They were not yet calling for outright independence, but they did clamor for at least more autonomy within the Ottoman construct, all of which became more pronounced during the even more repressive policies of the Young Turk triumvirate during World War I.

World War I in the Middle East

World War I is the most important period in the history of the modern Middle East.[11] Most of the important issues in the Middle East during the twentieth century and into the twenty-first century, such as Arab nationalism, Islamic extremism, the Arab–Israeli conflict, and even Iraq's Saddam Hussein, trace their origins back to the events that transpired in the region during and immediately after the "war to end all wars." This is the case even though the epicenter of the war was always in Europe, and events in the Middle East were always of secondary concern to the course of the war on the continent to the primary European combatants; nonetheless, to the countries and peoples of the region, it had a direct and long-lasting effect.

The Middle East in the World War I period was tremendously complex, comprised of the establishment of new states, the end of the Ottoman Empire, the evincing of nationalist and territorial goals on the part of Arabs and Zionists, and the intervention of European interests and intrigue, in addition to crisscrossing, ambiguous, changing, and often contradictory promises, pledges, and declarations. As such, this is also a period in modern Middle East history that is quite difficult to comprehend for the relatively uninitiated. The most efficient way to understand the complexities of the period is to first and foremost examine the British role. Britain was by far the prime mover of events in the Middle East during and immediately after the war. It was London that had the most influence in the region of all of the European powers; it was London that largely initiated and engaged in the diplomatic machinations resulting in such infamous documents as the Sykes-Picot agreement, the Hussein-McMahon correspondence, and the Balfour Declaration, not to mention the postwar negotiations that led to the redrawing of the map in the Middle East that has essentially remained geographically unaltered to this day.

If World War I is the most important period in modern Middle East history, the most important single decision may have been the Ottoman Empire's entrance into the war on the side of Germany and the Central Powers, a decision that until the summer of 1914 could have gone the way of siding with the Allied powers or neutrality. The Ottoman Empire had certainly shown some gumption that belied the "sick man of Europe" caricature. Socioeconomically speaking, however, the Empire could ill-afford to be drawn into an extended European conflict, even if when the "guns of August" sounded in 1914 it was thought the conflict would be of short duration, certainly not a largely static four years of unprecedented death and destruction. But the lure of reacquiring lands from and reordering the relationship with countries such as Russia, Britain, and France was ultimately too much to pass up. Germany had incrementally built up its economic and military position with the Ottomans, and certainly the choice was made that much easier when Russia, which had for over a century pressured the sultanate, positioned itself opposite the Kaiser following the chain of events emanating from the assassination of Archduke Ferdinand of the Austrian-Hungarian empire in Serbia. From the point of view of the triumvirate of CUP leaders, the Central Powers (Germany, Austria-Hungary, and Bulgaria) had at least as much chance to emerge victorious as the nascent coalition of Entente powers (Britain, France, Russia, Italy, and later Greece).

For Britain, the decision by Istanbul instantly transformed its policy toward the Ottoman Empire. For over a century it had been British policy to maintain the integrity of the Ottoman Empire so as to ensure the lifeline to India and create a buffer to Russian expansionist designs toward the heartland of the Middle East. Now the Ottomans were the enemy, and their defeat became official policy; recognizing the growing danger of Imperial Germany, London buried the hatchet with St. Petersburg in the 1907 Anglo-Russian agreement (as they had with France earlier in 1904 with the Entente Cordiale). Great Britain in World War I was now an ally of the Russian czar, whose friendship and interests were of the utmost importance upon the outbreak of the conflict. It was imperative that Russia stay in the war to force Germany to fight on multiple fronts in Europe. Despite the fact that many European diplomats envisioned the Ottoman Empire surviving the war, albeit most likely in a truncated fashion, plans began to emerge early regarding the disposition of Ottoman territories, particularly those regions in the Middle East that were still under Ottoman control such as Syria, Palestine, and Iraq.

In the immediate sense once hostilities commenced, British policy in the Middle East revolved around the strategic necessity of defeating the Ottoman Empire and the creation of a pro-British bulwark in the Arab territories of the empire that most believed would be detached from Istanbul in some form or fashion. These new Arab entities, whether independent or as protectorates, would serve the same function as had the Ottomans: to maintain the lifeline to India and buffer

British strategic interests in the region. And to accomplish both of these objectives while not upsetting London's allies, France and Russia, in a way that would deleteriously affect their abilities to carry on the war in Europe, especially as they were bearing the brunt of the German offensives. This was a tall order, and as we shall see, in order to achieve their goals in the Middle East the British expediently constructed, amended, and reversed their policies depending upon the exigencies of the diplomatic and military situation at any given moment, producing in the end what seemed to be contradictory pledges to a variety of states and groups as well as setting up unrealistic parameters for success in the region that would shape the course of modern Middle East history.

When the Sublime Porte formally allied itself with the Central Powers in August 1914, there were distinct differences among British policymakers in London and in the field as to whether or not the Entente powers should engage the Ottoman Empire militarily. There was a general consensus that the Ottoman Empire was weak and that it could be defeated relatively easily—a complacency that would come back to haunt them—but there were initial fears that the war effort in Western Europe could be negatively affected by diverting much-needed men and materiel to the East. Although Britain declared war on the Ottoman Empire on November 5, 1914, scant military action directed against Ottomans had been considered. This view began to change by early 1915. The main reason for this was that the war in Europe had clearly reached a virtual draw by then, characterized by static trench warfare. The war cabinet in the Asquith government began to listen to those who had long argued for opening up another front in the south—with little strategic movement in Europe, perhaps a quick strike through the underbelly of the Central Powers could bring about a swift and conclusive end to the war. To do this, however, first necessitated a military confrontation with the Ottomans. Prime Minister Herbert Henry Asquith, who had been particularly sympathetic to Russian interests, also saw an advantage to taking the strategically prized Turkish straits (Bosphorus and Dardanelles) and holding them as a carrot to ultimately award the Czar for maintaining a zealous effort in the war.

This was the origin of what would become the disastrous, ill-timed, and ill-planned Gallipoli campaign led by British, Australian, and New Zealander forces beginning in February 1915, which was intended to quickly move up the peninsula astride the Dardanelles toward Constantinople and swiftly knock the Ottomans out of the war. The Gallipoli campaign brought the Ottoman Empire front and center into the international war effort and international diplomacy. By doing so, its disposition, including the Arab Middle East after the Ottomans' presumed defeat, scaled the bureaucratic morass to become an item of increasing importance in London, Paris, and St. Petersburg as the war dragged on.

The British-led onslaught at Gallipoli, while intended to acquire the carrot of the straits in exchange for the Czar's continued involvement in diverting German resources on the eastern front (and utilizing other Ottoman territories as inducement to countries such as Italy and the Balkan states to enter the fray on the side of the Entente powers), also raised fears in St. Petersburg, expecting a quick Ottoman collapse, that Britain might just keep the straits. Therefore, Prime Minister Asquith felt the need to allay Russian concerns regarding the disposition of the Turkish prize. This manifested itself in the Constantinople agreement of March 1915, what Churchill termed a "convulsive gesture of self-preservation," as it essentially awarded the Turkish straits to Russia, something the British had ardently worked to deny to a succession of Czars for over a century. But the expediency of war dictated a radical shift in traditional British policy. With the Constantinople agreement the Arab Middle East formally entered the diplomatic scene, and places such as Syria and Palestine suddenly became strategic ground to be bartered and negotiated among a bevy of great powers and interested groups, the latter including Arabs and Zionists (secular Jewish nationalists seeking Palestine as the national home for Jews).

The ultimate failure at Gallipoli, which became apparent by the fall of 1915, compelled the British to seek an alternative route toward defeating the Ottomans in the Middle East, a path that would ultimately lead to a campaign directed by British General Sir Edmund Allenby from Egypt up through Palestine toward Damascus. It also forced the British to recognize that they might need some assistance not only in this task but also in the postwar strategic situation in the region, which would lead various British representatives to negotiate with groups of Arabs and Zionists competing to convince London that they could serve its interests better than anyone else. Even if the British had been more successful at Gallipoli there is no doubt that London would have had to deal with vexing issues regarding the Arab territories of the Ottoman Empire after the war, but what failure meant was that Britain now had to deal with these complex issues during the military and diplomatic flux of wartime—for virtually the entire duration. As such, a whole host of complicating factors entered the diplomatic equation that might otherwise have remained on the sidelines.

France, for its part, was becoming a bit concerned that while it was bearing the brunt of the war on the western front, Great Britain was in the process of stealing away with the Middle East. The fact that the British were militarily engaged at both ends of the Ottoman Empire early in the war at Gallipoli as well as in Mesopotamia (Iraq) informed Paris that it had best barter for its claims in the region before the British were in such a strong military position as to dictate the terms. As with Russia, British officialdom comprised two views: that of accommodation with the French in the Middle East for the sake of strategic cooperation in Europe, or exclusion of France from the region as much as possible in order to better advance British interests. Those who favored the latter position anticipated that the prewar imperial game with France, which many of them had experienced firsthand in the 1898 Fashoda crisis in the Sudan, would resume after the war.[12]

The British began to listen more intently to French interests by late 1915, when it became clear that the Gallipoli campaign was lost. They would not be able to impose their designs on the Middle East at will. The diplomatic battleground in the Middle East between the two European powers would revolve around Syria, including present-day Israel/Palestine and Lebanon. The French believed that Syria was practically its birthright, dating back to its involvement in this part of the region beginning with the Crusades. Paris also had a direct interest in the disposition of the Ottoman realm, as it provided 45 percent of the private sector foreign capital in the empire and assumed 60 percent of the Ottoman public debt.[13]

There were some practical reasons beyond Gallipoli that compelled the British to negotiate concessions to the French in the Middle East. If the British were to continue to militarily engage the Ottoman Empire, even via an alternative route, they would have to divert resources from the western front. This would require French acquiescence, and Paris would only do so for a price; British diplomat Sir Mark Sykes understood this. Another plan that was being hatched to aid the British cause in the Middle East—involving a possible Arab revolt led by the Sharif Hussein, the leader in the Hijaz and Guardian of the Two Holy Places (Mecca and Medina)—might be scuttled because it was thought that if British and Arab military action was not taken quickly, that the Ottomans might depose or otherwise get rid of Hussein before the rebellion could be launched. Concurrently with British negotiations with representatives of the sharif (to be discussed shortly), the British hastened to meet with French diplomats to find mutual accord between London and Paris so that plans could move forward in the region.

The French sent Francois Georges Picot as their representative, and negotiations began in November 1915. After negotiations stalled by December, Sykes was then designated as the lead British representative. What came to be called the Sykes-Picot agreement was consummated in May 1916, and it consisted of dividing the heartland of the Arab world into spheres of influence. The French could assume direct control over the coast of Syria west of a line running north–south from Aleppo through Hama and Homs to Damascus (including present-day Lebanon, which at the time consisted of a large and economically important Arab Christian population that had long-standing ties with France), while the interior of Syria would be a "sphere of influence" subject to some level of indirect control. The French also received the province of Mosul within their sphere of influence in what is now northern Iraq, while the British would retain the Ottoman provinces of Baghdad and Basra to the south down to the Persian Gulf. From the British perspective this would not only allay French concerns, but would also construct a French buffer between Russia and British-controlled territories in the Middle East. Palestine was a different story, however; both Britain and France wanted it within their respective spheres of influence. The intensity of the debate is revealed by the fact that no definitive agreement could be reached on the matter, and what was finally agreed to—more for the sake of expediency than anything else—was that

neither the British nor the French would receive Palestine. Instead, most of the territory, including Jerusalem, would fall under some sort of international administration that would presumably be delineated by an undetermined mechanism following the war. Otherwise in this part of the Arab world, the remaining territory would form some sort of Arab state or confederation of states that would be at least nominally independent, essentially Arabia minus the Persian Gulf shaykhdoms in which the British had established themselves and had a dominant position since the early 1800s. The extent to which most British officials actually thought of Arab independence as a reality is a different question, since many viewed the Arabs as incapable of statehood in the short term and as a vehicle through which Britain could exert its influence in the region. In addition, British officials, especially those in Cairo, believed that it would just be a matter of time before they were able to establish facts on the ground through military action in order to secure Palestine.

The Sharif Hussein was a Hashemite and therefore a direct descendant of the family of the Prophet Muhammad. He was the Guardian of the Two Holy Places, Mecca and Medina, in the Hijaz region of Arabia, which accorded him a certain amount of religious and political legitimacy. He was an opportunist who in the years preceding World War I had come to the conclusion that he needed a patron in order to realize his ambitions of expanding his realm throughout not only Arabia against rival clans, such as the Saudis, but also across the Arab world in the Fertile Crescent region. He had not had the best of relations with Ottoman sultans, and he constantly feared that he might be forcibly removed.[14] It is under these circumstances that he began his first halting steps toward establishing a relationship with the British.

Early in the war Hussein began to explore whether he could launch a genuine Arab revolt of the sort that the British wanted. One of the sharif's sons, Faisal, stopped at the hotbed of nascent Arab nationalism in Damascus in March 1915 on his way to Constantinople. There he met with representatives of Arab secret societies such as al-Ahd (The Covenant) and al-Fatat, who were bent on at least obtaining more autonomy from Ottoman rule, to discuss the possibilities of drawing up a program of action with the Hijazis. To both the British and the Hashemites the fact that most of the Ottoman military divisions in the Middle East were made up of Arabs, including many secret-society cohorts, was very appealing. While Faisal was in the Ottoman capital, members of the secret societies drew up what came to be called the Damascus Protocol, which outlined Arab demands to the British in return for rebelling against the Turks. It essentially called for British recognition of Arab independence in Syria (including present-day Lebanon, Israel, and Jordan), Iraq, and Arabia. Faisal brought the Damascus Protocol to his father, whereupon it was adopted as the basis for Hashemite policy with the British. It is under such conditions, armed with the apparent means to deliver a real rebellion, that the sharif initiated what came to be known as the Hussein-McMahon correspondence, the latter part named after the British High Commissioner in Egypt, Sir Henry McMahon (London had declared Egypt as its protectorate in 1914 just before the outbreak of the war).

In July 1915, prior to the commencement of the Sykes-Picot negotiations, Hussein sent off the first salvo in the correspondence to the British high commissioner of Egypt demanding recognition of the territorial assertions as outlined in the Damascus Protocol in addition to agreeing to an Arab caliphate. As many have pointed out, this was quite ironic: a Muslim asking a representative of the Christian West to consecrate the caliphate. McMahon's response was lukewarm at best, believing as did other British officials in Cairo that the Arabs had little to offer, especially considering the fact that a good many of them had obviously chosen the German side and were at that very moment battling British forces at Gallipoli.[15] The troubles the

British were encountering in Gallipoli, however, brought on a dramatic change of policy in Cairo regarding Hussein's offer; British military commanders at Gallipoli were apparently appealing to McMahon to do something to dilute the Arab forces in the Ottoman army on the Dardanelles. Not only was a diversion desired, but it had also become clear with the failure of the Gallipoli campaign that an alternative route to defeating the Ottoman Empire in the Middle East was needed, and for this Arab compliance and assistance would be necessary. From the start, the British had overestimated the potential of any Arab revolt. Arab secret societies and the percolating Arab nationalist movement had already been crushed in Syria by CUP leader Jamal Pasha, including scores of executions, and Arab units in Ottoman armies had already been scattered across the empire. What the British eventually got in terms of an Arab revolt was considerably less than they expected.

A letter from the Egyptian high commissioner dated October 24, 1915 was sent to the sharif. In it McMahon, in return for a Sharifian-led Arab revolt, offered independence to the Arabs along the lines of the Damascus Protocol with three reservations—and there was a passive nature to the note as shown in the documents, which did not specify the borders of an independent Arab state but qualified a nebulous offer with restrictions. The Arabs would gain independence with the exception of the following: 1) those the British decided were not "purely Arab," which meant the eastern Mediterranean coast, or west of the line in Syria that goes from Aleppo in the north through Hama, Homs, and then Damascus in the south; 2) those where the special interests of France limited Britain, which pertained especially to the interior of Syria east of the aforementioned line as delineated in Sykes-Picot; and 3) those in which Britain already had existing treaties, referring primarily to long-standing agreements between London and the Persian Gulf Arab shaykhdoms.

The first two reservations would cause most of the consternation and bitter debate that has ensued ever since regarding what actually was included in an independent Arab state that might emerge out of the war. The different interpretations surrounding the first reservation would become particularly relevant with the onset of the Arab–Israeli conflict, because it dealt with the disposition of Palestine.[16]

The reference to French interests has also come under intense scrutiny, especially regarding the interior of Syria. It seems as though Hussein was aware of British concern for French interests and the paramount position France had in British strategic calculations, as was made clear to him in McMahon's final letter in the correspondence of January 1916, but it is unclear how much Hussein knew (or was told) about the extent to which they were being met.

One of the problems with the Hussein-McMahon correspondence is that it was just that—a correspondence, not an officially recognized treaty. It was presumably the prelude to a negotiated settlement regarding an Arab revolt. But the Arab revolt launched by Faisal in June 1916 and assisted by the British liaison officer T. E. Lawrence, known as "Lawrence of Arabia," came and went, yet no specific border discussions ensued during the war. McMahon's language in his letters has been variously described as flowery and ambiguous, and purposely so since he knew of the simultaneous negotiations with the French over much of the same land. In strict diplomatic language, certainly along accepted Western standards of the day, there was no legal contradiction since there was no official document to stand up to Sykes-Picot, which itself did not survive the war unscathed and unaltered. The British were quite adept at always making sure, as good diplomats do, that there was an out if necessary regarding specific and legal commitments—something the Zionists would find out for themselves a few years after the Balfour Declaration.

SPOTLIGHT
Lawrence of Arabia

Born Thomas Edward Lawrence in north Wales in 1888, Lawrence of Arabia, as he came to be known, emerged out of World War I as one of the most celebrated, almost mythic figures of the British military campaign in the Middle East and the Arab fight for independence. Lawrence wrote his thesis at Oxford University on Crusader castles in the Levant, and he traveled to the region a number of times on an archeological dig in northern Syria for the British Museum. While there he became enamored with Arab culture, and he took to learning Arabic. When the war broke out in 1914, Lawrence was commissioned as a lieutenant in the British army and was assigned in 1915 to the Military Intelligence Department in Cairo.

Lawrence quickly impressed his superiors with his intellect, energy, and understanding of the region, and he was promoted to captain in early 1916. But he longed for more action and adventure, especially as his two brothers had been killed on the western front in Europe. He was sent on a mission to Iraq to secure the release of British troops surrounded by Ottoman Turkish forces at Kut al-Amara. He was unsuccessful, but his valiant efforts and his knowledge of indigenous elements won him praise. He seemed destined to become involved in bigger events. It was at this time that, per the Hussein-McMahon correspondence, the Sharif Hussein launched the Arab revolt in the Hijaz on June 5, 1916. Lawrence was assigned to report on the nature and development of the revolt.

While in Arabia, Lawrence met with all four sons of the Sharif Hussein but he came to respect Faisal bin Hussein the most, describing him in his epic account of his Arabian exploits *Seven Pillars of Wisdom* as "the man I had come to Arabia to seek—the leader who would bring the Arab Revolt to full glory."[1] For the next two years Lawrence would act as an adviser to and British liaison with Faisal. The initial object of the Arab revolt was to kick the Ottomans out of Medina and other cities in Arabia. However, Faisal and Lawrence quickly altered the plan to that of bypassing, thus bottling up the Turks in Arabia and setting out toward Damascus, and aiding General Allenby's Palestine campaign by raiding Ottoman trains, supplies, and depots associated with the 700-mile Hijaz railway from Medina to Damascus. The Arab revolt's most spectacular feat was the taking of the important coastal port of Aqaba on the Gulf of Aqaba. Surprise was the key element, as the Arabs attacked from the direction of the desert behind the fortifications and guns of the Ottomans. Getting enough Bedouin Arab warriors was always an ongoing concern, and Faisal and Lawrence continuously struggled to acquire and maintain a minimum force level; in this, Lawrence's role was crucial in gaining the trust and participation of certain Bedouin shaykhs. Although the Arab warriors were hardy, they were also independent-minded and fickle. As Colonel Pierce C. Joyce, one military colleague who fought with Lawrence, commented, "It was not, as is often supposed, by his individual leadership of hordes of Bedouin that he achieved success, but by the wise selection of tribal leaders."[2] Lawrence wrote that "after the capture of Aqaba, things changed so much that I was no longer a witness of the Revolt, but a protagonist in the Revolt."[3] The Ottomans offered a reward for his capture.

Lawrence continued to direct raids against Ottoman positions throughout 1917, although on one occasion while reconnoitering he was captured by Turkish forces. He apparently successfully convinced his captors that he was a light-skinned Circassian, but that did not prevent him from being beaten and, according to some speculation, sexually molested. It was an event that he obviously never forgot, the torment of it probably reaching depths of which even he was unaware. But he secured his release, rejoined the revolt, and pushed onward toward Damascus, which was captured by the Arabs under British auspices in 1918. Describing his entrance into the city on October 1 amid a jubilant population, Lawrence later wrote that "I drank as deeply as any man should do, when we took Damascus: and was sated with it."[4] Two days later he returned to England.

Back in England, gladly away from it all, he began work on his memoirs. Celebrity caught up with him as American journalist Lowell Thomas, who had spent some time with Lawrence during the war, began a series of popular lectures that focused upon—and embellished—Lawrence's role in the Arab revolt, labeling him at one point the "uncrowned king of Arabia." It was at this juncture that T. E. Lawrence became "Lawrence of Arabia." But Lawrence utilized this newfound celebrity to reengage in the complex politics surrounding the disposition of the Arab lands after the war. He traveled to Paris in 1919 as part of the British delegation to the postwar talks, meeting again with and interpreting for Faisal. On behalf of Arab postwar claims and offering cogent warnings to the British imperial position in the Middle East, Lawrence wrote a series of letters in *The Times*. He also joined the British Colonial Office headed by Winston Churchill in 1920 and was instrumental in the decision to bring Faisal to Iraq as king after the would-be Arab monarch was so unceremoniously ejected from Damascus by the French.

Lawrence spent the remainder of his life writing more books, corresponding with politicians and artists, and even joining up with the Royal Air Force

T. E. Lawrence, known as Lawrence of Arabia, 1917.
Fremantle/Alamy Stock Photo

under an alias for a time. He seemed to be haunted by his fame, however, and he remained a troubled soul until the end, which came as a result of a motorcycle accident in May 1935.

[1] T. E. Lawrence, *Seven Pillars of Wisdom* (Hertfordshire: Wordsworth Editions Limited, 1997), p. 76.
[2] O'Brien Browne, "The Enigmatic Lawrence of Arabia," *Military History* (October 2003): 29.
[3] Ibid., 30.
[4] Ibid., 32.

The moral obligation of the British in terms of intent and deception may be quite another matter. It seems as though the British never really took the idea of true Arab independence seriously during the wartime negotiations. This was a combination of the low regard British officials had for the capabilities of the Arabs to govern themselves, and the strategic interests of London in the Middle East—something, it was soon realized, that would require some level of British influence in order to fill the vacuum created by the Ottoman retreat. The offer to Hussein also appears to have been something of a convulsive reaction to the military disaster at Gallipoli. When responding to a British representative in India who was becoming a bit concerned that what McMahon was offering the Arabs could infringe upon the British India Office's purview in Mesopotamia, the High Commissioner of Egypt wrote the following:

> I do not for one moment go to the length of imagining that the present negotiations will go far to shape the future form of Arabia or to either establish our rights or to bind our hands in that country. . . . What we have to arrive at now is to tempt the Arab people into the right path, detach them from the enemy and bring them to our side. . . . This on our part is at present largely a matter of words and to succeed we must use persuasive terms and abstain from haggling over conditions—whether about Baghdad or elsewhere.[17]

On the other hand, there was also certainly deception going in the other direction as well. The Sharifian revolt was primarily a ragtag conglomeration of Bedouin Arab Hijazis and some Arab allies they picked up along the way. It was not an all-Arab rebellion against the Ottomans—not even close—but more of a guerilla warfare outfit (contrary to the general depiction of the revolt in the award-winning film *Lawrence of Arabia*) that accompanied the British along the right flank of General Allenby's Palestine campaign. As we shall see, it became politically desirable for the British to trumpet the Arab role in the campaign in order to secure pro-British allies in the interior of Syria in the hopes of warding off the French by rewriting Sykes-Picot with facts on the ground. As became apparent in the June 1918 Declaration to the Seven, a number of leading Arabs in Syria essentially disavowed Hashemite claims, marking the beginning of a process that would become manifest in the postwar years; the British themselves became progressively disenchanted with Hussein, viewing him as a bombastic, self-aggrandized would-be dynast, and they more and more turned to a rising force led by Abd al-Aziz ibn Abd al-Rahman Al Saud in Arabia, allowing the latter to effectively jettison Hussein into exile soon after the war. From the British perspective, since the sharif did not deliver a revolt of the magnitude that they were led to believe (and ignorantly assumed), then any promises made to the Arabs, whether implicit or explicit, were essentially null and void—they had not delivered, so they did not necessarily deserve even what was inferred in the Hussein-McMahon correspondence. Only self-interest militated against further extortion with continued British support of the Arab cause in Syria for a brief spot of time during the Faisali period.

Under the Sykes-Picot plan, Palestine was to be administered after the war as an international condominium—joint sovereignty run by the British, French, and Russians, the latter having also been a signatory to the agreement. The port city of Haifa was excluded from this, and it was to be set aside for the British as a naval base. It had become clear to the British, especially after David Lloyd George assumed the position of prime minister from Asquith in December 1916, that Palestine had climbed up the ladder of strategic importance. The powers that be in Egypt ever since the Pharaonic period had almost always concluded that a certain level of control over the land east of the Sinai Peninsula north to Syria was an essential security requisite in order to act as a buffer to invaders from the east. In this case the British were concerned about the relative proximity of the French in the anticipated postwar atmosphere, as they were expected to be in Syria and Lebanon.[18] Palestine would be the final piece in the strategic puzzle that linked British dominions from the Mediterranean to India and on into Southeast Asia. If facts could be established on the ground, through Allenby's Palestine campaign as well as securing allies for the British position in Palestine, Sykes-Picot could be for all intents and purposes rewritten—something that Lloyd George was in favor of, since he and a number of other British officials believed too much had been conceded to the French.

Negotiations between British officials and leading Zionists in England that would culminate in the Balfour Declaration began in February 1917. Ideas for using the Jews to advance British interests in Palestine had been put forth prior to this, but nothing came of them under the Asquith government.[19] By 1917, however, British officials were desperate to seek any and every advantage they could in the war given that the outcome was still seriously in doubt despite the fact that the United States, officially as an "associate" and not as an ally, had declared war against Germany (though not against the Ottomans) on the side of the Entente powers in April. It would not be until early 1918 that the United States could mobilize and marshal its enormous resources onto the battlefield; 1917 was a year full of serious reverses for Britain and France, including the Bolshevik revolution in Russia in November that led to its withdrawal from the war in 1918. Germany and its allies had hoped to end the war in terms favorable to them before the United States would inevitably turn the tide, and they almost succeeded in doing so. One almost gets the sense that the British were seeking any and all potential allies in the region, promising anything in order to win the war, and would worry about the repercussions and possible contradictions later, particularly if they emerged from the war in such a position of power that what was agreed to or promised earlier did not matter. The Zionists were a potential ally that could not only help secure the British position in Palestine, but could also aid the British war effort globally—thus the attention they received from British policymakers by 1917. The Zionists had been in search of a great power patron that could translate their desires for a Jewish national homeland into reality, and what country was better placed for this task than Great Britain? The negotiations that resulted in the Balfour Declaration were a marriage of strategic necessity, timing, and opportunity.

One of the more interesting aspects of the Balfour Declaration is that the same kind of anti-Semitic myths surrounding the idea of the all-encompassing power of world Jewry now worked in favor of the Zionist movement. A pro-Zionist British policy was now viewed as essential to keep Russia in the war and to garner full and immediate support from the Americans, even if just a few years earlier only about one percent of the world's Jews were acknowledged Zionists. In so doing it would prevent world Jewry from siding with Germany, which was constantly rumored as being on the verge of enacting a similar pro-Zionist policy.[20] The Zionists had done an excellent job of convincing British officials that world Jewry was solidly behind the movement, when in fact it was not. Anti-Zionist Jews based their opposition upon religious reasons, as well as the fear that support for a Jewish state could produce an anti-Jewish backlash in their home countries that could lead to an untenable situation and effective expulsion. They were as vociferously against the Balfour Declaration as were those British officials in the Middle East who were concerned about the reaction of the Arabs and potential negative repercussions for British strategic interests in the region. The knowledge that there were Jews (presumably pro-Zionist) in high places in both the Menshevik and Bolshevik revolutionary circles as well as among the closest advisers to President Woodrow Wilson (such as Felix Frankfurter and Louis Brandeis) had powerful policy repercussions regarding the fate of Palestine. Chaim Weizmann, one of the leaders of the Zionist movement in Britain, was quick to recognize the evolving British ideas regarding the importance of the Zionists and how that could be leveraged into British recognition of a Jewish position in Palestine.[21] The Zionist movement had concentrated on Palestine for the creation of a Jewish state since 1904—and the exigencies of the war now seemed to be close to making this a reality.

One cannot also discount pro-Zionist sympathies based on humanitarian concerns regarding the centuries of persecution Jews have had to endure. This harsh reality was often present in the minds of those British policymakers who also had a religious basis for supporting the creation of a Jewish entity in Palestine. This is related to the strongly held Protestant belief in biblical prophecy that the Parousia, or second coming of Christ, cannot occur until the Holy Land is in the hands of the Jewish people. Support for the Jews in this sense is almost a religious obligation, and it continues to act as the basis for the strong support for present-day Israel by the so-called Christian right in the United States (often referred to as "Christian Zionists"). Lloyd George and Arthur James Balfour (who became foreign secretary in 1916) were devout Christians who tended to believe in the literal meaning of the Bible, so it is entirely possible this also influenced their pro-Zionist sympathies, along with all of the other aforementioned factors. It was also thought that President Wilson, known for his anti-imperialist and anti-colonialist philosophy, might object at a critical moment in the war to any British move to exert direct control over Palestine. As such, the Declaration was floated past Wilson, whose nonresponse was taken as tacit approval.[22]

As to the language of the document itself, the final product was the result of a series of negotiations. The Zionists had pressed for a statement advocating the establishment of a Jewish state in Palestine, but persistent opposition from some British officials forced a compromise in the Zionist position, amending the demand for a state to that of some sort of national home for the Jews in Palestine. The Zionist draft submitted in July 1917 had asked His Majesty's Government to recognize Palestine as the "National Home for the Jewish People." Often the most important words in diplomatic correspondence and agreements are the smallest; the most ardent diplomatic wrangling frequently revolves around the definite versus the indefinite article, the latter usually providing for more diplomatic wiggle room or a more liberal interpretation to suit all parties concerned. In this case, the discomfort expressed by some British officials eventually modified the declaration to say that "His Majesty's Government views with favor the establishment in Palestine of *a* National Home for the Jewish People" (italics mine). This implied a more ambiguous commitment to an actual Jewish state in Palestine, since it could be interpreted as some sort of Jewish autonomous presence in a Palestinian state. As an indirect reference to the Arabs already living in Palestine and to protect Jews living outside of Palestine, the following phrase was also included: "Nothing being done which may prejudice the civil and religious rights of existing non-Jewish communities in Palestine, or the rights and political status enjoyed by Jews in any other country."

The Balfour Declaration was a tremendous boon to the Zionist movement. Despite the fact that the Zionists did not get everything they wanted in the note from Lord Balfour to Baron Edmond de Rothschild in terms of explicit denotation of a state with boundaries and a timetable, they did garner the support of the strongest military power in the world at the time. Regardless of how much the British tended to backtrack from their commitment in Balfour in the interwar years, the declaration would receive international sanction through the League of Nations as well as official approval from the United States, therefore opening the door wider for continued Jewish immigration to and land acquisition in Palestine, the twin pillars of the Zionist movement.

The Balfour Declaration did not really achieve its objectives from the viewpoint of London. It probably had little, if any, effect on the United States in terms of accelerating its mobilization in the war. Most importantly, it did not keep Russia in the war. By the end of 1917, the new Bolshevik regime had not only withdrawn from the conflict, but also—even more embarrassingly to its erstwhile Entente allies—it published the secret wartime agreements, most damaging of which was Sykes-Picot. The apparent contradictions in the various pledges from Britain started to become manifest, but with approximately one million troops on the ground in the Middle East theater by war's end, the British appeared not to care. They had gone a long way toward establishing facts on the ground. General Sir Edmund Allenby's Palestine campaign had taken Jerusalem by December 1917 and Damascus, Beirut, and Aleppo by October 1918; had effectively secured Palestine for the British; and seemed to be on the verge of making good on most of what the sharif had demanded in the Hussein-McMahon correspondence, particularly concerning the interior of Syria (but noticeably not Palestine), all of which kept the French at bay.[23]

The Sharifian revolt, launched in June 1916, had been something of a disappointment to British authorities. But with only an estimated 3,500 maximum troops at any one time in Faisal's army, there were built-in limitations as to what it could actually accomplish. By 1918, however, its main purpose had become more political than military. The taking of Damascus became enmeshed in postwar diplomacy before the war was even over. There were myriad questions facing British politicians and military officers in the last year of the war and into the postwar diplomatic environment: Just how much should the British honor French interests as articulated in Sykes-Picot? How much should the British honor an apparent pledge to the Arabs as articulated in the Hussein-McMahon correspondence, and could this be an indirect way to keep the French boxed in along the Syrian coast rather than allow them to extend their influence into the interior of Syria? How much could the British dictate and if necessary reshape the terms of the postwar order in the Middle East with troops abounding across the region? And how would the commitment to the Zionists made in the Balfour Declaration fit into the mix? There was anything but a uniform response to these questions, for there were definite divisions between British officials in London (who themselves did not speak with one voice) and British officials and military officers in the field.

By early 1918 British officials attempted to build up Faisal as a viable alternative to Hussein, to the distress of Faisal's father, who claimed the British were manipulating

General Allenby enters Jerusalem, 1917.
World History Archive/Alamy Stock Photo

his son against him. The Declaration to the Seven made in June 1918, which was an attempt by the British to shore up their position with the Arabs and reinforce their commitment to Arab independence with seven Arab nationalist representatives from Syria following the publication of the secret agreements, clearly indicates an attempt to find an alternative to Hussein. The British had been negotiating with Syrian Arabs in Cairo since early 1918 in an attempt to find an accommodation with the Balfour Declaration. Sykes was the one British official who tried to keep everyone happy; he believed that the agreement bearing his name could be reconciled with Hussein-McMahon and Balfour—but he was about the only one who did.

The British were attempting, as Sykes stated in 1917, to combine "Meccan Patriarchalism with Syrian Urban intelligentsia."[24] This was the intent of the Declaration to the Seven. It declared as independent all lands already under control of the Arabs and those lands liberated by the Arabs, while those areas under Entente control would be subject to negotiation. This opened the door ever so slightly for the Sharifian army, if the "conquest" of Syria could be arranged for them by the British. Faisal was the least objectionable of the Hijazis to the Syrians, especially since the latter began to realize that independence could not come without the former. In this way, Sykes could maintain some semblance of Hussein-McMahon while those British officials who had utter disdain for the concessions made to the French intimated in Sykes-Picot could utilize the Arabs to prevent Paris from extending its control beyond the Syrian coast.

Faisal's forces were allowed to enter Damascus first by the British, even though the Turks had long evacuated the city in anticipation of Allenby's advance to the north from Palestine. Whether via Lawrence's and probably Faisal's interpretation of the Declaration to the Seven or British officialdom's conclusion that wherever Faisal's banners flew would constitute the independent Arab state, it was important that Arab forces entered Damascus first. This would ameliorate French concerns that the British intended to take Syria while at the same time place someone in Damascus through whom the British could extend their influence while keeping the French effectively locked up on the coast. These first months of Arab rule in Damascus were quite chaotic, amid British and French machinations to secure the interior of Syria through Arab surrogates, with the French hoping they could control Faisal as much as the British appeared to be doing.

To Lloyd George, obtaining his strategic objectives in the Middle East (and elsewhere) in the last stages of the war was a race against what he perceived would be Wilsonian pressure to abide by the American president's stated principles of self-determination and anti-colonialism in the postwar diplomatic environment. While there were certainly those such as Foreign Secretary Balfour, who sincerely hoped for direct American involvement in a Middle East settlement, even to the point of exploiting Wilson's principles to secure an Arab veneer in the Middle East against French designs, the British prime minister saw the United States as a looming albatross.

Postwar Agreements and Mandate System

The victorious Entente powers met in Paris in January 1919 to begin to discuss the postwar environment. It was a venue in which the United States, particularly President Woodrow Wilson, made a celebrated, albeit brief, appearance into the maelstrom of international diplomacy, dominating the direction of negotiations on the surface due to his country's putative economic power and newfound military strength. But Wilson was inexperienced—if not naïve—in the ways of European diplomacy, which severely hampered the president's ability to implement his vision of a new world order set against the behind-the-scenes machinations of the allies attempting to achieve their diplomatic objectives. Nowhere was this more apparent than in what became known as the King-Crane commission. Even the name of the commission itself reveals the reason for its failure; it is only named after the two Americans who led the mission rather than the Council of Four Entente powers in Paris (Britain, France, Italy, and the United States) that at first jointly indicated their support for the enterprise. Wilson's intent was to help resolve potential British and French differences over the disposition of the Arab territories of the Ottoman Empire by sending a commission to the region itself in order to ascertain the desires of the indigenous populations.

Henry Churchill King, president of Oberlin College, and Charles R. Crane, a businessman from Chicago and Democratic party activist, led a group of Americans to Palestine, Syria, Lebanon, and Anatolia in the summer of 1919. In Syria, the commission found that public opinion there preferred no mandate (and no separation of Syria and Palestine); if a mandate was imposed on them, that it would first be supervised by the United States; and if not an American one, then a British one—by no means did they indicate any desire for a French mandate. The King-Crane commission report, even in the best of circumstances, would be nonbinding—it was simply informational in an attempt to shore up Wilson's position. Lloyd George was hoping to use Wilsonian anti-imperialism to grease the wheels for British influence in the Middle East through surrogates while minimizing the French position. The commission report was essentially ignored by the Europeans. Wilson, having been chastened by European diplomacy as well as US domestic politics in the interim, basically lost interest in it and focused more on the great questions of the day with regard to Europe, such as the League of Nations.[25]

In the negotiations regarding the Middle East, Lloyd George was quick to point out that Britain had over one million troops stationed in Ottoman lands. Despite economic and political realities in Britain that would force upon the government a severe demobilization in due course, British military dominance in the region at the time gave London a very strong bargaining hand. If anything, the military overextension and postwar economic problems back home only doubled Lloyd George's negotiating pace before reality weakened his position. At the peace conference, French Prime Minister Clemenceau would doggedly try to at least acquire the measure of supervision over the interior of Syria that had been mentioned in Sykes-Picot. Faisal also attended the conference, and he just as doggedly tried to hold onto Syria. He displayed a willingness to exclude Palestine from an independent Arab state, which, according to a number of officials at the time, he was never truly interested in to begin with—a concession on Palestine, which he suspected the British would retain in light of its dominant military position and commitment to the Zionists, might provide him more leverage vis-à-vis Syria. The French were not assuaged by Britain's support for Arab independence since they knew Faisal was beholden to the British financially, politically, and militarily. Syria was essentially the only bone of contention left to be negotiated out of the rump of the Ottoman Empire. The British had instituted direct rule in Mesopotamia (Iraq), first a military administration out of the British India office and a civilian administration soon thereafter. Britain's position in Egypt after the war received continued international recognition, and their position in the Persian Gulf was not questioned, nor was their influence with the Saudi and Hashemite families reexamined. The problem was that even though much of the Arab provinces of the Ottoman Empire had already been allotted, final and official acknowledgment of such was the last element of the overall post–World War I negotiations to be settled; this was especially the case in Syria. Events regionally and internationally began to negatively affect Britain's ability to achieve its initial objectives.

The regional and international environment was quite different by the fall of 1919 and into 1920. Russia had withdrawn from the war and the specter of Bolshevism cast a shadow over the Paris negotiations; the United States had begun to adopt a less internationalist posture that would come to characterize its interwar diplomacy, especially as Wilson suffered a debilitating stroke in September 1919. With the internationalist wing's most vocal and influential advocate sidelined, and a Republican-controlled Congress that was tired of the president's unilateral diplomacy and leery of entangling the country in European diplomatic perfidy and in international organizations that would usurp American sovereignty, Congress would not ratify the Treaty of Versailles nor US participation in the League of Nations. Britain, as economic problems mounted and the military remained overextended, would be forced into retrenchment mode in the Middle East that would lessen its bargaining leverage; by 1920, British troop levels in the Middle East had been reduced to about 300,000.[26] Together these were compelling reasons for Lloyd George to make concessions to France regarding Syria. He could no longer count on the United States to play an active role in Europe and contain Germany—in an ironic twist of fate, he realized he had to rely more on the French for balance of power politics on the continent, and the British prime minister would tellingly comment that "France is worth ten Syrias."[27] In addition, his colleague in Paris, with whom he had been able to negotiate directly and with whom a trust had been built, fell from office in January 1920. Alexandre Millerand became the new French president, and he was someone who was much less inclined to make any concessions on Syria and more willing to take advantage of Britain's decreasing leverage.

It was these conditions that compelled the British to announce in September 1919 that they would withdraw their troops from the Syrian region, thus leaving Faisal to fend for himself against the French. With Millerand as president and Faisal's supporters in Damascus defiant, the die was cast; it would just be a matter of time. With the British out of the way in Syria, Paris and London could finally close the diplomatic book with regard to the disposition of the Ottoman Empire. On December 21, 1919, the British and the French came to an agreement regarding the apportionment of oil rights in Mesopotamia: France would receive a 25 percent share of the British-controlled Turkish Petroleum Company while Paris would allow Britain to traverse its Middle East holdings with oil pipelines from Iran and Mesopotamia to the Mediterranean. And at the Conference of London in February 1920, the borders of the Palestine mandate were delineated along British designs, while the French got in return their interpretation of the border between Turkey and Syria.

By April 1920 British and French claims seemed to be settled, and in that month at San Remo, Italy, the Entente powers apportioned the Arab world between Britain and France, assigning mandates that would later be formalized by the League of Nations in September 1922. Britain obtained Palestine (including present-day Jordan) and Iraq, and its status in Egypt and in the Persian Gulf was confirmed. The French were assigned the Syrian mandate, including Lebanon. Arabia remained independent, soon to be taken over by the Saudi family supported by Wahhabi Islamists, resulting in statehood by 1932 with the birth of Saudi Arabia. Sharif Hussein would go into exile in Cyprus soon after the war, where he lived out his life watching his sons continue the Middle East game as the soon-to-be monarch of Iraq (Faisal, after being kicked out of Syria) and Transjordan (Abdullah). The term "mandate" was another bone thrown to Wilsonian sensitivities regarding imperialism. In other words, these were not protectorates or colonies in the Middle East; they were supposed to be more like international trusteeships. The mandates were to be supervised by the mandatory powers, ostensibly preparing them for eventual independence. While Britain and especially France only gave lip service to the intent of the mandate system, treating their mandates more as colonies than anything else, at least they were officially committed to granting independence.

By the summer of 1920, Faisal was living on borrowed time in Syria. The French, after quickly dispatching armed resistance outside of Damascus with their force of some 90,000 troops, ended the Hashemite Kingdom of Syria in July 1920 in a brief battle outside of Damascus, taking direct charge of what would become their Syrian mandate. Faisal's withdrawal from Syria had important repercussions for Palestine. Up until that time a number of Palestinians worked in high-level positions in Faisal's administration, and for the most part Palestinians supported a greater Syria under Faisal's rule, one obviously that would include Palestine.[28] Faisal seemed to be the horse on which to ride toward at least some semblance of independence. As evidence of this, the first two Palestinian national congresses were

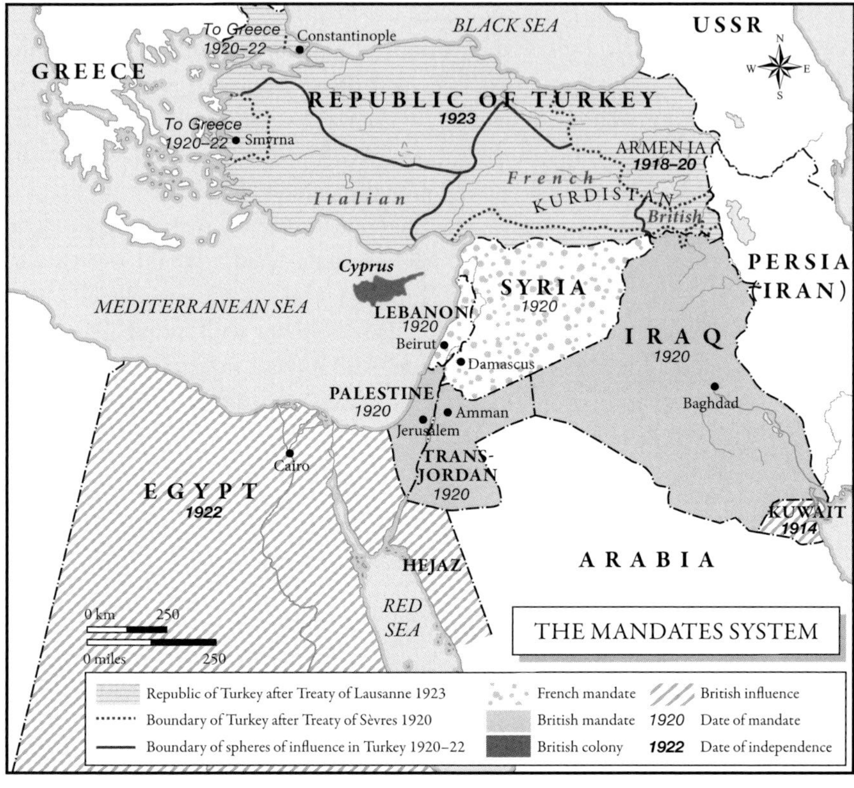

held in Damascus; the third, however, after Faisal's expulsion, was held in Haifa in December 1920. In retrospect, as mentioned earlier, the British abandonment of Faisal in Syria may have had repercussions far beyond the issue of betraying Arab interests to the French. It may have crystallized the contentious issues developing in Palestine more quickly, particularly focusing Palestinian Arab opposition to not only the British presence but also growing Jewish influence and claims via continued immigration and land acquisition. It made "Palestine" Palestine.

Hashemite dreams would not be totally lost, however, following Faisal's exit from Syria and his father's exile a few years later from the Hijaz. The British feared that Transjordan, the roughly 75 percent of mandated Palestine that lay east of the Jordan River (and corresponding in the main to present-day Jordan), would be claimed by the French as a kind of inheritance after taking control of Damascus from Faisal. This was certainly an area within the Greater Syria aspired to by Faisal and his Arab nationalist supporters as well as being wholly within the territory allotted to the Arabs under Hussein-McMahon. In addition, there were Arabs in Transjordan who were intent on returning Faisal to Damascus, something the French could utilize as an excuse to move troops into the arid region in order to quell potential countercoup movements. If the British were not careful, they could fall into a military conflagration with the French in the Middle East and potentially lose the contiguous land corridor from the Mediterranean to the Persian Gulf that was of such strategic importance, especially as London envisioned oil pipelines rather than trade caravans traversing the route. The British were unable to keep the French bottled up along the Syrian coast, but they certainly did not want French influence to extend beyond Syria itself. In order to meet this potential strategic threat at a time of British retrenchment in the region, it was decided at a conference in Cairo in March 1921, dealing primarily with Transjordan and Iraq, to make Abdullah (Hussein's third son and the great-great grandfather of the current King Abdullah of Jordan) the sovereign of Transjordan. Since Abdullah at that very moment had entered Amman with the apparent intent of liberating Syria for his brother, Faisal, it seemed like the proper thing to do at the time in order to ward off a potential conflict with the French. Abdullah was officially recognized as Emir of Transjordan by the British in December 1921. In this way, as the British typically did, London could work through a surrogate beholden to British interests and reliant upon British force to maintain its influence in the region, keep the French out and hopefully assuage the Arabs. For good measure, and as much an attempt at restitution as political or strategic motivation, at the conference it was agreed that Faisal would be made the king of the newly stitched-together entity now called Iraq, supported by a number of former Arab nationalist Ottoman officers who had been with him in Damascus. He officially assumed his new position in August 1921. Thus while one Hashemite "kingdom" was on its way out in the Hijaz (Hussein abdicated and went into exile in the face of Saudi pressure in 1924), two more were being created elsewhere in the Middle East.

Palestine had been under British military administration since Allenby's successful campaign to take Jerusalem in December 1917. British officers on the ground during this time tended to oppose London's policy as announced in the Balfour Declaration. To them, Zionist aspirations in Palestine were inconsistent with British interests in securing overall Arab support in the postwar environment. As happened in other areas of the Middle East throughout 1920, there were riots in Palestine in April. The nature of some of these riots in the region revolved around protestations to the British or French presence, but they were also the result of indigenous societal fissures created by the interregnum between Ottoman rule and the mandate system. In Palestine, the emerging Arab-Jewish dynamic added fuel to the fire. Even Winston Churchill, who had been an avid pro-Zionist, wrote to Lloyd George on June 13, 1920 that "Palestine is costing us 6 million a year to hold. The Zionist movement will cause continued friction with the Arabs. The French . . . are opposed to the Zionist movement & will try to cushion the Arabs off on us as the real enemy. The Palestine venture . . . will never yield any profit of a material kind."[29] Lloyd George, however, reacted to the increased disturbances by reiterating his commitment to the Zionist cause as delineated in the Balfour Declaration. As a result, in July 1920 he replaced the military administration in Palestine with a civilian one, headed by Sir Herbert Samuel as high commissioner.

For the Anatolian and European rump of the Ottoman Empire, a different set of agreements in Europe attended to its disposition. Ironically, the war did not directly end the empire; instead, it was a Turkish nationalist movement led by Mustafa Kemal Ataturk (the Kemalist movement). Ataturk was a very popular military leader, as he had been with the Third Army at Gallipoli. He was a Young Turk, more of the nationalist bent rather than liberal constitutionalist variety; nonetheless, he was a secularist who wanted to bring the Turks into the modern European world and get rid of the burdens of empire and Islamic baggage that accompanied it. Operating out of Ankara, he was supported by a broad coalition at first, including Islamic religious leaders. Ataturk initially aimed his arrows at external interference and not at the person of the sultan-caliph. Despite the fact that the position had fallen into disrepute, it still had led the Ottoman Empire for over six hundred years, so it was a familiar institution that could not be easily abolished.

But two things boosted Ataturk's cause. First was the Greek invasion of western Anatolia in May 1919 to secure claims made to Greece as part of World War I's secret agreements in order to get the Greeks into the war on the side of the Entente powers—and if there is one thing that would unite the Turks, it was an invasion by Greece. Next was the Treaty of Sevres (outside of Paris) in August 1920, which from the Turkish point of view, was humiliating. Among other aspects, the Entente powers established international control of the Turkish straits, created an independent Armenia and Kurdistan in eastern Anatolia, awarded the Dodecanese islands to Italy, and reinstituted the Capitulations. However, Ataturk was able to turn both of these humiliations around, thus providing him with the legitimacy and wherewithal to move against the sultan-caliph. His forces were able to expel the Greeks from Anatolia by September 1922, so he saved the Turks when the sultan could not.

It was not a surprise that he felt empowered enough to abolish the sultanate on November 17, 1922. Since the European powers were in no mood or position following a debilitating world war to enforce the provisions of the Treaty of Sevres, they caved in to the inevitable and renegotiated the terms with Ataturk—basically reversing Sevres completely with the Treaty of Lausanne in July 1923, still considered to this day one of Turkey's greatest diplomatic achievements. The Straits were returned to Turkish control, the Capitulations ended, and there would be no independent Armenia or Kurdistan. The Republic of Turkey was proclaimed in October, and the caliphate was abolished in March 1924. There has been no generally acknowledged caliph in the Islamic world ever since. Ataturk's goal was a modernized, secularized Turkey that would become part of Europe, the ultimate manifestation of which eventually would be to join the European Union. It was not an easy process; there were many growing pains, and the military became the final arbiter of power for decades despite his desire for a working parliamentary democracy. But he was on the whole successful, largely because the Tanizmat, which had failed in its primary purpose, had established a foundation of modernization on which Ataturk could build. It is important to mention here the tragic circumstances of Turkish nationalism run amok during the war. Armenians had previously been repressed in the Ottoman Empire, particularly in eastern Anatolia, but not to the extent of what happened in 1915. At that time it seems that Armenians, even those serving in the Ottoman army, were scapegoated for the mounting military defeats, all of which fed into existing sentiments among Turks against Armenians. As a result, most historians estimate that around 1.5 million Armenians were killed in what most countries now call the Armenian genocide.[30] Turkish governments over the years do not deny the deaths of many Armenians during the war, but they have claimed that it was more the product of the chaos of war than any intentional policy.

Much of the rest of the Middle East did not fare as well as Turkey with regard to European interference. The mandate system itself—the British and French position in the heartland of the Middle East—was a rather strange arrangement that did not really advance the prospects of true independence for these newly formed Arab states. Article 22 of the League of Nations Covenant referred to the inhabitants of the colonies taken from the defeated Central Powers as "people not yet able to stand by themselves under the strenuous conditions of the modern world." In an even more condescending fashion the article went on to state that "tutelage of such peoples should be entrusted to advanced nations who, by reasons of their resources, their experience, or their geographical position, can best undertake this responsibility." The "colonies" were not equal, however. The Entente powers divided them up into A, B, and C categories. Category A countries were those carved out of former German and Austrian-Hungarian territory in Europe that by virtue of being European were ready for immediate independence (Czechoslovakia, Hungary)—and did become independent; the Arab territories of the Ottoman Empire were in Category B, meaning they needed guidance and supervision from the mandate powers before independence; and in truly prejudiced fashion, Category C countries were those primarily in sub-Saharan Africa, which were viewed as so undeveloped and primitive that independence now or in the near future was not even a consideration.

Most analyses examine the mandate system in the Middle East as the beginning of the European-imposed nation-state system that established the foundation for subsequent events in the region. But it is important to note, as Middle East historian Michael Provence poignantly writes in his book *The Last Ottoman Generation*, that the end of the Ottoman Empire was just as, if not more, challenging for the indigenous population than the attempted imposition of new European-based institutions—even beyond the severe dislocations and hardships caused by the war itself. Despite the flaws in the Ottoman system, for many peoples long under the suzerainty of the Sublime Porte, it suited them better than the nation-state structure. As Provence writes, "As mandate citizens proclaimed repeatedly, Ottoman rule had delivered an imperfect but superior semblance of rights, justice, and representation to the majority of the population and petitioners viewed the Ottoman state as more legitimate and representative than the colonial regimes that replaced it. The Mandate state was afflicted by an immediate crisis of legitimacy, and continual opposition and challenges to its authority required violent suppression of the population."[31] Quite to the contrary of the publicly pronounced goal to develop representative parliamentary governments in the mandated territories—in and of themselves liberal facades at best—the absolute power of the High Commissioners and other local officials implanted by the British and French to run the mandates, supplemented by autonomous military and intelligence bureaucracies, actually did more to create the template of the military dictatorship in the region than any "orientalist" notion that this was the natural order of things to which the area reflexively reverted to upon independence following the mandate years.

The mandate years between World War I and shortly after World War II were similar in French-mandated Syria (and Lebanon), and in British-controlled Iraq, Egypt, and Palestine, although the latter situation was further complicated by the presence of a Palestinian Arab population mixed with an increasing number of Jewish settlers (**Yishuv**) who as part of the Zionist movement had been migrating to Palestine since the 1880s. Essentially, Britain and France tried to adjust and readjust their relationship with the ruling class in each of these countries—be it the monarch or the landed aristocracy leftover from the Ottomans—in a kind of triangular relationship, making concessions and proclamations that provided the illusion of empowerment to indigenous authorities without really giving it. The new Western-style parliamentary systems were dominated by the landed aristocracies and other notables who engaged in what the Syrian version called "honorable cooperation" with the mandate authorities. All the while, a mostly younger

Syrian women demonstrating against the French Mandate in 1925 in Damascus.
Syrianhistory.com

generation of Arabs becoming politically aware during the mandate years viewed all this with bewilderment and increasing frustration at the continuing inability, if not unwillingness, of the ruling Arab classes—the older generation—to obtain true independence from the European powers.

One of the first indications of postwar local opposition to the new arrangement imposed from the outside was the 1919 Egyptian revolution. When Britain declared Egypt a protectorate in 1914, thus officially severing the pretense of Ottoman sovereignty, it was done so, at least from the Egyptian perspective, with the promise of independence after the war's end—and with the idea that Egypt might be spared involvement in the war. As mentioned earlier, this did not happen as a result of the British loss at Gallipoli. The deprivations of war hit Egypt hard, as it had elsewhere in the Middle East (Syria lost about a quarter of its population to war, disease, and famine). Britain stationed thousands of troops in Egypt, disrupting society among all classes of the population. Moreover, the British conscripted hundreds of thousands of Egyptians, mostly from rural areas, into the Egyptian Labor Corps and tasked them with doing much of the dirty work to support the British effort. The Egyptians came to see this as a form of slavery, imbued with racism.[32] A rising nationalist response was the result, cutting across class lines, including Muslims and Christians and Egyptian men and women. Led by Saad Zaghlul, opposition to the British was organized by the *Wafd* ("delegation," so-called because it formed from a proposed Egyptian delegation to attend the Paris peace talks), which became the dominant political party in Egypt until World War II. The British administration in Cairo, fearing the rising distress, arrested and exiled Zaghlul in March 1919, which elicited an eruption of protests, demonstrations, and violence across the country. The British put down the "revolution" harshly by July, with some eight hundred Egyptians killed and much destruction.

SPOTLIGHT

Huda Sharawi (Shaarawi)

Huda Sharawi (1879–1947) was a leading Egyptian feminist and nationalist who dedicated her adult life to women's rights, establishing a number of organizations for the cause. She is considered to be the founder of the women's movement in Egypt and made her mark globally as well. She grew up in a wealthy family, where her father was a landowner who took an active role in Egyptian politics, becoming a member of the Chamber of Delegates in 1876. Sharawi was raised in a harem system as a member of an upper-class family, so she was confined to a certain part of her home and wore veils when venturing outside. This was a formative period in her life that she later memorialized in her book *Harem Years: The Memoirs of an Egyptian Feminist*. She became well-educated through private schooling at home and then at age thirteen was married off to her cousin, who was over thirty years her senior. In the early 1900s they had two children together.

Sharawi founded a variety of organizations staffed by women that were designed to help underprivileged women and children. She was strongly affected by the 1919 Egyptian revolution, and along with her husband became an outspoken advocate for Egyptian independence from Great Britain. Her husband, Ali Sharawi, was one of the founding members of the nationalist Wafd (delegation) party that dominated the Egyptian parliament and worked assiduously for more independence from the British in the interwar years. In 1920 Huda Sharawi founded and served as the president of the Women's Central Committee of the Wafd. This was emblematic of the increasing role of women in Egypt's nationalist movement and overall political activism; she played a central part in organizing a protest march of middle- and upper-class women against the British in 1919. Her husband died shortly after she took up her role in the Central Committee, whereupon Huda shifted her efforts more toward fighting for the equality of women in Egyptian society and left the Committee in 1924.

In 1923 she founded and became president (for the rest of her life) of the Egyptian Feminist Union, which fought for reforms to personal status laws, women's suffrage, and increased educational pathways for women. Also in 1923, in a signature moment of the Egyptian feminist movement, upon her return from a conference in Rome of the International Women Suffrage Alliance, she removed her face veil at a train station in Cairo. This caused a commotion at the station, although wearing a veil was really only an issue for wealthy women in Egypt, since they were the only ones who wore them.

In 1945 Sharawi became the founding president of the Arab Feminist Union. Both feminist unions published magazines that reflected their efforts, *Al-Misriyyah* (The Egyptian) in 1925 and *Al-Marah al-Arabiyyah* (The Arab Woman) in 1946. She was instrumental in connecting the Egyptian Feminist Union with the International Women Suffrage Alliance (later called

Huda Sharawi in Cairo in 1927.
Wikipedia

the International Alliance of Women), although she became somewhat disillusioned by its efforts as it tended to be dominated by European and North American feminists, and the agenda of feminists in Asia, Africa, and Latin American tended to be minimized. Sharawi gave a speech at the 1923 International Women Suffrage conference in which she argued that women in pharaonic Egypt had equal status to men and that Islam also granted equal rights to women, but in the latter case the Quran had been repeatedly misinterpreted by men to the disadvantage of equality for women in the Islamic world. Toward the end of her life she became a passionate supporter of Palestinian rights, and as a result focused more on pan-Arab nationalist causes.

Sources: Jennifer Jaffer, "Huda Sharawi," *Encyclopedia Britannica*, December 8, 2021, https://www.britannica.com/biography/Huda-Sharawi; also, https://scholarblogs.emory.edu/postcolonialstudies/2014/06/12/shaarawi-huda/.

In response to this the British appointed the Milner commission to investigate, after which it was decided the protectorate could not be maintained. Following even more protests and demonstrations after the San Remo conference, Britain would unilaterally declare Egyptian independence in February 1922. In true British form there were some reservations: security of communications, i.e. the Suez Canal; defense of Egypt against foreign aggression, which would come into play in the 1956 Suez war; and protection of foreign interests and minorities. In effect this was not true independence, but the strength of Egyptian nationalism reared its head. Britain did something similar in Iraq with a Treaty of Alliance in October 1922. Perhaps seeing the writing on the wall, especially as the Great Depression began in 1929 and with tensions rising in Europe in the 1930s, Britain made some further concessions to local interests with the 1930 Anglo-Iraqi treaty proclaiming full independence (again with some reservations), and the 1936 Anglo-Egyptian treaty that was negotiated with Egyptians and also proclaimed full independence. The French never really gave any pretense that their mandated territories were anything but colonies, and they ruled as such. They employed divide-and-rule tactics in populations that were religiously and ethnically fragmented in attempts to make sure no unified coalition of forces could adequately oppose them. Depending upon the nature of the government back in Paris, there were movements afoot in Syria to make concessions regarding independence along the lines of what the British were doing. Frequent changes of government in France often reversed things, however, damaging the credibility of the Syrian ruling class desperately hoping for progress while maintaining their political and economic positions of power—and further angering the disenfranchised groups of new and younger classes of Syrians.

In Palestine, the British tried to make the Arab-Jewish experiment work, even arranging for mixed legislative councils to promote a cooperative relationship, but in the end it failed.[33] At the end of World War I there were about 50,000 Jews in

Palestine, along with 800,000 Arabs. Most of the Jews in Palestine were either a few thousand who had been in Jerusalem for religious reasons for generations, or those who had come in the first two of many Zionist organized migrations (**aliyahs**) to Palestine since 1881. The second one (1904–1914), mostly comprised of Jews from Eastern Europe and Russia, was by far the most important of all the aliyahs, as many of the early leaders of Israel (such as David Ben-Gurion, the head of the Yishuv in Palestine and Israel's first prime minister) arrived as well as the secular, socialist ideological tinge they brought to the movement, or what was called Labor Zionism.

Jewish immigration to Palestine grew by leaps and bounds in the 1930s when Adolph Hitler came to power in Germany. Between 1933–1936 the Jewish population in Palestine doubled to about 400,000, and grew to about 700,000 by 1947. The twin pillars of the Zionist movement, immigration and land acquisition, were succeeding from the point of view of the Yishuv, especially as the Great Depression in the 1930s made land owned by Arabs more available to Jewish interests entering into land speculation and willing to pay premium prices. The Palestinian Arab population by World War II was about 1.2 million. The enhanced Jewish presence made for a more volatile situation, as the local Arab population began to better organize its opposition to both the British and the Yishuv, leading to violent riots in 1929 and then what came to be called the Arab Revolt in Palestine in 1936–1939, which reflected the growing anger and frustration of the younger generation of Palestinians who lived their lives under British occupation and increasing Jewish ownership.

The British had to send 20,000 troops to Palestine to quell the revolt. Their harsh suppression of Palestinians really diminished the latter's ability to confront the Yishuv after World War II, especially as their leadership was dismantled or exiled, leading to a vacuum of power that was filled by other Arab states and leaders who did not necessarily have the best interests of the Palestinians at heart. With the specter of World War II on the horizon and therefore the need to curry more Arab support in the region, the revolt compelled the British to essentially reverse the Balfour Declaration with the 1939 White Paper, which called for limitations to Jewish immigration and land acquisition while declaring that the Yishuv should exist within an independent Palestinian state to come into being over the next ten years. This really made no one happy, but now the British were increasingly the target of Jewish violence, all of which would lead London after World War II to get out of Palestine altogether. The first Arab-Israeli war in 1947–1949 and the emergence of the State of Israel would soon follow.

In the mandates in general, urban notables, intellectuals, and professionals, raised on the Western-inspired notions of parliamentary systems and constitutions and buoyed by the heritage of constitutional movements in the Ottoman Empire, worked for independence within the British and French-imposed systems.[34] However, as referred to earlier, there was a young generation who instead of reading the Locke, Voltaire, and Mill that had inspired their parent's generation, were reading

Marx and Engels—or for Islamists the Quran, leading in Egypt to the formation of the **Muslim Brotherhood** in 1928, founded by Hassan al-Banna. There were variable responses to the European presence. By the 1930s they could be patient no longer; the older generation had not delivered. They were seen to be a self-interested, self-aggrandizing, and corrupt barrier to true independence and economic justice. It would be this generation of Arab nationalists who would begin to organize themselves into independent socialist parties and organizations such as the **Baath** (Resurrection) party in Syria or the Free Officers movement in Egypt, who would eventually push aside the *ancien regimes* and their European masters after World War II. The final delegitimizing straw of the older generation, at least in the eyes of their younger counterparts, was its utter and abject failure in the 1947–1949 Arab–Israeli war, when they could not even defeat what was perceived to be a ragtag lot of Jews in Palestine, allowing Israel to come into being in the heart of the Arab world.

SPOTLIGHT

Naguib Mahfouz

Egyptian writer Naguib (Najib) Mahfouz (1911–2006) was the most famous and influential novelist in the Arab world in the twentieth century. In 1988, he was the first Arab writer to win the Nobel Prize in Literature. The Nobel committee credited Mahfouz with the "creation of an Arabian narrative art that applies to all mankind." He is known as one of the first contemporary writers of Arabic literature to explore themes of existentialism (along with Egyptian novelist Taha Hussein). He published over thirty books and hundreds of short stories as well as movie scripts, plays, and op-eds. His best-known books are probably *The Cairo Trilogy* (1956), which details the lives of three generations of families in Cairo from World War I through the 1952 Egyptian revolution that effectively brought Gamal Abd al-Nasser to power, and the *Children of Gebelawi* (1959), a controversial novel that portrayed a Cairene patriarch and his children living the lives of famous religious figures, such as Cain and Abel, Moses, Jesus, and Muhammad. American journalist Ben Lynfield, at the time working for the *Jerusalem Post*, interviewed Mahfouz on a number of occasions in the late 1980s and 1990s. Soon after Mahfouz's death, Lynfield penned an essay memorializing the late novelist in which he wrote that "Mahfouz was a master of allegory, a keen observer of human nature and politics who wrote books both popular and profound, distinctly Egyptian and yet universal."[1]

Many of Mahfouz's writings reflected his life in Egypt, his lower-middle-class upbringing in Cairo, the years of British control of the country, the Nasserist era, and the tensions and subsequent rapprochement with Israel. Many of his stories were set in the streets and homes of heavily populated urban areas of Cairo, and his characters were typically ordinary people dealing with twentieth-century issues such as modernization, Westernization, and the socioeconomic challenges of their lot in an allegorical writing style. Even though he was very young, the Egyptian revolution of 1919 protesting British rule had a profound effect on him, as he witnessed some of the violence perpetrated by British troops against demonstrators. Graduating from Cairo University in 1934, Mahfouz started his writing career as a journalist, whereupon he also began contributing short stories to the *Al-Ahram* and *Al-Hilal* newspapers. In addition, he worked at times in Egyptian government ministries as a civil servant, ending as a consultant to the Ministry of Culture in 1971.

As Lynfield points out, Mahfouz was also very much the political novelist. Although he published his most stinging criticism of Nasser after the latter died in 1970, he indirectly criticized the Egyptian leader in the 1960s, as he was very disappointed in the promise of Nasser and the 1952 revolution, especially following Egypt's devastating defeat in the 1967 Arab–Israeli war. As more of an Egyptian nationalist, he believed that Nasser misspent Egypt's assets frivolously on quixotic Arab nationalist or pan-Arabist ventures rather than on domestic development. Having lived through five Arab–Israeli wars, Mahfouz became an ardent advocate of peace with Israel, having supported President Anwar Sadat's path toward the 1979 Egyptian-Israeli peace treaty. Eventually the Egyptian novelist became disenchanted in the halting progress of peace, for the most part blaming Israeli policies for the disappointing results after so much potential for true normalization had frittered away.

Winner of the Nobel Prize for Literature in 1988, Egyptian novelist Naguib Mahfouz sits in the courtyard of Beit Suheimi in Cairo.
Barry Iverson/Alamy Stock Photo

As Mahfouz wrote, "After the peace agreement, our nation opened its heart to every Israeli, but the Israelis threw this away."[2]

In 1994 Mahfouz was stabbed in the neck by an Islamic militant, a reflection of the novelist's secular leanings and what Islamists believed were his blasphemous portrayals of the prophets. His injuries inhibited his ability to speak and write, but that did not stop him from doing so, although he slowed down considerably in his later years. Israeli scholar Menahem Milson, who befriended Mahfouz and wrote a biography of the Egyptian writer, captured his enormous legacy, saying the following after his death in 2006: "He really wrote excellent modern Egyptian novels in the Arabic language that were read all over the Arab world. The values infused through these novels are very important, such as the equality of women, the human dignity of women, the criticism of social conventions, compassion for human beings and the importance of people taking their fate into their hands and doing things rather than brooding idly at home."[3]

Fortunately for the rest of the world, after Mahfouz won the Nobel Prize, many of his novels were translated and published outside of the Middle East.

---

[1] Ben Lynfield, "Remembering Najib Mahfouz," *Tikkun*, January/February 2007, p. 49.

[2] Quoted in ibid., p. 50.

[3] Quoted in Ben Lynfield, "Egyptian laureate's legacy still resonates in Israel 10 years after death," *Jerusalem Post*, September 11, 2016, https://www.jpost.com/arab-israeli-conflict/egyptian-laureates-legacy-still-resonates-in-Israel-10-years-after-death-467430. Milson's biography is *Najib Mahfouz: The Novelist-Philosopher of Cairo* (New York: St. Martin's Press, 1998).

Arab nationalism became the language of the younger generation: an Arab nation that wanted a nation-state comprised of Arabs. It was a secular movement conceived mostly during the mandate years that saw an Arab nation cemented together by one common language, culture, and history. Islam was a major component of this cement but not the main one, especially as a number of Arab nationalists, such as one of the founders of the Baath party, Michel Aflaq, were Christian. Islam comprised many more people than just the Arabs, and the Arab nation predated the rise of Islam. Islam was always important, as it was a prerequisite for popular support, but while they cooperated to expel the mandate powers, Islamist groups such as the Muslim Brotherhood were always suspicious of the Arab nationalists, and they would go in different and competing directions after independence. Arab nationalists, however, viewed Arab history as one that was infected by tribal solidarity (*asabiyya*) over national solidarity; therefore, the Byzantines and Sassanians kept the Arabs at bay before the Prophet Muhammad, but the rise of Islam united the Arabs and led to the Arab conquests. But Islam was not enough, and tribalism soon prevailed, allowing foreigners to dominate yet again, as had the Persians, Turks, Mongols, the Turks again, and finally the Europeans. Many referred to this as a second **jahiliyya**, another age of ignorance. The Arabs needed to develop a national asabiyya, culling together the Arab nation to achieve true independence and greatness.

This response to the mandate system would become one of the dominant forces in the Middle East following World War II, as we shall see. The mandate system as a whole did not prepare the Arabs well for statehood, as was its intended purpose. All one has to do is look at the corrupt and uncoordinated Arab effort in the first Arab–Israeli war to understand this.[35] Although they often had the built-in advantage of preferential European support, the Yishuv did a much better job at state-building, making sure to develop a Hebrew nation with an institutional foundation before acquiring statehood. And it showed on the battlefields of Palestine. For the newly independent Arab states, state-building was a much more wrenching process. Arab polities, for the most part artificially constructed after the Great War, were politically immature and fragmented, subnational identities coming to the fore with just a scant feeling of national identity. Along with continued interference by external powers and a developing Arab–Israeli conflict, this matrix of internal and external pressures led to frequent political instability that often only came to an end under the watchful eye of a military dictatorship.

Chapter 10 Timeline

1876–1878	First Ottoman Constitutional Period
1876–1909	Rule of Sultan Abd al-Hamid (Hamidian era)
1882	British occupation of Egypt
1908–1909	Young Turk (CUP) revolution restores constitution and deposes Abd al-Hamid II
1914–1918	World War I; Ottomans enter on Germany's side
1916	Sykes-Picot agreement signed
1917	Balfour Declaration issued by British government
1920	San Remo Conference and the establishment of the mandate system
1921	Kingdom of Iraq and Emirate of Transjordan established under Hashemite rulers
1923	Establishment of Republic of Turkey under Mustafa Kemal Ataturk
1928	Hasan al-Banna founds the Muslim Brethren in Egypt
1936–1939	Arab revolt in Palestine caused by Jewish immigration and land acquisition
1940s	The Free Officers movement comes into being in Egypt
1947	The Baath Party (Arab Socialist Baath Party) officially forms in Syria
1947–1949	First Arab–Israeli War and the establishment of the state of Israel

Primary Sources

Negib Azoury: Program of the League of the Arab Fatherland

THERE IS NOTHING more liberal than the league's program.

The league wants, before anything else, to separate the civil and the religious power, in the interest of Islam and the Arab nation, and to form an Arab empire stretching from the Tigris and the Euphrates to the Suez Isthmus, and from the Mediterranean to the Arabian Sea.

The mode of government will be a constitutional sultanate based on the freedom of all the religions and the equality of all the citizens before the law. It will respect the interests of Europe, all the concessions and all the privileges which had been granted to her up to now by the Turks. It will also respect the autonomy of the Lebanon, and the independence of the principalities of Yemen, Nejd, and Iraq.

The league offers the throne of the Arab Empire to that prince of the Khedivial family of Egypt who will openly declare himself in its favor and who will devote his energy and his resources to this end.

It rejects the idea of unifying Egypt and the Arab Empire under the same monarchy, because the Egyptians do not belong to the Arab race; they are of the African Berber family and the language which they spoke before Islam bears no similarity to Arabic. There exists, moreover, between Egypt and the Arab Empire a natural frontier which must be respected in order to avoid the introduction, in the new state, of the germs of discord and destruction. Never, as a matter of fact, have the ancient Arab caliphs succeeded for any length of time in controlling the two countries at the same time.

The Arab fatherland also offers the universal religious caliphate over the whole of Islam to that sherif (descendant of the Prophet) who will sincerely embrace its cause and devote himself to this work. The religious caliph will have as a completely independent political state the whole of the actual vilayet of Hijaz, with the town and the territory of Medina, as far as Aqaba. He will enjoy the honors of a sovereign and will hold a real moral authority over all the Muslims of the world.

One of the principal causes of the fall of the vast empire of the Arabs was the centralization in a single hand of the civil and the religious powers. It is also for this reason that the caliphate of Islam has become today so ridiculous and so contemptible in the hands of the Turks. The successor of the Prophet of Allah must enjoy an incontestable moral prestige; his whole life must be of unblemished honor, his authority suffering no diminution, his majesty independent [of anything other than itself]. His power also will be universal; from his residence he will rule morally over all the Muslims of the universe who will hurry in pilgrimage to the sanctuaries of Mohammed. [About the position of the caliph, Azoury offers a word of explanation.]

The caliph of Islam must be either the sovereign of all the Muslims of the earth united in a single state, which has always proved impossible, even under the first caliphs, or, quite simply, the sovereign of a country entirely Islamic. There is indeed no country more Islamic than the Hijaz, and there are no towns more suitable than Medina and Mecca to receive the Supreme Head of the believers.

Source: Negib Azoury, *Le Réveil de la Nation Arabe dans l'Asie Turque en Présence des Intérêts et des Rivalités des Puissance Étrangères, de la Curie Romaine et due Patriarcat Oecuménique* (Paris, 1905), 245–247, 248, as quoted in Sylvia G. Haim, *Arab Nationalism: An Anthology* (Berkeley: University of California Press, 1952), 81–82.

Excerpts from the Hussein-McMahon Correspondence, July 14, 1915–January 25, 1916

Letter from the Sharif Hussein of Mecca to Sir Henry McMahon, His Majesty's High Commissioner at Cairo, July 14, 1915

Whereas the whole of the Arab nation without any exception have decided in these last years to accomplish their freedom, and grasp the reins of their administration both in theory and practice; and whereas they have found and felt that it is in the interest of the Government of Great Britain to support them and aid them in the attainment of their firm and lawful intentions (which are based upon the maintenance of the honour and dignity of their life) without any ulterior motives whatsoever unconnected with this object;

And whereas it is to their (the Arabs') interest also to prefer the assistance of the Government of Great Britain in consideration of their geographic position and economic interests, and also of the attitude of the above-mentioned Government, which is known to both nations and therefore need not be emphasized;

For these reasons the Arab nation sees fit to limit themselves, as time is short, to asking the Government of Great Britain, if it should think fit, for the approval, through her deputy or representative, of the following fundamental propositions, leaving out all things considered secondary in comparison with these, so that it may prepare all means necessary for attaining this noble purpose, until such time as it finds occasion for making the actual negotiations:

> Firstly.—England will acknowledge the independence of the Arab countries, bounded on the north by Mersina and Adana up to the 37th degree of latitude, on which degree fall Birijik, Urfa, Mardin, Midiat, Jezirat (Ibn 'Umar), Amadia, up to the border of Persia; on the east by the borders of Persia up to the Gulf of Basra; on the south by the Indian Ocean, with the exception of the position of Aden to remain as it is; on the west by the Red Sea, the Mediterranean Sea up to Mersina. England to approve the proclamation of an Arab Khalifate of Islam.

> Secondly.—The Arab Government of the Sherif will acknowledge that England shall have the preference in all economic enterprises in the Arab countries whenever conditions of enterprises are otherwise equal.
> Thirdly.—For the security of this Arab independence and the certainty of such preference of economic enterprises, both high contracting parties will offer mutual assistance, to the best ability of their military and naval forces, to face any foreign Power which may attack either party. Peace not to be decided without agreement of both parties.
> Fourthly.—If one of the parties enters into an aggressive conflict, the other party will assume a neutral attitude, and in case of such party wishing the other to join forces, both to meet and discuss the conditions. . . .
> Fifthly.—England will acknowledge the abolition of foreign privileges in the Arab countries, and will assist the Government of the Sherif in an International Convention for confirming such abolition.
> Sixthly.—Articles 3 and 4 of this treaty will remain in vigour for fifteen years, and, if either wishes it to be renewed, one year's notice before lapse of treaty is to be given.

Consequently, and as the whole of the Arab nation have (praise be to God) agreed and united for the attainment, at all costs and finally, of this noble object, they beg the Government of Great Britain to answer them positively or negatively in a period of thirty days after receiving this intimation; and if this period should lapse before they receive an answer, they reserve to themselves complete freedom of action. Moreover, we (the Sherif's family) will consider ourselves free in work and deed from the bonds of our previous declaration which we made through Ali Effendi.

Letter from McMahon to the Sharif Hussein, August 30, 1915

. . . We have the honour to thank you for your frank expressions of the sincerity of your feeling towards England. We rejoice, moreover, that your Highness and your people are of one opinion—that Arab interests are English interests and English Arab. To this intent we confirm to you the terms of Lord Kitchener's message, which reached you by the hand of Ali Effendi, and in which was stated clearly our desire for the independence of Arabia and its inhabitants, together with our approval of the Arab Khalifate when it should be proclaimed. We declare once more that His Majesty's Government would welcome the resumption of the Khalifate by an Arab of true race. With regard to the questions of limits and boundaries, it would appear to be premature to consume our time in discussing such details in the heat of war, and while, in many portions of them, the Turk is up to now in effective occupation; especially as we have learned, with surprise and regret, that some of the Arabs in those very parts, far from assisting us, are neglecting this their supreme opportunity and are lending their arms to the German and the Turk, to the new despoiler and the old oppressor. . . .

Letter from the Sharif Hussein to McMahon, September 9, 1915

With great cheerfulness and delight I received your letter dated the 19th Shawal, 1333 (the 30th August, 1915), and have given it great consideration and regard, in spite of the impression I received from it of ambiguity and its tone of coldness and hesitation with regard to our essential point . . .

Your Excellency will pardon me and permit me to say clearly that the coolness and hesitation which you have displayed in the question of the limits and boundaries by saying that the discussion of these at present is of no use and is a loss of time, and that they are still in the hands of the Government which is ruling them, &c., might be taken to infer an estrangement or something of the sort.

As the limits and boundaries demanded are not those of one person whom we should satisfy and with whom we should discuss them after the war is over, but our peoples have seen that the life of their new proposal is bound at least by these limits and their word is united on this.

Therefore, they have found it necessary first to discuss this point with the Power in whom they now have their confidence and trust as a final appeal, viz., the illustrious British Empire.

Their reason for this union and confidence is mutual interest, the necessity of regulating territorial divisions and the feelings of their inhabitants, so that they may know how to base their future and life, so not to meet her (England?) or any of her Allies in opposition to their resolution which would produce a contrary issue, which God forbid. . . .

With reference to your remark in your letter above mentioned that some of our people are still doing their utmost in promoting the interests of Turkey, your goodness (lit. "perfectness") would not permit you to make this an excuse for the tone of coldness and hesitation with regard to our demands, demands which I cannot admit that you, as a man of sound opinion, will deny to be necessary for our existence; nay, they are the essential essence of our life, material and moral.

. . . In order to reassure your Excellency I can declare that the whole country, together with those who you say are submitting themselves to Turco-German orders, are all waiting the result of these negotiations, which are dependent only on your refusal or acceptance of the question of the limits and on your declaration of safeguarding their religion first and then the rest of rights from any harm or danger. . . .

Letter from McMahon to the Sharif Hussein, October 24, 1915

. . . I regret that you should have received from my last letter the impression that I regarded the question of the limits and boundaries with coldness and hesitation; such was not the case, but it appeared to me that the time had not yet come when that question could be discussed in a conclusive manner.

I have realised, however, from your last letter that you regard this question as one of vital and urgent importance. I have, therefore, lost no time in informing the Government of Great Britain of the contents of your letter, and it is with great pleasure that I communicate to you on their behalf the following statement, which I am confident you will receive with satisfaction:—

The two districts of Mersina and Alexandretta and portions of Syria lying to the west of the districts of Damascus, Homs, Hama and Aleppo cannot be said to be purely Arab, and should be excluded from the limits demanded.

With the above modification, and without prejudice of our existing treaties with Arab chiefs, we accept those limits.

As for those regions lying within those frontiers wherein Great Britain is free to act without detriment to the interest of her ally, France, I am empowered in the name of the Government of Great Britain to give the following assurances and make the following reply to your letter: . . .

1. Subject to the above modifications, Great Britain is prepared to recognize and support the independence of the Arabs in all the regions within the limits demanded by the Sherif of Mecca.
2. Great Britain will guarantee the Holy Places against all external aggression and will recognise their inviolability.
3. When the situation admits, Great Britain will give to the Arabs her advice and will assist them to establish what may appear to be the most suitable forms of government in those various territories.
4. On the other hand, it is understood that the Arabs have decided to seek the advice and guidance of Great Britain only, and that such European advisers and officials as may be required for the formation of a sound form of administration will be British.
5. With regard to the vilayets of Bagdad and Basra, the Arabs will recognise that the established position and interests of Great Britain necessitate special administrative arrangements in order to secure these territories from foreign aggression, to promote the welfare of the local populations and to safeguard our mutual economic interests. . . .

Letter from the Sharif Hussein to McMahon, November 5, 1915

. . . 1. In order to facilitate an agreement and to render a service to Islam, and at the same time to avoid all that may cause Islam troubles and hardships-seeing moreover that we have great consideration for the distinguished qualities and dispositions of the Government of Great Britain-we renounce our insistence on the inclusion of the vilayets of Mersina and Adana in the Arab Kingdom. But the two vilayets of Aleppo and Beirut and their sea coasts are purely Arab vilayets, and there is no difference between a Moslem and a Christian Arab: they are both descendants of one forefather. . . .

2. As the Iraqi vilayets are parts of the pure Arab Kingdom, and were in fact the seat of its Government in the time of Ali ibn Abu Talib, and in the time of all the Khalifs who succeeded him; and as in them began

the civilisation of the Arabs, and as their towns were the first towns built in Islam where the Arab power became so great; therefore they are greatly valued by all Arabs far and near, and their traditions cannot be forgotten by them. Consequently, we cannot satisfy the Arab nations or make them submit to give us such a title to nobility. But in order to render an accord easy, and taking into consideration the assurances mentioned in the fifth article of your letter to keep and guard our mutual interests in that country as they are one and the same, for all these reasons we might agree to leave under the British administration for a short time those districts now occupied by the British troops without the rights of either party being prejudiced thereby (especially those of the Arab nation; which interests are to it economic and vital), and against a suitable sum paid as compensation to the Arab Kingdom for the period of occupation, in order to meet the expenses which every new kingdom is bound to support; at the same time respecting your agreements with the Sheikhs of those districts, and especially those which are essential. . . .

4. The Arab nation has a strong belief that after this war is over the Turks under German influence will direct their efforts to provoke the Arabs and violate their rights, both material and moral, to wipe out their nobility and honour and reduce them to utter submission as they are determined to ruin them entirely. The reasons for the slowness shown in our action have already been stated.
5. When the Arabs know the Government of Great Britain is their ally who will not leave them to themselves at the conclusion of peace in the face of Turkey and Germany, and that she will support and will effectively defend them, then to enter the war at once will, no doubt, be in conformity with the general interest of the Arabs.
6. Our letter dated the 29th Shaual, 1333 (the 9th September, 1915), saves us the trouble of repeating our opinions as to articles 3 and 4 of your honoured last letter regarding administration, Government advisers and officials, especially as you have declared, exalted Minister, that you will not interfere with internal affairs. . . .

Letter from McMahon to the Sharif Hussein, December 14, 1915

. . . I am gratified to observe that you agree to the exclusion of the districts of Mersina and Adana from boundaries of the Arab territories.

I also note with great pleasure and satisfaction your assurances that the Arabs are determined to act in conformity with the precepts laid down by Omar Ibn Khattab and the early Khalifs, which secure the rights and privileges of all religions alike.

In stating that the Arabs are ready to recognise and respect all our treaties with Arab chiefs, it is, of course, understood that this will apply to all territories included in the Arab Kingdom, as the Government of Great Britain cannot repudiate engagements which already exist.

With regard to the vilayets of Aleppo and Beirut, the Government of Great Britain have fully understood and taken careful note of your observations, but, as the interests of our ally, France, are involved in them both, the question will require careful consideration and a further communication on the subject will be addressed to you in due course.

The Government of Great Britain, as I have already informed you, are ready to give all guarantees of assistance and support within their power to the Arab Kingdom, but their interests demand, as you yourself have recognised, a friendly and stable administration in the vilayet of Bagdad, and the adequate safeguarding of these interests calls for a much fuller and more detailed consideration than the present situation and the urgency of these negotiations permit.

We fully appreciate your desire for caution, and have no wish to urge you to hasty action, which might jeopardise the eventual success of your projects, but, in the meantime, it is most essential that you should spare no effort to attach all the Arab peoples to our united cause and urge them to afford no assistance to our enemies.

It is on the success of these efforts and on the more active measures which the Arabs may hereafter take in support of our cause, when the time for action comes, that the permanence and strength of our agreement must depend.

Under these circumstances I am further directed by the Government of Great Britain to inform you that you may rest assured that Great Britain has no intention of concluding any peace in terms of which the freedom of the Arab peoples from German and Turkish domination does not form an essential condition. . . .

Letter from the Sharif Hussein to McMahon, January 1, 1916

. . . With regard to what had been stated in your honoured communication concerning El Iraq as to the matter of compensation for the period of occupation, we, in order to strengthen the confidence of Great Britain in our attitude and in our words and actions, really and veritably, and in order to give her evidence of our certainty and assurance in trusting her glorious Government, leave the determination of the amount to the perception of her wisdom and justice.

As regards the northern parts and their coasts, we have already stated in our previous letter what were the utmost possible modifications, and all this was only done so to fulfill those aspirations whose attainment is desired by the will of the Blessed and Supreme God. It is this same feeling and desire which impelled us to avoid what may possibly injure the alliance of Great Britain and France and the agreement made between them during the present wars and calamities; yet we find it our duty that the eminent minister should be sure that, at the first opportunity after this war is finished, we shall ask you (what we avert our eyes from to-day) for what we now leave to France in Beirut and its coasts.

I do not find it necessary to draw your attention to the fact that our plan is of greater security to the interests and protection of the rights of Great Britain than it is to us, and will necessarily be so whatever may happen, so that Great Britain may finally see her friends in that contentment and advancement which she is endeavouring to establish for them now, especially as her Allies being neighbours to us will be the germ of difficulties and discussion with which there will be no peaceful conditions. In addition to which the citizens of Beirut will decidedly never accept such dismemberment, and they may oblige us to undertake new measures which may exercise Great Britain, certainly not less than her present troubles, because of our belief and certainty in the reciprocity and indeed the identity of our interests, which is the only cause that caused us never to care to negotiate with any other Power but you. Consequently, it is impossible to allow any derogation that gives France, or any other Power, a span of land in those regions. . . .

Letter from McMahon to the Sharif Hussein, January 25, 1916

. . . We take note of your remarks concerning the vilayet of Baghdad, and will take the question into careful consideration when the enemy has been defeated and the time for peaceful settlement arrives.

As regards the northern parts, we note with satisfaction your desire to avoid anything which might possibly injure the alliance of Great Britain and France. It is, as you know, our fixed determination that nothing shall be permitted to interfere in the slightest degree with our united prosecution of this war to a victorious conclusion. Moreover, when the victory has been won, the friendship of Great Britain and France will become yet more firm and enduring, cemented by the blood of Englishmen and Frenchmen who have died side by side fighting for the cause of right and liberty. . . .

Source: Available from the Jewish Virtual Library, https://www.jewishvirtuallibrary.org/the-hussein-mcmahon-correspondence.

The Sykes-Picot Agreement, 1916

It is accordingly understood between the French and British governments:

That France and Great Britain are prepared to recognize and protect an independent Arab state or a confederation of Arab states (a) and (b) marked on the annexed map, under the suzerainty of an Arab chief. That in area (a) France, and in area (b) Great Britain, shall have priority of right of enterprise and local loans. That in area (a) France, and in area (b) Great Britain, shall alone supply advisers or foreign functionaries at the request of the Arab state or confederation of Arab states.

That in the blue area France, and in the red area Great Britain, shall be allowed to establish such direct or indirect administration or control as they desire and as they may think fit to arrange with the Arab state or confederation of Arab states.

That in the brown area there shall be established an international administration, the form of which is to be decided upon after consultation with Russia, and subsequently in consultation with the other allies, and the representatives of the sherif of Mecca.

That Great Britain be accorded (1) the ports of Haifa and Acre, (2) guarantee of a given supply of water from the Tigres and Euphrates in area (a) for area (b). His majesty's government, on their part, undertake that they will at no time enter into negotiations for the cession of Cyprus to any third power without the previous consent of the French government.

That Alexandretta shall be a free port as regards the trade of the British empire, and that there shall be no discrimination in port charges or facilities as regards British shipping and British goods; that there shall be freedom of transit for British goods through Alexandretta and by railway through the blue area, or area (b), or area (a); and there shall be no discrimination, direct or indirect, against British goods on any railway or against British goods or ships at any port serving the areas mentioned.

That Haifa shall be a free port as regards the trade of France, her dominions and protectorates, and there shall be no discrimination in port charges or facilities as regards French shipping and French goods. There shall be freedom of transit for French goods through Haifa and by the British railway through the brown area, whether those goods are intended for or originate in the blue area, area (a), or area (b), and there shall be no discrimination, direct or indirect, against French goods on any railway, or against French goods or ships at any port serving the areas mentioned.

That in area (a) the Baghdad railway shall not be extended southwards beyond Mosul, and in area (b) northwards beyond Samarra, until a railway connecting Baghdad and Aleppo via the Euphrates valley has been completed, and then only with the concurrence of the two governments.

That Great Britain has the right to build, administer, and be sole owner of a railway connecting Haifa with area (b), and shall have a perpetual right to transport troops along such a line at all times. It is to be understood by both governments that this railway is to facilitate the connection of Baghdad with Haifa by rail, and it is further understood that, if the engineering difficulties and expense entailed by keeping this connecting line in the brown area only make the project unfeasible, that the French government shall be prepared to consider that the line in question may also traverse the Polgon Banias Keis Marib Salkhad tell Otsda Mesmie before reaching area (b).

For a period of twenty years the existing Turkish customs tariff shall remain in force throughout the whole of the blue and red areas, as well as in areas (a) and (b), and no increase in the rates of duty or conversions from ad valorem to specific rates shall be made except by agreement between the two powers.

There shall be no interior customs barriers between any of the above mentioned areas. The customs duties leviable on goods destined for the interior shall be collected at the port of entry and handed over to the administration of the area of destination.

It shall be agreed that the French government will at no time enter into any negotiations for the cession of their rights and will not cede such rights in the blue area to any third power, except the Arab state or confederation of Arab states, without the previous agreement of his majesty's government, who, on their part, will give a similar undertaking to the French government regarding the red area.

The British and French governments, as the protectors of the Arab state, shall agree that they will not themselves acquire and will not consent to a third power acquiring territorial possessions in the Arabian peninsula, nor consent to a third power installing a naval base either on the east coast, or on the islands, of the red sea. This, however, shall not prevent such adjustment of the Aden frontier as may be necessary in consequence of recent Turkish aggression.

The negotiations with the Arabs as to the boundaries of the Arab states shall be continued through the same channel as heretofore on behalf of the two powers.

It is agreed that measures to control the importation of arms into the Arab territories will be considered by the two governments.

I have further the honor to state that, in order to make the agreement complete, his majesty's government are proposing to the Russian government to exchange notes analogous to those exchanged by the latter and your excellency's government on the 26th April last. Copies of these notes will be communicated to your excellency as soon as exchanged. I would also venture to remind your excellency that the conclusion of the present agreement raises, for practical consideration, the question of claims of Italy to a share in any partition or rearrangement of Turkey in Asia, as formulated in article 9 of the agreement of the 26th April, 1915, between Italy and the allies.

His majesty's government further consider that the Japanese government should be informed of the arrangements now conduded.

Source: Available from the Avalon Project, Lilllan Goldman Law Library, Yale Law School, http://avalon.law.yale.edu/20th_century/sykes.asp.

The Balfour Declaration, 1917

November 2nd, 1917

Dear Lord Rothschild,

I have much pleasure in conveying to you, on behalf of His Majesty's Government, the following declaration of sympathy with Jewish Zionist aspirations which has been submitted to, and approved by, the Cabinet.

"His Majesty's Government view with favour the establishment in Palestine of a national home for the Jewish people, and will use their best endeavours to facilitate the achievement of this object, it being clearly understood that nothing shall be done which may prejudice the civil and religious rights of existing non-Jewish communities in Palestine, or the rights and political status enjoyed by Jews in any other country."

I should be grateful if you would bring this declaration to the knowledge of the Zionist Federation.

Yours sincerely,
Arthur James Balfour

Source: Available from the Avalon Project, Lillian Goldman Law Library, Yale Law School, http://avalon.law.yale.edu/20th_century/balfour.asp.

British Declaration to Seven Arab Spokesmen

16 June 1918

His Majesty's Government have considered the memorial of the seven with the greatest care. His Majesty's Government fully appreciate the reasons why the memorialists desire to retain their anonymity, and the fact that the memorial is anonymous has not in any way detracted from the importance which His Majesty's Government attribute to the document.

The areas mentioned in the memorandum fall into four categories—

1. Areas in Arabia which were free and independent before the outbreak of war;
2. Areas emancipated from Turkish control by the action of the Arabs themselves during the present war;
3. Areas formerly under Ottoman dominion, occupied by the Allied forces during the present war;
4. Areas still under Turkish control.

In regard to the first two categories, His Majesty's Government recognise the complete and sovereign independence of the Arabs inhabiting these areas and support them in their struggle for freedom.

In regard to the areas occupied by Allied forces, His Majesty's Government draw the attention of the memorialists to the texts of the proclamation issued respectively by the General Officers Commanding in Chief on the taking of Baghdad and Jerusalem. These proclamations embody the policy of His Majesty's Government towards the inhabitants of those regions. It is the wish and desire of His Majesty's Government that the future government of these regions should be based upon the principle of the consent of the governed and this policy has and will continue to have the support of His Majesty's Government. . . .

Source: Available from the United Nations Information System on the Question of Palestine, https://www.un.org/unispal/.

NOTES

1. Eugene Rogan, *The Fall of the Ottomans: The Great War in the Middle East* (New York: Basic Books, 2015), p. 2.
2. The French, under the direction of Ferdinand de Lesseps, built the 120-mile-long canal with mostly Egyptian labor beginning in 1854. It is estimated that 100,000 Egyptian peasants died in the process. American cotton production plummeted during the US Civil War (1861–1865) when the North blockaded the South, thus driving up the price on Egyptian cotton during that time. Egyptian Viceroy Ismail borrowed huge amounts of money at high interest rates from European banks, obviously thinking Egyptian cotton prices would continue in perpetuity. They did not, and when the Civil War ended cotton prices in general leveled out, and Egypt could not repay its debts. Ismail then felt compelled to sell Egypt's shares in the Suez Canal Company to the British government in 1875, with Britain now along with France owning the majority shares in the company. See Joel Beinin, "The Long Struggle Over the Suez," *Tribune Magazine* (London), March 30, 2021.
3. M. E. Yapp, *The Making of the Modern Near East, 1792–1923* (London: Longman, 1987), p. 181.
4. See Sylvia G. Haim, *Arab Nationalism: An Anthology* (Berkeley: University of California Press, 1962), pp. 6–9.
5. Muhammad Abduh, an Egyptian thinker who was instrumental in promoting Islamic modernism in the late nineteenth century, actually argued that Islam was "basically gender-egalitarian and that unequal treatment of women came from later corruptions of the religion." Nikki R. Keddie, *Women in the Middle East Since the Rise of Islam* (Washington, DC: American Historical Association, 2007), p. 22.
6. For this discussion see James L. Gelvin, *The Modern Middle East: A History* (Oxford: Oxford University Press, 2005), p. 129.
7. For this discussion on the Young Turk revolution, see Rogan, *Fall of the Ottomans*, pp. 4–9.
8. Quoted in ibid., p. 5.
9. Ibid., p. 22.
10. From *Jamiyya al-Arabiyya al-Fatat*, the Young Arab Society, *fatat* meaning "young." A similar group of Syrian ex-pats founded the Ottoman Decentralization Party in 1912 to protest against the centralizing policies of the Young Turks, although not yet calling for Arab independence. An amalgam of these groups convened the First Arab Congress in Paris in 1913 to discuss all of these concerns. Although nothing much concrete came out of the meeting amid divisions within the group, it laid the foundation for future meetings and actions on the part of these Arab secret societies and compelled the Young Turks to take notice with some reforms for fear that the Arabs might seek out European help.
11. Much of the material in this and the next section of this chapter is drawn from David W. Lesch, *The Arab-Israeli Conflict: A History* (Oxford: Oxford University Press, 2019).

12. Reflecting this sentiment, Lord Curzon said the following near the beginning of the war: "A good deal of my public life has been spent in connection with the political ambitions of France, which I have come across in Tunis, in Siam, and in almost every distant region where the French have sway. We have been brought, for reasons of national safety, into an alliance with the French, which I hope will last, but their national character is different from ours, and their political interests collide with our own in many cases. I am seriously afraid that the great Power from whom we may have most to fear in the future is France." Quoted in Margaret MacMillan, *Paris 1919: Six Months that Changed the World* (New York: Random House, 2003), p. 373.
13. David Fromkin, *A Peace to End All Peace* (New York: Henry Holt and Company, 1989), p. 95.
14. Michael J. Cohen, *The Origins and Evolution of the Arab-Zionist Conflict* (Berkeley: University of California Press, 1987), p. 10.
15. Many of the Arabs fighting at Gallipoli were the ones that made up the Ottoman divisions in Syria; the Porte, fearing that they may cause unrest in Syria, had the bulk of them transferred to the Gallipoli front, where they were needed much more urgently anyway.
16. There have been volumes of dispute and discord over whether or not the west of the Aleppo to Damascus line meant the inclusion of Palestine. It all may come down to inadequate translations, but as in any diplomatic correspondence or agreement, individual words can cause decades of conflict. The dispute centers on the use of the term "vilayet" (*wilayat* in Arabic), which was an official Ottoman term meaning "province," the largest administrative unit below that of the empire itself, as it was translated into Arabic in the letter to Hussein. Usually a number of districts (sing., *sanjak*) constituted a province, the latter led by a provincial governor appointed by Constantinople. The confusion begins with the fact that oftentimes provinces, such as the Syrian province, were known more colloquially by the main city located in a particular province; therefore, the province of Syria was often simply called "Damascus." If this is the case, then the province of Syria/Damascus extended from around Hama just south of the vilayet of Aleppo all the way down to the Gulf of Aqaba. West of the *suriyya vilayet* was the special sanjak of Jerusalem (which constituted about the southern half of present-day Israel) and the vilayet of Beirut (which was made up of the northern half of present-day Israel, Lebanon, and up to the northern coast of present-day Syria west of Aleppo). Under this interpretation, "west" of the Damascus/Syria province certainly included Palestine, and it therefore should be excluded from an independent Arab state. This tended to be the position adopted by the British, especially after the Balfour Declaration of November 1917 added a new group, the Zionist movement, to the list of claimants for the land of Palestine. On the other hand, upon closer examination, this is clearly not what was meant. If vilayet does refer to the province of Syria, then how could the same term be utilized to refer to Hama or Homs, both of which were districts within the Syrian province? It is more likely that the British, when referring to those

four cities, meant west of the general region of those locales—more of a geographic designation. If this is the case, then the area they outlined as not being purely Arab consists of what is basically present-day Lebanon—definitely not Palestine. Under this interpretation—one that for obvious reasons has been championed by most Arabs ever since—Palestine, including the holy city of Jerusalem, should have been included in an independent Arab state under the apparent terms of the Hussein-McMahon correspondence.

17. Quoted in Cohen, *Origins and Evolution*, pp. 22–23.
18. In 1923 Lord Curzon, who had been an opponent of the Balfour Declaration, now justified Britain's position in Palestine by saying, "We cannot now recede. If we did the French would step in and then be on the threshold of Egypt and on the outskirts of the [Suez] Canal. Besides Palestine needs ports, electricity, and the Jews of America were rich and would subsidise such development." Quoted in Cohen, *Origins and Evolution*, p. 63.
19. A November 9, 1914, memo from Herbert Samuel, then a member of the British Cabinet, stated the following: "British influence ought to play a considerable part in the formation of a [Jewish] state, because the geographical situation of Palestine, and especially its proximity to Egypt, would render its goodwill to England a matter of importance." Chaim Weizmann, the leader of the Zionist movement in Britain, recognized immediately that this strategic desire could work to the Zionists' advantage. In a letter from March 1915, Weizmann said that "a strong Jewish community on the Egyptian flank [in Palestine] is an efficient barrier for any danger likely to come from the north . . . England would have in the Jews the best possible friends." Quoted in Lesch, *The Arab-Israeli Conflict*, p. 60.
20. As an example of this line of thought, a March 13, 1916, memo from the British embassy in Russia to the Russian foreign minister stated that "it is very clear that by utilizing the Zionist idea, important political results can be achieved. Among them will be the conversion, in favor of the Allies, of Jewish elements in the Orient, in the United States, and in other places, elements whose attitude at the present time is to a considerable extent opposed to the Allies' cause." Quoted in Lesch, *The Arab-Israeli Conflict*, p. 61.
21. Dr. Weizmann was a noted chemist. He discovered a way to extract acetone from maize, which is used in the manufacture of explosives. He was officially a member of the British Zionist Federation, elected as president of this organization in February 1917. Born in Russia, he became a naturalized British citizen.
22. Wilson would publicly endorse the Balfour Declaration in a letter to the American Jewish community in September 1918. Congress would later formally endorse the Balfour Declaration in 1922 as defining US policy on the matter.
23. The British had finally turned things around in the Mesopotamian campaign after some initial reverses, capturing Baghdad in March 1917.
24. Quoted in Fromkin, *A Peace to End All Peace*, p. 330.
25. For more on the King-Crane commission, see James Gelvin, "The Legacy of the King-Crane Commission," in David W. Lesch, ed., *The Middle East and the United*

States: A Historical and Political Reassessment, 3rd edition (Boulder, CO: Westview Press, 2003), pp. 13–29.

26. Churchill, as head of the Colonial Office, advocated returning the Arab lands to Ottoman control.
27. Quoted in David W. Lesch, *The Arab-Israeli Conflict,* p. 71
28. Cohen, *Origins and Evolution*, p. 67. Two General Syrian Congresses, one held in mid-1919 and the other in March 1920, both passed resolutions proclaiming an independent Syria that comprised present-day Syria, Lebanon, Jordan, and Israel, under the rule of Faisal. Traditional Syrian elites as well as Faisal were more willing to work with the French, especially when Clemenceau was in power, but with Millerand in Paris by January 1920 Faisal was caught between a more resistant French president and Arab nationalists in Damascus who refused to cave into French demands. Ultimately, Faisal was forced to join with his Arab cohorts against the French. The British had already made the decision to allow Faisal to fend for himself, but as Fromkin points out (*A Peace to End All Peace*, p. 438), Syria's claims to British mandates in Palestine and Mesopotamia only helped isolate Syria that much more from the British. The British seemingly could not win with Faisal, as Fromkin states, "The French blamed them for putting Feisal up and the Arabs blamed them for letting Feisal down" (p. 440).
29. Quoted in Fromkin, *A Peace to End All Peace*, p. 448.
30. On April 24, 2021, US President Joe Biden became the first president of the United States to call it a genocide. April 24 is referred to as Armenian Genocide Remembrance Day among those who observe it, as it is the day in 1915 when about 250 Armenian leaders and intellectuals were rounded up and killed, in many ways launching what was to come, including forced marches to concentration camps. On July 16, 1915, Henry Morgenthau Sr., who was the US ambassador to the Ottoman Empire and witnessed some of the atrocities, said in a memo to the State Department that "It appears that a campaign of race extermination is in progress." Quoted in Gillian Brockell, "The Massacre of Armenians: This Is What Happened in 1915," *Washington Post,* April 24, 2021, p. A24.
31. Michael Provence, *The Last Ottoman Generation and the Making of the Modern Middle East* (Cambridge: Cambridge University Press, 2017), p. 271.
32. On this, see Kyle J. Anderson's excellent book *The Egyptian Labor Corps: Race, Space, and Place in the First World War* (Austin: University of Texas Press, 2021).
33. For a more detailed discussion of the Palestine mandate, see Lesch, *The Arab–Israeli Conflict*, pp. 92–122.
34. David W. Lesch, *Syria: A Modern History* (Cambridge: Polity Press, 2019), p. 54.
35. Historian Josh Landis, commenting on the war, said, "From the beginning, the fight was over the balance of power in the region and the future of the Arab world; this was not a war waged to destroy the Jewish state." Quoted in Lesch, *The Arab-Israeli Conflict,* p. 142, from Joshua Landis, "Syria and the Palestine War: Fighting King Abdullah's Greater Syria Plan," in Eugene L. Rogan and Avi Shlaim, eds., *The War for Palestine: Rewriting the History of 1948* (Cambridge: Cambridge University Press,

2001), p. 178. Landis even suggests (p. 200) that since several of the Arab states fighting in the war seemed to be more concerned with the movements of their fellow Arab combatants than with that of the Jews that the war could be equally characterized as an inter-Arab rather than an Arab–Israeli conflict. In his chapter in this edited volume ("Israel and the Arab Coalition in 1948"), Shlaim writes the following about the Arab combatants, "All these states . . . only sent an expeditionary force to Palestine, keeping the bulk of their army at home [in large part for fear of internal coup attempts]. The expeditionary forces were hampered by long lines of communication, the absence of reliable intelligence about their enemy, poor leadership, poor coordination, and very poor planning for the campaign" (p. 81).

KEY TERMS

aliyah p. 318
Baath p. 319
Committee of Union and Progress (CUP) p. 288
jahiliyya p. 321
Muslim Brotherhood p. 319
salafiyya p. 287
Yishuv p. 314

For additional digital learning resources please go to www.oup.com/he/lesch-middleeast-1e

11 THE SHAPING OF THE MODERN MIDDLE EAST

Cold Wars

Given the fact that the first Arab–Israeli war ended with the signing of armistice agreements and not peace treaties, the unleashing of Arab–Israeli enmity as a result of the hostilities, and the existence of a burgeoning Palestinian refugee problem, it would not have been difficult to envision at the time that there would be an early resumption of the conflict—another war within the next few years. The next Arab–Israeli war would not occur until the 1956 Suez war, and even this was precipitated as much by external machination (British and French) and regional politics as by the Arab–Israeli dynamic. But there were a number of intervening processes at work at different levels in the Middle East that tended to focus the potential Arab–Israeli combatants' attentions away from each other toward more immediate goals.

The 1950s might be the most complex decade in modern Middle East history, with compelling forces at the domestic, regional, and international levels coming into play and creating an almost incomprehensible multidimensional matrix that is as difficult to decipher in retrospect as it was at the time. In the immediate post–World War II period, there was the European decolonization movement combined with the rise of Third World nationalisms. A number of Arab states—and Israel—had recently escaped or were in the process of escaping from the shackles of imperial control and had embarked on what became for the most part a painful journey toward true independence and state-building. Many of these Arab states engaged in a heated competition for regional leadership in what has been called the Arab cold war.[1] Focusing more international attention on the region was the result of the increasing share of world oil production coming from the Middle East as well as its share of estimated world oil reserves. From 16.7 percent of world oil production in 1950, the Middle East's share rose to 21.2 percent by 1955; in addition, its estimated oil reserves rose from 45 percent of the world total in 1950 to 75 percent in 1956. Finally, superimposed on all of this was the emerging superpower Cold War between the United States and the Soviet Union, a battle that increasingly began to be fought by proxy in the Third World. And winding its way into the jetties created by these turbulent waters was the Arab–Israeli conflict, quickly becoming a legitimate dimension in and of itself, affecting in a direct way the other levels of the Middle East matrix.

There were a few events and circumstances in the early 1950s that mitigated against an early resumption of conflict in the Arab–Israeli arena. First was the May 1950 Tripartite agreement between Britain, France, and the United States in which they pledged to ration the supply of arms to the Arab states and Israel so as to prevent the development of an arms race that could create an unfavorable imbalance of power between them, which in turn could entice one side or the other to initiate hostilities. They also became guarantors of the armistice borders negotiated at the end of the 1947–1949 war, committing to prevent any attempt to alter them by force. Next was the so-called July Revolution in Egypt in 1952 that brought elements of the Free Officers movement, led by Gamal Abd al-Nasser, to power in Cairo, overthrowing King Farouk, whose lineage dates back to Muhammad Ali. The Free Officers established a Revolutionary Command Council that acted as a kind of politburo decision-making body, led by Nasser. Since the Free Officers were relatively young and unknown, General Muhammad Naguib was chosen as the new president of Egypt. Although Naguib was a bit more assertive than the Free Officers would have liked, Nasser assumed full control as president by 1954.

The reason the July or Egyptian Revolution was a mitigating factor is that anytime the Arab countries are distracted by internal or inter-Arab discord, it makes it less likely that their attentions will be turned toward Israel; Israel very much likes it when the Arab states are busy looking elsewhere, especially in this case, with the most populous and powerful Arab nation. The revolution brought about a great deal of change domestically in Egypt. There were three main shifts of power there and in a number of other Arab countries that had also recently broken free from European control. First was a movement away from foreign-owned to nationally owned businesses, a point of pride with many states in the region to build, own, and profit from their own resources. Next was a shift from landed interests (the landed aristocracy) to industrial, financial, and commercial interests; in Egypt as in a number of other Arab countries, once these newly empowered governments of the next generation of Arab leaders came to power, typically one of the first domestic programs they enacted was that of land reform in order to reduce the political and economic clout of the landed aristocracy. Much of the reallocated land would go to rural areas, cementing an alliance with the rural population to counter the powerful urban notables who had been running the show during the mandate and immediate post–World War II years. Finally, there was a shift from the private sector to the state, the public sector. Private capital in a Western oriented capitalist economic system provided the wealth and power to the landed aristocrats, who were seen as corrupt and exploitative tools of the West who created an unequal distribution of wealth. A state capitalist economy, with the government—rather than the hidden hand—engaging in economic planning (manifest in five-year plans) would provide for a more equitable distribution of wealth. The Baath party in Syria, while not coming formally to power there until 1963, used the decade preceding it to maneuver itself into an influential political force on the scene. Its mantra was freedom, unity, and socialism, all of which was designed to oppose Western imperialism: freedom from Western control, Arab unity to fend off predations from the West, and socialism in order to reduce the power of the capitalist class that facilitated Western economic imperialism. This did not mean that the landed aristocrats were done for. The private sector still provided the bulk of the gross domestic product, but the trend steadily moved in the direction of these shifts, causing a good bit of economic adjustment and political jostling in a number of countries in the Arab world—growing pains the Israelis were all too happy to see.

One final significant mitigating factor against an early resumption of war was the presence in Egypt of some 80,000 British troops in their Suez Canal base, the largest military base in the world at the time. It would be difficult for Egypt under these conditions to initiate a war with Israel, and if Egypt was not going to war against Israel, no other Arab country would either. The maintenance of this British buffer, from the Israeli perspective, became very important in short order. From the Egyptian perspective, the British presence at Suez was a sore reminder that they were not yet truly independent. It would become an overriding concern for Nasser to arrange for the evacuation of these troops; otherwise, he could be seen in the same light as the monarchy and majority Wafd (delegation) party that was dominated by the older generation and who could never truly get rid of British rule.

However, as often happens in the Middle East, things can change abruptly, in this case a series of events between 1954 and 1956 that would heighten tensions in the region leading to the 1956 Suez crisis and war. First was the Anglo-Egyptian accord signed in October 1954 that arranged for the withdrawal of those 80,000 British troops from the Canal Zone in 1955, therefore removing the buffer between Egypt and Israel that the latter so much wanted to stay in place. This agreement was pushed hard by Washington, which wanted to utilize Egypt to help bring about an overall Arab-Israeli peace, which was a much less complicated thing to do at this point rather than after 1967, as well as include Egypt in a pro-West defense alliance in the region. Nasser was not going to budge on any of these two issues until British troops were out of the country. The United States, seeking entry points of its own in the Middle East, tended to form associations with military officers in countries of interest, such as Nasser in Egypt, because most of the other leading classes, the royal family and the landed aristocracy, were tied to the British. Officials in Washington figured that military men might better understand the strategic threat posed by Soviet communism and thus be more willing to enter into pro-West defense alliances—or so it was thought.[2]

The Israelis were concerned about the deal. They very much wanted the British troops to stay in order to continue to play the role of buffer. Moshe Sharrett was now the Israeli prime minister, and he was known as more dovish than David Ben-Gurion, who had earlier stepped down into self-imposed retirement. The defense minister, Pinhas Lavon, was an acolyte of Ben-Gurion. The two of them concocted a plan, unbeknownst to Sharrett, whereby Egyptian Jews who had immigrated to Israel soon after independence would surreptitiously reenter Egypt, dress up as Egyptian soldiers, and then attack British installations. This they did. The idea was that London would conclude that it could not withdraw its troops because the situation was too unstable—thus the buffer would remain. The Israelis also thought that it might scuttle any momentum the United States may have been building to include Egypt in a pro-West defense alliance. What later became known as the Lavon Affair was a spectacular failure, as a number of the spies were captured and executed in early 1955. However, at the time most of the Israeli government and the entire Israeli public were unaware of the covert scheme, and they concluded that the charges were fabricated by Nasser to deflect attention from some domestic problems with which he was dealing. He survived an assassination attempt in late 1954 by members of the Muslim Brotherhood; subsequently, the government engaged in an all-out effort to suppress the Islamist organization.

Israel was outraged by the executions. Ironically, there were calls for Ben-Gurion to return to the government. What was needed was a dose of classic Ben-Gurionism— disproportionate Israeli response to Arab provocations in order to deter future attacks. Ben-Gurion returned as defense minister, and less than two weeks later he put his stamp on Israel's response. On February 28, Israel launched a military raid on an Egyptian military outpost located in the Gaza Strip near the border with Israel, ostensibly because the Egyptians were casting a blind eye to Palestinian *fedayeen* (self-sacrificers) raids into Israel that had been occurring periodically since the 1947–1949 war. The fedayeen were Palestinians living in UN administered refugee camps in the Gaza Strip and elsewhere, after having been made refugees by the war. Over forty Egyptian soldiers were killed (the Israelis lost eight). The effect of the raid on Nasser was profound. He was humiliated by it, having promised the Egyptian population that the military had been reformed under his watch. This was not yet the Nasser that would soon become a god-like figure in the Arab world; he was tenuously holding onto power at the time. He felt he had to dramatically respond.

Another blow to Nasser occurred less than a month later. The idea for a pro-West defense pact in the Middle East had gone through several permutations, cutting across the administrations of Harry S. Truman and Dwight D. Eisenhower. One finally did come into being, however, that did not include Egypt: the Baghdad Pact (officially CENTO, the Central Treaty Organization). It was cobbled together in February and March of 1955. To understand the origins of the Baghdad Pact, one must understand the strategic background of the emerging superpower Cold War that would trickle down to the Middle East.

The Eisenhower administration came to power in January 1953 with the intention of implementing its New Look foreign policy in an attempt to correct what it viewed as the deficiencies inherent in the approach of the Truman administration, defined in the April 1950 policy paper commonly referred to as "NSC-68" (National Security Council Resolution 68). Containing the Soviet Union (and the People's Republic of China after the communist revolution in 1949) from expanding its influence beyond that which already existed was the paramount foreign policy objective in both administrations; however, the means by which this was to be accomplished changed when Eisenhower became president. This change had an important impact upon the Middle East, affecting the political dynamics that had already produced tensions in the area at the regional and domestic levels.

NSC-68 was loosely based on George F. Kennan's theory of containment of the Soviet Union and postulated that the United States should meet any communist advances anywhere in the world with a direct reciprocal response. US entrance into the Korean War in June 1950 can be seen in this light. The Republican party, however, in the runup to the 1952 presidential elections, castigated the Truman administration for "losing China" as well as what had become a stalemate in Korea. It accused Truman's strategic conception of giving the communists the initiative in fomenting trouble, requiring a costly American military posture in order to symmetrically respond to these advances in a timely fashion. The budget-conscious and economically conservative Republican platform in 1952 preached a foreign policy that would more effectively meet the communist threat at less cost. As former commander of the allied forces in the European theater in World War II, Eisenhower was one of the few people who could get away with such policy admonitions; the public trusted that he would not sacrifice security for the sake of cost.

To meet the combined need of global defense against communist expansion and a more economically efficient foreign policy, Eisenhower and his secretary of state, John Foster Dulles, formulated the New Look. It was based on the proposition that the American people should not and would not suffer the debilitating effects of a lower standard of living just to maintain the high military profile ordained under NSC-68. To address this problem the idea of asymmetrical strategic deterrence was adopted, or as it is more popularly termed, "massive retaliation." This portended a greater reliance on nuclear weapons to retaliate directly against the perpetrator of communist aggression in order to deter such aggression rather than be placed in a defensive position by being forced to react via the much more costly means of conventional forces sent halfway across the globe (as in Korea) to meet communist advances *after* they had been initiated. In this fashion, conventional force levels could be reduced at the same time, since the focus was on maintaining, at much cheaper cost, a nuclear deterrent ("more bang for the buck").

The focus on nuclear weapons tended to overlook two other legs of the New Look: establishing strategic alliances (or military pacts) to share the burden of containment and covert operations to fill the gaps in the strategic design of the New Look, countering indirect aggression or subversion engineered through nonmilitary means. Both of these aspects of the New Look would be directly applied to the Middle East. The North Atlantic Treaty Organization (NATO) had been formed in 1949 under Truman, an alliance that Turkey joined in 1952. The Southeast Asian Treaty Organization was constructed in 1954, in which Pakistan was a member, so the fringes of the Middle East were part of pro-West defense pacts. But there was a strategic gap in the belt surrounding the two communist behemoths, the Soviet Union and China—the heartland of the Middle East, which happened to border the underbelly of the Soviet Union and contain about 75 percent of the world's proven oil reserves. Soon after coming to power, Dulles traveled to the Middle East and South Asia to sound out the leaders of various countries as to their willingness to join a pro-West defense pact. The US secretary of state found in the Arab world a distinct unwillingness to become members of an organization that would include the two European states from which most of them had just achieved independence. Dulles prudently concluded that a Middle East defense pact would best be achieved without the inclusion of any Arab states. This would also allow Washington to not be drawn into Arab–Israeli or inter-Arab disputes related to the pact. Dulles thus proposed in 1954 the Northern Tier approach, a military alliance composed of states along the northern and eastern periphery of the Middle East that were non-Arab: Turkey, Iran, and Pakistan.

Britain, however, was not at all pleased to see the United States further expand its influence in the region at London's expense. Already out of Palestine and on their way out of Egypt by the end of 1954, the British were concerned lest they lose their influence in Iraq, one of their last remaining significant areas of ingress in the Arab world. If Dulles's Northern Tier approach could be attached to Iraq in the formation of a military pact, London could maintain its level of influence in the region. If Iraq could become the linchpin to a defense pact, with corresponding access to advanced Western weaponry, it could become the dominant player in the inter-Arab arena, eclipsing Egypt's natural spot at the top of the pecking order.

The inclusion of an Arab state went against the Northern Tier approach. However, by this time Dulles was becoming more and more disenchanted with Nasser. The secretary of state began to see the Egyptian president, whose regional interests were in conflict with US global interests, as more of an enemy than a potential friend. The hope in London and Washington was that other Arab states, namely Jordan, Syria, and Lebanon, would soon join the pact, thus isolating Egypt and compelling it to come to terms with the West. Dulles's worst fears came to pass, however. With the inclusion of Iraq, Nasser correctly felt his position threatened at the inner-Arab level, and he launched a heated propaganda campaign against Baghdad for becoming a lackey of Western imperialism. An Arab cold war began. As a result of this new threat, coming on top of the Gaza raid, Nasser was desperate for a countermove. He went to the Soviet Union. For Moscow, this was a godsend. Not only could it leapfrog the containment belt that had been drawn around it in the Middle East, but it also would do so with the most powerful and populous Arab state. The Soviets grabbed the opportunity, and an arms deal was consummated in

September 1955 through its Eastern Bloc client Czechoslovakia. The Baghdad Pact had totally backfired: instead of containing the Soviets, it helped facilitate their first significant entry into the Arab world.

Nasser was an all-Arab hero overnight. Finally, it seemed an Arab state had acquired the wherewithal to confront Israel. The Egyptian president would utilize this momentum to turn the tables on Iraq, isolating Baghdad in the inter-Arab arena rather than the other way around. Nasser had won this inter-Arab contest. The Eisenhower administration was certainly taken aback by this development. But instead of trying to punish Nasser, in December 1955 it offered, along with the British, to fund the Aswan High Dam project in Egypt. This was a very important project for Nasser. Not only would it control the flooding of the Nile River in Egypt that periodically caused agricultural havoc, but it would also increase the area of cultivable land and provide hydroelectric power for a rapidly growing population. For Israel, one of its biggest fears had become reality: Egypt had access to arms from one of the superpowers. This was well before the United States became the primary supplier of military aid to Israel. Given the opportunity to cut Nasser down to size, especially if it could be done before Egypt assimilated Soviet weaponry into its military, Israel would jump at the chance.

The strategic interests of Britain and France vis-à-vis their waning positions in the Middle East, and even the United States vis-à-vis the Cold War, could not be reconciled with Egyptian nationalist interests and Nasser's own regional objectives. It is no surprise, then, that exhortations from London and Paris increasingly began to paint Nasser as an obstruction to peace in the Middle East. Even worse, he was beginning to be compared to Hitler, which meant that he must be removed from power—following World War II, no Hitler-like figure could be allowed to remain in power. British Prime Minister Anthony Eden insisted that "Nasser was the incarnation of all the evils of Arabia who would destroy every British interest in the Middle East unless he himself were speedily destroyed."[3]

The final straw for Dulles occurred in May 1956, when Nasser recognized communist China, which the secretary of state saw as a direct slap in the face of the United States given the known position of Washington toward Beijing at the height of the Cold War struggle against communism. This also added the so-called China lobby of mostly Republican congresspersons who were adamantly opposed to Beijing to the growing list of those who pressured Dulles to rescind the offer to fund the dam. While Nasser must have certainly known that recognition of China would have severe repercussions in Washington, many have also speculated that his action was simply the culmination of his growing role in the nonaligned movement. Nasser attended the Bandung meeting in Indonesia in April 1955 that sparked the nonaligned movement, allied with neither the West nor the Eastern Bloc. In reaction to this, Dulles abruptly withdrew the offer to fund the Aswan High Dam on July 19, 1956. From this point on events would move swiftly, leading inexorably to the Suez war.

President Gamal Abd al-Nasser addresses the crowd where he proclaimed the nationalization of the Suez Canal, Cairo, Egypt, July 31, 1956.

In reaction to Dulles's withdrawal, on July 26 Nasser nationalized the Suez Canal Company, owned by British and French shareholders. Nationalization of foreign owned assets is legal as long as the shareholders are compensated, an amount usually predetermined through an arbitration process. But Nasser was the new Hitler, and Anthony Eden, steeped in the Munich mentality of not appeasing dictators (as much of Europe had to Hitler at the Munich conference in 1938), and perhaps a bit unsettled from the drugs he was taking to deal with a botched gall bladder operation, was determined to teach Nasser a lesson. While Egypt showed a willingness to diplomatically resolve the crisis, the British and the French were having none of it. Running out of excuses to take the Canal by force, British and French officials concocted one with the help of Israel, itself eager to get at Nasser. In what might be the last significant case of European gunboat diplomacy, Britain and France recruited Israel to invade the Sinai Peninsula and head to the canal. Britain, as planned, would activate the 1922 reserve clause in the treaty announcing Egypt's independence, the one that said Britain reserved the right to come to Egypt's defense if it was attacked by a third party. The tripartite invasion of Egypt began on October 29, 1956. It went as planned for the invaders, except that they did not count on the vehement opposition of the Eisenhower administration, which had been pretty much kept in the dark by its erstwhile allies. The administration was not pro-Nasser, but it was definitely against this type of European imperialism that would make life more difficult for the United States and open up opportunities for the Soviet Union. Ironically, the tripartite invasion was such a farce that at the height of the superpower Cold War, it compelled the United States and Soviet Union to cooperate in the UN to bring about a cease-fire on November 8.

The results were disastrous for Britain and France, their last hurrah of any sort of influential position in the region, quickly being replaced, if they were not already as outside powers, by America and Russia. For Nasser it was an unqualified, if unplanned, success. He snatched political victory from the jaws of military defeat, as he took on the traditional imperialist powers and Israel—and survived. His popularity in the region soared tremendously. It was no longer Arab nationalism or pan-Arabism; it was Nasserism. He was a bigger threat to Israel and the evaporating positions of the British and French than ever before. For Israel it was a mixed bag. Its actions confirmed Arab suspicions that it was a tool of the West, and already strained relations with the Eisenhower administration worsened; however, the war did, through international fiat, open up the Gulf of Aqaba to Israeli shipping, which had been blockaded since 1949, and placed the **United Nations Emergency Force** (**UNEF**) into a now demilitarized Sinai Peninsula. It was not the 80,000 British troops, but at least it was an internationally recognized tripwire, so the buffer, of sorts, remained.

The Suez Crisis also brought the United States more directly into the region. To fill what was perceived to be a vacuum of power in the Middle East, the Eisenhower Doctrine was announced in early 1957. It offered US military and economic aid to any country in the region that requested it in order to fend off the advances of "international communism." This left many in the Arab world bewildered. Had they not just been attacked by Britain, France, and Israel? They had not been attacked by communist forces; the Soviet Union ostensibly came to their aid. Washington now seemed to many to simply be taking up the mantle of Western imperialism. It was confirmed by subsequent US actions, particularly in the so-called American–Syrian crisis of August–October 1957, when the United States unsuccessfully attempted to overthrow a government in Damascus that was deemed to be too pro-Soviet.[4] It unleashed a regional—then international—crisis as the United States and Soviet Union eventually faced off against one another, the latter protecting its assets in Syria. Amid the superpower standoff Nasser swooped in to support his own assets in Syria, namely the emerging Baath party. With his sky-high popularity, the momentum toward Arab unity was intense. Nasser became captive to his own rhetoric and stature in the region, and he reluctantly gave in to an integral union with Syria, which he deemed necessary to keep it within his orbit and away from his inter-Arab competitors, such as Iraq. The result was the February 1958 formation of the **United Arab Republic (UAR)**, a merger of Syria (northern province) and Egypt (southern province), with Nasser as the president and Egyptian civilian and military officials dominating the top posts in the new state.

For the pro-British Hashemite monarchy in Baghdad, gamely hanging on to power, this was the death blow. Nasserism was rampant, and the internal pressure from many quarters had been building. It erupted in the violent Iraqi revolution of July 17, 1958, with what appeared to be an Arab nationalist junta led by Colonel Abd al-Karim Qassim sweeping aside the monarchy. It was thought that it would join the UAR, as the Arab nationalist dream seemed to be on the precipice of realization. But this was not the case. Qassim turned out to be more of an Iraqi nationalist than an Arab nationalist.[5] He was of the same ilk as Nasser, but he did not dance to the same beat of the drum as the Egyptian president. And why would he want to be a second or third vice president in the UAR when he was president of Iraq? The Arab cold war only intensified, but it did so at two levels. First, there was the more overt competition between the so-called progressive, neutralist Arab states of Egypt, Iraq, and Syria on one side, and the Arab monarchies of Saudi Arabia, Jordan, and Kuwait (independent from Britain in 1961) on the other. The latter group was deemed by the former to be anachronistic lackeys of the West. But there was actually a more lethal Arab cold war on one side of the equation, between Egypt, Iraq, and Syria, all vying for leadership in the Arab world (usually Syria and Iraq trying to counter Nasser) with each adopting a "more anti-Israeli than thou" position than the others to win points in the region and on the Arab street.

A series of events occurred in the Middle East that transferred these heightening tensions in the inter-Arab arena to the Arab–Israeli conflict, which had been fairly dormant while the Arab states were at each other's throats. First was the January 1964 emergency Arab League summit meeting in Cairo convened to craft a response to Israel's provocation of getting near its completion of the diversion of the headwaters of the Jordan River to increase arable land as part of the National Water Carrier Project. The Arab riposte was twofold: create the **Palestine Liberation Organization (PLO)** to represent the Palestinian cause, and empower Syria to attempt to divert the tributaries in the Golan Heights bordering Israel that fed into the Jordan River, which led to low-level military confrontations between the Syrians and Israelis. The next event was the action of the Soviet Union. Moscow thought it was sitting pretty after the Iraqi revolution, with the three most powerful Arab states looking to Russia rather than America. But the Soviets got caught in the middle of the Arab cold war between Egypt, Iraq, and Syria. Relations between them had deteriorated even more so after Syria seceded from the UAR in September 1961 and the Baath party came to power formally in both Iraq and Syria in early 1963. Both the Iraqis and Syrians high-tailed it to Cairo for unity talks, which failed amid mutual recriminations. As such, Moscow began to focus more and more of its diplomatic attention and propaganda trying to convince the Arab world that Israel and the United States were the source of their problems and were the real threats. By doing so Russia was playing a dangerous game, helping to shift tensions to the Arab-Israeli arena that might possibly blow up into a war—and it did.

The third event was the intra-Baath coup in February 1966 that brought perhaps the most radical and anti-Israeli regime to power in Damascus. The so-called

Neo-Baath adopted an increasingly aggressive posture against Israel, primarily by indirectly supporting Palestinian raids into Israel and intensifying its activities along the Israeli border, placing Nasser in the rather uncomfortable position of being seen as doing relatively little by comparison. Finally, Moscow orchestrated the November 1966 Egyptian-Syrian mutual defense pact, committing each to the defense of the other if attacked by Israel. While the Kremlin hoped that this might calm things down between Israel and Syria, by making the Israelis think twice about precipitate action against Damascus for fear of Egypt, it was done primarily to get Nasser more in control of the situation rather than the unpredictable Neo-Baath leadership in Syria. To the Israelis, however, it had the opposite effect. The last thing Israel wanted to see was any sort of coordinated Arab military front building up against it, much less Egypt and Syria right on its borders. Many Israelis believed this was an existential threat against which, if given the opportunity, they would have to act. They did in the 1967 Arab–Israeli war.

Arab–Israeli Conflict

"Zion" is a traditional Jewish synonym for Jerusalem and Israel. Zionism emerged primarily as a secular Jewish nationalist movement in the second half of the nineteenth century, inspired by nationalist trends sweeping across Europe at the time. Anti-Semitism in Russia was prevalent in the 1880s (especially when Jews were mistakenly blamed for the assassination of Czar Alexander II in 1881), and led to calls among Jews to leave. Leo Pinsker's *Auto-Emancipation* was published in 1882, calling on Russian Jews to essentially free themselves, a number of whom formed the first significant Zionist organization called **Hovevei or Hibbat Zion** (lovers of Zion). With philanthropic help from wealthy European Jews such as the Baron Edmond de Rothschild, the first Aliyah to Palestine began in the 1880s. The person many call the father of Zionism, Theodore Herzl, wrote what became a Zionist manifesto in 1896, *Der Judenstaat* or *The Jewish State*, which called for the establishment of a state for the Jews. Herzl was an Austrian Jew, a journalist who at first advocated for Jews in Europe to assimilate or fit into the dominant Christian society and environment around them. It was the so-called Dreyfus Affair in France in 1895 that changed his mind. Covering the trial and initial conviction for treason of Lieutenant Dreyfus, a French officer who happened to be Jewish, Herzl witnessed the rampant anti-Semitism in Paris surrounding the proceedings. Although Dreyfus was later acquitted, Herzl concluded that there was an innate "Judeophobia" in Europe that could not be overcome. Herzl believed that there were several locations in which to settle, at least as an initial step for this Jewish state, such as Argentina or Uganda. Palestine was the goal, but Herzl believed that because of the complexity of international politics regarding the area, the fact that there was already an existing Arab population living there who might vigorously resist, and the urgency of getting Jews to safety, that perhaps another locale should come first.

Herzl was indefatigable in organizing the embryonic Zionist movement, especially in creating the World Zionist Organization (WZO) in 1897 that began to raise funds for Jewish emigration to Palestine, which officially became the preferred location for a Jewish state. We have already seen the consequential second Aliyah from 1904 to 1914, which brought the idea of a self-contained, self-sufficient,

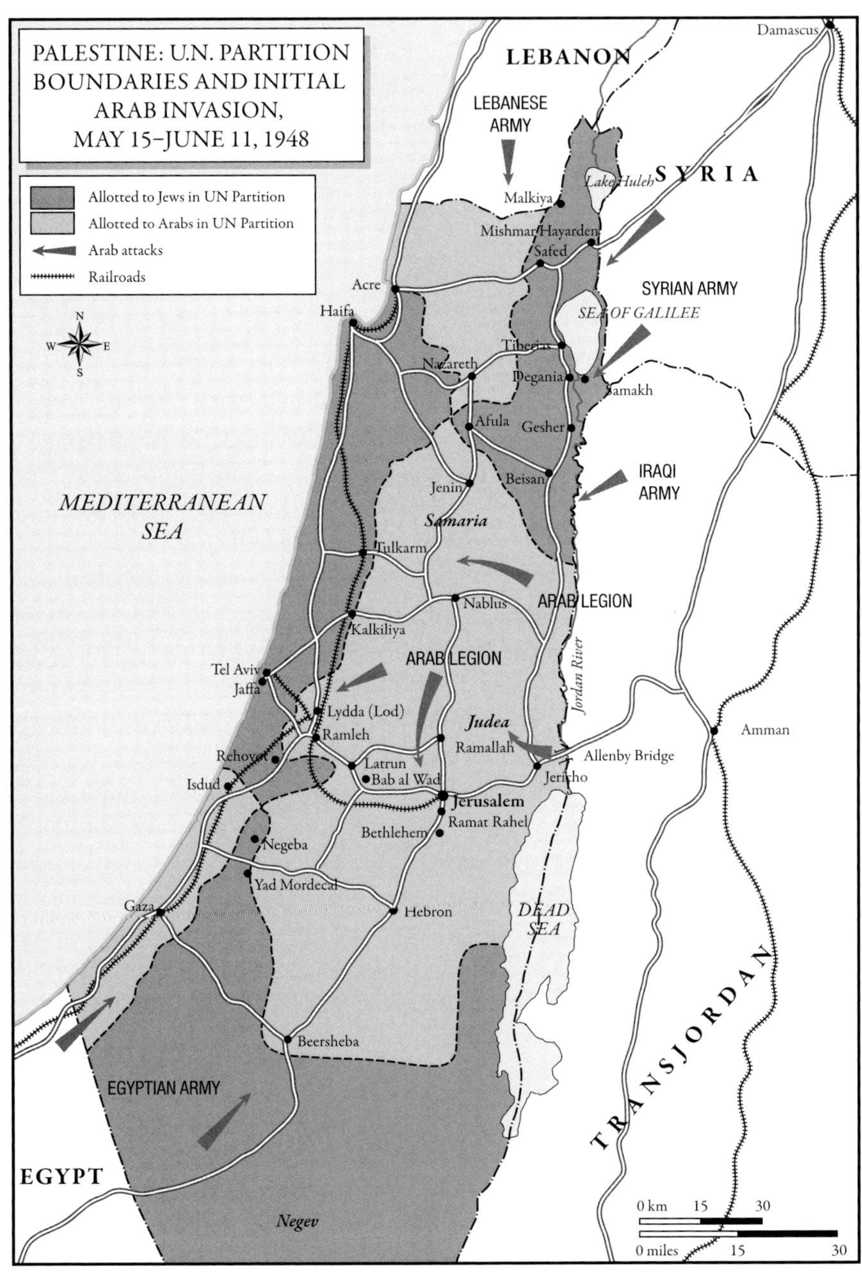

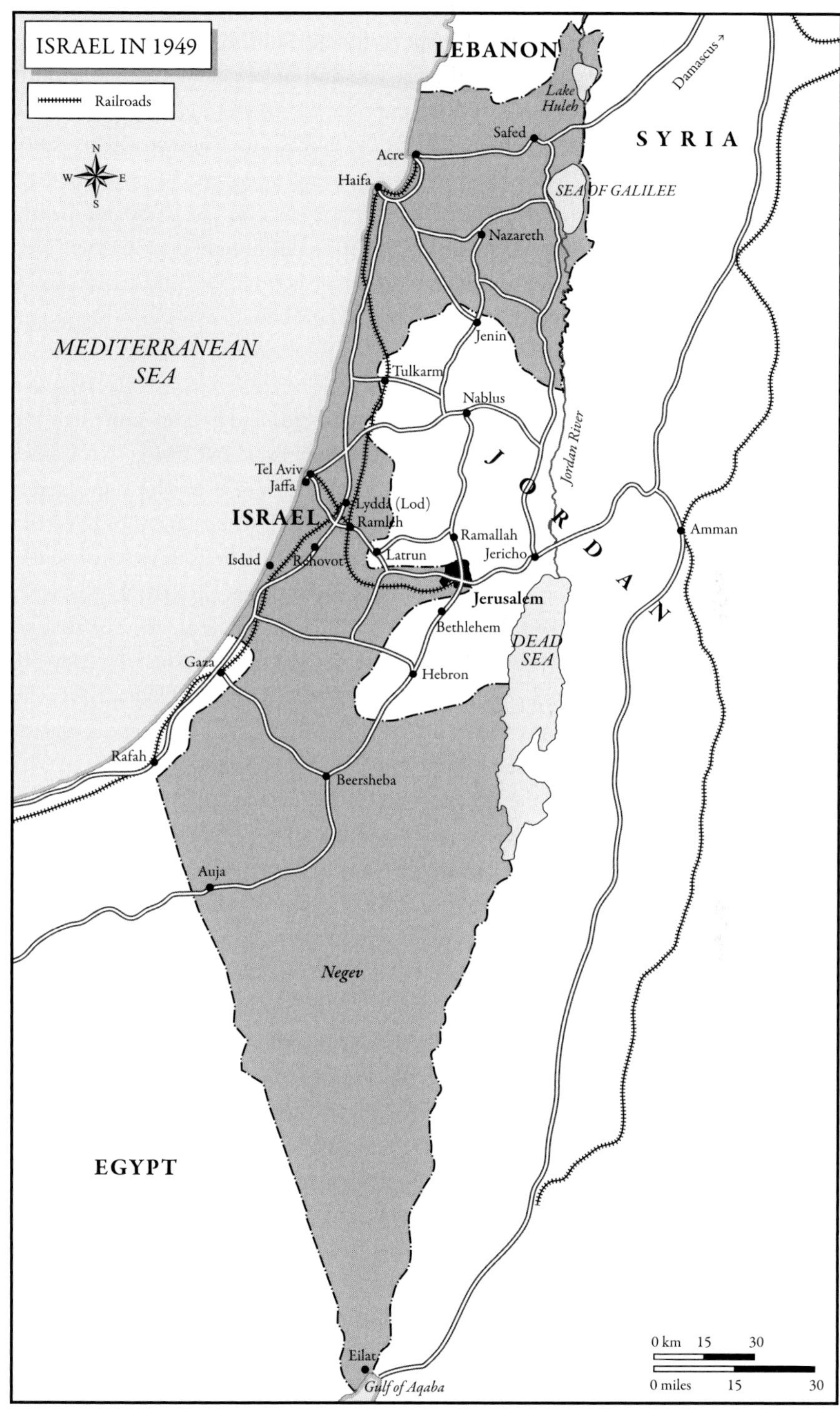

ISRAEL IN 1949
Railroads
N
W
E
S
LEBANON
Lake Huleh
Damascus
SYRIA
Safed
Acre
Haifa
SEA OF GALILEE
Nazareth
MEDITERRANEAN SEA
Jenin
Tulkarm
Nablus
Jordan River
JORDAN
Tel Aviv
Jaffa
Lydda (Lod)
ISRAEL
Ramleh
Ramallah
Amman
Isdud
Rehovot
Latrun
Jericho
Jerusalem
Bethlehem
DEAD SEA
Gaza
Hebron
Rafah
Beersheba
Auja
Negev
EGYPT
Eilat
Gulf of Aqaba
0 km 15 30
0 miles 15 30

all-Jewish state to the fore in the Zionist movement. Labor Zionism (or what some call cultural or social Zionism) became the dominant ideological strand: to build a culturally and institutionally strong Hebrew nation before acquiring the nation-state, so as to be adequately prepared when the time came for statehood.[6] As we saw in the previous chapter, they were indeed ready, as was shown in the 1947–1949 Arab–Israeli war, out of which Israel was born in May 1948.

The Arab–Israeli conflict was somewhat in abeyance in the 1950s and early 1960s, as the cold wars in the Middle East and state-building deflected attentions in other directions for a time. As discussed in the last section, however, direct Arab-Israeli tensions started to significantly rise by late 1966 and into 1967, creating a facilitating environment for war unless cooler heads prevailed. They did not. In response to a series of back-and-forth provocations between Syria and Israel, Egypt's Gamal Abd al-Nasser, with Soviet encouragement, attempted to gain control of the situation in order to prevent war. But Nasser was never shy about trying to translate a crisis into political gain—after all, he did so after the Suez war. Through a series of escalating moves, especially the one on May 22, 1967, when he announced the closure of the Gulf of Aqaba to Israeli shipping, something the Israelis consistently said would be a *casus belli*, Nasser invited a near certain direct confrontation with Israel—the kind he had worked hard to avoid in previous years.[7] It appears that he convinced himself that he had Israel on the defensive, especially when, by May 30, Jordan had joined the Egyptian-Syrian defense pact and countries from all over the Arab world were sending contingents of troops to Egypt. If he had miscalculated, the international community, as in 1956, would come bail him out.

By the first week of June, the Israeli government had a hawkish war cabinet in place to deal with the crisis. They were not going to let Nasser off the hook this time. If war came, Israel would try to quickly achieve victory before international diplomacy forced the Jewish state to prematurely stand down. Israel struck first in an audacious air campaign initially focused on Egypt; in Israel this war is often called the Six-Day War (June 5–June 11), but it was really over in about three hours. In about the first three hours of the air assault on Egypt, Israel almost completely destroyed Egypt's air capabilities. Without air cover, Egyptian ground forces were at Israel's mercy in the Sinai Peninsula. One by one, Israel dealt with Jordan and then Syria. In the end Israel had captured the Gaza Strip and Sinai Peninsula from Egypt; the West Bank, including Arab East Jerusalem, from Jordan; and the Golan Heights from Syria. In the Sinai, Israel itself was now the buffer.

Israel's stunning victory was a seismic event in modern Middle East history, the effects of which we are still dealing with today. The Occupied Territories situation was created, along with the land for peace formula embodied in UN Security Council Resolution 242 of November 1967; Israel would return some or all of the occupied lands in exchange for peace with its Arab neighbors. A bargaining situation was created, but the problem was that it was asymmetrical or unequal. Israel held all of the land and was in a very strong position compared to the Arab combatants,

ISRAEL AND THE OCCUPIED TERRITORIES, 1967
Lands captured during the Six-Day War
N
W
E
S
Beirut
LEBANON
Sidon
Tyre
SYRIA
Golan Heights
Acre
Safed
Haifa
SEA OF GALILEE
Yarmuk River
Nazareth
MEDITERRANEAN SEA
Irbid
Jenin
Nablus
Jarash
West Bank
Jordan River
Tel Aviv
Jaffa
Lydda
Salt
Amman
Jericho
Ramleh
Jerusalem
ISRAEL
Bethlehem
Gaza
Hebron
DEAD SEA
Khan Yunis
Port Said
Rafah
Port Fuad
Beersheba
Al Arish
Suez Cannal
Qantara
Negev
Ismailia
Petra
Suez
Port Tawfiq
JORDAN
Sinai
Aqaba
Eilat
EGYPT
GULF OF SUEZ
GULF OF AQABA
St. Catherine's Monastery
SAUDI ARABIA
Sharm el-Sheikh
Strait of Tiran
Tiran
0 km 30 60
0 miles 30 60
RED SEA

who had just lost a war so decisively. Divisions began to develop among Israelis themselves over the question of whether the occupied territories should be kept in full or in part for security or religious reasons (the latter having to do with a united Jerusalem and the West Bank—Judea and Samaria to the more conservative parties in Israel—being a part of Biblical Israel), or whether the lands should be returned in full or in part to their former owners in exchange for peace and normalization of relations. The devastating loss meant that the war effectively ended Nasserism, and by doing so it also effectively ended Arab nationalism as a viable ideology. In its wake, Islamism, or what many call Islamic fundamentalism, experienced a resurgence that continued for decades, as clearly the more secular alternatives had failed. Finally, the war brought the two superpowers more intimately into the Arab-Israeli arena, with all of the inherent dangers of a regional conflict leading to a superpower confrontation, something that almost happened in the 1973 Arab–Israeli war.

SPOTLIGHT

Umm Kulthum and Fairuz

Umm Kulthum of Egypt and Fairuz (Fairouz, Fayrouz) of Lebanon are two of the most iconic singers in the Arab world over the last century. Their music has enriched the lives of millions in and outside of the Middle East over multiple generations. Their influence extended far beyond their music. They were cultural phenomena, and whether they wanted to or not, they influenced politics and society at home and abroad.

The first time I visited Egypt was in 1984, staying the summer along with a group of students in a program led by one of my dear friends and mentors, Professor Lou Cantori. When we traveled between cities in our bus, oftentimes the hour or hour-and-a-half ride would be accompanied by only one song on the radio. It was sung by Umm Kulthum. At first it was frankly kind of annoying to a Western-trained musical ear. But as I learned more about her music and her technique—she repeated lines in different ways, seemingly never singing one the same way twice; and her jazz-like exploration of *maqamat*, or Arabic scales, which is why many of her songs and performances were so lengthy—and her emotional effect on Egyptians as a whole, I came to enjoy and respect Umm Kulthum by the end of the summer. It is a good thing, because to this day anyone who travels in Egypt will still hear her omnipresent voice over the radio, in cafes, hotel lobbies, and on television, almost fifty years after her passing.

Known as the "Star of the East," "mother of the Arabs," or "Egypt's fourth pyramid," Umm Kulthum was born in 1904 in rural Egypt (Tummay al-Zahayrah). Her father was a village imam who sang traditional religious songs, a talent she obviously inherited. After recognizing her gift he took his daughter with him, dressed as a boy, to perform together, and she made a name for herself in the Egyptian delta region. The family moved to Cairo in 1923, where she became a sought-after singer in salons and the private homes of the wealthy. She moved on to theaters and cabarets, until by the end of the decade she had achieved a level of fame—and consequent pay—in Cairo. Umm Kulthum leveraged this increasing popularity into appearing in her first film, *Wedad*, in 1936, playing the title character. It would be one of six films that featured her.

She recorded over three hundred songs over her sixty-year career, ranging from religious and sentimental songs to those that were nationalistic. Her music helped many Egyptians get through the trials and tribulations they endured in the twentieth century, from the Great Depression and British colonial dominance through World War II and the rapturous and tumultuous years under the leadership of Gamal Abd al-Nasser, culminating with the pain of the disastrous loss to Israel in the 1967 Arab–Israeli war. Umm Kulthum remained a staunch supporter of Nasser and the 1952 Egyptian revolution (one of her songs became the national anthem of the United Arab Republic)—something that brought her some criticism, and she was accused at times of being an unwitting tool of the Egyptian president. She also became a vocal critic of Israel and supporter of the Palestinians. She said on one occasion that she wanted to tell "each European face to face that every centime, pence or cent they give to Israel is transformed into a bullet killing an Arab person."[1]

She has been admired by many Western musical artists, including Bob Dylan, Beyoncé, and Led Zeppelin's Robert Plant, who once said he was "driven to distraction" by her voice when he was in Marrakesh, Morocco in 1970: "When I first heard the way she would dance down through the scale to land on a beautiful note that I couldn't even imagine singing, it was huge, somebody had blown a hole in the wall of my understanding of vocals."[2] Umm Kulthum suffered from a variety of health problems from the 1950s on, especially with her eyes, which later in life led to her signature look of heavy sunglasses for protection against the stage lights. She died of kidney failure in 1975, with her funeral procession attended by some four million Egyptian mourners. In 2001, cementing her iconic status, the Egyptian government established in Cairo the Kawkab al-Sharq Mathaf, the Star of the East Museum.

I can say something similar about Fairuz, as the first time I visited Syria in 1989, staying for a couple of months, I became as familiar with her folkloric music as I did with Umm Kulthum's in Egypt; Fairuz is just as or even more popular in Syria than in her native Lebanon. Born in 1934 under the name of Nuhad al-Haddad to Christian parents in Beirut, her talents were noticed early on, and she enrolled in a music conservatory in the city. She gave her first performance on Radio Lebanon in the 1940s, whereupon she adopted the stage name of "Fairuz," or "Turquoise." While at the radio station she met Assi and Mansur Rahbani (the Rahbani brothers), who wrote and composed many of her songs. Fairuz married Assi in 1954. They recorded their first song, "Itab" (Blame), for Radio Damascus in the 1950s. She rose to stardom by performing in 1957 at the Baalbek International Festival, where she performed annually until it was suspended due to the outbreak of the Lebanese civil war in 1975. Her songs evolved into long performances, even skits or plays, accompanied by singers, musicians, and dancers of the traditional *dabkah*, all of whom reflected Lebanese folklore.

Even though Fairuz was a Greek Orthodox Christian, her music cut across religious sects in Lebanon, even during the divisive and destructive civil war that lasted until 1990. Even though she often performed abroad she kept Lebanon as her residence during the war, to the great appreciation of the Lebanese people. She advocated for peaceful resolution of the war and for unity while adopting an impartial position between the conflicting groups. As with Umm Kulthum, the 1967 Arab–Israeli war tremendously influenced her art, as it did with artists, musicians, filmmakers, and authors across the Arab world. Her songs in the aftermath of the war brought her acclaim throughout the Middle East, particularly one song, "Zahrat al-Madain" (Flower of the Cities), written and performed during the summer of 1967. Fairuz is still active, recording new studio albums in 2010 and in 2017. Over her career she has sold over 80 million albums across the globe.[3] Her international appeal reached American shores when Madonna employed one of Fairuz's songs in her hit "Erotica" in 1992, for which she was almost brought to court because

Umm Kulthum, over four decades after her death, is still widely regarded as one of the greatest Arabic singers ever.
CPA Media Pte Ltd / Alamy Stock Photo

Fairuz at The Olympia in Paris, France in May 1979.
Photo by Jean-Claude FRANCOLON/ Gamma-Rapho via Getty Images

she did not obtain proper permission ahead of time. The matter was settled outside of court, but both Madonna's song and album were banned in Lebanon, where Fairuz rules.[4]

[1] Quoted in Hossein Kamaly, *A History of Islam in 21 Women* (London: Oneworld Publication, 2019), p. 200.
[2] Quoted in Tom Faber, "She Exists Out of Time: Umm Kulthum, Arab Music's Eternal Star," *The Guardian*, February 28, 2020, https://www.theguardian.com/music/2020/feb/28/she-exists-out-of-time-umm-kulthum-arab-musics-eternal-star.
[3] On Fairuz, see Christopher Stone, "Fairouz," *Encyclopedia Britannica*, November 16, 2021, https://britannica.com/biography/Fairouz.
[4] Khaoula Ghanem, "Fairouz Turns 85: Here Are 7 Facts About the Legendary Singer," *Vogue*, November 21, 2020, https://en.vogue.me/culture/fairouz-facts-singer-birthday/.

The next six years consisted of Egypt primarily trying to insert some symmetry into the bargaining situation. It was clear that Israel was now here for good and that it could not be pushed into the sea militarily, so accumulating more chips with which to bargain became the order of the day. First was the so-called War of Attrition (March 1969–August 1970) initiated by Nasser. As the name suggests, this was intended to wear down Israel through low-level warfare that took advantage of Egypt's greater resources, whereas Israel, because of its relatively small size and population, preferred to engage in quick, mobile warfare. While it worked to re-activate international diplomacy by bringing in the United States to arrange for a limited cease-fire after things threatened to spiral out of control by August 1970, the overall repercussions of this war were far out of proportion to the actual level of conflict. First, more radical branches of the PLO, not wanting to see if a limited cease-fire between Egypt and Israel could potentially lead to a peace treaty, hijacked several European passenger airliners to an airbase outside of Amman, Jordan, where the PLO was headquartered. The planes—minus the passengers—were blown up, all of which was an affront to King Hussein of Jordan, who already feared that the PLO had become a state within a state in his country. The king responded militarily against the PLO, thus igniting the Jordanian civil war, or what became known to Palestinians as Black September.

While successfully negotiating an end to the civil war in September, Gamal Abd al-Nasser died of a heart attack and was succeeded as president by his Free Officer comrade, Anwar al-Sadat, who would eventually take Egypt in a bold new direction. In Syria, turmoil within the leadership of the Baath government over differences of how much it should intervene in Jordan to back the PLO and possibly get rid of a pro-Western monarch led to an intra-Baath coup by November 1970. This brought the more moderate Hafiz al-Assad to power, who would rule Syria for three decades; he too would take his country in different directions. Finally, the Richard M. Nixon administration, particularly National Security Advisor (and soon-to-be Secretary of State) Henry Kissinger, recognized the positive role

Israel played in indirectly protecting King Hussein while staring down the Syrians in a way that compelled Hafiz al-Assad, as minister of defense and commander of the air force, to stand down, disobeying orders from his more radical Baathist colleagues to intervene more assertively. The United States for a generation had been looking for a Middle East ally to help to contain the Soviets. Israel, by containing Soviet ally Syria in this instance, proved its worth, thus beginning a much more fruitful US-Israeli partnership that led to exponentially more US military aid to Israel, strengthening—and hardening—Israel's position. It seemed as if the asymmetry was getting even worse.

This is the backdrop to Anwar Sadat's decision to get the Sinai Peninsula back at all costs, either through diplomacy or war. He needed it for his own political legitimacy as well as for the economic value (Suez Canal tolls, oil production) of the Sinai. This time, Egypt and Syria would work more in concert with each other. Their use of deception combined with a bit of Israeli complacency and lack of politic imagination allowed the two Arab states to enjoy initial success when they launched the 1973 Arab-Israeli war on October 6. The Israelis never imagined the Arabs would go to war because they knew the Arabs could not defeat Israel. But Sadat was not out to defeat Israel; he simply wanted to improve his bargaining position by bloodying Israel for a change as well as reactivating international diplomacy. He succeeded in accomplishing this, though not without some serious drama. For instance, while the Soviets started almost immediately massively resupplying Syria and Egypt, the United States waited for a few days, with Kissinger not wanting a repeat one-sided affair as in 1967, which would hamper prospects for an overall peace deal. All the while, Israel was suffering some losses to the extent it hinted that it might have to resort to its unofficial nuclear arsenal, a small nuclear capability the Israelis had built up with primarily the help of the French in the early 1960s. Israel did turn it around, placing both Damascus and Cairo on the clear defensive, which compelled Moscow to make some serious threats about intervening, which then prompted the Nixon administration to put US nuclear forces on their highest alert since the Cuban missile crisis in 1962. Meanwhile, to help its Arab brothers, Saudi Arabia led the Arab members of the **Organization of Petroleum Exporting Countries (OPEC)** to announce an oil embargo against those states (mainly the United States, the world's largest consumer of oil) who supported Israel. This helped accelerate diplomacy, but not before almost quadrupling the price per barrel of oil from $3.01 before the war to $11.65 by January 1974, leading to a global oil shortage and economic recession as well as perhaps the greatest transfer of wealth in history from consumers to producers of oil.

The war was brought to a close via a UN-negotiated cease-fire and Security Council resolution on October 25. But one can say that the heightened destructive levels of the conflict, both actual and potential, scared most everyone straight. What would the next Arab–Israeli war look like? Immediately after the cease-fire, Kissinger engaged in his famous shuttle diplomacy to engineer limited agreements between Israel and Egypt on the one hand, and Israel and Syria on the other. The former produced two disengagement agreements, Sinai I of January 1974 and Sinai II of September 1975, that arranged for a partial Israeli withdrawal from the Sinai in return for UN monitoring devices and peacekeeping forces accompanied by some Egyptian concessions. The latter ended with its own disengagement agreement regarding the Golan Heights in May 1974, the two armies separated by UN peacekeeping forces. Kissinger, with his step-by-step approach, was able to do this while keeping the Soviets out, which to him was the key to his efforts, while prying Egypt out of the Soviet and into the US camp, which was something Sadat preferred so that he could open up Egypt's economy to the West.

The stage seemed to set for a comprehensive Arab-Israeli peace brokered by the United States. This was very high on President Jimmy Carter's agenda when he came into power in January 1977. It was determined that the step-by-step approach had exhausted itself because of what Washington had to promise both sides just to get limited concessions—and for the Israelis to only withdraw a few dozen miles. The resulting 1979 Egyptian-Israeli peace treaty was something short of Carter's ultimate objective.

1979 and Its Aftermath

My 2000 book *1979: The Year That Shaped the Modern Middle East* discussed the efficacy of examining a year through the concept of change and cause and effect analysis informed by physics, biology, and philosophy. I determined in the end that the seminal events that occurred in the Middle East in 1979 constituted separately and together bent rails, and the course of history was unalterably changed—the train went in a different direction—due to these events, the repercussions of which in succeeding years only proved the point. Then I turned to the events themselves. I focused on what I believed at the time were the three primary events in the Middle East region in 1979: the culmination of the Iranian revolution in February; the signing of the Egyptian-Israeli peace treaty in March; and then the Soviet invasion of Afghanistan in December. I had the taking of the Grand Mosque in Mecca by Sunni militants in November as a secondary event; however, if I were to write the book today, I would probably move that up to a primary event as well, given what history has shown since.

The Iranian revolution that culminated in the departure of the Shah of Iran and the landing at Teheran airport of the Ayatollah Ruhollah Khomeini on February 1, 1979, is a true revolution. Many coups masquerade as revolutions, but this one was a transfer of power from one class to another and an almost completely altered political system based on a new prevailing ideology—the Islamic Republic of Iran. The causes of the revolution are complex and multifarious. Various explanations draw from the historical experiences of Iran dating back to the Safavid empire, the decentralized rule of the Qajar dynasty (1796–1925), British and Russian imperialism in Iran in the nineteenth century, and the ravages of World War I, which paved the way for the Pahlavi dynasty to come to power formally in 1925 with the ascension to the Peacock Throne of Reza Shah, the father of Muhammad Reza Shah, the monarch overthrown in 1979. Other explanations focus on the post–World War II period, just after Reza Shah was removed from power during the war by the British for his pro-Nazi sympathies. His young and untested son was then placed in power in 1945, beholden to the British and soon the Americans, facing a host of challenges, in particular from an austere intellectual liberal constitutionalist, Muhammad Mussadiq, whose overthrow by US covert action in 1953 foreshadowed what would be a widening gulf between the regime and the Iranian people, especially as the shah's dependence on the United States increased.

Virtually all explanations touch as least to some degree on the overly rapid modernization process that father and son embarked upon. The changes that occurred as a result had economic, political, and social ramifications, accelerating what Iran historian Nikki Keddie called the "dual culture" nature of Iranian society.[8] It had begun under Reza Shah, who implemented his own Ataturk-inspired modernization program in the 1920s and 1930s, only he did not have the advantage of the foundation the Tanzimat provided the Turkish leader on which he could build his modern state apparatus, the lack of which only fragmented society that much more. The Qajar dynasty that ostensibly ruled over Iran from the late eighteenth century until 1925 was weak overall, subject to the vicissitudes of European powers, primarily the British and the Russians, who did not want to see a strong central government that could implement serious reform measures; when the Qajars made a move in one direction, the other European power would counter accordingly. After further depredations from World War I, the Cossack (Kazakh) military led by Reza Khan easily cast aside the Qajars, thus making him Reza Shah. His ambition got the better of him, and he tried to fit the square peg of modernization into the round hole of a very traditional society. Whenever there is change of a significant order there are those who benefit from it and those who do not. Suffice it to say that the environment for revolution tends to become much more propitious when the bulk of the population consider themselves in the latter category.

In the 1960s and especially in the 1970s, with the available capital from the increased oil revenues from changes in the global oil economy in 1970–1971 in favor of producers as well as the oil price hike due to the 1973 Arab–Israeli war, Muhammad Reza Shah embarked upon an economic program of import-substituting industrialization (ISI). We have seen the pitfalls of ISI before, except that with Iran's oil and natural gas revenues, the shah could continue to pour money into the program without going bankrupt as happened in most other countries that attempted it. As a result, from the outside it looked as though things were moving forward in Iran with a growing gross national product. But on the inside the Iranian population became increasingly stratified, with an elite Westernized class divorced from the reality of much of the rest of the struggling population. It was this

Muhammad Reza Shah, last Shah of the Pahlavi dynasty in Iran from 1941 until his overthrow during the Iranian Revolution in 1979.
Jimmy Carter Library and Museum

Portrait of Ayatollah Ruhollah Khomeini: Leader of the Islamic revolution and founder of the Islamic Republic of Iran in 1979 until his death in 1989.
World History Archive / Alamy Stock Photo

disenchantment and disenfranchisement that opponents of the shah tapped into, especially the Ayatollah Khomeini.

The shah was a megalomaniac out of touch with Iranian society, and he was obsessed with making Iran not only a regional power but a global one. Perhaps no single event indicated this more than his $300 million party (a Guinness Book world record at the time for the most expensive) he hosted in 1971 to commemorate the 2,500th anniversary of the Achmaenid dynasty, held at the ancient site of Persepolis, one of the capitals of the dynasty. Not only was the lavishness and prodigality an affront to many Iranians living in poverty, but the celebration of a pre-Islamic entity was deeply offensive to the religious classes and mostly traditional Muslim population. The shah's subsequent adoption of the Persian calendar to replace the Islamic one only reinforced the view that he had an utter disregard and ignorance of the sensitivities of most Iranians. Along with the repressive apparatus put in place by the shah, this only positioned the religious opposition more toward the mainstream of discontent and brought diverse opposition groups closer together.

The shah's close relationship with the United States (and indirectly with Israel) also weakened his monarchy by emboldening the opposition. The strategic nature of the US–Iran relationship grew by leaps and bounds with the Vietnam-induced Nixon Doctrine of 1969, which called on US allies to shoulder more of the burden of defense against Communist aggression while the United States was bogged down in the Vietnam War. In the Middle East, this meant more support for Iran to act as Washington's gendarme in the Persian Gulf—and for Israel in the heartland of the region, which naturally produced Iran-Israel strategic ties, especially since both shared Iraq as a common enemy. For this the United States armed the shah to the teeth, giving him access to almost everything in the US arsenal; it was said that it was like giving the "keys to the largest liquor cabinet in the world to a confirmed alcoholic." So many more weapons were purchased than were necessary, but the shah wanted to look the part. He was seen as doing the bidding of the United States and Israel, the puppeteers who directed the shah's repression and neglect. One only has to scan the speeches of Khomeini to see how effectively he tied the shah to the United States and Israel as focal points of the opposition.[9]

A series of events, some of them bloody, or what I call flashpoints in 1977 and 1978, complicated the situation for the shah and elevated Khomeini within the growing opposition movement. As a result, many Iranians began to see the value of Khomeini's uncompromising stand on the shah: that he must go, and an Islamic republic must be formed. More moderate alternatives, such as a constitutional monarchy, had very little chance of succeeding because of the growing demonstrations and widespread strikes. By the time the shah appointed Shahpour Bakhtiar prime minister in December 1978, it was too little too late. Seeing the writing on the wall, the shah effectively abdicated by leaving the country on January 16, 1979, weak from the cancer that would soon take his life. All that was left was for Khomeini to triumphantly return on February 1 from his exile in Paris, forcing the Bakhtiari government to dissolve itself and begin the task of consolidating power—and changing Middle East history.

When Israeli Prime Minister Menachem Begin and Egyptian President Anwar Sadat met at the White House on March 26, 1979, and signed the Egyptian-Israeli peace treaty with President Jimmy Carter presiding over the ceremony, most everyone knew that the Middle East had changed in a profound manner. What people did not know quite yet was the direction of that change and whether it would be for better or worse. As mentioned earlier, Carter came to office in January 1977 with Middle East peace high on the agenda. The problem is that he had an unexpectedly tight window to get something done, because in May 1977, the right-wing Likud party won a majority in the Israeli Knesset for the first time, and its leader, Menachem Begin, became prime minister. Begin was a prominent member of the **Irgun Zevai Leumi**, a right-wing militia dedicated to forcing the British out of Palestine. Many in and outside of the mandate viewed the Irgun as a terrorist organization. He led two famous terrorist attacks, one in 1946 that blew up much of the King David Hotel in Jerusalem, a wing of which served as the headquarters of the British mandate authority. Scores of British, Arabs, and Jews were killed. He also led an attack against a Palestinian Arab village, Dayr Yaseen, in 1948, in which a couple hundred men, women, and children were killed, in a brutal scare tactic aimed at compelling more Palestinians to leave Palestine. This was not the man Carter wanted to see in power.

SPOTLIGHT

Water in the Middle East

Water is obviously vital for human survival, important not only for daily consumption but also in terms of agricultural and industrial productivity and growth. The United Nations Commission on Sustainable Development noted in 1997 that by 2025 two-thirds of the world's population will suffer from moderate to severe water stress resulting from overdemand and pollution. Today, 3.5 billion people live on less than 50 liters per day, only one-seventh of the quantity used by the average American. The Middle East is experiencing severe water stress in many areas; despite the fact that some countries, such as Turkey and Lebanon, enjoy relatively plentiful water supplies, the region as a whole entered a water-deficit phase by 1970. The Middle East and North Africa (MENA) is the most water-scarce region in the world, comprising about 6.3 percent of the world's population yet containing only 1.4 percent of the world's renewable fresh water.

The combination of water scarcity (limited surface and subsurface resources) with territorial disputes, historical antagonisms, refugee and immigration flows, and rapid population growth has produced a potentially volatile situation in the region, to the point where the phrase "water wars" has entered the lexicon of possible characterizations of the future for the Middle East. Water has already entered into the calculations of combatants in the region. As noted, Israel's diversion of the headwaters of the Jordan River in the early 1960s (and Arab attempts at preventing it) raised the level of tension in the Arab–Israeli arena leading up to the 1967 Arab–Israeli war, and in that war the Israeli takeover of the Golan Heights was driven as much by the desire to control the tributaries feeding into the Jordan River as by strategic necessity. In addition, questions concerning water ownership and management have exacerbated relations among a host of riparian states associated with the Tigris–Euphrates river system, the Nile River with the Grand Ethiopian Renaissance Dam (GERD) affecting the Sudan and Egypt, and the Jordan River basin, all three of which cross international borders and demand diplomatic cooperation and resolution of competing claims. The issue of adequate water-sharing and water ownership greatly complicates a resolution to the Israeli–Palestinian conflict because vital underground aquifers that feed into Israel's National Water Carrier are located in the West Bank, together providing about 50 percent of Israel's total water consumption. A water-stressed country is one defined as having less than 1,700 cubic meters of water per capita, while a water-scarce country is one with less than 1,000 cubic meters per capita, which cannot for long meet even the basic needs of an organized society on its own. In 1945, Bahrain, Jordan, and Kuwait were considered to be water-scarce countries. By 1990, eight more joined the list (Algeria, Qatar, Saudi Arabia, Somalia, Tunisia, the United Arab Emirates, Yemen, and the Occupied Territories/Palestine). UN studies estimate that by the year 2025 Egypt, Ethiopia, Iran, Libya, Morocco, Oman, and Syria will join the ranks of water-scarce nations. Studies indicate that by 2025 the per capita water availability in the MENA region will be 700 cubic meters, half of what it was in the 1990s. By contrast, the United States has almost 9,000 cubic meters of water per capita.

It is not only the quantity of water that is at issue but also the quality, in terms of whether downstream riparian states receive enough sweet, as opposed to salinated, water for productive agricultural utilization. To deal with these water shortages, countries in the region have attempted a variety of short-term expedients and long-term plans from water-sharing agreements, high-yield agriculture, and conservation to high-cost alternatives such as desalinization plants and water transport—or simply fixing leaky pipes (in Damascus, it is estimated that 30 percent of the water is lost due to leaky pipes, whereas in Israel the figure is 12 percent, about what it is in most places in the United States). Whatever may come of the water situation in the Middle East, it is a tremendously complex problem that involves economics, geography, ecology, politics, and international relations—and maybe most importantly, flexibility and imagination.

Noria waterwheel on the Orontes River in Hama, Syria.
David Lyon / Alamy Stock Photo

Source: David W. Lesch, *The Arab-Israeli Conflict*, pp. 377–78.

Begin greatly accelerated the Jewish settlement process in the Occupied Territories, hoping to create facts on the ground that would make it difficult, if not impossible, for any future Israeli government to withdraw from the territories. With domestic and congressional forces resisting Carter's push for a comprehensive Arab-Israeli land-for-peace deal, a stalemate on the negotiating front ensued. But Sadat had committed himself to get the Sinai Peninsula back. As he had in 1973 with the bold move of going to war, Sadat made another equally bold move: he flew to Israel in November 1977, met Begin on the airport tarmac, and spoke in the Israeli Knesset. It had been a long-standing Israeli foreign policy imperative to pursue a separate peace deal with Egypt, without which the Arab world could not ever hope to confront Israel militarily. Begin would drive a hard bargain, but he could not pass on this opportunity. But the Israeli prime minister held all the cards. Sadat had given up his greatest leverage, recognition of Israel, before getting anything in return. Begin, however, would remain in power and popular in many circles whether he got a deal (on his terms) or not.

The momentum slowed considerably, so to reactivate diplomacy President Carter, who also had committed the weight of the US office to a deal, intervened by inviting Begin and Sadat to the presidential retreat in Camp David, Maryland, in September 1978 for thirteen days of intense and often dramatic negotiations. What emerged became known as the Camp David Accords, which consisted of two frameworks for peace. One was titled "A Framework for the Conclusion of a Peace Treaty between Egypt and Israel," which dealt with bilateral Egyptian-Israeli issues, including the phased Israeli withdrawal from the remainder of the Sinai Peninsula in return for the establishment of full normal diplomatic relations between the two countries. The second framework was titled "A Framework for Peace in the Middle East," which was intended to provide for a comprehensive settlement to the Arab–Israeli conflict based on **United Nations Security Council (UNSC)** 242, including a resolution to the Palestinian problem. After several more months of haggling on all sides, the treaty was signed on March 26, 1979. It essentially reflected the Camp David Accords and the two frameworks. As the critics of the treaty (and there were many) quickly pointed out, the two frameworks were not linked; that is, progress on the one track, the Egyptian-Israeli bilateral agreement, would not necessarily have to be matched by progress on the other track. While the former framework came to fruition, the second one made very little progress, as Begin adopted a very narrow view of it and continued the settlement process. Without negotiating leverage, Sadat and Carter basically only had a wish and a prayer on their side to compel Begin to make concessions on the Palestinian issue. In essence, Egypt signed a separate peace with Israel in what turned out to be the final step in the Egyptian-Israeli negotiations that began soon after the 1973 war.

In 1902, Abd al-Aziz Abd al-Rahman ibn al-Saud (often just known as Ibn Saud) led a group of puritanical Sunni Muslims, the *Ikhwan* (Brethren), to victory in Riyadh against another tribe in central Arabia.[10] By the mid-1920s he ruled over

On March 26, 1979, on the North Grounds of the White House, Presidents Carter and Sadat and Prime Minister Begin joined hands in celebration of the signing of the "Treaty of Peace Between the Arab Republic of Egypt and the State of Israel."
Peter Probst / Alamy Stock Photo

most of Arabia, and in 1932 his domain was recognized by the international community as Saudi Arabia. We think of Saudi Arabia as a monarchy, but in reality it is a diarchy ruled by the Saudi family and the descendants of Muhammad ibn Abd al-Wahhab (1703–1792), the Wahabbis, who make-up the rigid, neo-Hanbali religious establishment in the country. As of this writing, all of the Saudi monarchs have been the offspring of its founder after his death in 1953. Some of the southern tribes of the original Ikhwan became too fanatical, however, for Ibn Saud's tastes. He defeated them in the battle of Sbala in 1929. One of those Ikhwan was Muhammad bin Seif al-Uteybi, who seven years later had a son by the name of Juhayman. By the 1970s, with the influx of oil wealth, modernization, and foreign workers, many Saudis such as Juhayman al-Uteybi became more and more agitated at the liberal ideas entering the country and saw a large gap between Islamic theory and Saudi practice. Many of the young Saudi Bedouins felt displaced physically, mentally, economically, and spiritually by modernization, and they embraced piety to cope with it. Juhayman led a small group who decided to take action.

The Saudis did not expect what happened. After facing off against the secular Arab nationalists and socialists of Nasser and the Baath party for the better part of two decades, the religious right in the country was simply not on their radar screen; similar to what happened to the Shah of Iran after the Mussadiq crisis and after the Iranian revolution in February, the royal family seemed to see everything through an Iranian prism and growing Shiite threat in the Gulf. But Juhayman and his followers audaciously took over Islam's holiest site, the Grand Mosque in Mecca, on November 20, 1979 and they held it until Saudi special forces, supported by French commandoes, forcibly recaptured it on December 4. Driven by prophecy that declared one of their lot (actually Juhayman's brother-in-law) as the Mahdi to auger in the end of times and Day of Judgement, the rebels also called for the overthrow of the House of Saud. This was a grave threat to the Saudis, for their job, first and foremost, is Guardians of the Two Holy Sites (Mecca and Medina)—so if they can't even do that, their legitimacy is severely undermined.

The uprising failed, but its ripple effects were profound, which is now much more apparent than when I originally wrote my *1979* book. The writings of Juhayman inspired Khalid Islambouli, the Egyptian who organized and led the assassination of Anwar Sadat in 1981 for abandoning Jerusalem (Islam's third holiest site) and the Palestinian cause by signing the peace treaty with Israel. Sadat never saw the final portion of the Sinai Peninsula returned to Egypt in April 1982. Juhayman's movement also inspired those who would later lead and join al-Qaida, as well as Abu Musab al-Zarqawi, who created al-Qaida in Iraq and from which sprung the Islamic State (ISIS or the Islamic State of Iraq and Syria). The Saudi rulers reacted to the uprising by stepping up adherence to sharia law in the country and further empowering the religious establishment, especially in terms of financially

Insurgents who seized the Grand Mosque in November 1979.
UtCon Collection / Alamy Stock Photo

supporting the latter's efforts to spread Wahabbi thought and practice throughout the Muslim world. This would lead to much more fertile ground for the growth of radical Islamic movements thereafter—one notable example of where this occurred is Afghanistan.

It was geographically fated that the history of Afghanistan, bordering the underbelly of Czarist Russia and then the Soviet Union, would be indelibly linked to its larger neighbor to the north. The great game between Great Britain and Russia had been played out in large measure in Afghanistan in the nineteenth century. Many say, perhaps wrongly, that Afghanistan was a country that was essentially formed by default from whatever was left between the borders of its neighbors. It is an ethnically diverse country, with Pashtuns, Tajiks, and Uzbeks accounting for the three largest groups. This heterogeneity, compounded by the mountainous geography of the country, has engendered little to no national consciousness and has made it extremely difficult for any Afghani ruling regime to control the country in anything more than a loose confederation of powerful tribes. As long as the regime was bland and somewhat indifferent, Afghanistan could exist in relative stability. This accounts for the long reign of King Muhammad Zahir from 1933 to 1973—he basically stayed out of everyone's way. Whenever a government attempted to assert itself by instituting far-reaching reforms or some political ideology, it invariably encountered reflexive resistance from the tribal-based countryside.

This would all change in 1973, when a member of the royal family, Muhammad Daoud, ousted King Zahir from power, declaring an end to the monarchy and establishing the Republic of Afghanistan. He enacted wide-ranging reforms to lift Afghanistan out if its isolated and impoverished condition. To help do so, he also improved relations with the West as well as pro-US neighbors such as Iran and Pakistan. This Moscow did not like, as it sees Afghanistan as a key buffer state to the south. A bloody coup in April 1978 resulted, probably encouraged and supported by the Soviet Union. A revolutionary council was established, led by the triumvirate of Muhammad Taraki as president and prime minister, Hafizullah Amin as foreign minister, and Babrak Karmal as vice president and deputy prime minister, all of whom would vie with each other for real power. The country was now called the Democratic Republic of Afghanistan, similar to other Soviet client-states with pretensions of communism. The new regime attempted to implement a wide-ranging, communist-inspired reform program, which was akin to Reza Shah in Iran trying to fit a square peg into the round hole of a traditional, Sunni Muslim, and tribal-based society. The opposition led by the tribes was immediate and pervasive, resulting in uprisings and civil war in 1978 and 1979.

It is into this maelstrom in Afghanistan that the Kremlin sent 80,000 Soviet troops in late December. Amin, who had become alienated from Moscow, was killed, along with members of his family, by Soviet special forces on December 27. Babrak Karmal then became the Soviet designated ruler. Moscow did not want the unrest in Afghanistan to spread to other Muslim Soviet republics in Central Asia nor an anti-Soviet Islamist regime to come to power (especially on the heels of the galvanizing Iranian revolution), as the opposition was dominated by fighters who simply became known as the mujahideen, holy warriors. Soviet doctrine held that once a state becomes communist it stays communist, lest other countries in the Soviet bloc be tempted to break away. The fact that the United States had lost its ally in Iran, the shah, made the decision a bit easier; the Kremlin understood that Washington would be less able to respond militarily. The Carter administration saw things much differently: that the Soviets were more offensive- rather than defensive-minded, and were using the vacuum of power in the Persian Gulf as a result of the fall of the shah to make a push further into the Middle East. The United States therefore responded in kind in January 1980 with the Carter Doctrine, which drew a line in the sand by stating that "Any attempt by any outside force to gain control of the Persian Gulf region will be regarded as an assault on the vital interests of the United States of America, and such an assault will be repelled by any means necessary, including military force." The United States had now become the gendarme of the Gulf and the superpower Cold War was reignited, which facilitated the rise of an old Cold Warrior, Ronald Reagan, to a resounding presidential victory in 1980. Far from Afghanistan acting as a launching pad for further expansion, however, the Soviets became bogged down in a prolonged quagmire until their troops were forced to retreat by 1989. It was Moscow's Vietnam, which together with a habitually underperforming state-planned economy helped bring about the end of the Soviet Union itself in 1991.

The repercussions of the events of 1979 were profound and lasting. Saddam Hussein, long the strongman in Iraq who assumed the formal role of president in July 1979, ordered the invasion of his neighbor Iran in September 1980. He had defensive and offensive reasons for doing so. Iraq at the time was a Shiite Arab majority country ruled by a Sunni Arab minority. When Ayatollah Khomeini, the Supreme Guide of the Shiite Islamic Republic of Iran, wanted to export the revolution around the Middle East, Iraq became a natural target. He was fond of saying that he was going to liberate Jerusalem through Baghdad. Saddam thought perhaps the best defense is a good offense; additionally, it was clear the United States was not going to come to the aid of Iran, not after Khomeini's Iranian Revolutionary Guards Corps stormed the US embassy in Teheran in November 1979 and held fifty-two US hostages for 444 days. Not only did this place the United States and Iran at loggerheads, but the action also alienated much of the international community. Most countries would not and did not mind if Khomeini was cut down to size. And all of those US weapons provided to the shah were pretty much vestigial, without ammunition, spare parts, training, and resupply from the United States. The ambitious Iraqi ruler saw an opportunity to fill two vacuums in the Middle East with one stone. With improved relations with the Reagan administration, Saddam could perhaps become the new gendarme of the Gulf, filling the shoes of the shah, while at the same time leading a moderate Arab consensus toward peace with Israel, thus filling the shoes of Sadat. Emblematic of Saddam's intentions, the two emergency Arab League summit meetings convened to first condemn the Camp David Accords and then to ostracize and isolate Egypt after the Egyptian-Israeli peace treaty—and kick Egypt out of the Arab League—were held in Baghdad and chaired by the Iraqi dictator. As seen through the prism of two succeeding US wars against him, it is difficult to think of Saddam in any sort of positive manner, but at the time he was something of a darling in US foreign policy circles, especially when compared to the Ayatollah, who was then the Middle East evil du jour in Washington.

The bloody war ebbed and flowed for eight years, with the United States helping both sides on occasion, but ultimately it sided with Iraq. With the Cold War winding down and Moscow needing Western investment to help its ailing economy, Washington was able to work through the UN to get a cease-fire to end the war in August 1988. Even though Iran had launched successful counteroffensives after the initial Iraqi thrust into Iran—and held a not inconsiderable amount of Iraqi land, while Iraq held no Iranian territory by the end of the war—Saddam claimed victory, simply because Teheran cried uncle first. The results of this war led to the 1990–1991 Gulf crisis and war (or what many in the region simply call the Second Gulf War).

Saddam was at it again. Deeply in debt with a great deal of reconstruction to do following the damage of the Iran–Iraq war, amid some specific beefs with his Persian Gulf neighbor, Saddam saw this bank to the south called Kuwait, a country with which Iraq had irredentist ideas ever since the small shaykhdom gained independence from the British in 1961. Getting control of Kuwait's oil wells and adding it to its own would put Iraq almost on par with Saudi Arabia in terms of proven oil reserves. Strategically, it would also give Iraq better access to the Persian Gulf by increasing its coastline, something that proved to be a strategic liability when Iran fairly easily cut Iraq off from the Gulf in the Iran–Iraq war. Most importantly, Saddam thought he could get away with it—and he almost did. He knew that the only country in the world that could stop him would be the United States, but despite his thuggish behavior at times, the new administration of President George H. W. Bush saw Saddam in much the same way as his predecessor—as a potential partner. In addition, Saddam and many of his US-educated advisors determined that the only time the United States sent thousands of troops halfway around the globe since World War II was to fight Soviet and communist advances (Korea and Vietnam). The superpower Cold War was clearly over, so the takeover of Kuwait was just as clearly not a communist or Soviet sponsored putsch. As long as the oil flowed at a reasonable price, why would Washington care? Finally, the Iraqis surmised that the United States public and Congress were still hamstrung by the Vietnam syndrome—the fear of getting caught in a military quagmire without any clear exit strategy.

The problem for Saddam was that President Bush was not of the Vietnam War generation. He was a decorated air force pilot who had fought in World War II, and his conceptual paradigm was shaped by the Munich mentality. In Bush's view, one does not let dictators snatch up even the smallest of neighbors, because it will only whet their appetite for more. They must be rolled back. It was also a critical time for many countries in Eastern Europe emerging out from under Soviet control and communist party dominance, transitioning to fledgling democracies. The last thing the new democratic governments needed was a difficult global economy from high oil prices due to Middle East instability. That instability was Saddam Hussein, a man who invaded two of his neighbors in a decade. If allowed to incorporate Kuwait, right on Saudi Arabia's doorstep, he would be an unpredictable power-hungry dictator at the head of the Persian Gulf. The global markets did not favor this. As the sole superpower left, the Bush administration could reinforce the continued utility of the United States in what he termed a New World Order, where the international community would work together to prevent and turn back what was often called at the time "naked aggression."

The international community played its part on this occasion, as the United States led a constellation of countries in a UN-mandated effort to liberate Kuwait in early 1991. Both Saddam's army and country were severely circumscribed in the war as Iraq was forced out of Kuwait, but he survived to fight another day. The Bush administration hoped the ignominy of decisive defeat would cause Saddam's fall from power, but the US-led UN force could not exceed the UN mandate to liberate Kuwait—it was not to effect regime change in Iraq, which would have alienated a number of coalition partners, especially the Arab countries who were on board. In addition, the Bush team presciently concluded that as the face of the UN force, the United States would be seen as an occupier over time in Iraq rather than a liberator from a military dictator. The United States would have to own the reconstruction and nation-building efforts, which was expensive in terms of dollars and manpower, and would only produce long-term opposition. There was a clear path to victory and an exit strategy—the anti–Vietnam War doctrine—but it left Saddam entrenched in Baghdad.

While the Egyptian-Israeli peace treaty emboldened Saddam, it also did so to Israel. Many of the critics of the treaty, not least of whom was Syria's President Hafiz al-Assad, were saying that if Israel was secure to the south, at peace with Egypt, this freed it up to pursue its strategic objectives to the north, directly or indirectly aimed at Damascus. In June 1982, only a couple of months following the final portion of the Sinai Peninsula returned to Egypt, Israel launched an invasion of Lebanon. Ostensibly it was to counter continued attacks against Israel sponsored and carried out by the PLO, which had moved its headquarters from Amman to Beirut following the Jordanian civil war in 1970. Much as it had in Jordan, the PLO had become something of a state within a state in Lebanon, controlling much of the country's majority Shiite-populated south. But Menachem Begin and his defense minister, Ariel Sharon, had a secret agenda. The goal was to rid Lebanon of the PLO and Syrian troops entirely, and put in place a Maronite Christian president (Bashir

Gemayel), who would then sign a peace treaty with Israel. This would outflank Damascus and put Assad on the clear defensive. Lebanon could no longer be used as a launching pad for anti-Israeli action, and the Syrian-Israeli proxy battle there would come to an end. To make a very complicated story short, it was a disaster for Israel. Lebanon became its Vietnam; as the offensive slowed, Israeli forces were not eager to fight house-to-house battles in the labyrinth of Beirut. And although the PLO was forced to move yet again, this time to Tunisia, Yasser Arafat was still around, although by the late 1980s the PLO's weakened condition compelled the PLO chairman to reluctantly recognize Israel and renounce terrorism—and Syria was anything but gone from Lebanon. The level of destruction also caught the attention of the international community, and the United States led a multinational force (MNF) into Lebanon to help stabilize the situation following the assassination of Gemayel in September 1982 and the subsequent massacre by vengeful Christian Phalangists of hundreds of defenseless Palestinians at the refugees camps of Sabra and Shatila in south Beirut. The MNF was a disaster as well, as they soon became targets themselves, especially as the Reagan administration tried to achieve through diplomacy what the Israelis could not do militarily. Syria's back was against the wall, and Hafiz al-Assad fought tooth and nail to make sure his country's strategic and economic interests in Lebanon were not lost. If there was a winner to this ugly historical episode, it was Assad.

In the end, Israel was compelled to withdraw to a salient along the border, which it kept until fully withdrawing in 2000, and the MNF withdrew altogether by early 1984. The conflict deepened Lebanon's ongoing civil war and Syria's influence in Lebanon. But perhaps the most long-standing result of the conflict was that it led to the creation of Hizbullah (Party of God), the Shiite Islamist group that today is the strongest single party in Lebanon politically and militarily. I remember seeing striking footage of Shiite villages in southern Lebanon actually welcoming Israeli soldiers when they invaded. To these Shiites, Israel was liberating them from the control of the PLO, who from their point of view only brought down Israeli bombs as reprisal raids that killed more Shiites than PLO soldiers. But in a monumental strategic error, Israel stayed in the buffer zone in the south along the border. To the Shiites living there, Israel now was an occupier. This opened the door for Syrian and Iranian support to enter Lebanon to make life as difficult for Israel as possible. Iran, looking to pad its Middle East credentials on the front line with Israel, eagerly entered the fray by financially and militarily helping to build and establish Hizbullah, which is today the biggest single strategic threat to Israel in the heartland of the Middle East.

On the other side of the Middle East, the Reagan administration, aided and abetted by Pakistan and Saudi Arabia, among others, engaged in a huge program of military aid to support the mujahideen fighting the Soviets. Turnabout was considered fair play for what the Soviets had done to the United States in Vietnam. Unfortunately, as many have commented since, the United States helped create

Frankenstein's monster: the legitimation of a radicalized strata of Muslims in Afghanistan and other Muslims traveling there to help fight the evil empire. One of these was a Saudi, Osama bin Ladin, who eventually formed al-Qaida. The mess left behind by the Soviet withdrawal led to more conflict and chaos, with only the extremist Sunni movement called the Taliban offering any semblance of security after taking Kabul in 1996. To the distaste of most Muslims in and outside of Afghanistan, the Taliban went on to implement a socioculturally puritanical form of Islam in areas under its control. The new Taliban government was content to allow al-Qaida to operate within its borders under its effective protection.

While the Soviet Union was becoming a second-rate power following its Afghani imbroglio, the United States became what many in the 1990s called a hyperpower. In the Middle East, following the successful eviction of Iraq from Kuwait, people were saying that the region was now living under a Pax Americana. Even the Syrians, bereft of Soviet backing and in need of Western investment, decided to send a mostly symbolic military force as part of the US-led UN coalition to liberate Kuwait. This apparent reordering of things created the opportunity for the Madrid peace process, jointly sponsored by the United States and a crumbling Soviet Union in the fall of 1991. It indirectly produced an accord between Israel and the PLO in 1993, again signed on the White House lawn, and it directly produced the Israeli-Jordanian peace treaty in 1994 as well as ongoing direct negotiations brokered by the United States between Israel and Syria that came tantalizingly close to a peace treaty just before Hafiz al-Assad died in June 2000—one of the enduring what-ifs, at least in my mind, of modern Middle East history. There were multilateral talks associated with the Madrid peace process discussing everything from water-sharing to region-wide economic development, and conferences were held where Arabs and Israelis mingled together to discuss potential business cooperation.

But as often happens in the Middle East, things can unravel quickly. PLO-Israeli negotiations stalled, with a last-gasp attempt brokered by US President Bill Clinton in 1999–2000 that only led to mutual recriminations and frustration on both sides. The frustration boiled over in the West Bank and Jerusalem into a Palestinian uprising, or **intifada**. Many Israelis, seeing this as the result of a decade of failed talks, along with the Palestinian branch of the Muslim Brotherhood, Hamas, establishing itself in control of the Gaza Strip in direct opposition to Israel, started to wonder if the so-called two-state solution was a fantasy. Many Palestinians were wondering the same thing. The Syrian-Israeli rapprochement ended abruptly, as Hafiz al-Assad's son, Bashar, took power formally in July 2000, backing the intifada and trying to chart out his own course amid efforts to consolidate his power in Syria. A new US president, George W. Bush, was voted into office in 2000, with neo-conservative ideas in his administration lurking just beneath the surface.

There was still a well of hope for peace in the region despite the less-than-expected overall returns of the Madrid peace process. Then came September 11, 2001, and all bets were off.

Chapter 11 Timeline

1952	Overthrow of Egyptian King Farouk by Free Officers movement
1954–1970	Gamal Abd al-Nasser in power in Egypt
1956	Suez crisis and war
1958–1961	Union of Egypt and Syria as the United Arab Republic
1960	The Organization of Petroleum Exporting Countries (OPEC) is formed
1967	Arab–Israeli war, also known as the Six-Day War
1970	Anwar al-Sadat succeeds Nasser as president of Egypt; Hafiz al-Assad comes to power in Syria
1973	Arab–Israeli war, often referred to as the October war or the Ramadan war; during the war, oil embargo imposed by the Arab members of OPEC
1979	Iranian Revolution; Egyptian-Israeli peace treaty signed; Sunni militants occupy Grand Mosque in Mecca; Soviet Invasion of Afghanistan
1980–1988	Iran–Iraq War
1982	Israeli invasion of Lebanon
1988–1989	First Palestinian *Intifada* (uprising)
1989	Fall of the Berlin Wall and symbolic end to the Cold War
1990–1991	Second Gulf War initiated by Iraq's invasion of Kuwait
1991	Beginning of Madrid peace process; dissolution of the Soviet Union
1993	PLO and Israel sign Declaration of Principles
1994	Israeli-Jordanian peace treaty
2000	Death of Syrian President Hafiz al-Assad (his son, Bashar al-Assad, assumes power)

Primary Sources

United Nations General Assembly Resolution 181

November 29, 1947

The General Assembly, having met in special session at the request of the mandatory Power to constitute and instruct a Special Committee to prepare for the consideration of the question of the future Government of Palestine at the second regular session;

Having constituted a Special Committee and instructed it to investigate all questions and issues relevant to the problem of Palestine, and to prepare proposals for the solution of the problem, and

Having received and examined the report of the Special Committee (document A/364) (1) including a number of unanimous recommendations and a plan of partition with economic union approved by the majority of the Special Committee,

Considers that the present situation in Palestine is one which is likely to impair the general welfare and friendly relations among nations;

Takes note of the declaration by the mandatory Power that it plans to complete its evacuation of Palestine by 1 August 1948;

Recommends to the United Kingdom, as the mandatory Power for Palestine, and to all other Members of the United Nations the adoption and implementation, with regard to the future Government of Palestine, of the Plan of Partition with Economic Union set out below;

PLAN OF PARTITION WITH ECONOMIC UNION

Part I. Future Constitution and Government of Palestine

A. Termination of Mandate, Partition and Independence

The Mandate for Palestine shall terminate as soon as possible but in any case not later than 1 August 1948.

The armed forces of the mandatory Power shall be progressively withdrawn from Palestine, the withdrawal to be completed as soon as possible but in any case not later than 1 August 1948.

The mandatory Power shall advise the Commission, as far in advance as possible, of its intention to terminate the mandate and to evacuate each area. The mandatory Power shall use its best endeavours to ensure that an area situated in the territory of the Jewish State, including a seaport and hinterland adequate to provide facilities for a substantial immigration, shall be evacuated at the earliest possible date and in any event not later than 1 February 1948.

Independent Arab and Jewish States and the Special International Regime for the City of Jerusalem, set forth in Part III of this Plan, shall come into existence in Palestine two months after the evacuation of the armed forces of the mandatory Power has been completed but in any case not later than 1 October 1948. The boundaries of the Arab State, the Jewish State, and the City of Jerusalem shall be as described in Parts II and III below.

The period between the adoption by the General Assembly of its recommendation on the question of Palestine and the establishment of the independence of the Arab and Jewish States shall be a transitional period.

. . .

F. Admission to Membership in the United Nations

When the independence of either the Arab or the Jewish State as envisaged in this plan has become effective and the declaration and undertaking, as envisaged in this plan, have been signed by either of them, sympathetic consideration should be given to its application for admission to membership in the United Nations in accordance with article 4 of the Charter of the United Nations.

Part II. Boundaries

A. The Arab State

The area of the Arab State in Western Galilee is bounded on the west by the Mediterranean and on the north by the frontier of the Lebanon from Ras en Naqura to a point north of Saliha. From there the boundary proceeds southwards, leaving the built-up area of Saliha in the Arab State, to join the southernmost point of this village. There it follows the western boundary line of the villages of 'Alma, Rihaniya and Teitaba, thence following the northern boundary line of Meirun village to join the Acre-Safad Sub-District boundary line. It follows this line to a point west of Es Sammu'i village and joins it again at the northernmost point of Farradiya. Thence it follows the subdistrict boundary line to the Acre-Safad main road. From here it follows the western boundary of Kafr-I'nan village until it reaches the Tiberias-Acre Sub-District boundary line, passing to the west of the junction of the Acre-Safad and Lubiya-Kafr-I'nan roads. From the south-west corner of Kafr-I'nan village the boundary line follows the western boundary of the Tiberias Sub-District to a point close to the boundary line between the villages of Maghar and 'Ellabun, thence bulging out to the west to include as much of the eastern part of the plain of Battuf as is necessary for the reservoir proposed by the Jewish Agency for the irrigation of lands to the south and east.

The boundary rejoins the Tiberias Sub-District boundary at a point on the Nazareth-Tiberias road south-east of the built-up area of Tur'an; thence it runs southwards, at first following the Sub-District boundary and then passing between the Kadoorie Agricultural School and Mount Tabor, to a point due south at the base of Mount Tabor. From here it runs due west, parallel to the horizontal grid line 230, to the north-east corner of the village lands of Tel Adashim. It then runs to the northwest corner of these lands, whence it turns south and west so as to include in the Arab State the sources of the Nazareth water supply in Yafa village. On reaching Ginneiger it follows the eastern, northern and western boundaries of the lands of this village to their south-west corner, whence it proceeds in a straight line to a point on the Haifa-Afula railway on the boundary between the villages of Sarid and El-Mujeidil. This is the point of intersection. The south-western boundary of the area of the Arab State in Galilee takes a line from this point, passing northwards along the eastern boundaries of Sarid and Gevat to the north-eastern corner of Nahalal, proceeding thence across the land of Kefar ha Horesh to a central point on the southern boundary of the village of'Ilut, thence westwards along that village boundary to the eastern boundary of Beit Lahm, thence northwards and northeastwards along its western boundary to the north-eastern corner of Waldheim and thence north-westwards across the village lands of Shafa 'Amr to the southeastern corner of Ramat Yohanan. From here it runs due north-north-east to a point on the Shafa 'Amr-Haifa road, west of its junction with the road of Ibillin. From there it proceeds north-east to a point on the southern boundary of Ibillin situated to the west of the Ibillin-Birwa road. Thence along that boundary to its westernmost point, whence it turns to the north, follows across the village land of Tamra to the north-westernmost corner and along the western boundary of Julis until it reaches the Acre-Safad road. It then runs westwards along the southern side of the Safad-Acre road to the Galilee-Haifa District boundary, from which point it follows that boundary to the sea.

The boundary of the hill country of Samaria and Judea starts on the Jordan River at the Wadi Malih south-east of Beisan and runs due west to meet the Beisan-Jericho road and then follows the western side of that road in a north-westerly direction to the junction of the boundaries of the Sub-Districts of Beisan, Nablus, and Jenin. From that point it follows the Nablus-Jenin Sub-District boundary westwards for a distance of about three kilometres and then turns north-westwards, passing to the east of the built-up areas of the villages of Jaibun and Faqqu'a, to the boundary of the Sub-Districts of Jenin and Beisan at a point northeast of Nuris. Thence it proceeds first northwestwards to a point due north of the built-up area of Zir'in and then westwards to the Afula-Jenin railway, thence north-westwards along the District boundary line to the point of intersection on the Hejaz railway. From here the boundary runs south westwards, including the built-up area and some of the land of the village of Kh. Lid in the Arab State to cross the Haifa-Jenin road at a point on the district boundary between Haifa and Samaria west of El-Mansi. It follows this boundary to the southernmost point of the village of El-Buteimat. From here it follows the northern and eastern boundaries of the village of Arara rejoining the Haifa-Samaria district boundary at Wadi 'Ara, and thence proceeding south-south-westwards in an approximately straight line joining up with the western boundary of Qaqun to a point east of the railway line on the eastern boundary of Qaqun village. From here it runs along the railway line some distance to the east of it to a point just east of the Tulkarm railway station. Thence the boundary follows a line half-way between the railway and the Tulkarm-Qalqiliya-Jaljuliya and Ras El-Ein road to a point just east of Ras El-Ein station, whence it proceeds along the railway some distance to the east of it to the point on the railway line south of the junction of the Haifa-Lydda and Beit Nabala lines, whence it proceeds along the southern border of Lydda airport to its southwest corner, thence in a south-westerly direction to a point just west of the built-up area of Sarafand El-Amar, whence it turns south, passing just to the west of the built-up area of Abu El-Fadil to the north-east corner of the lands of Beer Ya'aqov. (The boundary line should be so demarcated as to allow direct access from the Arab State to the airport.) Thence the boundary line follows the western and southern boundaries of Ramle village, to the north-east corner of El Na'ana village, thence in a straight line to the southernmost point of El Barriya, along the eastern boundary of that village and the southern boundary of Innaba village. Thence it turns north to follow the southern side of the Jaffa-Jerusalem road until El-Qubab, whence it follows the road to the boundary of Abu-Shusha. It runs along the eastern boundaries of Abu Shusha, Seidun, Hula to the southernmost point of Huida, thence westwards in a straight line to the north-eastern corner of Umm Kalkha, thence following the northern boundaries of Umm Kalkha, Qazaza and the northern and western boundaries of Mukhezin to the Gaza District boundary and thence runs across the village lands of El-Mismiya El-Kabira, and Yasur to the southern point of intersection, which is midway between the built-up areas of Yasur and Batani Sharqi.

From the southern point of intersection the boundary lines run north-westwards between the villages of Gan Yavne and Barqa to the sea at a point half-way between Nabi Yunis and Minat El-Qila, and south-eastwards to a point west of Qastina, whence it turns in a south-westerly direction, passing to the east of the built-up areas of Es Sawafir, Esh Sharqiya and Ibdis. From the south-east corner of 'Ibdis village it runs to a point southwest of the built-up area of Beit 'Affa, crossing the Hebron-El-Majdal road just to the west of the built-up area of Iraq Suweidan. Thence it proceeds southward along the western village boundary of El-Faluja to the Beersheba Sub-District boundary. It then runs across the tribal lands of 'Arab El-Jubarat to a point on the boundary between the Sub-Districts of Beersheba and Hebron north of Kh. Khuweilifa, whence it proceeds in a south-westerly direction to a point on the Beersheba-Gaza main road two kilometres to the north-west of the town. It then turns south-eastwards to reach Wadi Sab' at a point situated one kilometer to the west of it. From here it turns northeastwards and proceeds along Wadi Sab' and along the Beersheba-Hebron road for a distance of one kilometer, whence it turns eastwards and runs in a straight line to Kh. Kuseifa to join the Beersheba-Hebron Sub-District boundary. It then follows the Beersheba-Hebron boundary eastwards to a point north of Ras Ez-Zuweira, only departing from it so as to cut across the base of the indentation between vertical grid lines 150 and 160.

About five kilometres north-east of Ras Ez-Zuweira it turns north, excluding from the Arab State a strip along the coast of the Dead Sea not more than seven kilometres in depth, as far as 'Ein Geddi, whence it turns due east to join the Transjordan frontier in the Dead Sea.

The northern boundary of the Arab section of the coastal plain runs from a point between Minat El-Qila and Nabi Yunis, passing between the built-up areas of Gan Yavne and Barqa to the point of intersection. From here it turns south-westwards, running across the lands of Batani Sharqi, along the eastern boundary of the lands of Beit Daras and across the lands of Julis, leaving the built-up areas of Batani Sharqi and Julis to the westwards, as far as the north-west corner of the lands of Beit-Tima. Thence it runs east of El-Jiya across the village lands of El-Barbara along the eastern boundaries of the villages of Beit Jirja, Deir Suneid and Dimra. From the southeast corner of Dimra the boundary passes across the lands of Beit Hanun, leaving the Jewish lands of Nir-Am to the eastwards. From the south-east corner of Beit Hanun the tine runs south-west to a point south of the parallel grid line 100, then turns northwest for two kilometres, turning again in a southwesterly direction and continuing in an almost straight line to the north-west corner of the village lands of Kirbet Ikhza'a. From there it follows the boundary line of this village to its southernmost point. It then runs in a southerly direction along the vertical grid line 90 to its junction with the horizontal grid line 70. It then turns south-eastwards to Kh. El-Ruheiba and then proceeds in a southerly direction to a point known as El-Baha, beyond which it crosses the Beersheba-El 'Auja main road to the west of Kh. El-Mushrifa. From there it joins Wadi El-Zaiyatin just to the west of El-Subeita. From there it turns to the north-east and then to the south-east following this wadi and passes to the east of 'Abda to join Wadi Nafkh. It then bulges to the south-west along Wadi Nafkh, Wadi 'Ajrim and Wadi Lassan to the point where Wadi Lassan crosses the Egyptian frontier.

The area of the Arab enclave of Jaffa consists of that part of the town-planning area of Jaffa which lies to the west of the Jewish quarters lying south of Tel-Aviv, to the west of the continuation of Herzl street up to its junction with the Jaffa-Jerusalem road, to the south-west of the section of the Jaffa-Jerusalem road lying south-east of that junction, to the west of Miqve Yisrael lands, to the northwest of Holon local council area, to the north of the line linking up the north-west corner of Holon with the northeast corner of Bat Yam local council area and to the north of Bat Yam local council area. The question of Karton quarter will be decided by the Boundary Commission, bearing in mind among other considerations the desirability of including the smallest possible number of its Arab inhabitants and the largest possible number of its Jewish inhabitants in the Jewish State.

B. The Jewish State

The north-eastern sector of the Jewish State (Eastern Galilee) is bounded on the north and west by the Lebanese frontier and on the east by the frontiers of Syria and Trans-jordan. It includes the whole of the Huleh Basin, Lake Tiberias, the whole of the Beisan Sub-District, the boundary line being extended to the crest of the Gilboa mountains and the Wadi Malih. From there the Jewish State extends northwest, following the boundary described in respect of the Arab State. The Jewish section of the coastal plain extends from a point between Minat El-Qila and Nabi Yunis in the Gaza Sub-District and includes the towns of Haifa and Tel-Aviv, leaving Jaffa as an enclave of the Arab State. The eastern frontier of the Jewish State follows the boundary described in respect of the Arab State.

The Beersheba area comprises the whole of the Beersheba Sub-District, including the Negeb and the eastern part of the Gaza Sub-District, but excluding the town of Beersheba and those areas described in respect of the Arab State. It includes also a strip of land along the Dead Sea stretching from the Beersheba-Hebron Sub-District boundary line to 'Ein Geddi, as described in respect of the Arab State.

C. The City of Jerusalem

The boundaries of the City of Jerusalem are as defined in the recommendations on the City of Jerusalem. (See Part III, section B, below.)

Part III. City of Jerusalem

A. Special Regime

The City of Jerusalem shall be established as a corpus separatum under a special international regime and shall be administered by the United Nations. The Trusteeship Council shall be designated to discharge the responsibilities of the Administering Authority on behalf of the United Nations.

B. Boundaries of the City

The City of Jerusalem shall include the present municipality of Jerusalem plus the surrounding villages and towns, the most eastern of which shall be Abu Dis; the most southern, Bethlehem; the most western, 'Ein Karim (including also the built-up area of Motsa); and the most northern Shu'fat, as indicated on the attached sketch-map (annex B).

. . .

ADOPTED AT THE 128TH PLENARY MEETING:

In favour: 33

Australia, Belgium, Bolivia, Brazil, Byelorussian S.S.R., Canada, Costa Rica, Czechoslovakia, Denmark, Dominican, Republic, Ecuador, France, Guatemala, Haiti, Iceland, Liberia, Luxemburg, Netherlands, New Zealand, Nicaragua, Norway, Panama, Paraguay, Peru, Philippines, Poland, Sweden, Ukrainian S.S.R., Union of South Africa, U.S.A., U.S.S.R., Uruguay Venezuela.

Against: 13

Afghanistan, Cuba, Egypt, Greece, India, Iran, Iraq, Lebanon, Pakistan, Saudi Arabia, Syria, Turkey, Yemen.

Abstained: 10

Argentina, Chile, China, Colombia, El Salvador, Ethiopia, Honduras, Mexico, United Kingdom, Yugoslavia.

Source: Available from the Avalon Project, Lillian Goldman Law Library, Yale Law School, http://avalon.law.yale.edu/20th_century/res181.asp.

Speech by President Nasser on Nationalization of the Suez Canal

September 15, 1956

In these decisive days in the history of mankind, these days in which truth struggles to have itself recognized in international chaos where powers of evil domination and imperialism have prevailed, Egypt stands firmly to preserve her sovereignty. Your country stands solidly and staunchly to preserve her dignity against imperialistic schemes of a number of nations who have uncovered their desires for domination and supremacy.

In these days and in such circumstances Egypt has resolved to show the world that when small nations decide to preserve their sovereignty, they will do that all right and that when these small nations are fully determined to defend their rights and maintain their dignity, they will undoubtedly succeed in achieving their ends. . . .

I am speaking in the name of every Egyptian Arab and in the name of all free countries and of all those who believe in liberty and are ready to defend it. I am speaking in the name of principles proclaimed by these countries in the Atlantic Charter. But they are now violating these principles and it has become our lot to shoulder the responsibility of reaffirming and establishing them anew. . . .

We have tried by all possible means to cooperate with those countries which claim to assist smaller nations and which promised to collaborate with us but they demanded their fees in advance. This we refused so they started to fight with us. They said they will pay toward building the High Dam and then they withdrew their offer and cast doubts on the Egyptian economy. Are we to declaim [*sic,* disclaim?] our sovereign right? Egypt insists her sovereignty must remain intact and refuses to give up any part of that sovereignty for the sake of money.

Egypt nationalized the Egyptian Suez Canal company. When Egypt granted the concession to de Lesseps it was stated in the concession between the Egyptian Government and the Egyptian company that the company of the Suez Canal is an Egyptian company subject to Egyptian authority. Egypt nationalized this Egyptian company and declared freedom of navigation will be preserved.

But the imperialists became angry. Britain and France said Egypt grabbed the Suez Canal as if itwere part of France or Britain.The British Foreign Secretary forgot that only two years ago he signed an agreement stating the Suez Canal is an integral part of Egypt.

Egypt declared she was ready to negotiate. But as soon as negotiations began threats and intimidations started. . . .

Eden stated in the House of Commons there shall be no discrimination between states using the canal. We on our part reaffirm that and declare there is no discrimination between canal users. He also said Egypt shall not be allowed to succeed because that would spell success for Arab nationalism and would be against their policy, which aims at the protection of Israel.

Today they are speaking of a new association whose main objective would be to rob Egypt of the canal and deprive her of rightful canal dues. Suggestions made by Eden in the House of Commons which have been backed by France and the United States are a clear violation of the 1888 convention, since it is impossible to have two bodies organizing navigation in the canal. . . .

By stating that by succeeding, Abdel Nasser would weaken Britain's stand against Arab nationalism, Eden is in fact admitting his real objective is not Abdel Nasser as such but rather to defeat Arab nationalism and crush its cause. Eden speaks and finds his own answer. A month ago he let out the cry that he was after Abdel Nasser. Today the Egyptian people are fully conscious of their sovereign rights and Arab nationalism is fully awakened to its new destiny. . . .

Those who attack Egypt will never leave Egypt alive. We shall fight a regular war, a total war, a guerrilla war. Those who attack Egypt will soon realize they brought disaster upon themselves. He who attacks Egypt attacks the whole Arab world. They say in their papers the whole thing will be over in forty-eight hours. They do not know how strong we really are.

We believe in international law. But we will never submit. We shall show the world how a small country can stand in the face of great powers threatening with armed might. Egypt might be a small power but she is great inasmuch as she has faith in her power and convictions. I feel quite certain every Egyptian shares the same convictions as I do and believes in everything I am stressing now.

We shall defend our freedom and independence to the last drop of our blood. This is the staunch feeling of every Egyptian. The whole Arab nation will stand by us in our common fight against aggression and domination. Free peoples, too, people who are really free will stand by us and support us against the forces of tyranny. . . .

Source: Available from the Modern History Sourcebook, Fordham University, http://www.fordham.edu/halsall/mod/1956Nasser-suez1.html.

Remarks by Golda Meir to President Sadat in the Knesset, November 21, 1977

Mr. President, I'm sure that from the moment your plane landed at Lydda Airport, and as you drove through the streets of Jerusalem, you must have felt, in all your encounters with the many people who turned out to meet you—the little children; the mothers with babies in their arms; the old people; the people who were born in this country, the second, third, fourth and fifth generations, and those who have come recently—that all, without exception, were overjoyed to see you in our Land.

When asked, many years ago, when I thought that peace would come to this region to our country and to our neighbouring countries—I said: I do not know the date, but I do know under what conditions it will come—when there will be a leader, a great leader of an Arab country. He will wake up one morning and feel sorry for his own people, for his own sons who have fallen in battle, and that day will be the beginning of peace between us.

Mr. President, we have a saying in Hebrew: "zchut rishonim." In English, this means "the privilege of being the first." I congratulate you, Mr. President, that you are privileged to be the first great Arab leader of the greatest country among our neighbours to come to us, with courage and determination, despite so many difficulties, for the sake of your sons, as well as for the sake of our; for the sake of all mothers who mourn sons that fell in battle. No mother should have to give birth to a son in the fear that he may fall in battle. For the sake of all our sons and all our children, not only those who are alive today but also those to be born in future generations—you have come to us and said: let us have peace; let the war of 1973 be the last war between us.

You have come telling us that, from now on, you are prepared to live in peace with us. I can assure you, Mr. President, that as far as we are concerned, the desire for peace, the hope of peace and the dream of peace have never left the hearts of a single one of us. We have come back to this country to live in peace. We have come back to this country to live. We have come back to this country to create. In this room, you will see people who, for the first time in their lives, have climbed hills and planted trees in this country; who, for the first time, have gone down to the desert—it was considered a desert, a God-forsaken land and have made it green, so that our children can live and play everywhere in it. Many of these children—very many of them—also enjoy the privilege of having been the first, after centuries upon centuries, to bring life to the desert, to the swamps and to the hills of this country. All this we have done for peace—to live in peace; to live, but to live in peace.

Mr. President, we listened to you last night and we heard your appeal for peace. When I was in office, and I am sure this was true for everyone who preceded me and for those who succeeded me in office—I hope that the day would come when we could meet with a leader of one of the Arab countries and hold a discussion with him. Not that we ever imagined that, at the very first meeting, we would come with pens in our hands, ready to sign a peace treaty. But our hope was that we would hold discussions on points of disagreement, and that we would discuss these points face-to-face, rather than through intermediaries for, no matter how successfully intermediaries may report to both of us, it is not the same. As I sit here and look at you, and as I heard you in person last night, it is not the same.

Of course, we must all realize that the path leading to peace may be a difficult one, but not as difficult as that path which leads to war. What Israel wants—what this group with which you are meeting today has wanted, from the very beginning, is territorial compromise, in accordance with the programme it adopted immediately after the war of 1967. As a matter of fact, Israel has made and accepted compromises ever since 1947. I can say, in all sincerity, that we have desired additional territory. We have always been prepared to live within our existing boundaries.

We will not go into history today, but what we want to tell you is that we were, and are, prepared for territorial compromise on all our borders—with one condition: these borders will give us security, and protect us from danger, so that we will never be in need, God forbid, at any time, of help from abroad in order to defend ourselves. We have never sought such help from others; nobody has ever come to defend us. The blood that has been shed, to our sorrow, has been our own. We don't want to shed the blood of others.

With us today is Mr. Rabin. After the war of 1967, he was awarded an Honorary degree by the Hebrew University of Jerusalem and, in his words of acceptance, as Chief of Staff, he said: "Here is the Israeli army that came back victorious. It came back a sad army, despite its victory; sad because of our men who fell, but also because of our sons who were compelled to shoot others." These two things we do not want: we do not want to be shot at—and, believe me—we do not want to shoot others.

Therefore, we want borders within which, when we do sign peace treaties, all Israelis will be assured that they live in security, without having to rely on international guarantees. I do not think we will need these when we have peace -neither we shall need them, nor you. But we must have borders that will enable us—if, God forbid, something should happen in the future—to defend ourselves. Territorial compromise—yes, but not compromise with our security! Each country, each nation, will decide its security requirements. When we talk of territorial compromise, it is essential that we remember this.

Mr. President. We, the People of Israel, are the last to be insensitive to the sorrow of others. We have never said that we want the Palestinian Arabs to remain as they are—in camps, in misery, dependent on charity. We do not wish to be dependent upon others, nor do we wish them to be dependent upon others. Had is been within our power, there would never have been a problem of this kind. Of course, we realize that there are Palestinian Arabs and we believe there is a solution, one that is both good for them and safe for us.

Because we believe this, we believe also that there is no connection between our opposition to another state between us and Jordan—a Palestinian state which would be small, probably not viable and perhaps forced to expand—and between our awareness of the need to solve the problem of the Palestinian Arabs. Our opposition to another state is based on Israel's most vital security requirements. Mr. President, should we agree to the establishment of such a state, there would be only ten miles between the Mediterranean and the borders of this state. You cannot expect us to feel secure within such borders.

Of course, we favour a solution for the Palestinian Arabs, and believe that in the programme of this group gathered here today with you, such a solution exists. This programme, formulated prior to the elections and still valid to this day, states that in our peace treaty with Jordan, there must be a solution for the Palestinian Arabs, so the camps may be wiped out and become a thing of the past. But not at the expense of Israel's security. If there were no solution, it would be a terrible problem for us. But there is a solution to this problem too.

Therefore, we say to you, Mr. President, that, while we do not agree with everything you said last night—surely, this does not surprise you—we deeply appreciate your call for peace, and believe in your sincere desire for it, just as I hope you believe in our sincere desire for it. Now, let us go forward. Even if we do not reach agreement on everything this morning, let us, at least, conclude one thing: the beginnings that you have made, with such courage and with such hope for peace, must go on, continuing face-to-face between ourselves and you, so that even an old lady like myself will live to see the day—yes, you always call me an old lady—and regardless of whoever signs on Israel's behalf, I want to live to see that day—that peace reigns between you and us, peace between ourselves and all our neighbours.

And, Mr. President, as a grandmother to a grandfather, may I give you a little present for your new grand-daughter, and thank you for the present you have given me.

Source: Available from the Jewish Virtual Library, https://www.jewishvirtuallibrary.org/remarks-by-golda-meir-to-president-sadat-in-the-knesset.

Excerpts from speech by Egyptian President Anwar Sadat to the Israeli Knesset, November 20, 1977

In the name of God, the Gracious and Merciful.

Mr. Speaker, Ladies and Gentlemen:

Peace and the mercy of God Almighty be upon you and may peace be for us all, God willing. Peace for us all on the Arab land, and in Israel as well, as in every part of this big world, which is so complexed by its sanguinary conflicts, disturbed by its sharp contradictions, menaced now and then by destructive wars launched by man to annihilate his fellow man. Finally, amid the ruins of what man has built and the remains of the victims of Mankind, there emerges neither victor nor vanquished. The only vanquished remains man, God's most sublime creation, man whom God has created—as Ghandi the apostle of peace puts it: to forge ahead to mould the way of life and worship God Almighty.

I come to you today on solid ground, to shape a new life, to establish peace. We all, on this land, the land of God; we all, Muslims, Christians and Jews, worship God and no one but God. God's teachings and commandments are love, sincerity, purity and peace.

I do not blame all those who received my decision—when I announced it to the entire world before the Egyptian People's Assembly—with surprise and amazement. Some, gripped by the violent surprise, believed that my decision was no more than verbal juggling to cater for world public opinion. Others, still, interpreted it as political tactics to camouflage my intention of launching a new war. I would go as far as to tell you that one of my aides at the Presidential Office contacted me at a late hour following my return home from the People's Assembly and sounded worried as he asked me: "Mr. President, what would be our reaction if Israel should actually extend an invitation to you?" I replied calmly, I will accept it immediately. I have declared that I will go to the end of the world; I will go to Israel, for I want to put before the People of Israel all the facts.

I can see the point of all those who were astounded by my decision or those who had any doubts as to the sincerity of the intentions behind the declaration of my decision. No one would have ever conceived that the President of the biggest Arab State, which bears the heaviest burden and the top responsibility pertaining to the cause of war and peace in the Middle East, could declare his readiness to go to the land of the adversary while we were still in a state of war. Rather, we all are still bearing the consequences of four fierce wars waged within thirty years. The families of the 1973 October War are still moaning under the cruel pains of widowhood and bereavement of sons, fathers and brothers.

As I have already declared, I have not consulted, as far as this decision is concerned, with any of my colleagues and brothers, the Arab Heads of State or the confrontation States. Those of them who contacted me, following the declaration of this decision, expressed their objection, because the feeling of utter suspicion and absolute lack of confidence between the Arab States and the Palestinian People on the one hand, and Israel on the other, still surges in us all. It is sufficient to say that many months in which peace could have been brought about had been wasted over differences and fruitless discussions on the procedure for the convocation of the Geneva Conference, all showing utter suspicion and absolute lack of confidence.

But, to be absolutely frank with you, I took this decision after long thinking, knowing that it constitutes a grave risk for, if God Almighty has made it my fate to assume the responsibility on behalf of the Egyptian People and to share in the fate-determining responsibility of the Arab Nation and the Palestinian People, the main duty dictated by this responsibility is to exhaust all and every means in a bid to save my Egyptian Arab People and the entire Arab Nation the horrors of new, shocking and destructive wars, the dimensions of which are foreseen by no other than God himself.

After long thinking, I was convinced that the obligation of responsibility before God, and before the people, make it incumbent on me that I should go to the farthest corner of the world, even to Jerusalem, to address Members of the Knesset, the representatives of the People of Israel, and acquaint them with all the facts surging in me. Then, I would leave you to decide for yourselves. Following this, may God Almighty determine our fate.

Ladies and Gentlemen, there are moments in the life of nations and peoples when it is incumbent on those known for their wisdom and clarity of vision to overlook the past, with all its complexities and weighing memories, in a bold drive towards new horizons. Those who, like us, are shouldering the same responsibility entrusted to us, are the first who should have the courage to take fate-determining decisions which are in consonance with the circumstances. We must all rise above all forms of fanaticism, self-deception and obsolete theories of superiority. The most important thing is never to forget that infallibility is the prerogative of God alone.

If I said that I wanted to save all the Arab People the horrors of shocking and destructive wars, I most sincerely declare before you that I have the same feelings and bear the same responsibility towards all and every man on earth, and certainly towards the Israeli People.

Any life lost in war is a human life, irrespective of its being that of an Israeli or an Arab. A wife who becomes a widow is a human being entitled to a happy family life, whether she be an Arab or an Israeli. Innocent children who are deprived of the care and compassion of their parents are ours, be they living on Arab or Israeli land. They command our top responsibility to afford them a comfortable life today and tomorrow.

For the sake of them all, for the safeguard of the lives of all our sons and brothers, for affording our communities the opportunity to work for the progress and happiness of man and his right to a dignified life, for our responsibilities before the generations to come, for a smile on the face of every child born on our land—for all that, I have taken my decision to come to you, despite all hazards, to deliver my address.

. . . First: I have not come here for a separate agreement between Egypt and Israel. This is not part of the policy of Egypt. The problem is not that of Egypt and Israel. Any separate peace between Egypt and Israel, or between any Arab confrontation State and Israel, will not bring permanent peace based on justice in the entire region. Rather, even if peace between all the confrontation States and Israel were achieved, in the absence of a just solution to the Palestinian problem, never will there be that durable and just peace upon which the entire world insists today.

Second: I have not come to you to seek a partial peace, namely to terminate the state of belligerency at this stage, and put off the entire problem to a subsequent stage. This is not the radical solution that would steer us to permanent peace.

Equally, I have not come to you for a third disengagement agreement in Sinai, or in the Golan and the West Bank. For this would mean that we are merely delaying the ignition of the fuse; it would mean that we are lacking the courage to confront peace, that we are too weak to shoulder the burdens and responsibilities of a durable peace based on justice.

I have come to you so that together we might build a durable peace based on justice, to avoid the shedding of one single drop of blood from an Arab or an Israeli. It is for this reason that I have proclaimed my readiness to go to the farthest corner of the world.

Here, I would go back to the answer to the big question: how can we achieve a durable peace based on justice?

In my opinion, and I declare it to the whole world from this forum, the answer is neither difficult nor impossible, despite long years of feud, blood vengeance, spite and hatred, and breeding generations on concepts of total rift and deep-rooted animosity. The answer is not difficult, nor is it impossible, if we sincerely and faithfully follow a straight line.

You want to live with us in this part of the world. In all sincerity, I tell you, we welcome you among us, with full security and safety. This, in itself, is a tremendous turning point; one of the landmarks of a decisive historical change.

We used to reject you. We had our reasons and our claims, yes. We used to brand you as "so-called" Israel, yes. We were together in international conferences and organizations and our representatives did not, and still do not, exchange greetings, yes. This has happened and is still happening.

It is also true that we used to set, as a precondition for any negotiations with you, a mediator who would meet separately with each party. Through this procedure, the talks of the first and second disengagement agreements took place.

Our delegates met in the first Geneva Conference without exchanging a direct word. Yes, this has happened.

Yet, today I tell you, and declare it to the whole world, that we accept to live with you in permanent peace based on justice. We do not want to encircle you or be encircled ourselves by destructive missiles ready for launching, nor by the shells of grudges and hatred. I have announced on more than one occasion that Israel has become a fait accompli, recognized by the world, and that the two superpowers have undertaken the responsibility of its security and the defence of its existence.

As we really and truly seek peace, we really and truly welcome you to live among us in peace and security.

. . . I have come to Jerusalem, as the City of Peace, which will always remain as a living embodiment of coexistence among believers of the three religions. It is inadmissible that anyone should conceive the special status of the City of Jerusalem within the framework of annexation or expansionism, but it should be a free and open city for all believers.

Above all, the city should not be severed from those who have made it their abode for centuries. Instead of awakening the prejudices of the Crusaders, we should revive the spirit of Ornar ibn el-Khattab and Saladdin, namely the spirit of tolerance and respect for rights. The holy shrines of Islam and Christianity are not only places of worship, but a living testimony of our uninterrupted presence here politically, spiritually and intellectually. Let us make no mistake about the importance and reverence we Christians and Muslims attach to Jerusalem.

Let me tell you, without the slightest hesitation, that I did not come to you under this dome to make a request that your troops evacuate the occupied territories. Complete withdrawal from the Arab territories occupied in 1967 is a logical and undisputed fact. Nobody should plead for that. Any talk about permanent peace based on justice, and any move to ensure our coexistence in peace and security in this part of the world, would become meaningless, while you occupy Arab territories by force of arms. For there is no peace that could be in consonance with, or be built on, the occupation of the land of others. Otherwise, it would not be a serious peace.

Yes, this is a foregone conclusion which is not open to discussion or debate—if intentions are sincere and if endeavours to establish a just and durable peace for ours and the generations to come are genuine.

As for the Palestinians cause, nobody could deny that it is the crux of the entire problem. Nobody in the world could accept, today, slogans propagated here in Israel, ignoring the existence of the Palestinian People, and questioning their whereabouts. The cause of the Palestinian People and their legitimate rights are no longer ignored or denied today by anybody. Rather, nobody who has the ability of judgement can deny or ignore it.

It is an acknowledged fact received by the world community, both in the East and in the West, with support and recognition in international documents and official statements. It is of no use to anybody to turn deaf ears to its resounding voice which is being heard day and night, or to overlook its historical reality. Even the United States, your first ally which is absolutely committed to safeguard Israel's security and existence, and which offered and still offers Israel every moral, material and military support—I say—even the United States has opted to face up to reality and facts, and admit that the Palestinian People are entitled to legitimate rights and that the Palestinian problem is the core and essence of the conflict and that, so long as it continues to be unresolved, the conflict will continue to aggravate, reaching new dimensions. In all sincerity, I tell you that there can be no peace without the Palestinians. It is a grave error of unpredictable consequences to overlook or brush aside this cause.

I shall not indulge in past events since the Balfour Declaration sixty years ago. You are well acquainted with the relevant facts. If you have found the legal and moral justification to set up a national home on a land that did not all belong to you, it is incumbent upon you to show understanding of the insistence of the People of Palestine on establishing, once again (sic) a state on their land. When some extremists ask the Palestinians to give up this sublime objective, this, in fact, means asking them to renounce their identity and every hope for the future.

. . . Conceive with me a peace agreement in Geneva that we would herald to a world thirsty for peace, a peace agreement based on the following points:

> First: ending the Israeli occupation of the Arab territories occupied in 1967.
> Second: achievement of the fundamental rights of the Palestinian People and their right to self-determination, including their right to establish their own state.
> Third: the right of all states in the area to live in peace within their boundaries, which will be secure and guaranteed through procedures to be agreed upon, which provide appropriate security to international boundaries, in addition to appropriate international guarantees.
> Fourth: commitment of all states in the region to administer the relations among them in accordance with the objectives and principles of the United Nations Charter, particularly the principles concerning the non-resort to force and the solution of differences among them by peaceful means.
> Fifth: ending the state of belligerency in the region.

Ladies and Gentlemen, peace is not the mere endorsement of written lines; rather, it is a rewriting of history. Peace is not a game of calling for peace to defend certain whims or hide certain ambitions. Peace is a giant struggle against all and every ambition and whim. Perhaps the examples taken from ancient and modern history teach us all that missiles, warships and nuclear weapons cannot establish security. Rather, they destroy what peace and security build. For the sake of our peoples, and for the sake of the civilizations made by man, we have to defend man everywhere against the rule of the force of arms, so that we may endow the rule of humanity with all the power of the values and principles that promote the sublime position of Mankind.

Source: Available from the Jewish Virtual Library, https://www.jewishvirtuallibrary.org/address-by-egyptian-president-anwar-sadat-to-the-knesset.

Camp David Accords: The Framework for Peace in the Middle East

Muhammad Anwar al-Sadat, President of the Arab Republic of Egypt, and Menachem Begin, Prime Minister of Israel, met with Jimmy Carter, President of the United States of America, at Camp David from September 5 to September 17, 1978, and have agreed on the following framework for peace in the Middle East. They invite other parties to the Arab–Israel conflict to adhere to it.

Preamble

The search for peace in the Middle East must be guided by the following:

- The agreed basis for a peaceful settlement of the conflict between Israel and its neighbors is United Nations Security Council Resolution 242, in all its parts.
- After four wars during 30 years, despite intensive human efforts, the Middle East, which is the cradle of civilization and the birthplace of three great religions, does not enjoy the blessings of peace. The people of the Middle East yearn for peace so that the vast human and natural resources of the region can be turned to the pursuits of peace and so that this area can become a model for coexistence and cooperation among nations.
- The historic initiative of President Sadat in visiting Jerusalem and the reception accorded to him by the parliament, government and people of Israel, and the reciprocal visit of Prime Minister Begin to Ismailia, the peace proposals made by both leaders, as well as the warm reception of these missions by the peoples of both countries, have created an unprecedented opportunity for peace which must not be lost if this generation and future generations are to be spared the tragedies of war.
- The provisions of the Charter of the United Nations and the other accepted norms of international law and legitimacy now provide accepted standards for the conduct of relations among all states.
- To achieve a relationship of peace, in the spirit of Article 2 of the United Nations Charter, future negotiations between Israel and any neighbor prepared to negotiate peace and security with it are necessary for the purpose of carrying out all the provisions and principles of Resolutions 242 and 338.
- Peace requires respect for the sovereignty, territorial integrity and political independence of every state in the area and their right to live in peace within secure and recognized boundaries free from threats or acts of force. Progress toward that goal can accelerate movement toward a new era of reconciliation in the Middle East marked by cooperation in promoting economic development, in maintaining stability and in assuring security.

- Security is enhanced by a relationship of peace and by cooperation between nations which enjoy normal relations. In addition, under the terms of peace treaties, the parties can, on the basis of reciprocity, agree to special security arrangements such as demilitarized zones, limited armaments areas, early warning stations, the presence of international forces, liaison, agreed measures for monitoring and other arrangements that they agree are useful.

Framework

Taking these factors into account, the parties are determined to reach a just, comprehensive, and durable settlement of the Middle East conflict through the conclusion of peace treaties based on Security Council resolutions 242 and 338 in all their parts. Their purpose is to achieve peace and good neighborly relations. They recognize that for peace to endure, it must involve all those who have been most deeply affected by the conflict. They therefore agree that this framework, as appropriate, is intended by them to constitute a basis for peace not only between Egypt and Israel, but also between Israel and each of its other neighbors which is prepared to negotiate peace with Israel on this basis. With that objective in mind, they have agreed to proceed as follows:

- **West Bank and Gaza**

  Egypt, Israel, Jordan and the representatives of the Palestinian people should participate in negotiations on the resolution of the Palestinian problem in all its aspects. To achieve that objective, negotiations relating to the West Bank and Gaza should proceed in three stages:

1. Egypt and Israel agree that, in order to ensure a peaceful and orderly transfer of authority, and taking into account the security concerns of all the parties, there should be transitional arrangements for the West Bank and Gaza for a period not exceeding five years. In order to provide full autonomy to the inhabitants, under these arrangements the Israeli military government and its civilian administration will be withdrawn as soon as a self-governing authority has been freely elected by the inhabitants of these areas to replace the existing military government. To negotiate the details of a transitional arrangement, Jordan will be invited to join the negotiations on the basis of this framework. These new arrangements should give due consideration both to the principle of self-government by the inhabitants of these territories and to the legitimate security concerns of the parties involved.
2. Egypt, Israel, and Jordan will agree on the modalities for establishing elected self-governing authority in the West Bank and Gaza. The delegations of Egypt and Jordan may include Palestinians from the West Bank and Gaza or other Palestinians as mutually agreed. The parties will negotiate an agreement which will define the powers and

responsibilities of the self-governing authority to be exercised in the West Bank and Gaza. A withdrawal of Israeli armed forces will take place and there will be a redeployment of the remaining Israeli forces into specified security locations. The agreement will also include arrangements for assuring internal and external security and public order. A strong local police force will be established, which may include Jordanian citizens. In addition, Israeli and Jordanian forces will participate in joint patrols and in the manning of control posts to assure the security of the borders.

3. When the self-governing authority (administrative council) in the West Bank and Gaza is established and inaugurated, the transitional period of five years will begin. As soon as possible, but not later than the third year after the beginning of the transitional period, negotiations will take place to determine the final status of the West Bank and Gaza and its relationship with its neighbors and to conclude a peace treaty between Israel and Jordan by the end of the transitional period. These negotiations will be conducted among Egypt, Israel, Jordan and the elected representatives of the inhabitants of the West Bank and Gaza. Two separate but related committees will be convened, one committee, consisting of representatives of the four parties which will negotiate and agree on the final status of the West Bank and Gaza, and its relationship with its neighbors, and the second committee, consisting of representatives of Israel and representatives of Jordan to be joined by the elected representatives of the inhabitants of the West Bank and Gaza, to negotiate the peace treaty between Israel and Jordan, taking into account the agreement reached in the final status of the West Bank and Gaza. The negotiations shall be based on all the provisions and principles of UN Security Council Resolution 242. The negotiations will resolve, among other matters, the location of the boundaries and the nature of the security arrangements. The solution from the negotiations must also recognize the legitimate right of the Palestinian peoples and their just requirements. In this way, the Palestinians will participate in the determination of their own future through:

   i. The negotiations among Egypt, Israel, Jordan and the representatives of the inhabitants of the West Bank and Gaza to agree on the final status of the West Bank and Gaza and other outstanding issues by the end of the transitional period.
   ii. Submitting their agreements to a vote by the elected representatives of the inhabitants of the West Bank and Gaza.
   iii. Providing for the elected representatives of the inhabitants of the West Bank and Gaza to decide how they shall govern themselves consistent with the provisions of their agreement.
   iv. Participating as stated above in the work of the committee negotiating the peace treaty between Israel and Jordan.

v. All necessary measures will be taken and provisions made to assure the security of Israel and its neighbors during the transitional period and beyond. To assist in providing such security, a strong local police force will be constituted by the self-governing authority. It will be composed of inhabitants of the West Bank and Gaza. The police will maintain liaison on internal security matters with the designated Israeli, Jordanian, and Egyptian officers.
vi. During the transitional period, representatives of Egypt, Israel, Jordan, and the self-governing authority will constitute a continuing committee to decide by agreement on the modalities of admission of persons displaced from the West Bank and Gaza in 1967, together with necessary measures to prevent disruption and disorder. Other matters of common concern may also be dealt with by this committee.
vii. Egypt and Israel will work with each other and with other interested parties to establish agreed procedures for a prompt, just and permanent implementation of the resolution of the refugee problem.

- **Egypt-Israel**

1. Egypt-Israel undertake not to resort to the threat or the use of force to settle disputes. Any disputes shall be settled by peaceful means in accordance with the provisions of Article 33 of the U.N. Charter.
2. In order to achieve peace between them, the parties agree to negotiate in good faith with a goal of concluding within three months from the signing of the Framework a peace treaty between them while inviting the other parties to the conflict to proceed simultaneously to negotiate and conclude similar peace treaties with a view the achieving a comprehensive peace in the area. The Framework for the Conclusion of a Peace Treaty between Egypt and Israel will govern the peace negotiations between them. The parties will agree on the modalities and the timetable for the implementation of their obligations under the treaty.

- **Associated Principles**

1. Egypt and Israel state that the principles and provisions described below should apply to peace treaties between Israel and each of its neighbors—Egypt, Jordan, Syria and Lebanon.
2. Signatories shall establish among themselves relationships normal to states at peace with one another. To this end, they should undertake to abide by all the provisions of the U.N. Charter. Steps to be taken in this respect include:

   a. full recognition;
   b. abolishing economic boycotts;
   c. guaranteeing that under their jurisdiction the citizens of the other parties shall enjoy the protection of the due process of law.

3. Signatories should explore possibilities for economic development in the context of final peace treaties, with the objective of contributing to the atmosphere of peace, cooperation and friendship which is their common goal.
4. Claims commissions may be established for the mutual settlement of all financial claims.
5. The United States shall be invited to participate in the talks on matters related to the modalities of the implementation of the agreements and working out the timetable for the carrying out of the obligations of the parties.
6. The United Nations Security Council shall be requested to endorse the peace treaties and ensure that their provisions shall not be violated. The permanent members of the Security Council shall be requested to underwrite the peace treaties and ensure respect or the provisions. They shall be requested to conform their policies and actions with the undertaking contained in this Framework.

For the Government of the Arab Republic of Egypt: Muhammed Anwar al-Sadat
For the Government of Israel: Menachem Begin
Witnessed by: Jimmy Carter, President of the United State of America

Camp David Accords: Framework for the Conclusion of a Peace Treaty between Egypt and Israel

In order to achieve peace between them, Israel and Egypt agree to negotiate in good faith with a goal of concluding within three months of the signing of this framework a peace treaty between them:
It is agreed that:

- The site of the negotiations will be under a United Nations flag at a location or locations to be mutually agreed.
- All of the principles of U.N. Resolution 242 will apply in this resolution of the dispute between Israel and Egypt.
- Unless otherwise mutually agreed, terms of the peace treaty will be implemented between two and three years after the peace treaty is signed.
- The following matters are agreed between the parties:

  1. the full exercise of Egyptian sovereignty up to the internationally recognized border between Egypt and mandated Palestine;
  2. the withdrawal of Israeli armed forces from the Sinai;
  3. the use of airfields left by the Israelis near al-Arish, Rafah, Ras en-Naqb, and Sharm el-Sheikh for civilian purposes only, including possible commercial use only by all nations;
  4. the right of free passage by ships of Israel through the Gulf of Suez and the Suez Canal on the basis of the Constantinople Convention of 1888 applying to all nations; the Strait of Tiran and Gulf of Aqaba are

international waterways to be open to all nations for unimpeded and nonsuspendable freedom of navigation and overflight;
5. the construction of a highway between the Sinai and Jordan near Eilat with guaranteed free and peaceful passage by Egypt and Jordan; and
6. the stationing of military forces listed below.

Stationing of Forces

- No more than one division (mechanized or infantry) of Egyptian armed forces will be stationed within an area lying approximately 50 km. (30 miles) east of the Gulf of Suez and the Suez Canal.
- Only United Nations forces and civil police equipped with light weapons to perform normal police functions will be stationed within an area lying west of the international border and the Gulf of Aqaba, varying in width from 20 km. (12 miles) to 40 km. (24 miles).
- In the area within 3 km. (1.8 miles) east of the international border there will be Israeli limited military forces not to exceed four infantry battalions and United Nations observers.
- Border patrol units not to exceed three battalions will supplement the civil police in maintaining order in the area not included above.
- The exact demarcation of the above areas will be as decided during the peace negotiations.
- Early warning stations may exist to insure compliance with the terms of the agreement.
- United Nations forces will be stationed:

    1. in part of the area in the Sinai lying within about 20 km. of the Mediterranean Sea and adjacent to the international border, and
    2. in the Sharm el-Sheikh area to insure freedom of passage through the Strait of Tiran; and these forces will not be removed unless such removal is approved by the Security Council of the United Nations with a unanimous vote of the five permanent members.

- After a peace treaty is signed, and after the interim withdrawal is complete, normal relations will be established between Egypt and Israel, including full recognition, including diplomatic, economic and cultural relations; termination of economic boycotts and barriers to the free movement of goods and people; and mutual protection of citizens by the due process of law.

Interim Withdrawal

Between three months and nine months after the signing of the peace treaty, all Israeli forces will withdraw east of a line extending from a point east of El-Arish to Ras Muhammad, the exact location of this line to be determined by mutual agreement.

For the Government of the Arab Republic of Egypt: Muhammed Anwar al-Sadat
For the Government of Israel: Menachem Begin
Witnessed by: Jimmy Carter, President of the United State of America

Author's note: In addition to this text there was an "Annex to the Framework Agreements" consisting of "Exchanges of Letters" between Carter, Sadat, and Begin further delineating and clarifying various aspects of the accords.

Source: The Jimmy Carter Presidential Library and Museum, https://www.jimmycarterlibrary.gov/research/camp_david_accords.

Annual State of the Union Message (the Carter Doctrine), 1980

Appendix C

This last few months has not been an easy time for any of us. As we meet tonight, it has never been more clear that the state of our Union depends on the state of the world. And tonight, as throughout our own generation, freedom and peace in the world depend on the state of our Union.

The 1980s have been born in turmoil, strife, and change. This is a time of challenge to our interests and our values and it's a time that tests our wisdom and our skills.

At this time in Iran, 50 Americans are still held captive, innocent victims of terrorism and anarchy. Also at this moment, massive Soviet troops are attempting to subjugate the fiercely independent and deeply religious people of Afghanistan. These two acts—one of international terrorism and one of military aggression—present a serious challenge to the United States of America and to all the nations of the world. Together, we will meet these threats to peace.

I'm determined that the United States will remain the strongest of all nations, but our power will never be used to initiate a threat to the security of any nation or to the rights of any human being. We seek to be and to remain secure—a nation at peace in a stable world. But to be secure we must face the world as it is.

Three basic developments have helped to shape our challenges: the steady growth and increased projection of Soviet military power beyond its own borders; the overwhelming dependence of the Western democracies on oil supplies from the Middle East; and the press of social and religious and economic and political change in the many nations of the developing world, exemplified by the revolution in Iran.

Each of these factors is important in its own right. Each interacts with the others. All must be faced together, squarely and courageously. We will face these challenges, and we will meet them with the best that is in us. And we will not fail.

In response to the abhorrent act in Iran, our Nation has never been aroused and unified so greatly in peacetime. Our position is clear. The United States will not yield to blackmail.

We continue to pursue these specific goals: first, to protect the present and long-range interests of the United States; secondly, to preserve the lives of the American hostages and to secure, as quickly as possible, their safe release, if possible, to avoid bloodshed which might further endanger the lives of our fellow citizens; to enlist the help of other nations in condemning this act of violence, which is shocking and violates the moral and the legal standards of a civilized world; and also to convince and to persuade the Iranian leaders that the real danger to their nation lies in the north, in the Soviet Union and from the Soviet troops now in Afghanistan, and that the unwarranted Iranian quarrel with the United States hampers their response to this far greater danger to them.

If the American hostages are harmed, a severe price will be paid. We will never rest until every one of the American hostages are released.

But now we face a broader and more fundamental challenge in this region because of the recent military action of the Soviet Union.

Now, as during the last 3 1/2 decades, the relationship between our country, the United States of America, and the Soviet Union is the most critical factor in determining whether the world will live at peace or be engulfed in global conflict.

Since the end of the Second World War, America has led other nations in meeting the challenge of mounting Soviet power. This has not been a simple or a static relationship. Between us there has been cooperation, there has been competition, and at times there has been confrontation. . . .

We superpowers also have the responsibility to exercise restraint in the use of our great military force. The integrity and the independence of weaker nations must not be threatened. They must know that in our presence they are secure.

But now the Soviet Union has taken a radical and an aggressive new step. It's using its great military power against a relatively defenseless nation. The implications of the Soviet invasion of Afghanistan could pose the most serious threat to the peace since the Second World War.

The vast majority of nations on Earth have condemned this latest Soviet attempt to extend its colonial domination of others and have demanded the immediate withdrawal of Soviet troops. The Moslem world is especially and justifiably outraged by this aggression against an Islamic people. No action of a world power has ever been so quickly and so overwhelmingly condemned. But verbal condemnation is not enough. The Soviet Union must pay a concrete price for their aggression.

While this invasion continues, we and the other nations of the world cannot conduct business as usual with the Soviet Union. That's why the United States has imposed stiff economic penalties on the Soviet Union. I will not issue any permits for Soviet ships to fish in the coastal waters of the United States. I've cut Soviet access to high-technology equipment and to agricultural products. I've limited other commerce with the Soviet Union, and I've asked our allies and friends to join with us in restraining their own trade with the Soviets and not to replace our own embargoed items. And I have notified the Olympic Committee that with Soviet invading forces in Afghanistan, neither the American people nor I will support sending an Olympic team to Moscow.

The Soviet Union is going to have to answer some basic questions: Will it help promote a more stable international environment in which its own legitimate, peaceful concerns can be pursued? Or will it continue to expand its military power far beyond its genuine security needs, and use that power for colonial conquest? The Soviet Union must realize that its decision to use military force in Afghanistan will be costly to every political and economic relationship it values.

The region which is now threatened by Soviet troops in Afghanistan is of great strategic importance: It contains more than two-thirds of the world's exportable oil. The Soviet effort to dominate Afghanistan has brought Soviet military forces to within 300 miles of the Indian Ocean and close to the Straits of Hormuz, a waterway through which most of the world's oil must Row. The Soviet Union is now attempting to consolidate a strategic position, therefore, that poses a grave threat to the free movement of Middle East oil.

This situation demands careful thought, steady nerves, and resolute action, not only for this year but for many years to come. It demands collective efforts to meet this new threat to security in the Persian Gulf and in Southwest Asia. It demands the participation of all those who rely on oil from the Middle East and who are concerned with global peace and stability. And it demands consultation and close cooperation with countries in the area which might be threatened.

Meeting this challenge will take national will, diplomatic and political wisdom, economic sacrifice, and, of course, military capability. We must call on the best that is in us to preserve the security of this crucial region.

Let our position be absolutely clear: An attempt by any outside force to gain control of the Persian Gulf region will be regarded as an assault on the vital interests of the United States of America, and such an assault will be repelled by any means necessary, including military force.

During the past 3 years, you have joined with me to improve our own security and the prospects for peace, not only in the vital oil-producing area of the Persian Gulf region but around the world. We've increased annually our real commitment for defense, and we will sustain this increase of effort throughout the Five Year Defense Program. It's imperative that Congress approve this strong defense budget for 1981, encompassing a 5 percent real growth in authorizations, without any reduction.

We are also improving our capability to deploy US military forces rapidly to distant areas. We've helped to strengthen NATO and our other alliances, and recently we and other NATO members have decided to develop and to deploy modernized, intermediate-range nuclear forces to meet an unwarranted and increased threat from the nuclear weapons of the Soviet Union.

We are working with our allies to prevent conflict in the Middle East. The peace treaty between Egypt and Israel is a notable achievement which represents a strategic asset for America and which also enhances prospects for regional and world peace. We are now engaged in further negotiations to provide full autonomy for the people of the West Bank and Gaza, to resolve the Palestinian issue in all its aspects, and to preserve the peace and security of Israel. Let no one doubt our commitment to the security of Israel. In a few days we will observe an historic event when Israel makes another major withdrawal from the Sinai and when Ambassadors will be exchanged between Israel and Egypt.

We've also expanded our own sphere of friendship. Our deep commitment to human rights and to meeting human needs has improved our relationship with much of the Third World. Our decision to normalize relations with the People's Republic of China will help to preserve peace and stability in Asia and in the Western Pacific.

We've increased and strengthened our naval presence in the Indian Ocean, and we are now making arrangements for key naval and air facilities to be used by our forces in the region of northeast Africa and the Persian Gulf.

We've reconfirmed our 1959 agreement to help Pakistan preserve its independence and its integrity. The United States will take action consistent with our own laws to assist Pakistan in resisting any outside aggression. And I'm asking the Congress specifically to reaffirm this agreement. I'm also working, along with the leaders of other nations, to provide additional military and economic aid for Pakistan. That request will come to you in just a few days. . . .

Finally, we are prepared to work with other countries in the region to share a cooperative security framework that respects differing values and political beliefs, yet which enhances the independence, security, and prosperity of all.

All these efforts combined emphasize our dedication to defend and preserve the vital interests of the region and of the nation which we represent and those of our allies—in Europe and the Pacific, and also in the parts of the world which have such great strategic importance to us, stretching especially through the Middle East and Southwest Asia. With your help, I will pursue these efforts with vigor and with determination. You and I will act as necessary to protect and to preserve our Nation's security. . . .

Source: Available at Office of the Historian, Foreign Service Institute, United States Department of State, https://history.state.gov/historicaldocuments/frus1977-80v01/d138

"Palestinians, America and the U.N." Op-ed in the *New York Times*, January 20, 2011, by Hanan Ashrawi

Palestinians are well within their rights to bring the issue of Israeli settlements and their illegality before the United Nations Security Council. Our decision to do so follows both Israel's refusal to cease all settlement activity in the occupied Palestinian territory, and America's failure to ensure Israel's compliance with international law and existing agreements. The United States should support such a move, not block it.

It is universally recognized that Israeli settlements are illegal under international law, and that without a full cessation of all settlement activity, Palestinian-Israeli negotiations and the two-state solution are both doomed. In spite of the dilution of American public statements, the United States still recognizes settlements as illegal. Not only are they a violation of the Fourth Geneva Convention; under the Rome Statute, they are considered a war crime.

With America unwilling to hold Israel accountable to international law and existing agreements, Israel has remained intransigent in the face of international efforts to revive genuine negotiations. A Security Council resolution would reaffirm today's international consensus in support of the two-state solution by recognizing the threat posed by illegal settlements.

This is not rocket science. Settlements are built on occupied Palestinian land. They also entail the exploitation of Palestine's natural resources, including water. Both belong to a future Palestinian state. Without them, no Palestinian state can be viable.

The true impact of Israeli settlements is measured not only by the way they undermine the two-state solution; it is also the enormous damage they inflict on countless Palestinian communities.

Settlements superimpose a colonial grid over the West Bank, including East Jerusalem. They constitute an illegal exercise of Israeli extraterritoriality in Palestine. Built on the expropriation and theft of Palestinian land, they dominate the surrounding hilltops of the occupied West Bank, encircling and besieging Palestinian towns and villages below.

They stand at the heart of an ever expanding web of checkpoints, walls, roadblocks and settler-only bypass roads that marginalize Palestinian realities and render all normal life impossible. Palestinian farms, businesses and homes have all been destroyed to make way for settlement expansion, while Palestinian lives and livelihoods have been shattered in the process.

The rights and protections enshrined under international law apply as much to Palestinians as to anyone else. Indeed, at the very heart of the Palestinian struggle is a determination to win back these very rights and protections long denied us by Israel. This applies as much to the rights of Palestinian refugees living in exile for the last 60 years, as it does to the many Palestinians who have suffered for over four decades under the brutality of an Israeli military occupation.

Settlements are a fundamental part of this. Given that they continue to expand in flagrant violation of international law, it is perfectly reasonable for Palestinians to turn to the United Nations as a forum in which to pursue their legitimate rights.

The question is not whether or not Palestinians should approach the United Nations. We have every right to pursue all legal avenues available to us, whether in the absence of or parallel to negotiations, just as the African National Congress did in its struggle to overthrow apartheid in South Africa. Rather, the question is why the United States should oppose such a move, particularly given that its own attempts to revive Palestinian-Israeli negotiations have been thwarted time and again by Israel's refusal to stop building settlements.

Negotiations are not a substitute for international law. Rather, they should be guided by international law, which alone establishes the benchmarks for a just peace. Nor are settlements a bilateral issue whose illegality is up for discussion.

It is just such a message that the Obama administration is in danger of sending by opposing a Security Council resolution reaffirming the illegality of Israeli settlements. It sets up a false opposition between negotiations and international law, substituting one for the other. And it closes down what few avenues are open to Palestinians, in the absence of negotiations, to continue our national struggle through nonviolent means.

The U.N. charter explicitly references its "faith in fundamental human rights" and the need to uphold "conditions under which justice and respect for the obligations arising from treaties and other sources of international law" be respected. What could be more applicable than the damage done by Israeli violations, in particular unilateral measures like settlement activity?

Hanan Ashrawi is a former Palestinian peace negotiator and an elected member of both the Palestine Liberation Organization's executive committee and the Palestinian Legislative Council.

Source: "Palestinians, America and the U.N." Op-ed in the New York Times, Jan. 20, 2011. By Hanan Ashrawi. Source: New York Times online. By permission of Dr. Hanan Ashrawi.

NOTES

1. The phrase "Arab cold war" has long been associated with Malcolm Kerr's book *The Arab Cold War: Gamal Abd al-Nasir and His Rivals, 1958–1970* (Oxford: Oxford University Press, 1971).
2. For an examination of Nasser's mercurial relationship with the United States, see David W. Lesch, "Abd al-Nasser and the United States: Enemy or Friend?" in Elie Podeh and Onn Winckler, eds., *Rethinking Nasserism: Revolution and Historical Memory in Modern Egypt* (Gainesville: University Press of Florida, 2004), pp. 205–229.

3. Anthony Nutting, *Nasser* (London: Constable, 1972), p. 123. Quoted in David W. Lesch, The *Arab–Israeli Conflict: A History* (Oxford: Oxford University Press, 2019), p. 175.
4. For more on this, see David W. Lesch, *Syria and the United States: Eisenhower's Cold War in the Middle East* (Boulder: Westview Press, 1992).
5. It has been said that the mandate system both spawned and killed Arab nationalism, in that over time Arabs began to think of themselves more as Egyptian, Iraqi, Syrian, and so on.
6. See Bernard Avishai, *The Tragedy of Zionism* (New York: FSG, 1986), p. 48.
7. For a more detailed analysis of Nasser's moves, see Lesch, *The Arab–Israeli Conflict*, pp. 191–211.
8. Nikki Keddie, *Roots of Revolution: An Interpretive History of Modern Iran* (New Haven, CT: Yale University Press, 1981), pp. 93–112.
9. See Hamid Algar, *Islam and Revolution: Writings and Declarations of Imam Khomeini* (Berkeley: Mizan Press, 1981).
10. Much of this discussion on Saudi Arabia and the taking of the Grand Mosque in Mecca is based on the book by Yaroslav Trofimov, *The Siege of Mecca: The Forgotten Uprising in Islam's Holiest Shrine and the Birth of Al Qaeda* (New York: Doubleday, 2007), which is simply an outstanding, impeccably researched, and riveting examination of the event.

KEY TERMS

Hibbat Zion or Hovevi Zion p. 349
intifada p. 373
Irgun Zevai Leumi p. 362
Organization of Petroleum Exporting Countries (OPEC) p. 358
Palestine Liberation Organization (PLO) p. 348
United Arab Republic (UAR) p. 347
United Nations Emergency Forces (UNEF) p. 347
United Nations Security Council (UNSC) p. 365

For additional digital learning resources please go to www.oup.com/he/lesch-middleeast-1e

12 MIDDLE EAST AGONISTES

9/11

What do we call it? In the West it is most often referred to as Islamic fundamentalism; however, the religious application of the word "fundamentalism" actually has its origins in the United States. American fundamentalism arose in response to two movements in the late nineteenth and early twentieth centuries: modernization and the social gospel movement.[1] Followers of the social gospel movement were not unlike the Islamic modernists who epitomized the Salafiyya movement in the Middle East toward the end of the nineteenth century. They too advocated for an accommodation with science and technology to deal (in the case of the United States) with the ravages of industrialization and urbanization. Many, mostly Protestants, arguing against the social gospel movement, said that too many Americans had strayed from the principles of Christianity due to modernization, and felt they needed to go back to the basics. Christians needed to understand that it was the literal interpretation of original Christian sources—the Bible—that would set straight the wayward elements in society. This type of thinking, no matter the religion—Christianity, Islam, Hinduism, Judaism—is often called fundamentalism, and the general objectives of going back to original sources in both thought and application are quite similar in all of them.

Slapping an American label on something that has its own origin story in the Middle East was seen as typically arrogant, particularly by those in academia, who are often more sensitive to such nomenclature than the people themselves in the Middle East. Soon enough a preferred reference emerged during my academic lifetime: Islamism or Islamicism, and the practitioners were termed Islamists or Islamicists, respectively. But this too is misleading, as there are many different levels of Islamism or fundamentalism. There are also those Muslims who are so designated in name only; they are secularized and generally do not practice the faith. And then there are the many practicing Muslims who do not consider themselves fundamentalist in any shape, fashion, or form.

Of the Islamists, there are different types. There are those who simply want their religion respected and followed more closely, and who peacefully advocate for this through education, social works, and the ballot box when they are allowed to do so. Then are those who have been called Islamic militants or extremists (often Jihadists), whose moral absolutism in their beliefs makes it difficult if not impossible for any sort of compromise. They have a sense of urgency that dictates a more militant tone and action before the situation becomes irreversible. In their view, trying to bring about a morally just society through peaceful means either takes too long or is easily suppressed and manipulated by authoritarian ruling structures. There is no political space (i.e., legitimate elections) to bring about change via the ballot box, so more assertive action is necessary. As Georgetown University professor of religion John Esposito wrote: "Many Muslims today believe that the conditions of their world require jihad. They . . . see a world dominated by corrupt authoritarian governments and a wealthy elite, a minority concerned solely with its own economic prosperity rather than national development, a world awash in Western culture and values in dress, music, television, and movies. Western governments are perceived as propping up oppressive regimes and exploiting the region's human and natural resources, robbing Muslims of their culture and their options to be governed according to their own choice and to live in a more just society."[2] As a result, there is a radicalized minority of Muslims who "combine militancy with messianic visions to inspire and mobilize an army of God whose jihad they believe will liberate Muslims at home and abroad."[3]

What we have witnessed over the past fifty years or so is only the latest manifestation of Islamism. Fundamentalist movements have occurred throughout Islamic history from almost the very beginning. The Kharijites, a few decades after the death of the Prophet Muhammad, rebelled against and broke away from what they believed had become a corrupted Islam. The Abbasid revolution, the Wahabbis in the eighteenth century, and the Salafiyya movement were all to at least some degree fundamentalist movements. The Islamism/Islamic fundamentalism we have seen in the twentith and into the twenty-first centuries has been a reaction to Western interference at many different levels—political, economic, and sociocultural—as well as against the Muslim governments that allowed it to happen, who embraced Western ideologies and catered to the West for the sake of money and power. In many ways, as mentioned previously, it was a function of the recognition that the Salafiyya movement and the Islamic modernists had failed, which only led to more outside interference and control ultimately in the form of the mandate system. It was the merger of the traditional call for the implementation of Islamic law (*sharia*), the vehicle by which Muslims could restore the rule of law, justice, and the balance between rulers and ruled, with anti-imperialism and anti-Westernization. This dynamic has only been further charged by socioeconomic distress, restricted political space, and what Islamists see as cultural poisoning due to globalization that threatens traditional Muslims' cultural identity.

From the point of view of many Muslims, the imported Western ideologies of socialism and capitalism did not deliver the goods. They only led to the exhaustion of the state, corruption, repression, and a grossly unequal distribution of wealth. Together with the demographic pressures (such as high birth rates, characteristic of the region, where typically 60 to 75 percent of a country's population is under the age of thirty), it has been a recipe for frustration, disillusionment, and unrest. Population growth rates consistently outstripped economic growth rates. By the 1970s this confluence of factors created what historian Philip Khoury called the gap between mobilization and assimilation, between Western-style consumerist expectations and Third World production and per capita income.[4] The social welfare compact the state typically made with the population in the 1960s and 1970s provided what was (and still is in many cases) free education through the university years, so an ever-increasing number of young people were mobilized—educated—to expect decent paying jobs once they graduated. But dilapidated and corrupt economies were not able to adequately absorb the youth by providing jobs, or at least well-paying ones; many were underemployed and had to work two or three smaller jobs to attempt to make a living. They were not assimilated.

Three of the most important Muslim ideologues of the twentieth century were key to the evolving brand of a militant response to increasing political, economic, and cultural encroachment from the West. First is Hassan al-Banna, who founded the Muslim Brotherhood in Egypt in 1928 under the noses of the British and the British-supported Egyptian monarchy. In many ways, the Muslim Brotherhood reflected the search for an organizational capacity for Muslims following the abolition of the caliphate in Turkey by Mustafa Kemal Ataturk four years earlier. Next, Sunni Islamism advanced ideologically with the theory of modern Jahiliyya developed by Maulana Maudoodi in India in 1939, again during the period of British colonial rule.[5] Maudoodi equated modernity with Jahiliyya; Muslims were living in a new age of ignorance, a deplorable and dangerous situation that required an immediate and forceful response to counter. He was one of the first Muslim thinkers to arrive at a sweeping condemnation of modernity—Westernization—and its incompatibility with Islam. The compromise between modernity and Islam hoped for by the Islamic modernists of the Muhammad Abduh school during the Salafiyya was impossible, so another course of action was needed.

Finally, the signature development of this new course of action was guided by the writings of Sayyid Qutb, who has been called the godfather of twentieth-century Sunni Islamic militancy. Qutb, an Egyptian and member of the Muslim Brotherhood in the 1950s, was a disciple of Maudoodi.[6] He did not start out this way. Ironically, he began his professional life as a modernist literary critic, who seemed to deepen his Islamism following a two-year stint (1948–1950) in New York City. He was directly exposed to modernity, which he viewed as corrupt and decadent, and he believed this was the future that awaited the Muslim world unless something was done immediately to prevent what seemed to be at the time an inevitable progression toward Westernization—hence the urgency and violent tone of his message. The theory of modern jahiliyya started to gain a wider audience following the devastating defeat suffered by the Arabs during the 1947–1949 Arab–Israeli war that produced the State of Israel. Qutb expanded upon Maudoodi's teachings.

Commenting on how Muslims veered off course, he wrote: "Jahiliyya signifies the domination (*hakimiyya*) of man over man, or rather the subservience to man rather than Allah. It denotes rejection of the divinity of God and the adulation of mortals. In a sense, jahiliyya is not just a specific historical period, but a state of affairs."[7] Qutb believed this was the most "insidious" period in modern Islamic history because the threat was not just from the outside, but also it emanated from the inside, within the citadel. This was a reference to the secular Arab nationalists, the Baathists and Nasserists, who dominated discourse in the Arab world of his day. Reflecting this thought, another Indian Muslim thinker, Ali Nadvi, wrote that "the [Arab] nationalists are sincere and serious; they have been driven into these erroneous theories merely by an excess of zeal, by a desire to glorify the Arab cause. Unwittingly, they became agents of destructive Western ideas . . . building up a national movement devoid of an Islamic dimension."[8]

The Muslim Brotherhood and the secular Arab nationalists worked together for a time in Egypt to oust their common enemy, the British; however, Qutb would call for the end of this marriage of convenience. To deal with the external and internal challenges, Qutb and his cohorts developed a methodology to deal with the multiple threats: begin with a diagnosis, develop a cure, and then come up with a way to administer the cure.[9] The diagnosis was that modernity equals jahiliyya. The cure was rebellion, first internally and then externally. Qutb's major contributions to the development of Sunni Islamic militancy came in the form of legitimately and effectively administering the cure. According to Qutb, true Muslims needed to establish a countersociety or micro-society so as to cordon themselves off from jahili society. They could construct a micro-society even in the heart of jahili society, much as Muhammad and the first Muslims did in Mecca prior to the Hijra. Following this stage or even as a first stage in and of itself, Muslims should separate themselves from jahili society and establish a countersociety, the ideal example being that of Medina following upon the Hijra. In this way one could better preserve one's purity and then have the time and space to prepare adequately for jihad. In this sense, the formula was as follows: hijra, education, jihad—in this order.

SPOTLIGHT

Sayyid Qutb

Ibrahim Hussein Shadhili Sayyid Qutb was born near Asyut, Egypt in 1906. Before being executed in Cairo by the Egyptian government of President Gamal Abd al-Nasser in 1966, he would undergo a transformation intellectually to become one of the most important Islamist thinkers and writers of the twentieth century. His influence is directly linked to Osama bin Ladin and the establishment and growth of al-Qaida as well as other militant Sunni Islamic movements—and therefore the events of September 11, 2001.

Sayyid Qutb's first career centered around endeavors such as being a literary critic, poet, and social activist. He also worked in the Egyptian Ministry of Education. He was raised in a devout Muslim home, and it is reported that he had memorized the Quran by the age of ten. In 1948 he began to adopt an overtly Islamist outlook, which he first detailed in his book *Social Justice in Islam*. He spent a few years (1948–1951) in the United States, which only seemed to confirm his new path, for even though he recognized America's technological advances and economic and military might, he also thought it was a morally bankrupt country. He believed Americans looked down on the "Old World," deriding what others hold as sacred. He attended graduate school at the University of Northern Colorado (then Colorado State College of Education), as he took great interest in the evolution of the United States. On one occasion he said, "This great America: What is its worth in the scale of human values? And what does it add to the moral account of humanity?" His answer was "nothing." New was not necessarily improved in his mind.

Qutb returned to Egypt in 1951 following the assassination of Hassan al-Banna, the founder of the Muslim Brotherhood, of which he became a member soon after his return. At first, as were most Muslim Brethren, he was on pretty good terms with Nasser's secular and Arab nationalist Free Officers movement, for they shared the goal of ridding Egypt of British influence. It appears that Nasser had visited with Qutb prior to the Egyptian revolution in 1952 to receive his backing, and that Qutb even expected to be appointed to a post in the Egyptian government following the Free Officers takeover of power. He was not asked to join. He soon ran afoul, as did most Muslim Brethren, of the secular nature of the Nasserist government and its inability to totally get rid of the British. After a failed Muslim Brotherhood attempt to assassinate Nasser in December 1954, Qutb was among a number of Brethren who were arrested under the charge of sedition, and he was imprisoned.

During his prison years (1954–1964), though frequently tortured and living in terrible conditions, Qutb was able to prolifically write and smuggle his writings out of prison, maybe the most influential prison literature of its type in modern times. One of his books, *Signposts in the Road* (1964, sometimes translated as *Milestones* rather than *Signposts*) became the guidebook for twentieth-century Sunni Islamic militancy (his ideological and methodological contributions are outlined in this chapter). He was released from prison in 1964, but soon thereafter he was again arrested and tried for treason. Despite an offer of Nasser for clemency if he renounced his teachings—an offer Qutb refused—he was executed by hanging in 1966.

Qutb believed Muslims should not fear death if they were martyrs for the cause, which included protecting the sanctity of Islam from the pernicious activity of Jews and Christians. Reflecting on his interpretation of the Quran, he wrote the following: "Those who risk their lives and go out to fight, and who are prepared to lay down their lives for the cause of God are honorable people, pure of heart and blessed of soul. But the great surprise is that those among them who are killed in the struggle must not be considered or described as dead. They continue to live, as God Himself clearly states."[1] There is some debate, however, whether Qutb would have approved of al-Qaida's tactics of killing innocent civilians, especially in the events of 9/11. He was against that type of violence. One wonders, though, had he lived to experience the repercussions of the 1967 Arab–Israeli war and subsequent events leading up to the 1979 Egyptian-Israeli peace treaty, if his thinking would have changed over time and become even more militant. These events had that sort of effect on a number of Muslims, one of whom was Osama bin Ladin.

Whether or not Qutb would have advocated for the killing of innocents, those who were so influenced by him, such as Osama as well as his al-Qaida cofounder, the Egyptian physician Ayman al-Zwahiri, certainly believed it was justified; Qutb's brother, Muhammad, was able to escape the Muslim Brethren arrests, heading to Saudi Arabia where one of his students at King Abd al-Aziz University was Osama bin Ladin.

Sayyid Qutb on trial in 1966 in Cairo.
Historic Collection / Alamy Stock Photo

[1] Paul Berman, "The Philosopher of Islamic Terror," *New York Times Magazine*, March 23, 2003, Section 6, p. 24.

Perhaps Qutb's most lasting contribution is legitimizing the right for Islamists to use violence in general but specifically against those who also call themselves Muslims. For Shiite Muslims, having been oppressed and in the opposition for much of their history, the right to revolt is much more direct, and they see it as their duty to overthrow unjust rulers, even if they are Muslim. For Sunnis the task is more complicated, haunted as their history has been with civil war (*fitna*) and a hadith attributed to the Prophet Muhammad in which he stated that forty years of tyranny is better than one day of anarchy. But Qutb legitimized the right to revolt in terms of mainstream Sunni thought. He did so by basing his argument on the theories of Ibn Taymiyya (1268–1328), one of the most prominent medieval Islamic philosophers.[10] Taymiyya spent most of his life under Mamluk rule in Syria, and the Mamluks' greatest enemy at that time was the Mongol Ilkhanate. Although Taymiyya was not a big fan of the Mamluks, having spent time in and out of prison in Damascus, they were, in his mind, better than the Mongols. To make a long story short, the Mamluks wanted Taymiyya to come up with a rationale to legitimize the call for a jihad against the Ilkhanate. The problem was by that time the state religion of the Ilkhanate was Islam, therefore one theoretically could not proclaim a jihad against fellow Muslims. A jihad is what they wanted because it would better mobilize the population, allowing the government to levy troops, raise taxes, and expropriate property and resources to fight the infidels. Taymiyya's solution was to assert that the Mongols did not practice pure Islam nor fully apply sharia, Islamic law. Their version was a mix of preexisting religious traditions. Since they did not follow true Islam, they were therefore not Muslim, so the Mamluks could have at them.

Qutb brought Taymiyya's ideas into the modern world, thus providing the rationale for carrying out violence against those within the citadel who called themselves Muslim. Secular, single-party authoritarian leaders such as Nasser, Sadat, and Assad were fair game. And while they could ban Qutb's writings—and even kill him—they could not ban the thoughts of such a prominent Islamic thinker as Ibn Taymiyya. Three of Anwar Sadat's four assassins in Egypt did extensive readings of Taymiyya, particularly his landmark work, *The Absent Precept*.

Osama bin Ladin, a member of one of the wealthiest families in Saudi Arabia, was one of those Arab volunteers in the 1980s who went to Afghanistan to fight against the Soviets—and he was also one of those mujahideen supported by CIA operations. By the late 1990s, however, he became one of the most wanted terrorists by US authorities, having built up the transnational terrorist network al-Qaida.[11] He and his organization were accused of numerous terrorist attacks against American and other Western targets, including the bombing of US embassy compounds in Kenya and Tanzania in 1998 and the 2000 bombing of the USS Cole while it was being refueled off the coast Yemen. The incident that transformed bin Ladin into an international terrorist was the Western presence in Saudi Arabia during the 1990–1991 Gulf crisis and war. Many devout Muslims considered the presence of non-Muslim forces in a country that houses the two holiest sites in Islam to be an abomination, which only underlined what they viewed as the subservience of the House of Saud to the United States. Juhayman al-Otaybi's taking of the Grand Mosque served as an example of matching words with deeds. Bin Ladin left Saudi Arabia and stayed in the Sudan for a couple of years (1994–1995) following his return from Afghanistan, eventually making his way back there under the protection of the Taliban, where he established his al-Qaida (*the Base*) countersociety and from which he could recruit, build his organization, and plot his next attacks against both what he termed the near enemy (those in the Middle East) and the far enemy (such as the United States).[12]

This type of transnational terrorism, intertwined with international weapons smuggling and procurement financed by opium production in Afghanistan, Pakistan, and Lebanon and international money laundering from Russia through Europe and the United States, changed the nature of global terrorist threats in the post–Cold War environment. The battleground moved to the shores of the United States in 1993 in what in retrospect was a kind of warm-up for 9/11, when Islamic

World Trade Center, September 11, 2001.
KAKIMAGE / Alamy Stock Photo

militants trained in Afghanistan carried out the World Trade Center bombings in New York, killing six and injuring more than a thousand. But the Bill Clinton and early George W. Bush administrations in the late 1990s and into the years of 2000–2001 failed to adequately adjust, lacking the type of interagency coordination and imagination to detect what was to come, something that is especially difficult to establish during the interstice between administrations representing different political parties. On September 11, 2001 nineteen al-Qaida operatives (fifteen of them from Saudi Arabia) hijacked four US passenger jets, three hitting their targets: one plane hit each of the Twin Towers of the aforementioned World Trade Center, bringing both of them down, while another hit the Pentagon in Washington, DC, the total dead of the two attacks approaching three thousand; a fourth hijacked plane, probably intended to hit another national landmark in Washington, was brought down over Pennsylvania by the courageous actions of passengers who stormed the cockpit. It was the worst foreign attack on US soil since Pearl Harbor. The United States would respond forcefully.

The 2003 Invasion of Iraq

For Americans, the world definitely changed on September 11, 2001. The distance traveled from the secure, if not invincible, feeling Americans had prior to 9/11 to the sense of vulnerability following the attacks was enormous. There was worldwide sympathy for the United States in the immediate aftermath. As Gerard Baker noted, "When Iranian mullahs, French editorialists, and Chinese Communist party officials rush to express support for Americans, you know something large has happened in international relations."[13] Generally speaking, the post-9/11 foreign policy of the George W. Bush administration was frequently compared with the era of Manifest Destiny in the 1840s. It was almost a mystical religious belief in a divinely mandated mission to humankind for US expansion in the name of liberty. While critics point to Manifest Destiny as an arrogant rationalization of real-life territorial aggression, it seems to have provided a veneer of idealism that the American traditional exceptionalist view of itself demands, and that masked policies based on strategic and economic necessity. After 9/11, the perception in the United States was that there was a new force, most often identified as Islamic extremism, attempting to undermine the political, cultural, and economic hegemony of the country—and this threat had to be defeated.

The initial US response to 9/11 came in the form of invading Afghanistan in October 2001 to rid the country of the Taliban and al-Qaida presence. With considerable assistance from local Afghani factions that had opposed the Taliban regime for years, the United States, invoking Article 5 of the NATO charter that sanctioned military action in self-defense, did just that by early December. The war in Afghanistan elevated the influence of the Pentagon at the White House. As the war was considered such a rousing military success story at the time, the so-called

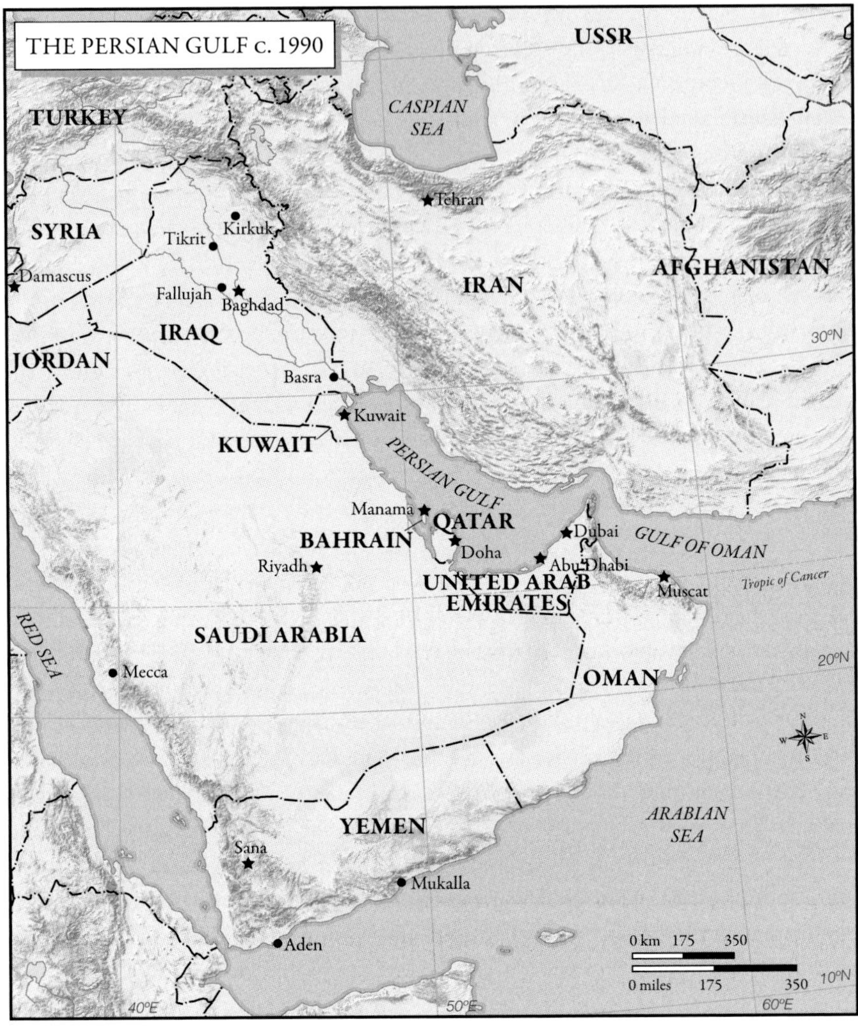

neo-conservatives, who formed an important ideological base for the administration, trumpeted the advantages and utility of power to achieve foreign policy objectives. Strategic power was seen as an asset, and in this sense Israel was always viewed quite favorably by the "neo-cons."

As such, the old wound of Iraq vaulted to the top of the policy priority list even before the overthrow of the Taliban had been completed.[14] Important voices right after 9/11 were pushing for an initial invasion of Iraq instead of Afghanistan. With all of the chaotic propaganda invading the airwaves in the aftermath of 9/11, a large majority of the US population mistakenly believed Saddam Hussein's Iraq was behind the terrorist attacks. Iraq suddenly became part and parcel of the global war against terror, as it was not only linked to 9/11 but also was suspected of developing **weapons of mass destruction (WMD)** in violation of UN resolutions and sanctions. President Bush's State of the Union address in January 2002 appeared to be the capstone of this policy shift, when he grouped Iraq with Iran and North Korea as the "axis of evil." As Middle East scholar Rashid Khalidi noted at the time, the neo-cons had moved from the conservative think tanks in the 1990s to the policymaking corridors in Washington when the Bush administration came to power. The shock of 9/11 brought this neo-con policy that was lurking in the policymaking corridors front and center in the Pentagon and at the White House. Two ideological factions in the Republican foreign policymaking apparatus merged in the administration: the neo-cons (or what some called the "democratic imperialists") and the so-called assertive nationalists, among whom were Secretary of Defense Donald Rumsfeld and Vice President Dick Cheney. The realist or internationalist wing of the Republican Party was present primarily in the State Department, led by Secretary of State Colin Powell, who for the most part was outflanked by Rumsfeld and Cheney and marginalized in the run-up to the war in Iraq in 2003 and in the immediate postwar period.

Both the neo-cons and the assertive nationalists had a unilateral bent in terms of utilizing (or not utilizing) international institutions such as the UN, in opposition to the US-led UN coalition that evicted Iraq from Kuwait in 1991. The assertive nationalists employed their unilateralism as a protective shield to guard the United States from various threats, and they were absolutely opposed to nation-building—they would deal with the threat, diminish or get rid of it, and then pull out. The neo-cons, on the other hand, were positively Wilsonian in their outlook, viewing a unilateralist approach as the most efficient way to remake the world—or as Wilson famously stated regarding US involvement in World War I, "make the world safe for democracy"—although without the support and engagement of the international institutions that Wilson envisioned. The neo-cons saw this as the best antidote to Islamic extremism: eliminating the facilitating environments of authoritarianism, corruption, and socioeconomic distress that spawns it. These two factions shared the same idea on the need to go to war in Iraq in 2003, but they differed dramatically on determining the ultimate objectives and how best to achieve them, which as it turned out was one of the main problems in developing a coherent and workable postwar reconstruction plan in Iraq.

The United States shifted its strategic modus operandi in the post-9/11 era to that of preventive war as articulated in the administration's National Security Strategy of September 2002, or what became known as the Bush Doctrine. It is a strategy that advocates when necessary a preventive war through preemptive military action against what are determined to be imminent threats to US security—there would be no more 9/11s. The use by al-Qaida of the failed state environment in Afghanistan to build up its terrorist network convinced policymakers that the United States could no longer wait for a threat to become manifest. It was now compelled to deal with countries that from the viewpoint of Washington facilitated terrorism before the actual threat emerged. The war in Afghanistan was retributive.

The war in Iraq was the first application of the Bush Doctrine, although many would say it was also part and parcel of a cathartic American response to 9/11, especially as Iraq was low-hanging fruit; in other words, it was doable, an easy foe to defeat. Even before the war began in March 2003, two-thirds of the country had been overflown by US, British, and French aircraft on a daily basis ever since the end of the 1991 Gulf War; it had been debilitated by severe, if imperfect, UN sanctions for a dozen years; and its military had been ravaged by war, purges, and neglect.

Neither the UN inspection teams prior to the war nor the US investigating teams after the initial conflict found WMD in Iraq. The way Saddam Hussein was playing a shell game with the UN teams made one think the US teams would find at least some caches of WMD. It may be that Saddam wanted the United States to think that Iraq had them because he thought ultimately in 1991 that was the reason the American-led UN coalition did not go farther into Iraq and up to Baghdad for fear of Iraq using WMD, especially chemical weapons. Perhaps he thought the same trick could work twice; little did he know that by pretending to have WMD he played right into the hands of Bush administration officials pushing for war. When WMD were not found, the Bush administration began to tout a different reason for the invasion: to bring democracy to Iraq and by doing so, spark a domino effect that would spread across the region. Importantly, the coalition forces spent so much time and resources on trying to find the WMD that would have justified the war, it created opportunity costs in the form of paying less attention to detecting what was a growing anti-US insurgency in the country.

As is well known, things did not go as planned for the United States and its allies (mainly Britain) in Iraq following the toppling of Saddam Hussein's government and the capture of the former dictator. They got bogged down in exactly what George H. W. Bush administration officials had feared: a quagmire, whereby US forces, originally seen as liberators by many Iraqis, were increasingly seen as occupiers and were actively opposed. First of all, there were not enough US troops in Iraq to secure pertinent sites, such as government buildings, power stations, and weapons depots. The scaled-down military presence replicated that which was implemented in Afghanistan, except that the much more urban environment of Iraq required hundreds of thousands of additional troops to properly stabilize the country. The Bush administration also relied heavily on Iraqi exiles for information, many of whom advanced the war option out of self-interest, but they lacked on the ground knowledge because most had not spent time in Iraq in decades, ultimately misleading the United States on what it could expect by invading.

In retrospect, a number of bad decisions were made by the US-dominated Coalition Provisional Authority (CPA) that was charged with overseeing the postwar administration and recovery. For instance, the CPA disbanded the Iraqi army. Many of these soldiers, particularly the officers, were contacted via social media, leaflets, and even phone calls by US military personnel to stand down in the war—to not fight—and if they did so, they would have a future in the new Iraq moving forward.

Iraqi President Saddam Hussein's statue in Baghdad's al-Fardous Square is pulled down with the help of US Marines during the Iraq war in April 2003.
Trinity Mirror / Mirrorpix / Alamy Stock Photo

Whether they did or did not, many felt betrayed by the United States when the army was disbanded; furthermore, a number of trained soldiers with weapons were all of a sudden out of work and they became brigands, increasingly joined a growing insurgency arrayed against the coalition forces and ultimately many joined up with the Islamic State. The lack of an indigenous security force—one that took months if not years to build back up by the United States—put an American face on the occupation, with US personnel coming under attack by those opposed to the US presence in principle and those lashing out in frustration and disillusionment.

The CPA furthermore dismembered the Baath party in Iraq, as this was seen as the political vehicle through which Saddam ruled—and it could not be trusted. In fact, it was a de-Baathification of the country; however, many Iraqis originally joined the Baath party not so much out of fealty to Saddam or belief in Baathist ideology, but simply to advance their career prospects and salaries. This included university professors, schoolteachers, and civil service workers. When they were kicked out of their positions because they were Baath party members, the country lost key occupational components and skill sets of those who essentially operated Iraq, which added to the postwar confusion and chaos of simply trying to get the country half-way working again. Finally, US officials did not adequately negotiate with the very powerful (mostly Sunni) tribes in the critical areas to the west of Baghdad toward the border with Syria. American officials thought it to be bad form for their democratizing efforts to deal with decidedly undemocratic and anachronistic tribal elements in the country; ironically, it is only when US military personnel began to negotiate with the Sunni tribes a few years later that the insurgency began to die down.

The combination of lack of preparation for the postwar condition of Iraq, as well as a slew of questionable decisions, led to years of political instability in the country that continues as of this writing. Soon enough many Iraqis, originally pleased to see Saddam fall from power, began to long for the days, even under Saddam, when there were ample amounts of such things as food and electricity, and there was relative stability as long as one knew what lines not to cross. Just because elections are held doesn't mean a country has become democratic; there is more to it than that, such as literacy rates, building a civil society, and establishing a functioning economy with sound political institutions. The holding of relatively free elections, however, brought the majority Shiite Arabs to power in Iraq. On the surface this was long overdue, but the political culture of Iraq has traditionally been quite violent. Often when one party or group is removed from power, whether through legitimate means or not, the victorious party or group engages in violence—if not revenge—against the outgoing party or group. This led to a number of bloody massacres in twentieth-century Iraq. The long-ruling Sunni Arabs in the country were not going to take this lying down; if they did, they risked being totally marginalized if not imprisoned or killed. This was the initial impulse that fed the insurgency—and eventually led to the creation and establishment of the hardline Islamic State in Iraq, which by 2014 took over Mosul (and Raqqa in Syria) and about a third of the country territorially before Iraqi forces, supported by the United States and other countries, helped defeat them by 2018.

With Shiite parties in a predominant political power position, Iran's influence in the country naturally increased by leaps and bounds. This was one of the reasons the George H. W. Bush administration had not wanted to unseat the Sunni Arab ruling class in Iraq in 1991, even though it hoped Saddam would fall. By doing so, they feared it would create a vacuum of power in Iraq that Iran was best poised to fill. This is exactly what happened, which also facilitated enhanced Iranian influence in Syria and Lebanon to the point where some Sunni rulers, most notably Jordan's King Abdullah, feared the creation of a Shiite crescent from Iran to the Mediterranean. This development realigned Middle East politics and alliances in the region, as many Sunni Arab states, led by Saudi Arabia, began to see Iran as their primary strategic threat.

Today, Iraq is still struggling along in the aftermath of the 2003 invasion. The northern Kurdish-dominated third of the country has essentially become autonomous, and in many ways successfully so, although it still has to deal with the remnants of the Islamic State as well as the regional political competition of Iran and Turkey on its border. The United States still has a contingent of troops in Iraq, although they are largely unwelcome. Iraq hesitatingly moves forward with political maturation, but this is anything but a stable or functioning state at this point and could easily slide back into chaos and instability.

The Arab Spring

It was the self-immolation of a young man in Tunisia in late 2010 that began what came to be called the Arab Spring. Twenty-six-year-old Muhammad Bouazizi worked a fruit and vegetable cart in the Tunisian town of Sidi Bouzid. Police confiscated his produce because he supposedly lacked the proper permit to sell his merchandise. On December 17, he set himself on fire in what appears to be a final act of despair and anger at his lot in life, dying shortly thereafter due to his injuries. Little did he know that he would light a fire under the entire Middle East.[15]

The Arab world was—and still is—full of predominantly male, urban twenty-somethings who are either unemployed or underemployed. They cannot make ends meet. Those who are married and have children often cannot provide adequately for their families, while those who do manage to scrape by usually need to hold down two or three jobs. Young single men do not earn enough to provide a dowry or even have the merest glimmer of hope of a financially secure future. They were promised more than this, especially the throngs who acquired a college education.

As discussed previously in this chapter regarding the rise of Islamism in the 1970s and 1980s, in the 2000s the disaffected youth have been similarly mobilized but not assimilated. The vehicle by which anger and frustration are expressed matters less than the cause. Youths all over the Arab world were led to believe that a university education would lead to a decent job. But the contracting, faltering, and corrupt economies combined with political repression are not providing enough jobs for the demographic time bomb that was brought about by decades of high birth rates. The moribund, socialist-inspired, state capitalist economies, especially in the non–oil rich Arab states, could not provide enough growth to keep up with the population growth. The public sector then became the employer of last resort, in the process turning into bloated vessels of civil servant purgatory.

By 2011, the vestiges of long-standing authoritarian governments in the Arab world born in the 1950s and 1960s had been haltingly trying for decades to shift to a more market-oriented economy. It was a wrenching process of neoliberalism ordained by the International Monetary Fund that led regimes to adopt a zigzag approach: if they reformed too quickly the economy would tank (for instance, privatization of public sector companies generates an initial unemployment spike as they streamline). The economy might generally improve down the road, but not before there was political unrest due to the downturns and disruption of the initial stages of economic reform, which then could lead to their fall (or removal) from power before experiencing an economic upturn. Reform was implemented in bits and pieces by Arab governments, leading to kleptocracies rather than market-oriented democracies. Remaining in power was the paramount objective. Though this led to some GDP growth, some easing of the flow of capital, and some infrastructural improvement, these incomplete market reforms also exacerbated the unequal distribution of wealth, widespread corruption, and relative poverty. Thus the gap between mobilization and assimilation widened. It is this gap that in large measure produced the level of societal anger and frustration that fueled the Arab Spring. Combined with the lack of any real political space—free and legitimate elections, and decades of political repression—this created a highly combustible mixture.

The events of the Arab Spring were not the first manifestations of anger and frustration by the masses against entrenched, corrupt regimes. There had been episodes of this in the past in a number of states in the region, such as the bread riots in the 1970s and 1980s, when subsidies for basic foodstuffs were reduced; however, a combination of state repression and strategic backtracking usually kept regimes in power. The seminal Arab Human Development Report (AHDR) issued originally in 2002 under the auspices of the UN Development Programme found a number of problems in the Arab world, most particularly a widespread "knowledge deficit" in the region that did not produce the necessary skill set in most of the respective populations to act as the foundation for economic growth and innovation. There was not nearly enough investment by governments in research and development nor on education in general, while there was an overabundance of expenditure on the military in many countries.[16]

The governments in general were able to muddle through the muck for decades—but not in 2011. The demonstrations were larger and angrier, fueled by a perfect storm of higher commodity prices and lower investment bought on by the 2008 global financial crisis; a youth bulge that had been expanding for years, resulting in 60 percent of the Arab world being under the age of thirty; and the new instrument of protest: social media.[17] The 2008 financial crisis hit many countries, and it led to changes in government in places such as Great Britain, Greece, Spain, Poland, Portugal, Ireland, Italy, and the United States. But these changes occurred peacefully through elections. In the Middle East, popular representatives could not be turned out of office because there were really very few popular representatives. There was restricted political space where elections, if they occurred at all, were heavily controlled in favor of the ruling regime if not outright rigged. As a result, protestors, bereft of the ballot box, hit the streets demanding change. In the year or so after the beginning of the Arab Spring in Tunisia in December 2010, long-entrenched authoritarian regimes were removed from power either by the force of popular protest or military force in Tunisia, Egypt, Yemen, and Libya. There were large protests in Bahrain, Jordan, Morocco, and Algeria, with stirrings of discontent in Saudi Arabia as well, but through a combination of repression, largesse, some political concessions, and historical legitimacy in a few long-ruling monarchies, these regimes have been able to mitigate most of the dissatisfaction and remain in power—for now.

SPOTLIGHT

Middle East Activists

As we have already seen with Huda Sharawi, women played important roles in the Middle East over the last century in feminist movements, human rights organizations, political parties and salons, and by becoming vocal advocates for democracy. The spotlight could shine on many, many more, but I am going to focus on the following three individuals whose accomplishments are noteworthy in any setting and at any time: Shirin Ebadi from Iran, Tawakkol Karman from Yemen, and Alaa Salah from the Sudan.

Shirin Ebadi was the first Iranian and first Muslim woman to receive the Nobel Peace Prize in 2003 for her efforts to promote democracy and human rights in Iran, which frequently brought her into conflict with the Iranian government. She was born in Hamadan, Iran and studied law at Teheran University, soon thereafter becoming a judge in 1970. Under the more secularist and pro-Western regime of the Shah of Iran, she advanced quickly, becoming the first female president of the Teheran city court. She and other female jurists were forced to resign upon the 1979 Iranian revolution and creation of the Islamic Republic of Iran.

Compelled to enter a private law practice by 1992, she took on a number of human rights and freedom of expression cases that challenged the government authorities. She was targeted by government officials, receiving a suspended jail sentence and a professional ban, and her Human Rights Center in Teheran, founded in 2001, was closed by state fiat in 2008. By 2009 she was forced into exile, moving to Great Britain. Her important memoir *Until We Are Free: My Fight for Human Rights in Iran* was published in 2016. In awarding the Nobel Prize, the selection committee stated that she was chosen because "as a lawyer, judge, lecturer, writer and activist, she has spoken out clearly and strongly in her country, Iran, and far beyond." She wrote in 2006 that "from the day I was stripped of my judgeship to the years of doing battle in the revolutionary courts of Teheran, I had repeated one refrain: an interpretation of Islam that is in harmony with equality and democracy is an authentic expression of faith. It is not religion that binds women, but the selective dictates of those who wish them cloistered. That belief, along with the conviction that change in Iran must come peacefully and from within, has underpinned my work."[1]

Yemen's Tawakkol Karman once said, "behind every great revolution, there are brave women." She won the Nobel Peace Prize in 2011 (along with two Liberian women, Ellen Johnson Sirleaf and Leymah Gbowee) "for their non-violent struggle for the safety of women and for women's rights to full participation in peace-building work." Karman was born in 1979 in Mekhlaf, Yemen, growing up in a political family just outside of Taiz. She began her career as a journalist after receiving her master's degree in political science at Sanaa University. She wrote controversial articles and produced documentary films advocating for women's rights and democracy, upon which she began to encounter threats and constraints from the Yemeni government. She was one of the leaders in staging sit-ins in Sanaa beginning in 2007 demanding political reform, for which she was arrested several times. A member of the Islamist opposition party in Yemen, Islah (Reform), she clashed as well with the party's conservative members on more than one occasion—for instance, against the party's opposition to legislation raising the legal marriage age for women to seventeen.

During the early moments of the Arab Spring, in January 2011, Karman was again arrested after leading a protest against the government of President Ali Abdullah Salih, all of which sparked larger youth-driven pro-democracy protests that morphed into Yemen's Arab Spring revolution, eventually forcing Salih to leave the country. As such, she became known in Yemen as "the mother of the revolution," "the iron woman," and "the lady of the Arab Spring." Her role models are Martin Luther King and Mahatma Gandhi, and she promoted change through peaceful and nonviolent means. Since 2011 Yemen, already a poor country, has devolved into a protracted civil war that became a proxy battle ground between Saudi Arabia and the United Arab Emirates on one side and Iran on the other. Karman continues to preach her nonviolent methodology, calling on all sides to enter into a political dialogue that could bring a peaceful conclusion to the conflict.

It is an indelible image that went viral in and outside of the Sudan. There is Alaa Salah, standing on top of a car in a traditional Nubian white *toub* dress, leading the protestors in 2019 in chants against the authoritarian regime of long-serving President Omar al-Bashir. It was a critical moment that helped launch the movement that toppled him from power after thirty years of dictatorial rule. Salah is the youngest of our featured activists, born in 1997. When the protests began, she was studying engineering and architecture at Sudan International University in Khartoum.

Her role in the protests highlighted the fact that women often outnumbered men in many of them. As she stated in a landmark speech to the UN Security Council in 2019 on behalf of the NGO Working Group on Women, Peace, and Security: "Women led resistance committees and sit-ins, planned protest routes and disobeyed curfews, even in the midst of a declared state of emergency that left them vulnerable to security forces. Many were teargassed, threatened, assaulted, and thrown in jail without any charge or due process. However, despite this visible role, despite their courage and their leadership, women have been sidelined in the formal political process in the months following the revolution."[2] Salah emphasized that concurrent anti-government demonstrations in Hong Kong and Lebanon energized Sudan's protests, and vice-versa; "every revolution inspires another revolution," she said.[3] In her speech to the UN in October 2019, she said that in the Sudan, "for the last thirty years, women's bodies and our rights have been policed; backlash has been swift and violent when patriarchal norms have been challenged. Women activists, politicians, human rights defenders, and peacebuilders continue to be, systematically attacked and targeted, including through sexual violence, which has forced many out of the country entirely."[4]

If anything, the situation in the Sudan has become more complicated of late, as a military junta removed the transitional civilian government in 2021. As of early 2022, the various sides are trying to come to some sort of peaceful transition to civilian government amid continuing protests and international diplomacy. No doubt Alaa Salah is in the middle of this in a way that someday soon may be recognized by the Nobel Prize committee. A line she quoted from a poem was repeatedly chanted at the rallies, "The bullet does not kill. What kills is the silence of people."

Alaa Salah addresses protesters against Sudanese President Omar al-Bashir during a demonstration in front of the military headquarters in the capital of Khartoum on April 10, 2019.
AFP via Getty Images

[1] Quoted in BBC Profile, November 27, 2009, http://bbc.co.uk/2/hi/middle_east/3181992.stm.
[2] Quoted in article by Katie Reilly in *Time Magazine*, October 30, 2019, https://time.com/5712952/alaa-salah-sudan-women-protest/.
[3] Ibid.
[4] Quoted in "Statement by Ms. Alaa Salah at the UN Security Council Open Debate on Women, Peace and Security," October 29, 2019, Working Group on Women, Peace and Security, https://www.women-peacesecurity.org/resource/statement-unsc-wps-open-debate-october-2019/.

Then there is Syria. With the barrier of fear broken by the fall of regimes in Tunisia and Egypt, large swaths of the long-suppressed population in Syria began to rise up. What largely began in March 2011 as peaceful protests demanding political reform and an end to rampant corruption within months turned increasingly violent, and within a year they had morphed into a full-fledged civil war that has lasted over a decade; environmental historians also look at climate change as a possible causal factor, as the prolonged drought in Syria led to decreased agricultural production and employment in rural areas, which just happened to be the initial breeding ground for the uprising.[18]

The civil war quickly devolved into a regional and international proxy battleground, particularly between Saudi Arabia, Turkey, and their regional and international allies (supporting the rebels/revolutionaries against the Bashar al-Assad government) on the one hand, and Iran and its regional and international allies on the other, supporting the Assad government. Into the space created by the failing state arose ISIS (variably meaning the Islamic State in al-Shams or the Islamic State in Iraq and Syria; also ISIL, the Islamic State in the Levant, or its local acronym, Daesh). Founded and led at first by Abu Bakr al-Baghdadi, this was an extremist Sunni Islamic movement that emerged out of al-Qaida in Iraq. Finding support among segments of increasingly frustrated populations in both Iraq and Syria, who tended to retreat into their sectarian identities to better guard against the debilitations and rapaciousness of the broken-down state, ISIS was able to establish a caliphate in a large swath of territory crossing the Iraqi-Syrian border, taking the northern Iraqi city of Mosul in 2014 and establishing its capital soon thereafter in Syria, in Raqqa. Jihadist and like-minded recruits from all of the world flocked to the caliphate, but ultimately its puritanical and brutal style of rule alienated local populations, much less the rest of the world. Even al-Qaida was compelled to denounce and distance itself from ISIS. In the end, local military forces, supported by the United States and its allies, defeated ISIS, the latter losing both Mosul and Raqqa by 2017. ISIS thereafter disintegrated into small patches of decentralized but still dangerous cells amid the continuing instability in Syria.

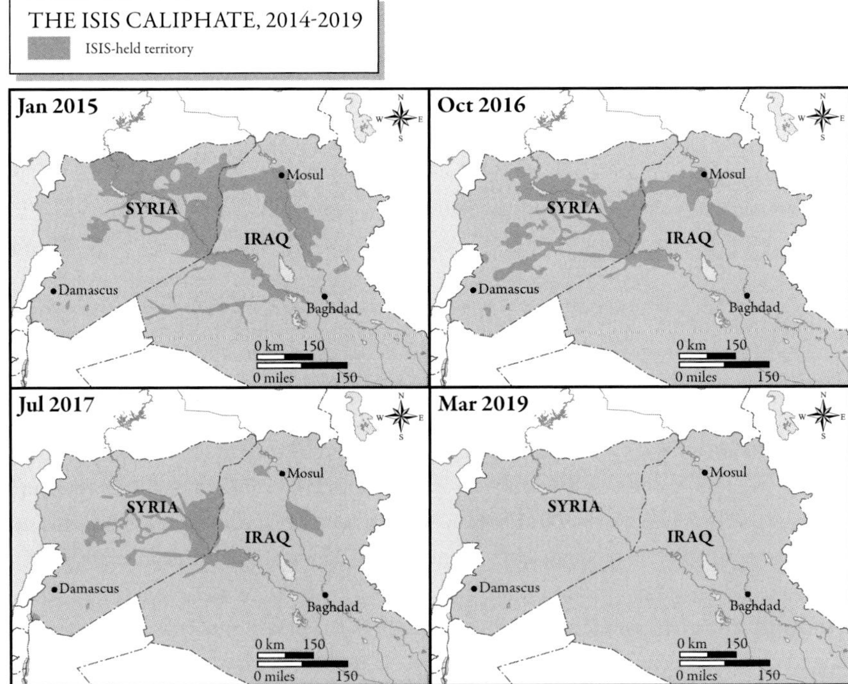

Russia's direct military intervention in September 2015 on behalf of Assad turned the tide of the conflict, to the point where within a few years the Syrian government had essentially won the war and controls most of the population centers against a largely fragmented opposition whose external patrons were also rarely on the same page. In May 2021 Assad ran—and unsurprisingly won—his fourth seven-year term in office, first coming into power in 2000 soon after his father, Hafiz al-Assad, died following his own thirty-year run in office. But it is a country where an estimated 500,000 people died during the conflict, half of the population is displaced either internally or externally, much of the country—including many cities—are devasted with a conservative overall price tag of $300 billion for reconstruction (much less the emotional recovery of the population at large), and extreme poverty and unemployment are widespread amid a war economy largely controlled by rapacious warlords. It will be a generation or more before the country returns to something approaching normalcy.[19]

But the authoritarian regimes and systems in the Middle East have proved to be quite resilient, to the point where many said that the Arab Spring was followed by an Arab Winter. Tunisia was thought to be the only country where a change of government brought on by the initial protests somewhat stabilized and grew into a functioning democracy. Even here, though, by the summer of 2021 there was a rise in political unrest and instability in Tunis due to being hard hit by economic challenges and the COVID-19 pandemic. This resulted in an increasingly authoritarian turn by Tunisian President Kais Saeed, who accumulated more and more executive power, capped off when he dissolved parliament in April 2022. The Syrian civil war has mercifully wound down, but it continues in Libya and Yemen amid tireless UN and international efforts to broker compromise. Other countries have been periodically racked by protests against deteriorating socioeconomic conditions, especially after the COVID-19 pandemic in 2020–2021 hit the Middle East particularly hard. On the Israeli-Palestinian front there have been four so-called Gazan wars since 2008 primarily between Israeli forces and Hamas, which dominates the Gaza Strip, with any sort of equitable and sustainable Israeli-Palestinian settlement along the lines of the two-state solution envisioned in UNSC 242 in 1967 increasingly remote.

Things seem pretty bleak in the Middle East. There are stagnant economies and corrupt political systems across the region. While social media use is high in the region, as seen during the Arab Spring, digital platforms are lagging, particularly in monetary transactions, because of a general lack of trust in government and the financial system as a whole.[20] In this sense, while poised for a potential digital revolution, the region has some significant catching up to do in terms of creating useful digital ecosystems and a mindset of trust in state institutions. Another wave of Arab Spring–like protests could very well occur, and the demonstration effects of the initial protests this time around could be much more widespread. This is not to even speak of the very serious—and related—problems of water scarcity and climate change, both of which affect the Middle East more than any other region in the world, with some areas, especially around the Persian Gulf, predicted to be virtually uninhabitable within the next fifty years or so if global temperatures continue to rise. And finally, the Russian invasion of Ukraine in February 2022 has forced a number of countries in the region to walk a fine line between condemning the invasion outright, as the United States and most of Europe has done, or casting something of a blind eye toward it, encouraging an end to hostilities and calling for a peaceful resolution to the conflict (or even openly supporting Russia in the case of Syria and Iran). It is a reminder that a new kind of international cold war—no doubt this time having to factor China into the equation—could develop once again, which Middle East states must once again navigate.

However, I am an eternal optimist; one has to be when specializing in the Middle East. With the proper alignment of political willpower at the domestic, regional, and international levels, great things can happen. Israel has expanded the number of Arab countries with which it has established diplomatic relations beyond Egypt (1979) and Jordan (1994). Although one can argue against the rationale for doing so, the Trump administration negotiated the so-called Abraham Accords in 2019–2020, whereby the United Arab Emirates, Bahrain, Morocco, and the Sudan have made peace with Israel, although these countries are on the fringes of the Arab-Israeli conflict. More could be in the offing, with Israel finally feeling secure enough that perhaps it can make the difficult compromises that will bring about a just and

Egyptian demonstrators protest in Cairo's Tahrir Square next to a tank in a bid to topple the government of President Husni Mubarak in Cairo, Egypt on January 29, 2011.
UPI / Alamy Stock Photo

lasting settlement with the Palestinians, a dispute still important to overall peace and stability in the Middle East. Israelis could also go in the opposite direction, feeling so secure and strong that they by and large believe they do not need to make any concessions. Even "Islamist terrorism" has dropped off considerably, falling by 59 percent in 2021 from its high in 2014 in terms of total deaths globally, whereas far-right terrorism has increased by 250 percent during the same span of time.[21] Most Islamist terrorism has become more localized, with political Islam itself falling out of fashion. As Islamic politics professor Nader Hashemi points out, "The popular prestige of political Islam has been tarnished by its experience with state power."[22] On the other hand, the Taliban came back into power in Afghanistan in August 2021. The failure of the US nation-building exercise in Afghanistan for two decades can be measured by the rapidity with which the Afghan government and military disintegrated in the face of consistent Taliban advances. This has no doubt given like-minded groups (such as Hayat Tahrir al-Sham, a conglomeration of Sunni jihadist groups in Syria that is affiliated with al-Qaida) a boost of confidence. When there continues to be socioeconomic distress, extremist movements can find fertile ground. Where the Middle East is going seems to be more and more of a confusing proposition.

One has to remember, however, that most of the countries in the region are relatively young. The United States itself is still a work in progress, having experienced the brutality of the industry of slavery of black Africans and their progeny, the subsequent devastating civil war fought primarily over slavery, another hundred years of institutionalized discrimination against African Americans and other people of color, the decimation of the Native American population, and even this day the political, class, and racial divisions represented and produced by Trumpism—and historically America was much more remote from and much less coveted by other countries than the Middle East has been with its oil, geostrategic location, and history as the epicenter of three world religions. The Middle East is still going through the growing pains of modernization, globalization, and identity politics; does someone identify themself first as an Arab, a Kurd, a Muslim (Sunni or Shiite), a Christian, a Syrian, an Egyptian, a Turk, or an Iranian? Consider Europe. If one stood in the center of Europe toward the end of the years 1815, 1848, 1918, or 1945, one might conclude that there was no possible way that it would develop into one of the more stable and prosperous regions in the world after so much death, destruction, political instability, and revolution. But it did, even though it, too, still encounters new and ongoing challenges. Maybe the Middle East can as well. In the 1990s it came close, and with political will it can happen again, perhaps this time all the way to fruition. Progress is not a linear process. It unpredictably moves in fits and spurts in all sorts of directions. While it may not be inevitable, it is, in my opinion, likely.

Many moons ago the commander of NATO, who was from a small European country, mentioned to me in conversation that "every country or region has their time on top"; even his little country had its time, in the early modern European period. The Middle East had its time at or near the top for a number of centuries during its medieval and early modern period, at the center of things in terms of power, scientific discovery, and cultural florescence. It may not get back to that level in the foreseeable future, but there are different ways of being on top. Maybe it's not just about being the most powerful country militarily or having the most robust economy. If general happiness of the citizenry is a measure of success, then the Scandinavian countries are currently leading the pack. I suspect most in the Middle East would be quite satisfied with that. But there is still much work to be done—and more fitful history to witness.

Chapter 12 Timeline

1906–1966	Sayyid Qutb, prominent Egyptian Islamist Thinker
1990s	Osama bin Ladin builds up al-Qaida network
2000	Second Palestinian Intifada
2001	Al-Qaida directed attack on World Trade Center and Pentagon; United States responds to attack by invading Afghanistan
2003	US-led coalition invades Iraq and topples Iraqi President Saddam Hussein
2008	Global financial and economic crisis
2010	Self-immolation of Muhammad Bouazizi in Tunisia sparks Arab Spring
2011	Tunisian, Egyptian, Yemeni, and Libyan leaders either leave or are removed from office as a result of Arab Spring protests; Protests begin in Syria and soon turn into a civil war
2014–2018	The Islamic State (ISIS) establishes a territorial caliphate in large swaths of Syria and Iraq
2021	Taliban return to power in Afghanistan

Primary Sources

Excerpt from President George W. Bush's State of the Union Speech, January 2002

Thanks to the work of our law enforcement officials and coalition partners, hundreds of terrorists have been arrested. Yet, tens of thousands of trained terrorists are still at large. These enemies view the entire world as a battlefield, and we must pursue them wherever they are. (Applause.) So long as training camps operate, so long as nations harbor terrorists, freedom is at risk. And America and our allies must not, and will not, allow it. (Applause.)

Our nation will continue to be steadfast and patient and persistent in the pursuit of two great objectives. First, we will shut down terrorist camps, disrupt terrorist plans, and bring terrorists to justice. And, second, we must prevent the terrorists and regimes who seek chemical, biological or nuclear weapons from threatening the United States and the world. (Applause.)

Our military has put the terror training camps of Afghanistan out of business, yet camps still exist in at least a dozen countries. A terrorist underworld—including groups like Hamas, Hizbollah, Islamic Jihad, Jaish-i-Mohammed—operates in remote jungles and deserts, and hides in the centers of large cities.

While the most visible military action is in Afghanistan, America is acting elsewhere. We now have troops in the Philippines, helping to train that country's armed forces to go after terrorist cells that have executed an American, and still hold hostages. Our soldiers, working with the Bosnian government, seized terrorists who were plotting to bomb our embassy. Our Navy is patrolling the coast of Africa to block the shipment of weapons and the establishment of terrorist camps in Somalia.

My hope is that all nations will heed our call, and eliminate the terrorist parasites who threaten their countries and our own. Many nations are acting forcefully. Pakistan is now cracking down on terror, and I admire the strong leadership of President Musharraf. (Applause.)

But some governments will be timid in the face of terror. And make no mistake about it: If they do not act, America will. (Applause.)

Our second goal is to prevent regimes that sponsor terror from threatening America or our friends and allies with weapons of mass destruction. Some of these regimes have been pretty quiet since September the 11th. But we know their true nature. North Korea is a regime arming with missiles and weapons of mass destruction, while starving its citizens.

Iran aggressively pursues these weapons and exports terror, while an unelected few repress the Iranian people's hope for freedom.

Iraq continues to flaunt its hostility toward America and to support terror. The Iraqi regime has plotted to develop anthrax, and nerve gas, and nuclear weapons for over a decade. This is a regime that has already used poison gas to murder thousands of its own citizens—leaving the bodies of mothers huddled over their dead children. This is a regime that agreed to international inspections—then kicked out the inspectors. This is a regime that has something to hide from the civilized world.

States like these, and their terrorist allies, constitute an axis of evil, arming to threaten the peace of the world. By seeking weapons of mass destruction, these regimes pose a grave and growing danger. They could provide these arms to terrorists, giving them the means to match their hatred. They could attack our allies or attempt to blackmail the United States. In any of these cases, the price of indifference would be catastrophic.

We will work closely with our coalition to deny terrorists and their state sponsors the materials, technology, and expertise to make and deliver weapons of mass destruction. We will develop and deploy effective missile defenses to protect America and our allies from sudden attack. (Applause.)

And all nations should know: America will do what is necessary to ensure our nation's security.

We'll be deliberate, yet time is not on our side. I will not wait on events, while dangers gather. I will not stand by, as peril draws closer and closer. The United States of America will not permit the world's most dangerous regimes to threaten us with the world's most destructive weapons. (Applause.)

Our war on terror is well begun, but it is only begun. This campaign may not be finished on our watch—yet it must be and it will be waged on our watch. . . .

Source: Available from the White House Archives, https://georgewbush-whitehouse.archives.gov/news/releases/2002/01/20020129-11.html.

Statement by President Trump on Jerusalem, December 2017

Thank you. When I came into office, I promised to look at the world's challenges with open eyes and very fresh thinking. We cannot solve our problems by making the same failed assumptions and repeating the same failed strategies of the past. Old challenges demand new approaches.

My announcement today marks the beginning of a new approach to conflict between Israel and the Palestinians.

In 1995, Congress adopted the Jerusalem Embassy Act, urging the federal government to relocate the American embassy to Jerusalem and to recognize that that city—and so importantly—is Israel's capital. This act passed Congress by an overwhelming bipartisan majority and was reaffirmed by a unanimous vote of the Senate only six months ago.

Yet, for over 20 years, every previous American president has exercised the law's waiver, refusing to move the US embassy to Jerusalem or to recognize Jerusalem as Israel's capital city.

Presidents issued these waivers under the belief that delaying the recognition of Jerusalem would advance the cause of peace. Some say they lacked courage, but they made their best judgments based on facts as they understood them at the time. Nevertheless, the record is in. After more than two decades of waivers, we are no closer to a lasting peace agreement between Israel and the Palestinians. It would be folly to assume that repeating the exact same formula would now produce a different or better result.

Therefore, I have determined that it is time to officially recognize Jerusalem as the capital of Israel.

While previous presidents have made this a major campaign promise, they failed to deliver. Today, I am delivering.

I've judged this course of action to be in the best interests of the United States of America and the pursuit of peace between Israel and the

Palestinians. This is a long-overdue step to advance the peace process and to work towards a lasting agreement.

Israel is a sovereign nation with the right like every other sovereign nation to determine its own capital. Acknowledging this as a fact is a necessary condition for achieving peace.

It was 70 years ago that the United States, under President Truman, recognized the State of Israel. Ever since then, Israel has made its capital in the city of Jerusalem—the capital the Jewish people established in ancient times. Today, Jerusalem is the seat of the modern Israeli government. It is the home of the Israeli parliament, the Knesset, as well as the Israeli Supreme Court. It is the location of the official residence of the Prime Minister and the President. It is the headquarters of many government ministries.

For decades, visiting American presidents, secretaries of state, and military leaders have met their Israeli counterparts in Jerusalem, as I did on my trip to Israel earlier this year.

Jerusalem is not just the heart of three great religions, but it is now also the heart of one of the most successful democracies in the world. Over the past seven decades, the Israeli people have built a country where Jews, Muslims, and Christians, and people of all faiths are free to live and worship according to their conscience and according to their beliefs.

Jerusalem is today, and must remain, a place where Jews pray at the Western Wall, where Christians walk the Stations of the Cross, and where Muslims worship at Al-Aqsa Mosque.

However, through all of these years, presidents representing the United States have declined to officially recognize Jerusalem as Israel's capital. In fact, we have declined to acknowledge any Israeli capital at all.

But today, we finally acknowledge the obvious: that Jerusalem is Israel's capital. This is nothing more, or less, than a recognition of reality. It is also the right thing to do. It's something that has to be done.

That is why, consistent with the Jerusalem Embassy Act, I am also directing the State Department to begin preparation to move the American embassy from Tel Aviv to Jerusalem. This will immediately begin the process of hiring architects, engineers, and planners, so that a new embassy, when completed, will be a magnificent tribute to peace.

In making these announcements, I also want to make one point very clear: This decision is not intended, in any way, to reflect a departure from our strong commitment to facilitate a lasting peace agreement. We want an agreement that is a great deal for the Israelis and a great deal for the Palestinians. We are not taking a position of any final status issues, including the specific boundaries of the Israeli sovereignty in Jerusalem, or the resolution of contested borders. Those questions are up to the parties involved.

The United States remains deeply committed to helping facilitate a peace agreement that is acceptable to both sides. I intend to do everything in my power to help forge such an agreement. Without question, Jerusalem is one of the most sensitive issues in those talks. The United States would support a two-state solution if agreed to by both sides.

In the meantime, I call on all parties to maintain the status quo at Jerusalem's holy sites, including the Temple Mount, also known as Haram al-Sharif.

Above all, our greatest hope is for peace, the universal yearning in every human soul. With today's action, I reaffirm my administration's longstanding commitment to a future of peace and security for the region.

There will, of course, be disagreement and dissent regarding this announcement. But we are confident that ultimately, as we work through these disagreements, we will arrive at a peace and a place far greater in understanding and cooperation.

This sacred city should call forth the best in humanity, lifting our sights to what it is possible: not pulling us back and down to the old fights that have become so totally predictable. Peace is never beyond the grasp of those willing to reach.

So today, we call for calm, for moderation, and for the voices of tolerance to prevail over the purveyors of hate. Our children should inherit our love, not our conflicts.

I repeat the message I delivered at the historic and extraordinary summit in Saudi Arabia earlier this year: The Middle East is a region rich with culture, spirit, and history. Its people are brilliant, proud, and diverse, vibrant and strong. But the incredible future awaiting this region is held at bay by bloodshed, ignorance, and terror.

Vice President Pence will travel to the region in the coming days to reaffirm our commitment to work with partners throughout the Middle East to defeat radicalism that threatens the hopes and dreams of future generations.

It is time for the many who desire peace to expel the extremists from their midst. It is time for all civilized nations, and people, to respond to disagreement with reasoned debate—not violence.

And it is time for young and moderate voices all across the Middle East to claim for themselves a bright and beautiful future.

So today, let us rededicate ourselves to a path of mutual understanding and respect. Let us rethink old assumptions and open our hearts and minds to possible and possibilities. And finally, I ask the leaders of the region—political and religious; Israeli and Palestinian; Jewish and Christian and Muslim—to join us in the noble quest for lasting peace.

Thank you. God bless you. God bless Israel. God bless the Palestinians. And God bless the United States. Thank you very much. Thank you.

(The proclamation is signed.)

Source: Available from the US Embassy, https://it.usembassy.gov/statement-president-trump-jerusalem-december-6-2017.

Palestinian Authority President Mahmoud Abbas Reacts to Trump's Announcement

We are here today, and behind us all our nation and peoples, all Muslims and Christians in our region and the world, in order to save and protect Al-Quds Al-Sharif (Jerusalem) and to confront all plots against it to falsify its identity and change its character, especially after those recent US decisions that challenge the feelings of Muslims and Christians everywhere.

We are here today, for all of us to speak in a clear language: Jerusalem has been, and will remain forever, the capital of the State of Palestine and its crown without which there will be no peace, nor stability.

President Trump's declaration that Jerusalem is the capital of Israel and his instructions to move the US embassy to it is a flagrant violation of international law and signed agreements, especially Security Council resolutions, and a provocation to the international community, whose various countries and peoples and political and spiritual leaderships and regional and international organizations have expressed their rejection of this declaration and who expressed support for the Palestinian people and their aspirations for freedom and independence.

I would like to assure you that we have rejected these unilateral, illegitimate and unjust US decisions, which the American administration shocked us at the time we were involved in the political process in order to reach a just and comprehensive peace in the region. This has raised our astonishment and deep disapproval of the disregard of the peoples' feelings in our region and the world, the Security Council and international law. Thus the United States has chosen to lose its eligibility as an intermediary and to have no role in the political process.

These unilateral steps by President Trump will not give any legitimacy to Israel in Jerusalem. It is a Palestinian Arab Muslim Christian city, the eternal capital of the state of Palestine. There can be no Palestinian state without the city of Jerusalem as its capital and there will be no peace in the region and in the world without it.

There is no doubt that these unilateral steps will encourage extremist groups to transform the conflict from political conflict to religious conflict, and this is what we have always warned against.

Our role in the fight against terrorism in our region and the world is known to all. We have forged partnerships and agreements with many countries, including the United States. So we reject the decisions of the US Congress, which considers the PLO a terrorist organization and demand its cancellation.

We have complied with all understandings between us and successive US administrations, including this administration, but these illegal resolutions on Jerusalem have crossed all red lines, which will not make it possible to keep our commitments unilaterally. We have agreed with them that we do not join international organizations on condition the US does not recognize Jerusalem nor move its embassy and demands that Israel stop settlements.

—Dec. 13, 2017, speaking at a summit for the Organization of Islamic Cooperation, according to and translated by http://english.wafa.ps/.

Excerpts from Speech by Syrian President Bashar al-Assad to the Syrian Parliament Addressing the Mounting Protests, March 30, 2011

I know that the Syrian people have been waiting for this speech since last week, and I intentionally postponed it until I had a fuller picture in my mind . . . our enemies work every day in an organized, systemic and scientific manner in order to undermine Syria's stability. We acknowledge that they had been smart in choosing very sophisticated tools in what they have done, but at the same time we realize that they have been stupid in choosing this country and this people, for such conspiracies do not work with our country or our people.

. . . Syria is not isolated from what is happening in the Arab world. We are part of this region. We influence and are influenced by it, but at the same we are not a copy of other countries . . . We in Syria have certain characteristics which might be different internally and externally from others. Our foreign policy has been based on holding to our national rights, holding to pan-Arab rights, to independence, to supporting Arab resistance when there is occupation. The link between domestic and foreign policies has always been the Syrian citizen. When the Syrian citizen is not the heart of domestic and foreign policies, this is a deviation, and it is the job of the country's institutions to correct this deviation. The net outcome of these policies has been an unprecedented case of national unity which has been the real force which has protected Syria during the past years when pressures intensified against Syria . . . We have been able to maintain Syria's central role and position. But this has not deterred the enemies. Of course, I have just started to talk about this conspiracy, and then I will move to the internal situation so that satellite TV stations will not say that the Syrian president considered all that has happened a foreign conspiracy.

. . . And I am sure you all know that Syria is facing a great conspiracy whose tentacles extend to some nearby countries and far-away countries [a less than subtle reference primarily, but not exclusively, to Israel and the United States], with some inside the country. This conspiracy depends, in its timing not in its form, on what is happening in other Arab countries . . . Some satellite TV stations actually spoke about attacking certain buildings an hour before they were actually attacked. How did they know that? Do they read the future? This happened more than once . . . They will say that we believe in the conspiracy theory. In fact there is no conspiracy theory. There is a conspiracy . . . What we are seeing today is a stage . . . the last stage for them is for Syria to get weaker and disintegrate because this will remove the last obstacle facing the Israeli plans.

. . . In the beginning they started with incitement, many weeks before trouble started in Syria. They used the satellite TV stations and the Internet but did not achieve anything. And then, using sedition, started to produce fake information, voices, images, etc., they forged everything. Then they started to use the sectarian element . . . We have not yet discovered the whole structure of this conspiracy. We have discovered part of it but it is highly organized. There are support groups in more than one governorate linked to some countries abroad . . . Deraa is on the frontline with the Israeli enemy, and it is the frontline of defense for the hinterland.

. . . [Part] of what has happened is similar to what happened in 2005. It is a virtual war. I said at the time that they want us to surrender . . . using the media and Internet, although the Internet was not as widespread as it is today . . . The United States wanted to impose on us reform and democracy. We fought against this project in the Arab summit and it failed.

. . . I am not adding new things, but when you know how we think we harmonize our visions. So, did we make these reforms because there is a problem or because there is sedition? If there was no sedition wouldn't we have done these reforms? If the answer is yes, it means that the state is opportunistic, and this is bad. If we say that these things were made under the pressure of certain conditions or popular pressure, this is weakness. And I believe that if the people get the government to bow under pressure, it will bow to foreign pressure . . . The things I announced Thursday [24 March] were not decisions because those were the decisions of the Baath Party Regional Conference in 2005 . . . When we proposed these ideas in 2005 there was no pressure on Syria [actually there was tremendous pressure, the most there had been prior to the 2011 unrest] . . . This does not justify lagging behind on other issues, but we did not focus much on political issues like the emergency law and the party law. The reason is that when there are human issues at stake, they cannot be postponed. We can postpone a party statement for months or even years, but we cannot postpone providing food for children for breakfast . . . The measures announced last Thursday did not start from square one . . . The former government started these studies and they will be a priority for the new government . . .

Source: David W. Lesch, *Syria: The Fall of the House of Assad* (London: Yale University Press, 2013), pp. 76–79.

Shirin Ebadi, 2003 Nobel Peace Prize Laureate, Nobel Lecture, December 10, 2003

In the name of the God of Creation and Wisdom

Your Majesty, Your Royal Highnesses, Honourable Members of the Norwegian Nobel Committee, Excellencies, Ladies and Gentlemen,

I feel extremely honoured that today my voice is reaching the people of the world from this distinguished venue. This great honour has been bestowed upon me by the Norwegian Nobel Committee. I salute the spirit of Alfred Nobel and hail all true followers of his path.

This year, the Nobel Peace Prize has been awarded to a woman from Iran, a Muslim country in the Middle East.

Undoubtedly, my selection will be an inspiration to the masses of women who are striving to realize their rights, not only in Iran but throughout the region—rights taken away from them through the passage of history. This selection will make women in Iran, and much further afield, believe in themselves. Women constitute half of the population of every country. To disregard women and bar them from active participation in political, social, economic and cultural life would in fact be tantamount to depriving the entire population of every society of half its capability. The patriarchal culture and the discrimination against women, particularly in the Islamic countries, cannot continue forever.

Honourable members of the Norwegian Nobel Committee!

As you are aware, the honour and blessing of this prize will have a positive and far-reaching impact on the humanitarian and genuine endeavours of the people of Iran and the region. The magnitude of this blessing will embrace every freedom-loving and peace-seeking individual, whether they are women or men.

I thank the Norwegian Nobel Committee for this honour that has been bestowed upon me and for the blessing of this honour for the peace-loving people of my country.

Today coincides with the 55th anniversary of the adoption of the Universal Declaration of Human Rights; a declaration which begins with the recognition of the inherent dignity and the equal and inalienable rights of all members of the human family, as the guarantor of freedom, justice and peace. And it promises a world in which human beings shall enjoy freedom of expression and opinion, and be safeguarded and protected against fear and poverty.

Unfortunately, however, this year's report by the United Nations Development Programme (UNDP), as in the previous years, spells out the rise of a disaster which distances mankind from the idealistic world of the authors of the Universal Declaration of Human Rights. In 2002, almost 1.2 billion human beings lived in glaring poverty, earning less than one dollar a day. Over 50 countries were caught up in war or natural disasters. AIDS has so far claimed the lives of 22 million individuals, and turned 13 million children into orphans.

At the same time, in the past two years, some states have violated the universal principles and laws of human rights by using the events of 11 September and the war on international terrorism as a pretext. The United Nations General Assembly Resolution 57/219, of 18 December 2002, the United Nations Security Council Resolution 1456, of 20 January 2003, and the United Nations Commission on Human Rights Resolution 2003/68, of 25 April 2003, set out and underline that all states must ensure that any measures taken to combat terrorism must comply with all their obligations under international law, in particular international human rights and humanitarian law. However, regulations restricting human rights and basic freedoms, special bodies and extraordinary courts, which make fair adjudication difficult and at times impossible, have been justified and given legitimacy under the cloak of the war on terrorism.

The concerns of human rights' advocates increase when they observe that international human rights laws are breached not only by their recognized opponents under the pretext of cultural relativity, but that these principles are also violated in Western democracies, in other words countries which were themselves among the initial codifiers of the United Nations Charter and the Universal Declaration of Human Rights. It is in this framework that, for months, hundreds of individuals who were arrested in the course of military conflicts have been imprisoned in Guantanamo, without the benefit of the rights stipulated under the international Geneva conventions, the Universal Declaration of Human Rights and the [United Nations] International Covenant on Civil and Political Rights.

Moreover, a question which millions of citizens in the international civil society have been asking themselves for the past few years, particularly in recent months, and continue to ask, is this: why is it that some decisions and resolutions of the UN Security Council are binding, while some other resolutions of the council have no binding force? Why is it that in the past 35 years, dozens of UN resolutions concerning the occupation of the Palestinian territories by the state of Israel have not been implemented promptly, yet, in the past 12 years, the state and people of Iraq, once on the recommendation of the Security Council, and the second time, in spite of UN Security Council opposition, were subjected to attack, military assault, economic sanctions, and, ultimately, military occupation?

Ladies and Gentlemen,

Allow me to say a little about my country, region, culture and faith.

I am an Iranian. A descendent of Cyrus the Great. The very emperor who proclaimed at the pinnacle of power 2500 years ago that "he would not reign over the people if they did not wish it." And [he] promised not to force any person to change his religion and faith and guaranteed freedom for all. The Charter of Cyrus The Great is one of the most important documents that should be studied in the history of human rights.

I am a Muslim. In the Koran the Prophet of Islam has been cited as saying: "Thou shalt believe in thine faith and I in my religion". That same divine book sees the mission of all prophets as that of inviting all human beings to uphold justice. Since the advent of Islam, too, Iran's civilization and culture has become imbued and infused with humanitarianism, respect for the life, belief and faith of others, propagation of tolerance and compromise and avoidance of violence, bloodshed and war. The luminaries of Iranian literature, in particular our Gnostic literature, from Hafiz, Mowlavi [better known in the West as Rumi] and Attar to Saadi, Sanaei, Naser Khosrow and Nezami, are emissaries of this humanitarian culture. Their message manifests itself in this poem by Saadi:

> "The sons of Adam are limbs of one anotherHaving been created of one essence."
> "When the calamity of time afflicts one limbThe other limbs cannot remain at rest."

The people of Iran have been battling against consecutive conflicts between tradition and modernity for over 100 years. By resorting to ancient traditions, some have tried and are trying to see the world through the eyes of their predecessors and to deal with the problems and difficulties of the existing world by virtue of the values of the ancients. But, many others, while respecting their historical and cultural past and their religion and faith, seek to go forth in step with world developments and not lag behind the caravan of civilization, development and progress. The people of Iran, particularly in the recent years, have shown that they deem participation in public affairs to be their right, and that they want to be masters of their own destiny.

This conflict is observed not merely in Iran, but also in many Muslim states. Some Muslims, under the pretext that democracy and human rights are not compatible with Islamic teachings and the traditional structure of Islamic societies, have justified despotic governments, and continue to do so. In fact, it is not so easy to rule over a people who are aware of their rights, using traditional, patriarchal and paternalistic methods.

Islam is a religion whose first sermon to the Prophet begins with the word "Recite!" The Koran swears by the pen and what it writes. Such a sermon and message cannot be in conflict with awareness, knowledge, wisdom, freedom of opinion and expression and cultural pluralism.

The discriminatory plight of women in Islamic states, too, whether in the sphere of civil law or in the realm of social, political and cultural justice, has its roots in the patriarchal and male-dominated culture prevailing in these societies, not in Islam. This culture does not tolerate freedom and democracy, just as it does not believe in the equal rights of men and women, and the liberation of women from male domination (fathers, husbands, brothers . . .), because it would threaten the historical and traditional position of the rulers and guardians of that culture.

One has to say to those who have mooted the idea of a clash of civilizations, or prescribed war and military intervention for this region, and resorted to social, cultural, economic and political sluggishness of the South in a bid to justify their actions and opinions, that if you consider international human rights laws, including the nations' right to determine their own destinies, to be universal, and if you believe in the priority and superiority of parliamentary democracy over other political systems, then you cannot think only of your own security and comfort, selfishly and contemptuously. A quest for new means and ideas to enable the countries of the South, too, to enjoy human rights and democracy, while maintaining their political independence and territorial integrity of their respective countries, must be given top priority by the United Nations in respect of future developments and international relations.

The decision by the Nobel Peace Committee to award the 2003 prize to me, as the first Iranian and the first woman from a Muslim country, inspires me and millions of Iranians and nationals of Islamic states with the hope that our efforts, endeavours and struggles toward the realization of human rights and the establishment of democracy in our respective countries enjoy the support, backing and solidarity of international civil society. This prize belongs to the people of Iran. It belongs to the people of the Islamic states, and the people of the South for establishing human rights and democracy.

Ladies and Gentlemen

In the introduction to my speech, I spoke of human rights as a guarantor of freedom, justice and peace. If human rights fail to be manifested in codified laws or put into effect by states, then, as rendered in the preamble of the Universal Declaration of Human Rights, human beings will be left with no choice other than staging a "rebellion against tyranny and oppression". A human being divested of all dignity, a human being deprived of human rights, a human being gripped by starvation, a human being beaten by famine, war and illness, a humiliated human being and a plundered human being is not in any position or state to recover the rights he or she has lost.

If the twenty-first century wishes to free itself from the cycle of violence, acts of terror and war, and avoid repetition of the experience of the twentieth century—that most disaster-ridden century of humankind, there is no other way except by understanding and putting into practice every human right for all mankind, irrespective of race, gender, faith, nationality or social status.

In anticipation of that day.

With much gratitude Shirin Ebadi

Source: Shirin Ebadi – Nobel Lecture. NobelPrize.org. Nobel Prize Outreach AB. Copyright © The Nobel Foundation 2003.

NOTES

1. For this see James L. Gelvin, *The Modern Middle East: A History* (New York: Oxford University Press, 2005), pp. 294–295.
2. John L. Esposito, *Unholy War: Terror in the Name of Islam* (New York: Oxford University Press, 2002), p. 27.
3. Ibid., p. 27.
4. Philip S. Khoury, "Islamic Revivalism and the Crisis of the Secular State in the Arab World: A Historical Approach," in Ibrahim Ibrahim, ed., *Arab Resources: The Transformation of Society* (Washington, DC: Contemporary Center for Arab Studies, 1983).
5. Emmanuel Sivan, *Radical Islam: Medieval Theology and Modern Politics* (New Haven, CT: Yale University Press, 1985), pp. 22–23. For a lengthier discussion on Qutb's use of jahiliyya, see Sayyid Qutb, *Milestones* (Beirut: Holy Koran Publishing House, 1980), pp. 242–263. Qutb writes, "The foremost duty of Islam is to depose Jahiliyya from the leadership of man, and to take the leadership into his own hands and enforce the particular way of life which is its permanent feature." (p. 245). He further writes that "Jahiliyya is evil and corrupt, whether be of the ancient or modern variety. Its outward manifestations may be different during different epochs, yet its roots are the same" (p. 247).

6. It is interesting that a brother of Qutb, Muhammad Qutb, was one of Osama bin Ladin's teachers in Saudi Arabia, which frequently imported Egyptians to teach in the new schools that were being built across the kingdom. Osama bin Ladin was the founder and leader of al-Qaida, which planned and carried out the 9/11 attacks.
7. Quoted in Sivan, *Radical Islam*, pp. 23–24. Also see Qutb, *Milestones*, pp. 103–107 for more of Qutb's thoughts on this.
8. Quoted in Sivan, *Radical Islam*, p. 36.
9. Ibid., p. 186.
10. See ibid., pp. 95–107.
11. I will go with Jessica Stern's definition of terrorism, which she defines as "an act or threat of violence against noncombatants with the objective of exacting revenge, intimidating, or otherwise influencing an audience." Jessica Stern, *Terror in the Name of God: Why Religious Militants Kill* (New York: Ecco, 2003), p. xx.
12. In one of his writings in 1998, Osama bin Ladin stated the following: "To kill Americans and their allies—civilians and military—is an individual duty incumbent upon every Muslim in all countries, in order to liberate the al-Aqsa Mosque [the 'farthest' mosque, located on the Haram al-Sharif/Temple Mount in Jerusalem] and the Holy Mosque [Grand Mosque in Mecca] from their grip, so that their armies leave all the territory of Islam, defeated, broken, and unable to threaten any Muslim." Bruce Lawrence, ed., *Messages to the World: The Statements of Osama bin Ladin* (New York: Verso, 2005), p. 61. He also wrote in 2005: "As I speak, our wounds have yet to heal from the Crusader wars of the last century against the Islamic world, or from the Sykes-Picot Agreement of 1916 between France and Britain, which brought about the dissection of the Islamic world into fragments. The Crusaders' agents are still in power to this day, in light of a new Sykes-Picot Agreement, the Bush-Blair Axis, which has the same banner and objective, namely the banner of the Cross and the objective of destroying the looting of our beloved Prophet's *umma*." Ibid., p. 102.
13. Quoted in David W. Lesch, *The Arab-Israeli Conflict: A History* (London: Oxford University Press, 2019), p. 389.
14. To the point where foreign policy officials from both Bush administrations were sniping at each other at the time, the latter criticizing the former for not finishing the job in 1991. Some have even suggested that George W. Bush's support for the war in 2003 stemmed in part on his need to move out of his father's shadow.
15. For more on the origins and course of the Arab Spring, see Mark L. Haas and David W. Lesch, eds., *The Arab Spring: The Hope and Reality of the Uprisings* (Boulder, CO: Westview Press, 2017).
16. For instance, according to the AHDR, the expenditure on education in Syria stood at an average of 11.1 percent of total government spending during the years 1999–2001, while it was at 17.3 percent in 1990, a 35 percent drop in ten years. David W. Lesch, *The New Lion of Damascus: Bashar al-Asad and Modern Syria* (New Haven, CT: Yale University Press, 2005), p. 205. A clear demonstration of the imbalance in

budget allocation on education versus the military was detailed in the World Health Organization's *World Health Report 2000*, in which it was stated that the Southeast Asian country of Burma (Myanmar) spent over 200 percent more on military expenditure than on health and education. The only countries with a worse ratio at the time were Iraq and Syria. Ibid.

17. The higher commodity prices on top of the fact that the Middle East was already more dependent on imported foodstuffs than any other region in the world. For instance, at the time of the Arab Spring 63 percent of household spending in Morocco goes to food, whereas in the United States it is 7 percent. See James L. Gelvin, *The Arab Uprisings: What Everyone Needs to Know* (New York: Oxford University Press, 2012).
18. See Andrea Duffy, "What the Ottoman Empire Can Teach Us About the Consequences of Climate Change—and How Drought Can Uproot Peoples and Fuel Warfare," *The Conversation*, June 8, 2021, https://source.colostate/what-the-ottoman-empire-can-teach-us-about-the-consequences-of-climate-change-and-how-drought-can-uproot-peoples-and-fuel-warfare/.
19. For more on the civil war, see David W. Lesch, *Syria: The Fall of the House of Assad* (New Haven, CT: Yale University Press, 2013). Despite the title of the book, I concluded that the most likely outcome of the Syrian civil war was Bashar al-Assad surviving and staying in power. Also see David W. Lesch, *Syria: A Modern History* (London: Polity Press, 2019) for a more general narrative of Syrian history, the last chapter focusing on the civil war. For an excellent book on the regional and international dimensions of the Syrian civil war, see Christopher Phillips, *The Battle for Syria: International Rivalry in the Middle East* (New Haven, CT: Yale University Press, 2016).
20. Al-Monitor Staff, "World Bank Says Mideast, North Africa Ripe for Digital Transformation," *Al-Monitor*, March 18, 2022, https://www.al-monitor/originals/2022/03/world-bank-says-mideast-north-africa-ripe-for-digital-transformation/0Mideast%20North%20Africa%20rpie%20for%20digital%20transformation.
21. Fareed Zakaria, "Ten Years Later, Islamist Terrorism Isn't the Threat It Used to Be," *Washington Post*, April 29, 2021, https://www.washingtonpost.com/opinions/global-opinions/ten-years-later-Islamist-terrorism-isn't-the-threat-it-used-to-be/2021/04/29/deb88256-a91c-11eb-bca5-048b2759a489_story.html.
22. Quoted in ibid.

KEY TERM

weapons of mass destruction (WMD) p. 412

For additional digital learning resources please go to www.oup.com/he/lesch-middleeast-1e

FOR FURTHER READING

Abdullah, Thabit A. J. *A Short History of Iraq: From 636 to the Present*. New York: Pearson-Longman, 2003.

Ahmed, Leila. *Women and Gender in Islam: Historical Roots of a Modern Debate*. New Haven, CT: Yale University Press, 1992.

Algar, Hamid. *Islam and Revolution: Writings and Declarations of Imam Khomeini*. Berkeley: Mizan Press, 1981.

Allen, S. J., and Emilie Amt, eds. *The Crusades: A Reader*, 2nd ed. Toronto: University of Toronto Press, 2014.

Anderson, Kyle J. *The Egyptian Labors Corps: Race, Space, and Place in the First World War*. Austin: University of Texas Press, 2021.

Avishai, Bernard. *The Tragedy of Zionism*. New York: FSG, 1986.

Bakhash, Shaul. *The Reign of the Ayatollahs: Iran and the Islamic Revolution*. New York: Basic Books, 1984.

Barkan, Omer Lutfi, and Justin McCarthy. "The Price Revolution of the Sixteenth Century: A Turning Point in the Economic History of the Near East." *International Journal of Middle East Studies* 6, no. 1 (January 1975): 3–28.

Bennison, Amira K. *The Great Caliphs: The Golden Age of the Abbasid Empire*. New Haven, CT: Yale University Press, 2009.

Billig, Michael. *Banal Nationalism: Theory, Culture, and Society*. Thousand Oaks, CA: SAGE Publications, 1995.

Bonine, Michael E., Abbas Amanat, and Michael Ezekiel Gaspar, eds. *Is There a Middle East?: The Evolution of a Geopolitical Concept*. Stanford: Stanford University Press, 2011.

Bowen, Harold. *The Life and Times of Ali ibn Isa: The Good Vizier*. Cambridge: Cambridge University Press, 1928.

Brundage, James A. *The Crusades: A Documentary Survey*. Milwaukee, WI: Marquette University Press, 1962.

Catlos, Brian A. *Kingdoms of Faith: A New History of Islamic Spain*. New York: Basic Books, 2018.

Cleveland, William L., and Martin Bunton. *A History of the Modern Middle East*, 5th ed. Boulder, CO: Westview Press, 2013.

Clover, Frank, and R. Stephen Humphreys, eds. *Tradition and Innovation in Late Antiquity*. Madison: University of Wisconsin Press, 1989.

Cohen, Michael J. *The Origins and Evolution of the Arab–Zionist Conflict*. Berkeley: University of California Press, 1987.

Cole, Juan. *Napoleon's Egypt: Invading the Middle East*. New York: Palgrave Macmillan, 2008.

Cooperson, Michael. *Al Ma'mun*. Oxford: Oneworld Publications, 2012.

Cox, Harvey. "Understanding Islam." *Atlantic Monthly*, January 1981, 73–80.

Crone, Patricia. *Meccan Trade and the Rise of Islam*. Piscataway, NJ: Gorgias Press, 2004.

Crowley, Roger. *Empires of the Sea: The Final Battle for the Mediterranean, 1521–1580*. London: Faber and Faber, 2008.

Darke, Diana. *Stealing from the Saracens: How Islamic Architecture Shaped Europe*. London: Hurst, 2020.

Diamond, Jared. *Guns, Germs, and Steel: The Fates of Human Societies*. New York: Norton, 1999.

Donner, Fred M. *Muhammad and the Believers: At the Origins of Islam*. Cambridge, MA: Harvard University Press, 2010.

Esposito, John L., ed. *The Oxford Dictionary of Islam*. Oxford: Oxford University Press, 2003.

Esposito, John L. *Unholy War: Terror in the Name of Islam*. New York: Oxford University Press, 2002.

Fierro, Maribel. *Abd al-Rahman III: The First Cordoban Caliph*. Oxford: Oneworld Publications, 2005.

Finkel, Caroline. *Osman's Dream: The History of the Ottoman Empire*. New York: Basic Books, 2005.

Fisher, Sydney Nettleton, and William Ochsenwald. *The Middle East: A History*. New York: McGraw Hill, 2011.

Fletcher, Richard. *Moorish Spain*. Berkeley: University of California Press, 1992.

Fowden, Garth. *Before and After Muhammad: The First Millennium Refocused*. Princeton, NJ: Princeton University Press, 2014.

Freedman, Robert O. *Soviet Foreign Policy Toward the Middle East Since 1970*. New York: Praeger, 1982.

Fromkin, David. *A Peace to End All Peace*. New York: Henry Holt and Company, 1989.

Gabrieli, Francesco. *Arab Historians of the Crusades*. Berkeley: University of California Press, 1969.

Gani, Jasmine K. *The Role of Ideology in Syrian–US Relations: Conflict and Cooperation*. New York: Palgrave-Macmillan, 2014.

Gause, F. Gregory. *Oil Monarchies: Domestic and Security Challenges in the Arab Gulf States*. New York: Council on Foreign Relations Press, 1994.

Gelvin, James L. *The Arab Uprisings: What Everyone Needs to Know*. New York: Oxford University Press, 2012.

Gelvin, James L. *The Modern Middle East: A History*. Oxford: Oxford University Press, 2005.

Gordon, Matthew S. *The Rise of Islam*. Indianapolis: Hackett Publishing Company, 2005.

Guthrie, Shirley. *Arab Social Life in the Middle Ages: An Illustrated History*. London: Saqi Books, 1995.

Haas, Mark L., and David W. Lesch, eds. *The Arab Spring: The Hope and Reality of the Uprisings*. Boulder, CO: Westview Press, 2017.

Haim, Sylvia G. *Arab Nationalism: An Anthology*. Berkeley: University of California Press, 1962.

Halm, Heinz. "Al-Andalus und Gothic Sors." *Welt des Oriens* 66 (1989): 55–72.

Halm, Heinz. *The Fatimids and their Traditions of Learning*. New York: I. B. Tauris, 1997.

Halm, Heinz. *The Shiites: A Short History*. Princeton, NJ: Markus Weiner Publishers, 2007.

Hanioglu, M. Sukru. *A Brief History of the Late Ottoman Empire*. Princeton, NJ: Princeton University Press, 2008.

Hassani, Salim T. S. Al-, ed. *1001 Inventions: The Enduring Legacy of Muslim Civilization*. Washington, DC: National Geographic Society, 2012.

Hawting, G. R. *The First Dynasty of Islam*. Carbondale: Southern Illinois University Press, 1987.

Henninger, Joseph. "Pre-Islamic Bedouin Religion." In *Studies on Islam*, edited by Merlin L. Schwartz, 3–22. Oxford: Oxford University Press, 1981.

Hinnebusch, Raymond. *The International Politics of the Middle East*. Manchester, UK: Manchester University Press, 2015.

Hodgson, Marshall G. S. *The Order of the Assassins*. The Hague: Mouton & Co., 1955.

Hodgson, Marshall G. S. *The Venture of Islam, Volume 1: The Classical Age of Islam*. Chicago: University of Chicago Press, 1974.

Hodgson, Marshall G. S. *The Venture of Islam, Volume 2: The Expansion of Islam in the Middle Periods*. Chicago: University of Chicago Press, 1974.

Holt, P. M. *The Age of the Crusades: The Near East from the Eleventh Century to 1517*. New York: Longman, 1986.

Hourani, Albert. *A History of the Arab Peoples*. Cambridge, MA: Harvard University Press, 1991.

Humphreys, R. Stephen. *Mu'awiya ibn Abi Sufyan: From Arabia to Empire*. Oxford: Oneworld Publications, 2006.

Ibrahim, Ibrahim, ed. *Arab Resources: The Transformation of Society*. Washington, DC: Contemporary Center for Arab Studies, 1983.

Itzkowitz, Norman. *Ottoman Empire and Islamic Tradition*. Chicago: University of Chicago Press, 1972.

Jackson, Peter. *The Mongols & the Islamic World*. New Haven, CT: Yale University Press, 2017.

Kaegi, Walter E. *Byzantium and the Early Islamic Conquests*. Cambridge: Cambridge University Press, 1992.

Kamaly, Hossein. *A History of Islam in 21 Women*. London: Oneworld Publications, 2019.

Keddie, Nikki R. *Roots of Revolution: An Interpretive History of Modern Iran*. New Haven, CT: Yale University Press, 1981.

Keddie, Nikki R. *Women in the Middle East Since the Rise of Islam*. Washington, DC: American Historical Association, 2007.

Kennedy, Hugh. *The Prophet and the Age of the Caliphates: The Islamic Near East from the Sixth to the Eleventh Century*. New York: Longman, 1986.

Kennedy, Hugh. *When Baghdad Ruled the World: The Rise and Fall of Islam's Greatest Dynasty*. Cambridge, MA: De Capo Press, 2004.

Kerr, Malcolm. *The Arab Cold War: Gamal Abd al-Nasir and His Rivals, 1958–1970*. Oxford: Oxford University Press, 1971.

Khaldun, Ibn. Translated by Franz Rosenthal, edited by N. J. Dawood. *The Muqaddimah: An Introduction to History*. Princeton, NJ: Princeton University Press, 1994.

Khalidi, Rashid. *Resurrecting the Empire: Western Footprints and America's Perilous Path in the Middle East*. New York: Beacon Press, 2005.

Khan, Muhammad Mushin, trans. *The Translation of the Meanings of Sahih Al-Bukhari, (Arabic-English) Volume 4*. Riyadh: Darussalam Publishers & Distributers, 1997.

Kidwai, Abdur Raheem. *Women in Islam: What the Qur'an and Sunnah Say*. Leicester, UK: Kube Publishing Ltd., 2020.

Kirsch, Jonathan. *God Against the Gods: The History of the War Between Monotheism and Polytheism*. New York: Penguin, 2004.

Kritzeck, James. *Anthology of Islamic Literature*. New York: Holt, Rinehart and Winston, 1964.

Kunt, Metin, and Christine Woodhead, eds. *Suleyman the Magnificent and His Age: The Ottoman Empire in the Early Modern World*. London: Longman, 1995.

Lambton, A. K. S. "The Internal Structure of the Seljuq Empire." In *The Cambridge History of Iran, Volume 5, The Saljuq and Mongol Periods*, edited by J. A. Boyle, pp. 203–283, Cambridge: Cambridge University Press, 1968.

Lawrence, Bruce, ed. *Messages to the World: The Statements of Osama bin Ladin*. New York: Verso, 2005.

Lesch, David W. *1979: The Year That Shaped the Modern Middle East*. Boulder, CO: Westview Press, 2000.

Lesch, David W. *The Arab–Israeli Conflict: A History*. Oxford: Oxford University Press, 2019.

Lesch, David W., ed. *The Middle East and the United States: A Historical and Political Reassessment*, 3rd ed. Boulder, CO: Westview Press, 2003.

Lesch, David W. *The New Lion of Damascus: Bashar al-Asad and Modern Syria*. New Haven, CT: Yale University Press, 2005.

Lesch, David W. *Syria: A Modern History*. Cambridge: Polity Press, 2019.

Lesch, David W. *Syria and the United States: Eisenhower's Cold War in the Middle East*. Boulder, CO: Westview Press, 1992.

Lesch, David W. *Syria: The Fall of the House of Assad*. New Haven, CT: Yale University Press, 2013.

Lewis, Bernard. *The Assassins*. Oxford: Oxford University Press, 1967.

Long, David E., Bernard Reich, and Mark Gasiorowski, eds. *The Government and Politics of the Middle East and North Africa*, 6th ed. Boulder, CO: Westview Press, 2011.

Maalouf, Amin. *The Crusades Through Arab Eyes*. New York: Schocken Books, 1989.

MacMillan, Margaret. *Paris 1919: Six Months That Changed the World*. New York: Random House, 2003.

Madden, Thomas F. *The New Concise History of the Crusades*. Lanham, MD: Rowman & Littlefield, 2006.

Madelung, Wilferd. *The Succession to Muhammad: A Study of the Early Caliphate*. Cambridge: Cambridge University Press, 1997.

Man, John. *Saladin: The Sultan Who Vanquished the Crusaders and Built an Islamic Empire*. New York: De Capo Press, 2016.

Mansel, Philip. *Constantinople: City of the World's Desire, 1453–1924*. New York: St. Martin's Press, 1995.

Marozzi, Justin. *Tamerlane: Sword of Islam, Conqueror of the World*. Cambridge, MA: De Capo Press, 2004.

Marsot, Afaf Lutfi Al-Sayyid. *A History of Egypt: From the Arab Conquests to the Present*. Cambridge: Cambridge University Press, 2007.

McAuliffe, Jane, ed. *The Qur'an*. New York: Norton, 2017.

McCarthy, Justin. *The Ottoman Turks: An Introductory History to 1923*. London: Longman, 1997.

McNeill, William H., and Marilyn Robinson Waldman. *The Islamic World*. Chicago: University of Chicago Press, 1973.

Mernissi, Fatima. *The Veil and the Male Elite: A Feminist's Interpretation of Women's Rights in Islam*. Reading, MA: Addison-Wesley, 1991.

Mitchell, Richard P. *The Society of the Muslim Brothers*. Oxford: Oxford University Press, 1993.

Morgan, David. *The Mongols*. New York: Basil Blackwell, 1986.

Morgan, Michael Hamilton. *Lost History: The Enduring Legacy of Muslim Scientists, Thinkers, and Artists*. Washington, DC: National Geographic Society, 2007.

Mottahedeh, Roy. *Loyalty and Leadership in an Early Islamic Society*. Princeton, NJ: Princeton University Press, 1980.

Neggaz, Nassima. "The Many Deaths of the Last Abbasid Caliph al-Musta'sim bi-Illan (d. 1258)." *Journal of the Royal Asiatic Society* 30, no. 4 (August 18, 2020): 585–612.

Nutting, Anthony. *Nasser.* London: Constable, 1972.
Parsa, Misagh. *Social Origins of the Iranian Revolution.* New Brunswick, NJ: Rutgers University Press, 1989.
Phillips, Christopher. *The Battle for Syria: International Rivalry in the Middle East.* New Haven, CT: Yale University Press, 2016.
Pierce, Leslie. *The Imperial Harem: Women and Sovereignty in the Ottoman Empire.* New York: Oxford University Press, 1993.
Podeh, Elie, and Onn Winckler, eds. *Rethinking Nasserism: Revolution and Historical Memory in Modern Egypt.* Gainesville: University Press of Florida, 2004.
Provence, Michael. *The Last Ottoman Generation and the Making of the Modern Middle East.* Cambridge: Cambridge University Press, 2017.
Quandt, William B. *Peace Process: American Diplomacy and the Arab–Israeli Conflict Since 1967.* Washington, DC: Brookings Institution Press, 2005.
Quataert, Donald. *The Ottoman Empire, 1700–1922.* Cambridge: Cambridge University Press, 2000.
Qutb, Sayyid. *Milestones.* Beirut: Holy Koran Publishing House, 1980.
Qutb, Sayyid. Translated by John B. Hardie and Hamid Algar. *Social Justice in Islam.* New York: Islamic Publications International, 2000.
Rashid, Ahmed. *Taliban: Militant Islam, Oil, and Fundamentalism in Central Asia.* New Haven, CT: Yale University Press, 2010.
Richards, Alan, and John Waterbury. *A Political Economy of the Middle East.* Boulder, CO: Westview Press, 1996.
Robinson, Chase. *Abd al-Malik.* London: Oneworld Publications, 2005.
Rogan, Eugene L., and Avi Shlaim, eds. *The War for Palestine: Rewriting the History of 1948.* Cambridge: Cambridge University Press, 2001.
Rogan, Eugene. *The Fall of the Ottomans: The Great War in the Middle East.* New York: Basic Books, 2015.
Roy, Olivier. *The Failure of Political Islam.* Cambridge, MA: Harvard University Press, 1994.
Safran, Nadav. *Israel: The Embattled Ally.* Cambridge, MA: Harvard University Press, 1982.
Said, Edward W. *Orientalism.* New York: Vantage Books, 1979.
Savory, Roger. *Iran Under the Safavids.* Cambridge: Cambridge University Press, 1980.
Schacht, Joseph. *The Origins of Muhammadan Jurisprudence.* Oxford: Oxford University Press, 1950.
Seale, Patrick. *The Struggle for Syria: A Study of Post-War Arab Politics, 1954–1958.* New Haven, CT: Yale University Press, 1987.
Shaban, M. A. *The Abbasid Revolution.* Cambridge: Cambridge University Press, 1970.
Shaban, M. A. *Islamic History: A New Interpretation, A.D. 600–750.* Cambridge: Cambridge University Press, 1971.

Shaban, M. A. *Islamic History: A New Interpretation 2, A.D. 750–1055*. Cambridge: Cambridge University Press, 1976.

Shaw, Stanford J. *History of the Ottoman Empire and Modern Turkey: Volume I: Empire of the Gazis; The Rise and Decline of the Ottoman Empire, 1280–1808*. Cambridge: Cambridge University Press, 1976.

Sivan, Emmanuel. *Radical Islam: Medieval Theology and Modern Politics*. New Haven, CT: Yale University Press, 1985.

Skalcup, Brenda. *The Crusades*. San Diego: Greenhaven Press, 2000.

Smith, Charles D. *Palestine and the Arab–Israeli Conflict*. New York: St. Martin's Press, 2001.

Sourdel, Dominique. *Medieval Islam*. London: Routledge & Kegan Paul, 1979.

Spuler, Bertold. *The Age of the Caliphs: History of the Muslim World*. Princeton, NJ: Markus Weiner Publishers, 1995.

Stern, Jessica. *Terror in the Name of God: Why Religious Militants Kill*. New York: Ecco, 2003.

Streusand, Douglas E. *Islamic Gunpowder Empires: Ottomans, Safavids, and Mughals*. London: Routledge, 2010.

Sugar, Peter F. *Southeastern Europe Under Ottoman Rule, 1354–1804*. Seattle: University of Washington Press, 1977.

Swartz, Merlin L. *Studies on Islam*. Oxford: Oxford University Press, 1981.

Tolan, John V. *Saracens: Islam in the Medieval European Imagination*. New York: Columbia University Press, 2002.

Trofimov, Yaroslav. *The Siege of Mecca: The Forgotten Uprising in Islam's Holiest Shrine and the Birth of Al Qaeda*. New York: Doubleday, 2007.

Tschanz, David W. "History's Hinge: Ain Jalut." *Aramco World* 58, no. 4 (July/August 2007): 24-33.

Vohra, Anchal. "The Middle East is Becoming Literally Uninhabitable." *Foreign Policy*, August 24, 2021. https://foreignpolicy.com/2021/08/24/the-middle-east-is-becoming-literally-uninhabitable/.

Voll, John. *Islam: Continuity and Change in the Modern World*. Boulder, CO: Westview Press, 1982.

Watt, W. Montgomery. *The Influence of Islam on Medieval Europe*. Edinburgh: Edinburgh University Press, 1994.

Watt, W. Montgomery. *Muhammad: Prophet and Statesman*. Oxford: Oxford University Press, 1964.

Weatherford, Jack. *Genghis Khan and the Making of the Modern World*. New York: Three Rivers Press, 2004.

Wellhausen, Julius. *Das Arabische Reich und Sein Sturz*. Berlin: De Gruyter, 1960.

Wiley, Peter. *The Castles of the Assassins*. London: George G. Harrap & Co., 1963.

Yapp, M. E. *The Making of the Modern Near East, 1792–1923*. London: Longman, 1987.

GLOSSARY

10 Muharram: The tenth day of the Islamic month of Muharram commemorated by Shiite Muslims as the day Hussein, the grandson of the Prophet Muhammad, son of Ali ibn Abu Talib, and the third imam in the Shiite line of imams, was martyred by Umayyad forces in the Battle of Karbala in present-day Iraq in 680 CE. Often called the *Ashura*, which in Arabic is the number 10, for the 10th day of the month.

abna (Arabic: sons): This is the plural of *ibn* (son), and in this book a reference to the *abna al-dawlah*, the Sons of the Revolution, the descendants of the original Khurasaniyya who played the key military role in the Abbasid revolution.

ahl al-kitab (related, **dhimmi)** (Arabic: People of the Book): A term found in the Quran, designating Jews, Christians, and Sabians as believers in a revealed book, specifically the Bible or Torah. Special protections were extended to those deemed *dhimmi* or protected ones under Muslim rule, in return for a tax paid (*jizya*).

Alids: Those who were followers of Ali ibn Abu Talib, something of a precursor to Shiite Muslims.

aliyah (Hebrew: ascent): Zionist term for the waves of Jewish immigration to Palestine and then Israel.

Amir al-mumineen: Arabic title translated as "Commander of the Faithful," one of the early references to the head of the Islamic community (*umma*), more frequently referred to as the caliph (successor) to the Prophet Muhammad.

amir al-umara: A senior military position in the Abbasid caliphate that came to surpass the civilian bureaucracy, effectively relegating the caliphs to ceremonial figureheads by 936. The term is translated as "commander of commanders."

amsar, singular **misr:** Garrison towns established by Muslim armies in conquered lands. Many of these established the foundation for or actually became major cities throughout the region over time.

Ansar (Arabic: the helpers): These helpers were residents of Medina who took the Prophet Muhammad and his followers (the *Muhajirun*) into their homes after the *hijra* from Mecca. They became an important interest group in early Islam.

asabiyya: The concept of group solidarity or social cohesion.

Ashraf, singular **Sharif:** Literally meaning "noble," it is a title often given to those who are descended from the family of the Prophet Muhammad, the Hashimites. It is also something of an honorific title given to tribal or religious leaders. In this book it is also a reference to the so-called latecomers in the early Islamic period, a group of tribal shaykhs and other nobles from Arabia who migrated to Iraq, but because they converted to Islam later than earlier groups felt somewhat disadvantaged, especially in terms of salary (*ata*) and position, which they resented.

Assassins: A relatively small Nizari Ismaili sect who, from the eleventh to the mid-thirteenth century, became infamous for their guerilla tactics of singling out enemy leaders (typically Sunni Muslims) and killing them. The term "assassin" is an English corruption of the Arabic word "hashishiyyun," those who smoke or ingest hashish, which the Assassins were said to do before going on their missions.

ata: Salary paid to the military and administrators in early Islam, often, at least in theory, determined by one's *sabiqa*, or precedence in Islam.

Auspicious Incident (1826): When Sultan Mahmud II in the Ottoman Empire moved militarily against the Janissary corps, effectively eliminating it.

ayan: Refers to a class of local notables in the Ottoman Empire particularly from the seventeenth through the nineteenth centuries. They were especially powerful in the provincial areas of the empire, and there frequently was tension between the ayan and the centralized authority of the Sublime Porte.

Baath (Arabic: renaissance or rebirth): Name of the pan-Arab party founded in the 1930s primarily by Syrians. According to its slogan, the Baath advocated freedom, unity, and socialism. It became the ruling party in both Syria and Iraq in 1963 and had small branches in a number of other Arab countries. As of this writing, it remains the ruling party of Syria; however, it was eliminated in Iraq with the removal of the regime of Saddam Hussein in the 2003 Iraq war.

beylerbeyik: A large territorial subdivision of the Ottoman Empire, the equivalent of a province, led by a provincial governor known as *beylerbey*. A province has also been termed *vilayet*, and if using this reference, the governor is called the *vali*.

caliph, alternate **khalifa:** Successor to the Prophet Muhammad as leader of the Muslim community.

Committee of Union and Progress (CUP): A largely covert revolutionary party in the late nineteenth and early twentieth century in the Ottoman Empire, its members mostly located in the Balkans. It was composed of and aligned with the Young Turks movement.

Coptic: Members of the Coptic Orthodox Church, the largest Christian religion in Egypt, or a more generic cultural term for Egyptian Christians.

devshirme: Literally meaning "a gathering or levying of youths," this was an Ottoman system of collecting and recruiting Christian children, usually between the ages of eight and thirteen, from within the empire (mostly in the Balkans), converting them to Islam and training them as soldiers and bureaucrats.

dihqan, plural **dahaqin:** Lesser aristocracy that included administrators and tax collectors in the Sassanian Empire, many of whom continued in their occupations even after the Islamic conquest.

Diophysite: Meaning "two natures," it is a reference to the Christian belief in the two natures of Jesus Christ, divine and human miraculously fused into one. It became the official religion of the Byzantine Empire at the Council of Chalcedon in 451 CE, in opposition to Monophysites.

Divan al-Humayun (Imperial Council): This was the top administrative body in the Ottoman Empire composed of leading government ministers, led by the sultan—and in his absence, the grand vizir (or *sadr al-azam*).

Gazi (Ghazi): From the word *gaza*, meaning going to war for the faith. Used especially by early Ottoman sultans to refer to their Muslim soldiers and is akin to the popular meaning of *mujahideen* or holy warriors.

Ghadir Khumm on 18 Dhu al-Hijja: This is the 18th day of the Islamic month of *Dhu al-Hijja* that Shiite Muslims celebrate. According to Shiite tradition, on this day in 632 CE the Prophet Muhammad, at the well of Ghadir Khumm outside of Medina, anointed Ali ibn Abu Talib as his successor or caliph. Sunni Muslims do not recognize this.

hadith: A collection of sayings of the Prophet Muhammad that are considered the most important religious guide for Muslims apart from the Quran. Essentially the documentation of the *Sunna* or custom of the Prophet.

hajj: Annual Islamic pilgrimage to Mecca, considered to be one of the Five Pillars of Islam. Muslims are expected to undertake the hajj at least once in their lifetime if they are physically and financially able.

Hanbalis: Followers of Ahmad ibn Hanbal in the ninth century CE, otherwise known as the Traditionalists. They resisted the doctrine of Mutazilism and asserted that the Quran is the final, unalterable Word of God and could not be reinterpreted. Hanbali Islam today is one of the legal schools (*madhabs*) of Sunni Islam, known as the most rigid of the generally acknowledged four madhabs.

haram: Sanctuary, often a religious sanctuary. Also a reference to forbidden areas.

Haram al-Sharif (Arabic: Noble Sanctuary): Muslim reference to what Jews call the Temple Mount in the Old City of Jerusalem. The platform consists of the al-Aqsa Mosque and the Dome of the Rock, which is the primary reason most Muslims consider Jerusalem to be the third holiest site in Islam after Mecca and Medina.

Hashimites: The family of the Prophet Muhammad. Today, the monarchies in Jordan and Morocco claim descent from the family of the Prophet and therefore are considered Hashimite kingdoms.

Hibbat Zion or **Hovevi Zion** (Hebrew: Lovers of Zion): Society formed primarily in Russia that organized the first aliyah to Palestine.

Hijra (Arabic: migration): The Prophet Muhammad's migration, along with his followers, from Mecca to Medina in 622.

ijtihad (related, **mujtahid**): The ability to interpret divine will, the Quran. A mujtahid is a recognized authority in applying reason in interpreting Islamic precepts.

Imam: Spiritual leader of a Muslim community.

intifada (Arabic: shaking off or uprising): Name used by Palestinians to refer to their uprising against Israeli occupation that began in late 1987. Also used in reference to another uprising (the al-Aqsa intifada) that began in September 2000.

iqta: Parcels of land in varying sizes awarded by the central government to military commanders—and sometimes administrators. The iqta holders would be responsible for local governmental duties such as tax collection, and also commit to providing a certain number of troops when called upon by the central government. This would relieve the central treasury of the burden of paying for a salaried or standing army.

Irgun Zevai Leumi (Hebrew: National Military Organization): Founded in 1937 and led by Menachem Begin in 1941. Often considered a terrorist organization, it was committed to taking almost any action that brought about the creation of the state of Israel. The Irgun particularly viewed the British as the major impediment to Jewish statehood, and it carried out a series of attacks against British interests, most spectacularly the blowing up of the British military headquarters in the King David Hotel in Jerusalem in 1946, as well as against Palestinians. It was dissolved by the Israeli government in 1948.

jahiliyya: The period before the advent of Islam in Arabia, referred to by Muslims as the "Age of Ignorance."

Janissary (Yeni Ceri or New Force): Slaves converted to Islam, educated in Turkish and Ottoman ways, then given military training and organized into what became an elite infantry.

Jazira: "Island" in Arabic, this is a reference to the geographic area across present-day north-central Syria and Iraq that fell between, like an island, the Tigris and Euphrates rivers.

jihad (Arabic: struggle): Often translated in the West as "holy war," it has come to refer to those who fight in the way of Islam, or *mujahideen* (holy warriors). In traditional Islam, it refers as much to an inner struggle to become a better Muslim.

jizya: A tax paid by non-Muslims.

Kaaba: The square shrine (draped in black silk embroidered with gold) that sits at the center of the Grand Mosque in Mecca, Saudi Arabia, and is considered the most holy site in Islam. It is the point of orientation for Muslim prayer.

kapikullari (slaves of the Porte, Sublime Porte): In the Ottoman Empire, these were slaves captured in battle or purchased outright by the Ottoman government. The slaves were then converted to Islam (if they were not already Muslim), trained, and taught the Ottoman way. Most of them would then fill the ranks of the Janissary corps and some went to work in the bureaucracy.

katib, plural **kuttab:** Literally meaning "secretary" in its singular form. The plural refers generally to the civilian bureaucracy in the Abbasid caliphate.

kharaja: Land tax paid based on the area of one's holdings and types of crops cultivated.

Khurasaniyya: Those from the province of Khurasan in northeast Iran who formed the military core in support of the Abbasid revolution and played a leading role in the state in the early Abbasid period.

Mahdi: Divinely guided messiah or savior who, according to Islamic belief, will appear at the end of times to rid the world of injustice.

mamluks: Non-Arab slaves, mostly Turkish, who originally were captured in battle or purchased. They were then converted to Islam, trained, manumitted, and often integrated into the ruling apparatus through military and administrative duties.

mawali, singular **mawla:** Non-Arab converts to Islam.

millet: Meaning "nations," these were horizontal divisions of the Ottoman Empire based upon religious affiliation. Typically, those in an official millet, such as Greek Orthodox, Armenian Orthodox, or Jewish would look to their own courts and officials in family and religious affairs. Islam itself was not a millet since it was the state religion.

Monophysite: Meaning "one nature," it is a reference to Christians who believe that Jesus Christ has one divine nature and not both human and divine, as in Diophysism.

Muhajirun: Those who followed Muhammad and accompanied him from Mecca to Medina in the Hijra in 622 CE.

munafiqun: The "doubters," this is a reference to those in Medina during the Prophet Muhammad's stay there who doubted the legitimacy of his religious claims and thus his political leadership.

Muslim Brotherhood (*Ikhwan al-Muslimun*)**:** Islamist party founded by Hasan al-Banna in Egypt in 1928. It became the largest and most influential Islamist (or Islamic fundamentalist) party in the Arab world, with branches or off-shoots established in many Muslim countries.

Mutazilism: Literally meaning "those who withdraw or separate themselves," it was a philosophical school that became significant during the Abbasid caliphates of al-Mamun and al-Mutasim in the early- to mid-ninth century. Considered to be religious rationalists influenced by Greek reason, Mutazilites believed in human freedom of action as well as the createdness of the Quran, therefore it was subject to interpretation at different times. It was mostly the ideology of the elite ruling class although it was harshly implemented by an inquisition during its heyday. Although not surviving long as a religious doctrine, it certainly influenced the development of certain evolving Shiite principles over the next century.

nass: Refers to the designation of an imam by the previous imam in Shiite Islam.

Nizam-i Jedid (1791): The "new order" or "new system/regulations," this is a reference to the reform program more along the European model inaugurated by Ottoman Sultan Selim I.

Organization of Petroleum Exporting Countries (OPEC): Founded in September 1960.

Palestine Liberation Organization (PLO): Created by the Arab League in 1964.

qibla: The direction of prayer for Muslims, which is toward the Kaaba, in the Grand Mosque in Mecca.

Quraysh: The tribe into which the Prophet Muhammad was born in Mecca. It controlled trade and dominated in Mecca during the time of the Prophet.

Ramadan: The name of the ninth month in the Islamic calendar, it is also the holy month of fasting (*sawm*), one of the Five Pillars of Islam (Arkan al-Islam), the basic duties of a Muslim.

Rashidun: The first four caliphs (Abu Bakr, Umar, Uthman, and Ali) of the Islamic community following the death of Muhammad. They are believed by Muslims to be the "rightly guided ones."

razzia: Raids or raiding among Bedouin Arabs.

sabiqa: A Muslim's standing or precedence in the community, which often determined one's salary (*ata*) and position.

salafiyya (Arabic: ancestors): Reference derived from the first generations of Muslims, called *al-salif al-salih* (the pious ancestors), this is an Islamic intellectual movement that emerged in the late nineteenth century that called for a return to the purity of the first Muslims and their foundational texts, namely the Quran and Hadith; however, the movement was also referred to as Islamic modernism because it was not incompatible with modern (European) innovation and thought.

salat: Daily prayers recited by Muslims and one of the Five Pillars of Islam.

Sawad: Located in central to southern Iraq, this was an area of rich alluvial plains fed by intricate canals and irrigation systems. It was critical to the financial health of the Abbasid caliphate.

sawafi: State or crown lands.

shahada: Sacred profession of Islamic faith, translated as "There is no God but Allah, and Muhammad is his Messenger." Muslims are called to recite this during each of their daily prayers, and it is one of the Five Pillars of Islam.

shahanshah: Title typically given to Persian leaders, literally meaning "king of kings."

sharia (Arabic: the way or path): Islamic law.

shura (Arabic: consultation): A committee or council, as well as the concept of "mutual consultation," which the Quran prescribes as the preferred method for decision-making in government.

sipahis: Ottoman cavalry.

Sublime Porte: Government of the Ottoman sultan.

sultan: Originally a moral authority, but came to denote a Muslim sovereign.

Sunna: Tradition or custom of the Prophet Muhammad based on his sayings (*hadith*). It is second only to the Quran in terms of its religious significance as a guide for Muslims.

Tanzimat (Turkish: regulations): Ottoman reform movement in the nineteenth century, officially launched in 1839.

timars: Land grants in return for service to the Ottoman Empire.

ulama, singular **alim:** Muslim religious scholars.

umma (Arabic: community): The collective community of Islamic people throughout the world.

United Arab Republic (UAR): The merger initially of Egypt and Syria into one country, established in February 1958 and lasted in this form until September 1961, when Syria seceded.

United Nations Emergency Force (UNEF): UN peacekeeping forces stationed in the Sinai Peninsula following the Suez war.

United Nations Security Council (UNSC): Voting body of fifteen member states of the United Nations, including the five permanent members (United States, Soviet Union/Russia, China, Great Britain, and France), where each of the five can veto proposed resolutions. The passed resolutions, which apply to events and circumstances worldwide, are consecutively numbered, such as UN Security Council Resolution 242, passed in November 1967 and pertaining to the 1967 Arab-Israeli war that occurred the previous June.

waqf: Assets that are donated or bequeathed for a charitable cause.

wazirs (*viziers*, singular vizir): usually a reference to government ministers, typically in Abbasid times a high ranking political official.

weapons of mass destruction (WMD): Usually taken to mean nuclear, biological, or chemical weapons.

Yishuv (Hebrew: settlement): Term used to refer to the Jewish community in Palestine before the creation of the state of Israel.

zakat: Giving of alms to the poor. It is one of the Five Pillars of Islam.

Zanj: A name given to the slaves, mostly of African origin, who worked in southern Iraq largely on agricultural land reclamation. They rose up in rebellion against the Abbasid caliphate in 869 CE, holding significant territory in present-day southern Iraq and southwestern Iran until their defeat by Abbasid forces in 883.

INDEX

Page numbers followed by *f* indicate a figure, map, or photograph on the designated page.